EUROPE AND THE ISLAMIC WORLD

EUROPE
AND THE
ISLAMIC
WORLD
A HISTORY

JOHN TOLAN, GILLES VEINSTEIN,
AND HENRY LAURENS

Translated by Jane Marie Todd
With a Foreword by John L. Esposito

PRINCETON UNIVERSITY PRESS
PRINCETON AND OXFORD

Second printing, and first paperback printing, 2016

Paperback ISBN: 978-0-691-16857-9

The Library of Congress has cataloged the cloth edition of this book as follows:

Tolan, John Victor, 1959–
[Europe et l'islam. English]
Europe and the Islamic world : a history / John Tolan, Gilles Veinstein, and Henry Laurens ;
translated by Jane Marie Todd With a Foreword by John L. Esposito.
p. cm.
Henry Laurens's name appears first on the original French ed.
Includes bibliographical references and index.
ISBN 978-0-691-14705-5 (hardcover : alk. paper)   1. Europe—Relations—Middle East.
2. Middle East—Relations—Europe.   3. Europe—Relations—Islamic countries.   4. Islamic
countries—Relations—Europe.   5. Europe—Civilization—Islamic influences.   6. Islamic
civilization—Western influences.   I. Veinstein, Gilles.   II. Laurens, Henry, 1954–
III. Todd, Jane Marie, 1957–   IV. Title.
DS63.2.E8L3813 2013
303.48'2401767—dc23
2012016021

British Library Cataloging-in-Publication Data is available

Cet ouvrage publié dans le cadre du programme d'aide à la publication bénéficie
du soutien du Ministère des Affaires Etrangères et du Service Culturel de l'Ambassade
de France représenté aux Etats-Unis.

This work received support from the French Ministry of Foreign Affairs
and the Cultural Services of the French Embassy in the United States
through their publishing assistance program.

This book has been composed in Minion Pro

Printed on acid-free paper. ∞

Printed in the United States of America

3 5 7 9 10 8 6 4 2

CONTENTS

FOREWORD

by John L. Esposito

CONTEMPORARY POLITICS and the media have too often produced a narrative of conflicting paradigms that sees the world and the history of relations between the West and Islam in terms of a clash of civilizations, Orientalism versus Occidentalism, fourteen centuries of jihad versus Crusades and colonialism, Islamophobia and anti-Westernism. Lost in the cultural crossfire are the religious, historical, political, and cultural diversity rather than monolithic nature of the West and the Muslim world and positive interactions and exchanges and cross-fertilization.

Despite common historical and theological roots and beliefs, Muslim-Christian relations have often been overshadowed by political and economic as well as religious conflict as the armies and missionaries of Islam and of Christendom have been locked in a struggle for power and for souls: from the fall of the Byzantine (eastern Roman) Empire before Muslim armies in the seventh century to the Crusades during the eleventh and twelfth centuries; the expulsion of the "Moors" from Spain and the Inquisition; the Ottoman threat to overrun Europe; European (Christian) colonial expansion and domination from the eighteenth to early twentieth centuries; the political and cultural challenge of the superpowers in the new colonialism or American "neocolonialism" since the latter half of the twentieth century; the creation of the state of Israel by Western "Christian" countries and Palestinian exile; the competition of Christian and Muslim missionaries today from Africa to Southeast Asia; and the contemporary reassertion of Islam in Muslim politics around the world.

Theologically, the very similarities of Christianity and Islam put the two on an early collision course. Islam belongs to the Abrahamic family of great monotheistic faiths. Muslims, like Jews and Christians, view themselves as the children of Abraham, as proclaimed in each of their sacred scriptures: the Old and New Testaments and the Qur'an. Despite specific and significant differences, Judaism, Christianity, and Islam share a belief in one God, the creator, sustainer, and ruler of the universe who is beyond ordinary experience. And all believe in angels, Satan, prophets, revelation, moral responsibility and accountability, divine judgment, and reward or punishment. Yet while Jews and Christians claim descent from Abraham and his wife, Sarah, through their son Isaac, Muslims trace their religious roots back to Abraham (Ibrahim) through Ismail, his firstborn son by Hagar, Sarah's Egyptian servant.

Both religions had a universal message and mission. Both possessed a supersessionist theology—that is, each community believed that its covenant with

God was the fulfillment of God's earlier revelation to a previous community that had gone astray. While Christians had little problem with their supersessionist views toward Judaism, a similar claim by Muslims to have the final revelation was unacceptable and, more than that, a threat to the uniqueness and divinely mandated role of Christianity to be the only means to salvation.

Christendom experienced the early conquests and expansion of Islam not only as a theological but also as a political and civilizational challenge to its religious and political hegemony. Muslim rule quickly spread from the Byzantine and Persian empires to Syria, Iraq, and Egypt, and swept across North Africa and into Europe, where Muslims ruled Spain and the Mediterranean from Sicily to Anatolia.

For non-Muslim populations in Byzantium and Persia, who had been subjugated by foreign rulers, Islamic rule meant an exchange of rulers rather than a loss of independence. Many in Byzantium willingly exchanged Greco-Roman rule for that of new Arab masters, fellow Semites, with whom they had closer linguistic and cultural affinities and to whom they paid lower taxes. Upon declaration of their allegiance to the Islamic state and payment of a poll (head) tax, these "protected" (*dhimmi*) peoples could practice their faith and be governed by their religious leaders and law in matters of faith and private life.

Islam often proved more tolerant than imperial Christianity, providing greater religious freedom for Jews and indigenous Christians; most local Christian churches had been persecuted as schismatics and heretics by a "foreign" Christian orthodoxy. As Francis Peters has observed:

> The conquests destroyed little: what they did suppress were imperial rivalries and sectarian bloodletting among the newly subjected population. The Muslims tolerated Christianity but they disestablished it; henceforth Christian life and liturgy, its endowments, politics, and theology, would be a private not a public affair. By an exquisite irony, Islam reduced the status of Christians to that which the Christians had earlier thrust upon the Jews, with one difference. The reduction in Christian status was merely judicial; it was unaccompanied by either systematic persecution or blood lust, and generally, though not everywhere and at all times, unmarred by vexatious behavior.[1]

The rapid spread and development of imperial Islam produced a rich Islamic civilization that flourished from the ninth to the twelfth centuries. Urban cultural centers emerged in Cairo, Baghdad, Cordova, Palermo, and Nishapur. With significant assistance from Christian and Jewish subjects, Muslims collected the great books of science, medicine, and philosophy from the West and the East and translated them into Arabic from Greek, Latin, Persian, Coptic, Syriac, and Sanskrit. The age of translation was followed by a period of great creativity as a new generation of educated Muslim thinkers and scientists made their own contributions to learning in philosophy, medicine, chemistry, astronomy, algebra, optics, art, and architecture. Towering intellectual giants dominated this period: al-Farabi (d. 950), Ibn Sina (known as Avicenna, 980–1037), Ibn Rushd (known as Averroes, d. 1198), al-Biruni (973–1048), and al-Ghazali (d. 1111). The cultural traffic pattern was again reversed when Europeans, emerging from the Middle Ages, turned to Muslim centers of learning to regain their lost heritage and to learn from Muslim advances in philosophy, mathematics, medicine, and science. They retranslated the Greek philosophers and the writings of their great Muslim disciples: men like al-Farabi, who had come to be known as "the second teacher or master" (the first being Aristotle) and Ibn Rushd (Averroes), remembered as "the great commentator on Aristotle." Many of the great medieval Christian philosophers and theologians (Albert the Great, Thomas Aquinas, Abelard, Roger Bacon, Duns Scotus) acknowledged their intellectual debt to their Muslim predecessors.

FROM THE CRUSADES TO EUROPEAN COLONIALISM

Few events have had a more shattering and long-lasting effect on Muslim-Christian relations than the Crusades. For many in the West, the specific facts regarding the Crusades are but a dim memory. Few remember that it was the pope who called for the Crusades and that on balance the Crusaders lost.

For Muslims, the memory of the Crusades lives on as the clearest example of militant Christianity, an early harbinger of the aggression and imperialism of the Christian West. If many in the West have regarded Islam as a religion of the sword, Muslims down through the ages speak of the Christian West's Crusader mentality and hegemonic ambitions.

For Muslim-West relations, it is less a case of what actually happened in the Crusades than how they are remembered. Political and economic motives and incentives are often forgotten or overlooked as each community looks back with memories of its commitment to defend its faith and with heroic stories of valor and chivalry against "the infidel." Both Muslims and Christians saw the other as militant, somewhat barbaric and fanatic in religious zeal, determined to conquer, convert, or eradicate the other, and thus an enemy of God.

A second far-reaching and influential event affecting the relationship of Islam to the West is the experience of European colonialism. Its impact and continued legacy remains alive in Middle East politics and throughout the Muslim world today. No one who has traveled in and studied the Muslim world can be oblivious to the tendency of many to associate their past and current problems in large part with the legacy of European colonialism. European colonialism abruptly reversed a pattern of self-rule that had existed from the time of the Prophet. By the nineteenth century, Europeans had colonized many Muslim areas: the French in North, West, and Equatorial Africa and the Levant (Lebanon and Syria); the British in Palestine, Transjordan, Iraq, the Arabian Gulf, and the Indian subcontinent; and in Southeast Asia, the British in Malaya (Malaysia, Singapore, and Brunei) and the Dutch in Indonesia.

As the balance of power and leadership shifted to Europe, much of the Muslim world found itself either directly ruled or dominated by the "Christian West," threatened by "crown and cross." Many Europeans believed that modernity was not only the result of conditions producing the Enlightenment and the industrial revolution, but also due to the inherent superiority of Christianity as a religion and culture. The British spoke of the "white man's burden" and the French of their "mission to civilize" as they colonized much of Africa, the Middle East, and South and Southeast Asia.

The external threat to Muslim identity and autonomy from European Christendom raised profound religious as well as political questions for many in the Muslim world: What had gone wrong, and why had Muslim fortunes been so thoroughly reversed? Was it Muslims who had failed Islam or Islam that had failed Muslims? How were Muslims to respond?

ISLAM AND THE WEST: CHALLENGE OR THREAT?

Since the late 1990s, a growing chorus of voices have charged that Islam and the West are on a political, civilizational (or religiocultural), and demographic collision course. Immigrants and immigration have become an explosive political issue in Europe and America. The impact of religious extremism and terrorism—in particular 9/11, followed by attacks in London and Madrid and Osama Bin Laden's declaration of a global jihad against the West—have fed stereotypes and fears characterized as a war between Islam and the West.

After September 11, 2001, the clash of civilizations became part of a now-notorious set of Manichaean depictions of the forces arrayed in the "war on terror," routinely described in presidential addresses and editorial pages as a war between the civilized world and terrorists who "hate" Western democracy, capitalism, and freedom or as an existential struggle against "evil" and "the merchants of death." America's international pursuit of its broad-based war on terror, as well as the political rhetoric of the Bush administration—which spoke of the struggle as a "crusade" and initially dubbed the invasion of Afghanistan "Operation Infinite Justice," in a direct affront to Muslim believers, for whom only God can embody such a trait unto infinity—convinced many Muslims that the war was indeed against them and their religion.

The most influential proponent of a clash of civilizations was Samuel Huntington, who in his 1993 *Foreign Affairs* article "The Clash of Civilizations?" argued that cultural and religious differences were supplanting the struggle for ideological dominance that had characterized conflict in the cold war era. In his subsequent book, *The Clash of Civilizations and the Remaking of World Order* (New York: Simon and Schuster, 1996), he sounded a more urgent note, arguing that such cultural-cum-religious rivalries had emerged as the biggest threat to world peace. Western dominance and "universal" ideas, according to

Huntington, were going to be challenged by new rivals, in particular Muslim and Chinese ones. The September 11 attacks narrowed his focus further: in a December 2001 *Newsweek* piece, "The Age of Muslim Wars," he declared that the age had officially begun, presaging intensified battle between Islam and the West. Huntington's conclusion that "Islam's borders *are* bloody, and so are its innards," is a view that explicitly and simplistically attributes bloodshed to the religion of Islam—rather than to the actions of a minority of Muslim terrorists whose primary grievances are political.

This reasoning flattens cultural and historical forces into a template that distorts the true nature of the societies and religious traditions. In laying out a grand new theory of global conflict, he failed to appreciate the significant diversity that existed not only among but also between and *within* the countries and societies he grouped under the rubric of a given civilization to be Islamic or Western.

In the twenty-first century, understanding relations between the West and Islam is pivotal and critical both in foreign and in domestic policy in Europe and the United States. The failure of the conventional wisdom based on a paradigm that often questioned whether Islam was compatible with modernity and whether Islam and Arab culture were compatible with democracy has been discredited by the Arab Spring. At the same time, in Europe and the United States, where Islam is the second or third largest religion, integration and pluralism are challenged by the rise of Islamophobia and the threat of domestic terrorism.

As in the past, so too today a reductionist approach that sees the religion of Islam as the primary driver in Muslim-West relations and as a necessary source of conflict and a clash of civilizations is a dead end and dangerous. It obscures or downplays historical, political, and economic causes for conflict, posits a monolithic Islam and Muslim world as well as a monolithic Europe and America. *Europe and the Islamic World: A History* is a major antidote of this dangerous myopic worldview, offering a critical and balanced assessment of a historic encounter marked not only by religious competition and conflict but also by coexistence and cooperation in domestic politics and foreign relations, trade and commerce, science and culture. So too today, we face a world in which religion remains strong globally and as in the past is a source of guidance and morality, a source of conflict and violence but also of peace and conflict resolution and of interreligious and intercivilizational dialogue.

2

Europe and the Islamic World

GENERAL INTRODUCTION

As EVERYONE MUST KNOW, the relations between Europe and the Muslim world are very much in the news: European diplomacy with Iran or within the context of the Israeli-Palestinian conflict; Muslim immigration to European countries; the position of European oil companies in Arab economies; the economic trade agreements between the European Union (EU) and the countries of the Maghreb; Turkey's negotiations to join the EU; European reactions to the democratic revolutions sweeping the Arab world. All these pressing matters and many others as well, which could lead to cooperation, concord, or conflict, will remain key issues for European and Muslim societies throughout the twenty-first century and beyond.

This book explores the history of this rich and complex relationship, which began in the 630s, when the armies of Constantinople and Medina fought for control of Syria-Palestine. Since then, and for nearly fifteen centuries, there have been continuous and extremely varied forms of contact: wars, conquests, reconquests, diplomacy, alliances, commerce, marriages, the slave trade, translations, technological exchanges, and imitation and emulation in art and culture. Far from marginal curiosities within the history of the European and Muslim peoples, these contacts have profoundly marked them both.

The importance, richness, and scope of these relations, so apparent to anyone who knows the history of Europe or of the Muslim countries, are not obvious to everyone, however. The American political scientist Samuel P. Huntington claims that "during most of human existence, contacts between civilizations were intermittent or nonexistent."[1] According to him, it was only with the Portuguese and Spanish explorations and colonization at the turn of the sixteenth century that civilizations entered into permanent contact with each other. On the basis of that huge historical error, Huntington constructed his infamous thesis of the "clash of civilizations," which maintains that a limited number of distinct "civilizations" (the West, Islam, China, and so on) developed autonomously and then confronted each other.

How are we to address the relationship between Europe and the Muslim world without falling into Huntington's trap of placing two "civilizations," Islam and Europe, in opposition? Let us begin by defining our terms—that of "Europe" first and foremost. For the geographers of Greek and Roman antiquity, Europe was one of the three parts of the world, alongside Asia and Africa (or Libya). That idea can also be found in the Latin cartographers of the Middle Ages, who represented the world on "T and O" maps, so called because they depict the ocean as a circle surrounding the land mass, and the waters of the Mediterranean, the Nile, and the Tanais as a T dividing the world into three continents. But that long-lasting geographical tradition seems to have had little influence on real identities: people considered themselves Genoese or Normans, they were part of a kingdom or an empire, but they rarely called themselves "Europeans." The larger frame of reference was religious: the church, in theory, united all Christians. But the unity of the church was in fact fictive, since many theological and institutional issues divided the various Christian communities. By the ninth century, some Latin authors were speaking of *Christianitas* (Christendom) to designate all those who recognized the pope's authority and who used Latin as the liturgical language. But that entity was centered in Europe, which left out most of the world's Christians. And Latin Christendom was rapidly expanding, first within Spain and northeastern Europe and in the islands of the Mediterranean (Sicily, Corsica, the Balearics, Cyprus). It briefly seized control of a part of Palestine: Jerusalem was in the hands of the Crusader kings from 1099 to 1187, and the Latins held a section of the Palestinian coast until 1291. From the Portuguese and Spanish colonial ventures beginning in the late fifteenth century to Napoleon's expedition to Egypt, European expansion played out in other parts of the world.

Among Arab authors as well, "Europe" (*Arufa*), a term inherited from the Greek tradition, was presented in learned geography as one of the parts of the world. But it had a minimal role, since Arab geographers generally rejected the division into continents in favor of a different schema, also of Greek origin: they separated the world into climates, usually seven in number. They therefore considered Europe not a unit but rather distinct countries (*balad*): those of the *Rūm* (Byzantines), the *Ifranj* (Franks), the Slavs, and so on. That is, they viewed these regions in terms of plurality and diversity rather than as a "rival" civilization. In this book, we shall be content to use the term "Europe" to denote the continent's current delimitations, with all the ambiguity that implies as to its eastern boundaries.

What about the "Islamic world"? It can be assimilated to the term *dār al-islām*, widespread among the Arab authors, which literally means "house of Islam." This refers to all those territories where Islam is the dominant religion, and is not to be confused with the *umma*, the community of Muslim believers as a whole. The *dār al-islām* is not inhabited solely by Muslims. Also residing there are *dhimmis*, "protected" minorities (Jews, Christians, Mazdeans). And the *umma* includes Muslims who live outside the *dār al-islām*: captives or minorities living in regions ruled by non-Muslims, traders in the Indian Ocean or in sub-Saharan Africa, or (in the twentieth and twenty-first centuries) emigrants to Europe or America.

Clearly, the *dār al-islām* is no more stable a geographical entity than is Europe: it expanded rapidly throughout the Middle Ages. It came into being with a wave of lightning conquests that, over the century following Muhammad's death in 632, gave the Muslims control of an empire extending from the Indus and the Hindu Kush to the Atlantic coasts of Morocco and Portugal. Although that expansion slowed subsequently, it resumed later by other means: through the mass conversion of the Turks from the ninth century on and of the Mongols beginning in the thirteenth century, which brought Islam to central Asia and to China's doorstep. The Islamized Mongols went on to conquer a good part of northern India. Elsewhere, Islam spread through commerce: to the kingdoms of western Africa such as Mali, or to the Indian Ocean, from Zanzibar to Java. Between the thirteenth and fifteenth centuries, Christian kings of Northern Iberia conquered al-Andalus, or Muslim Spain. But during the same period, the Ottoman Empire extended its power into the heart of Europe. For the medieval period, we shall direct our interest primarily to the part of the *dār al-islām* that had close contacts with Europe, particularly the Mediterranean regions.

What was the European perception of the *dār al-islām*? The words "Islam" and "Muslim" entered European languages only belatedly: "Islam" was used in French for the first time in 1697, in English in 1818; "musulman" can be found in French from the mid-sixteenth century on, and "Moslim" in English as of 1615.[2] Before that time, the terms for Muslims generally referred to ethnic origin: "Arab," "Turk," "Persian," "Moor." There were also biblical terms: "Ishmaelites" or "sons of Ishmael," since, in the biblical and Qur'anic tradition, Ishmael was considered the forefather of the Arabs. Similarly, Muslims were called "Hagarenes," after Hagar, the mother of Ishmael. But the most commonly used term in the Middle Ages was undoubtedly "Saracen." For ancient geographers, that word of obscure origin referred to one of the peoples of Arabia. It then came to designate all Arabs, and then, more generally, Muslims. To denote Islam, the expressions "law of the Saracens" (*lex Sarracenorum*) or "law of Muhammad" (*lex Mahumeti*) were often used. With the rise of the Ottoman Empire in the fourteenth and fifteenth centuries, people spoke primarily of "Turks," or often, "*the* Turk" in the singular. If there was a Latin expression equivalent to *dār al-islām* in the Middle Ages, it was probably *terrae Sarracenorum* (lands of the Saracens). Many European authors of the time vacillated between a monolithic view of the Saracens, considered universally hostile to the Christians, and a more nuanced view sensitive to the great diversity of regions and peoples.

Were there, as Huntington claims, two rival civilizations—founded on universalist ideologies and competing in their expansionist aims—that clashed with each other, brandishing the banners of the Crusade and of jihad? Or rather, as the historian Richard Bulliet maintains, were these two branches of a single "Islamo-Christian" civilization, with deep roots in a common religious, cultural, and intellectual heritage: the civilization of the ancient Mediterranean and the Near East; biblical revelation; and Greek and Hellenistic science and philosophy? In Bulliet's view, that common heritage grew stronger over fifteen centuries, thanks to the uninterrupted exchange of goods, persons, and ideas.[3] If we view the Muslim world and Europe (or the West) as two branches of a single civilization, the idea of a "clash of civilizations" no longer makes any sense. And this is not simply a matter of words. For example, to see the Muslim conquest of Spain (711), the First Crusade (1099), the taking of Constantinople by the Ottomans (1453), the conquest of Granada (1492), Napoleon's Egyptian expedition (1798–1801), the French conquest of Algeria (1830–1847), and the U.S. interventions in Iraq (1991 and 2003) as so many manifestations, so much evidence, of a supposed "clash of civilizations" makes any search for more specific explanations superfluous. But no one, in delineating the wars within Europe or in Muslim countries, resorts to such an explanatory straitjacket. Whether discussing the Ottoman conquest of the Mamluks, the Wars of Religion in Europe, or the world wars that tore Europe asunder in the twentieth century, historians seek to explain events without appealing to some "clash of civilizations." France was often at war with its neighbors, particularly Great Britain and Germany, but no one claims it belonged to a "civilization" distinct from them.

Readers should therefore not be fooled by the title of this book: It will have less to do with relations between Europe and the Islamic world than with those between Genoese and Tunisians, Constantinopolitans and Alexandrians, Catalans and Maghrebis. It will deal not with the relations between two "civilizations" but with the complex and diverse relations between many individuals and groups that belong to what we lump together, with all the ambiguity already noted, under the umbrella terms "Europe" and "the Islamic world."

This book will also not be a theoretical argument or an ideological manifesto. The authors will not attempt systematically to refute Huntington's theses or the corresponding theses of those who have inspired the current Islamist movements promoting jihad. Similarly, Islam and Christianity will not be objects of study qua religions: we will not seek their common roots, their points of divergence or potential points of intersection. We will simply attempt to revive a long history, many aspects of which have fallen into oblivion, and to replace simplistic and reductive schemata with evidence of a richer and more complex history. Furthermore, it is not history itself that we will bring to light: historians can never provide anything but a reconstruction, within a discourse that imposes an order on the mass of raw material and that makes selections. That mass is so large in this case, given the long period we have embraced, the many angles from which the subject can be approached, and the variety of levels at which it can be grasped, that the authors have abandoned any idea of providing an exhaustive treatment. The pages that follow do not constitute a systematic treatise or even a textbook on the question. This book is closer in form to the essay, a more subjective and hence more arbitrary genre that privileges the significant event, the illustrative example, the telling quotation as a function of a few guiding ideas. Yet readers will encounter not *one* essay but three in succession, each divided into a series of chapters. The authors—the first dealing with the medieval period, the second with the fifteenth to eighteenth centuries, and the third with the contemporary period—have carried out their respective tasks in rather different ways. The reason no doubt lies in their individual personalities but also in more objective factors. The three periods belong to different historical fields, whether in terms of the quantity and quality of the available documentation, the status of the respective historiographies, and, last but not least, the historical circumstances themselves, which in each era bring different questions to the fore.

Part I of this book is devoted to the history of relations in the Middle Ages, that is, from the 630s to the fifteenth century. Chapter 1 examines how medieval Arab and European geographers perceived the world and the populations who lived in it. John Tolan pays particular attention to the image of Europeans in Arab geography and to that of the East in Latin geography. In both Christian and Muslim territories, ideologies of holy war were often used to justify conquest of the "infidels," as he demonstrates in chapter 2, devoted to the development of the concepts of jihad, Crusade, and *reconquista*. These ideologies glorified war waged for the "true" religion but rarely ruled out political and military alliances with princes belonging to rival faiths. Nor did they prevent princes from setting aside a protected but subaltern place for religious minorities. Chapter 3 examines the fate of the minority Christians in the Muslim countries of Europe and of minority Muslims in Christian countries. In the Mediterranean world, commerce established strong ties between the European seaport cities (such as Pisa, Venice, Genoa, and Barcelona) and ports in the Muslim world. Especially from the twelfth century on, trade had a profound impact on all the societies it touched, as Tolan shows in chapter 4. Last, chapter 5 deals with intellectual, cultural, and artistic exchanges, studying in particular the profound impact of Arab science and philosophy on the intellectual revival of Europe that began in the twelfth century.

Part II deals with what French historians call the "modern period," which extends from the late fifteenth to the late eighteenth century. Some may object that such a demarcation makes more sense for Western history (for which it was devised) than for the history of Islam. It is justified, however, inasmuch as, within the history of Islam itself, that period has certain identifying characteristics, such as the emergence and blossoming of several great empires, which replaced the political fragmentation of the previous phase: the empire of the Great Moguls in India, that of the Shiite Safavids in Persia, and the Ottomans. In recognizing that, with the advent of modernity, this period was marked by profound changes in Europe, we must acknowledge above all that the relationship between Europe and the Islamic world entered a new phase at that time. We will privilege the history of the Ottoman Empire, since its destiny is thoroughly interwoven with Europe, to such a degree that the two histories merge in part. Chapter 6 retraces that shared history. Focusing on the Ottoman conquest in Europe, Gilles Veinstein recites the litany of events by which the history of Europe became indistinguishable from that of its relationship, whether good or bad, with the principal Muslim power of the time. Chapter 7 details the characteristics of that "other Europe" resulting from the Ottoman conquest:

a multiethnic and multifaith Europe under the domination of the Crescent. The presence of the "infidels" in Europe and the threat it posed constituted the worst of scandals for Christendom. Chapter 8 delineates all the forms of antagonism that, at the ideological level, irremediably pitted the two protagonists against each other. The religious factor remained significant, as in the Middle Ages, usually taking the same forms as in medieval polemics. But that mutual rejection also took new forms, feeding on sources of exclusion that were not specifically religious. Chapter 9 highlights another consequence of the schism between the two Europes (unequally represented in contemporary European memory): the existence of an Islamic-Christian border running through the middle of the continent. That border was the site of permanent confrontations, both physical and symbolic, but also of mutual exchanges and influences. A striking expression of these influences can be found in the twin sociomilitary organizations that, under various designations and with characteristics proper to each, were a constant on both sides, along the entire length of the land and sea border. On that demarcation line dividing Europe, alternative societies arising from the social and religious tensions of the interior faced off: these adversaries resembled each other only to better enter into opposition. This space between, this world apart, tended to play by its own rules when negotiating the relationship between states and, when necessary, came to disrupt the *modus vivendi* these states set in place. Chapter 10 tempers the predominantly dark and negative image of the preceding chapters. Breaches existed in the wall of hostility, and centuries of coexistence can in no way be reduced to an uninterrupted succession of violent acts and confrontations. Ideological antagonism regularly yielded to political realism or commercial pragmatism, which, of course, did not eliminate the antagonism but at least bracketed it. Other temperaments, such as a taste for exoticism, intellectual curiosity, or philosophical speculation could more effectively break down the ideological barrier, but they undermined it only to a very limited degree during the period under consideration.

Part III begins with the major rupture of the second half of the eighteenth century, which historians used to call "the origin of the Eastern question." Henry Laurens examines the different phenomena that suddenly placed Europe in the position of a superpower with, as a corollary, plans to conquer the Old World. From the early nineteenth century on, it became clear to Muslim elites that, to survive, they would have to accept change. The agreed-upon plan was to form modern states, but that entailed fundamental transformations of society and of culture.

Those regions that succeeded in preserving formal independence were caught up in a race between European encroachment or interference and the establishment of a strong state, which also had to call on the Europeans for assistance. Because of that dynamic of change, it is difficult to determine what was borrowed pure and simple and what was the result of evolutionary synchronism: the complex question of the emancipation of non-Muslims in

Islamic territory is a case in point. Other regions had to face the "colonial night" of European domination, which in certain places eventually adopted the form of settlement colonies.

The Muslim world was far from passive when confronted with Europe's multifaceted advance. Rather, it entered a cycle of accelerated transformation, culminating in the adoption of the nationality principle as the new mode of social organization. The new forms of political expression contested both the imperial Islamic heritage and the modern colonial empires. Then, at the start of the twentieth century, the Muslim world entered the revolutionary era. Its emancipation increased with World War I, which, however, devastated its entire continental space, from Morocco to India.

Independence, won by armed struggle when necessary, has imposed new challenges on the Islamic world in its confrontation with Europe: nationalism and Islamism, development and dependency, modern states and religious or ethnic communities. The Muslim world was both the prize and the agent of the new cold war conflicts, which perpetuated the logic of involvement and interference introduced in the nineteenth century.

At the same time, migratory movements gave birth to a "European" Islam within the former colonial metropolises. Multiculturalism partly encompasses the colonial heritage but within an entirely new perspective. At a time when the "north bank" of the Mediterranean is coalescing into a European Union, Europe is called on to define its identity in terms of its proximity to the Muslim world. The culturalist discourses on both sides tend to want to deny the inner life they share as a result of fifteen centuries of common history.

—J. T., G. V., H. L.

PART I

Saracens and *Ifranj*: Rivalries, Emulation, and Convergences

by
John Tolan

CHAPTER 1

THE GEOGRAPHERS' WORLD

From *Arabia Felix* to the *Balad al-Ifranj* (Land of the Franks)

WHAT NOTION DID the men and women of the Middle Ages have of the world they lived in? What were their perceptions of the boundaries—geographical, religious, cultural, and so on—that separated what we moderns call the Islamic world from Europe? Clearly, the responses are many, and the perspective changes with one's point of view: from a Northumbrian monastery in the eighth century, from Baghdad in the tenth century, from the unstable border regions of Anatolia in the eleventh century, from a Genoese ship sailing off the coast of Egypt in the thirteenth century, from the Maghreb in the fourteenth century, or from Cape Sagres at the far southwest tip of Portugal in the fifteenth century. We are, moreover, obliged to rely on the reflections that a small literate elite, usually male, left behind regarding the geography and ethnography of the world they inhabited.

The geographical culture of these literati had a dual foundation: scriptures (the Bible and the Qur'an) and Greek geographical scholarship. Greek geography had undergone transformations, since medieval Europe received it through the filter of Latin geographical and encyclopedic works, texts dating primarily to the fifth to seventh centuries. In the Umayyad and then the Abbasid caliphates, translations of Greek works were supplemented by Persian and Hindu geographical traditions. For these geographers, there was no hard and fast distinction between physical geography, human geography, and religious explanation: mountains, for example, are sometimes presented as manifestations of divine power, and the excessively cold climate of the northern countries is cited as an explanation for why Slavs and Franks are unable to grasp the superiority of Islam.

SONS OF ISAAC, SONS OF ISHMAEL

Let us first examine the frameworks that the reading of scripture—the Bible and the Qur'an—imposes on geography and ethnography. The tendency is more pronounced in Latin scholarship than in Arabic, and for good reason: the Bible (unlike the Qur'an) provides geographical information that allows Christians to retrace the history of the chosen people from Adam to Jesus (though with a few gaps) and to situate a number of neighboring or enemy peoples within that history. Time is structured in the same way: the chroniclers divided history into six "ages," punctuated by the lives of the protagonists of divine history: Adam, Noah, Abraham, David, Nebuchadnezzar (the only "enemy" in the series), and then Christ.[1]

For Isidore of Seville, a Latin encyclopedist and contemporary of Muhammad, human geography was a consequence of human history: the diversity of peoples, languages, and customs in the world is the direct result of the Fall, the Flood, and the confusion of tongues at Babel. We all descend from Adam and Noah. Our ancestors all spoke the same language, Hebrew, until God destroyed the Tower of Babel. For Isidore, the astonishing diversity of humankind could be rationally explained; at least in theory, it was possible to go back to a unified origin, a common ancestor, in the person of Noah. Although Isidore integrates many details of the classical Roman ethnographic tradition, he places them within a biblical framework, imposing order on chaos.[2] He presents his vision of historical ethnography in various writings, particularly in book 9 of the *Etymologies*. The world has seventy-two or seventy-three peoples, each with its own language, and all can be traced back to one of the three sons of Noah: Shem, Ham, and Japheth. That schema allows Isidore and his readers to classify all peoples within an apparently rational and comprehensible framework. He designates various biblical figures as fathers of precise peoples, including a son of Abraham, "Ishmael, from whom arose the Ishmaelites, who are now called, with corruption of the name, Saracens [*Saraceni*], as if they descended from Sarah, and Hagarenes [*Agareni*], from Hagar."[3]

According to Genesis, Ishmael was Abraham's firstborn; his mother was Hagar, Sarah's servant. The angel of the Lord who announced the birth of Hagar's son told her he would be a "wild man; his hand will be against every man, and every man's hand against him; and he shall dwell in the presence of all his brethren" (Genesis 16:12, King James Version). Then Abraham's wife, Sarah, bore a son, Isaac. When Isaac was weaned, his parents gave a great feast, and Sarah saw Ishmael mocking his younger brother (Genesis 21:9). She then demanded of Abraham: "Cast out this bondwoman and her son: for the son of this bondwoman shall not be heir with my son" (Genesis 21:10). And God told Abraham to heed Sarah, consoling him by declaring that "also of the son of the bondwoman will I make a nation." That is the same message He sends to the desperate Hagar in the desert (Genesis 21:13, 18). Ishmael will live long enough to have twelve sons, "twelve princes according to their nations," who "dwelt from Haviläh unto Shur, that is before Egypt, as thou goest toward Assyria" (Genesis 25:16–18). Isaac, Abraham's legitimate son, was his heir; Ishmael was cast out into the desert. But his descendants remained a threat to those of

Isaac. From the first century C.E. on, Jewish and Christian authors identified the twelve sons of Ishmael with the twelve Arabian tribes.[4] In the early fifth century, Jerome claimed that they had usurped the name "Saracens," "falsely taking the name of Sarah in order to claim to be descendants of a free and sovereign woman."[5] These Hagarenes, the descendants of the slave Hagar, claimed to be the sons of Sarah, Abraham's legitimate wife; they insisted on being called "Saracens." In fact, no Arab called himself a "Saracen," a term originating in ancient Greek geography.[6] But Isidore borrows this passage from Jerome, and many Latin authors will repeat that false etymology, making the Saracens the usurpers of a legitimacy that belongs solely to Sarah's lineage.[7]

The Qur'an gives a very different account of Abraham and Ishmael. Abraham proclaims: "Praise be to God who has given me Ishmael and Isaac in my old age!" (14:39).[8] Ishmael is the firstborn; it is he who accompanies his father to Mecca, where father and son build the Kaaba together (2:125–27). Several times in the Qur'an, the faithful are entreated to declare that they worship the God of Abraham, Ishmael, and Isaac; sometimes the names of the prophets are added, especially Moses and Jesus.[9] Far from being an illegitimate child, Ishmael was "a man of his word, an apostle, and a prophet. He enjoined prayer and almsgiving on his people, and his Lord was pleased with him" (19:54–55). When the Qur'an describes how Abraham made ready to sacrifice his son, it does not specify whether that son was Ishmael or Isaac (37:101–7).

Arab geographers adopted these Qur'anic traditions. For Mas'ūdī in the tenth century, there is a clear hierarchy between the three sons of Noah: at the top, Shem and his descendants (including the Arabs and Hebrews); then Japheth (the ancestor of the Chinese, the Indians, the Franks, the Slavs, and the Turks, among others); and last of all, Ham (from whom the blacks were descended).[10] This is sometimes difficult to fathom: Mas'ūdī also distinguishes between the Yūnāniyyūn (Greeks), descendants of Japheth, and the Rūm (Byzantines), stemming from Shem.[11] But for Latin and Arab authors, both Christians and Muslims, the scriptural genealogies provide geographical and ethnographical information of the utmost importance.

THE ENDS OF THE EARTH: THE LAND OF THE FRANKS AS SEEN FROM MEDIEVAL BAGHDAD

André Miquel has described in detail the development of geography in the intellectual centers of the Muslim world, especially in Baghdad, the Abbasid capital, but also, as of 972, in Cairo, the new capital of the Fatimid caliphate. The geographers of the early centuries of Islam translated, adapted, and commented on Greek, Persian, and Hindu geographical works, and added to them new knowledge gleaned from travel narratives, dispatches, and government records. In the ninth and tenth centuries, that new science, called "jūghrāfia" after the

Greek, benefited from masterful encyclopedic works such as those of Masʿūdī, Ibn Hawqal, and al-Muqaddasī. Geographical knowledge became part of *adab*, the learned culture that every educated man had to possess.

The Muslim world claimed for itself the choicest part of that geography. Baghdad, a political and cultural capital, was in some sense the center of the world, though at times it shared that position with the holy cities of Mecca and Medina. Muslim authors attempted to establish and communicate knowledge of a world under the power of the caliphs by sketching mountainous reliefs, rivers, and trade routes by land and sea. Geographers described the populations of the different regions, their languages, habits, and economy. They drew a portrait of the cities, tallying up the mosques, hammams, and markets for the reader.

The world beyond the *dār al-islām* fascinated these geographers as well, especially the vast, populated, rich regions of India and China. China in particular inspired open admiration in the Arab geographers. Its administration, justice system, and economy all functioned impeccably, according to many of these authors, and everything seemed devoid of corruption. Beyond China and India, especially in the islands of the sea, geographers situated a fabulous world. Some islands abounded in gold or precious stones, while on others fruit trees grew on their own, sparing men the trouble of working the soil. Other islands were inhabited by cannibals, still others by women whose sexual appetites killed the poor sailors who dropped anchor there. In indulging in such fantasies of wondrous creatures and bizarre societies, Muslim geographers perpetuated the traditions of their ancient Greek predecessors. They populated the edges of the world with monstrous beings: headless men with faces on their chests, others with human bodies and dog's heads. There was the country of the Waq-Waq, where one tree bore a strange fruit in the shape of a naked woman. When ripe, the fruit opened its mouth, said "Waq Waq!" and fell; upon bursting on the ground, it gave off a nauseating odor.[12]

Unlike China or India, Europe occupied only a very small place within that vision of the world. The Greek word *Europa*, which in Arabic became *Arūfa*, certainly existed among these geographers: it is found in the tenth century, for example, in Hamdānī and Ibn Khurdādhbih, for whom the term designates the northwest quadrant of the habitable world.[13] But, as André Miquel points out, "except for these old recollections, the concept of Europe is nonexistent."[14] Arab scholars instead divided the world into climates (*iqlīm*): horizontal bands, normally seven of them but sometimes three or five, generally distributed between the equator and the arctic.[15] Each climate had its own characteristics (humidity, heat, and so forth) that determined the nature and behavior of its flora, fauna, and human inhabitants. Like the Greeks before them, the Arab geographers claimed that the climates most propitious for human habitation were those where they themselves lived. In these "central" climates, man could practice agriculture, build cities, and benefit from a physical and mental balance that allowed for intellectual reflection, erudition, and adherence to the true religion.

According to these geographers, things were very different for the unfortunate souls who lived in too hot or too cold a climate. Their agriculture was more rudimentary, their constructions were flimsily made of wood or straw, and the fragility of their health could be clearly discerned by the color of their skin—too dark for those who lived in excessively hot climates, too light for those who lived in the cold countries. The damaging effects of the climate also prevented them from reasoning clearly, depriving them of the benefits of philosophy, science, and the true religion. It was not at all astonishing that so few of them were Muslims!

Of course, the damaging effects of a frigid climate affected peoples other than those of Europe: the Turks especially, whose military feats the geographers admired but whom they portrayed as half-savages. The cold impelled them toward nomadism and war, but it reduced their sexual appetites. The same effects were also found among the Slavs and Franks (*Ifranj*), peoples who inhabited the extreme northwest of the inhabited world. That portrait of barbarians from the north corresponded to that of antiquity, whether Herodotus's Scythians or Tacitus's Germans. Hamdāni (d. 945) based that view on Ptolemy's astronomy. He enumerated the regions of the northwest quadrant of the world: Britain, Galatia, Germania, Italy, Gaul, Puglia, Sicily, the land of the Celts, Hispania, and the land of the Slavs, among others. The inhabitants of these regions are "little inclined to submission, love freedom, weapons, and fatigue, are hostile to peoples of law and order, and given to grand designs."[16] These traits are the effect of the distance from the sun but also of the greater influence of the planets Jupiter and Mars.

Other geographers went even further. Consider, for example, what the great encyclopedist Mas'ūdī (d. 956–957) says in his *Book of Notification and of Verification*:

> The inhabitants of the northern quadrant are those for whom the sun is far from the zenith—increasingly far the farther north they go—such as the Slavs, the Franks, and other nearby nations. Since, because of its distance, the sun has only a weak power over these regions, cold and humidity prevail, and snow and ice rarely disappear from them. The humors have little ardor there; the men are tall in stature, fierce, with crude manners, dull intelligence, halting speech; their complexion is so white that it turns from white to bluish; their skin is thin, their flesh thick; their eyes are also blue, matching the tone of their complexion; their hair is flowing and rust-colored, because of the water vapor. Their religious beliefs are without solidity, because of the nature of the cold and for lack of heat. Those who live farthest to the north are the coarsest, the stupidest, and the most brutish. These characteristics grow more prominent as they move farther away, in a northerly direction, as can be seen among the Turkish tribes that move deep into the northernmost regions. Being very far from the trajectory described by the sun as it rises and sets, they have abundant snow; cold and humidity invade their homes. Their bodies become soft and thick;

the vertebrae of their backs and the bones in their necks are so flexible that they can fire their arrows while twisting their torsos backward as they flee. They are so fleshy that dimples form at the joints; their eyes are small in round faces; the heat rises to their faces when the cold takes hold of their bodies. The cold humors, in fact, produce a great deal of blood and color the complexion, because the cold gathers up the heat and makes it appear on the outside. The men who live sixty some miles above that latitude are the tribes of Gog and Magog. They belong to the sixth climate and are counted among the beasts.[17]

Wherein lay the interest of that description for the Baghdad scholar and his reading public? No doubt it confirmed his sense of religious and cultural superiority: heavenly bodies themselves, especially the sun, procure significant benefits for those who have the good fortune to live in the central climates of the "ecumene," the inhabited world. Lack of heat is the cause of Northerners' peculiar characteristics: blue eyes, red hair, stupidity, and coarseness, and even of the Turks' ability to shoot arrows while turning backward in their saddles. Such is the sad fate that the Arabs escaped by being born in the center of the world. To be sure, it is not possible to speak of a vision of "Europe" here, only of the vision of a vague and vast north, with the borders between Franks, Slavs, and Turks remaining unclear. For Mas'ūdī, these peoples were the neighbors of Gog and Magog, savage nations who, according to the Bible and the Qur'an, would devastate the civilized world at the end of time. We have the impression that these ferocious men of the north are in some sense midway between "normal" men, those who inhabit the central climates, and the monstrous beings— Gog, Magog, cannibals, Waq-Waq—that haunt the periphery of the world. Nevertheless, the remote peoples elicit amazement: Ibn Rusteh, in his *Book of Precious Things* (903), describes whaling activity among the Irish and evokes islands inhabited by geese who feed solely on the flesh of shipwrecked sailors.[18]

The sources for these ideas about the peoples who inhabit the fringes of the earth were often Greek and Persian geographical works, but more recent information can also be found. An embassy left Baghdad in June 921, arriving almost a year later at the king of the Bulgarians on the banks of the Volga. The secretary of the group, Ibn Fadlān, described the journey, the talks, and the customs of the peoples they met: Khwārezmians, Turks, Oghuz, Bashkirs, Pechenegs, Bulgarians, Russians. He describes with astonishment the harsh climate of the Great North, where his beard froze when he left the hammam, and notes the stupor and terror inspired by his first experience of the aurora borealis. Ibn Fadlān has the eye of an ethnographer: for each people he meets, he describes their eating habits, clothing, cleanliness (or most often, lack of cleanliness), marriage customs and sexuality, funeral rites, and, of course, religion. He encounters Turks who worship phallus idols and who explain their belief as follows: "I came out of something similar to this, and I do not know any creator of myself other than it."[19] The Russians have idols sculpted from wooden stakes stuck into the ground, and they offer these idols presents to obtain their favor for trade or war. As for the king of the Bulgarians, he had converted to Islam: Ibn Fadlān lectured his muezzin about the proper way to make the call to prayer and tried in vain to compel Bulgarian women to veil themselves.

Ibn Fadlān's report could only confirm the climatic scheme that relegated the peoples of the north to an inferior status. In that border world, Gog and Magog were not far off. The Bulgarians supposedly told him of their encounter with a giant who belonged to that people: at the mere sight of it, children died and pregnant women miscarried. That giant caught men and strangled them; in the end, the king of the Bulgarians had him hanged, and he showed the grave to Ibn Fadlān. Of the peoples Ibn Fadlān met, he called the Russians "asses who have gone astray," partly because of their idolatry but also because they were "the dirtiest creatures of God."[20] They bathed rarely or not at all; they had sex with their slaves in view of everyone. But his ethnographer's gaze is apparent especially in the detailed description he gives of the funeral of a Russian chief. The people placed the deceased in a temporary grave while all the preparations were being made for his cremation. They erected tents around the grave and selected one of the young slave girls to share her master's death. For ten days, that victim celebrated with the deceased's loved ones, drinking with them and giving herself to all the men. On the tenth day, they built a pyre, on which was placed a boat containing a funeral chamber. They removed the deceased from his grave, dressed him sumptuously, offered him food and drink; they killed animals for him. Finally, they placed his slave next to him; four men held her, and an old woman, known as "the angel of death," stabbed her with a dagger. Then they lit the funeral pyre, and in the space of an hour everything was reduced to ashes. These reports would provide new material for geographical encyclopedias but would change none of the assumptions regarding the barbarians of the north.

In general, however, these peoples of the north occupy little place in the geographers' accounts. The encyclopedists, though they wanted to give an exhaustive description of the inhabited world, had few things to say about northern Europe. Are we to conclude, with Bernard Lewis, that medieval Arabs were lacking in curiosity about the world beyond the *dār al-islām*?[21] Not at all: we have already mentioned the important place occupied by China and India, and Byzantium too merits long descriptions.

Byzantium—*Rūm* in Arabic (literally, "Rome")—was a rival that inspired fear and envy in many Arab authors of the ninth and tenth centuries, at a time when the empire of Constantinople was regaining force and making conquests at the expense of its Muslim neighbors. These authors took an interest in the empire's military might and infrastructure: its networks of fortresses, the organization of its army into *themata*, and its fleet.[22] The capital of Constantinople, which the Arab troops had tried to take in the early decades of the conquest, remained invincible, proud behind its powerful walls. Hārūn Ibn Yahya, a prisoner of war who lived there (probably in about the late ninth century), offers a tableau rich in information, insisting particularly on the sumptuous decorations of the palaces and churches and on the pomp of the processions and rites during feast days, providing as an example a detailed description of the organ played during a banquet. The geographers would repeat that account. Byzantium was an object of anxiety and fascination. They wondered where its financial resources came from: they knew that the land tax was the basis for this wealth but sometimes suspected that the emperor possessed inexhaustible funds resulting from his knowledge of alchemy. In fact, whispered Ibn al-Faqīh in his *Kitāb al-buldān* (*Book of Lands*; ninth century), the emperor had in his treasury sacks of white powder that he turned into gold.[23]

Although Constantinople was the capital of *Rūm*, these geographers were well aware that there was another Rome, the first, in the West. Mas'ūdī points out the importance of that Mediterranean city and traces its history from Julius Caesar to Constantine, listing the emperors. He also describes how Christianity had replaced the cult of idols there. The city became the see of the patriarch, called *bāb*, or "pope."[24] For many authors, the description of the city was tinged with the supernatural: Ibn Khurdādhbih (in his *Kitāb al-masālik wa l-mamālik, Book of Roads and Kingdoms*, written in about 885) provides a description that would be largely adopted (and sometimes expanded) by his successors. He claims that Rome had 12,000 streets, each with 1,223 palaces; there were 95 markets and 40,000 baths (600,000 according to Ibn al-Faqīh in 903). But it is the ascendancy of the church that especially captured Ibn Khurdādhbih's imagination: 1,220 stylite monks were said to live perched on as many columns; there were supposedly 1,200 churches (24,000 according to Ibn al-Faqīh), more than 100,000 bells, 21,000 gold crosses, and so on. The largest of these churches was said to measure 3 kilometers long and was illuminated solely by the carbuncles inserted in the eyes of statues. In the Basilicas of the Apostles Peter and Paul, lamps burned with oil collected in a remarkable manner: the wind blew into a copper weathercock in the shape of a bird, which began to whistle. In response, every thrush in the area gathered a twig from an olive tree and came to deposit it in front of the church.[25]

Europe would occupy a much more important place for Abū 'Abdallāh Muhammad Idrīsī, who in the 1150s composed his *Book of Roger* for Roger II, Norman king of Sicily.[26] Idrīsī's avowed aim was to present an overarching and accurate view of the world. He drew a map of the world, for which the *Book of Roger* was in some sense a detailed commentary (figure 1). He used the texts of previous geographers, his own knowledge of the places he had seen (in Sicily, Spain, and the Maghreb), and also the eyewitness accounts of the travelers and merchants who frequented the Palermitan court, accounts he seems to have collected systematically. Idrīsī was no longer writing from the viewpoint of literary *adab*; he condensed the historical excursus and the descriptions of wonders that he found in his sources. He did not eliminate them completely, however: in

Figure 1. Idrīsī's world map, from a manuscript copied by 'Alī ibn Hasan al-Hūfī al-Qāsimī in Cairo in 1456, now housed in the Bodleian Library in Oxford, UK (MS Pococke 375 fol. 3v–4r). In this illustration, South is at the top and North is at the bottom.

his description of Rome, for example, there are again twelve hundred churches, a large canal made of copper and, in one church, twelve statues of pure gold whose eyes are made of rubies. In describing the churches of Rome, he relied more on Ibn Khurdādhbih than on the prelates in Roger's entourage.

Idrīsī retains the classic structure of the seven climates; he cuts each climate into ten cross-sections, west to east. Within each section, his description follows the traveler on his itinerary, sailing along the coast from port to port, or traveling on the rivers or overland routes. Sometimes he describes the countryside, the farmland, stock breeding, or fishing. He names the cities, some of which (Cordova and Tunis, for example) merit a relatively detailed description, while others are merely qualified as "remarkable" (Clermont) or "pleasant, famous, and very prosperous" (Thessalonica). The information on Europe contained in the *Book of Roger* surpasses by far that of its predecessors. It is possible, for example, to construct an itinerary from Mainz to Utrecht, or from Cologne to Ratisbon (Regensburg), since Idrīsī provides the name of each stopover city along the way. He gives abundant, well-understood information on Sicily and southern Italy. For the rest of Europe, his information is uneven; along with Henri Bresc and Annliese Nef, we may be surprised, for example, at the paucity of information on northern Italy.[27] No doubt some of his informants were Norman merchants, who provided him with knowledge of the coasts of Brittany (along with a poor opinion of the Bretons). Normandy occupies a place of choice in the description. Hence Bayeux is an "agreeable city, splendid and prosperous," whereas Paris is supposedly a city "of mediocre size."[28]

The *Book of Roger* remains unique in geography: written in Arabic at the court of a Norman king, it blends the Arab geographical tradition with information collected from interviews with European travelers and merchants. It is testimony to the cosmopolitan character of the court of the kings of Sicily—the patrons of Latin, Greek, and Arab scholars—that this work could be published. But that cosmopolitanism had its limits: the book was not translated in the Middle Ages and therefore exerted no influence on Europeans' knowledge of geography.

The World Seen from Latin Europe in the Twelfth Century: Geography and History According to Hugh of Saint Victor

The Greek geographers had made Delphi the navel (*omphalos*) of the world; the Arab geographers placed the center of the world sometimes in Baghdad, sometimes in the holy cities of Arabia. The European geographers of the Middle Ages, by contrast, never claimed to inhabit the center of the world. Beholden to the ancient traditions, they were aware that they lived on the northwest fringe of the earth. The center was Jerusalem, as can be seen on many medieval world maps. These geographers divided the world into three continents surrounded by the Ocean Sea: Asia, to the east, occupied half the habitable surface of the earth; Africa occupied the southwest quadrant; and Europe, the northwest.

Let us look at the world as seen from Paris in about 1130. Hugh of Saint Victor probably wrote his *Descriptio mappe mundi* shortly after 1130,[29] with the aim of teaching the art of reading a world map. A native of Flanders, Hugh entered the monastery of the Canons Regular of Saint Victor, just outside Paris, in about 1110 and stayed there until his death in 1141. Not content to produce a mere catalogue of the knowledge of geography he had learned from books, he tried to present clearly and systematically the different toponyms. His text is both traditional and innovative. It is traditional in that his vision of the world differs very little from that of Isidore and Bede, the great authors of the seventh and eighth centuries who had described the world with knowledge drawn from their readings of the ancient geographers, the Bible, and the church fathers. But Hugh displays an interest in pedagogy that these authors did not have: his *Descriptio* is in some sense a scholarly manual, showing us how, in the Paris of 1130, a map of the world could be used to teach geography. Neither of the two twelfth-century manuscripts that contain the *Descriptio* preserves the map that Hugh was annotating. Another map has been identified, however, also produced in northern France in the twelfth century, similar to the one used by Hugh (reproduced in figure 2, with a schematic rendering in figure 3).[30]

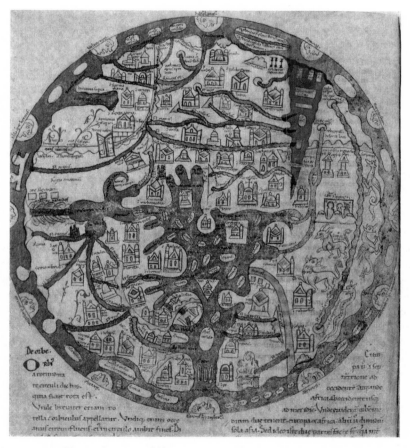

Figure 2. World map from a twelfth-century manuscript of Isidore of Seville's *Etymologies*. In this illustration, East is at the top and West is at the bottom. Munich, Bayerische Staatsbibliothek (MS CLM 10058 fol. 154v). Reprinted by permission of the Bibliothèque Nationale de France.

Figure 3. Schematic drawing based on world map in figure 2 from plate II of P. Gautier Dalché, *La 'Descriptio mappe mundi' de Hugues de Saint-Victor* (Turnhout, Belgium: Brepols, 1988). Reprinted by permission of the Institut d'Études Augustiniennes.

The organization of this text probably also reflects the order in which Hugh presented his geography lessons. He explains that he will begin with the description of the ocean, the twelve winds, and the islands found in the ocean. The map of the world located in the Bayerische Staatsbibliothek in Munich makes it clear that Hugh began from the outside. The ocean, in the tradition of ancient geography, surrounds the habitable world, and the names of the twelve winds are marked around it. And in fact, having explained the position of the ocean and the names of the winds, Hugh goes on to list the islands found in the ocean and in the different seas, offering a brief description of some of the islands and their inhabitants. He then explains the division of the earth: "The world is customarily divided into three parts, namely, Asia, Africa, and Europe, though there is a great inequality of size among the three. But anyone wishing to know the regions of these three parts [of the world] or their provinces and divisions should first know the different mountains, rivers, and streams that separate the regions and provinces. In Asia, which contains almost half the earth [in size], the rivers and streams are the following. . . ."[31] An enumeration of the rivers of the different regions of Asia follows: it is easy to imagine the gesture of the teacher, tracing with his hand the course of rivers on the map. Next, he does the same for the mountains of Asia. The map of the world tries to impose order, to make the world knowable, comprehensible; Hugh's reading of the map does likewise. The world is divided into three "parts." (Hugh does not use the word "continent.") Each of the three parts is divided into regions by mountains and rivers, natural boundaries created by God. The pedagogical approach is clear: it is first necessary to know these natural divisions before attempting to learn the names of the cities or kingdoms, which are human creations that follow the logic of natural geography delimited by the rivers and mountains. And so Hugh goes on to list the names of the "provinces and cities of Asia." Then he enumerates the different seas between the continents, before turning to "the part of the world called Africa" and finally, to Europe, "the third part of the earth."

A student who had attentively followed that geography lesson would have been able to say, for example, that the city of Echbathanis is located in India, on the banks of the Ganges, that the Cretan Sea is situated between the island of Crete and Alexandria, that Europe is divided in two by the Alps, and that Noah's ark came to rest on Mount Ararat in Armenia. But what is the aim of Hugh's pedagogy? What is its place in the curriculum of the school of Saint Victor? In the prologue to the *Descriptio*, Hugh declares, "we propose in this work not to draw the map of the world but to describe it, that is, to show not the things and images of things but rather their meanings."[32] Geographical knowledge is useful for understanding the names of places encountered in reading the Bible and the ancient authors. Note the difference from Arab geography. The geography of Hugh (and of other Latin authors) was produced in and for a monastic environment; it was based on the ancient authors and the Bible and served as a tool for the monk or canon, whose principal concern was to understand his biblical and patristic readings. Arab geography, by contrast, was produced in the court of the caliphs and other Muslim sovereigns; it was an integral part of the *adab*, the education of the worldly man, the man of culture. It relied on the same Greek tradition and incorporated information from the biblical and Qur'anic tradition, but it also incorporated information gleaned from administrative dispatches, travel narratives, and the reports of merchants. The aim was to accumulate the knowledge necessary for a man of the court. The case of Idrīsī (a contemporary of Hugh) was slightly different. Idrīsī, like Hugh, used a map as his starting point; both of their texts were in some sense presented as a commentary on a world map. But the result was quite different: Idrīsī wished to grasp the world *in itself*, whereas, in Hugh's view, geography was a science in the service of exegesis and theology.

For Hugh, before one can understand the spiritual meaning of Noah's ark (to which he devotes a treatise), one is well advised to know how to situate Noah and his ark in time (through the study of history) and space (through geography). Geography and history are very useful auxiliary sciences, which constitute a modest but important part of education. To understand a map of the world is to comprehend a portion of the logical organization that God gave to the universe. Hugh and the other Latin geographers have little or nothing to say about the Muslim inhabitants of Asia and Africa, partly because their knowledge was based primarily on the works of ancient geographers, written before the rise of Islam. There were travel narratives, written by pilgrims, merchants, and others who traveled to Islamic countries, but the information they provided was not incorporated into the maps of the world or into the geographical texts.

Hugh drew information from the works of previous Christian authors, who themselves had taken them from ancient authors, the Bible, and the writings of the church fathers. The names of the cities and regions (when they are not distorted) are identical to those found in fourth-century authors, as if the intervening eight centuries had changed nothing. From time to time Hugh does provide a new detail: he places Egypt in Africa and not Asia, trusting his map of the world rather than the textual authorities. He cites a few names of cities that are not found in the ancient authors: Maroch (Marrakech) in Africa, Bogdada (Baghdad) and Toflit (Tiflis) in Asia. The king of Georgia, an ally of the Crusaders, had conquered the city of Tiflis in 1122, and the map of the world therefore included some relatively recent information. Hugh seems to have made an effort to update his knowledge, as is evident for Europe: he names several European cities whose criterion for inclusion seems to have been their importance in the twelfth century. But Europe, including Gaul, which he describes in detail, is full of errors: the Garonne flows into the Loire, Toulouse is placed in Brittany, and so on. Hugh's view of the world does not correspond to reality.

This is even clearer in his descriptions of the Far East, where he combines outdated information, distorted names, and fantastic details. The divisions (ethnic and other) are obsolete, dating back to the time of the ancient authors, indirect sources for the world map. Hugh's attitude toward knowledge is very different from our own: for him, the ancient authors are trustworthy a priori, and ethnic groups are relatively stable over the course of time. Toponyms are sometimes distorted and places difficult to identify. Finally, everything is colored by the fantastic: like his Arab colleagues, faithful to the ancient and medieval tradition, Hugh populates the eastern and southern edges of the world with bizarre creatures. In reference to India, for example, he declares:

> In these regions are many marvelous monsters, if what is said is true. There are Pygmies, men a cubit tall, who live solely on [the sight of?] different colors. There are enormous bulls. There are Centaurs, half-man, half-horse. There are also Icthyophages [fish eaters], who eat eels thirty feet long. There are elephants and unicorns. There are midgets. Between the Coaspim River and the Red Sea, there are Himantipodes, who walk with their feet upside down, and Manticores, ferocious quadrupeds who have the heads and faces of women. There are Cenophales, who have men's bodies and dog's heads. There are Blemii, who have [men's] bodies with no heads and eyes on their thoraxes, and Monopods, who have only one eye and only one foot apiece.[33]

This passage tells us a great deal about the medieval culture drawn from books, even though Hugh expresses reservations, beginning his description with "if what is said is true." Yet he populates Africa with dragons and other monsters without the slightest hesitation. In the face of the rich menagerie haunting the ancient poems, which were still read in the Middle Ages, his reflex is not to call into doubt the existence of centaurs or sphinxes but rather to push them back to the remote edges of the habitable world. Ancient "scientific" authorities (such as Pliny the Elder) had already populated the Orient with these monsters; they would live on in the imaginations of sixteenth-century explorers, who baptized the new places they discovered with names borrowed from imaginary geography: Brazil, Thule, Amazonia. Jacques Le Goff writes that, for medieval Europe, "the Indian Ocean was a mental horizon, . . . the place where its dreams freed themselves from repression."[34] The Orient was the site of the bizarre and the unusual. It was therefore altogether normal that the worst of heresies surfaced in the Orient and that the decadent Orientals, not inclined toward rationality, embraced Islam.

The *Descriptio* is also filled with biblical names: Gog and Magog are relegated to an island in the ocean at the far northern end of the world. For Hugh, as for several other authors, the earthly paradise of Eden was located at the eastern extremity of the habitable world.[35] And he indicates the place where Noah's ark set down. His description of western Asia contains many biblical toponyms.

It would be all too easy to make fun of the paltry geographical knowledge of that Parisian canon—or, on the contrary, to excuse him by recalling that he had only inaccurate sources at his disposal. But what matters here is not the accuracy of his view of the world but the fact that he had one. For Hugh, the world was knowable, orderly, logical. Its natural divisions (continents, then regions delimited by mountains and rivers) were rational. They reflected supreme Reason, God as creator of the universe. The world's human divisions (peoples, cities) closely followed that natural logic, because human logic can understand (at least imperfectly) the divine logic that gives order to the world. Although in this text Hugh does not make explicit the moral and theological difference between East and West, he does so in his *Noah's Ark*.

Hugh of Saint Victor's geography is imbued with history: the places mentioned are often those that played an important historical role. Conversely, his conception of history is very geographical. He imagines a slow progression of the key historical events from the East (where God created Adam and Eve in earthly paradise) to the Holy Land, the location of the life and death of Christ, then to the West, where the final drama must unfold:

Divine Providence seems to have arranged everything so that what came to pass at the origin of time should occur in the East, as at the beginning of the world, and that then, as the course of time approached its end, all events should descend toward the West. We therefore recognize the approach of the end of days inasmuch as the course of things has already reached the ends of the world. The first man, created in the Garden of Eden, was thus placed in the East. . . . Similarly, after the Flood, the origin of empires and head of the world was located in the East, among the Assyrians, the Chaldeans, and the Medes. It then came to the Greeks. Finally, toward the end of time, supreme power passed to the West, to the Romans, living at the extremities of the world. The sequence of events thus follows a straight line descending from East to West.[36]

God is the supreme historian, the sublime geographer: he organizes space and time. For Hugh, history is not merely a disorderly and arbitrary succession of events. It is a drama orchestrated by its divine Author/Director, acted out on the stage he has created (the world), a drama full of meaning for any informed reader.

For the Christian and for the Muslim, history has a beginning (the creation), a middle, and an end (the Apocalypse and Last Judgment). God is the author of history; everything that takes place therefore reflects divine will. The Christian (or Muslim) author tries to understand and explain the unfolding of history, placing particular emphasis on the development of the "true" religion (Islam or Christianity) and its expansion in the world. He must also account for the success (temporary and illusory, he claims) of those who embrace religious "errors" (heretics, pagans, Jews, "Trinitarians," "Saracens"). Here Hugh attempts to do so by referring to a progression both temporal and spatial. History begins in the Far East (with the Creation) and "descends" to the West. For Hugh, the end of time had nearly arrived by the twelfth century, since the West was now at the center of history. That was a way of marginalizing the East, now Muslim. Of course, in biblical times Palestine was the center of the world, but now its true dramatic (if not geographical) center was located in Europe.

Hugh provides a particularly clear example of the *translatio* from East to West, but he is not alone: many medieval authors speak of the *translatio imperii*, the transfer of empire to the West's benefit, and also of the *translatio studii*, the transfer of knowledge. The European West, though at the margins of the world, was said to be the heir, the new "decentered center," of legitimate power, spirituality, and learning.

The geographical culture of the Islamic countries and of the Latin world drew from the same sources but took very different forms. Authors such as Mas'ūdī in the tenth century and Hugh of Saint Victor in twelfth-century Paris knew how to manipulate their geographical knowledge to assert the centrality of their culture and religion and to marginalize those of the Other. At the same time, their Arab and European contemporaries forged ideologies to justify the conquests being made at that other's expense.

CHAPTER 2

CONQUEST AND ITS JUSTIFICATIONS

Jihad, Crusade, *Reconquista*

THROUGHOUT THE MIDDLE AGES and well beyond, religion, whether Christian or Muslim, inspired or justified military conquests. Muslims waged jihad against the Christian infidel, *Rūm,* or the *Ifranj*: Christians called for Crusade against Saracens and for the reconquest of territories fallen to the infidels. But both sides also used the logic and vocabulary of holy war against internal enemies, claiming that victory came from God: for example, in the struggle of the "Orthodox" against "heretics" or "schismatics"; between the Sunni Seljuks and the Fatimid Shiites; between the Byzantines and the Normans; or between the papacy and the Hohenstaufen. Although the ideology of holy war served to justify or celebrate one victory or another, let us make no mistake: religion was often an a posteriori explanation for a conflict that had many other causes. These conflicts should not be viewed as avatars of a "clash of civilizations" between "Islam" and "the West." On the battlefield, on the Iberian Peninsula, in Palestine, in Sicily, or on the Maghrebian coast, Christians often allied with Muslims and vice versa, facing adversaries who were themselves mixed.

Yet religion was both an important motivation and an essential justification for war in the Middle Ages. I shall examine various examples, privileging two types of texts: chronicles and legal documents. Let us consider first the Muslim conquest, then the various forms of Christian conquest.

WAR AND CONQUEST IN ISLAM: FROM MUHAMMAD TO THE ABBASID CALIPHATE

The first century of Islam saw the astonishingly rapid conquest of an enormous part of the known world. From the Hegira of Muhammad in 622 to his death in 632, the Muslims were able to impose their dominion through conversion and conquest of the entire Arabian Peninsula. The caliphs, the Prophet's successors, conquered Syria, Iraq, Persia, and Egypt. Then they turned to North Africa, with the mass conversion of Berber tribes followed by the conquest, between

711 and 718, of most of the Iberian Peninsula. At the same time, Muslim troops conquered territories in Transoxiana (Afghanistan) and on the banks of the Indus.

Many factors account for these conquests—in particular, the political and religious unity of the Arab tribes and the weakness of the two great rival empires, Persia and Byzantium. The subjects of these empires were not inclined to fight to defend their masters; that was especially the case for the Monophysite Christians of Syria and Egypt, who were persecuted as heretics by Constantinople and offered little resistance to the Muslims. In negotiations during the siege of a city, Muslim conquerors guaranteed freedom of worship to the residents and offered them judicial autonomy, in exchange for the recognition of Muslim authority and the payment of an annual tribute. A century after the Hegira, the new Muslim empire extended from the Indus to the Atlantic: of the two empires that had dominated the Mediterranean world and the Middle East for centuries, Persia was completely integrated, as was a good part of Byzantium, though Constantinople still resisted all attempts at conquest.

Had not God shown his preference in granting Islam these astounding victories? A seventh-century Muslim, it seems, found it easy to declare to a Christian monk that "it is a sign of God's love for us and pleasure with our faith that he has given us dominion over all regions and all peoples."[1] Sophronius, the patriarch of Jerusalem, who had to surrender that city to Caliph 'Umar I in 638, complained that the Saracens boasted they had conquered the whole earth.[2] The meteoric rise of Islam appeared truly miraculous to Muslim authors: a handful of desert warriors had vanquished the richest and most populous parts of the most powerful empires in the world.

The Muslim was not supposed to force the "people of the book" (*ahl al-kitāb*, that is, Jews and Christians) to convert; he could, however, oblige them to recognize the superiority and the suzerainty of Muslim power. The Qur'an (9:29) is explicit: "Fight against such of those to whom the Scriptures were given as believe neither in God nor the Last Day, who do not forbid what God and His apostle [Muhammad] have forbidden, and do not embrace the true Faith, until they pay tribute [*jizya*] out of hand and are utterly subdued." The Muslim community was enjoined to conduct war and submit non-Muslims to its power. It was not to compel them to embrace Islam but only to obtain their submission to Muslim power and make them pay the *jizya*, a specific tribute or tax that constituted one of the principal legal obligations of the non-Muslim in Islamic territories. That war was part of the jihad, or effort on the path toward God, which every Muslim was supposed to make.[3] But according to the Qur'an, it was only one element: of the thirty-five occurrences of the word *jihād* and related terms in the holy book, only ten refer to war.[4] Usually, that "effort on the path toward God" was made by peaceful means. The Qur'an summons the Muslims to conduct the "greater jihad" against the infidels through preaching.[5] As Alfred Morabia has noted, all mentions of war refer to Muhammad's expeditions against specific enemies; no passage in the holy book speaks of war to spread Islam beyond the peninsula.[6] The Qur'an displays ambivalence toward war. Some passages exhort Muslims to spread the faith solely by peaceful means, while others authorize defensive war when the Muslims are attacked, and still others encourage war to submit the infidel enemies to Muslim power. Finally, many verses indicate disagreements within the early Muslim community regarding the use of violence, beginning in Muhammad's lifetime: some Muslims undertook an offensive expedition, whereas others refused to participate.[7]

But the view of jihad evolved in the generation following the death of the Prophet, a generation that saw great conquests, doctrinal quarrels with Judaism and Christianity, and, at the same time, the formation of Muslim doctrine, especially through the setting down in writing of the traditions, or Hadith. These traditions reflect a great diversity of viewpoints on jihad, as on many other subjects. Some of the compilers provide a particularly bellicose view of relations between the Muslims and the world beyond Islam. Muhammad is said to be not merely the prophet sent to the Arabs; his mission is universal in character. Jihad would supposedly consist primarily of expanding the domain of Islam (*dār al-islām*) by force of arms, until the whole world recognized its suzerainty. That gave rise to the distinction between the *dār al-islām*, the territories subject to Muslim power, and the *dār al-kufr*, the realm of infidelity, also called *dār al-harb*, the realm of war, territories that had not yet been won over to Islam but that must be sooner or later. That distinction, absent from the Qur'an, took root during the time of the great conquests.[8] As for the apparent contradictions in the Qur'an regarding war in the service of Islam, commentators resolved them by contextualizing the revelations, which were supposedly received in very specific situations: the passages counseling nonviolence, they claimed, were revealed at a time when the Muslim community of Mecca was weak and could not forcibly resist. The more militant passages came from the Medina period, when the Muslims asserted their power, and they abrogated the previous revelations, establishing the new norms that were to govern the community from then on. That interpretation, as Reuven Firestone has shown, was produced during Islam's rapid expansion, when the militant view was seeking firm support in the Qur'anic text.[9]

The theory and the practice of jihad continued to change, reflecting the preoccupations and needs of the Muslim community. Spiritual for the most part during Muhammad's Mecca period, more bellicose after the Hegira—when Muhammad became the leader of Medina and conducted military actions against pagan and Jewish tribes on the peninsula—jihad assumed a completely different dimension during the great conquests: it became an appeal to submit the earth as a whole to the power of God's religion. The divisions that marked the *dār al-islām* during the *fitnas* (civil wars) of 680 and 750 and the increased resistance of certain adversaries (especially the Byzantines) would lead to a further evolution in the concept. Jihad became primarily defensive: it was necessary to protect the community against the incursions of enemies, whether Byzantines, Turks (not yet Islamized), or "heterodox" currents within Islam.

Of course, those who felt most threatened by the Byzantine expansion tried to revive the sense of an obligation to jihad against the infidel. That was the case, for example, of Sayf al-Dawla, sultan of Aleppo from 945 until his death in 967, who employed a whole team of preachers. "It is you who should lead the offensive, not the infidels," exclaimed one of them, Qadi Tarsūsi.[10] But these appeals, coming from a border region that would be retaken by Byzantium between 974 and 987, only underscored that the time of the great conquests was over and that the war against the infidel was a priority only for the zones directly threatened. In the marches of the *dār al-islām*, jihad was also often invoked to justify raids in which religious motivations combined with the lure of booty. The most important element, because it was the most lucrative, may have been the slave trade: these raids on land or sea supplied captives to be sold everywhere in the Muslim world.

The "external" jihad, the fight to conquer the *dār al-harb*, was only rarely considered obligatory for Muslims. It was, however, meritorious, and some historians claim that jihad is the "monasticism" of Islam.[11] Consider the complex development of the term *ribat*, which originally meant preparation for battle and later came to designate fortified posts, usually near borders with the *dār al-harb*, where the *mujahidin* could earn glory and accumulate wealth by waging defensive or offensive war against the infidel.[12]

It is difficult to know how the Muslim conquerors of the seventh and eighth centuries perceived these wars, since most of the Arab sources that relate them date from the ninth century. It is clear that the conquests of that later time, such as Sicily by the Aghlabids of Ifrīqiya (present-day Tunisia), undertaken in 827, assumed a religious dimension.[13] But that did not prevent alliances between the Aghlabids and the cities of the southern Italian coast such as Amalfi—which discreetly remained neutral during the conquest of Sicily—or Naples, which allied itself with the Aghlabids against the Lombard prince of Benevento.[14]

In Spain, the accounts of the conquest—from the landing of the Berber general Tariq in 711 to the taking of Narbonne in 719 by Governor al-Samh ibn Malik al-Khawlānī—are all late texts: they betray a nostalgia for the heroic age of the great expeditions.[15] By 719, the advance into Europe was running out of steam. In 721, al-Samh besieged Toulouse but was attacked by Eudes, count of Aquitaine, who killed the governor and put the Muslim troops to flight. After that, confrontations were common, but they consisted of raids more than attempted conquests. The best known is that of 732: having pillaged Bordeaux and Poitiers, Muslims troops were attacked and dispersed by the forces of Charles Martel, and Governor ʿAbd al-Rahmān al-Ghāfiqī met his death. That Battle of Tours (also called the Battle of Poitiers), though its importance has been wildly exaggerated in historiography, did mark a serious setback for the Hispano-Arabs and an important milestone in the rise to power of the

Carolingian family. It in no way put an end to the raids in Gaul, however. They continued for more than a century, interrupted by truces or periods of calm.

A closer look indicates that, despite chronicles that readily speak of glorious jihad or the defense of Christianity, here too alliances were often established between Christians and Muslims. Count Eudes of Aquitaine feared his powerful neighbor to the north, Charles Martel, as much as he did the Andalusian governors. He therefore formed an alliance with a Berber chief, Munuza, installed in a castle in the Pyrenees not far from Puigcerdá. It is clear that what linked Eudes and Munuza was that both were trying to resist the power of a mighty coreligionist, while seeking to avoid an invasion of the "infidel" from across the Pyrenees. In vain: Munuza met his death at the hands of Cordovan troops in 729, and Charles Martel took advantage of his Poitiers victory in 732 to annex Aquitaine. This kind of alliance was common in the following decades, when Cordova tried to secure its power one way or another over the peninsula. A whole series of Muslim rebels on the northern peninsula crossed the Pyrenees to ally themselves with Charlemagne or his son Louis the Pious. The Banu Qasi of Aragon had an agreement with the Christians of Pamplona, and the rebels of Merida and Toledo frequently appealed to the kings of the Asturias and to the Frankish kings. As for the Franks, those who wished to free themselves from the tutelage of Louis the Pious and Charles the Bald naturally made deals with Cordova.

Between the mid-eighth and the mid-ninth centuries, four major powers asserted their authority around the Mediterranean: the Abbasid caliphate, the Byzantine Empire, the Umayyad emirate, and the Carolingian Empire. The Abbasids, who were fighting Byzantium in Anatolia and Syria and who saw the emirate of Cordova as the offshoot of an illegitimate regime they had suppressed in the East, turned to the Carolingians, their natural allies because they were enemies of these same Byzantines and Umayyads. Pepin the Short, therefore, sent an embassy to Baghdad in 765. It was probably well received by Caliph al-Mansūr, who sent back a mission with gifts for the king in 768. Charlemagne sent an embassy to Hārūn al-Rashīd in 797, and in 802 an Abbasid delegation arrived in Aix-la-Chapelle laden with gifts, the most cumbersome of them an elephant named Abū al-ʿAbbas, who did not fail to impress witnesses. In 831, Caliph al-Maʾmūn sent another delegation to Louis the Pious in Thionville.[16] Although these exchanges did not come to much, they do indicate that geopolitical interests, for the Carolingians and for the Abbasids, were much more important than any religious solidarity.[17]

On a more or less regular basis, the Umayyad emirs and caliphs of Cordova waged jihad year after year against the infidels of the north: their aim seems to have been booty and prestige more than the conquest of territories. These wars against the small northern kingdoms continued sporadically under the caliphs, allowing them to impose humiliating terms on the sovereigns of these kingdoms, which cast into relief the caliphs' theoretical suzerainty over their territories. True, the chamberlain al-Mansūr b. Abī 'Āmir (977–1002), under the theoretical authority of the caliph, invoked the ideology of jihad in order to conduct several devastating expeditions against the Christian states. The most notorious is the one that took him to Santiago de Compostela: the general brought back the church bells, both booty and a symbol of the humiliation he was able to inflict on the infidel enemies.[18] But these raids, catastrophic though they were for their victims, were short-lived; al-Mansūr seems to have used them primarily to assert his power in Cordova, and he did not try to establish a Muslim presence in the devastated territories. Furthermore, nothing indicates that this belligerent attitude toward the Christians led to a change of attitude toward the Mozarab *dhimmis* of the caliphate; Christian contingents remained an essential part of his army.

THE ARAB CONQUESTS SEEN BY EUROPEAN CHRONICLERS IN THE SEVENTH TO NINTH CENTURIES

How did the Christians of Europe react to the Muslim conquests? From Constantinople to Jarrow Monastery in Northumbria, various authors tried to explain as best they could the causes and consequences of the "Saracen" conquest. Let us examine in particular those works by chroniclers who tried to insert these conquests into a Christian view of history. That is, if God is the author of history, if He is just, why did He allow these "infidel" invaders to seize so much territory at the expense of the Christians? This was not the first time the question had arisen. In the fourth and fifth centuries, "barbarian" (especially Germanic) peoples, whether pagans or Arians, had conquered a good part of the Western Roman Empire. The Eastern Empire (what historians call the Byzantine Empire) had to endure the assault of many enemies: Slavs, Avars, and Persians. It was always hoped that these infidels would be defeated or would convert to Christianity. In the end, these hopes were often realized: most of the Slavic and Germanic invaders eventually joined the church.

It was from that point of view that some Christian authors presented the wave of "Saracen" invaders: as a scourge sent by God to punish the Christians for their sins, but a scourge that was not fundamentally different from previous attacks. The *Chronicle of Fredegar* (about 658), the very first Latin chronicle to mention the Arab victory over the Byzantines, describes the invasions in semiapocalyptic terms: astrologists warned Emperor Heraclius of his imminent defeat at the hands of a circumcised race; he opened the mythical north gates (built by Alexander the Great), to release a flood of barbarians from the north on the Saracens, but to no avail.[19]

For Bede (about 673–735), a monk in the Jarrow Monastery in Northumbria, the Saracens were a distant and vague threat.[20] In his *Ecclesiastical History of the English People*, in which he recounts the triumphant history of the growth of British Christianity and celebrates the lives of the monks, the distant incursions of non-Christian warriors on the European continent warrant only brief mentions, as a few small dark clouds on the horizon. Bede nevertheless noted the appearance, in the year 729, of two comets presaging the arrival of the barbarian invaders, before adding, "at this time a terrible plague of Saracens ravaged Gaul with cruel bloodshed and not long afterwards they received the due reward of their impiety [*perfidia*] in the same kingdom."[21] Some historians have suggested that Bede is alluding here to the defeat of 'Abd al-Rahmān al-Ghāfiqī by Charles Martel's forces in 732, but it is more likely an allusion to the Battle of Toulouse (721), in which Eudes, duke of Aquitaine, defeated Emir al-Samh. The Saracen incursion was a "terrible calamity" reminiscent of the ordeals and punishments of the Hebrews in the Old Testament, followed by a reversal that proved Christian superiority in a satisfying manner. In addition, Bede explains that the Saracens were punished for their *perfidia*, a word that other authors of the time generally used to designate religious error, whether pagan, Jewish, or heretical (though on occasion it could mean "treachery" without any religious connotations). It seems they were punished more for their religious error than for their devastating incursions into Christian Gaul. In reality, for Bede, the Saracens' brutality was probably the direct consequence of their *perfidia*. After all, his *Ecclesiastical History* speaks of other groups of *perfidi* who waged war relentlessly until their conversion: the residents of Kent before the arrival of Augustine of Canterbury, the Angles, the Picts, and others. In fact, in a Europe continually ravaged by war and invasions, the Saracens were only one group of infidel intruders among others. Christian European authors proved to be largely incurious about the religion of these invaders, whether Saracens, Vikings, or something else. They all seemed to be part of the terrible ordeals God was inflicting on His people, but no one had the sense that their religious beliefs and practices merited investigation, much less that they were the slightest bit legitimate.

The Saracens' advantage over other distant invaders, from the standpoint of a monk and scholar such as Bede, was that it was possible to learn about them by consulting the Bible. It is in his biblical commentaries that he appears aware of the scope and importance of the Saracen invasions. Genesis (16:12) describes Ishmael as a "wild man" with his "hand . . . against every man." Like a number of his contemporary Eastern brothers, Bede saw that as a transparent allusion to the Saracen conquests: "And here now is his hand against every man and the hand of every man against him, while they [the descendants of Ishmael] impose his authority over the entire length of Africa and occupy most of Asia and a part of Europe, in hatred and hostility toward all."[22]

From Constantinople, where Theophanes wrote his chronicle in about 815, things looked rather different. It was now clear that the new Muslim masters of the Middle East were there to stay, and it was therefore necessary to explain their successes within the context of Christian history. Theophanes devoted a brief biographical sketch to Muhammad, "the leader and false prophet of the Saracens."[23] He describes the marriage of Muhammad to the widow Khadīja, and his travels in Palestine in search of the writings of Jews and Christians. Muhammad had an epileptic seizure that aggrieved Khadīja, and he consoled her in these terms: "I keep seeing a vision of a certain angel called Gabriel, and being unable to bear his sight, I faint and fall down." Khadīja sought advice from a "certain monk living there, a friend of hers (who had been exiled for his depraved doctrine)."[24] That heretical monk—originating, perhaps, from the Muslim traditions concerning two Christians close to Muhammad, Waraqa and Bahira—explained to her that Muhammad was truly a prophet, to whom the angel Gabriel was manifesting himself in visions. After that excellent beginning, his "heresy" was soon spread by force. Muhammad, says Theophanes, promised all who fell while fighting the enemy a paradise full of sensual delights: food, drink, sex. He recounted "other things full of profligacy and stupidity."[25]

Fully aware of the religious motivations behind the Muslim conquests, Theophanes characterizes Islam as a heresy combining Jewish and Christian elements; later, he presents Mecca as the place of the Saracens' "blasphemy."[26] He is no less clear about the reasons why God allowed these Muslim heretics to conquer vast territories. It was because Heraclius embraced the Monothelite heresy (according to which Christ had only a single, unified will, rather than two distinct wills, one human, one divine) that the Christians began to lose their territories in favor of the Arabs. That disgrace was particularly tragic in that, in Theophanes' eyes, Heraclius had been the champion of Orthodoxy, the one who had crushed Constantinople's Avar and Persian enemies and recaptured the True Cross from them. God and the Virgin had watched over Heraclius and guaranteed his success, until the day the emperor inexplicably became a heretic, at which time they abandoned him to the Arab invaders. Moreover, if Heraclius had allowed himself to be drawn into the nets of heresy, the fault lay with the Syrian Monophysites.[27] How could the pillaging of Syria by the Arab armies be anything but a divine punishment, just and terrible?

In Latin Europe, by contrast, the Latin chroniclers said nothing about the religious dimension of the Muslim conquest. They continued to represent the Muslims as scourges sent by God to punish them for their sins and as formidable military adversaries, but *not* as religious adversaries. For the Carolingian chroniclers, the Goths lost Spain because of their sins, and it was quite natural that the hegemony over their former territory (Septimania, Catalonia) had passed over to the Franks. The *Chronicon moissiacense* presents the Arab conquest of Spain as punishment for the sins of the Visigoth king Witiza.[28] Nevertheless, whether they were reporting the sack of Benevento or the victory of Charles Martel in Poitiers, the chroniclers have nothing to say about the religious beliefs or practices of these "Saracens."[29] The same is true, in the tenth century, for Liutprand of Cremona's description of the depredations perpetrated by the Saracens of Fraxinetum.[30]

In the ninth century, many authors were preoccupied with the Aghlabid conquest of Sicily, then with the incursions on the Italian peninsula. But ecclesiastics also expressed the idea that the incursions of the "infidels" were a punishment sent by God against "bad Christians." That was the perspective of Adon, archbishop of Vienna, and of Pope John VIII.[31] These "Saracens" or "Arabs" were often called "pirates," "thieves," or "looters." Terms of opprobrium, no doubt, but ones that were applied to many Christians as well, which suggests these were small armed bands rather than disciplined armies.

At the same time, other texts speak of alliances between Christian princes and Muslim leaders. When Muslim troops sacked the city of Benevento, the soldiers of Emperor Louis II (855–875) portrayed the Saracens as avengers sent by God against the Beneventines, who had taken the emperor captive.[32] When Pope John VIII called for unity as a way to counter the depredations of the "infidels," it was in part to assert his influence in southern Italy. Naples and Amalfi therefore preferred to ally themselves with the Aghlabids of Tunisia and Sicily, despite the spiritual threats from Rome.[33] On the shifting borders between Byzantium and its Muslim neighbors, a number of Arab and Turkish leaders integrated the Byzantine elite, even as some members of the provincial Byzantine elite were forming alliances with their Muslim neighbors or suzerains.[34] The examples could be multiplied: people complained of the incursions of the "infidel Saracens" when they were the victims of their attacks, but that in no way prevented alliances between Christian and Muslim princes.

THE CRUSADE OF THE CHRONICLERS

Until the eleventh century, confrontations between Europeans and Arabs had usually taken place on European soil. But then the situation began to change: the Pisans and Genoese conducted pillaging expeditions in North Africa; then came the Christian conquest of Mediterranean islands such as Sicily, which the Normans conquered between 1061 and 1091; and then the First Crusade, launched in 1095, which culminated in the taking of Jerusalem in July 1099 and the formation of the Latin states in the East—the kingdom of Jerusalem, the county of Tripoli, the principality of Antioch, and the county of Edessa. We shall see in chapter 3 how the European leaders of these states imposed their power on a majority Muslim Arabophone peasantry. At this point, let us examine how the chroniclers of the Crusade justified that expedition.

It should be pointed out, first, that the troops who captured Jerusalem in 1099 were not aware that they were participating in a "Crusade"; it was not until the thirteenth century that canonists explicitly used the term *crociata*.[35] Contemporaries linked their expedition to a pilgrimage: they called it *iter* (journey), *via* (way), or *peregrinatio* (pilgrimage); the soldiers were usually *peregrini* (pilgrims), sometimes *cruce signati* (marked by the cross, or "Crusaders," hence the later term "Crusade").[36] In fact, when Pope Urban II launched his appeal in Clermont in 1095, he presented the expedition as an armed pilgrimage and offered participants the same indulgences that were granted to pilgrims going to Jerusalem. The vow to set off was also assimilated to a vow of pilgrimage; the "pilgrim" had a cross sewn into his or her clothing to mark that pledge. The chroniclers therefore have a tendency to present these mighty armies as bands of humble pilgrims headed for Jerusalem. At the same time, however, they call them "soldiers of Christ" (*milites Christi*) or "the army of God" (*exercitus Dei* or *militia Dei*). They present the Christian army as heir to the army of Israel in the Old Testament. The chronicler Robert the Monk relates that, after the decisive victory of Dorylaeum (1097), which opened eastern Anatolia to "God's army," the victorious soldiers sang a hymn to God, adapting the one Moses had uttered to thank him for destroying Pharoah's army: "Thy right hand, O Lord, is become glorious in power: thy right hand, O Lord, hath dashed in pieces the enemy" (Exodus 15:6–7).[37] Of course, the words of Exodus were more likely to flow from a monk's pen than from the lips of soldiers; but at least this passage says a great deal about how a certain monastic elite perceived the expedition. Robert was not alone: other chroniclers established a close parallel between the army of Israel and the *militia Dei* that set out to conquer Jerusalem.[38]

That view, of course, required that the adversary be portrayed as the enemy of God. In the Chronicle of Robert the Monk, Pope Urban II, launching the appeal for the First Crusade, painted a very dark picture: from the East news was arriving that the Persians, "a despised race," had invaded the lands of the Christians in those regions, sowing destruction, spilling blood, and spreading fire. In addition, these enemies of God were said to have destroyed churches, overturned altars, circumcised Christians by force, and poured the blood from these circumcisions onto altars and into baptismal fonts—not to mention their rape of Christian women.[39] In Robert the Monk's chronicle, the Turks have become Persians (the Romans' traditional enemy), and he readily attributes the worst atrocities to them. According to him, the goal of the expedition was to rescue these Eastern Christians and to avenge them, but also to recover the territories unjustly taken by the infidels and to return the sanctuaries profaned by them to the Christian faith.

Most of these authors knew nothing about Islam, but they made up for their ignorance by using their imaginations and their knowledge, acquired through books, of other discredited beliefs, those of the pagans of antiquity. For example, the chronicler Petrus Tudebodus sees the Saracens as "our enemy and God's . . . saying diabolical sounds in I know not what language."[40] He attributes to a Saracen chief an oath "by Machomet and by the names of all the gods."[41] These enemies were therefore idolatrous pagans, like those who had once persecuted the chosen Jewish people and then the early Christians. Hence Tudebodus depicts as martyrs the Christians who lost their lives at the hands of these infidels.

The most striking example of the use of the Turks' supposed idolatry to justify the Crusade appears in many chroniclers' descriptions of the sacrilegious worship of the Saracens of Jerusalem. According to Fulcher of Chartres, in the Temple of the Lord—that is, the Dome of the Rock—they had installed an idol of Muhammad, to whom they addressed their vain prayers, thus profaning that holy site.[42] Raoul of Caen reports that his patron, the worthy Tancred, had found the idol in the temple and had piously destroyed it.[43] Such sacrileges in the most holy places of the world could only bring glory to the undertaking of the soldiers of Christ. It hardly mattered that these acts were pure fiction.

Not all chroniclers depicted the Muslim adversary as an idolater, however. One of the chroniclers of the First Crusade provides a very different (though no less hostile) image of Muhammad. Guibert of Nogent declares that Muhammad is not the God of the Saracens as some think, but that the Saracens believe he is "a just man and their patron, through whom divine laws were transmitted."[44] Guibert inserts a short biography of Muhammad into his chronicle, *The Deeds of God through the Franks* (1109). He knows that the Saracens worship only God the Father, that they reject the Trinity, and that they believe Jesus was a man and a prophet but not God. According to Guibert, that "Mathomus," with the aid of a heretical Christian, compiled a law that "gave them free rein for every kind of shameful behavior."[45] To make the Arabs believe he was a prophet, Muhammad trained a dove to eat seeds from his ear, so that people would believe it was an angel from heaven. He attached the scrolls of his law to the horns of a cow, then celebrated its advent as a miracle. That new law, acclaimed by the crowd, encouraged excesses of the flesh: polygamy, prostitution, homosexuality. As a just punishment for his crimes, "Mathomus" endured a horrible death: first afflicted with epilepsy, he was later devoured by flatulent pigs. The stories of false miracles resemble those told about the heresiarchs: these deceptions, inspired by the devil, supposedly explain why the mob embraced the heresies.

The ideological function of that life of Muhammad, placed at the beginning of Guibert's chronicle, is clear: it serves as a justification for the Crusade. Guibert declares that the Eastern Christians were too clever and that their ratiocination led them to fall into every sort of heresy. Islam is said to be only the most recent and most catastrophic manifestation of these heretical tendencies. The message is simple: the Eastern peoples need Westerners to put their affairs in order. The denigration of the Prophet is a key element in the justification of the Crusade. Other Crusade chroniclers followed Guibert's lead. William, archbishop of Tyre, presents Muhammad as the "firstborn of Satan," a madman and liar who "seduced Arabia."[46] The disciples of such a man could have no political legitimacy in the land of Christ.

The Crusade of the Jurists

Whereas the chroniclers depict the Crusades as a reconquest of the patrimony of Christ unduly usurped by the infidels, canon law gave a legal framework to the war, which was waged under ecclesiastical authority to assert the rights of the church. The *Concordia discordantium canonum* (or *Decretum*) from the mid-twelfth century is an encyclopedic compilation, attributed to Gratian, that became the foundation for the entire system of canon law in the Middle Ages. The *Decretum* is divided into various *causae* (cases). The *causa* that interests us is the twenty-third, which deals with the legitimacy of war waged under church authority against the heretics. As in all the *causae*, Gratian first posits a hypothetical case, then presents conflicting opinions, which he tries to resolve by citing authoritative texts:

> Some bishops, along with the people in their charge, sank into heresy. By threats and torture, they began to force the Catholics in the region to embrace their heresy. The pope ordered the bishops of the neighboring regions, who had accepted civil jurisdiction from the hands of the emperor, to defend the Catholics against the heretics. These bishops, having accepted that apostolic mandate, summoned troops and began to fight the heretics, both openly and by ruse. Many heretics were killed, others despoiled of their own property and that of their churches; others were imprisoned or reduced to slavery, while still others were compelled to return to the unity of the Catholic faith.[47]

Many historians, with some justification, have seen this *causa* as an allusion to the First Crusade; this impression is confirmed by the many illuminated manuscripts of the *Decretum* that, beginning in the thirteenth century, illustrate *causa* 23 with scenes iconographically identical to the illuminations in the Crusade chronicles. The thirteenth- and fourteenth-century canonists make reference to this *causa* when they speak of the Crusades. The parallels between the First Crusade and the case at hand are too numerous to be fortuitous: they include the power of the pope to call the *milites* to arms for the defense of oppressed Christians, and the right of the victors to appropriate the property of the defeated and to establish their power over the conquered territories. There can be no doubt that Gratian is seeking to affirm the legitimacy of the First Crusade. But he also provides criteria for judging the legitimacy of any sort of military action, offensive or defensive, undertaken under the church's authority.

Gratian obviously does not intend to rule on the legality of the "Crusades" as such, since the concept of "Crusade" did not yet exist. He poses the problem much more broadly. For him, it seems, the legal precedent for the First Crusade was the fight against the Donatist heretics of North Africa in the fourth and fifth centuries. In both cases, the aim was to reestablish Roman authority (imperial or pontifical) over those who rebelled against it and to assist the Catholic Christians being persecuted by the heretics. If Gratian presents the bishops' adversaries as heretics, it is because, by the twelfth century, that was how the Muslims were viewed, as we have seen in the examples of Guibert of Nogent's and William of Tyre's chronicles. It is therefore possible to apply that *causa* dealing with heretics to the "Saracens."

As in each of Gratian's *causae*, the hypothetical case is followed by a series of questions proceeding from it—eight in this case. He considers, among other things, the legitimacy of the war, the duty of aiding one's comrades, the punishment for the guilty, and the authority of various individuals (popes, bishops, emperors, and so on) to call people to arms against the heretics. In his seventh question, Gratian asks whether the possessions of the heretics and their churches may be confiscated and whether "good Christians" may seize them. In his responses, he asserts the legitimacy of the conquest and of the appropriation of lands and other property. True to the incipient scholastic style of the twelfth century, Gratian cites authorities for and against each of his propositions: biblical passages, ecumenical councils, pontifical bulls, and church fathers— Ambrose, Jerome, Gregory the Great, and especially Augustine, who provides most of the citations. This preference for the bishop of Hippo is altogether logical. In his writings on the Donatists, Augustine justifies the use of arms in the service of the Catholic Church against the heretics. Augustine was not the first to refuse them civil rights. Under Constantine, heretics were already deprived of *privilegia*. By the fourth century, heresy was assimilated to a crime of lèse-majesté, even treason, in imperial legislation.[48]

In the four excerpts for *quaestio 7*, which articulates the right of Christians to appropriate the property of heretics, Gratian cites the bishop of Hippo exclusively. According to Augustine, the Donatists had placed themselves outside the law: having rebelled against both divine law and human law (that of the empire), they had no legitimate title to possess goods. Gratian follows Augustine and stipulates the right of Catholics to confiscate the heretics' possessions, thus offering a justification for conquest at their expense. That justification became authoritative and constituted the starting point for any reflection on the subject by twelfth- and thirteenth-century canonists. For the canonist Huguccio, who taught in Bologna in the late twelfth century (and who was probably the teacher of the future pope Innocent III), the war against the heretics was authorized by both human and divine law.[49] Canon 3 of the Fourth Lateran Council (1215) imposed on prelates the duty to combat heresy and to mobilize princes to drive out the heretics, granting Catholics the right to confiscate their personal property. The decretist Laurentius Hispanus (d. 1248) declared that *causa* 23 conferred legitimacy on any war against heretics or Saracens.[50] The theologians who addressed *causa* 23 were generally of the same opinion. For the Franciscan Alexander of Hales (d. 1245), the Crusaders' despoliation of heretics and Saracens was a meritorious act.[51]

Some jurists hesitated, however, to relegate the Saracens to the rank of heretics, especially since, like the Jews, many Muslims possessed the status of a subaltern minority, tolerated in Spain, Sicily, and the Latin states of the East. A few canonists presented the war against the Saracens rather as a restoration of legitimate Christian power, which the infidels had supposedly usurped. The thirteenth-century Dominican jurist Raymond of Penyafort, in his *Summa de casibus*, recognizes that the Saracens may legitimately reign, but not in territories they acquired at the expense of Christians. The Christian conquest of Muslim territories became legitimate when it was a reconquest of formerly Christian lands: the Holy Land, Spain, or other parts of the former Roman Empire. That is also the opinion of other thirteenth-century canonists, such as William of Rennes and Johannes de Deo, and of theologians such as Robert of Courçon. Pope Innocent IV confirmed the right to reconquest. Thomas of Aquinas goes even farther: for him, infidels cannot rule over Christians, and the church has the right to abolish that domination.[52] In their work, therefore, thirteenth-century jurists followed in Gratian's footsteps, declaring categorically the legitimacy of the reconquest of the Christian territories of the Roman Empire, where the heretics, including the Saracens, did not have the right to exercise power.

The *Reconquista* in Spain

While the Crusaders were carving out principalities in the East, the Christian kingdoms of the northern Iberian Peninsula launched conquests against the Muslim principalities. In the early eleventh century, the caliphate of Cordova, which had ruled the peninsula until that time and which represented the most powerful and richest state of Europe, sank into *fitna*, civil war, and ultimately broke into *taifas*, small rival emirates fighting among themselves. The Christian sovereigns of the north (the count of Barcelona and the kings of Castile, Aragon, León, and, as of the late eleventh century, Portugal) took the opportunity to conquer lands or to ask the emirs for tributes (*parias*). That was the case, for example, of Fernando I (1035–1065), king of Castile and León, who demanded *parias* from the emirs of Toledo, Badajoz, and Seville. His son Alfonso VI (1065–1109) continued and broadened that policy: the heavy burden of the tributes obliged the emirs to impose non-Qur'anic taxes on their subjects, which led to revolts. Alfonso took advantage of one rebellion against the emir of Toledo to seize that city in 1085. The emirs of other *taifas*, to deal with the threat represented by Alfonso, appealed to the Almoravids, a Berber dynasty ruling a good part of western Africa, from Mali to Algiers. The Almoravids intervened, inflicted a bitter defeat on Alfonso in Zallaka (1086), and imposed their rule over the *taifas*. In the 1140s, another Maghrebian dynasty, the Almohads, overthrew the Almoravids, conquered Andalusia, and launched attacks on Christian kingdoms of the north. But a coalition of Christian kingdoms finally inflicted a decisive defeat on the Almohads in 1212, at the Battle of Las Navas de Tolosa, opening the way to conquest. James I of Aragon seized Majorca (1229) and Valencia (1238), while Fernando III of Castile and León took Cordova (1236) and Seville (1248). Only the Nasrid kingdom of Granada remained in the hands of Muslim leaders until its conquest by Isabel of Castile and Fernando of Aragon in 1492.

Reconquista, or "reconquest," is the term traditionally used in historiography to designate these successive waves of conquests by Christian princes. The word implies a coherent ideological program: at issue is not merely a conquest but a return to normalcy, a reestablishment of a Christian order that was temporarily overthrown by Muslim domination. Although the term *reconquista* is for the most part an invention of nineteenth-century historiographers,[53] the concept is rooted in medieval historiography. In the ninth-century kingdom of Asturias, the idea was already taking shape that the Asturian kings were the heirs of the Visigoth kings of old and that the "Chaldeans" were merely a scourge sent by God, destined to vanish from the peninsula in favor of the Asturian king Alfonso III. That ideology would be elaborated by chroniclers in the entourage of his successors, kings of León and Castile. Two essential elements were joined together: first, the restoration of a dynasty stemming from the line of the Visigoths, and, as a result, the only legitimate power on the entire peninsula; and second, Christian restoration, a corollary of that Gothic restoration. Only the reign of Christian princes could be legitimate: the Muslim princes had no right to rule on Iberian soil. This idea is also found in the crown of Aragon, whose kings obviously did not subscribe to the notion of a Gothic restoration, which would have meant bowing to the monarchs of Castile and León.[54]

In the ninth century, when Cordova recovered its strength under the caliphate, the Christian kingdoms of the north could hardly claim to be launching a new "reconquest" of the peninsula. It was only in the eleventh century, when Alfonso VI took the offensive against the emirs of the *taifas,* that the Asturian idea of a restoration of "Gothic" legitimacy reemerged. The king managed to take the city of Toledo, former capital of the Visigoth kings, which added weight to his claim to their inheritance. That preoccupation was apparent in the titles he bestowed on himself: he was dubbed "Alfonso, emperor of all Spain by the grace of God" and "magnificent victor of the Toledan empire"; his power extended over "the whole empire of Spain and the kingdom of Toledo."[55] Curiously, that claim to a Gothic restoration appears most clearly not in Latin chroniclers of the time but in two Arab authors. 'Abd Allah, the last Zirid emir of Granada, recounts that Count Sisnando Davides, sent by Alfonso VI to Granada to demand payment of *parias,* told him: "In the beginning, al-Andalus belonged to the Christians [*Rūm*], until they were defeated by the Arabs, who pushed them back into Galicia. But now that it is possible, they wish to recover what had been stolen from them by force." Whether Sisnando said this or not, it is clear that 'Abd Allah was well aware of that ideology of Gothic and Christian restoration. Ibn Bassam (d. 1148) relates that Alfonso, after taking the city, turned the main mosque into a church. At that time, advisers suggested that he "assume the crown and put on the garments of the Christians who ruled the peninsula before the conquest."[56]

That ideology appears clearly in three chronicles from the thirteenth century: the *Chronicon mundi* (1236–1242) by Lucas of Tuy; *De rebus Hispaniae*

(1243–1246) by Rodrigo Jiménez de Rada, archbishop of Toledo and close adviser to King Fernando III of Castile and León; and the *Estoria de España*, written at the order of King Alfonso the Wise (1252–1284) and completed under the reign of his son Sancho IV (1284–1295).[57] The *Estoria* recounts the history of the various dynasties that ruled Spain: Greek, Carthaginian, Roman, Vandal, Visigoth, and Arab. Of all these groups, only two were legitimate, the Romans and the Visigoths. Alfonso X, king and emperor (since he claimed the imperial title), was the natural successor of both. The others were intruders, especially the invaders from Africa, Carthaginians and Moors.[58] The *Estoria de España*, like the chronicles preceding it, refused to recognize any legitimacy on the part of the Arab masters ("Chaldeans," "Saracens," or "Moors"). An anonymous Latin chronicle written in 754 set the tone: the "loss" of Spain by the Christian Visigoth kings was an unparalleled catastrophe, surpassing the destruction of Jerusalem and the sack of Rome.[59]

The other side of that political imposture by the "Moors" was their religious illegitimacy. Several authors insert a brief biography of Muhammad into their chronicles of the history of Spain. The *Prophetic Chronicle* (883) presents him as a "heresiarch," an "impious prophet" to whom the "spirit of error" (that is, the devil) appeared in the form of a golden-faced vulture, claiming to be the archangel Gabriel. Emboldened by the vulture's revelations, the chronicle maintains, Muhammad assumed the role of prophet and preached the total destruction of nonbelievers by the sword. The text describes the "pseudo-prophet" as a violent and lustful man who does not hesitate to take other men's wives. In addition to being a heresiarch, Muhammad bears the traits of the Antichrist: he supposedly predicted that the angel Gabriel would come to raise him from the dead after three days; but, "instead of angels, dogs came to devour his flank, attracted by the rank odor." That polemical biography serves to deny all religious or political legitimacy to the Moors, disciples of a false prophet.[60] Similar biographies appear in Lucas of Tuy, Rodrigo Jiménez de Rada, and in the *Estoria de España*. The portrait drawn by Rodrigo Jiménez de Rada, who uses Arabic sources, is less coarse, more nuanced and thorough, than that of the *Prophetic Chronicle*. But the conclusion is similar: "By a false revelation, the crafty Muhammad concocted a pestilential virus."

If the devil is on the side of the heresiarch and his thugs, God and his saints support the Christians. For the authors from León and Castile, Santiago (Saint James) was the first patron saint of the *reconquista*. At the Battle of Clavijo in 844 (whose historical existence is not clearly established), the saint, mounted on a white horse and carrying a white banner, intervened to give the victory to the Castilians against the Muslims. Similar legends developed around other battles: the apostle became a *miles* (soldier) fighting for Castile against its enemies. But he sometimes also intervened against Christian enemies, especially the Portuguese. The Military Order of Santiago, founded in 1170, adopted as its ensign *Rubet ensis sanguine Arabum*, "The sword is red with the blood of the Arabs."

Later, especially in the modern period, it became *Santiago matamoros*, "Saint James, Moor-slayer." Santiago is represented on horseback, sword in hand, with Moors lying on the ground around him. That iconography spread to Spain and to the Americas; cities in both Mexico and Texas are named "Matamoros."

James was not the only patron saint of the Christian armies. Isidore of Seville, whose remains were transferred to León in the twelfth century, was a favorite of authors from that region, particularly Lucas of Tuy. In his *Miracles of Saint Isidore*,[61] Lucas describes how the saint appeared to King Alfonso VIII in a vision during the siege of Baeza (1147), promising him victory over his Moorish enemies, even though they were much greater in number. Beside Isidore was Saint James, armed with a double-edged sword. On the eve of taking Cordova, the former capital of the caliphate, Fernando III prayed to Isidore, patron saint of the Spanish *reconquista*, to deliver up the city.

The integrity of places of worship was another key element used to justify the retaking of territory from the hands of the "infidels." If we are to believe the Christian chroniclers, the Moors, during their conquest of the peninsula, had destroyed churches; worse, they had converted them to mosques. The *Estoria de España* presents the matter as follows:

> The sanctuaries were destroyed, the churches demolished. In the places where God had been joyfully praised, [the Muslims] blasphemed and wreaked havoc. They hurled the crosses and altars out of the churches. The chrism, the books, and all things for the honor of Christianity were looted and trampled underfoot. Feasts and celebrations, all were forgotten. The honor of the saints and the beauty of the church were no longer anything but ugliness and abomination. In the churches and towers where God had been praised, there, in that same place, they invoked Muhammad.[62]

One of the aims of the reconquest was therefore to return these places to the true faith. After the conquerors took a city from the Muslims, there was often a ritual "purification" of the main mosque, which then became a church.[63] The churches returned to their original use; the proper hierarchy of priest, bishop, primate, and pope was reestablished, as was the righteous power of the heir to the Gothic kings of Spain.

More than in Castile and León, it was in Aragon that the kings embraced the ideology and legal frameworks of the Crusade. The first great conquest of King James I was of Majorca, in the Balearic Islands. In November 1229, Pope Gregory IX wrote to James that he was sending men, both laymen and clergy, to help the king in his expedition and that the pope "granted them the indulgence normally reserved for those who come to the aid of the Holy Land." Gregory was also very clear about the purpose of the Crusade: to return the territory to Christendom. James, he said, had taken up the cross "so that, once the enemies were captured or dispersed, the land could be restored to the divine Faith and the rites of the Church could be propagated."[64] That justification for conquest, as a Crusade to restore the Christian faith in usurped territories, was repeated in pontifical documents regarding James's later conquests, especially that of Valencia, which he took in 1238 after a long siege. Outside the walls of the besieged city, James held a mass baptism of Muslims newly converted to Christianity, an initiative with great symbolic value intended to discourage the Muslim defenders while allowing the Crusader king to display his moral and religious merit.

The Revival of Jihad against the "Franks" in the Eleventh to Thirteenth Centuries

In the West as in the East, the conquests of *Rūm* or of the *Ifranj* would revive the ideological rhetoric of jihad. This rhetoric had long existed, since the caliphs of Cordova had waged regular campaigns against the Christian principalities that refused to pay them tribute, invoking the ideology of holy war to justify and glorify what were primarily punitive expeditions or raids. The *hajib* al-Mansūr expanded that policy, conducting devastating raids on the northern peninsula. He sought thereby to deter those who might revolt against his usurpation of power from the caliph. In the East, the Seljuk Turks used the rhetoric of jihad to legitimate their conquests of Byzantium but also to oppose the Shiite (hence "heterodox") Fatimids of Egypt.

In Spain, it was primarily with the arrival of the Berber dynasties, the Almoravids in 1086 and the Almohads in 1174, that jihad became an essential element of political ideology.[65] It can be found in the letters from the Almohad chancery, which call the Christian enemies "infidels," "miscreants," or "associationists."[66] When Almohad troops surprised a raiding expedition conducted by the count of Avila in 1173, al-Qālamī, secretary to the Almohad caliph Abū Ya'qūb Yūsuf, presented the skirmish as a great victory of Islam over the infidel. The enemy was led off to the gates of hell, and the Almohad troops returned in glory to Seville, bearing "the humiliated flags of the Christians, on which appeared their images, their crosses, signs of their lies about God and of their impiety. They also brought the head of their reprehensible leader, their stoned Satan, persecutor of the believing people, the most insolent of all the infidels toward the Merciful One."[67] In a letter describing the taking of Almeria by the Almohads, another author speaks of the victorious troops as lions that "offered each other the blood of that mob of infidels to drink."[68] Yet these same Almohad caliphs, like the Almoravids before them, hired Catalan and Portuguese mercenaries and signed trade treaties with the Pisans and the Genoese.[69] In addition, the "infidels" they fought most doggedly, and those most vilified in their writings, were their Muslim rivals, the Almoravids, who were accused of the worst crimes: heresy, debauchery, infidelity, paganism. Ibn Tūmart, founder of the Almohad movement, said it clearly: "Know—God help you!—that fighting them is a religious obligation for most of you, for those who are able to fight. Devote yourself to jihad against the veiled infidels [the Almoravids, whose men wore veils], since it is at least twice as important to combat them as to combat the Christians and all the infidels. In fact, they have attributed a corporeal aspect to the Creator—may he be glorified!—have rejected the *tawhid* [the absolute unity of God], have rebelled against the truth!"[70]

To judge by the first Muslim reactions to the Crusades in the East, religious hostility had little place there. It was first believed that the Frankish troops were only mercenaries of Byzantium being used to lead a counterattack against the Turks, and the Egyptian Fatimids were not displeased with the early successes of the Crusades against their Seljuk enemies. They soon realized, however, that the Franks were acting on their own behalf, and they deplored the massacres being perpetrated. But the hostility they felt toward the Franks was not a *religious* hostility; after all, the Muslims knew Christianity well, thanks to the Byzantines and the *dhimmis*. The ferocity of the Franks seems to have had a completely different origin. The Muslims concluded alliances with them or made war on them, but war was not an expression of jihad.

Gradually, however, the Muslims of the region began to realize that the Franks were motivated by religious hostility. There were descriptions of the profanations of mosques that the Franks perpetrated, and in 1127, Muslims of Aleppo avenged themselves by attacking churches belonging to Christian *dhimmis*. In Damascus and Aleppo, pietists exhorted Muslims not to ally themselves with the infidel Franks and began to call for jihad against them. In 1125, they succeeded in delivering the city of Aleppo to the prince of Mosul, Bursuqī, who was succeeded by 'Imād al-Dīn Zengi in 1128. Zengi is often portrayed as the originator of jihad, of the Muslim counteroffensive. It was he who retook the city of Edessa in 1144, the first action of the Muslim reconquest. But it cannot be said that the war against the Franks was a high priority for the prince of Mosul, nor that he regularly resorted to jihad. It was rather his son, Nūr al-Dīn, who embraced and developed that ideology, marrying the "greater jihad" (the internal struggle against oneself) to the "lesser jihad" (the struggle against the external enemy). Nūr al-Dīn led an austere life, abolished non-Qur'anic taxes, surrounded himself with men of religion, and waged war against the Franks— and against any Muslim who did not embrace his dual jihad, especially the Shiite community of Aleppo. In presenting himself as a unique *mujāhid*, the only sovereign able to unite the Muslims against the Franks, he succeeded in unifying Syria. He imposed his power over Damascus through a propaganda war against its timorous princes, who were vacillating between truces and war with the Franks, as much as by his military force. The pietist circles of Damascus and public opinion were on Nūr al-Dīn's side, and in 1154 his troops took the city without a fight.

When Nūr al-Dīn died in 1174, his successor, Saladin, announced his intention to continue his work, using the appeal for unity and jihad to impose his power over Muslim rivals in Syria. Nevertheless, between 1174 and 1186

Saladin waged war primarily on other Muslims in northern Syria and Iraq, in order, he said, to unify his coreligionists before reconquering the lands under Frankish domination. When in 1187 Reginald of Châtillon attacked a Muslim caravan, thereby breaking the truce between the kingdom of Jerusalem and Saladin, the sultan decided that the time had come to attack the kingdom. The decisive victory of Hattin and the taking of Jerusalem followed. Henceforth, no one could contend with Saladin for the title of *mujāhid*; the praise and congratulations from the whole Muslim world were unanimous. Jerusalem's importance for Islam grew, and it was said that the Kaaba rejoiced at the deliverance of its brother al-Aqsa Mosque. The holy city was purified of the taint of the "pig eaters" and "polytheists." Saladin's biographer Imād al-Dīn describes how Taqī al-Dīn, the sultan's nephew, had the entire Dome of the Rock sanctuary cleansed with pure water, then with rose water, to "make that blessed ground pure until its purification is a certainty."[71]

The unity that Saladin built up with so much difficulty did not last long. Upon his death in 1193, his brother, sons, and nephews fought over his legacy. They were able to unite in the event of a crisis: when the forces of the Fifth Crusade seized Damietta in the Nile Delta in 1219, al-Muazzam, sultan of Damascus, and al-Ashraf, sultan of al-Jazira, came to the aid of their elder brother, al-Kāmil, and succeeded in inflicting a bitter defeat on the Frankish army. But a few years later, al-Kāmil concluded an alliance with Emperor Frederick II against his brother al-Muazzam, promising Jerusalem to the emperor. By the time the emperor came to the Holy Land in 1229, al-Muazzam had already died, but Frederick and al-Kāmil negotiated the Treaty of Jaffa, granting the entire holy city to the emperor, with the exception of the Esplanade of the Mosques. In 1239, a year after al-Kāmil's death, his nephew al-Nāsir Dāwūd retook the city. But he soon found it prudent to ally himself with the Franks: in 1240 or 1241, he granted them the right to buy weapons in Damascus proper, which provoked the anger of the ulemas.[72] Then, in 1243, believing he was well advised to form an alliance with the *Ifranj* against the Khwarezmians, he returned Jerusalem to them, without even demanding control of the mosques on the Esplanade, which were turned into churches, something al-Kāmil had carefully avoided in 1229.[73] For the Ayyubids—the dynasty Saladin had built on the ideological foundations of a jihad to recover Jerusalem—the holy city had become an asset that could either be retained or be readily granted to the Franks to obtain their alliance.

The Mamluks, who overthrew the Ayyubids during Louis IX's Egyptian Crusade in 1250, were imbued from the start with the ideology of jihad. They waged it against the Eastern Franks and against the Mongols, who conquered a good part of the Muslim world, notably sacking Baghdad in 1258. The Mamluks crushed a Mongol army in Ain Jalut, Syria, in September 1260 and were soon planning the expulsion of the Eastern Franks. In 1263, they undertook the slow and systematic conquest of the Frankish cities and fortresses of Syria. The conquest of Acre in May 1291 sounded the death knell of the Latin East.

From the *Reconquista* to Imperial Conquest:
The Iberians against the Moors in the
Fifteenth and Sixteenth Centuries

In the fourteenth and fifteenth centuries, when attempts to relaunch the Crusades failed and the Ottomans invaded eastern Europe, those in the Iberian kingdoms dreamed of new conquests at the expense of the Muslims of Granada and the Maghreb. Several fifteenth-century authors displayed growing intolerance for the presence of a Muslim power on the peninsula.[74] Calixtis III preached a new Crusade against Granada in 1457, a plan enthusiastically welcomed by the Franciscan polemicist Alonso de Espina (among others). In his *Fortalium Fidei*, Alonso took up the anti-Muslim polemics and historiographical traditions of the thirteenth-century chroniclers, asserting the illegitimacy of Muslim power. In 1482, Queen Isabel of Castile and her husband, King Fernando of Aragon, began the conquest of the emirate of Granada. On January 6, 1492, the couple entered the city as victors and annexed the emirate to Castile.

The Portuguese had already waged war on the "Moors" beyond the Strait of Gibraltar. On July 25, 1415, King João I of Portugal departed from Lisbon at the head of a fleet of 242 ships, accompanied by his four sons. On August 21, the Portuguese troops landed on the Moroccan coast, routed a Marinid army, and took the city of Ceuta. The Portuguese "purified" the mosque, turned it into a church, and hung bells in the minaret on Sunday, August 24. At the end of the mass, the king knighted his four sons. On September 2, the king returned to Portugal, leaving twenty-seven hundred men behind. Ceuta was now a commercial and military outpost of Portugal. João, the illegitimate son of King Pedro (1357–1367) and the founder of a new dynasty (the House of Avis), no doubt needed a real coup to demonstrate the legitimacy of his reign. He therefore revived the holy war against the infidels. In so doing, he launched Portugal on a new venture: exploration, conquest, and colonization of the territories outside the Iberian Peninsula.

One of João's four sons present at the taking of Ceuta was Enrique, known to history as Henry the Navigator (1394–1460).[75] That prince set up his residence in Sagres, on Cape St. Vincent at the southwest tip of Portugal (and Europe), where he nurtured a dual obsession: to conquer lands at the expense of the Moors and to find new commercial routes granting direct access to African gold and Asian spices. In Sagres, he used his considerable resources (several lordships, from which he drew revenues) to assemble cartographers and navigators around him. Between 1419 and 1427, Portuguese sailors discovered the uninhabited islands of Porto Sando, the Madeira, and the Azores, which Enrique arranged to have colonized. Agriculture developed there, especially the production of wine, wheat, and sugarcane. In the 1430s, the Portuguese caravels began to push farther and farther down the southern African coast, reaching Cape Bojador in 1434, Cape Branco in 1441, Sierra Leone in 1460, and finally, the Cape of Good Hope in 1487. That opened the way to the Indies, where Vasco da Gama arrived in 1498.

These navigators engaged in trade and fishing, and they also captured slaves. The chronicler Gomes Eanes of Zurara describes the many raids that occurred year after year.[76] A caravel would arrive on an island or an inhabited coast. The crew made land, usually at night. Without a sound, the Portuguese encircled a village. Then, to cries of "Portugal! Santiago! Saint George!" they attacked, killing any men who resisted and capturing the others. The battles, when there were any, were quickly won by the better-armed Portuguese, who had the advantage of surprise. Often they put to flight the men and captured only women and children, whom they bound and took on ship. After a few "fine catches," a caravel could proudly leave with a cargo of several hundred slaves. Zurara describes the undertaking with pride; it showed that God was on the side of the Christians and against the Moors. From time to time, he displays compassion for these slaves, especially when he describes how a group, upon its arrival in Portugal, was divided into lots to facilitate their sale, which had the effect of separating husbands from wives, children from parents. He evokes the cries and tears on all sides, the confusion when children ran back to the arms of their mothers, before being torn from them once again. But it was all for the best, he affirms: most of the captives became Christians (often better ones than the native Portuguese, he says). No doubt God reserved a great reward for those who led so many souls to eternal salvation.

In Christian as in Muslim territory, the ideology of holy war was often used to justify conquest of the "infidels." That in no way prevented political and military alliances with princes of the rival faith. It also did not keep Muslim and Christian societies from granting a large place to religious minorities.

CHAPTER 3

THE SOCIAL INFERIORITY OF
RELIGIOUS MINORITIES

Dhimmis and Mudejars

CHRONICLES OF HOLY WAR celebrated the feats of arms against the infidels and minimized those against coreligionists, except in cases where the latter were portrayed as heterodox. But once the conquest was achieved, the new subjects had to be integrated into the political and social order. These religious "minorities," who in actuality were often in the numerical majority immediately after the conquest, were usually granted a protected but subordinate place in society. Theologians and jurists justified their subordination, defining their role with reference to the founding texts (Qur'an, Hadith, Bible, or Roman law). From Barcelona to Baghdad, large minorities lived in Muslim and Christian societies. They were sometimes the victims of persecutions, acts of violence, and expulsions, but in general they enjoyed a status where their theoretical inferiority (religious and legal) did not prevent some of them from achieving clear economic and social success.[1]

PROTECTED AND INFERIOR: THE *DHIMMIS* IN THE MUSLIM
SOCIETIES OF EUROPE (AL-ANDALUS AND SICILY)

Let us first consider how Muslim law defined the status of the *dhimmi*, or protected person.[2] Although the Qur'an does not clearly establish the legal framework for non-Muslims within the *dār al-islām*, it declares that the Muslim must not force the "peoples of the book" (*ahl al-kitāb*, the Jews and Christians) to convert. By contrast, he may oblige them to recognize the superiority and suzerainty of Muslim authority and to pay "humbly" the *jizya*, the capitulation tax (Qur'an 9:29). During the great conquests, the victorious Muslims gave guarantees to the conquered peoples, granting them far-reaching legal autonomy and freedom of worship. According to certain chroniclers, restrictions were sometimes among the conditions of surrender applied to the defeated Christians. This is apparent in the Pact of 'Umar, which, according to Muslim tradition, the second caliph, 'Umar ibn al-Khattab (634–644), imposed on the Christians of Syria. In fact, these restrictions were imposed gradually, throughout the first century A.H. (beginning in 622 C.E.), and expanded under 'Umar II (717–720).[3] The first author to give us a full version of the Pact of 'Umar is the Andalusian traditionist al-Turtūshī (d. 1126) in his *Siraj al-mulūk*. In that text, the Christians of Syria send a missive to Caliph 'Umar to remind him of the pledge they made at the time of their surrender. They present a long list of prohibitions that they agreed to respect: on building new churches and monasteries, teaching the Qur'an, wearing "Muslim" clothing or turbans, bearing arms, and so on. A numbers of these measures were aimed at limiting or proscribing the public expression of Christianity. Hence the Christians pledged not to put crosses on their churches, not to display their scriptures in public, not to participate in certain public processions, not to pray in a noisy or ostentatious manner, not to ring their bells too loudly.[4]

The tradition attributed that pact to 'Umar, a great general during the conquests and the second caliph, probably to grant authority to a status that took definite shape only slowly in the early Muslim centuries. It was during the eighth and ninth centuries C.E. that the Umayyad, then the Abbasid, caliphs and jurists defined and circumscribed the status of the *dhimmi*. By paying the *jizya*, the *dhimmi* marked his submission to Muslim authority and as a result enjoyed its protection. If he owned lands, he also paid the *kharāj*, a property tax higher than the one the Muslim had to pay. At the same time, the *dhimmi* accepted his social inferiority. The theoretical restrictions were not uniformly respected, however. Far from it: many churches and synagogues were built in Muslim countries; the clothing prohibitions were applied very unevenly, and a number of Christians and Jews occupied positions of authority in the entourage of princes. There were times of tension, even persecution: the most notorious example was the reign of the Fatimid caliph al-Hākim (996–1021), who imposed on the Jews and Christians the wearing of distinctive clothing, prohibited them from drinking wine and from holding their processions and public feast days, and had many churches and synagogues razed.[5] But that policy was an aberration, and Christians and Jews were soon allowed to rebuild their places of worship and to practice their religions as before. The taxes could nevertheless be burdensome, especially on the most destitute. In Fatimid Egypt, for example, a Cairo artisan had to pay a *jizya* of about 1 2/3 dinars, the equivalent of two weeks (twelve days) of his salary, an altogether acceptable amount; by contrast, for a worker (for example, a peddler), the same sum represented twenty-two weeks (132 days) of work.[6]

In Europe, it was primarily the Christians and Jews of Sicily and the Iberian Peninsula who were under Muslim domination, beginning in the eighth century. The sources describing the conquest of Spain are all of late date, but we possess a curious document, a pact of surrender, dating to 713, between Theodomir (Tudmir in Arabic), a Visigoth lord of large territories in the southeast of the peninsula (in the region of the present-day city of Murcia), and 'Abd al-Aziz, governor of al-Andalus and son of the conqueror Musa ibn Nusayr. Tudmir surrendered the cities of the region to 'Abd al-Aziz and promised to pay a tribute in kind. In return, the governor recognized the lordship of Tudmir and guaranteed his security and that of his subjects, the enjoyment of their personal property, and their freedom to practice Christianity.[7]

Historians call the Christians of al-Andalus "Mozarabs," a word that may be derived from the Arabic must'arib, meaning "Arabized."[8] Throughout the nineteenth and twentieth centuries, historians inquired at length about them: How many were there at different times in the history of al-Andalus? How many had converted to Islam (and when)? Where and until when had their communities survived? The debate has sometimes been bitter because it is ideologically charged. For some nineteenth- and early twentieth-century Spanish historians, the Mozarabs represented the "true" Spaniards, forcibly subjected by the Muslim "outsider." The existence of the Mozarabs made it possible to justify the war as a reconquest (reconquista) waged by northern Christians to "liberate" their coreligionists from the yoke of Islam. For other historians, the near total disappearance of the Mozarabs before the thirteenth century demonstrated the widespread Arabization and Islamization of the peninsula; the invasion of men from the north was not a reconquest but quite simply a conquest. The lack of documentation has played a large role in the virulence of the debate, since historians are obliged to speculate.

What is certain is that the Mozarabs represented almost the totality of the population during the Muslim invasions of the eighth century, that they remained the majority for the rest of the eighth century, and that, by contrast, they were almost nonexistent by the mid-thirteenth century. If we are to believe Mikel de Epalza, their decline was rapid, less because of individual and voluntary conversions than for lack of ecclesiastical structures. In the absence of bishops and priests, the inhabitants of the rural zones of the peninsula were deprived of the essential sacraments of Christianity, especially baptism. Within the space of a few generations, they could no longer remain Christians and were considered Muslims.[9] The situation was different in large cities such as Toledo, Merida, Seville, and especially Cordova: there, the Umayyad authority maintained privileged relationships with the bishops and other prelates, often important figures in the court of the emirs (and later of the caliphs). For Christians, the presence of these prelates at court symbolized the Muslim authority's acceptance and reflected the universal power of the caliphs of Cordova (mirroring that of their predecessors in Damascus). A heavy tax burden fell on the dhimmis: it has been estimated that, in the mid-eighth century, a protected person had to pay the state about three and a half times what a Muslim owed.[10] That burden helps explain the reactions of Christians, many of whom converted to Islam, emigrated to the Christian kingdoms to the north, or joined revolts against the Umayyad authority within Andalusian society.

Religious differences were only one factor in a society riven by ethnic and regional divisions—between southern Arabs, northern Arabs, Berbers, and *muwalladun* (autochthonous peoples who had converted to Islam). The emirs attempted to deal with the revolts produced by these divisions, even as they manipulated them to prevent united opposition to their power. They therefore cultivated personal relationships with each community, including the Christians. For a long time, Muslims and Christians were thrown together even in their main place of worship: they shared the Cathedral of Cordova until ʿAbd al-Rahmān I (756–788), judging the place too cramped, purchased the building from the Christians and allowed them to construct churches in the new neighborhoods of the capital.[11] That emir and his successors named a Christian "count" (*comes* in Latin; *kumis* in Arabic), an intermediary between the Christians and the sovereign, responsible for taxation and the justice system in the Christian community.

Christian notables had a presence at the caliphal court of ʿAbd al-Rahmān in the tenth century: the caliph confirmed the nomination of bishops; and Christians served in the Umayyad administration, where they played an important role as ambassadors and translators in negotiations between Cordova and the Christian princes on both sides of the Pyrenees. The best-known example is no doubt that of Reccemundus, or Rabī b. Zayd: as indicated by his two different names, he, like a number of Mozarabs in the tenth century, lived between the Latin and Arab worlds. ʿAbd al-Rahmān III sent him as an ambassador to both the Byzantine and the Germanic emperors. For his trouble, the envoy received the bishopric of Elvira from the caliph. It was apparently he who compiled the *Calendar of Cordova* in a bilingual (Latin and Arabic) version, dedicating it in 961 to the new caliph, al-Hakam II. But the Mozarabs of the caliphal period generally left few traces in the documentation or among the chroniclers.

For the period of the *taifas* (1031–1090), the information about the Mozarabs is even rarer. The Christians who remained were increasingly Arabized: essential Christian texts were translated into Arabic for readers who no longer knew Latin. Those playing an important role in diplomacy or politics became rarer; with the disappearance of the caliphate, it seems, no emir felt the need to surround himself with representatives of the Christian community, whose political importance was minimal. By contrast, the presence of Christians within the *taifas* seems in general not to have provoked any anxiety. No one feared they might form an alliance with the *harbīs* (non-Muslim residents of the *dār al-harb*) to the north, who were becoming increasingly aggressive. This is particularly surprising when we realize that the Jews in certain *taifas* were sometimes accused of destabilizing the power structure, as was the case in Granada, where they were the victims of a massacre in 1066.

Under the Almoravids (1090–1147), the situation of the *dhimmis* on the peninsula grew grimmer. For Yūsuf b. Tāshfīn and his followers, one of the fatal flaws of the petty kings of the *taifas* was precisely their lack of steadfastness in their relations with the Christians, *dhimmis* and *harbīs*. There could now be no question of making peace with the *harbīs*, much less of their paying *parias*. As for the *dhimmis*, it was necessary to limit and scale back their role in Andalusian society and minimize their contacts with Muslims, while still respecting the rights that the Sharia granted them. Ibn 'Abdun's manual of *hisba* (urban law) reflected that new state of affairs: it specifies that no Muslim ought to do "lowly" tasks for a Jew or Christian—take care of his animals, dispose of his garbage, clean his latrines, and so on. It was the *dhimmi* who was to execute these tasks, which corresponded to his inferior status. Christians were morally inferior as well, according to Ibn 'Abdun: he advises prohibiting Christian women from going into churches except on days when mass is held, since it is well known, he says, that they go there to fornicate with the priests.[12]

In 1099, Yūsuf b. Tāshfīn, on the advice of his ulemas, had the main church of Granada razed. Later, the Christians of the city appealed to the Aragonese king Alfonso I, who conducted a campaign of raids in Andalusia in 1125–1126, bringing back a good number of Mozarabs with him to Aragon. The role played in that affair by the Christians of Granada led to the deportation of a fair number of Mozarabs to Morocco, where it would have been difficult for them to conspire with their northern coreligionists and where they could perform the function of collectors of non-Qur'anic taxes. Other Christians and Jews did not wait for these expulsions to leave al-Andalus: some departed for other, more tolerant Muslim countries. The Jewish philosopher Maimonides, for example, settled in Cairo. Others fled to Christian Spain, increasing the Jewish and Mozarab population in border cities such as Toledo. The repression of non-Muslims by the Almohads led to further mass departures of Christians and Jews. At the time of the taking of the chief Andalusian cities by Christian kings in the thirteenth century, there were almost no *dhimmis* left. The inhabitants of the Nasrid emirate of Granada were almost exclusively Muslim.

In Sicily, almost half the population remained Christian until the end of the Muslim period. Some Christian communities on the island remained independent until the tenth century, others simply paid a tribute to the Muslim rulers, while still others were under the authority of the Muslims as *dhimmis*. These *dhimmis* had nearly the same status as elsewhere in the Muslim world, including al-Andalus. But whereas the Visigoth kingdom had completely collapsed in Spain, the Christian Sicilians still maintained ties (religious, cultural, and sometimes political) with Constantinople. Those who rebelled against the Muslim authority placed their hopes in the Byzantine Empire, and various emperors tried in vain to reconquer the island.[13]

Many legal texts, especially *fatwas* (legal opinions) and manuals of *hisba*, deal with the everyday contacts between Muslims and *dhimmis*. Let us consider a few concrete examples of the problems raised by the coexistence of Muslims and *dhimmis*: sexuality and marriage, food (especially meat and wine), and social hierarchies.

From the early days of Islam, the laws governing marriage were relatively clear: a Muslim man could marry a Jewish or Christian woman, though certain jurists affirmed that marriage to a Muslim woman was far preferable. In any event, the children of a Muslim father were Muslims. A Muslim man could also have sexual relations with his female slaves, whether or not they were Muslim. By contrast, a Muslim woman could marry only a Muslim man, since a female believer was not to be placed in a position of inferiority in relation to a *dhimmi*.[14]

Food raised further problems. Islam imposed a whole series of rites on the slaughter of animals: it was necessary to cut the trachea, the esophagus, and the two veins in the neck while reciting the *tasmiya*, an invocation of God's name. At the same time, the vast majority of the jurists believed that it was permissible for a Muslim to purchase and consume meat slaughtered by the *dhimmis*. The Jews had slaughtering methods similar to those of the Muslims, but that was not at all the case among the Christians. The meat of Christians sometimes caused concern: some jurists prohibited Muslims from consuming it if they knew an invocation to Jesus had been uttered during the slaughter.[15] Ibn 'Abd al-Ra'ūf, an Almoravid jurist, acknowledged that the purchase of meat prepared by *dhimmis* was legitimate, but he strongly discouraged it, going so far as to declare that someone who purchased it was a "bad Muslim." Who knows whether the meat had been consecrated "for their churches, or in the name of the Messiah or the Cross, or for some other reason of the same kind?" He concluded that it was better to abstain.[16]

Wine could be a troublesome subject. Although at certain times and in certain parts of the *dār al-islām*, Muslims readily drank wine,[17] this practice often provoked the wrath of jurists. A mufti from Cordova in the first half of the eighth century declared that the house of every wine merchant should be burned down.[18] In the twelfth century, Ibn 'Abdun complained that Cordovan Muslims were crossing the Guadalquivir in boats at night, to go to the Christian neighborhood and buy wine. Ibn 'Abd al-Raūf recommended harsh punishments for the Muslim who drank wine and for the Christian who sold it to him, but also for the overzealous Muslim who tried to prevent the Christian from consuming it.[19]

The jurists endeavored to impose respect for social hierarchies, which relegated the *dhimmis* to an inferior place, and to discourage certain types of relations between Muslims and *dhimmis*. For example, a tenth-century Cordovan mufti railed against Muslims who participated in Christmas festivities and exchanged gifts with Christians, or who joined Christians in celebrating New Year's or the winter and summer solstices.[20] It is likely that his fulminations were wasted effort and that the practices he denounced were widespread. Another mufti of the same period prohibited the Muslims from teaching the Qur'an to Christian children.[21] A Cordovan mufti from the late ninth century declared that a *dhimmi* man who raped a Muslim woman would receive the death penalty, but if he embraced Islam in extremis, he could be pardoned, provided he paid the rape victim a dowry proportionate to her social status. Conversely, if his was a false conversion, he would be crucified.[22]

Large Christian populations could be found in Sicily until the end of the Muslim period. In Spain, by contrast, as in the nearby Maghreb, Christianity tended to disappear under the Almoravid and Almohad dynasties, as a result of conversions or emigration. At the same time, more and more European Muslims found themselves under the yoke of Christian princes.

MINORITY MUSLIMS IN CHRISTIAN STATES: LAW AND PRACTICE

In the eleventh and twelfth centuries, a large number of Muslims fell under Christian domination during the Norman conquest of Sicily (1072–1092), the First Crusade in the East (1098–1099), and the conquests by Christian princes of the Iberian Peninsula—the Castilian-Leonese conquest of Toledo (1085) and the Aragonese takeover of Huesca (1096) and Saragossa (1118). Later, large Muslim populations came under Christian authority following the major peninsular conquests of the thirteenth century, when James I of Aragon took Majorca (1229) and Valencia (1238), and Fernando III of Castile captured Cordova (1236) and Seville (1248). Although every conquest resulted in a different situation, most often the Christian princes granted the defeated a status similar to that of the *dhimmis* in Islamic territory, with the same legal and religious guarantees and the same fiscal and social constraints.[23]

At the time of the Norman conquest, Sicily had nearly 250,000 Muslims, slightly more than half the population, the rest of it composed primarily of Greek-speaking Christians and a few Jews.[24] During the conquest and in the years that followed, many Muslims left the island to return to the *dār al-islām*. It was principally merchants and the wealthy who could emigrate: peasants, whose minimal wealth was primarily in real property, had a hard time leaving their lands. The Norman military aristocracy imposed a feudal system on the majority Muslim peasantry. Count Roger I divided up the island into fiefs, which were distributed (along with the *villani*, dependent Muslim peasants) to his Norman and Italian vassals. Other Muslim communities possessed greater rights over their lands and paid only an annual tribute to the royal authority, but their semi-independent status deteriorated throughout the twelfth century. The Norman kings had no interest in seeing the Muslims of the island convert to Christianity. They were content to reproduce the system of *dhimmis* while reversing the roles: it was now the Muslims and Jews who had to pay the *jizya* (the Arabic word was retained by the Norman administration). Muslim peasants worked the land for their new masters and paid a royalty twice a year. Other Muslims enjoyed a more advantageous status, especially the residents of Palermo and other cities that had bowed to Norman authority relatively early on and had thus been able to negotiate certain rights, such as exemption from the *jizya*. They gradually lost these rights, however.

Although the Norman lords had an interest in protecting their Muslim peasants, some immigrants were less favorable toward them. Lombard peasants were sent to settle the eastern part of the island, a sparsely populated zone that needed a labor force; and it was these immigrants who massacred the Muslim peasants in the surrounding villages in 1160–1161, obliging the survivors to take refuge in the western parts of the island. On the island as a whole, the Muslims' traditional farming method, an intensive polyculture, gradually gave way to cereal monoculture, no doubt because wheat was easier to sell on the Italian and Ifrīqiyan markets, but also because of the decline and exodus of the Muslim peasantry. In the cities, Muslim artisans and merchants, essential to economic activity, increasingly found themselves in competition with immigrants—Lombards, Genoese, Pisans, Catalans, and others—who had every interest in seeing their rivals lose their privileges. In that extremely divided society, where the alliances between different parties were multiple and shifting, religious differences did not account for everything, though they remained important. The Sicilian Muslims' increasingly precarious status owed less to the rise of religious intolerance than to a game of shifting and complex interests in which Muslims more often than not lost ground.

One of the most fascinating accounts about the Muslims of Norman Sicily was penned by the Andalusian traveler Ibn Jubayr, who was shipwrecked off the coast of the island in December 1184 and who remained there until March 1185.[25] In his *Rihla*, or travel narrative, he painted a very mixed picture of the state of Sicilian Islam: he was amazed at the survival and piety of the Muslims he met on the island but also worried about the difficulties they faced. In theory, a Muslim, according to the Sharia, should not live under the jurisdiction of an infidel but should emigrate to a Muslim country if he can. Some jurists acknowledged extenuating circumstances, however: the mufti al-Māzarī (d. 1141) set forth various reasons that might justify a Muslim living in Norman Sicily.[26] Ibn Jubayr agreed entirely, going so far as to say that the eunuchs in the royal palace of William I, obliged to conceal their religion, were in a state of continual jihad, since they were working for their faith and the well-being of their Muslim brothers. He was delighted to see the importance the monarch granted to his Muslim advisers. But he felt there was also a danger there: Could the kindness of the Christians of Palermo and the beauty of the Christian women be a lure? Charmed by the Christmas mass sung in the Church of the Martorana, dazzled by the beauty of the light coming through the stained-glass windows, Ibn Jubayr confesses that everything "provoked a conflict in my soul, from which I seek refuge in God." Children threatened their parents with converting to Christianity, and far-sighted parents married their daughters to Muslim travelers, so that the women could live in Islamic countries.

For many reasons, Muslims were on their way to losing their status in 1184–1185: intrigues at court pitted Muslim *qā'ids* against Christian counts, and Lombard peasants rioted against the Muslims on the eastern part of the island. Then there was the geopolitical climate. So long as the Normans were conquering the African coast (as they had done during the first half of the twelfth century), the

Sicilian Muslims did not constitute a threat; but when the Almohads embarked on the reconquest, and especially after they took Mahdiyya in 1160, the loyalty of the Muslim subjects began to be called into question. In Palermo, their weapons were taken from them, exposing them to even more violence.

But the final blow to the Sicilian Muslim community would be dealt by a prince whose enemies often presented him as an Islamophile: Frederick II Hohenstaufen, king of Sicily and German emperor. In the struggles that marked his contested succession, many Muslims on the island allied themselves with German rebels. Frederick crushed these revolts, not without difficulty, between 1221 and 1224, then decided to put an end to Muslim Sicily. He had about sixteen thousand rebels transported to Lucera in Puglia, where he established an exclusively Muslim colony. Some Muslim communities persisted on the island, but they were small and few in number, and they have left almost no traces in the documentation. All that is mentioned is the embassy sent by al-Kāmil, sultan of Egypt, asking Frederick to leave the Sicilian Muslims in peace or at least to let them go to Egypt. The founding of Lucera served a dual objective. Far from their lands and coreligionists, the Muslims could no longer revolt; they were dependent on the emperor's goodwill. In addition, by installing them in Italy, Frederick could use them to assert his power against the Italian barons. In the years that followed, Frederick authorized Dominican missionaries to preach to the city's Muslims, who, it was said, spoke good Italian. It was only when popes Gregory IX and Innocent IV were seeking polemical arguments against Frederick (and against his son Manfred) that they presented Lucera as evidence of the emperor's tepid faith, his penchant for Saracen culture and women, and even for the Muslim religion. When Charles I of Anjou, at the pope's instigation, defeated Manfred and took the crown of Sicily, he promised to liquidate Lucera, and his son Charles II did so in 1300. Muslims who did not agree to be baptized were sold as slaves.[27]

In the East following the First Crusade, the Europeans imposed their suzerainty on their Eastern subjects: Melkite, Syriac, or Jacobite Christians as well as Jews and Muslims.[28] There are few data that permit us to estimate the proportions of these different groups. It seems, however, that Eastern Christians lived primarily around Jerusalem, while most of the Muslims lived in the other, rural regions of the kingdom; Europeans probably did not represent more than a quarter of the population. The villages retained their own structures of government: the notables of the village governed it under the leadership of the village chief, or *ra'is*, who meted out justice. Often the village was granted to a member of the Frankish nobility, or in some cases to an ecclesiastical institution. In the East and in Sicily, the feudal system was superimposed on autochthonous village structures. The Eastern peasant (whether Christian or Muslim) generally paid a percentage of his harvest, roughly the equivalent of the *kharāj* that the *dhimmi* peasant had to pay under Muslim authority. His status was often equivalent to that of a serf in the West, though with a few differences: for example, he had almost no corvées, since demesne lands were almost nonexistent. Ibn Jubayr, who traveled in the region of Acre, believed that the Muslim peasants under Frankish jurisdiction were actually less exploited than their brothers in Islamic countries. That was likely not the result of "tolerance" on the part of their masters, but an indication that these masters needed to hold on to their labor force.[29]

In Spain, every conquest led to large-scale emigration to territories still under Muslim control, especially Granada and the Maghreb, in accordance with the prescriptions of the Sharia, which discouraged the Muslim from living under the yoke of the infidel. But a good number of Muslims remained, and the kings did their best to encourage them, sometimes going so far as to establish new Muslim settlers in underpopulated regions (such as the island of Minorca). It would be difficult to draw general conclusions about the size of these Mudejar communities (as they were called in Christian Spain), which varied enormously from one region to another. In Castile and León in the eleventh and twelfth centuries, Muslim populations were often expelled from the conquered cities.[30] Toledo was an exception: Alfonso VI is said to have allowed the Muslims who wished to remain there after the conquest of 1085 to do so, but the vast majority emigrated.[31] In the Ebro Valley, by contrast, a good number of Muslim peasants stayed after the conquest of the region (Alfonso I of Aragon captured Saragossa in 1118). These Muslims actively participated in the local economy, selling and buying lands and other property; their new Aragonese lords were usually content to live off their seigneurial revenues. Hence the Aragonese saying: "Quien no tiene Moro no tiene oro" (he who has no Moor has no gold).[32] During the major Castilian conquests of the thirteenth century, the Muslims from the cities who offered strong resistance were generally expelled, whereas those who negotiated their surrender were granted guarantees allowing them to remain. Some Muslim princes who accepted the suzerainty of the king of Castile had their titles and powers confirmed.[33]

In Catalonia, few Muslims remained after the Christian conquest, except in the city of Lérida, where there was a large community until the sixteenth century. The major expeditions of King James I of Aragon added a large number of Muslim subjects to the Crown. During the conquest of Majorca (1229), a good part of the Muslim population, especially the social and economic elite, left the island; only a "headless" Muslim peasantry remained. The Muslims on the neighboring island of Minorca mounted such fierce resistance that the king, when he finally took the island in 1235, reduced the entire population to slavery. In the kingdom of Valencia, a significant Muslim population remained; in many surrender treaties, James guaranteed legal autonomy and religious freedom to the *aljamas* who recognized his sovereignty.[34]

There was always the risk that these Muslims would form alliances with potential invaders: Mudejars allied themselves with various Muslim princes from Granada and the Maghreb and revolted against Christian authority. That was especially the case during an uprising orchestrated by two Muslim vassals of Alfonso X of Castile and León, Ibn al-Ahmar, emir of Granada, and Ibn Hud, emir of Murcia, in 1264–1265. (Rebel Christian vassals participated as well.) The Muslim populations revolted in several Andalusian cities, proclaiming their allegiance to Ibn al-Ahmar. They were aided by a contingent of three thousand Moroccan warriors. With some difficulty, Alfonso X succeeded in reasserting his authority and then in expelling the Muslim populations from certain hotbeds of rebellion, especially Jerez and Cadiz. In the region of Denia, which was now part of the kingdom of Valencia, al-Azraq led a major uprising against James I in 1247–1248. James managed to regain control and drove out many Muslims. In 1276, some Mudejars of Valencia revolted to such an extent that the king resolved to expel a good number of them. But his son Peter III of Aragon did not implement that decision.

In the twelfth and especially the thirteenth century, a large number of legal texts came to define the status of Muslims in Christian territory: treaties of capitulation, municipal or royal *fueros*, ecclesiastical councils. These documents demonstrate that the Muslims from Christian kingdoms could be slaves, free peasants, artisans, or mercenaries in the royal armies. The Muslims' right to practice their faith was generally guaranteed. Religious conversions had to be voluntary—and only to Christianity, of course. The laws tried to maintain a certain level of segregation: marriage and sexual relations between Muslims and Christians were forbidden, public baths were not to accept Muslims and Christians at the same time, and so on. In theory, the Mudejar was supposed to be socially inferior to the Christian, just as the *dhimmi* in Islamic countries was inferior to the Muslim. Since the laws concerning the Muslims in Christian lands have been the object of many studies,[35] I shall simply give a few examples, by way of comparison, of the legal provisions introduced to define and circumscribe the place of Muslims in Christian societies.

First of all, the Muslims, like the Jews, were granted the right to practice their religion and to have places of worship. Alfonso X, for example, declared that the Moors could live "observing their law without insulting our own." Their mosques were royal property; the king could therefore do with them as he pleased. Implicitly, that provision entailed the possibility of turning them into churches, or conversely, of setting some aside to continue to serve as mosques.[36] This tolerance tended to erode over time. A good example is the right to perform the *adhan*, the call to prayer issued by the muezzins, which was often among the concessions granted. In 1311, the Council of Vienne barred the *adhan* in any Christian territory. But that prohibition was respected in the breach: in Valencia, various fourteenth- and fifteenth-century kings and lords granted exceptions to that ban or declined to enforce it, sometimes drawing the wrath of church authorities.[37]

Muslim subjects were kept in check by specific legal institutions. In the Latin kingdom of Jerusalem, all Eastern subjects (Christians, Jews, and Muslims) fell under the jurisdiction of the Court of the Fronde, composed of two Frankish magistrates and four Eastern Christians—but no Muslims or Jews.[38] Matters of justice within the Muslim community were normally left to the Muslim procurator, the qadi (*alcalde* in Castilian, *alcaide* in Portuguese). Some Christian sovereigns guaranteed their Muslim subjects the right to elect their own qadi. Others preferred to name him themselves, but it is likely that, in such cases, the sovereign's choice was made through negotiations with his Muslim subjects.[39]

In legal matters involving both Muslims and Christians, it was the Christian justice system (municipal, royal, or other) that prevailed. A Muslim witness sometimes had to swear on the Qur'an, just as the Jew swore on the Torah and the Christian on the Gospels. The *Siete partidas* of Alfonso X of Castile established a precise and elaborate rite: the oath had to be taken at the door of the mosque; the Muslim witness had to swear in the name of Muhammad and his law and had to declare that, if his testimony was not truthful, he agreed to be deprived of all the goods belonging to Muhammad and the prophets and to suffer all the punishments that the Qur'an destined for the infidels.[40] The court placed more faith in Christian witnesses than in Muslims or Jews: a Muslim could not testify against a Christian, except in cases of treason.[41] Penalties and fines often reflected the Muslim's inferior status. The *Leyes de estilo*, compiled in Castile in the early fourteenth century, stipulated that the fine for the murder of a Moor should follow local custom but that it had to be lower than that levied for the murder of a Christian.[42]

The legislation relating to Muslim minorities was derived from the traditional laws that limited the place of Jews in Christian society: in accordance with canon law, Jews could not have the slightest power over Christians. In particular, they were not allowed to own Christian slaves or to hold public office. Later laws extended these principles to the Muslims. The Third Lateran Council (1179) prohibited the Jews and Saracens from owning Christian slaves, a prohibition often repeated in royal legislation (for example, in the *Siete partidas*).[43] Various *fueros* in Iberian cities prohibited the Jews and Muslims from being judges in cases relating to Christians.[44]

That legal inferiority did not always translate into true social inferiority. Muslims and Jews could in fact be found at every level of society. Mudejar contingents from Valencia played an important role in the army of the Aragonese kings: during the French invasion of Catalonia in 1285, for example, six hundred Valencian Mudejars, crossbowmen in particular, took part in the defense of Girona. Many Jewish and Muslim doctors were also in the service of princes and commoners. They sometimes provoked jealousy or distrust: William of Tyre complained that the wives of Frankish nobles preferred Jewish or Saracen doctors, and his translator added that these doctors were poisoning the grandees of the kingdom.[45]

Many laws were aimed at prohibiting all sexual relationships between Christians and Muslims. Interfaith marriage was outlawed, except in cases where an already-married Muslim or Jew converted to Christianity. Such a person had the right to remain married to a non-Christian spouse, according to Gratian's *Decretum*, and Pope Gregory IX confirmed that right in 1234.[46] In Christian Spain generally, the Christian woman and Muslim man who had sexual relations faced great risks, but that was not the case for the Muslim woman and her Christian lover. The *Fuero de Sepúlveda* decrees that a Muslim man who sleeps with a Christian woman will be thrown from a cliff and his lover burned; in the *Fuero de Béjar*, they are both to be burned. The *Siete partidas* is slightly more lenient toward the Christian woman: the Muslim or Jewish lover is to be stoned, while his accomplice loses half her possessions. If she is married, she faces the death penalty; if a prostitute, the two lovers are whipped together throughout the city. In all cases, the penalties for repeat offenders are harsher.[47] By contrast, no mention is made of sexual relations between a Christian man and a Muslim or Jewish woman, which seem to have been tacitly accepted. To judge by municipal jurisprudence, especially the *fueros* granted to Iberian cities by Christian sovereigns, it appears that sexual relations between Christian men and Muslim slave girls were commonplace. In the Crown of Aragon of the fourteenth century, a Christian prostitute ran the risk of being burned alive if she slept with a Jewish or Muslim man, and the Muslim authorities often demanded the death penalty for a Muslim woman who slept with a Jewish or Christian man. Nevertheless, the woman could escape punishment either by converting to Christianity or by becoming a slave—often of her Christian lover.[48] In law as in literature, sexual conquest became the metaphor for conquest generally. The pretty Muslim woman was not only a literary topos, she could also be found in the bed of many a Christian knight. A few authors did criticize or discourage these practices: The *Castigos e documentos para bien vivir ordenados por el rey don Sancho IV* tried to persuade the future king Fernando IV of Castile that having sexual relations with a Moorish woman was like sleeping with a dog, since she followed the irrational law of Muhammad.[49] Such views, one suspects, had little influence on the sexual practices of the prince and his entourage.

Contact with the religious adversary was often seen as an element of corruption or pollution to be avoided. Some *fueros* banned non-Christians from going to the public baths on the same days as Christians.[50] Christian wet nurses were prohibited from breastfeeding Jewish or Muslim children, Christians from using Muslim or Jewish wet nurses for their offspring.[51] It was also in an attempt to better enforce the sexual prohibitions that the law imposed (or tried to impose) clothing restrictions. As early as 1120, the Council of Nablus followed its many sexual prohibitions with a ban on Muslims dressing as "Franks."[52] These clothing restrictions were supposed to help Christians identify Muslims and thus avoid any needless contact with them. In the same spirit, in 1215 the Fourth Lateran Council decreed that Saracens and Jews were to wear distinctive garb to prevent sexual relations with Christians, or rather, to prevent Christians from pleading ignorance to justify their affairs with non-Christians. These measures were in principle to be imposed on all Christendom, but they were unevenly applied. Sumptuary laws requiring distinctive signs for Muslims and prohibiting them from wearing "Christian" clothing can in fact be found in various eras: at the Cortes of Seville in 1252, at that of Valladolid in 1258, and again at that of Seville in 1261, proof that the measure taken by the council of 1215 was not respected to any great extent.[53]

Not only sexual corruption but also spiritual corruption provoked fear. Innocent III and the Fourth Lateran Council strove to defend the Christians from the mockeries and blasphemies of the "infidels." In order to protect the Holy Week rituals from such contamination, the council did not hesitate to ban Muslims and Jews from public places during that period, as legislation in Spain would later do.[54] Muslims and Jews were lumped together because of their supposed hostility toward the Christians. Both were "blasphemers," according to the council, which claimed that members of these two groups paraded during Holy Week in gaudy clothes, making fun of the Christians who were ritually expressing their sorrow at the Passion of Christ. That hostility was specifically invoked to justify the ban on their holding public office: a "blasphemer" could not be granted the slightest power over a Christian. A polemical view of Islam fed these decisions of the Fourth Lateran Council: the council did not enumerate or distinguish the different "blasphemies" of the Muslims or Jews, but it declared that they were sufficient to justify their exclusion from any position of authority.

Alfonso X devoted one of the sections (*títulos*) of the seventh *Partida* to those who insulted "God, Mary, and the other saints."[55] The last of the six chapters of the *título* has to do with the Jews and Moors who utter such insults. It notes that the Jews and Moors were allowed to live in "our country" even though they did not share "our faith," but that this permission was granted them only if they did nothing to insult Christ, his mother, or the other saints. In addition to the ban on verbal insults, it was forbidden to spit on crosses, altars, and images of saints; to strike a holy object with the hand, foot, or another object; and to throw stones at churches.[56]

The problem of conversion recurs often in legal documents. Alfonso the Wise made it the main subject of *título* 7.25 of the *Siete partidas*, called "De los moros": seven of the ten laws are devoted to it. Five laws have to do with the punishments to be inflicted on the Christian who converts to Islam. The apostate shall lose all his possessions, which become the property of his heirs who have remained Christian; he can be accused of that crime until five years after his death. If an apostate returns to Christianity, he still loses the right to be a public official or a witness, and to enter into sales or purchasing contracts. The political and military context of thirteenth-century Castile instilled a fear of converts to Islam. It was a very real danger: conversions often occurred during captivity in Islamic territory or accompanied an act of treason.[57] By contrast, the conversion of a Muslim to Christianity was desirable, according to the *Siete partidas*, but always had to be voluntary: Christians had to try to persuade

Muslims by reason and example, not by violence or constraint. No one had the right to prevent a Muslim from converting to Christianity, or to call the convert a *tornadizo* (renegade or traitor), or to insult him. According to Alfonso, it was the fear of being the object of such insults, as well as force of habit, that would keep Muslims from converting. Kings James I and Peter of Aragon decreed similar laws to protect converts from insults and the loss of their inheritance.

Conversion to the dominant religion was often motivated by social considerations. That was especially the case for slaves: baptism resulted in liberation, as specified, for example, in the *Siete partidas* or in the *Furs* of Valencia. But slave owners were naturally opposed to that principle and tried to prevent the evangelization of their slaves: Jacques de Vitry, bishop of Acre in the thirteenth century, complained that the Christians of the Holy Land did not allow him to preach to their slaves. Pope Gregory IX ultimately decreed that the conversion of a slave would not result in liberation, hoping that masters would thereby allow slaves wishing to convert to do so.[58]

CAPTIVES AND SLAVES

In the Middle Ages, slavery was an integral part of Mediterranean societies, both Muslim and Christian. Slaves were often captives taken during a siege, sailors and passengers of a commandeered ship, or peasants from coastal regions rounded up by corsairs. The captive faced one of three fates. If he had wealthy or influential relatives, he was ransomed: from the point of view of his abductors, that was the most profitable operation. He could also be used as currency of exchange to secure the liberation of captives held by the adversary. Or the abductor could reduce him to slavery, either to profit directly from his services or to sell him on the international market in the extensive slave trade.

In the wars between the caliphal and the Byzantine armies, the many prisoners taken by each side had first and foremost a propaganda value: they were paraded about, displayed in public, because they embodied the victory over the infidel enemy. In about 900, for example, the emperor of Constantinople held a banquet for his Muslim prisoners on Easter: his "guests" were solemnly reassured that they would be served no pork. He also had a mosque built for the prisoners and for visiting Muslim diplomats.[59] These captives were later exchanged for Byzantines held by the Muslims. The Qur'an stipulates the fate of prisoners of war taken by the Muslims: "Grant them their freedom or take ransom (*al-fidā'*) from them, until War shall lay down her burdens" (the term *al-fidā'* would later be used to designate both ransom and exchange).[60] In addition, the redemption of Muslim prisoners was considered an obligation and was one of the authorized uses for the *zakat*, alms that had become an obligatory tax for every Muslim. Many exchanges of captives between the Byzantine emperors and the Abbasid caliphs took place between 769 and 969.[61]

In the Holy Land in the age of the Crusades, many were taken captive on both sides. 'Imād al-Dīn, a chronicler in Saladin's entourage, claimed that Saladin had redeemed twenty thousand Muslims from captivity among the Franks: an exaggerated figure no doubt, but other sources on both sides confirm that many were freed. In 1263, the Mamluk sultan Baybars is reported to have proposed a large exchange of captives to the Franks of Acre; the military orders refused, however, because their Muslim slaves were talented artisans whom it would have been impossible to replace.[62] When Charles II of Anjou reduced the Muslims of Lucera to slavery in 1300, about ten thousand were sold on the markets of Naples, Bari, and other cities of the kingdom.

The owner of a perfume shop successfully purchased five hundred slaves in Spain after the Muslim conquest and brought them back to Syria, if we are to believe a chronicle written three centuries after the events. The same text speaks of a Visigoth slave purchased in Medina for a handful of pepper.[63] The summer raids by Umayyad troops into northern Spain in the ninth and tenth centuries often procured large quantities of slaves.[64] Sometimes the northern kings responded in kind, as in summer 913, when Ordoño II of León attacked Alentejo and took four thousand women and children captive.[65] Almohad chroniclers claim (exaggerating no doubt) that Caliph Abū Yūsuf Ya'qūb al-Mansūr took as many as twenty-five thousand captives during his victory at Alarcos in 1195. Other sources speak of five thousand captives, reportedly exchanged for five thousand Muslim captives.[66] During the great conquests of the Spanish Christian kings (such as the taking of Majorca in 1229, of Minorca in 1235, or of Granada in 1492), captives were plentiful on the markets of Iberian and Italian cities.

More common were captures during actions on a smaller scale: small raids on border regions, where attackers quickly seized objects of value (including cattle, women, and children); and acts of piracy, with pirates commandeering a ship or making a rapid incursion into a coastal zone. When Muslims of Spain conquered Crete in the ninth century, they used it primarily as a base for conducting raids against the Byzantine Empire, enriching themselves with the booty and ransoming captives or selling them on the slave markets. Greek corsairs did the same on the coasts of Syria, Palestine, and Egypt.[67]

Some of these actions were illegal, which in theory prevented the perpetrators from selling the booty, including slaves. In the case of those captured during a war, the purchaser was assured that captives were "fair game" (de bona guerra) and that, as a result, the purchase did not risk being voided. Otherwise, the legality of the sale was not assured. In fourteenth-century Catalonia, for example, if someone who was purchased as a slave turned out to be a Christian prince's Mudejar subject, unjustly deprived of his freedom, or the subject of a Muslim ally of the king of Aragon taken during an illegal raid, the buyer could be obliged to free the slave, often without financial compensation.[68] That may be part of the reason that in Genoa young Tatar or Greek women were preferred to Maghrebis; the Genoese controlled the trade, without being overly moved that the Greek women were Christians. Over time, the enslavement of Christians raised fewer and fewer objections, provided they could be considered heretics, schismatics, or simply rebels. Two popes (in 1294 and then in 1305) threatened to reduce their Italian political adversaries to slavery.[69]

Raids represented humiliation for those who were reduced to slavery and for their families, fellow citizens, and coreligionists. Many initiatives were therefore taken to liberate the captives, usually in exchange for ransom. In the early tenth century, the patriarch of Constantinople sent a pound of gold to the residents of Amalfi, who had commercial and political relations with the Aghlabids of Ifrīqiya, in order to redeem Christian captives.[70] Bequests (often in wills) have been found dating to late tenth-century Catalonia for the redemption of captives taken by al-Mansūr in 985.[71] In the twelfth century, some *fueros* established that Christians had a right to purchase Muslim slaves at the market price, in order to use them as ransom for Christian captives in Muslim hands.[72] In 1182, King Alfonso VIII of Castile captured the castle of Santafila and took seven hundred prisoners; the Muslims of Seville redeemed them for twenty-seven hundred gold dinars.[73] In the documents, the redemption of captives sometimes looks like one commercial practice among others, profitable for the merchant involved. In eleventh-century Egypt, the ransom for a captive varied between twenty-four and one hundred gold dinars, depending on the circumstances. One hundred dinars for three captives seems to have been more or less the "standard" price[74]—it was, for example, what Greek corsairs selling Muslim captives in the Palestinian ports asked in the tenth century.[75] That commerce benefited the abductors but also the retailers, such as the Amalfitans who purchased Egyptian Jewish captives from their *Rūm* (Byzantine or Italian) captors, brought them back to Egypt, and then offered the Jewish community of Alexandria the chance to redeem them.[76] Many examples exist, such as a contract concluded in 1454 in Genoa, by the terms of which two captives, Ahmet Mazus and Mohammed Zamai, acknowledged that they were in the power of a certain Giovanni Raibaldi, "who purchased us from the hands of our enemies." They pledged to pay Raibaldi's brother in Tunis 161.5 gold doubloons and a half-length of cloth within twenty days after their return to North Africa. Similarly, Italian, Catalan, and Marseillais merchants redeemed Christian captives in North Africa, in exchange for the promise of payment after their return to Europe.[77] The redemption of captives became a profession: the *fakkāk*, Hispanized to *alfaqueque*, collected funds, crossed the Mediterranean, redeemed Muslim or Christian captives, and brought them home. By the thirteenth century, various Christian kings of Spain had named *alfaqueques* who acted in the state's behalf.[78]

Family initiatives, the pursuit of profit, state interests, and religious motivations all play their part in the accounts of the liberation of captives.[79] Usāma ibn Munqidh tells of his missions to purchase Muslim captives from the hands of the Franks.[80] Ibn Jubayr was moved by the sight of chained Muslim prisoners in the streets of Acre. He writes that the princes and other Muslims of the region made abundant gifts to free these captives.[81] And it was not only their coreligionists whom people took it upon themselves to ransom: Ibn Taymiyya says he paid a ransom to the Mongols for the liberation not only of the Muslim prisoners but also of the *dhimmis*, who were "under the protection" of the Muslims.[82] In Spain, the gifts offered for the liberation of captive Christians in Muslim territory sometimes went through the intermediary of the *alfaqueques*, but increasingly they passed through religious institutions. These could be military orders (like that of Santiago) or new orders created specifically to work for the liberation of the captives: the Order of the Holy Trinity (founded in 1198) and the Order of Our Lady of Mercy (1218).[83] Monks collected funds from the faithful and traveled to meet with Muslim princes in Spain and North Africa to redeem Christian prisoners, whom they brought back to Europe.

Slaves remained numerous in most Mediterranean societies of the Middle Ages. Slavery was fostered not only by raids and roundups but also by international trade or trafficking extending from the Mongol Empire to western Africa.[84] Slaves were omnipresent in the Byzantine Empire: in the workshops of Constantinople, in the homes of owners of large rural demesnes, in the mines, in the imperial palace.[85] In Muslim territories, many slaves were imported from the *dār al-harb*: Slavs (pagan or Christian) from northern Europe, mamluks (often pagan Turks) from the Asian steppes, blacks from eastern and western Africa. These slaves occupied a not insignificant place in Muslim societies. Slave women and young girls were destined to perform household tasks and sometimes to become the concubines of their masters. The men formed large military contingents within the caliph's or sultan's armies: from Iraq to al-Andalus, the power of various princes rested on the military strength of their Slavic, black, or mamluk contingents. The princes used them as counterweights to Arab or Berber forces. For example, the *Saqāliba* (Slavs) played an important role in the armies of the caliphate of Cordova in the tenth century and in the palatine administration.[86] The strategy was dangerous, however, and sometimes gave rise to armed slave revolts, assassinations (a number of Cordovan leaders were killed in the first third of the eleventh century), and even coups d'état, such as the one that overthrew the Ayyubids of Egypt in favor of the Mamluks in 1250.

Other men were subjected to castration and became eunuchs. They were assigned to guard the princely harems and were given tasks of an administrative nature. The owners of the extensive domains in certain parts of Europe used large numbers of Muslim slaves. In Cyprus and Sicily, for example, the slaves cultivated sugarcane. The introduction of sugar to the kingdom of Valencia, and then to Portugal, encouraged the growth of agricultural slavery, which was already well established. These practices spread to the Portuguese islands of the Atlantic in the fifteenth century and to the American colonies in the sixteenth.[87] Other intensive farming, such as that of mulberries (for silkworms) also relied on slavery, especially in the region of Genoa.[88] But most of the slaves in medieval Europe were domestics in aristocratic and bourgeois houses, responsible for the cooking, the housework, and the care of children. Some served as wet nurses: a young nursing woman had a much greater value on the market. In Genoa and Venice, girls were purchased from the Maghreb, or more often (beginning in the thirteenth century), from the lands bordering the Black Sea. Slaves could be found even in modest quarters, in the shops of artisans of Italian or Portuguese cities, for example; a young apprentice or a free servant girl would have been much more costly.[89] In the marriage contracts of aristocratic Italian families, a slave girl was often part of the dowry provided by the bride's parents. It is difficult to estimate the slave population, but there were reportedly 13,750 "Slavs" (Saqāliba), slaves and freedmen, in Cordova in the tenth century,[90] and 1,225 slaves were counted in Barcelona in 1431. In mid-fifteenth-century Genoa, there may have been 3,000 slaves (the vast majority of them women and girls), representing about 3 percent of the city's population as a whole but 10 percent of the female population under thirty.[91]

Although narrative sources on these slaves are few, normative texts are abundant, ranging from the Bible and the Qur'an to treatises on municipal laws, sales contracts, and acts of manumission. In Roman and Byzantine law, the child of a slave mother or any captive taken during a war was a slave. In theory, punitive slavery was also recognized, but that practice became increasingly less common in the Middle Ages. A master who wanted to marry his slave had to free her beforehand. Muslim law prohibited reducing a Muslim or a dhimmi to slavery; these prohibitions were generally respected, except in rare cases of those considered heterodox, sometimes judged unworthy of their freedom.[92] The child born of a slave mother was considered the slave of its mother's master, unless the master himself was the father, in which case the child was free and legitimate and the slave mother became umm al-walad (mother of children): she retained her slave condition, but her master no longer had the right to sell her, and she became free upon his death. The son of such a union had the same rights to inheritance as the sons of free wives, and it was not uncommon for the son of a slave to reach the highest echelons of power.[93] The mother of the grand caliph of Cordova, 'Abd al-Rahmān III, was a Frankish captive, his paternal grandmother a Gascon.[94]

Jews, Christians, and Muslims practiced slavery in the Middle Ages. It was broadly accepted, including by men of faith and religious institutions such as monasteries and military orders, which owned many slaves. In Byzantium, the monks and nuns of aristocratic origin kept the personal slaves in their service at the convent.[95] Sometimes religious scruples impelled masters to treat their slaves with indulgence or even to free them. According to various Hadith, Muhammad reminded the faithful that God, who gave them authority over their slaves, could also have reversed the roles, and that they should therefore be gentle and fair to their slaves. According to several Christian authors, slavery is a punishment for human imperfection that must be endured with humility and patience. Hagiography, moreover, often portrays the captivity of Byzantine Christians raided by Muslim corsairs as an ordeal allowing the saint to display his virtues, and sometimes to perform miracles leading to his liberation or the conversion of his abductors.[96] For many Jews, Christians, and Muslims, liberating one's slaves was an act of piety. The Qur'an encourages the Muslim to liberate his war captives, either for ransom, in an exchange of prisoners, or freely, without compensation. This last initiative was for many jurists a good way to receive forgiveness for one's misdeeds and be reconciled with God.[97] One Hadith declares that anyone who frees a Muslim slave will be liberated from the torments of hell; another says that the Muslim man who educates a young slave girl, frees her, then marries her honorably, will obtain a dual reward in paradise.[98] Byzantine hagiography mentions various cases of saints who freed their slaves in order to then devote themselves to a pious life. There it was less the institution of slavery than worldly possessions (human or other) that were an obstacle to a holy life.[99] In Constantinople and in Italian cities such as Genoa and Venice, many acts of manumission are recorded, either to allow a slave woman who has served her master well to enter into marriage with a free man, or to free slaves upon the master's death (though often the will containing the act stipulates that one or two slaves remain in the service of his widow). Acts of manumission readily cite reasons of a religious order: the love of God or of his saints, the desire to be forgiven of one's sins or to obtain eternal salvation. Similar manumissions in extremis were carried out by Jewish merchants in Cairo.[100] In the large Italian and Iberian cities, religious institutions emerged specifically to attend to these liberated slaves.[101]

Manumission was sometimes granted as a reward for services, past or future, given to one's master. A number of Muslim captives in Constantinople eventually converted to Christianity, married Christian women, and settled in the empire, where they often served in the army. If we are to believe the tenth-century geographer Mas'ūdi, the empire had a contingent of twelve thousand Christianized Arab cavalrymen. Byzantine and Frankish captives, only some of whom had converted to Islam, also served in the armies of Muslim princes.[102]

The laws of Italian and Iberian cities tried to regulate the sex lives of slaves (especially women). In the large agricultural estates, the issue at hand was primarily unions between slaves, whose children were slaves like their parents, while in the cities it was more often a matter of liaisons between slave women and free men. In Genoa, any man who acknowledged impregnating someone else's slave had to pay a fine to make amends to the master; the children born of such unions, usually free, were given to orphanages or adopted by their fathers. In Spain, by contrast, the child generally remained the property of the mother's master. The *Fuero* of Teruel (1176 or 1177) imposed a fine of twenty gold coins on any man who raped a Moorish slave not his own; there was no punishment, however, for raping one's own slave. If a slave gave birth and the master was not the father, the child would be the master's slave until the father purchased it. Only children who were redeemed, and then freed, could inherit from their fathers. The provisions were similar in other *fueros*.[103]

Slaves and captives sometimes tried to escape. This was not a major problem in Italian cities, where slaves were far from their native lands and could not count on the aid of the local population. In Byzantium, fugitive slaves could take refuge in monasteries and become monks. Hagiography provides various examples of saints, such as Saint Faith of Conques or Saint Dominic of Silos, who focused particularly on the miraculous liberation of Christian captives from the hands of the infidels.[104] But other saints, especially Theodore Tiron and John the Soldier, actually helped Christian masters recover their fugitive slaves.[105] In Spain, near the border, Malekite jurists tried to establish procedures for capturing the escaped slaves and returning them to their Muslim masters.[106] In the Christian kingdoms, fugitive Muslim slaves were sometimes aided or hidden by free Mudejars. It seems, in fact, that in certain areas of Spain there was a sort of underground railroad that helped escaped slaves flee to Muslim lands. In the mid-twelfth century, the *Usatges de Barcelona* established monetary rewards for returning fugitive slaves to their masters.[107] In the fifteenth century, the king of Aragon founded an obligatory insurance fund for slave owners, who paid an annual premium for each slave and received indemnities for each fugitive. The money collected was used not only to pay compensation but also to maintain a dedicated police force and to give rewards to those who helped recover the escaped slaves. Once captured, these slaves were auctioned off, and the money from the sale returned to the fund.[108]

Religious coexistence in Europe is not the result of twentieth-century immigration: it existed in European Christian and Muslim societies throughout the Middle Ages. Religious minorities—Jewish, Christian, or Muslim—played a key role at that time, as they still do today, in the transmission of knowledge and culture and also in commerce.

CHAPTER 4

In Search of Egyptian Gold

Traders in the Mediterranean

THE HISTORY OF DIPLOMATIC, military, and cultural relations in the Mediterranean has always been tied to that of commerce. The Arab world was located on the major axes of world trade, linked to India, China, Byzantium, Africa, and Europe. In the tenth century, Latin Europe was only a minor partner in these exchanges, but over the following centuries, commercial relations developed and contributed to an economic boom for both civilizations, turning the Mediterranean region into a single economic unit.

CITY AND COUNTRY IN EUROPE AND THE MUSLIM WORLD

At the time of Muhammad's death in 632, Constantinople was the only large city in Europe.[1] As the cultural, political, and economic center of an empire, albeit one weakened by its recent wars with Persia and the invasions of the Slavs and Avars, it remained the great metropolis, the driving force behind commerce with the rest of the empire: namely, the cities around the Aegean Sea (Thessalonica, Ephesus, Smyrna, Miletus), those in the West (Rome, Ravenna, Carthage), and the two other major cities in the empire, Alexandria and Antioch. In the seventh century, both of these cities were taken by Muslim armies, which also twice besieged Constantinople without success (in 674–678, and then in 717–718). The largest city in Europe remained Byzantine until its conquest by the Venetians and the Crusaders during the Fourth Crusade in 1204.

In the seventh century, the Muslims seized the most populous and wealthy cities of the Byzantine and Persian empires, with the exception of Constantinople. From Isfahan to Lisbon, the autochthonous elites (now *dhimmis*) continued to govern the cities and the rural regions of what was now a Muslim empire. In the cities, where peoples and traditions mingled, a Muslim culture and civilization developed. The Umayyad caliphs (680–750) were the first to make urban culture and urban monuments central to Islam and to caliphal authority. This was apparent in Palestinian and Syrian cities, especially Jerusalem, where the

Dome of the Rock was built in 692, and al-Aqsa Mosque some twenty years later, and Damascus, which was turned into a major capital befitting caliphal ambitions, with a great mosque and a palatine complex. The Damascene palace was sacked during the Abbasid coup d'état of 750, and the walls of the city dismantled; Baghdad, the capital of the new dynasty, took inspiration both from Damascus and, to a lesser degree, from Ctesiphon, the former Persian capital nearby. A dense urban network emerged, linking Roman and Persian cities to the new cities arising from Arab military encampments and to other new entities.[2] The model for a medieval Muslim city took shape: the great mosque with its minarets dominating the city; the palace of the prince (caliph, emir, or sultan), often next to the mosque; baths, souks, and small neighborhood mosques. Surrounding it all were the ramparts, whose height and solidity served first and foremost as military defense, but which also reflected the power and wealth of the city and its prince. "The most beautiful jewels of the Muslim Middle Ages were its cities," declares André Miquel.[3] At a time when Europe was composed primarily of rural societies, Islam became the urban civilization par excellence. The sites of power in Latin Europe were usually castles; in Islam, they were cities. The places for education and writing in Europe (before the twelfth century) were for the most part monasteries; in Islam, they were the mosques and madrasas of the major cities. In the famous tripartite division of European feudal society (those who pray, those who wage war, and those who work the land) invented by monks in about the year 1000, the rural world dominated, whereas Muslim jurists tended to view society as a city, distinguishing rich merchants or financiers from workers and artisans. The peasants (*fellahin*), like the Bedouins, were considered outside civilized society, and the great Maghrebian historian Ibn Khaldūn even combined the two groups.[4]

It is therefore not surprising that, as of the ninth century, it was in Muslim Europe—that is, in the emirate and then the caliphate of Cordova—that the only large European cities outside Constantinople were located. Cordova was the first, the seat of the Umayyad dynasty in the West, perpetuating the memory of the fallen Damascus and rivaling Abbasid Baghdad.[5] That capital, if we are to believe the tenth-century geographer Ibn Hawqal, "has no equivalent in all the Maghreb, or in Mesopotamia, Syria, or Egypt, in terms of the size of its population, its land area, the vast space occupied by its markets, the cleanliness of the place, the architecture of its mosques, and the large number of baths and caravansaries."[6] The economic vitality of many Andalusian cities besides Cordova was dependent on artisanship and commerce. Almeria was the most important port, the "key" of al-Andalus, according to the twelfth-century geographer Ahmad al-Rāzī. The city produced silk and built ships, and several contracts in the Geniza of Cairo mention Almeria. That same al-Rāzī describes other ports on the Mediterranean coast (especially Valencia, Denia, and Málaga), and then depicts Seville as one of the best ports of al-Andalus, even though, to reach it from the Mediterranean, one had to cross the Strait of Gibraltar, then travel more than eighty kilometers up the Guadalquivir. Before the year 1000, commercial thoroughfares linked al-Andalus, first, to the Maghreb, then to Egypt and Syria; exchanges with Europe north of the Pyrenees were less common.[7]

In a Mediterranean dominated by the confrontations and rivalries between Byzantines, Umayyads, and Abbasids, the rest of Europe played a minor role. In the eighth century, the Italian and Provençal coastal regions were more the victims of plunder than economic actors, which led the Belgian historian Henri Pirenne to argue, in his *Mahomet et Charlemagne*, that the Muslim domination of the Mediterranean sounded the death knell of the ancient Roman world and obliged Europe to recenter itself to the north. It was not until the ninth century, when the Christian states acquired the military advantage in the Mediterranean, that, Pirenne claims, they were once more able to engage in major trade. For Maurice Lombard, conversely, it was precisely contact with a more economically developed Muslim world that allowed Europe to enrich itself and to take part in commerce, which it finally came to dominate. Although the sources remain few, archaeology and numismatics have made it possible to qualify such claims.[8] Europe retained a role in the Mediterranean economy, as attested by the Arab, and especially Andalusian, coins found in Gaul, England, and Scandinavia and dating to the eighth to tenth centuries. It is true that these coins did not circulate solely through commerce: they could also be gifts or booty. But they nevertheless suggest the existence of trade and at times point to odd convergences: for example, a silver coin found in Poland bore, on one side, an Arabic inscription with the name of the Cordovan caliph Hishām II (976–1009) and, on the other, a Latin inscription in the name of the German emperor Henry II (1002–1024).[9] Although it is hard to see who could have struck such a coin or for what reason, it clearly attests that relations, probably diplomatic as well as economic, existed between the two sovereigns.

Historians insist on the important role that the exchange of gifts played in consolidating political and social ties in Europe in the early Middle Ages, whether between husband and wife, vassal and lord, or two allied kings. From that point of view, the lists of objects exchanged during embassies, between Cordova, Constantinople, Aix-la-Chapelle, and Baghdad are of interest here. For example, during negotiations for an anti-Umayyad alliance between the Frankish king Pepin the Short and the Abbasid caliph al-Mansūr in the 760s, the ambassadors on both sides were "laden with presents."[10] In 802, when a new Abbasid embassy arrived at the court of Charlemagne in Aix-la-Chapelle, it brought linen and silk, perfumes and spices, a bronze clock, a brass candelabra, and exotic animals, including an elephant named Abū al-'Abbas, which impressed the court and whose death eight years later was noted with sadness.[11] It is not known exactly what gifts Charlemagne sent to Baghdad, but he likely would have had trouble creating the same sensation in that city. By contrast, Abbasid caliphs and Byzantine emperors tried to outdo one another in the extravagance of the gifts they sent with embassies between the two capitals.

Caliph Maʿmūn, having received sumptuous gifts from Emperor Theophilus (829–842), ordered: "Give him a present a hundred times more precious than his own, so that he will know the power of Islam and the blessings God has bestowed on us."[12]

More prosaically, for the Mediterranean economy Europe represented an important source of raw materials: wood and iron especially, and also hides and furs. But its most important and most lucrative export between the eighth and tenth centuries was undoubtedly slaves.

FROM A "MUSLIM LAKE" TO AN ITALIAN *MARE NOSTRUM* IN THE ELEVENTH TO FOURTEENTH CENTURIES

After the year 1000, as the caliphate of Cordova was collapsing, Fatimid Egypt became the true hub of world commerce, for three reasons. First, located between the Mediterranean and the Red Sea, Egypt stood at the crossroads of major world trade routes. Second, it was one of the most prosperous regions of the Muslim world: the Nile irrigated and fertilized it and also provided a crucial artery of communication. And third, the leaders of the country, the Fatimid caliphs (969–1171) and then the Ayyubid sultans (1171–1250), understood the importance of commerce for their country and generally did not impose excessive tax burdens or restrictions on personal travel. The historian Shlomo Goitein even calls the Mediterranean of the time a "free trade community."[13]

The letters of Jewish merchants found in the Geniza attached to the synagogue of al-Fustāt (Old Cairo) indicate the scope of activity of the Egyptian traders, present on the Atlantic coasts of Morocco and Portugal and even in the ports of India. It was in India that spices (pepper, cinnamon, ginger, and others) were purchased, to be taken to a port on the Red Sea: either Qulzum (present-day Suez), from whence merchandise was transported via caravan as far as Cairo; or ʿAydhāb, in Upper Egypt, from which traders crossed the desert to Aswān and then sailed down the Nile. The annual caravan returning from the pilgrimage to Mecca frequently offered an opportunity to bring back Eastern goods to the capital. From Cairo, ships transported merchandise to one of the Mediterranean ports: Rosetta, Damietta, or especially, Alexandria. From these ports, spices from the East as well as Egyptian products, the most important of them being linen, were transported to Palestine, Cyprus, Byzantium, the Maghreb, and Europe. This linen could be in the form of flax (exported to the Maghreb or Sicily, where it was woven) or of finished cloth. In Egypt, as elsewhere in the Mediterranean world, the textile industry was one of the most important economic activities; according to Goitein, it involved, in one way or another, most of the active population of Cairo. Linen cloth—garments, sheets, cushions, rugs, or other products—represented a large share of the wealth in each house.[14] But not everyone worked for the textile industry: the Geniza mentions 265 manual occupations, from peddler to dyer and from bead piercer to maker of kohl sticks.[15] A number of these artisans fabricated export articles, especially glass, or gold and silver jewelry. Some also produced foodstuffs, sugar first and foremost, and many an Egyptian trader invested in refineries. Ports such as Alexandria especially were the site of all sorts of activities related to the production of provisions for sea journeys: biscuit, salted fish, and so on.

The letters in the Geniza, most of them from Tunisian, Sicilian, and Egyptian merchants, show that there was frequent communication and that these merchants crossed the sea back and forth between Palestine, Cyprus, Constantinople, Spain, Sicily, and the Maghreb. Merchants generally did not specialize in a particular product but bought and sold a large diversity of goods. One of the many examples is Nahray b. Nissīm, who traveled the Mediterranean for fifty years (1045–1096): he bought linen in Egypt and resold it in Tunisia or Sicily; imported Spanish silk, Maghrebian felt, and Byzantine cotton to Egypt; purchased olive oil, soap, and wax in Tunisia or Palestine; exported Egyptian sugar; purchased dried fruit in Syria; and bought and sold shoes, hides, jewelry, books, paper, and many products used in dye works, as well as pharmaceuticals, cosmetics, and perfumes.[16] The documents in the Geniza mention roughly two hundred products, about forty of which were the object of regular and intense trade.[17] A large part of society participated in commerce: more than one traveler, whether pilgrim or ambassador, rabbi or ulema, took advantage of his travels to engage in trade. Those who did not travel often played the role of financial backers or producers. In al-Andalus and Sicily, it was possible to invest small or large amounts in the silk trade, just as people now invest in the stock market.

By contrast, the Egyptian merchants who criss-crossed the Mediterranean between Cyprus and Seville did not go to Italy or Provence. It was the Italians who went to Egypt, especially Alexandria—certainly in small numbers in the tenth century, but increasingly in the following centuries. Sometimes they were called simply *Rūm*, "Romans," a term normally used for the Byzantines, but more and more often they were called "Franks" (*Faranj* or *Ifranj*).[18] The arrival of *Ifranj* merchants in an Arab port was an important event for Muslim merchants. As soon as someone caught sight of their ships or heard a rumor of their arrival, prices on certain goods climbed, to the joy of sellers and the despair of potential buyers. In the eleventh century, many merchants were delighted at the presence of the Europeans, who paid high prices even for poor-quality goods. The Europeans sold wood, cheese, and wine (its consumption was not forbidden during the Fatimid era).[19] They also brought silver, a rare product in the Muslim East before the eleventh century, when gold coins were primarily in use. And they brought slaves.

Until the tenth century, two European regions in particular were involved in these networks of international trade: the empire of Constantinople and the caliphate of Cordova. The rest of Europe profited somewhat from the boon of that commerce: there were Frankish merchants in the cities of al-Andalus, and Italian—especially Venetian— merchants in Constantinople. But gradually, beginning in the tenth century, Italian merchants headed to the East, especially Egypt, to gain direct access to Arab markets.[20]

Amalfi, from the ninth century until its conquest by the Normans in 1073, was the chief Italian city trading with North Africa.[21] This port city south of Naples established peaceful relations with the Aghlabids of Ifrīqiya (modern-day Tunisia) in the ninth century, which kept it from becoming a target during the Ifrīqiyan maritime raids on the Italian coast, and allowed it to retain its independence from the Lombard princes of Benevento. Although the city nominally recognized the suzerainty of Constantinople, with which it maintained fruitful diplomatic and economic contacts, that did not prevent it from enjoying de facto independence, and especially, from participating in trade with Muslim Ifrīqiya and Sicily. It established good relations with the Fatimids soon after the creation of the Shiite caliphate in 909. The Amalfitans participated in the Fatimid conquest of Egypt in 969 by conveying food and wood for the conquerors. The new lords of Egypt showed their gratitude by granting the Amalfitans significant fiscal privileges. Their presence in Egypt is confirmed by the report of an incident in 996: rumors spread in Cairo of a Byzantine invasion, and Amalfitan merchants suspected of being in league with the *Rūm* were massacred. If we are to believe the chronicles, about a hundred died, and losses amounted to about 84 pounds of gold. That event shows the dangers that foreign merchants faced in Egypt and elsewhere, but it does not seem to have discouraged the Amalfitans for long: the caliph ratified their privileges and compensated them for their material losses. These merchants exported wheat, wood, linen, wine, and fruit from Italy to North Africa; in Ifrīqiya, they obtained olive oil, wax, and gold; in Egypt, spices and gold. Amalfi and its neighbors Salerno and Naples adopted the *tari*, a Fatimid gold coin, as the principal currency, a good indication of the importance of these contacts in the region's economy. Gold fueled Amalfitan trade with Byzantium and Italy, thanks to which Italian princes and popes could obtain luxury articles. Amalfitan commerce suffered when the Normans conquered the city in 1073 (the Norman kings favored Palermo and Naples), then again when the Fatimids fell from power in 1171.

Venice, built on an archipelago at the headwaters of the Adriatic, also turned resolutely toward the sea.[22] Its primary resources were salt and fish. After the decline of Ravenna, it served as the chief Byzantine port in northern Italy. Like Amalfi, Venice benefited from its privileged relationship with Constantinople, while at the same time enjoying great autonomy. A Byzantine protectorate, it became a naval ally of Constantinople against the Slavs in the Adriatic, then against the Normans in southern Italy. The Venetians therefore obtained a series of privileges in the imperial capital, especially in 992 and in 1082, that allowed them access to the Constantinople market with reduced customs duties.

At first, the Venetians bought primarily in Constantinople itself, but increasingly they established themselves directly in the ports of the Levant. In addition to salt and fish, they brought wood, iron, and slaves. According to a hagiographical legend, Venetian merchants in Alexandria stole the body of Saint Mark the Evangelist in 828, hiding it in a pork barrel to thwart the vigilance of Muslim customs officers. But it was primarily from the twelfth century on that they settled long-term in the East: in Tyre, after the Crusaders' conquest of that city in 1124, and in Alexandria. Venice also became a privileged partner of the Ayyubids in Egypt. The aim of the Fourth Crusade of 1204, financed in large part by the Venetians, was to conquer Egypt; diverted from that aim, it ultimately sacked Constantinople.[23] Venice drew a considerable profit from that conquest. It played an important role in the government of the new Latin empire in the East and established many colonies or trading posts in the Aegean and Black seas. It did not overlook Egypt, however: between 1205 and 1217, Venice and the Ayyubids concluded a series of six peace and trade treaties. The first of these mentions a delegation of Venetian high dignitaries coming to Egypt to negotiate the accord. To mark the new alliance, Sultan al-'Ādil freed Venetian captives and sent balm to the doge of Venice. The accords granted the Venetians the right to engage in trade anywhere in Egypt, to transport wine, to keep a *funduq* (a sort of inn and warehouse) in Alexandria; each side promised not to attack the lands or ships of its partner.[24]

In contrast to the slow progress of Venice and Amalfi, Pisa and Genoa seem to have come out of nowhere in the eleventh century, taking control of the western Mediterranean basin within a generation. From the eighth to the tenth century, the Italian coast had often been the victim of Ifrīqiyan raids: Genoa, for example, was sacked by a Fatimid expedition in 935.[25] In the eleventh century, the disappearance of the caliphate of Cordova, the only naval power in the western Mediterranean, left a void that was immediately filled by pirates and adventurers. Naval war and privateering became the norm, and some islands, such as Corsica, Sardinia, the Balearics, and Djerba were lairs for Arab privateers. Pisans and Genoese also engaged in piracy, launching raids against the islands and the ports of the African coast: Sardinia in 1015–1016, Annaba in 1034, Palermo in 1064, Mahdia in 1087, Tortosa, Spain, in 1092, and the Balearics in 1113–1115.

The Pisans and the Genoese fought over Corsica and Sardinia and concluded peace and trade accords with the Muslim cities they had previously sacked. According to Abū Shāma, a thirteenth-century chronicler, these ferocious pirates and plunderers had become merchants who now sold to Muslims the arms with which they had previously threatened them. To avoid the risk of raids and to attract trade, the Muslim princes gave privileges to both cities, often managing to play up the rivalry between the two. Hence many peace treaties were signed in the twelfth and thirteenth centuries between Italian cities and Muslim princes, with each side promising not to engage in acts of plunder or piracy against the other. At the same time, the merchants of the Italian city obtained access to the market in the Muslim prince's territory at preferential customs rates.[26]

Pisa and Genoa often contributed toward the conquests of the Christian princes in Spain, Sicily, and in the Crusader states, offering their assistance in exchange for booty and tax privileges in the conquered cities. In the twelfth century, the two cities vied for control of the western Mediterranean, without any other real pretender: the Almoravids did not have a significant fleet. The Almohads did manage to form a navy, which participated in their conquests and for several decades controlled the Strait of Gibraltar. The importance of that fleet became apparent when Saladin asked Caliph al-Mansūr for the navy's aid in Acre, which had been besieged by Philip Augustus and Richard the Lion-Hearted. But these same Almohads conceded major fiscal privileges to the Pisans, recognizing the commercial hegemony of the Italian maritime cities.

The Catalan ports, with the backing of the kings of Aragon, became important economic and military actors in the Mediterranean in the thirteenth century. In the twelfth century, the counts of Barcelona and the kings of Aragon were still appealing to Pisan or Genoese fleets to aid them, for example, in undertaking maritime actions against the Muslim princes of the Balearics or al-Andalus, but by the next century, the Catalans had become a true sea power. It was from Barcelona that James I launched the conquest of the Balearic Islands (1229–1235), and the Catalan fleet also played an important role in the conquest of Valencia (1238). By midcentury, merchants from the three major Catalan ports—Barcelona, Majorca, and Valencia—were present nearly everywhere in the Mediterranean: they obtained privileges in Tunis, Bougie, Alexandria, and elsewhere. Thanks to a matrimonial alliance with the Hohenstaufen and a shrewd exploitation of the Sicilian Vespers of 1282, the House of Aragon took over Sicily, then added the conquest of Corsica and Sardinia in the fourteenth century, and finally, the kingdom of Naples in the fifteenth. Aragon thus became the great unrivaled power of the western Mediterranean. In the late fifteenth century, it merged with Castile, an emergent sea power in the Atlantic.[27]

Competition was keen between these commercial cities, taking the form of piracy, violent attacks on the property or persons of the rival city, and sometimes open warfare. For example, four wars erupted between Genoa and Venice between 1256 and 1381. Many Muslim princes were able to benefit from the rivalry between these cities by offering the potential ally privileged access to their markets. Although traders continued to frequent Mamluk Egypt in the thirteenth and fourteenth centuries, the competition between Genoese, Venetians, and Catalans was increasingly intense in the Aegean and Black seas. In the Crimea, where the Silk Road passing through Mongol territories reached its end, the Genoese established a trading post in Caffa and the Venetians one in Tana. Silk was imported to Europe from these ports, but so too were slaves bound for Europe and Mamluk Egypt. It was from Caffa that the Genoese brought back to Europe the Black Plague, which ravaged both Europe and the

Arab world in 1347–1348. The plague accelerated a demographic and economic decline that had already begun in Europe in the early fourteenth century. That tendency, coupled with the rise of the Ottomans, decimated European trade in the East. The fifteenth and sixteenth centuries were marked by a series of setbacks, with the European cities losing one by one their trading posts and colonies in the Black and Aegean seas. The Mediterranean went from a "Muslim lake" in the ninth century to an increasingly Italian sea (*mare nostrum*, it was called) from the twelfth century on—becoming, in the fifteenth and sixteenth century (as described by Fernand Braudel), a sea increasingly dominated by two great powers: the Ottomans in the East and the Spaniards in the West.

Modalities of Trade: Contracts, Technologies, Port Institutions

The modalities of trade—contracts, technologies, and institutions—changed and became more diverse throughout the Middle Ages. There was continuity in that gradual change, however. In general, Italian merchants of the twelfth to fifteenth centuries used the same procedures and institutions as their Jewish and Muslim counterparts and predecessors, and the European languages of the Mediterranean basin adopted several of the Arabic terms designating these practices and institutions.

Equipping a ship, loading it with merchandise, and taking it across the Mediterranean involved considerable costs and risks. In addition to storms and shipwrecks, there was the danger of war and piracy. The line between war and privateering, between piracy and commerce, was fuzzy. As we have already seen, there were frequent raids on land and at sea, inflicted to avenge affronts suffered and to obtain booty. Some of these expeditions were led by rulers as part of a declared war, but most of the attacks were makeshift operations in which religious or military confrontation was merely a pretext. Of the many examples, consider that of Jabbāra, emir of Barka (in modern-day Libya) in the eleventh century. A supporter of the Fatimids of Cairo at a time when Ifrīqiya had liberated itself from the Shiite caliphate, he waged holy war against both the Byzantines and the Western Sunnis. Thus he attacked the ships doing business between Ifrīqiya and Egypt that sailed past Barka. In Alexandria and Cairo, the emir had agents to whom the merchants could pay a ransom if their property or employees were seized. Jabbāra provides a good example of economic diversification: in Egypt, he sold slaves procured through the commandeering of Byzantine ships, and he made those trying to get past Barka without being attacked pay a high price for his "protection" service. He exemplified flexibility as well: in 1051, Jabbāra became a vassal of the Ifrīqiyan Sunni Muʿizz b. Bādis and henceforth conducted his raids against Fatimid Egypt.[28] There were dozens of Jabbāras in the Mediterranean at any given moment (though most of them had less power to cause harm): small adventurers who, on the pretext of defending the true religion (Greek or Latin Christianity, Sunni or Shiite Islam) or a legitimate prince, attacked passing ships. To discourage them, the ships formed convoys. Such was the case in Alexandria in the eleventh century, especially in wartime: ships heading for the Maghreb left the port together, accompanied by armed ships belonging to the caliph.[29] And such was also the case in the Italian cities, especially for the Venetians, who organized a series of annual convoys for different destinations.

A whole series of contracts and organizations were set in place in the Middle Ages to share costs, risks, and profits.[30] The most simple, the *shirka* or *khulta* in Arabic, consisted of a partnership in which everyone invested a share of the funds and obtained a corresponding percentage of the gains or losses. Another type of contract was the *qirad* between a financial backer, who provided the capital, and a merchant who transported and sold the merchandise. Italian merchants adopted that type of contract in the eleventh century, calling it a *commenda*. Profits were usually divided as follows: 75 percent to the investor, 25 percent to the trader who delivered the merchandise. Yet another type was the *societas*, in which the traveling merchant provided a share of the capital, often a third, and the financer the remaining two-thirds; they then shared the profits. The financial backer could be a group of people: Genoese women and men, for example, sometimes invested small sums in maritime enterprises.

To facilitate payments, merchants in the Mediterranean world developed banking instruments. They were attempting to circumvent two problems: the transportation of metal currency and the prohibition on usury in Muslim and Christian law, a prohibition often interpreted as a ban pure and simple on interest-bearing loans. Italian merchants often used bills of exchange: a merchant or banker would pay an entrepreneur in the local currency in Pisa, for example, and the entrepreneur would promise to reimburse the banker's agents elsewhere, in Alexandria, say, in the local currency at a later date. That allowed the merchant to have the capital he needed to purchase the merchandise he was going to transport and to avoid the problem of transporting and changing money. This operation constituted a hidden interest-bearing loan, since the rate of exchange was always set in such a manner as to provide the lender with a profit. Islamic countries used a *sakk* (the origin of the English word "check"), which authorized payment on an account.[31]

The seacraft that crossed the Mediterranean in the Middle Ages were many and varied, as reflected in a rich lexicon of Arabic, Latin, Italian, and Catalan terms. They ranged from small boats for one or two people to large galleys with a crew of two hundred to three hundred seamen. Western ships were for the most part built on the model of Byzantine and Muslim ships, with a lateen sail that shifted to take advantage of the winds and a double lateral rudder; this until the second half of the thirteenth century, when ships from the Atlantic appeared, with a single rudder aft and a combination of lateen and square sails.

After the conquests of the eleventh and twelfth centuries, the Islamic countries along the Mediterranean had few forests that could provide sufficient wood for shipyards. Sardinia and Corsica, by contrast, provided wood to the Genoese shipyards, along with a labor force to build and man the ships. Barcelona made good use of the Catalan forests. This situation contributed to the growing domination of Latin sea power, especially since many synods of the twelfth and thirteenth centuries prohibited selling ships to the Muslims. The prohibition, however, did not prevent the Genoese and others from doing so.

For navigation, Arab pilots had astrolabes that allowed them to measure latitude. By the late eleventh century, they could orient themselves by a magnetized needle, precursor to the compass (which appeared in the second half of the thirteenth century). They also probably had nautical charts, forerunners of the portolans of fourteenth-century Italian navigators. Commercial ships could readily become war vessels: as soon as the captain came across an enemy ship, he could decide, often with the agreement of the crew and merchants, to attack in the hope of seizing the rival ship, its merchandise, and its crew. If he succeeded, he shared the booty with merchants and crew. Many letters from travelers express the fear of being taken in such actions. That is why passengers were often torn between the desire to sail within sight of the coast (to better keep their bearings and to be able to return to terra firma in case of a problem) and the desire to distance themselves from it, in order to be out of sight of potential corsairs. Letters from Egyptian and Tunisian traders speak of the relief everyone felt when the coast was no longer visible.[32]

In addition to merchants and the crew, which could also include soldiers and oarsmen, the ships often transported passengers: Crusaders, mercenaries, emigrants, pilgrims to Jerusalem or Mecca. Passenger lists and contracts survive, but few descriptions of life on board. Ibn Jubayr traveled on a Genoese craft, stopping in Christian ports. He describes the festivities of All Saints' Day, when the ship shone with the candles of Christians, who listened to sermons from their priests.[33] But he gives the impression that, in general, contacts on board were limited. All remained with their own party, spoke their own language, ate their own food that they had brought with them, and, when a storm hit, implored God in keeping with their own religion.

When travelers arrived in a port, they normally had to report to agents of the port *dīwān* (the Arabic word that gave the Italian *dogana* and the French *douane*, customs), to whom they were obliged to pay duties (called *'ushr*, tithes) on the value of the goods they brought with them. According to Muslim law, a pilgrim to Mecca was exempt, but every other Muslim had to pay 2.5 percent; the *dhimmi*, 5 percent; and the *harbī*, 10 percent. In reality, these payments varied greatly. In Fatimid and Ayyubid Egypt, it seems that Jewish merchants did not pay more than Muslims. They were simply obliged to carry on their persons an attestation that they had paid the *jizya*. Saladin tried to impose a higher rate on non-Muslim merchants but later changed his mind.[34] Ibn Jubayr, upon his arrival in Alexandria, was scandalized that pilgrims were obliged to pay the 'ushr, as well as non-Qur'anic taxes. He deplored the humiliation that the customs officers inflicted on travelers.[35] The Italian cities negotiated the amount of their 'ushr: in 1161, the Almohads granted the Genoese a rate of 8 percent, which gave them an advantage over the Pisans, who still had to pay 10 percent. Elsewhere, Christian merchants paid more, sometimes as much as 25 or 30 percent. The Italian ports adopted similar laws. In general, local merchants enjoyed an advantageous rate, while merchants from foreign cities paid a higher rate, as a function of their nationality. In the ports, on the roads, and alongside rivers and streams, local authorities often tried to take advantage of passing merchants by collecting tolls and taxes. In Islamic countries as in the Latin world, that often led to conflicts and negotiations between the local powers, the central powers, and the merchants.

Once the merchant had been through customs, he took lodgings in a *funduq*, sometimes called a *khan*, a sort of inn for merchants and travelers.[36] These institutions were numerous: if we are to believe thirteenth-century geographers, there were sixteen hundred in the city of Cordova (these figures may be for the caliphal period, however); most must have been very modest establishments. Italian cities often arranged to have *funduqs* in the port cities of Muslim countries or in the Latin East. These *funduqs* sometimes formed small, semiautonomous communities protected by walls, often run by a consul with administrative and judicial powers. They had wells, warehouses, ovens, baths, taverns, and chapels. These centers were very active in summer, but in winter only a small population of expatriates remained. In return, the Italian cities granted *funduqs* to foreign merchants, such as the *fondaco tedesco* (German *funduq*) in Venice.

Local authorities sought to control the sale of imported products, in order to make a profit on them, and at times they held a monopoly on the trade in certain products. In Alexandria, the port authorities organized an auction in the port itself. Italian merchants could be found in the interior of Egypt—Amalfitans in the tenth century, Pisans in the twelfth—but that remained the exception. In Spain, conversely, foreign merchants moved into the urban markets: *fueros* in favor of the Christian cities guaranteed and regulated the access of Muslim merchants, whereas in the Muslim West *hisba* treaties did the same for Christian merchants in Muslim cities. In both cases, to be able to enter the city or to sell at the market, the merchant had to pay duties, which could vary a great deal.

Despite the taxes, storms, pirates, thieves, and swindlers, commerce could be highly profitable. In the mid-eleventh century, pepper was twice as expensive in Tunis as in Cairo: someone who purchased it in Egypt to resell in the Maghreb could hope for an 80 percent profit if all went well.[37] To understand how that trade worked, let us follow, with the historian Shlomo Goitein, a bundle of "purple" (clothing dyed red) weighing 474 pounds from Cairo to Sfax (Tunisia), via

Alexandria, in about the year 1100. The bundle, which cost sixty-six dinars in Cairo, would be sold for ninety-four dinars in Sfax; the merchant paid three dinars in customs duties in Egypt, one dinar for transportation from Cairo to Alexandria, and four dinars for transportation by ship to Sfax. That allowed him to realize a profit of twenty-one dinars, that is, almost a third of his investment.[38] True, it was also possible to lose money, especially since "prices are in the hands of God," according to an Arabic saying attributed to Muhammad and often found in the writings of Jewish and Muslim merchants of Egypt.[39]

THE IMPACT OF TRADE ON ECONOMIES AND MENTALITIES

Trade changed the ways of life of the inhabitants of Europe and the Islamic countries. It influenced eating habits and habits of dress: Europe discovered oranges, bananas, rice, sugar, pepper, and many spices, as well as silk and henna. The Islamic countries especially took away raw materials (iron, wood) but also wool clothing. The volume of such trade remained limited: in the Middle Ages, only a very small portion of the European population could eat sugar or exotic spices and dress in silk. But that meager transformation of habits of eating and dress in the Latin and Arab worlds would only grow stronger in the centuries that followed. Often these goods from the "Muslim" world were actually produced by Muslim or Jewish minorities in Spain or Sicily, and Christian sovereigns encouraged Muslim farmers practicing intensive horticulture and silk production to stay on. For both merchants and sovereigns, conquest and commerce were two ways of acquiring the wealth desired.

How are we to distinguish between the exchange of goods and the appropriation of ideas, technologies, and modes of thought that accompanied it? The intermediaries were the slaves, immigrants, *dhimmis*, or Mudejars who provided their services and expertise, whether in navigation, metallurgy, or architecture. Medicine provides a good example: the diffusion and translation of pharmacological treatises required commerce in pharmaceutical products; without the ingredients, the formulas served no purpose, and vice versa. But let us consider in more detail the impact of commerce in a few products of foremost importance: slaves, weapons, paper, gold, silver, and woolen textiles.

One of the chief export products from Europe between the seventh and twelfth centuries was slaves.[40] We have seen how pirates and corsairs—Arabs, Greeks, Italians, Catalans, and others—engaged in raids and enriched themselves at the expense of captives, who were either ransomed or sold into slavery. There was also significant commerce in slaves from northern and eastern Europe, captured by Ottonian, Byzantine, or Slavic armies, or sold by their parents. We have seen the important role played by the *Saqāliba* (Slavs) in Arab countries, especially in the Umayyad armies of Spain. They were so numerous in Europe that the classic word to designate a slave, *servus*, was replaced by *esclavus*. Pope Zachary (741–752) learned that the Venetians were purchasing slaves on the Roman market to resell them to the Muslims; outraged, he closed the market and redeemed many slaves, then liberated them.[41] That was no doubt only a local and temporary impediment to a very profitable business. Constantinople tried to regulate the trafficking in slaves for its own profit, barring the export of certain kinds of slaves (for example, those who worked in silk weaving shops) and attempting to prohibit the Italians from selling slaves to the Muslims, a ban that Pope Adrian I communicated to Charlemagne in 776. The aim of these measures was both to guarantee a labor pool and to keep the strength of Muslim rivals in check. But that very lucrative trade skillfully found a way around the Byzantine obstacle: the Venetians played a large role, and sellers circumvented the empire to the west (through Germania and Gaul) and to the east (through the Caucasus) to reach Muslim markets.[42]

Many written accounts indicate the European merchants' involvement in the slave trade. In 836, the Neapolitans promised the Lombard prince Sicard that they would no longer sell Lombard captives to Arab merchants—a promise they likely did not keep.[43] In 845, the Council of Meaux took note of Christian and Jewish merchants from the kingdom of West Francia who were transporting pagan (probably Slavic) slaves through the kingdom to sell them to "the enemies of the faith" (the Muslims of Spain). For the council, that was harmful in two ways: first, the pagans did not have an opportunity to accept the Christian faith; and second, the enemy's strength thereby increased. The council therefore proclaimed that merchants had to sell their human merchandise within the Frankish kingdom and not export it. There is little chance that the measure was respected; the "enemies of the faith" undoubtedly paid more attractive prices.[44] This traffic would only increase in the following century, fed by the Ottonian emperors' conquests in Slavic lands.[45] Verdun emerged as an important hub for that trade and specialized in the castration of slaves, since the price of a eunuch was about four times that of an uncastrated man on the Byzantine or Muslim markets, and Byzantine law prohibited the castration of slaves (but not the importation of eunuchs).[46]

Before the year 1000, therefore, slaves were an export product for Europe: European merchants sold them on the markets of al-Andalus or North Africa. The archives of the Cairo Geniza attest to the purchase of European slaves.[47] That began to change in the eleventh century. First, the conquests of the Christian princes, from Portugal to Sicily to the Holy Land, placed a large number of Muslim captives in the hands of European Christians, who were able to ransom or resell them. From the eleventh, and especially, the twelfth century on, Iberian *fueros* allude to specific taxes on the transport and sale of *moros* (Muslim slaves).[48] Beginning in the twelfth century, the Catalans sold slaves in Catalonia or Genoa. Slave markets could be found from one end of the Mediterranean to the other: slaves were auctioned at the Rialto in Venice, at the markets in Andalusian cities, and in the East.

Beginning in the thirteenth century, the Genoese and Venetians competed in the trafficking of slaves, the most important source of which was the Black Sea region, where they purchased pagan and Christian slaves. The Genoese exported the male slaves to Mamluk Egypt, where they would be integrated into the army, and the females to Italy, where they would serve as household servants.[49] The slave trade, for the Italian or Catalan merchants who participated in it, was one activity among others: the captives or slaves (rarely more than twenty to forty at a time) traveled in ships loaded with various import goods. About ten thousand slaves a year may have been sold in Venice in the fifteenth century.[50] Slave traders paid close attention to the religious affiliations of slave and buyer: in Christian territory, it was forbidden to sell a Christian to an infidel, just as, in the *dār al-islām*, a Muslim could not be sold to a *dhimmi*. That sometimes led to odd practices: in the thirteenth century, it was in Tunis that some European merchants sold Christian slaves to the Muslims; others sold Muslims there, whom they passed off as Christians. These practices, reported to the pope by Franciscans and Dominicans living in Tunis, drew a sharp condemnation, which probably had no effect on that commerce.[51]

War was an omnipresent danger in the medieval Mediterranean, but it also presented attractive commercial opportunities. The sale of weapons, military materiel, and foodstuffs to the armies was very lucrative in the Middle Ages, as it still is today. Within a context of holy war, efforts were sometimes made to prohibit commerce with the "infidel" enemy, but these prohibitions themselves attest to the ubiquity of such trade.[52] The chronicler Maqrīzī recounts, for example, that a Mamluk vizier was convicted of selling arms to the Franks. Christian kings of Jerusalem and popes tried to bar European merchants from selling strategic products (arms, wood, iron) to the Crusaders' enemies. In a treaty concluded with Pisa in 1154, the Fatimids reserved the right to buy all iron, pitch, and wood that the Pisans brought to Egypt. Two years later, Baldwin III, king of Jerusalem, in granting economic privileges to the Pisans, prohibited them from conveying iron or wood to Egypt. These bans were likely not respected to any great extent. In 1179, the Third Lateran Council railed against the Christians who were selling arms, iron, or wood to the Saracens or who served as captains on their ships. These Christians were to be excommunicated, their possessions confiscated, and, once captured, they were reduced to slavery. Here again, such draconian punishments seem to have been ineffective. During the Fourth Lateran Council of 1215, at a time when preparations were being made for a new Crusade against Egypt, the prohibitions were reiterated, with the additional ban on providing assistance or advice to the Crusaders' enemies. But the council introduced a distinction between aid offered to the declared enemies (the Ayyubids), which was expressly prohibited, and commerce with other Muslim princes, which was still allowed. Throughout the Middle Ages and well beyond, popes and other ecclesiastical authorities fulminated in vain against those who did business with the enemy.

One of the products that arrived in Europe through the Muslim world and that completely altered European society was paper, which had been produced in China since antiquity and was common in the Muslim world from the ninth century on. Spain became one of the major paper producers; Egypt imported Andalusian paper in the eleventh and twelfth centuries. One of the chief centers of production in the Muslim West was Xátiva (south of Valencia), conquered in 1244 by James I of Aragon, who seized the paper factory and turned it into a state monopoly. Xátiva paper, much less costly than parchment, spread (slowly, it is true) to northern Europe and encouraged imitations. It is no coincidence that the reign of James I is particularly well documented: the paper from Xátiva allowed him to develop his chancery. Without paper, a Chinese invention that crossed over to the Islamic countries and was adopted in Aragon, the development of modern bureaucratic states would be unthinkable.[53]

But it may be the wool trade that best demonstrates the profound and reciprocal effect of commerce between the Latin world and Islamic countries. Here is how that industry operated near the end of the thirteenth century: wool production occurred almost everywhere in Europe and the Maghreb, but increasingly in Castile, England, and Scotland. The wool was transported to Italy, or especially, to Flanders, where workers processed and dyed it (often with colors imported from the Muslim world along with a fixative, alum, at first primarily from Egypt, then from Phocea in Anatolia) and then wove it into cloth. The finished cloth was sold to Italian merchants, who resold it in Italy, elsewhere in Europe, and in ports across the Mediterranean. The cloth industry fostered commerce and vice versa. It changed habits of dress in Islamic countries, as well as the economy of the wool-producing countries: the Castilian *mesta* (a professional guild of sheep farmers) emerged at that time to regulate transhumance and to ensure profits for this very lucrative trade. Some lords in northern England and Scotland turned their lands into sheep grazing grounds, which they found more profitable than the agricultural work of peasants. During the same period, the Egyptian textile industry foundered in the face of competition from European imports.

Commerce led to changes in the monetary system of both civilizations. Previously, the coinage in Latin Europe was primarily made of silver, often in a copper alloy. In Islamic countries and in Byzantium, gold remained the standard currency of exchange, though silver and copper coinage also existed. Thanks to exchanges with the Maghreb, Europe had access to African gold at a time when its merchants needed it for their large transactions. They used Muslim gold coins or imitations fabricated in Sicily and Spain; the Florentines and Genoese finally minted gold coins beginning in 1252. The silver from European mines, especially in central Europe, financed the products of Italian merchants, who reused the silver to pay for their purchases in the East. Egypt turned the silver into coins, which promoted retail trade. Since gold was relatively overvalued in Europe and silver overvalued in the Maghreb, Maghrebis often paid in gold to buy European products, while Europeans used silver in Maghrebian markets. Toward the end of the twelfth century, the Maghreb, like the East, began to strike coins with European silver. These were square dirhams bearing Muslim inscriptions: "God is great," "Muhammad is his prophet." These dirhams, which the Europeans called *millares*, were so popular that Europeans began to strike *millares* of their own, used for trade with the Maghreb and bearing these same Muslim inscriptions, which shocked Pope Clement IV and the French king Louis IX.

It is impossible to enumerate all the many effects of commerce on European and Muslim societies of the Middle Ages. Sometimes, these effects were perceived as negative: when Jewish fishermen from Alexandria frequented the bars of Acre and drank beer with Christians, they elicited the contempt of some of their coreligionists.[54] Beginning in Italy in the eleventh century, then in the rest of Europe in the twelfth century, cities developed as a result of demographic growth and commerce. In all the participating Mediterranean cities, trade favored the expansion of artisan crafts oriented toward exportation. One of the social effects of commerce was the emergence of urban classes of artisans and merchants. In a large number of European cities, especially in Italy, merchants would ultimately take (that is, buy) power, whereas in the Muslim countries, power remained in the hands of the politico-military elite.[55]

In Islamic countries, various princes skillfully manipulated the privileges they granted to foreign merchants, Europeans in particular. No one did so better than the Fatimids, and then their Ayyubid successors: in the eleventh and twelfth centuries, Egypt consolidated its position as the richest country in the Mediterranean world and in the Islamic world, the crossroads of world trade. Although that preeminence faded in the Mamluk period (1250–1517), this was in large part because the Mongol conquests of the thirteenth century had opened a new overland trade route, the Silk Road, which competed with the sea route controlled by the Egyptians.

From the fifteenth century on, it was through the Atlantic that Portuguese and Castilians vied to circumvent the control of their rivals—Mamluks, Italians, and Catalans—and to obtain the fruits of commerce without intermediaries: slaves, gold, sugar, spices. Slaves the Portuguese rounded up on the African coast. Gold they obtained from African princes. Sugar they produced and refined in Madeira and the Azores in the fifteenth century, as they would do in Brazil and the Caribbean in the sixteenth. As for spices, Christopher Columbus would go on a futile search for them in the Caribbean, and Vasco da Gama would purchase them when he finally arrived in India in 1498.

CHAPTER 5

ON THE SHOULDERS OF GIANTS

Transmission and Exchange of Knowledge

TRADE IS INSEPARABLE from political, diplomatic, and military relations. The mingling of people and goods traveling back and forth across the Mediterranean was accompanied by a mingling of ideas, technologies, and texts—of cultures, in short. All the various players adopted the technologies, institutions, and tools of the merchants and sailors—whether banking instruments, contracts, *funduqs*, compasses, or portulans—modified them to fit their own needs and culture, and perfected them when necessary.

Exchanges of ideas and technologies in the Mediterranean basin were not limited to commerce and navigation. They occurred in all areas: agricultural, hydraulic, architectural, and military technologies; the knowledge and practice of medicine and pharmacology; artistic, musical, and literary tastes and expertise; scientific and philosophical scholarship. It would clearly be impossible to provide a complete list of these activities here; I can give only a brief outline and focus on a few examples.

GRECO-ARAB SCIENCE AND PHILOSOPHY IN LATIN EUROPE

Latin and Arab geographers differed significantly in their training and learning, as we saw in chapter 1, and that contrast was even more marked in the fields of science and philosophy, which were much more developed in the Arab world than in Latin Europe.[1] The cultural and intellectual mixing of Greek, Persian, and Arab elements, well under way with the Umayyads of Damascus (680–750), continued under the Abbasids. In addition, "Greek" science was already the product of a hybrid civilization, Hellenistic and then Roman, marked by Babylonian, Egyptian, Persian, and other sciences. That was the case in the second century for Galen's medicine and Ptolemy's astronomy, for example.[2] Caliph al-Maʾmūn (813–833) established the Bayt al-Hikma, or House of Wisdom, to promote the translation of Persian, Syriac, Sanskrit, and especially Greek scientific works. According to the tenth-century Baghdad author Ibn al-Nadīm, Aristotle appeared to the caliph in a dream and inspired his plan. The caliph, Ibn al-Nadīm relates, asked for and obtained Greek manuscripts from the Byzantine emperor.[3] It is likely that the caliph was able to find most of the texts and translators in the caliphate itself. Translations were done—to cite only the best-known authors—of Euclid and Archimedes in geometry, Ptolemy in astronomy, Galen and Hippocrates in medicine, and of course, Plato and Aristotle. Also translated were works of Hindu mathematics and astronomy. From the eighth century on, many Arab authors studied and annotated that rich panoply of texts, adding to it their own contributions in the sciences, philosophy, and theology.

It has often been said that, as the Abbasid caliphs were transforming Baghdad into a new world capital of science, Charlemagne and his successors were laboriously learning to write their own names. In Byzantium, scholars continued to study the classics of antiquity; but in Latin Europe, from the Carolingian period to the twelfth or thirteenth century, few read Greek, and only one of Plato's dialogues had been translated into Latin. No text by Aristotle, Euclid, Hippocrates, Galen, or Ptolemy was available in Latin translation. True, there were Latin vulgarizers dating from Late Antiquity and the early Middle Ages: Macrobius, Boethius, Isidore. But their works provided only scant remnants of Greek thought. Between the eighth and eleventh centuries, a few traces of the influence of Arab science survived in Latin Europe. Then, in the eleventh and especially the twelfth century, many Europeans began to learn Arabic, especially in Spain, to study science and philosophy and, if need be, to translate texts into Latin. In the twelfth and thirteenth centuries, these translations would have a profound impact on intellectual life in Europe. By way of example, let us consider the field of medicine.

In medicine as in so many other disciplines, Arab science rested on a Greek theoretical base, combined with significant Persian and Indian elements. Many Arab authors introduced additions to these foundations, whether from medical theory, clinical practice, or pharmacopoeia. In 987, for example, when Ibn al-Nadīm compiled his *Fihrist*, a sort of *catalogue raisonné* of works written in the Arabic language, he listed 430 medical texts, 174 of which were translated from other languages (primarily Greek). For the Middle Ages as a whole, there may have been a thousand or so Arabic texts in medicine.[4]

Hunayn ibn Ishāq was one of the major figures in the movement aimed at assimilating Greek medicine. Born into a Christian family from the Euphrates valley, the son of a pharmacist, Hunayn immigrated to Baghdad, where he was involved in the work of the Bayt al-Hikma. He learned Greek and did many translations, producing Syriac and Arabic versions of texts in astronomy, philosophy, mathematics, the divinatory sciences, and especially medicine. In a letter written in 856, he mentions 129 treatises by Galen that he knew, and a good share of which he and his collaborators had translated.[5] Thanks to that work, the Arab world appropriated the Greek medical heritage. In 850, a contemporary of Hunayn's, ʿAlī b. Rabban al-Ṭabarī, completed an encyclopedia of medical knowledge, the *Firdaws al-Ḥikma* (*Paradise of Wisdom*), in which Greek, Persian, and Indian traditions blended together.[6] Although in al-Ṭabarī, as in later authors, Greek thought dominated and structured Arab medicine, Eastern contributions remained significant. The *Firdaws* describes in detail Indian medical practices, based on Sanskrit texts translated under the caliphate of Hārūn al-Rashid (786–809); in its chapters on pharmacopoeia, Persian terms predominate. Hence there emerged in the mid-ninth century a true theoretical and practical Arab medicine, a blending of various traditions.

Such were the foundations on which Arab physicians of the Middle Ages were working. They adapted or honed ancient hypotheses about the origins of illnesses, which generally rested on a theory positing a balance or imbalance of the four elements (earth, water, air, fire), the four corresponding humors (black bile, phlegm, blood, yellow bile), and their respective properties (hot/cold and dry/wet). When the great Greek thinkers were not in harmony—for example, when Galen's medical theories contradicted Aristotle's notions of physics—the Arab authors provided arguments for choosing between the two or for constructing syntheses.

Although the theoretical structure stemming from classical antiquity predominated, practices continued to evolve, and medical writers did not hesitate to correct Galen's errors. This is particularly well demonstrated in the prolific writings of Abū Bakr Muḥammad al-Razī (d. 925 or 935); 61 of his 184 known works are devoted to medicine.[7] This Persian physician, a discriminating connoisseur of ancient medical texts, claims that he surpassed the ancients since, after integrating their knowledge acquired over thousands of years, he made his own discoveries and contributed to the development of science. A modern who applies himself, he says, necessarily sees farther than the ancients. His medical works reflect this conviction: he carefully lists descriptions of one illness or another and its treatment by his predecessors (Greek, Syriac, Persian, Indian, Arab), then offers his own ideas, the result of extensive clinical experience, which might confirm or on the contrary invalidate the theses of the ancients. When his experience revealed the weakness of an argument of Galen's (on the healing process of arterial wounds, for example, or the treatment of ulcers), he clearly sets out its refutation. Al-Razī provides the most brilliant example of that critical attitude toward the ancients, but he was not alone. In about 1200, ʿAbd al-Laṭīf al-Baghdādī, after observing skeletons, showed that the description given by Galen of the structure of the jaw was wrong; he wrote ironically of the excessive regard that modern scholars displayed toward Greek medicine.[8]

In terms of medical theory, one of the most remarkable syntheses is the *Canon* by Ibn Sīna, Avicenna for Europeans (980–1037), a text destined for unparalleled success, since for several centuries it was the most widely used manual in medical schools from India to Oxford.[9] There is nothing to indicate that Avicenna ever practiced medicine; his knowledge, unlike that of al-Razī, came almost exclusively from books. But the strong points of the *Canon* are its clear organization and its effort to make medicine a true rational science. Avicenna tried to apply the principles of logic to medicine, in order to show the correspondences between an illness, its symptoms, and its treatment.

Until the eleventh century, Latin Europe stood at a remove from that medical science: it was not familiar with either the Greek or the Arabic texts. There are some scattered indications of a trade in pharmaceutical products, however. In the Carolingian Rhineland, there were medicinal formulas in the 790s that very clearly displayed knowledge of Arab remedies and a commerce in medical products from the East, such as camphor.[10] But between the Arab world and Latin Europe, the gap in medical theory and practice remained great. Usāma ibn Munqidh, a twelfth-century Syrian author, describes Frankish medical practitioners with disdain and contempt, depicting them as inept, superstitious, and arrogant.[11]

In eleventh-century southern Italy, a push began, associated with Constantine the African, to translate Arabic medical texts into Latin. Constantine's life, transmitted through more or less improbable legends, remains obscure.[12] It seems, however, that he was originally from Ifrīqiya and that he settled in southern Italy, where he died in 1087. Constantine is reputed to have translated a dozen medical works from Arabic into Latin. As often in the Middle Ages, these were adaptations rather than exact translations. They reveal an ignorance of superior works, such as those of al-Rāzi. Compared to what had previously been available in Latin, however, they represented an important advance in medical theory. It was primarily in Salerno of the eleventh century that these translations were used in the teaching and practice of medicine.

More essential and long-lasting were the translations done in Toledo under Gerard of Cremona between 1145 and 1187. If we are to believe the list drawn up by his colleagues, Gerard translated seventy-three works, probably with the aid of his associates.[13] That list, inserted into the preface to a translation of a work by Galen, shows that Gerard's work shone not only for its quantity but also for its quality and variety. The text describes how Gerard, a native of Cremona, Italy, quickly reached the limits of the scientific knowledge available in Latin in the twelfth century. The work of his predecessors had awakened his curiosity, and he came to Toledo impelled "by the love of the *Almagest*" by Ptolemy, a fundamental astronomical text. When he arrived, he was astonished by the number of scientific texts available in Arabic, an abundance he contrasted to the scarcity of Latin texts. He began to learn Arabic, then undertook the translation of works chosen in advance, in order to offer a "wreath" of the most beautiful flowers of Arab wisdom. The quality of the works selected clearly stands out: in medicine, for example, he translated ten texts by Galen and one by Hippocrates, thus offering the Latin world the complete theoretical foundations of the ancient science. He added ten works by Arab medical authors, in particular, three texts by al-Rāzi and Avicenna's *Canon*.

Figure 4. Manuscript of al-Razi's *Continens*, 1282. The four scenes show the different phases in the translation of the work: Charles I sends an embassy to the emir of Tunis to request a copy of the work (top left); the emir gives the Arabic manuscript to the king's emissaries (top right); the translator Faraj bin Salem at work (bottom half of lower image); Faraj bin Salem presents his Latin translation to the king (top half of lower image). Bibliothèque Nationale de France (MS Latin 6912, fol. 1). Reprinted by permission of the Bibliothèque Nationale de France.

Yet only a small number of medical texts were translated from Arabic into Latin in the Middle Ages—about forty of the thousand or so texts available. To be sure, medical texts continued to be translated in the thirteenth and fourteenth centuries, though they did not manage to compete with Galen or Avicenna. Charles I of Anjou, king of Sicily, having heard of the *Kitāb al-Hāwī*, al-Rāzi's encyclopedic work, sent an embassy to the emir of Tunis, who sent back a copy of the Arabic text, which the king ordered translated in 1279 (figure 4).[14] In the fourteenth century, the Montpellier school of medicine was influenced by the work of Arnald of Villanova, a practicing physician, professor, and translator of medical texts from the Arabic. He sharply criticized his contemporaries for their excessive dependence on Avicenna and attacked Averroes (Ibn Rushd). For Arnald, the two philosophers were less reliable in medicine than the true masters, Galen and al-Rāzi (whom Arnald called the "second Galen").[15]

We could similarly trace the history of the different sciences in the Arabo-phone world and that of the translations and adaptations to which they gave rise in Europe. In astronomy, for example, the contribution of Arab science through translations, most of them done in the twelfth and thirteenth centuries, was essential to the development of that science in Europe.[16] Arab astronomy, like medicine, came into being in ninth-century Baghdad; knowledge and ideas of Persian, Sanskrit, and then Arab origin were brought to bear on an essentially Ptolemaic structure. The Latin world, meanwhile, had only a few vulgarizations of Greek astronomy (Macrobius, Martianus Capella), until, at the start of the twelfth century, a certain number of astronomers (Petrus Alfonsi, Adelard of Bath, Raymond of Marseilles) promoted Arab astronomy and began a transla-tion movement, which took on greater scope mid-century.[17]

Thanks to the work of Gerard and the other translators, Greco-Arab thought arrived in the major intellectual centers of Europe in the thirteenth century and completely altered learning and thinking. Aristotle—"the Philosopher," as he was most often called—entered Europe wearing a turban: in most cases, the Latin translations of his works were from the Arabic, often accompanied by glosses or commentaries also translated from the Arabic, such as those of Mai-monides and Averroes, which were still recent. They would have a profound in-fluence on intellectual life in Latin Europe, an influence perceptible, in the first place, in the sharp reaction they produced in the newly created universities. In 1215, when the pontifical legate Robert de Courçon set forth the regulations for the University of Paris, he specified that the metaphysical and scientific works of Aristotle were not to be taught in the faculty of arts. It appears, therefore, that not everyone was fond of the new fruits offered by the translators. We must not overstate the importance of such bans, however: other works by Ar-istotle, especially in logic, were taught, and the prohibitions were merely local. In 1229, when the new University of Toulouse wanted to attract students, it boasted that they could study there the works of Aristotle that were banned in Paris. Further bans, in 1231, 1245, 1263, 1270, and 1277, were intended to pro-scribe the teaching of certain doctrines that supposedly attacked the Christian faith, including ideas from Aristotle, Averroes, and Thomas Aquinas. But the Aristotelian works banned in 1215 were by now an integral part of the univer-sity curriculum.

Various theologians sought a middle way between the unbridled enthu-siasm of some people for that new philosophy and the absolute rejection of others. The chief authors of that compromise were Albertus Magnus (1193–1280) and his student Thomas Aquinas (1225–1274), who declared that the truths of philosophy or science could not be used to prove those of faith, but that it is possible to demonstrate that these truths do not contradict one another. In his scientific and theological works, Albertus forged an imposing synthesis of Arab, Greek, biblical, and patristic knowledge, attempting to eliminate or minimize disagreements between these different sources and to dismiss ideas considered heterodox (for example, that the world is eternal, as Aristotle and Averroes claimed, and not created). It was upon these foundations that Thomas built a monumental system of thought, which historians often compare to a Gothic cathedral, with solid foundations in Genesis and Aristotle, Augustine and Averroes, Moses and Maimonides. Yet the controversies continued, and some Parisian scholars were accused of being "Averroists," of teaching, among other erroneous doctrines, that there were two independent truths, one based in revelation and the other in philosophy. Ibn Rushd had never formulated such a doctrine, but the accusation of "Averroism" was an easy way to cast aspersions on intellectual enemies. The canonization of Thomas Aquinas in 1323, however, marked the triumph of his synthesis of Greco-Arab philosophy and Christian theology, a synthesis that would dominate religious teaching for centuries.[18]

ARTISTIC AND CULTURAL EXCHANGES

Artistic contacts and influences were also numerous and far-reaching. Architecture in the Umayyad period generally followed the Persian and Byzantine traditions, but there were also innovations, especially for palaces and religious buildings. For the construction of the Dome of the Rock in Jerusalem (692), the first great monument of Islam, Caliph 'Abd al-Malik appealed to Greek architects and mosaicists: the gold-covered dome, the mosaics, and the colored marble evoke Byzantine churches. But its octagonal form is unique, and the mosaics represent not holy figures (as in Byzantine churches) but plant motifs rendered abstractly. Its greatest novelty, however, was the use of Qur'anic inscriptions in Arabic, done in a sumptuous calligraphy, making the divine word of the Qur'an an object of decoration as well as instruction.[19] That mix of Byzantine tradition and innovation can also be found in others monuments of the time, such as the great mosques of Medina (705–709) and Damascus (706–715) or al-Aqsa mosque in Jerusalem (about 715).

In the following centuries, the eastern Mediterranean became such a cultural melting pot that sorting out the artistic "influences" would be difficult. Different ethnic and religious groups shared a largely undifferentiated material culture: looking at a ceramic cup from the twelfth century or a piece of silver jewelry from the thirteenth, you would be hard pressed to say whether the maker or user was Jewish, Christian, or Muslim, Turkish, Arab, Armenian, or Frankish.[20]

In Europe, it is first in the territories captured from the Muslims, in Spain and Sicily, that one finds the use and appropriation of elements of Arab culture. The Norman kings of Sicily, for example, struck coins bearing legends in Greek, Latin, and Arabic. Roger II struck gold *taris* that displayed a central cross on the reverse, with a legend in Greek: *IC/XC NI/KA*, "Jesus Christ is victorious." The obverse bears an inscription in Arabic, with the mint mark (for Palermo) and the king's motto in Arabic: *al-Muʿtazz bi-llāh*, "he who finds his strength and glory in God" (figure 5). In architecture, the same mix is found in the representations of kings in Palermo churches. In the Church of Martorana, for example, a mosaic shows Roger II crowned by Christ, the adaptation of a model common in the Byzantine world. And on the ceiling of the palatine chapel, the painted image of a crowned king depicts him in the guise of an Arab potentate, sitting cross-legged, a cup in his hand, flanked by servant girls who fan him. Roger also ordered a coronation mantle on which was represented, on either side of a palm tree, a lion (symbol of royal power) bringing down a camel; the Arabic inscription bordering it celebrated the king's virtues (figure 6).[21]

Byzantine and Arab architecture in Europe enjoyed a clear influence and prestige. In Italy, art objects and artisans arrived from the Muslim world along the trade routes. The monk and chronicler Amato de Montecassino explains that, in the last quarter of the eleventh century, when his abbot wished to decorate the abbey with new mosaics, he brought in Greek and Arab artisans from Constantinople and Alexandria.[22] It was no doubt Amalfitan merchants, patrons of the abbey, who arranged for these artisans to come. Twelfth-century Pisa enjoyed a craze for ceramics from Andalusia and the Maghreb, which were even incorporated into the façades of the city's churches as decorative

Figure 5. Golden Tari struck by Roger II, king of Sicily (1130–1154), minted in Palermo, 1140–1154. Left (obverse): The words "al-malik Rujar al-Muʿtazz billāh" appear around an inner circle decorated with six pellets and containing a pellet in the center; the mint mark and date are in the outer margin. Right (reverse): "IC/XC NI/KA" (Jesus Christ is victorious) appears in two lines across a field flanking a central cross; the mint mark and date are in the outer margin.

Figure 6. Coronation mantle of Roger II (Kunsthistorisches Museum, Vienna). A lion (symbol of royal power) subjugates a camel. On the fringe is the following Arabic inscription: "Here is what was created in the princely treasury, filled with luck, illustration, majesty, perfection, longanimity, superiority, welcome, prosperity, liberality, shine, pride, beauty, the achievement of desires and hopes, the pleasure of days and nights, without cease or change, with glory, devotion, preservation, protection, chance, salvation, victory and capability, in the capital of Sicily, in the year 528 H. [1133-1134]."

elements.[23] In the Romanesque churches of southern France from the eleventh and twelfth centuries, both the forms of Muslim architecture (polylobe or horseshoe arches) and its techniques (polychrome stones, ceramic) are apparent. Even the Qur'anic text on view in the mosques could become a source of inspiration: "inscriptions" in kufesque (pseudo-Kufic) characters, an approximate imitation of Arabic letters, were engraved in the stone of churches purely as decoration. Sometimes there were true Arabic inscriptions, which attest no doubt to the presence of Arab artisans from Spain. For example, the doors of the Cathedral of Puy bear the words *ma shalla*, "it was God's will."[24]

The Christian kings of Spain appropriated the palaces of the Muslim princes they had defeated. These ranged from the Aljafería in Saragossa, an eleventh-century palace that became one of the favorite residences of the kings of Aragon with Alfonso I's conquest of the city in 1118, to the Alhambra of Granada, which Isabel and Ferdinand seized during the conquest of 1492. When the kings built their own palaces, they were often inspired by the Arab models around them. One of the most beautiful examples is the palace built by Pedro I of Castile (1350–1369) inside the Alcázar of Seville. Laborers sent by Emir Muhammad V of Granada worked on it alongside local artisans. The decorations for that palace belonged to a pure Arab tradition: walls covered with *azulejos*, or sculpted stucco panels, coffered ceilings, and even Arabic inscriptions that proclaimed, among other things, "There is no other victor but God."

The palace of Pedro I is a jewel of so-called Mudejar art, a style also omnipresent in the religious architecture of the thirteenth and fourteenth centuries, especially in Aragon and Toledo. The Toledo church of Santiago del Arrabal (thirteenth century) seems to have sprung forth from a union between a Romanesque church and a Maghrebian mosque: the plan and the shape of the apses are Romanesque, but the material (brick) and the shape of the arches are reminiscent of Arab architecture. The nearby Church of San Román from the same period is in a similar Mudejar style, mixing Arab and European forms. Even more striking is the interior decoration: abstract frescoes in the pure Arab tradition stand side by side with portraits of saints, identified by inscriptions in both Arabic and Latin. Around the arches as well, inscriptions in the two languages alternate.

The Arab influence in literature is also clear in Italy, Christian Spain, and Provence. The cultural diversity of al-Andalus at the time of the *taifas* is evident in, among other things, the large quantity of poetry produced in both Arabic and Hebrew. It is a hybrid and innovative poetry, entailing two new forms: the *zajal*, a poem in dialectical Arabic with the inclusion of words borrowed from the vernacular proto-Spanish; and the *muwashshaha*, a poem in classical Arabic with a refrain in proto-Romance. These songs became very popular throughout the Arab world and remain so among Arab singers today. They also influenced the development of courtly poetry in Occitan, though the channels and degree of that influence continue to elicit spirited debates among specialists. The chronicler Ibn Hayyan enumerates, among the fabulous booty falling to the Provençal knights at the time of the taking of Barbastro in 1064, a large number of women singers, who did not fail to charm their ravishers. One of the participants in that expedition was Duke William VIII of Aquitaine; his son, William IX, was the first great troubadour. Could the *zajal* and *muwashshahat* that William heard from his father's slaves have inspired that first great Provençal poet?[25]

The Arab literature of the Middle Ages was also a success with European writers and readers. Various stories from the *Thousand and One Nights*, from *Kalīla wa Dimna*, and from other texts were transmitted orally or in written translation, and then adapted by European authors. In the twelfth century, Petrus Alfonsi composed his *Disciplina clericalis*, an anthology of aphorisms accompanied by brief fables of Arab origin. That work enjoyed great popularity in the Middle Ages: many authors borrowed its tales, from preachers in the thirteenth century to Boccaccio and Chaucer in the fourteenth. Other Christian authors from the peninsula, writing in Latin, Castilian, Catalan, or Portuguese, took up Arabic stories, translating them or taking inspiration from them. Among the most illustrious examples were Juan Manuel's *Conde Lucanor* and Juan Ruiz's *Libro de Buen Amor* in the fourteenth century, Fernando de Rojas's *Celestina* in the fifteenth, and Cervantes's *Don Quixote* in the seventeenth century, all influenced by the Arabic narrative tradition.

One of the European sovereigns most taken with Arab culture and science was undoubtedly Alfonso X the Wise of Castile, who surrounded himself with Jewish and Muslim scholars and oversaw the production of a vast library of Eastern and Western scholarship in Castilian. Some of the sumptuous miniatures in these works strikingly depict him as the king of all three religions: he is playing chess with a Muslim subject; listening to music with Christian and Muslim musicians; or, book in hand, directing his staff of Christian, Jewish, and Muslim scholars. The king in fact ordered the translation from the Arabic of several scientific and practical works: treatises in astronomy and astrology, divination, hunting, and chess. For centuries, his *Alfonsine Tables* remained the standard reference for European astronomers.[26] He also had literary works translated—notably, the *Kalīla wa Dimna*—as well as religious writings—a version of the *Miʿrāj*, or *Heavenly Journey of Muhammad*, and the Qur'an (that translation is now lost). In some sense, Alfonso was the counterpart of the Abbasid caliph al-Maʾmūn, who in the ninth century oversaw the translation of Greek and Persian works, which were Arabized and Islamized. The result was an enormous library that henceforth constituted the foundation of Arab culture and scholarship. Although the king of Castile's project was less vast, his ambition was similar: to found a rich library of scientific and literary works in his own language, in his case, Castilian. Alfonso sought to Hispanize Arab culture, just as al-Maʾmūn and his translators had Arabized Greek and Persian knowledge.

RELIGIOUS CONFLICTS AND CONVERGENCES

In the area of religion, doctrinal differences gave rise to conflicts and polemics among Jews, Christians, and Muslims. Just as, in the early centuries of Christianity, Christian doctrine had taken shape in competition and dialogue with Judaism and ancient paganism, the dogmas and practices of nascent Islam were marked by the rival forms of monotheism and by ancient philosophy and science. In Damascus and Baghdad, debates with Jewish and Christian scholars impelled the Muslims to define their orthodoxy and to defend their practices and sacred texts. A deep ambivalence toward Judaism and Christianity took root, one that was already present in the Qur'an. The holy book claimed in fact that the three great prophets (Moses, Jesus, and Muhammad) had revealed the word of God (the Torah, the Gospels, and the Qur'an) to their respective peoples. At the same time, it expressed sharp criticisms of certain Jewish and, especially, Christian practices and doctrines: the Christians worshipped a man, Jesus, as God; they compromised monotheism through the doctrine of the Trinity. Muslim scholars in Baghdad accused the Jews and Christians of having corrupted, intentionally or not, the sacred texts that their prophets had revealed to them. That "corruption" (*tahrīf*) supposedly discredited the arguments of Jews and Christians and marked the decline of their religions.[27]

One of the polemical texts from Baghdad religious circles was destined to become well known in Europe between the twelfth and sixteenth centuries: the *Risâlat al-Kindî*.[28] It is presented as an exchange of letters between two eminent members of the Abbasid court. A Muslim introduces Islam to a Christian friend and invites him to convert; in response, the Christian sets forth a long and meticulous refutation of Islam, accompanied by a defense of Christianity, and in turn asks his Muslim friend to convert. In reality, both letters were probably the work of a single Christian author. The *Risâlat al-Kindî* is both polemical and apologetic: it attacks Muslim doctrine and presents a defense of the fundamental Christian doctrines that particularly offended the Muslims. The author accuses Muhammad of being a libidinous false prophet who faked his revelations in order to impose his power on the Arabs and to satisfy his sexual desires. Muhammad himself composed the Qur'an, claims the *Risâlat* with the cooperation of a heretical Christian monk and two Jews. As for the Muslim rites, the Christian author finds them meaningless. Ritual ablutions? "You wash your bodies, but your hearts are impure and tainted by sin," like the hypocrites Christ denounces in the Gospel of Matthew. For similar reasons, the author attacks the Ramadan fast, circumcision, Muslim laws relating to marriage and divorce, and the prohibition on eating pork. He then launches into a long diatribe against the pilgrimage rite to Mecca, which he compares to the idolatrous rites of India. He adds an extensive tirade against holy war, explaining that it contradicts the Qur'anic injunctions denouncing the use of force in matters of religion. Those who die in wars will not go to heaven as martyrs; the only true martyrs are those who have given their lives for God peaceably and of their own free will. This diatribe, supposedly sent from a Christian to a Muslim friend, was no doubt actually intended for Christian *dhimmi* readers, to dissuade them from converting to Islam. It would be a notable success in Europe: first, in the Arabic-speaking Christian circles of the Iberian Peninsula; then, once it was translated into Latin in about 1143, throughout the rest of Europe.

In the East, a multitude of apologetic and polemical texts circulated, written by Christian, Muslim, and Jewish authors. In the West, by contrast, few polemical works were in evidence before the eleventh century, at which time the fall of the caliphate led to an ideological as well as a military confrontation between the Muslims of the *taifas* and the Christians from the northern kingdoms. One of the best-known examples is Ibn Hazm of Cordova (994–1064), who, probably in the 1050s, completed his *Fisal*, a polemical encyclopedia against Judaism, Christianity, and heterodox currents of Islam.[29] Some Muslim authors in the early centuries of Islam reproached the Christians and Jews for no longer respecting the precepts of their religion and for having falsified their holy writings. Ibn Hazm was the first to study the Torah and the Gospels in detail, and he did so in order to base these accusations on a critical reading of the Bible.

By pointing out the internal contradictions of the scriptures and the passages that seem illogical or blasphemous, Ibn Hazm aspires to prove that Jews and Christians falsified the revelations they had received from God. In Genesis and in the Gospels, for example, there are sometimes two versions of the same event, with small differences in the geographical, chronological, and genealogical information. Ibn Hazm uses these discrepancies to support his view and also catalogues passages in which God is described anthropomorphically: walking, eating, becoming angry. In addition, the Torah attributes the worst sort of behavior to the leaders of the chosen people: Abraham marries his half-sister, Jacob sleeps with his sister-in-law, Lot is seduced by his daughters, Solomon is led by his many wives to practice idolatry, and so on. All that shows not only that the writings were falsified but also that the Jews or Christians who accepted them were entirely lacking in morality, critical acumen, and rationality.

Ibn Hazm's father had been an official at the court of al-Mansūr in Cordova, and it may have appeared for a time that the son was also destined to play an important political role. But after the collapse of the caliphate, Ibn Hazm withdrew from political life and devoted himself to scholarly pursuits. He was one of the most remarkable and most prolific writers from al-Andalus, the author of poetry, chronicles, and legal, scientific, and theological treatises. His most widely read and best-known work today is no doubt his book on love, *The Ring of the Dove*. From his *Fisal*, we get the impression of a well-read man convinced that his Islamic culture and erudition placed him well above the despicable Christian (and Jewish) *dhimmis*, not to mention the barbarian *harbīs* from the northern Iberian Peninsula. But a growing insecurity can also be detected. The caliphate has fallen apart, and the Andalusian Muslim must now defend himself, militarily and ideologically, against the infidel.

It was in the context of *reconquista*, which changed the balance of powers between Muslims and Christians of the Iberian Peninsula, that a revival of anti-Muslim texts in the Arabic language occurred. They were written by Christian authors, some of them recent converts from Islam or Judaism. The authors of these texts attempt to defend Christianity against the objections that the Muslims raised: they assert the integrity of the Gospels in face of the accusations of *tahrīf*; they defend the Trinity against the charge of polytheism and seek to demonstrate its existence through arguments founded on reason; and they similarly defend the Incarnation. They also take the offensive, arguing against Muhammad and the Qur'an: they try to demonstrate that Muhammad was not a true prophet; that his law, in glorifying the pleasures of the flesh, showed itself to be irrational; and that Muslim rites, such as the pilgrimage to Mecca, were tainted by the remnants of paganism.

That apologetic and polemical tradition spread to Europe in the twelfth century by two means: the diffusion of Petrus Alfonsi's *Dialogues against the Jews* in 1110; and that of the Qur'an and other Arabic texts (including the *Risâlat al-Kindī*), translated into Latin at the initiative of Peter, abbot of Cluny (1142–1143). Petrus Alfonsi, a Jew who converted to Christianity, devotes a chapter of his anti-Jewish text to refuting Islam.[30] He adapts in abridged form the arguments of the *Risâlat al-Kindî*, which he probably knew in its Arabic version. Petrus Alfonsi's work was extremely successful, and the anti-Islamic chapter of the *Dialogues* was read and recopied. Humbert of Romans, master general of the Dominican order (1254–1263), in his *On the Formation of Preachers of the Crusade*, advises preachers to read two books so as to know the Muslim adversary: the Qur'an and the anti-Islamic chapter of Petrus Alfonsi.

During a trip to Spain in 1142–1143, Peter of Cluny formed the plan to have the Qur'an translated into Latin, along with other Arabic texts about Islam. He therefore hired Robert of Ketton, a translator of astronomical works, and a whole staff of scholars.[31] The aim of that project was to get to know the adversary thoroughly, in order to better combat him. Peter of Cluny, thanks to the information gleaned from these translations and from Petrus Alfonsi's *Dialogues*, could now fight the doctrine of Muhammad, whom he characterized as the worst of heresiarchs. He sought to produce a learned refutation of "the diabolical heresy of the Saracens," just as the church fathers had done against Arianism and other heresies. He uses the Qur'an to show that the Muslims ought to accept the Gospel; then he appeals to the Gospels to attack Muhammad and Islamic doctrines. The anti-Muslim polemics of Peter of Cluny caused little stir in the Middle Ages, but the translations he commissioned, especially that of the Qur'an, were recopied and reread—and finally published in Basel in the sixteenth century.

The relations between Christians, Muslims, and Jews cannot be reduced to conflicts and polemics, however. The three religions have common roots, and their doctrines, rites, and venerated sites are often similar. Hence there are many accounts of shared worship, common religious festivities, sites venerated together. Not surprisingly, these convergences, marks of the rapprochement between the faithful of different religions, sometimes elicit disapproval in the sources. We know, for example, that Muslims in ninth-century Spain celebrated Christmas, New Year's, and the summer solstice alongside the Christians only because muftis criticized that promiscuity and tried to ban it.[32] No doubt few heeded the prohibitions, since the muftis were obliged to reiterate them.

Many sites, associated with biblical and Qur'anic figures, were frequented by Christians, Muslims, and Jews. Such was the case for Hebron, where pilgrims visited the graves of the patriarchs Abraham, Isaac, and Jacob. In two sanctuaries dedicated to the Virgin Mary, the joint devotion of Christians and Muslims was particularly marked: at al-Matariyya, near Cairo, Egypt; and at Saydnāyā, near Damascus. Al-Matariyya has a spring in the middle of a grove of balsams; tradition has it that, during the flight into Egypt, the holy family stayed at that place and that the Virgin washed Jesus' diapers in the spring, conferring therapeutic properties on it. Various medieval authors (Copts, European Catholics, and Muslims) speak of it. Burchard of Strasbourg, who visited the site in about 1175, claims that Christians and Muslims came there and washed themselves in the spring. He adds that near Cairo was a date tree that had bent over to give its fruit to the Virgin, and that it too was an object of veneration for Christians and "Saracens."[33]

Several writers, including Burchard of Strasbourg, describe Saydnāyā, the site of a monastery dedicated to the Virgin. Here the object of veneration was an icon that was supposedly "incarnated" and that exuded oil smelling of balm. Burchard maintains that the miraculous oil cured many Christians, Muslims, and Jews. Clearly, Burchard's Virgin made no theological distinctions among her faithful: Saracens from the provinces in fact participated in the Christian feasts of the Nativity and of the Assumption of the Virgin and performed "their ceremonies with great devotion."

Muslims and Christians both, at times, demonstrated open admiration for the piety of those of other faiths. Usāma ibn Munqidh praises the devotion of the Christian monks. Riccoldo da Montecroce, a Florentine Dominican, admires the zeal of the Muslims of Baghdad: their respect for the rites, the fervor of their prayers, their love and compassion for their neighbor. Usāma and Riccoldo, like many other authors, were able to praise the zeal of their religious rival even while declaring that he embraced erroneous doctrines. In addition, these manifestations of admiration often had a rhetorical aim. As Riccoldo says, "We have recounted the preceding less to praise the Saracens than to embarrass certain Christians, who refuse to do for a living law what the damned do for a dead law."[34]

Other texts, though these are in the minority, show a greater openness, even an astonishing relativism. The pilgrim Burchard of Mount Sion wrote *Description of the Holy Land* in 1283. While describing a church dedicated to Saint John the Baptist, he explained that the Saracens venerated John as a holy prophet. They too believed that Jesus, born of the Virgin Mary, was the Word of God, but they did not recognize him as God, "and they say that Muhammad is the messenger of God and that God sent him *only to them*; I read it in the Qur'an, which is their book."[35] He places the emphasis on the fundamental compatibility of Christian and Muslim doctrines. Burchard begins with the idea that Muhammad was sent specifically to the Arabs (an idea indeed found in the Qur'an),[36] reaching the (erroneous) conclusion that, according to the Muslims, Islam is not universal. The Saracens, he suggests, have a revealed religion proper to them and make no claim for its superiority. Burchard confirms that sentiment in another passage from his *Description*, where he presents the various nations of the Holy Land. The Saracens form one group among many others: Latins, Greeks, Syrians, Armenians, and so forth, neither better nor worse than the others. Actually, according to Burchard, the worst of them are the Latins.[37]

That relativism finds literary expression in the legend of the three rings, first set down in writing in Italian in the thirteenth century and later repeated many times—by Boccaccio in particular, and even by Gotthold Ephraim Lessing in the eighteenth century, in *Nathan the Wise*.[38] In Boccaccio's version, Saladin, wanting to seize the riches of a Jew named Melchizedek, sets a trap for him by asking him which of the three religions is best: if he replies "Judaism," the sultan can declare himself insulted and seize Melchizedek's property; if he replies that Islam is better, the sultan can force him to convert. But the Jew replies with a tale: a king had three sons, whom he loved very much. Unable to choose among the three, he had two perfect copies made of his gold ring, the symbol of his power. Having arrived at death's door, the king called for his sons one by one and gave each a ring, declaring he had chosen that son as his heir. After his death, all three brothers, each brandishing his ring, laid claim to the paternal inheritance. And, concludes Melchizedek, we are like the three sons: Jews, Christians, and Muslims, we all claim the inheritance of our Father, God, but He alone knows which one He has chosen. At this, Saladin, filled with remorse, showered Melchizedek with presents, and the two became lifelong friends. Boccaccio has the Jewish character express that relativism. Menocchio, a sixteenth-century Friulian miller, read Boccaccio's tale and was inspired to declare openly that the Jews, the Christians, and the Turks could all have access to eternal joy by means of their own religion if they respected its precepts. Judged a heretic by the Inquisition tribunals, Menocchio was executed for that and other assertions.[39]

In the thirteenth century, a missionary movement appeared in Christian Europe, spearheaded primarily by the two new mendicant orders, the Franciscans and the Dominicans. Well before that date, Baghdad, Constantinople, and Rome had competed to convert Slavic and Turkish peoples around the periphery of the Black Sea, sending missionaries to them. But it was the thirteenth-century mendicant orders that lauched missions to Islam. The founder of the Order of Friars Minor, Francis of Assisi (1182–1226), traveled to Egypt in 1219, as the troops of the Fifth Crusade were besieging Damietta, and set out to meet Sultan al-Kāmil.[40] Francis, who was seeking to lead an apostolic life, wished to follow through to the end: like the apostles, he wanted to preach the faith to the infidels and, if he could not convert them, to suffer glorious martyrdom (figure 7). But al-Kāmil apparently had no desire to make a martyr of Francis; he listened patiently and sent him back to the Crusader camp, safe and sound. After that mission, martyrdom became the goal of several thirteenth-century Franciscans. Wishing to lead a life of poverty and asceticism like the apostles and to preach following their example, the Franciscans obviously aspired to die like them as well.

The first of these martyrs (1220) were five Franciscans who went to Seville (which was still Muslim), then to Marrakech. In both cities, they entered mosques, preached, insulted Muhammad and the Muslim religion—all gestures that would theoretically merit the death penalty according to the Sharia. But the Muslim authorities responded with prison and exile. It was only after several further infractions that the Almohad sultan granted them what they were fervently seeking: death. The news of their martyrdom spread; it filled Francis with joy and induced Anthony of Padua to become a Franciscan friar.

Figure 7. Bardi Dossal, ca. 1245, now in the Bardi Chapel in Santa Croce, Florence. Francis preaches to the Saracens. Reprinted by permission of akg-images, Paris.

In 1221, the *Regula non bullata*, the rule of the Franciscan order, encouraged missions among the infidels, specifying that superiors must not stand in the way of friars who were qualified to go, and that the friars must not fear death. Several Franciscans therefore set out in search of martyrdom: two met their deaths in Ceuta in 1227, five in Marrakech in 1232. Agnellus, bishop of Fez, also died in that city in 1246. Then ten Franciscans were martyred in the East between 1265 and 1269, and seven more in Tripoli in 1289. Other Franciscans lived more discreetly in Islamic countries, serving the Latin Christian communities (merchants, mercenaries, captives, slaves). But for many Franciscans, the Islamic countries were a stage on which the confrontation between apostles and "pagans" was being reenacted, and where the apotheosis of the former and the perdition of the latter were reproduced.

Other Franciscan missionaries endeavored to convert the Mongols. Giovanni dal Piano Carpini went to Karakorum between 1245 and 1247; Ascelin, to Tabriz (1246–1247); and then William of Rubruck, also to Karakorum (1253–1255).[41] These friars did not seek out martyrdom but tried to use logical arguments, inspired by the apologetic and polemical textual traditions, to bring the Mongol chiefs to Christianity. William of Rubruck in particular attempted to convert various Mongol sovereigns, not by insulting their religious traditions but by engaging in debate with the followers of rival religions. He therefore participated in a debate before Möngke Khan in person, between representatives of Christianity, Islam, Buddhism, and Uyghur paganism.[42] Not without pride, William describes his role in the debate. Having declared that there was only one God, he asked the Buddhist what he believed. The Buddhist replied that the gods were many: a supreme god in heaven and many lower gods. William then asked him whether one of these gods was all-powerful. The Buddhist sat in silence for a good while, until the khan's scribes ordered him to reply. He acknowledged that no god was all-powerful: "Then all the Saracens erupted in a great burst of laughter." William had scored one point for monotheism against Buddhism. Seen from Kharakorum, the Muslims were decidedly allies as much as rivals.

The Dominicans had their own missionary strategy, whose great promoter was Raymond of Penyafort, superior general of the order (1238–1240), then adviser to James I, king of Aragon.[43] He founded a language school so that the missionary friars could learn Arabic and Hebrew and read the sacred Muslim and Jewish texts. Embracing a textual critique of rival scriptures, they sought arguments that could both undermine the religion of their adversaries and confirm the truth of Christianity. Ramón Martí, a friar in Raymond of Penyafort's entourage, produced a diptych for evangelizing the Muslims: the *De seta Machometi*, composed before 1257, and the *Explanatio simboli apostolorum*, written in 1257.[44] The first text is devoted almost entirely to the life and deeds of Muhammad, whom Martí makes a scapegoat: it is the Prophet and his false law he attacks, not the wisdom of later Muslims. He tries to bring Arab philosophers into the Christian camp by turning their philosophical arguments against Muhammad. For example, he cites Averroes to demonstrate that a true prophet must produce miracles. Muhammad thus becomes Martí's sole, but formidable, adversary: reason, natural law, philosophy, and even a good part of Muslim doctrine, he strives to demonstrate, are on the side of the Christians. In his *Explanatio simboli apostolorum*, Martí seeks to prove the truth of Christianity by presenting the main Christian doctrines and by providing explanations and justifications, while at the same time attempting to refute the Muslim objections to these doctrines. It is not known to what extent the Dominican missionaries actually used Martí's arguments before a Muslim public. Laws promulgated under James I obliged the Jews and Muslims to listen to the sermons of the missionary friars in their synagogues and mosques. Ramón Martí, according to some of these contemporaries, traveled to Tunis and presented his *Explanatio simboli apostolorum* to the sultan.[45]

Riccoldo da Montecroce, a Florentine friar, went to Baghdad in about 1290 to learn Arabic and to attempt to convert Muslims.[46] He describes his amazement at the city of Baghdad (which, however, was no longer what it had been before the Mongol sack of 1258): the sumptuousness of its houses, the beauty of its gardens, the devotion and generosity of its residents, the learning of its ulemas. Riccoldo studied the Qur'an in Arabic, and the book greatly perplexed him. For him, it was full of "lies," such as the allegations that Jesus is not God, and that Jesus and his apostles were Muslims. What most troubled Riccoldo was that God should allow the "blasphemies" of the Qur'an. Hence he addresses a complaint directly to Jesus: "My heart stung to the quick, in unbearable pain while reading the Qur'an in Arabic, often, as you know, I have set the book down open upon your altar, in front of your image and that of your very holy mother, and have said: 'Read, read what Muhammad says!' And I have the impression that you do not want to read."[47] Far from punishing the "Saracens" for their "blasphemies," God appears to favor them, granting them victory after victory over the Christians, especially during the capture of Acre by al-Ashraf Kahlil, Mamluk sultan of Egypt.

Riccoldo returned to Italy in about 1300 and there composed his *Against the Law of the Saracens*, a refutation of the Qur'an. The friar was very familiar with the Qur'anic text, which he considered an out-and-out fabrication by Muhammad, whose incoherence, impiety, and irrationality Riccoldo denounces. In the Qur'an, Riccoldo declares, Muhammad teaches Christian truth without understanding it. To prove the existence of the Trinity, Riccoldo adopts the arguments of earlier polemicists, which are based on the fact that God is designated by plural nouns and pronouns. He also cites passages that, if we are to believe him, prove the existence of the Holy Spirit and of Christ, the Word of God. Observing that the Qur'an praises the Torah and the Gospels, he asks why, in that case, Muslims do not study them. If they were to do so, they would soon discover their error. But to avoid being confronted with the truth, they have banned the study of the Bible, just as they have forbidden that of philosophy. In truth, declares Riccoldo, the Saracens use four tricks to prevent their error from becoming glaringly obvious: they kill anyone who attacks the Qur'an; ban all religious disputes; put the Saracens on their guard by telling them not to believe what the non-Saracens say; and proclaim, "your law is for you, mine is for me."[48] It is nevertheless astounding in Riccoldo's view that the Saracens prefer the Qur'an to the Gospels. Once again, it must have to do with their irrationality, for which there is only one remedy: "As a result, when certain doubts arise in the Qur'an, and certain questions to which the Saracens cannot reply, we must not only invite them but *compel* them to take part in the Banquet of Truth."[49] Since our rational arguments cannot persuade them, Riccoldo seems to be saying, we must force them to join the church. When dialogue fails, he recommends force. His book would become one of the most widely read anti-Islamic treatises between the fourteenth and the sixteenth centuries. Martin Luther would translate it into German. Riccoldo's image of violent and irrational Saracen zealots, impervious to reason, and against whom only force would be effective was destined for a long career.

HUMANISM AND THE REJECTION OF ARAB CULTURE

The intellectual ties between Arab and European culture weakened in the fourteenth and fifteenth centuries. The golden age of translations was past, though a few continued to appear, in medicine, for example. A new humanist movement, founded on reverence for antiquity, which developed in large part in the courts of the great princes of Italy, opposed the clerical culture of the universities. In their infatuation with the ancient world and their rejection of university culture, some humanists displayed their contempt for everything they disdainfully called "Gothic" or "medieval," and in particular everything that was supposedly a Germanic or an Arab aggregate of the culture of antiquity.

The Florentine poet Petrarch (1304–1374), a friend of Boccaccio and passionate supporter of the Crusade, railed against the influence of Arab authors on his contemporaries' ways of thinking. In his *Letters of Old Age*, Petrarch claims that the Greeks laid the foundations for medicine and that the Arabs, mediocre doctors, ought to be kept "in banishment" from it. "I hate the entire race" of the Arabs, he declares. Although he undoubtedly never read any Arabic poetry, he considers them bad poets. He accuses European doctors of worshiping Averroes as a demigod, of preferring him even to Christ. He calls Averroes a "mad dog . . . who barks against his Lord, Christ" and infects his Christian admirers with his poison. He calls Muhammad an impostor, the inventor of absurd fables, and the object of a revolting cult at his tomb in Mecca (Muhammad's tomb is actually in Medina).[50] In the *Divine Comedy*, Dante places Averroes and Avicenna in the circle of the "good pagans," next to the great teachers Plato and Aristotle. On many occasions, Boccaccio shows his sympathy and admiration for Arab figures, especially Saladin, and expresses a certain religious relativism in the fable of the three rings. There is nothing of the sort in Petrarch, who hated the Arabs and wanted to banish them.

He was not alone. In the late fifteenth century, Marineo Siculo believed that the reason Arabic was so rarely studied was that it was a barbarous language. A debate raged in the field of medicine in the fifteenth and sixteenth centuries: Should the Arabs be banished in an attempt to return to the "purity" of Greek medicine, to Galen and Hippocrates? Symphorien Champier (1471–1538), who taught medicine in Montpellier, acknowledged the value of Avicenna's work but warned his readers against the bad influence that the "empty and barbarous philosophy" of that "impious apostate" could have on the Christian doctor. He cursed the doctors from European medical schools who allowed their university curriculum to be dominated by "Arabs, Persians, Indians, and Mahometans." In his *Three Books of the Medical Paradoxes* (1535), Leonhart Fuchs affirms that the Arabs invented nothing; rather, like the Harpies, they plundered the Greeks and contaminated everything they touched.[51]

But other authors defended Avicenna and, more generally, the Arab authors' contribution to science. The *Canon* remained a standard manual for medical education in Europe until the eighteenth century.[52] Two friends, major figures of fifteenth-century humanism, Marsilio Ficino and Pico della Mirandola, express their admiration for the great Arab thinkers such as al-Farabi, Avicenna, and Averroes. Pico had read the Qur'an in Latin and tried to learn Arabic so that he could read the original. He concludes that each of the great religions contains a share of truth. In his *Oration on the Dignity of Man*, he cites approvingly a declaration of Muhammad's, according to which the man who distances himself from divine law falls into bestiality.[53] But at a time when the Ottomans were making major conquests in central Europe and in the Mediterranean, few humanists showed the open-mindedness of Ficino and Pico.

In certain fields, the effects on the level of knowledge were perceptible. Fifteenth-century cartographers were mad for Ptolemy, whom they considered the great ancient authority on the matter. Cartography regressed as a result, especially in the Mediterranean, where maps based on Ptolemy were much less precise than the portolan charts established on the basis of the concrete knowledge of navigators in the Mediterranean.[54] The rejection of the Turk and the cult of Greco-Roman antiquity led to a refashioning of the European historical and cultural imagination. The rich common heritage of a shared Mediterranean civilization was denied. People began to think of "Islam" as a civilization foreign and hostile to Europe.

PART II

The Great Turk and Europe

by
Gilles Veinstein

INTRODUCTION TO PART II

Continuity and Change in Geopolitics

HISTORIANS SPECIALIZING IN regions outside Europe, and especially in the Islamic world, have plenty of reasons to criticize the traditional periodization of European history when it is applied to their objects of studies. The label "modern period," which designates the eras from the Renaissance to the French Revolution, is the most problematic. Depending on the country, it begins in the fifteenth or sixteenth century and ends in the late eighteenth. The modern period can therefore be distinguished both from the Middle Ages and from the so-called contemporary period, the nineteenth to twenty-first centuries. What meaning can that designation have outside European history? What equivalent could there be, for example, in the Islamic world of the fifteenth and sixteenth centuries, to the intellectual, artistic, political, and religious changes that imposed the notions of "Renaissance" and "Reformation" in Western historiography? In many respects, during that same period in the Muslim world, continuity predominated over breaks. For a time, the year 1453 was proposed as the turning point between the Middle Ages and the Renaissance. But that was less because of the Ottoman sultan Mehmed II's Islamic conquest of Constantinople than because of the flow of scientists and ancient manuscripts from Byzantium into Italy as a result of the threat of that event—or of the event itself. That is, the conquest was seen as one of the sources of the return to antiquity proclaimed by the humanists. As for 1492, which is often preferred as the starting point for the modern period, it is certainly more beholden to Christopher Columbus's first expedition to America than to the fall of Granada, the last Muslim stronghold surviving in Spain.

Nevertheless, though the sixteenth century did not entail a cultural break in Islam on the same order as that posited for the West, there is one realm where that century was, for Islam as well, synonymous with rupture: that of geopolitics. New political structures appeared at the time within the Muslim world, and new territorial divisions came into being between Islam and Christendom.

THE GREAT EMPIRES OF THE MODERN AGE

The sixteenth century witnessed the establishment of the three great empires that transformed the political landscape of Islam and would continue to mark its fortunes in the following centuries. In 1523, the Turco-Mongol Babur, descendant of both Genghis Khan and Tamerlane, having left his small Afghan kingdom, seized the Punjab and Lahore, the beginning of the empire of the Great Moguls of India. That empire would shine brightest under his grandson Akbar (1556–1605) and would have its maximum territorial extension under Aurangzeb in the second half of the seventeenth century.

Two decades earlier, in 1501, Shah Esmāʿīl (1487–1524), the young heir to the Turkoman spiritual leaders of the Safaviyya (the powerful heterodox brotherhood from Ardebīl, Azerbaijan), seized Tabrīz and proclaimed himself shah, thus inaugurating the Safavid Empire, which unified Iran and imprinted on it the mark of Twelver Shiism. It was under Shah ʿAbbas the Great (1587–1629), who made Isfahan his capital in 1598, that this empire would complete its Iranization and reach its apogee.

As for the Ottoman Empire, the third empire of the "modern" period, it had come into being two centuries earlier but it too was at its zenith in the sixteenth century, under the reign of Süleyman the Magnificent (1520–1566), nearly achieving its maximum extension at that time. For though it benefited from several territorial additions in the following century, these remained relatively minor. The Ottoman Empire was also the most long-lasting of the three, ending only in 1923. Above all, it was by far the most important in the relations of all kinds between Europe and the Islamic world in the period under consideration. It is not enough to say that, of the three empires, it was the closest to Europe, since it was *in* Europe itself. It occupied a third or a fourth of that continent and, as of the fifteenth century, its capital, Edirne and then Istanbul, was located there. To be sure, these three empires in themselves did not represent the totality of the Muslim world. Other states (the Uzbek khanates of central Asia, for example, or the Sharifian kingdom of Morocco, not to mention the sultanates of sub-Saharan Africa or Indonesia) managed to survive independently, thanks to their geographical distance or as a function of the rivalries between empires that they were able to exploit. But compared to the fragmentation of the post-Abbasid or post-Mongol periods, the political simplification of the Muslim world that these empires introduced—restricting that world almost entirely to a few large units—and the relative unification they represented, despite the intense politico-religious antagonisms (between the Ottoman and Safavid empires, for example), are still striking. These mighty empires, so long as they remained strong and unified, were a rampart against any potential European penetration.

Toward an Islamic-Christian Division

Another characteristic of that "modern" period, closely linked to the preceding, lies in the evolution of the territorial division between Islam and Christianity. In the early Middle Ages, as a result of the great conquests that accompanied the beginnings of Islam, that religion had penetrated deeply into Europe: in Spain and Portugal, the Mediterranean islands (Sicily, Crete, Malta, Cyprus, the Balearics), and southern France. But that presence was relatively short-lived everywhere but in Spain, where the process of *reconquista* was much more gradual. As a result, the Muslim presence continued there for centuries, until the threshold of the modern age. In eastern Europe, however, in the southern regions of Russia within the part of the Mongol Empire called the "Golden Horde," Islam arrived much later, as a result of the Islamization of the Golden Horde in the fourteenth century. In that respect, these regions followed an opposite course when compared to the general process of Europe's resorption of Islam.

European princes and knights went even further in changing the geopolitics of the respective regions, by attempting to seize those in the Near East acquired by Islam from its beginnings, at the expense of Byzantine Christianity. That was the aim of the Crusades, which had initially retaken the Holy Sepulchre from the Infidels between 1099 and 1187, leading to the constitution of the kingdoms of Jerusalem and Cyprus, the county of Tripoli, and the principality of Edessa (as well as the formation of a Latin empire of Constantinople). But that shift did not last long in the face of the Muslim reaction, and by 1291 nothing remained of the Latin overseas states except Cyprus. It was now clear that neither of the two great monotheistic religions with universalist ambitions, in competition by their very nature, had managed to eliminate the other. Rather, they seemed to be heading toward a territorial division: to Christianity would fall Europe, which would therefore be identified with *Christianitas*; to Islam, the overseas regions, that is, the Middle East and the Maghreb. There the effects of the first wave of Muslim expansion would be long-lasting. Christian communities did survive in these regions, which had witnessed the birth of Christianity, but they remained under the domination of the Crescent, and the chasm separating them from Western Christendom, that is, from Rome, only grew wider. To what extent did the modern period confirm that pattern, and in what ways did it contradict it?

MAMLUKS AND PORTUGUESE

Let us first consider the Mashriq, that is, Egypt and Syria. In the last three centuries of the Middle Ages, that essential part of the Muslim world had been saved from the threat of both the Crusaders and the Mongols by the Mamluk regime. With wealth and power behind it, that dynasty had for the same reason been the protective suzerain and benefactor of the holy sites of Mecca and Medina and of the annual great pilgrimage. Nevertheless, in the late fifteenth and early sixteenth centuries, the Mamluks had to contend with the ambitions of new rising powers within Islam (the Ottomans, the Ak Koyunlu) and with an infidel peril of a new kind: indeed, when the Portuguese opened the sea route to India circumventing Africa, they dealt a fatal blow to Mamluk finances, diverting spice traffic from the eastern Mediterranean. It has been calculated that, between 1496 and 1506, imports from Alexandria fell by two-thirds and those from Beirut by five-sixths (the Venetian traffic in spices from the Levant would resume later in the sixteenth century).[1] But that was not all: the presence of the Portuguese fleet, an infidel force in the Indian Ocean and near the entrance to the Red Sea, was perceived as a threat to the holy sites. In 1505, the Portuguese had appeared outside Jidda. Aided by the Ottomans (who cooperated with them before eliminating them) and by the Venetians (for whom the Portuguese innovation had no less catastrophic consequences), the Mamluks sent a fleet to the Indian Ocean, defeating the Portuguese in Chaul in March 1508 and driving them from the coast of Gujarat. But a fatal setback quickly obliterated the Mamluk success: in 1509, the Portuguese crushed the Egyptian fleet in Diu and earned the cooperation of the sultan of Gujarat. The Mamluks were eliminated from the Indian Ocean.

OTTOMANS AND PORTUGUESE

These developments brought to light the Mamluk decline and thereby the weakening capacity for Islamic resistance in that essential zone. But it did not take the Ottomans long to step into the breach and replace the Mamluks. In the preceding decades, the Ottomans' rise to power had already introduced friction between them and the Mamluks, and especially, territorial rivalries in the eastern part of Asia Minor.[2] Nevertheless, Sultan Bayezid II and his successor, Selim I (early in his reign), had supported the Mamluk resistance against the Portuguese. Whatever their ulterior motives may have been, they were thereby conforming to the imperatives of Islamic solidarity. It was then that Selim I, who in 1514 had defeated the heretical sovereign of Persia, the Shiite Shah Esmāʿīl, at Chaldiran, turned his weapons against his former ally, the Mamluk sultan Kansawh al-Ghawri. The only justification Selim could give for his reversal and for that act of aggression (which in theory was illegal) against an irreproachably religious Sunni coreligionist, was the pretext that the Mamluks had formed a secret alliance with the Persian heretics against him. During a triumphant campaign, marked by the victory of Marj Dabiq (August 24, 1516), which gave him Syria, and then by the victory of Raydaniyya (January 23, 1517), near Cairo, which made him lord of Egypt, the Ottoman took the place of the Mamluk sultans. It appears that he himself was surprised by the relative ease of his successes, attributable in great part to the superiority of his artillery and firearms, or at least to better handling of them. In addition, Selim obtained the support of the sharif of Mecca, who had no other choice, given the persistent aggressiveness of the Portuguese. A few days after the Ottoman victory of Raydaniyya, the Portuguese Lopo Soares left Goa with a fleet that, in mid-April, arrived close to Jidda and hence on the doorstep of the holy sites.[3] The only thing the sharif could do was to make official the talks that, in all likelihood, had been secretly initiated several months earlier, by sending his son on an embassy to Cairo to see Selim. Under the terms of the agreement concluded, Selim I became in turn "servant of the two holy sanctuaries," that is, protector of the holy sites of Islam and of the pilgrimage. His successors took that title very seriously, in terms of both the duties it imposed on them and the justifications it was able to provide for their actions. Selim's achievement was in fact only the first act in the Ottomans' takeover of the Arab world. His son, Süleyman the Magnificent, active primarily on the western front, that is, in Europe, continued his father's work. In his major campaign against his Safavid adversary Shah Tahmasp in 1534–1536, Süleyman seized Tabrīz and Mesopotamia, along with the former caliphal capital of Baghdad. Subsequently, the Ottomans and Safavids continued to fight over Baghdad and Azerbaijan. The obstacles that the Ottomans' great rivals mounted against them in these regions did not prevent them from keeping the Portuguese infidels away from the Red Sea and the Persian Gulf; they were relatively effective in this regard, or at least fared better than the Mamluks had been able to do before them. They managed by conducting naval campaigns, whose results, as was generally the case for sea ventures, were often uncertain. In 1538, the Ottoman governor of Egypt, the eunuch Süleyman Pasha, who had dreamt for years of fighting the Portuguese fleet, finally set out on the Red Sea with seventy-four ships. He succeeded in seizing Aden and consolidated the Ottoman presence in Yemen, but he failed to fulfill his primary objective, which was to take the new fortress the Portuguese had built in Diu in 1535–1536. The Portuguese attempted to eliminate that maritime threat by launching an expedition in 1541 in the northern Red Sea. Conducted by Vasco da Gama's son Dom Estêvão, it was intended to destroy the Ottoman fleet based in Suez. But it was a failure. In 1552, the Ottomans again undertook a maritime expedition against the Portuguese, this time entrusted to Pīrī re'īs, a most experienced seaman who has remained famous for the atlas named after him. On that occasion, he received the lofty title "captain of the Indies."[4] He left Suez with twenty-five galleys and four galleons, taking aboard 850 soldiers, with the aim of capturing Ormuz, a gulf port occupied by the Portuguese since 1515, and also, if possible, Bahrain. Along the way, he pillaged Masqat, then besieged Ormuz. Pīrī re'īs did not succeed in taking the island and failed even to bring back his galleys, a dual setback that resulted in his execution. Another captain, Seydī 'Alī reīs, was sent out to replace him, leaving Basra in 1554. He sailed down the Persian Gulf without mishap, following the coast of Arabia via Bahrain, then twice clashed with Portuguese ships when he arrived at the Sea of Oman. In the second encounter, in Mascat, he lost several of his galleys, which were ill-suited for navigation in the ocean, conditions being very different there from those on the Red Sea. After that, he endured a terrible storm off the coast of Makran. He finally found refuge in Surat, on the coast of Gujarat, where the remains of his fleet dispersed.

The Ottomans were not content to face the Portuguese in maritime actions, which were always hazardous. Simultaneously, they made territorial advances along the coasts. They did not confine themselves (as the Portuguese would do) to acquiring bases for commercial and strategic purposes, such as Dakhla, Aden, Massawa, Suakin, Beilul, or Mascat. Aided by an expanse of continuous territory, which their Portuguese rivals obviously lacked, they penetrated farther into the hinterland and constituted actual provinces, or *beylerbeyilik*: for the Red Sea, the *beylerbeyilik* of Yemen, constituted in 1540, and of Habesh (Abyssinia), formed in 1555; for the Persian Gulf, the *beylerbeyilik* of Bassora, formed in 1546 following the conquest of the *beylerbey* of Baghdad, Ayas Pasha; and, on the northeast coast of the Arabian Peninsula, that of Lahsa. The motivations behind these conquests remain hypothetical, at least in part, though it is clear that economic and fiscal interests played a role. So too did religious interests, given the threat that the Zaydis of Yemen, heretics in the Ottomans' eyes, posed for the nearby holy sites. There are also many indications that these ventures, far from stemming solely from a deliberate plan that the central authority pursued coherently and continuously, were often the result of local initiatives.[5] That said, however, in the conflict with the Portuguese, the Ottomans saw territorial conquest as a substitute for naval confrontations and as ultimately more reliable than they. All the same, these two kinds of actions combined did not allow Süleyman and his successors to eradicate the Portuguese presence in the Sea of Oman and northwestern India. They failed to put a definitive end to commercial competition or to assure the freedom and security of the sea routes between Muslim India and the holy sites of the Hejaz. Realistically assessing his relative powerlessness, Süleyman the Magnificent attempted on two occasions to reach a compromise of sorts, first, in 1541–1544, with King John III, and then, in 1564, with King Sebastian. These negotiations led nowhere, however. Although the ventures were only a partial success, the Ottomans at least succeeded in containing the Portuguese peril. Moreover, in the 1530s and 1540s, a certain flow of Far Eastern spices resumed via the Red Sea and then Damascus, or via the Persian Gulf and then Baghdad. But that traffic remained limited, satisfying only the needs of Mideastern consumption, without giving rise to new exports to the West. These would in turn resume in the years 1545–1552.[6]

CHRISTENDOM AND ISLAM IN THE MAGHREB

In the Maghreb, which directly faced southern Europe and was thus particularly vulnerable to its expansionism at the beginning of the modern age, Muslim rulers nevertheless succeeded in holding onto their positions. The Ottoman presence again played a role in that geopolitical stronghold, but in this case the role was not exclusive and assumed very specific forms.

In the fifteenth century, the Maghreb was divided among local dynasties, which had had their hour of glory but had then weakened: the Hafsids of Ifrīqiya (Tunisia), Abd al-Walid of Tlemcen, the Marinids and then the Wattasids of Morocco. Portuguese and Spaniards had urgently set their sights on that weakened zone. This was, in short, a natural continuation of the *reconquista*. The Portuguese seized Ceuta in 1415, Arzila and Tangier in 1471. The Spaniards took Melilla in 1497. By the terms of the treaty of Tordesillas, Spain and Portugal divided the Maghreb into zones of influence: Morocco for Portugal; Algiers and Tunisia for Castile. The Spaniards seized Tripoli in 1510. In 1530, Charles V entrusted the fortress to the Knights of Malta. That movement undermining Muslim domination in the Maghreb would quickly be halted, however. Against the Spanish threat, the residents of Algiers appealed for aid from two corsair leaders, the Barbarossa brothers, 'Arūj and Khayr ad-Dīn. 'Arūj had himself proclaimed sultan and conquered several strongholds in Algeria, including Tlemcen. He died in that city in 1518, besieged by a Spanish army. His brother Khayr ad-Dīn succeeded him, understanding that his salvation depended on protection from the Ottoman Empire, whose Muslim presence was now growing in the east. He gave his states as a tribute to Sultan Selim I, to whom he became a sort of vassal. He continued his progress in Algeria, taking Bona, Constantine, and Cherchell. In 1529, he obtained the surrender of Peñón, a fortress held by the Spaniards on a small island near Algiers. Integration into the Ottoman Empire advanced further in 1553, when Barbarossa became grand admiral of Süleyman the Magnificent's fleet. At the same time, the seaman was an essential architect of the Franco-Ottoman rapprochement, a complementary aspect of his anti-Spanish policy. Algeria was now an Ottoman province, the *Jeza'ir beylerbeyliği*. It would quickly assume a special form, however, one common to the other Ottoman provinces of the Maghreb and which set them apart from the rest of the empire. The power of the governor, or *beylerbey*, then of the pasha, representative of the central Ottoman state, was soon eclipsed by that of the corps of local Janissaries (some of whom continued to be recruited from the central provinces of the empire) and its leader, the agha. Another entity shared the leadership of that principality of sorts (the Europeans would call them "Barbary regencies"): the guild of corsair captains (*ta'ifat al-ru'asā*). As of 1671, a higher authority took over, that of the dey, which survived until the French conquest of 1830. Nonetheless, the allegiance to Istanbul was never broken. The Ottoman sultan therefore perceived the French conquest as an assault.

Extending his takeover of the Maghreb to the east, Barbarossa seized Tunis in 1534. But the following year, in a formal expedition in which Charles V personally took part, and which he hoped would have the greatest repercussions possible, the emperor recaptured Tunis. He presented that success as a triumph, an expression of divine will, and as the prefiguration of decisive victories against the Ottomans. For the time being, however, he was content to reestablish the

Hafsids under his protectorate, placing the fortress of La Goulette under Spanish control. It was not until the winter of 1569–1570 that the Ottoman governor of Algiers, Uluj Ali Pasha, advanced overland to Tunis, seized the city, and set up a garrison there, the Hafsid prince having found refuge in La Goulette. John of Austria rushed in with a fleet from Sicily to reestablish Spanish authority in October 1573. But, in July of the following year, Uluj Ali Pasha reappeared outside Tunis, this time accompanied by a large fleet and, after a brief siege, he seized the city, as well as the fortress of La Goulette. That new episode established Ottoman domination in a lasting manner. At that relatively late date, the duel for control of the Maghreb between the Ottomans and Spain—and, more broadly, between Islam and Christendom—was decided in favor of the Muslims.

The evolution of the Tunisian province was rather similar to that of Algiers. Although the bond of allegiance was never broken, Tunis acquired a growing autonomy from Istanbul, to the benefit of the Janissaries and corsairs, who enjoyed a golden age in the first half of the seventeenth century. But, as in Algiers, a higher authority, a principate of sorts, was imposed after some time: by the end of the sixteenth century, it would be the regime of the deys. Later, in the mid-seventeenth century, Murad, a former slave from Corsica, installed the dynasty of the Muradite beys, which lasted until 1702. At that time, the new bey, Husayn bin Ali, founded a dynasty, the Husaynites, which were placed under the French protectorate in the late nineteenth century. Christian power, represented by the Knights of Malta, did not last in Tripoli either. In 1551, the expedition commanded by Koja Sinān Pasha made Tripoli the seat of a new Ottoman province, which evolved like its Maghrebian neighbors. In the seventeenth century, the activities of its corsairs reached their paroxysm, leading to a reaction on the part of the French and English, who bombarded the stronghold in 1676 and 1685. In 1711, the Karamanli dynasty was established with Istanbul's consent. It lasted until 1835.

The domination of Europe—in this instance, the Iberian states for the most part—was thus kept in check in the sixteenth-century Maghreb. The Spaniards held on to only a few isolated presidios. In their rivalry, neither Islam nor Christendom had formed a united front. Charles V was the ally of the Hafsids against Barbarossa. Morocco defended itself both against the Ottoman advance to the east and against the encroachments of the Christians from the north. When a new dynasty from the region of Sousse, bearing the name *chorfa*—that is, "descendants of the Prophet," the Saadians—took up the torch of holy war, they did not look askance at the cooperation of European adventurers and renegades, and they opposed both the Wattassids of Fez and the Portuguese, from whom they recaptured a series of fortresses. In the famous Battle of the Three Kings in Ksar el-Kebir (1578), which marked the elimination of the Portuguese from Morocco and the triumph of the *chorfa*, the Saadian Ahmad al-Mansūr was victorious over both King Sebastian of Portugal and the king of Fez.

Under the circumstances, it was in Europe itself that the greatest changes in the territorial division between Islam and Christendom took place in the modern period. That was not the case, however, for the western part of the continent. On the contrary, re-Christianization, already well under way in the Late Middle Ages, continued ineluctably. The capitulation of the Nasrids of Granada, the last Muslim sovereigns of Spain, to the "Catholic monarchs," Isabel of Castile and Ferdinand of Aragon, on January 1, 1492, was followed more than a century later, after many episodes of discrimination and persecution, by the expulsion of the "Moriscos": 350,000 Muslims were driven out toward the Maghreb.

In the Northeast: Russians and Tatars

Far away, in the northeastern part of the continent, the successes of the grand prince of Moscow were moving in the same direction. He shook off the tutelage of his Muslim suzerain, the Mongol khan of the Golden Horde, causing a reversal in power relations. The Horde, weakened and falling apart, fragmented into several small independent khanates in the first half of the sixteenth century. Ivan the Terrible, however, conquered two of these khanates, one after the other: the Kazan khanate on the Middle Volga in 1552 and the khanate of Astrakhan at the mouth of that great river in 1556. A third, more southern khanate, Crimea, did manage to resist Moscow. It owed that success to its own strength, which was not insignificant, but also to the protection of the great state whose orbit it had entered in 1475 and which, once again, was none other than the Ottoman Empire.

A New Muslim Wave in Europe

In Europe, not everything was heading in the same direction, however. Another part of the continent, the southeast, had for several centuries been undergoing a diametrically opposed evolution. There the Ottoman conquest had established the political domination of Islam. In that region, the identification of Europe with *Christianitas*, toward which the entire medieval evolution seemed necessarily to be leading, was belied in the most scathing manner. Let us return to the origins and modalities of a historical process whose paradoxical nature now appears in full: the Ottoman conquest of Europe. The events must be recalled in some detail, for here the history of Islam and that of a part of Europe are completely entangled.

CHAPTER 6

THE OTTOMAN CONQUEST IN EUROPE

TURKS AND MUSLIMS IN EUROPE BEFORE THE OTTOMANS

During the early Middle Ages, eastern Europe was unaffected by the Muslim expansion, though that part of the continent, an extension of the Eurasian steppe, did not remain completely untouched by the presence of Turkic peoples (whether direct ancestors of the Ottomans or not) or by the Muslim presence. The European parts of the Byzantine Empire had to deal with several of these invaders of the steppe, such as the Pechenegs, the Cumans, and the Uzes, all of whom the Byzantine literati assimilated to the Scythians of antiquity. Byzantium clashed with these peoples or used them against other "barbarians." Ultimately, in the second half of the thirteenth century, Turkish populations fleeing the Mongol advance in Asia Minor, under the leadership of the Anatolian Seljuk sultan Izz al-Dīn Kaykā'ūs, settled south of the Lower Danube, in Dobruja, a Byzantine province at the time. Their spiritual guide, Sarı Saltuk, is still the object of a cult in the popular piety of eastern European Muslims.[1] Turkish elements, integrated into the general population and especially the army, had also long been present in Byzantine territory, in Constantinople or other European strongholds. Beginning in the eighth century, Byzantium, like the Abbasid caliphate, put a call out to mercenaries of Turkish origin, some of whom reached the highest ranks. For example, Anna Comnena writes that a lieutenant of Emperor Alexius Comnenus (1081–1118) by the name of Tatikios "had under his orders Turks living in the region of Achrida [and] was a very courageous and intrepid man in battle." The emperor gave him the title of "protoproedros." John Comnenus named another Turk, Axouch, "great servant of the East and West."[2] In addition, the capital of Constantinople counted various Islamized Turks of sorts, whose numbers continued to grow in the eleventh century: these were soldiers but also merchants, beggars, and dervishes, as well as ambassadors of the Seljuk sultans of Anatolia, Seljuk princes in exile, and other visitors. In his correspondence dating to the thirteenth century, the patriarch Athanasius expressed distress that these Muslims of Constantinople had complete latitude to call the faithful to prayer in the very heart of the city. Other Muslim or Christian sources—the latter often tinged with the same indignation—confirm that Muslim presence in the two centuries that followed. There is mention of a Muslim neighborhood in Constantinople, which an Arabic source describes as being walled in. In the late fourteenth century, the Ottoman sultan, Bayezid I, leader of the neighboring power, took the liberty of giving that community a qadi. "It was not fair," said the sultan, according to the chronicler Dukas, "that the Muslims involved in commerce who frequent Constantinople appear before a court of infidels for lawsuits and disputes."[3] It would fall to the Ottomans to establish a presence in these regions of a completely different nature from the immigration just mentioned: a conquest spread out over three centuries, culminating in a much longer occupation.

The Origins of the Ottomans

The Ottomans' beginnings were extremely modest. Osman, the founder of the dynasty, to which he gave his name (the Ottomans are *Osmanli,* "descendants of Osman"), then his son and successor, Orhan, were in charge of one of the many small Turkoman principalities (*beylik*) that had formed on the Aegean, Mediterranean, and Pontic periphery of the Seljuk sultanate of Konya. The sultanate had weakened and, in 1243, it came under the protectorate of the Mongol Ilkhans of Persia.

Located northwest of Anatolia, in a rich region north of ancient Phrygia on the border of Byzantine Bithynia, the Ottoman *beylik* initially grew at the expense of the last Byzantine possessions in western Asia Minor, which it bordered, and of the other Turkoman Aegean *beyliks,* with which it was in competition. A first skirmish with a Byzantine force, the Battle of Bapheus on the southern coast of the Sea of Marmara, is attested for 1326. The Byzantines were defeated. Orhan conquered Brusa (Bursa) in 1326, and it became the capital of the young Ottoman state. In 1327 in Pelecanum, west of Nicomedia (Izmit), Orhan's archers clashed with the troops of the basileus Andronikos III, who was wounded. In 1331, Nicaea (Iznik) surrendered to Orhan after a siege lasting several years. Nicomedia fell in turn in 1337. Orhan, taking advantage of a dynastic crisis, took over the *beylik* of Karasi in 1346 and thus acquired the coast of the Dardanelles. That foothold in the strait zone opposite Byzantium and Europe was decisive for the future of the Ottoman state.

That dynasty of humble origins (and which would later endeavor to give more luster to them by inventing prestigious genealogies) was beginning to attract notice. It had only recently become Muslim, and its form of Islam was thoroughly mixed with previous central Asian beliefs and practices, which made it rather unorthodox. It is also clear that these first Ottomans owed a great deal of their success to the cooperation of local Christian elements. Nevertheless, the nascent state, like the other neighboring *beyliks,* was Islamic. The bey attributed to himself, at a still modest scale, all the characteristics of a Muslim sovereign of the time: he minted money, had his name pronounced at the sermon during the Friday great prayer, established pious foundations (*vakf*), named qadis in the conquered cities, and set up Islamic secondary schools (*medrese*) and mosques there. Some of these mosques were former churches, while others were newly constructed buildings. The oldest Ottoman mosque, Haji Ozbek in Iznik, dates to 1333–1334.

By virtue of its geographical location, that emirate, like the nearby *beyliks*, was an integral part of a complex regional policy that combined Christian and Muslim entities. Orhan especially was called on to intervene in the activities of rival Byzantine factions. During the Ottomans' first inroads into Europe, the Byzantines provided the pretext and the Genoese the ships to cross the Bosphorus.

Inroads into Europe

The Byzantine emperor, John Cantacuzenus (1341–1355), having usurped the throne of John V Palaeologus, whom he had served as minister, sought support among the Turkoman beys. He initially appealed to a bey from the region of Smyrna (Izmir), Umur Pasha of Aydin, but when Umur was busy fighting a Christian coalition, Cantacuzenus had to fall back on Orhan. The emperor brought him to Europe and in 1346 gave him his daughter Theodora in marriage. Close ties were established between the two men, and commercial contacts were made with Genoa, culminating in a first Ottoman-Genoese treaty in 1352. Orhan entrusted his son and putative heir, Süleyman Pasha, with operations in Europe, the "new frontier." In 1352, Süleyman Pasha went to Adrianople, Thrace, to assist John Cantacuzenus against the Serbs and Bulgarians. A band of "Turks," previously established by Byzantium, had a stronghold called Tzympe on the Isthmus of Gallipoli near Bolayir, northeast of Gelibolu. (Tzympe has since disappeared.) These Turks joined Süleyman Pasha, who took the opportunity to make the stronghold his first base in Europe. Then, despite Cantacuzenus's insistence, he refused to evacuate it, instead reinforcing that beachhead with troops freshly arrived from Anatolia. Shortly thereafter, during the night of March 1, 1354, Süleyman Pasha seized Gallipoli (Kallipolis, Gelibolu), thanks to an earthquake that damaged the fortress walls. There he established a garrison. The West realized the gravity of the event. Pope Urban V (who was still in Avignon) reacted by launching a first anti-Ottoman Crusade. The official aim was still holy war, but the real worry was the direct threat posed to the Latin states of Greece and Constantinople. In effect, the conquest of the last Byzantine territories of eastern Europe had begun. But Süleyman Pasha's achievement was cut short by his accidental death in 1357. When his father, reportedly inconsolable, died in turn in 1362, the Ottomans occupied a good part of southern Thrace, along with Didymoteicho (Dimetoka), which succeeded Bursa as the new seat of the bey. The emirate's center of gravity had shifted to the north.

FIRST WAVE OF CONQUESTS IN EASTERN EUROPE

Another of Orhan's sons succeeded him under the name Murad I. The advance into Europe, and simultaneously, Asia Minor, continued under his long reign (1360–1389). Along with the early Ottomans' military capacities and diplomatic skill, one of the causes of their success lay in the fragmentation and political weakness of eastern Europe at that time. Powerful states had appeared there more or less recently and were poised to succeed the Byzantine Empire. It had long been in decline, having been dealt a fatal blow in 1204 by the Latin conquest of Constantinople during the Fourth Crusade. In addition, the divisions among the members of the dynasty, the Palaeologi, offered their adversaries ample opportunities to act. The Bulgarian tsardom had reached its maximum extension in the Balkans and the apogee of its power under the reign of Tsar Ivan Asen II (1218–1241), but it had fallen apart just after his death. The kingdom of Serbia had replaced it in the mid-fourteenth century, spurred on by a great sovereign, Stephen Dušan. He had exploited the rich mining revenues to carve out an empire at the expense of Byzantium. In 1346, in Skopje, Macedonia, Stephen Dušan had himself proclaimed tsar of the Greeks, the Serbs, and the Bulgarians. He attempted to seize Constantinople, considering himself the best suited for providing protection against the Turks, but he died shortly thereafter, in 1354, the same year Süleyman Pasha took Gallipoli. His empire was immediately dismembered, and the pieces passed into the hands of princes independent of one another and divided among themselves.

Of the many dominions that parceled up that section of Europe, which was politically very fragmented—to which should be added the Republic of Venice and the various Frankish principalities, Italian or Catalan in origin, that were present in Greece—only the kingdom of Hungary was able to contain the Turkish advance in a lasting way. That "rampart of Christendom," as it called itself, did not collapse until the threshold of the modern age.

At first, Murad I was unable to intervene in Europe. Kept occupied in Anatolia by difficulties of succession that remain obscure even today and by an active appropriation policy vis-à-vis the neighboring Turkish emirates—a policy he would continue throughout his reign— he could no longer travel to Europe, where he had lost his indispensable crossing point. In fact, Pope Urban V's call for a Crusade against the Turks after the fall of Gallipoli, though it fell short in terms of attracting followers, at least spurred on Count Amadeus VI of Savoy, cousin of Basileus John V. He had managed to retake Gallipoli in August 1366. The following May, he also retook Enneakossia (Küçükçekmece) from the Turks. Murad would be unable to set foot again in Europe until 1376–1377, when Basileus Andronikos IV, one of John V's sons, returned his beachhead, in exchange for his aid in a civil war against his father and brothers. In the meantime, Turkish beys, acting autonomously, continued to fight and to have success in eastern Europe. Murad would be the ultimate beneficiary of these conquests.

It is impossible to retrace all these events with perfect clarity, however. The date of the taking of Adrianople (Edirne) is a matter of controversy, though it probably occurred in 1369.[4] The occupation of that stronghold dominating the valleys of the Maritsa and Tundzha rivers opened the way to many other conquests in Bulgaria, western Thrace, and Macedonia, with the latter two regions serving as the field of action for one of the most famous of these autonomous Turkish leaders, Evrenos Bey. To repel the danger, Vukašin of Ohrid and Prilep formed an alliance with his brother Uglesa of Serrai (Serres). These two Serbian despots of Macedonia, petty kings who had emerged with the decomposition of Dušan's empire, attempted to stop the Turkish advance on the Maritsa. A bloody battle known as "Chirmen" or "the Maritsa" unfolded on September 26, 1371, and both Serbian princes perished. Conquests in Macedonia and Serbia followed as a result. As a Byzantine chronicle notes, from that moment on, the Muslims began to invade the empires of the Christians.[5] Serres was taken in 1383, Niš in 1386, and Thessaloniki (Salonika) in 1387, though it was not occupied until 1394 and was definitively conquered only in 1430.

In the meantime, Bulgaria had begun to be vassalized. Upon his death in 1362, Tsar Alexander had two successors, his sons Shisman and Stratsimir. It seems that Stratsimir, the prince of Vidin on the Danube, accepted Hungarian suzerainty; as for Shisman, prince of Tarnova, he had to accept the suzerainty of Murad, who forced him to give Murad his sister in marriage. But in the following years, Shisman shook off that tutelage, refusing to send troops to Murad's army. He was joined in his opposition by Ivanko, son of Dobrotich, the lord of another part of Bulgaria, Dobruja. In 1388, Murad ordered an expedition against these rebels, and Shisman was forced to submit once more and also to give up the fortress of Silistra on the Danube.

KOSOVO: THE BATTLE AND THE MYTH

Simultaneously, Murad had run into resistance from another sovereign of the region, Tvrtko, king of Bosnia. Tvrtko's troops, commanded by one of his generals, Vlatko Vuković, had defeated an Ottoman officer, Lala Shahin, in Bileća, Serbia, northeast of Dubrovnik. That setback may have been the cause of the famous Battle of Kosovo. Murad may have undertaken a campaign against the Serbian sovereign, Knez Lazar, to avenge Belića, suspecting that Lazar was involved in the affair.[6] The battle took place on June 15, 1389, on the Kosovo plain (Kosovo Polje), slightly northwest of the city of Priština, at the confluence of the rivers Lab and Sitnica. Serbian national mythology portrays it as a disaster that for several centuries put an end to the unity and independence of Serbia, which was now plunged into the "Ottoman night." In reality, apart from the fact that Serbia was already fragmented before 1389, almost nothing is known about that battle, how it unfolded, or even its precise outcome. The Serbian side was represented by at least three elements: first, the contingent of Knez

Lazar Hrebeljanović, who at the time ruled central Serbia and part of eastern Kosovo and whose army included Hungarians and Albanians; second, that of Vuk Branković, who controlled most of Kosovo; and finally, as in Bileća, Tvrko's Bosnian troops, commanded by Vlatko. Murad had attached to his troops contingents of his Greek, Bulgarian, and Albanian vassals. It seems that after the battles, which were bitter and bloody, the Turks held the terrain, but their victory did not necessarily extend beyond it. In any case, two events likely to cause a stir marked the encounter. First, Sultan Murad was assassinated by an individual named Miloš Kobilić, about whom little is known. And second, Knez Lazar also perished, having been executed after he was captured, according to tradition: hence the aura of the martyred saint that surrounded him in Serbian history. The immediate consequences of the battle were very limited, however. Murad's successor, Bayezid, called away to Anatolia by a revolt of neighboring beys, hastily left the site. Lazar's young son, Stefan, succeeded his father but became the sultan's vassal only in 1392, on the advice of his mother, Queen Mother Milica. The sultan married Stefan's sister. Vuk Branković also waited until 1392 to accept the sultan's suzerainty. He did so with such bad grace, in fact, that he probably ended his days in one of Bayezid's prison. His two sons, Gregory and George, having come into possession of their father's personal property, recognized the sultan's suzerainty.[7]

BAYEZID I, "THE THUNDERBOLT"

Bayezid I continued the Ottoman conquest, both in Anatolia and in Europe, with a speed of execution, determination, and brutality that earned him the nickname "the thunderbolt" (*yıldırım*). In Europe, he reacted to the insolence of Mircea, voivode (military leader) of Wallachia, who, with the aid of Hungarian protection and his alliance with the bey of Kastamonu, an Anatolian adversary of the sultan, had installed himself on the south bank of the Danube, in Silistra. In 1393, Bayezid crossed the Balkans and took up a position against Mircea. Bayezid defended his private preserve by annexing a part of Dobruja, taken from a local lord, the despot Ivanko, son of Dobrotich. On July 17 of the same year, to stop the raids coming from north of the Danube, he annexed Tirnova, putting an end to the existing small Bulgarian vassal state of Shishman. The following winter, presenting himself as overlord of the Balkans, he assembled in Serres all his Christian vassals, to demonstrate his supremacy to them and to prepare for his fight against the Palaeologi. The members of the ruling Byzantine family were in fact making a show of independence by seeking the support of Venice. In 1394, Bayezid again occupied Salonika, which the Byzantines had previously recovered, and launched raids of privateers (*akınjı*) into Peloponnesus. To increase the pressure, he even attempted a blockade on Constantinople. Then, resuming the struggle to the north against Wallachia and Hungary, he crossed the Danube for the first time. He personally conducted an expedition that devastated the southern part of Hungary, then penetrated into Wallachia, where he had a great victory over the Wallachian army in Curtea de Argesh. Upon his return, he crossed back over the Danube to Nicopolis and had Shisman, the former king of Tarnova, arrested and executed.

These advances in Europe, particularly in the Lower Danube zone, alarmed the king of Hungary, Sigismund of Luxembourg, who had his sights set on the same region. He put pressure on the two popes, Benedict XIII in Avignon and Boniface IX in Rome, to proclaim a new Crusade. Venice, though it maintained with the Turks the relations necessary for its commerce, was obliged to cooperate. Basileus Manuel II and the Knights Hospitaller of Rhodes would also do their part. Alongside these directly affected protagonists, others would join out of loyalty to the medieval ideal of Crusade: Burgundian knights under the leadership of the count of Nevers, the future Fearless John, son of Duke Philip the Bold; English and French knights (the count of Eu, constable of France, Admiral Jean de Vienne, and Marshal Boucicaut), freed by the extension of the truce between France and England; as well as Germans and Italians. A wave of fervor spread across Europe, sustained by preachers, the most famous of them Vincent Ferrer, who brought new life to the "flagellant" movement. Departing from Dijon, that army arrived at Buda. Then all the Crusaders traveled down the Danube, seizing on the way Vidin, which was defended by Bayezid's vassal, Stratsimir, and then another city, Rahova, whose population they massacred. During this time, the Venetian fleet was guarding the Dardanelles. In early September 1396, the Crusaders laid siege to Nicopolis (Nikopol in Bulgaria, or Niğbolu). Bayezid then abandoned the blockade on Constantinople, which he had undertaken against the besiegers, joined along the way by his Serbian vassal, his brother-in-law Stefan Lazarević. The clash occurred on September 25, 1396. The losses were heavy on both sides, but they hit the Christian knights, who were clumsy, reckless, and undisciplined, especially hard. Crusader prisoners of war were massacred in cold blood. The only ones spared were those for whom a ransom could be expected, such as the count of Nevers; these ransomed captives returned home in 1397. Through that memorable victory, Bayezid consolidated his control over the Balkans and increased Ottoman prestige in the Muslim world. One immediate consequence was the annexation of the last Bulgarian state, Vidin, which was replaced by the two *sanjak* of Vidin and Niğbolu.

THE BATTLE OF ANKARA IN 1402 AND THE GREAT INTERREGNUM

Emboldened by his successes, Bayezid took the war to the Anatolian front, destroying the emirate of Karaman and other surviving Turkoman principalities. Then, pushing farther east, he attracted the Mamluks' hostility by encroaching on their territory and aroused the resentment of Tamerlane (Timur Lenk) by penetrating into the sphere of influence of that formidable Asian conqueror.

That last challenge would prove fatal: Timur decided to come settle the score in Anatolia, benefiting in that undertaking from the support of the Anatolian beys, whom the Ottoman had brutally dispossessed. The battle took place near Ankara on July 28, 1402. Bayezid's forces, very inferior in number despite the loyal assistance of his contingents of Christian vassals (especially the Serbs), were crushed. The victor took the sultan and one of his sons, Musa, as his prisoners.

That catastrophe marked a counterattack on the Ottoman conquest and placed the state's very survival in peril. An interregnum lasting about ten years followed, marked by civil war, perils from the outside, and even social and religious subversion.[8] Three of Bayezid's sons, Süleyman, Isa, and Mehmed, had escaped captivity. The eldest, Süleyman, presenting himself as the legitimate heir, took refuge in Europe, and settled in Edirne, accompanied by his father's grand vizier, Chandarly Ali Pasha, and other high state dignitaries. By the terms of a treaty concluded in Gelibolu in 1403, he had to make concessions to his European vassals to prevent a more serious reversal. The Byzantine emperor, Manuel II, seized the opportunity to recover Salonika and the southwestern coast of the Black Sea.

Having recovered his courage, he went so far as to drive the Ottoman merchants from Constantinople and to order the destruction of the mosque built for them. In addition, Venetians and Genoese obtained commercial concessions in Süleyman's territories. The empire's borders reverted to those existing at the end of Murad I's reign; Bayezid's conquests were obliterated.

Civil war erupted among the three rival brothers. Isa, based in Bursa, was quickly eliminated. A duel followed between Mehmed, retrenched in the region of Amasya, and Süleyman. Süleyman seemed on the verge of victory, but then Mehmed acquired a new advantage, the reappearance of his younger brother, Musa. After being liberated by Tamerlane in 1403, Musa had been the hostage of the emir of Germiyan, who decided in 1409 to hand him over to Mehmed. Mehmed sent him to Rumelia, where Musa formed an alliance with Mircea, the voivode of Wallachia, and married Mircea's daughter. He formed a second alliance with Stefan Lazarević of Serbia. These two Christian allies provided him with troops. Musa's successes in Rumelia forced Süleyman to return hastily from Anatolia and to cross over the Bosphorus. He did so with the aid of Manuel II, who had an interest in prolonging the fratricidal struggle. After several setbacks, Musa managed to have Süleyman assassinated. He was now in control of Süleyman's possessions in Anatolia and Rumelia. He ruled these territories for two years, conducting a brutal policy against the former elites and an offensive against his neighbors. After Süleyman's son Orhan took refuge with Basileus Manuel II, Musa attempted a siege on Constantinople in 1411, but without success. A first confrontation between Mehmed's troops and those of Musa took place in Thrace, near Chatalja. Musa was victorious, compelling Mehmed to return to Anatolia. But Musa's situation became more difficult. His former allies in Anatolia and Europe abandoned him in favor of Mehmed, who, at least at first, seemed less worrisome. Stefan Lazarević appealed to Mehmed to return to Rumelia to fight and placed his troops at Mehmed's disposal. Manuel II once again facilitated Mehmed's crossing of the Bosphorus by procuring the necessary ships and also provided him with troops. The two brothers' armies faced off in Chamurlu, in the mountains south of Sofia. At the end of the battle, Musa was forced to flee, but one of Mehmed's officers caught up with him and killed him. As the last man standing, Mehmed was in a position to restore the former unity of the empire under a single scepter.

THE REVIVAL UNDER MEHMED I

Mehmed reunited the empire only after overcoming two additional obstacles: his nephew Orhan and a certain Mustafa, known by the designation Düzme Mustafa (the Pseudo-Mustafa). Manuel II tried to use Orhan against Mehmed, but the sultan finally managed to have his nephew blinded, in accordance with Byzantine practice. As for Mustafa, he passed—rightly or wrongly—for one of Bayezid's sons captured at the battle of Ankara and later liberated by Shāh Rokh, successor of Tamerlane (d. 1405). He was initially defeated but would play a further role under Mehmed's successor, Murad II. Mehmed also had to deal with a powerful social and religious movement, an expression of the traumas the population had suffered following the Battle of Ankara and the civil wars. This movement was led by Sheikh Bedreddin, an eminent ulema, born to a Greek mother and a Muslim father in Simavna (Kyprinos), southwest of Edirne. Musa had made him his "qadi of the army" (kadi'asker), that is, supreme judge. The sheikh was also a mystic imbued with the doctrine of the "unity of being," who drew from it subversive conclusions, promoting the suppression of social differences between rich and poor as well as the barriers between the different forms of monotheism. He had thus moved toward a creed of social revolution and of syncretism of the various religions. The movement, born in Rumelia, underwent further development in western Anatolia. That charismatic leader was finally captured and hanged in Serres in 1416.[9]

With Mehmed I's premature death, the restored state remained fragile and the early days of his successor, Murad II, were uncertain. He had to eliminate definitively the "Pseudo-Mustafa," whom the Byzantines had once again attempted to use against his nephew, the new sultan, in the hope of recapturing Gallipoli. To avenge this most recent plot, Murad II mounted another siege on Constantinople (June 2–September 6, 1422). He lifted the siege to go put down a revolt by the Anatolian princes his father had conquered. The rebels were inciting another rival against him, his younger brother, also named Mustafa, whom they enthroned in Iznik. These Anatolian principalities, always ready to seize the opportunity to dispute the Ottoman takeover, were suppressed, with the exception of Jandar and Karaman, saved by the protection of Shāh Rokh, Tamerlane's successor.

MURAD II AND THE CHRISTIAN COALITION

Murad II, who had made the city of Edirne in Thrace his capital, was now free to resume the fight in Europe against Byzantium and the other Christian states that had benefited from the Ottoman retrenchment. Byzantium, which had recovered Salonika in 1402, handed it over to Venice, which was better able to hold onto it, in 1423. Murad reacted by waging war on Venice, not without difficulty, hindered as he was by the inadequacy of his fleet. He ultimately retook Salonika in 1430.

Hungary had also turned the Ottoman interregnum to its advantage, asserting its authority over the former Ottoman vassals, Wallachia and the despotate of Serbia, which was in the hands of George Branković. By the terms of the Treaty of Tata (1426), the king of Hungary, Sigismund of Luxembourg, ordered Branković to hand over the fortress of Belgrade, gateway to the Hungarian plain.

As a precaution, Murad postponed the attack on Hungary until the death of Sigismund, emperor and king of Hungary, in 1437. In 1438, Murad personally took his place at the head of his army, which crossed the Danube and advanced as far as Transylvania. Along the way, Murad conquered the despotate of Serbia, which he had vassalized in 1435 upon marrying Mara, Branković's daughter, and made it an Ottoman province. The next year, he attempted but failed to seize Belgrade. The raids he launched on Transylvania in 1441 and 1442 also met with failure, given the strong resistance of a formidable adversary, the voivode of Transylvania, John Hunyadi (Hunyadi Ianos; Iancu of Hunedoara); Ladislas III, king of Poland and the newly elected king of Hungary, had entrusted Hunyadi with the fight against the Turks. The Turkish victims counted in the thousands. Hungary and Christendom as a whole recovered hope at these setbacks on the sultan's part, combined with the eruption of a major revolt in Albania, led by Skanderbeg (George Kastrioti), a local lord who had previously joined with the Ottomans. That revolt, lasting twenty-three years, was not quashed until the reign of Mehmed II.[10] In 1443, a large Christian army headed by Hunyadi took Niš and Sofia; then, crossing the Balkans, it threatened Edirne. But Murad managed to halt the advance of the army, which was weakened by the cold, at the Battle of Izladi (Zlatica) on November 24, 1443. The sultan, obliged to introduce the enemy's new military technologies (artillery and firearms) into his own armies, cautiously took the path of conciliation. He concluded a peace treaty with Hungary and with George Branković, promising to restore the Serbian despotate to him. When his old Anatolian adversary, Ibrahim Bey, bey of Karaman, took advantage of the situation to attack him, Murad also signed a treaty with him, ceding the principality of Hamid. Once these gestures of reconciliation had been made, in 1444 Murad abdicated in favor of his son Mehmed II, only twelve years old, who thereby began a first reign. That abdication, unprecedented at the time in the Ottoman dynasty, caused universal surprise. Grand Vizier Chandarly Halil Pasha was assigned to be the young sultan's guide. The Ottomans' adversaries—Ladislas, king of Hungary and of Poland; John Hunyadi, voivode of Transylvania, in charge of the war against the Turks; and the pope himself—decided the time was ripe to launch a decisive Crusade against the Turks, even though it meant violating the ten-year truce pledged shortly before by Ladislas and Hunyadi. In early 1443, an encyclical of Pope Eugenius IV had imposed on all bishops and abbots a tithe on their revenues to finance the Crusade. The appeal had little effect in the West, however, where the attention of the princes, the French and English especially, was absorbed by their conflicts with one another. A Hungarian-Wallachian army crossed the Danube, while a Crusader fleet under Venetian command was sent to the Dardanelles to prevent the former sultan Murad II from reaching Europe from Anatolia. George Branković, however, remained outside the coalition, the sultan having promised to restore his state. Branković may even have prevented the Albanian rebel, Skanderbeg, from joining the allies. Given the gravity of the peril, Murad II, urgently called back from his Anatolian retreat of Manisa, managed to cross the Bosphorus with the aid of ships rented from the Genoese, which were equipped with a strong artillery. The Venetians, who were responsible for the surveillance of the Dardanelles, may have been playing a double game. Murad took command of an Ottoman army very superior in numbers to that of the Crusaders. Under the leadership of Hunyadi and the pope's legate, Giuliano Cesarini, the Crusaders had crossed the Danube, avoiding the dangerous mountain passes of the Edirne route, then headed for the Black Sea, plundering all along the way. They arrived in Vidin and Nicopolis, where they were joined by the voivode of Wallachia, Vlad II Dracul. The confrontation took place not far from Varna, on the Black Sea, on November 9, 1444. King Ladislas and Cardinal Cesarini perished in battle. The stunning victory Murad had achieved, though not without losses, sounded the death knell of Christian attempts to drive the Turks out of Europe.[11] After an appeal by the Janissaries, whom Mehmed had alienated through his manipulation of the monetary system, Murad took the throne a second time in May 1446. He thus put an end to that premature and brief first reign of his young son, who only grudgingly allowed himself to be shunted aside. Murad again had to confront Hunyadi, who was seeking to take his revenge at the head of a Hungarian-Wallachian army, in a second battle of Kosovo Polje, on October 18–19, 1448. Although inferior in firearms, which resulted in great losses, the Ottoman army was superior in numbers (especially since the Wallachian contingent deserted) and ultimately forced Hunyadi to flee. Murad died suddenly a few years later, on February 13, 1451.

THE TAKING OF CONSTANTINOPLE

Ascending to the throne a second time after a disastrous first reign that had ended with a humiliating expulsion, Mehmed II, now twenty-one, needed to impose his authority within his own state.[12] The Janissaries had violently rejected him, and from the beginning he attempted to appease them: he granted them a gift of joyous accession in Bursa upon his return from a first Anatolian expedition against Ibrahim Bey of Karaman. He also had to take the upper hand against Grand Vizier Chandarly Halil Pasha, who, in accordance with Murad's will, had been the young sultan's guardian during his first reign and had opposed his own advisers, secretly fanning the Janissaries' opposition. Finally, Mehmed had to assert his control over the empire's traditional adversaries, who were showing him no regard. Byzantium in particular, with the utmost arrogance, demanded an increase in the pension of Süleyman's son Orhan, whom the emperor consented to keep with him. A great military feat, a prestigious conquest would serve as the appropriate remedy to what would today be called his credibility gap. In addition, his big idea, the conquest of Constantinople (not a new idea among the Ottomans, and the object of several previous attempts among Mehmed's predecessors since the reign of Bayezid I), was a strategic necessity. Modest as the remains of the Byzantine Empire now were, reduced to the city of Constantinople—in large part depopulated and in ruins—and a part of Greece, the Ottoman takeover of southeastern Europe remained incomplete. Furthermore, the Byzantine capital controlled an essential point in the strait zone and, as the case of Prince Orhan aptly illustrated, remained an inextinguishable hotbed of anti-Ottoman intrigues, based especially on the "instrumentalization" of members of the dynasty, who could always be incited to oppose a reigning sultan. In addition, the "new Rome," diminished though it was, was the capital of a millennial empire and had long been the quintessential city. It remained an incomparable symbol in the eyes of both Muslims and Christians. The Muslims had attempted unsuccessfully to take Constantinople several times during the most sacred era of Islam, the first Arab conquests in the seventh to eighth centuries. For them, the capture of the city would win extraordinary glory for its instigator, whose exploit was foretold in Hadith and other prophecies. On this matter, Louis Massignon has spoken of the Muslims' "transhistorical desire for Constantinople."[13] The conqueror of Constantinople would stand as champion of the "combatants for the faith," the gāzi of all gāzis. For the Christians, by contrast, the conquest of "the city" by the infidel would be a catastrophe of eschatological dimensions, since in certain discourses the conqueror was assimilated to the Antichrist. Christendom ought therefore to have rushed to the aid of the symbolic city, but instead it set down conditions. Rome required the union of churches, that is, the end of the Great Schism, in actuality the submission of the Eastern church to the papacy. Emperor John VIII, pressured by the urgency of the peril, ultimately consented and, after a year and a half of intermittent discussions, the Council of Ferrara-Florence proclaimed union in July 1439.

The results of that decision remained unsettled, however, since it led to the most vehement opposition of the Orthodox clergy and of a large part of the

Byzantine population. Riots broke out in the streets of Constantinople. The patriarchs of Alexandria, Jerusalem, and Antioch also disavowed the union. Later, when the city was besieged, the last emperor, Constantine XI, in an ultimate effort to obtain help, handed over the stronghold of Nessebar on the northwest coast of the Black Sea to John Hunyadi, and the island of Lemnos to the king of Naples, Alfonso of Aragon. But neither Hungary nor Naples would intervene. Under the circumstances, the only external aid came from Genoa, which sent troops under the command of Giovanni Giustiniani Longo. The emperor made that shrewd general commander in chief in defense of the city.

All these weaknesses were not sufficient to make the taking of Constantinople an easy operation. Mehmed II prepared for it by constructing, within a brief span of time (between April 15 and August 31, 1452), the formidable fortress of Rūmeli Hisārı, on the European bank of the Bosphorus. It stood opposite the small Anatolian castle (Anadolu Hisārı), previously built by Bayezid I. The chosen site was where Darius had once built a bridge over the Bosphorus. With control of the strait thereby assured, in autumn Mehmed sent Turahan Pasha to conduct a preemptive campaign in Morea: the emperor's two brothers, the despots Thomas and Demetrios, had to be prevented from coming to the aid of the capital.

The besiegers numbered some 160,000 men, if we are to believe a Venetian account, while the besieged and their Latin auxiliaries totaled only a few thousand. To break down the walls that had braved the centuries, Mehmed had also taken care to equip himself with a powerful artillery, including a formidable cannon cast by a Hungarian renegade. He also ordered the construction of a giant siege tower, higher than the walls. In addition, adopting a bold stratagem, he got his vessels through the Golden Horde, closed off by a boom chain, by having them hoisted up, then brought back down to earth, from the Dolmabahche Valley.

The siege began on April 6 and did not end until fifty-four days later, on May 29, 1453, with a final assault in three successive waves. In conformity with Islamic law, the city, having been taken by force, was plundered. But the conqueror immediately showed that he did not intend to allow the infidel metropolis to disappear. On the contrary, by practicing a systematic settlement and construction policy, he sought to make it a great city once more. Did he immediately conceive the idea of making it his capital, and did he accept at once all the consequences of that decision? A few stumbles and reversals in the first years of the occupation suggest that things occurred more gradually in his mind, or at least, that the sultan threw off his mask only bit by bit. In fact, it was not until winter 1458–1459 that Mehmed II clearly made Istanbul his capital, abandoning Edirne. The chronicler Enveri wrote on the subject: "The sovereign came to Istanbul because he had made it his capital."[14] Henceforth, Mehmed fully exploited the Byzantine idea that the man in control of that city was the legitimate leader of the empire, styling himself the heir to the Roman Empire. Several Italian princes assented to that claim, hoping thereby to attract his favor, as he moved closer and closer to the peninsula. Some theorized that these princes were acting primarily out of opportunism or Machiavellianism, but that they placed a condition on their recognition of that *translatio imperii*: the sultan's conversion to Christianity. That was the thesis of George of Trebizond, a professor at the Pontifical University and an indefectible supporter of the Ottoman sultan (which would cause him some troubles), and especially of Pope Pius II, in his epistle to Sultan Muhammad II—a bewildering text that may actually have been a form of provocation addressed to Christendom itself.[15]

MEHMED II's OTHER CONQUESTS

The brilliant stroke that inaugurated Mehmed II's reign was followed by a series of further conquests, both in Asia and in Europe. The small Greek kingdom still called the empire of Trebizond would fall in Asia, and the great eastern rival Uzun Hassan, sovereign of the Turkoman confederation of the Ak Koyunlu, would be defeated, though not without difficulty. In Europe, in 1454 and 1455, the conqueror conducted two campaigns against the principality of Serbia, to consolidate its takeover (Murad II had had to restore Serbian independence in concluding the peace of 1444) and to counter the Hungarian influence. In doing so, Mehmed II seized the rich mining district of Novo Brdo. Then, in 1456, he besieged Belgrade, but a relief army commanded by John Hunyadi liberated the stronghold. The Christian troops' religious zeal had been fanned by the fiery sermons of the monk John of Capistrano. The sultan's retreat raised enormous hopes in Christendom. But the illustrious Hunyadi, hero of Christendom, died of the plague shortly thereafter. His son, Matthias Corvinus, became king of Hungary. As for the old despot of Serbia, George Branković, he had passed away in 1456, leaving a void in the principality, where a Hungarian party and an Ottoman party were at odds. Michael Angelović, the brother of Mahmud Pasha, Mehmed II's distinguished grand vizier, headed the Ottoman party.[16] After two further expeditions in 1458 and 1459 and the surrender of the Danube fortress of Smederevo, Mehmed put an end to the independence of Serbia, which became an Ottoman province.

The sultan now focused his attention simultaneously on Peloponnesus and Morea, where he was in competition with Venice. Two Palaeologi princes, Demetrios and Thomas, brothers of the deceased emperor Constantine XI, were still installed there. The two were engaged in an inexpiable struggle, with Demetrios supported by the Turks, Thomas by Venice. After two expeditions, in 1458 and 1460, Mehmed II occupied Morea. But Venice retained major bases there: Nauplia, Modon, and Coron, where the Most Serene Republic would build impressive coastal fortresses that could be resupplied by sea. In 1455, a raid by a border governor, Ömer Bey, son of Turahan, wrested Athens from the domination of minor Latin lords, the Florentine family of the Acciajuoli.

Competition with Venice was not confined to Peloponnesus. The threat increased for the republic, this time in the Adriatic, as a result of another of the sultan's acquisitions, which completed his hold over the Balkans: Bosnia. The king of Bosnia, Stefan Tomašević, until that time the sultan's vassal but unwilling to pay the obligatory tribute, had finally obtained a fifteen-year truce with Mehmed II. Notwithstanding that truce, Grand Vizier Mahmud Pasha, who had reduced the rebel voivode of Wallachia, Vlad the Impaler, the previous year, replacing him with Radu, a more docile vassal, launched a campaign in 1463 that culminated in the conquest of Bosnia. Stefan was put to death, despite assurances that he would be spared. The next year, 1464, the grand vizier seized Herzegovina.

Since these new Ottoman encroachments were detrimental to Hungary (which had designs on Bosnia and Wallachia) as well as to Venice, that republic counted on the cooperation of King Matthias Corvinus and did not hesitate to launch a major offensive against the Ottomans in July 1463. It held the Isthmus of Corinth and managed to retake control of a large part of Peloponnesus, while Matthias invaded Bosnia. That Ottoman-Venetian war lasted intermittently until 1479. At the end of that long conflict, an ordeal for both sides, Venice asked for peace. The sultan was granted the possession of Scutari, Croia, and the islands of Lemnos and Euboea. Venice grieved the loss of Euboea, one of the pearls of its colonial empire. In the meantime, the Ottoman-Venetian conflict had reignited the Albanian rebellion. In 1458, upon the death of his protector, Alfonso of Aragon, king of Naples, Skanderbeg had prudently placed himself under Ottoman suzerainty once more. But then, having rallied behind Venice, he again chose the path of sedition. Mehmed decided to get rid of him. He launched a first major campaign in 1466, and, in the summer of that same year, within the space of twenty-five days, he had the formidable fortress of Elbasan built on the Albanian plain, on the route of the old Via Egnatia. Then the Ottomans laid siege to the fortress of Krujë, last keep of the resistance. In 1467, Skanderbeg managed to lead an army against the besiegers of Krujë. That attack provoked the sultan's second Albanian campaign, which culminated in the conquest of most of the country, with the Venetians keeping only a few bases on the Adriatic. After taking refuge in Venetian territory, Skanderbeg died in 1468. Ottoman control over the mountains of the "land of eagles" would remain indirect and relatively light.

In his desire to secure complete control of the Aegean Sea and also to take advantage of his dominance of the straits to extend his influence over the Black Sea, Mehmed II clashed with another adversary, Genoa. He would take over its last colonial possessions: in 1455, he seized the old and the new Phocea, the center for alum production, as well as Aenos (Enez) in Thrace, at the mouth of the Maritsa in the Aegean Sea. In 1458, the Genoese islands of Lesbos and Chios were obliged to pay him a tribute (like the Venetian island of Naxos). The next year, the sultan reached the Pontic port of Amastris (Amasra) by land and captured it.

The growth of the Ottoman fleet following Mehmed II's establishment of an arsenal on the Golden Horn, which succeeded the first Ottoman arsenal of Gelibolu, gave a great deal of importance to the naval war in the conquests that followed. In the Black Sea, it was after the maritime expedition commanded by Grand Vizier Gedik Ahmed Pasha in 1475 that the Ottomans took over Caffa and the other ports of southern Crimea, which together had constituted the "Genoese Gazaria." They were united into the *sanjak* of Kefe, to which two other bases would be added northeast of the Black Sea: Kopa (Kuba), at the mouth of the Sea of Azov, and Anapa, on the coast east of Crimea. In 1478, moreover, the pro-Ottoman party was victorious in the struggles among the sons of Haji Giray for the succession of the khanate of Crimea. Mengli Giray became khan, and the khanate became a vassal state of the Ottoman Empire, as it would remain, with greater or lesser docility depending on the era, until 1774.

In the Mediterranean, Mehmed II launched an expedition in summer 1480 against the island of Rhodes, a possession of the Knights Hospitaller of Saint John of Jerusalem. The knights, who represented the last Latin power in the eastern Mediterranean, were threatening the coasts of southern Anatolia and constituted an obstacle to the sea route to Egypt. Mesih Pasha, a Byzantine renegade, headed the Ottoman fleet. The siege of Rhodes dragged on and on, its walls resisting successive assaults. The arrival of aid sent by the king of Naples, in anticipation of a possible mobilization of Christendom, induced Mesih Pasha to beat a retreat. At the same time, another fleet, also headed by Gedić Ahmed Pasha, successfully landed in Otranto. What did that Ottoman intrusion into southern Italy signify? A desire to strike a blow to the king of Naples, the Ottomans' old adversary? Or a plan by the sultan, after he had seized the "new Rome," to march on the old Rome and capture the papal see? Whatever the underlying motivations of the Otranto expedition, it was sufficiently troubling that the pope considered fleeing to France. The sudden death of Mehmed II in 1481, however, removed the threat. On May 3 of that year, the sultan, age forty-nine, had just crossed the Bosphorus to undertake a new campaign. Following his habit, he had not declared its objective, but the assumption was that it would be directed against Egypt. But he unexpectedly expired in his camp. Understandably, poison was suspected, but that suspicion remains hypothetical: complications from his long-deteriorating state of health cannot be ruled out.

BAYEZID II AND THE "JEM AFFAIR"

Under Mehmed's successor, Bayezid II, the conquests did not continue at the same pace. That sultan was at first hindered in his actions by the struggle for succession with his younger brother, Jem Sultan. Then, Jem asked for asylum from the Knights of Rhodes in 1482 and, as a result, found himself in France and then in Italy. The presence of that rival, liable to be used against him, in the hands of potential adversaries was a sword of Damocles hanging over Bayezid II's head. In the words of Theodōros Spandouginos, so long as the sultan's brother was still alive, Bayezid "was never entirely sure of his empire."[17]

No military undertaking of any great scope could be considered. The delicate situation caused by Jem's detention abroad also obliged the Ottomans to learn more about their neighbors to the west and to develop diplomatic relations with them. The first act in Franco-Ottoman relations, destined for such a great future, played out at that time. In any event, to have some peace, Bayezid had to wait until Jem died in 1495 and, to be even safer, until the sultan had recovered Jem's body, proof that his brother was truly dead. He did so, after a great deal of haggling, only in 1499. But the peace he found on that side was offset by the rival ambitions of his many sons, which would soon overwhelm him with more worries.

Difficulties in succession, which affected that reign more than others, did not entirely prevent continuing hostilities in Europe, albeit in the form of devastating raids in Hungary, Croatia, and even the Austrian provinces (Carniola, Styria, and Carinthia), at the initiative of the border beys. In 1484, moreover, while his brother was still a captive in Europe, Bayezid did not hesitate to personally conduct a campaign against Stephen the Great, voivode of Moldavia. On July 15, 1484, he took from Stephen the city of Kili, on the Danube estuary. Then, on August 9, with the aid of the cavalry of Mengli Giray, khan of Crimea, Bayezid captured the city of Akkerman, at the mouth of the Dniester. Stephen then secured the support of Casimir IV, king of Poland, acknowledging his suzerainty. But the voivode could not recapture his two cities, which, as stops on the major trade routes linking the Mediterranean to northeastern Europe, were of great strategic and commercial importance.[18] In 1487, he resolved to send the sultan a tribute once more. As for Poland, in 1489 it concluded a truce with the Turks, which would be extended in 1492 and again in 1494. But shortly thereafter, war resumed with Poland, which refused to have its access to the Black Sea cut off by the establishment of the Ottoman presence between Crimea and the Danube Delta. In the end, the truce would not be renewed until 1499. At that time, Bayezid needed to have a free hand to resume the fight against Venice, which the previous sultan had left unfinished. Many points of friction remained between the two states, both in Morea and on the Dalmatian and Albanian coasts of the Adriatic. The war lasted until 1502, with Venice benefiting from an alliance with the French king Louis XII, and then from a Hungarian alliance. Lepanto, in the Gulf of Corinth, which the sultan besieged in person, surrendered on August 29, 1499. The Turks took Coron, Modon, and Navarino in August 1500. In October 1501, French and Venetian fleets conducted a joint attack against Mytilene that would end in defeat.[19] Raids by Ottoman privateers, led by Mihaloğlu Iskender Pasha, reached Friuli and Venetian territory proper, opposite Vicenza. Finally, by the terms of the treaty of December 14, 1502 (ratified in August 1503), Venice gave up Lepanto, Coron, Navarino, and Durazzo; it evacuated the island of Sainte Maura and continued to pay a tribute for the possession of the island of Zante. Conversely, its possession of the island of Cephalonia was ratified and its prior commercial privileges in the Ottoman Empire restored. A new phase had begun in the gradual absorption of the Venetian empire.

Bayezid was forced to abdicate by his son, Selim, the ultimate victor in the competition between brothers to be the sultan's successor. That abdication came shortly before Bayezid's demise.

SELIM I AND THE TURNING POINT FOR THE NEAR EAST

Selim I's brief reign was a turning point in Ottoman history, because of his dazzling conquests in the Middle East. He first overcame Shah Esmāʿīl, the Shiite sovereign of Persia, for whom he felt an antagonism both political and religious, at the battle of Chaldiran, near Tabrīz, on August 23, 1514. He then went on to attack the Mamluks. The underlying conflict between the rising Ottoman power and their venerable Mamluk neighbors focused on the question of Cilicia and the boundary of the Taurus Mountains. It had already erupted twice, under Mehmed II and Bayezid II. After his successes in Azerbaijan, Selim resolved to lance the abscess. A two-year campaign resulted in 1516 and 1517, ending in the conquest of Syria after the Battle of Marj Dabik, near Aleppo, and the death on the battlefield of Sultan Qansuh al-Ghuri on August 24, 1516; the conquest of Egypt immediately followed. The last Mamluk sultan, Tuman Bay, Qansuh al-Ghuri's nephew, opted for resistance, despite the compromises proposed by Selim, and he was definitively defeated at the Battle of Ridaniyya on January 23, 1517. Finally captured, he was executed in Cairo on Selim's order the following April 13. That was the end of the Mamluk regime, which was replaced by the Ottomans. Egypt and Syria became Ottoman provinces, though these were initially entrusted to governors of Mamluk origin. Selim, by contrast, died prematurely on September 20, 1520, having run out of time to deal with the European front. He seems, however, to have been preparing to do so in his last years by constructing a large arsenal in Galata. A plan to finish off Rhodes, which had withstood his grandfather Mehmed II, has been attributed to him, though according to others sources, he judged the undertaking unrealistic.[20]

SÜLEYMAN THE MAGNIFICENT'S FIRST
SUCCESSES: BELGRADE AND RHODES

Selim's son and successor, Süleyman, nicknamed "the Magnificent" by Westerners and "the Lawgiver" in the Ottoman tradition, was the most illustrious of the Ottoman sovereigns, and his long reign (1520–1566) would be remembered as the "golden age" of an empire at the height of its power, wealth, and, for the most part, its territorial expanse. Dark moments were not absent, however, especially in the second part of his reign, beginning in 1540–1550.

A lawmaker and patron of the arts, Süleyman also distinguished himself through his conquests: on the eastern front, where he personally conducted three campaigns, including that of 1534, which resulted in his conquest of Baghdad and Iraq, and also in Europe, where he conducted no fewer than ten campaigns. It is primarily his European campaigns that I will consider here. Initially setting aside the struggle against Safavid Iran, in which his father had made his mark, Süleyman first sought strategic and symbolic successes to the west. His pretext was the mistreatment inflicted on his emissary Behram Chavush, officially sent to announce his accession to the king of Hungary, but probably also, less officially, to communicate to the king an offer to be vassalized, intended to divert him from his alliance with the Habsburgs. Launching a first campaign in Hungary, Süleyman took Sabac and Zemun, ravaged the regions between Sava and Drava, and above all, succeeded where Mehmed II had failed, seizing Belgrade on August 29, 1521. The next target too corresponded to a defeat on the part of his great-grandfather, a place whose strategic importance for the Ottomans had further increased since the conquest of Egypt: the island of Rhodes, held by the Knights of Saint John and serving as a base for active piracy in the eastern Mediterranean. Süleyman armed a fleet totaling perhaps 235 units and mobilized some 200,000 men. The siege continued into the winter, with the fleet going to seek shelter in the waters of Marmaris. The knights capitulated after five months, on December 21, 1522.

MOHÁCS: THE CRUSHING DEFEAT OF THE HUNGARIAN CAVALRY

When a second emissary sent to Louis of Hungary in 1524 met with no greater success, a new campaign was launched in April 1526. Louis II's army recklessly set out to meet the sultan's troops, who were greatly superior in number. The confrontation took place on August 29 on the Mohács plain, on the banks of the Danube. The Ottoman artillery carved the Hungarian heavy cavalry to pieces. The sultan's victory was all the more decisive in that the young Louis II drowned during his retreat, leaving no heir. But after occupying Buda, the Hungarian capital, for about ten days, Süleyman decided to return without delay, worried by news that had reached him of serious Turkoman revolts in Anatolia. Under the circumstances, the only result of that success, apart from the rich booty collected in Buda, was the annexation of two comitats south of the Danube, Szerém and Valkó. Thanks to the Ottoman retreat, two candidates in succession were elected king of Hungary by different diets: the most powerful magnate of the country, John Zápolya, voivode of Transylvania, was elected in Székesfehérvár on November 11, 1526; Charles V's brother, Ferdinand of Habsburg, archduke of Austria and soon the elected king of Bohemia, was enthroned in turn, by a smaller assembly in Bratslava on December 17, 1526. The sultan's preference quite naturally went to the weaker and therefore more manageable of the two, Zápolya, whom he made his vassal in February 1528.

THE FIRST SIEGE OF VIENNA: A CONCEALED FAILURE

But Ferdinand did not give up his ambitions, and his troops took possession of Buda. Süleyman therefore had to leave Istanbul on May 10, 1529, to begin a third Hungarian campaign, despite the difficulties of such undertakings: the cold and the rain, even in summer; the large waterways to be crossed; and the problems of provisions and logistics, given the great distances from the center of the Ottoman Empire. He reoccupied Buda without difficulty, then headed for Vienna, where, delayed from the outset by obstacles of all sorts, he did not arrive until September 27. So began the first Turkish siege of Vienna. Unable to take the city despite four successive assaults, Süleyman, facing the early arrival of winter, lifted the siege on October 14. The city and all Christendom felt enormous relief. For his part, Süleyman minimized his failure. In the victory report (in Greek) that he sent to the doge of Venice, he denied that he had ever had the intention of taking Vienna: he had simply set out in pursuit of a fleeing adversary, Ferdinand of Habsburg.[21]

SÜLEYMAN AND CHARLES V: THE EMPIRE AT STAKE

The rivalry between the Ottomans and the Habsburgs was at its height: beyond the control of Hungary, the imperial inheritance and hence the claim to universal domination were at stake. The sultan could not allow Charles V to be crowned emperor and his brother to become king of the Romans, since Süleyman believed that he himself was the only legitimate candidate for supreme sovereignty.[22] Under the circumstances, Süleyman directed his fourth campaign in Europe against Charles V in particular, who had styled himself the champion of the "Turkish war" at the diet of Ratisbon in April 1532. In the Ottoman tradition, that campaign is known as "Germany's campaign against the king of Spain." Modest in its results, that campaign of summer 1532 was marked especially by a laborious siege of the stronghold of Güns (Köszeg) and by devastating raids in Styria and Slavonia. The Habsburgs were sufficiently alarmed to request a truce, which the sultan readily granted them in June 1533, especially since the successes of the enemy fleet, which had seized Coron and Patras on the coast of Peloponnesus in 1532, gave him reason to worry. His attention, moreover, was now turning to Iran. By the terms of the accord, the status quo, that is, the division of Hungary between Ferdinand and Zápolya, was ratified, with the two rivals becoming tributaries of the sultan.

With the Baghdad campaign of 1534–1536, followed by the execution of Grand Vizier Ibrahim Pasha, whose influence had heretofore been preponderant,[23] the most spectacular phase of the young sultan's conquests came to an end. But his military activity was not suspended, either on land or on sea.

ADMIRAL BARBAROSSA AND THE FRANCO-OTTOMAN ALLIANCE

In 1533, the appointment of the corsair Khayreddin Barbarossa, leader of Algiers, to head the large imperial fleet was decisive for sea warfare. Diplomatic activity was occurring at the same time: a first permanent French embassy was sent to Istanbul in 1534, entrusted to Jean de la Forêt, an event that marked the officialization of the Franco-Ottoman alliance against the Habsburgs. The first fruit of the military collaboration between the two countries, which included concerted but separate land campaigns and joint sea campaigns, was a joint naval operation against Naples, a dependent of Spain and hence of Charles V. It took place in summer 1537. Nothing—or almost nothing—went off as planned. Francis I's fleet joined the sultan's at Avlonya only after a long delay. Süleyman for his part abandoned the idea of setting off for Naples, turning instead to the island of Corfu, a possession of Venice, with which relations had deteriorated in the meantime. Although the siege of Corfu was a failure, Barbarossa, continuing the struggle against the Most Serene Republic, managed to seize the majority of the Aegean Islands that were still in the hands of Venetian patrician families. In addition, on September 28, 1538, he had a major naval success in Preveza in the Gulf of Arta, putting to flight the joint fleets of Venice and Spain, commanded by the illustrious Genoese admiral Andrea Doria. Venice negotiated, always anxious to safeguard its commercial interests in the East. By the terms of the treaty of October 2, 1540, which Süleyman granted to Doge Pietro Lando, the Most Serene Republic agreed to new territorial sacrifices in the disputed zones between the two states: Nauplia and Monemvasia in Peloponnesus, Vrana and Nadin on the border of Bosnia, as well as a group of Aegean Islands, including Naxos, Paros, Santorini, and Andros.

THE MOLDAVIA CAMPAIGN

In that same summer of 1538, Süleyman personally conducted a campaign to call to order an intractable vassal, Petru Rareş, voivode of Moldavia. He was suspected of colluding with Vienna and of placing in peril the good relationship between the sultan and Poland. As a matter of fact, he had his sights set on a province claimed by Poland: Pokucia. After occupying Suceava between September 15 and 22, 1538, the sultan named a new voivode, then withdrew from Moldavia, but not without amputating the southeastern part of that country by annexing the zone between the Prut and the Dniester, the Bujak, with the fortress of Bender (Tighina in Romanian). Süleyman thus made his positions north of the Black Sea complete and assured overland connections with another vassal, the khan of Crimea.

Tripartition of the Kingdom of Hungary

In the following years, troubles continued in Hungary as a result of the pressure Ferdinand of Habsburg constantly exerted on his rival, John Zápolya. In 1538, Ferdinand imposed the secret treaty of Várad (Oradea), by which Zápolya pledged to transmit his right to the Hungarian crown to Ferdinand after Zápolya's death. But shortly thereafter, the wife of Zápolya, Isabella—daughter of Sigismund, king of Poland—whom he had married late in life, gave him a son. Zápolya died a few days later, in July 1540. The widow's chief adviser, George Martinuzzi-Utiešenović, bishop of Várad, had the then fifteen-day-old baby elected king of Hungary and secured the sultan's recognition of him. Ferdinand, who had rallied most of the Hungarian lords to his cause, ordered a siege on Buda in May 1541. That situation forced the sultan to intervene once again. Rushing in with his army, he reoccupied Buda in late July. The fumbling that followed attests to his hesitation about the fate to be reserved for Hungary. In the end, he annexed the center of the kingdom, which became an Ottoman province, the *beylerbeyilik* of Budun. In addition, he granted Zápolya's young son, for whom the bishop of Várad would serve as guardian, the "land of Transylvania," that is, not only the voivodate of Transylvania proper but the entire eastern part of the kingdom, including the Banat of Temesvár. But the sultan also recognized the special authority over the Banat of a Serb related to the Zápolyas, Peter Petrovics. In his role as regent, Martinuzzi navigated a careful path between the two parties, each of whom accused him of playing a double game. He was ultimately assassinated on Ferdinand's order in December 1551. The rest of Hungary, that is, the western and northern parts of the former kingdom, remained in Ferdinand's possession. It would be called "Royal Hungary."

The Continuing Advance in Hungary

Subsequently, Süleyman and his successors strove to expand their province and to strengthen its strategic position at the expense of Royal Hungary. In 1543, the sultan launched another major campaign, which required preparations at an unprecedented scale in terms of logistics and supplies. It culminated in the taking of a whole series of important fortresses (Valpó, Sziklós, Pécs, and especially Esztergom and Székesfehérvár, the former royal necropolis). But Ferdinand was still not definitively driven from Hungary. The sultan planned another large-scale campaign for the winter of 1544–1545, but finally canceled it in favor of a compromise that, after several truces, would lead to a treaty in June 1547. Peace was established for five years; the territorial status quo was maintained; and Ferdinand was to pay the Ottoman Porte a tribute of thirty thousand ducats a year. Süleyman thus had his hands free to conduct a campaign against Tahmasp, shah of Persia, in 1548–1549. Hostilities resumed to the west in 1551, after Ferdinand sent an army, led by Giovanni Battista Castaldo, into Transylvania and Hungary to fight the Turks. In 1552, the second vizier, Ahmed Pasha, waged another campaign, storming several fortresses of the Banat of Temesvár, which the Ottomans then annexed.

STABILIZATION OF THE OTTOMAN BORDERS

It was clear in the 1550s, however, that the expansion of the empire was reaching its limits and that its borders were becoming stabilized. That was true both for the eastern front, where the peace of Amasya in May 1555 established the respective zones of influence for the Ottomans and the Safavids, and on the western front in central Europe and the Mediterranean. In Europe, Süleyman had his final naval success in 1560, when his great admiral, Piyale Pasha, drove the troops of Philip II, king of Spain, off the island of Jerba. In 1566, the admiral also seized the island of Chios, the last Genoese possession in the Archipelago. By contrast, the previous year, the huge siege of Malta, where the Knights of Rhodes had found refuge, had ended in bitter defeat.

SZIGETVÁR: THE LAST CAMPAIGN

The following year, the sultan, now a sickly, irascible old man steeped in an austere piety, set out once more on a campaign, which he had not done in ten years. Again taking the Hungarian route, he besieged the fortress of Szigetvár beginning on August 4. He died outside its walls on the night of September 6, 1566; Szigetvár fell the day after his death. His demise was officially kept secret for forty-eight days as the army returned home, until they were approaching Belgrade. Süleyman's successor, his son Selim II, rushed to take charge of the troops and perhaps to continue the campaign. He was dissuaded by the poor disposition of the army, to which he had rashly refused the gift of joyous accession.[24]

FINAL CONQUESTS IN EUROPE IN THE LATE SIXTEENTH TO SEVENTEENTH CENTURIES

Cyprus

The last part of Süleyman's reign had been marked by a slower pace of conquests, with more laborious advances leading to more modest and more uncertain acquisitions. That tendency became more pronounced under Süleyman's successors until the late seventeenth century. Nevertheless, the conquest of the island of Cyprus was a significant addition during the reign of his son Selim II and a further painful amputation of Venetian "Romania," of which the island had been a part since 1489. The cautious grand vizier Sokollu Mehmed Pasha did not support provoking Christendom with such an undertaking, but he clashed with a "war party," a conflict very indicative of the factional struggles within the Ottoman power at the time. Among other pretexts, these "hawks" portrayed Cyprus as a sanctuary for pirates hindering the movements of pilgrims on their way to Mecca and of merchants. In March 1570, the Venetian senate, called upon to cede the island, responded with a negative vote, trusting in assistance from the outside. By September, the army had landed on the island and seized Nicosia.

The Battle of Lepanto

In reaction, a league was established at the instigation of Pope Pius V between Spain, the papacy, and Venice. The allied fleet, placed under the command of Don John of Austria, illegitimate son of Charles V and therefore the half-brother of Philip II, departed from Messina in September 1571. In the meantime, Famagusta, the second stronghold on the island, fell on August 1 after an eleven-month siege. On October 7, John of Austria's fleet encountered the sultan's armada off the coast of Lepanto, in the waters of the Gulf of Patras, at the mouth of the Gulf of Corinth. Most of the Ottoman vessels sank or burned, primarily as a result of the superiority of the allied artillery. There were reports that the sea was red with the blood of countless victims. That major Turkish setback caused an enormous stir in Christendom, becoming one of the symbols of the triumph of the Cross over the Crescent. The consequences were almost nil, however, both because of the divisions among the allies, who did not pursue their advantage, and because of the Ottomans' ability to bounce back. Spurred on by the grand vizier, they reconstituted their fleet over the following winter. Venice again negotiated: it agreed to give up Cyprus and paid a war indemnity of 300,000 ducats.

Hungary—Again

In the decades that followed, Royal Hungary also continued inexorably to be nibbled away. At the turn of the seventeenth century, during the Long War opposing the Habsburgs and the Ottomans (1591–1606),[25] further strongholds were taken: Bihać in 1592 and Györ in 1594. In 1596, restoring the tradition of combatant sultans that his two predecessors had abandoned, Mehmed III personally led his armies, but with limited success. At the most critical moment of the Battle of Keresztes, he put on the mantle of the Prophet, the most holy of relics, to attract the good fortune needed. The conquest of Eger (Erlau) was the only result of his efforts and his sole claim to glory. Finally, Kanizsa was taken in 1600 and Várad much later, in 1660. At the end of the Austro-Ottoman War of 1663–1664, even though the Ottomans suffered a grave defeat at the Battle of Saint-Gottard (Szentgotthárd) on the Raab, the truce of Varvár granted them favorable conditions, because Emperor Leopold was impatient to conclude the peace. As a result, the Hungarian border defense had to retreat farther, allowing for the constitution of one last Ottoman province in Hungary, the *eyālet* of Uyvár (Ujvár, Nové Zámky). The Austrians, forced to respond, set in place a new border front in 1665. Its centerpiece, constructed in accordance with the most modern principles of military architecture, would bear Leopold's name in its Hungarian form: Lipotvár.[26]

In general, the first decades of the seventeenth century saw a clear slowing of the empire's external activities: the Long War of Hungary, which dragged on for thirteen years at the turn of the century, culminated in a half-success. The Turks kept their possessions in the Banat of Temesvár and in Hungary, and even added to them somewhat. Their suzerainty over Moldavia, Wallachia, and Transylvania was also confirmed. But the Treaty of Zsitvatorok, which ended the conflict in 1606, marked a relative weakening of their position: again in a rush to have their hands free so as to turn against Persia, they had to negotiate as equals with their adversaries on the battlefield, in Hungary itself. In addition, the sultan consented—at least in the Hungarian version of the treaty—to give the title "Caesar" to the Habsburgs, thereby renouncing exclusive rights to imperial status. He also abandoned the demand for a tribute from the German sovereign.[27]

Subsequently, once another long war was over—this one with the Safavids (1603–1619)—the Ottoman government became absorbed in internal problems of all kinds. Fortunately for the Ottomans, Christian Europe could not take advantage of the situation, because it was mobilized by the Thirty Years' War.

Crete

Ottoman territorial expansion in Europe resumed somewhat in the 1650s, thanks to the recovery spearheaded with singular energy by the first two grand viziers of the Köprülüs: Mehmed Pasha (1656–1661) and then his son Fazıl Ahmed Pasha (1661–1676). In their ventures, they took advantage of the growing weakness of two European states: Venice and Poland.

For Venice, the loss of the "kingdom of Crete," its last jewel, at the end of a war that had been long and laborious for the conquerors, lasting from 1645 to 1669, sounded the death knell of its colonial empire. It was the end of a centuries-long, always unequal duel for domination of the eastern Mediterranean.[28]

Southern Poland and the Cossack Problem

The other European border where the situation was evolving in the seventeenth century was that of the steppes of the northern Black Sea, from the southern boundaries of Poland-Lithuania and Moscovy.[29] There, on the line between these two states, a new force emerged, which both states strove to control and exploit: the Cossacks. Between 1582 and 1638, they became a great military and naval power, increasingly provoking the Ottoman Empire directly: in about 1600, several of its Pontic ports were the object of surprise attacks by the Cossack fleets. In 1625, the Cossacks penetrated into the Bosphorus, advancing to the doorstep of the Ottoman capital.

Because of that new peril, combined with the persistent rivalry between Poland and the Ottomans for control of Moldavia, the very young and head-strong sultan Osman II decided in 1621 to undertake a campaign against Poland. At the head of his army, he, like his ancestors, crossed the Danube at the ford of Isaqça; then, in August, he laid siege to Chocim (Hotin) on the Dniester. After five fruitless assaults, and facing the arrival of winter and the scarcity of food, he had to turn back. But he left his army deeply disgruntled, a situation that would soon lead to disaster. The peace was concluded with Poland in October 1621.

A few decades later, the second of the Köprülüs, Fazıl Ahmed Pasha, undertook to constitute a buffer zone against the Polish and Russian advances on the coasts of the Black Sea. He wanted to take advantage of the weakness of the sovereign then ruling Poland, Michael Wiśniowiecki (1669–1673), and of the support of the Cossack leader, Peter Doroshenko. Doroshenko had in fact turned to the Turks because he was unhappy about the partitioning of the Ukraine, on which Poland and Russia had jointly agreed in the truce of Andrusovo (1667). The Dnieper served as a border between the respective parts of the two signatory countries.

In August 1672, Sultan Mehmed IV took the unusual measure of commanding the Ottoman armies, which seized the fortress of Kamieniec Podolski. The city's Gothic cathedral was turned into a mosque, where the sultan participated in the Friday great prayer. On the following October 18, the armistice of Buczacz with Poland ratified the reattachment of the province of Podolia to the Ottoman Empire. Mehmed IV was hailed as "the father of victory," "who tore down the edifice of unbelief and error."[30] That final conquest would be short-lived: Poland recovered Podolia with the Treaty of Karlowitz (1699).

The First Ottoman Retreats in Europe in the Late Seventeenth to Eighteenth Centuries

The retreat was slow and discontinuous. Within the chronological framework of the modern period, it also remained limited. It was only during the nineteenth century and the first years of the twentieth that the structure built up in Europe, primarily by the fourteenth- and fifteenth-century sultans, was truly dismantled.

The War of the Holy League and the Treaty of Karlowitz

A first significant retreat was recorded, however, at the very end of the seventeenth century, following the War of the Holy League (1683–1699), in which the Habsburg Empire, Poland, Russia, and Venice formed a coalition against the Turks and struck hard against them, pushing the Turkish empire to the brink of the abyss. The war began with the second Ottoman defeat outside Vienna. The siege had to be lifted after two months, given the arrival of German and Polish relief armies, which had a major victory under the command of John Sobieski, king of Poland, at Mount Kahlenberg on September 12, 1683. When the conflict was finally over in 1699, the Treaty of Karlowitz (Srmeski Karlovci) stipulated the end of Ottoman Hungary and of the empire's southern fringes between Sava and Drava. All these regions came under the sway of the Habsburgs. Only the Banat of Temesvár, that is, the territories between the Danube, the Tisza, and the Muresul, remained in the Ottomans' hands. The end had also come for Ottoman suzerainty over Transylvania, which dated back to Süleyman the Magnificent. In reality, the country had been able to conduct an independent policy with the Protestants within the context of the Thirty Years' War, under the voivodes Gabriel Bethlen (1613–1629) and George I Rackoczi (1630–1648). But then, under the grand viziership of the Köprülüs, the Ottoman Porte reasserted its authority over its vassal by imposing the voivodes of its own choosing. It was the appointment of Michael I Apafy, rejected by Leopold, that was the *casus belli* of the Austro-Turkish War of 1663–1664. Conversely, the first article of the Treaty of Karlowitz recognized Transylvania as belonging to the Habsburg emperor. Nevertheless, in conformity with the privileges Leopold I had granted to the country during the war (the *Diploma leopoldinum* of December 4, 1691), Transylvania remained an entity distinct from Hungary, possessing its own institutions—in line with the division made by Süleyman the Magnificent in 1541. In the following years, in fact, the Transylvanian opposition to the overly pro-Catholic policy of the Habsburg regime would seek refuge with the Ottoman Porte.

By the terms of the same treaties of 1699, Poland recovered Podolia; Venice, by way of belated compensation, received Peloponnesus, where it had formerly had large bases. During the war, Francesco Morosini, the same man who had not managed to keep Crete for the republic, had conquered the peninsula. Venice also occupied a large part of Dalmatia.

The first retreat, ratified by the treaties of 1699, did not end there. The dynamic set in motion continued into the first half of the eighteenth century, in conflicts still involving the Habsburgs and Venice but in which Peter the Great's Russia played an increasing role.

Appearance of the Russian Threat

It was Russia's designs on the south and on the "hot" waters of the Black Sea that brought the tsar into the game. After a first Russo-Ottoman war in 1695–1696 and the Treaty of Constantinople that followed, on June 13, 1700, the Ottomans had to give up their sovereignty over the north of the Sea of Azov, and lost the fortress of Azak and its territory, which they had held since the time of Mehmed II. The Russians then built the fortress of Taganrog there. Eleven years later, the Turks found an unexpected opportunity to take their revenge, when in July 1711 a Russian army, accompanied by Peter the Great and his wife, Catherine I, was surrounded on the Pruth by the Ottoman army, its ranks swelled by Tatar and Cossack reinforcements, under the command of Grand Vizier Baltajı Mehmed Pasha. Reduced to complete powerlessness, the tsar faced grave peril but managed to extricate himself under relatively favorable conditions. Catherine is said to have bought off the grand vizier, whose overly accommodating behavior earned him a prison term. In fact, by the terms of the Treaty of Pruth, Peter recovered his freedom, giving up only Azak and Taganrog.

The Treaty of Passarowitz

In Peloponnesus as well, the Ottomans wreaked their revenge, and the Venetians could not hold onto their conquest: the blunders of the Catholic hierarchy vis-à-vis the local Orthodox clergy had weakened their position. By 1715, Grand Vizier Damad 'Ali Pasha had recaptured the province, as the Treaty of Passarowitz would ratify.

The Austrians, conversely, under the leadership of Prince Eugene, continued their advance. Their overwhelming victory on August 5, 1716, at the Battle of Peterwardein (Petrovaradin), in which Grand Vizier Silahdar Ali Pasha met his death, left the road to Belgrade open to them. They conquered it the following summer. In the meantime, on October 12, 1716, Temesvár capitulated. The Treaty of Passarowitz, on July 21, 1718, ratified these conquests: Austria annexed Belgrade and northern Serbia as well as the Banat of Temesvár and western Wallachia, or Oltenia. Taking advantage of that position of strength, Vienna also obtained a treaty from the Ottoman Porte in 1719 granting its merchants freedom of trade on land and sea in the sultan's states.

The Peace of Belgrade

The Russians and the Austrians returned to war about fifteen years later, but with less success. This time, the Ottomans mounted a better resistance, and they would benefit from the effective mediation of the marquess of Villeneuve, French ambassador in Constantinople. With the Peace of Belgrade in 1739, Austria lost Belgrade and its acquisitions in Serbia; of its conquests north of the Black Sea, Russia kept only Azak.

The Treaty of Kuchuk Kaynarja

The Russian threat to the integrity of the Ottoman Empire began to come to light in all its gravity with the Russo-Ottoman War of 1768–1774. The empire's disorganization and the state of disrepair of its military forces, both on land and sea, now became fully apparent. The fleet was destroyed at the Battle of Chesma, surprised by the Russian ships, which had come into the Mediterranean after an impressive circumnavigation through the Baltic, the Atlantic Ocean, and the Strait of Gibraltar. The Greeks of Morea rose up in support of the Russians. The Treaty of Kuchuk Kaynarja (1774), which put an end to the conflict, stipulated an enormous war indemnity totaling 4,500,000 rubles, and contained several clauses of great consequence for the future. Crimea became independent, that is, its relationship of vassalage with the Ottomans was severed, a separation that could only favor its annexation by Russia, which in fact occurred in 1783. The Ottoman sultan retained only a religious bond with the Tatars, a situation that led diplomats to spell out and consecrate the notion of an Ottoman caliphate. At the territorial level, Russia recovered Azak and its territory, which would belong "in perpetuity to the Empire of Russia." Also attributed to Russia was a fortress at the mouth of the Dnieper, the castle of Kinburn (Kilburun) "with an adequate district on the left bank of the river," as well as a zone between the Dnieper and the Bug. In addition, the treaty recognized the right of the Russians to trade and navigate in the Black Sea and in the straits. Russian consulates were established in the Romanian capitals, Bucharest and Jassy. The treaty also declared the obligations of the Ottoman Porte vis-à-vis the Christians and their churches, in such a way as to establish a right of protection from the tsar (or tsarina) for the Sultan's Orthodox subjects. Catherine II stood as the champion of an Orthodox *reconquista* in eastern Europe, and Russia as the mortal enemy of the Ottomans.

CHAPTER 7

OTTOMAN EUROPE

An Ancient Fracture

THROUGHOUT MUCH of the modern age, a large part of Europe—a quarter or a third of the continent—was under the political domination of Islam. That fracture within the continent was not new. To a large extent, Ottoman Europe simply covered the *pars orientalis* of the continent, the religious and cultural sphere of influence of Constantinople, in opposition to that of Rome. Hence the Ottoman conquest ultimately followed a much more ancient cleavage, though, for some 150 years, between 1541 and the very end of the seventeenth century, it also crossed over that line, especially in Hungary.

The Ottoman Europe was far from homogeneous, however, and Istanbul's power was hardly of the same nature and the same strength everywhere. In actual fact—if not in the sultan's discourse—three circles could be distinguished. They did not always correspond to present-day national divisions.

THE THREE CIRCLES OF OTTOMAN DOMINATION IN EUROPE

Hungary, the Romanian Countries

The outer circle, the farthest from the capital and the most difficult to control, comprised the countries located north of the Danube and the Sava.

Moldavia and Wallachia were only tributary countries (*kharajgüzar*) of the sultan. They preserved their own social organization, dominated by the boyar aristocracy, and their own institutions, beginning with their princes, the voivodes, and their religious hierarchy. Their respective territories (after the successive amputations performed by the Turks for strategic reasons) were entirely closed off to the official Ottoman presence, whether it took the form of government agents (especially tax agents), garrisons, or representatives of the Muslim faith. The Ottomans did exert their influence, however: these countries annually paid the sultan a tribute, which grew in size over time and was supplemented by contributions called "gifts" (*pishkesh*). In addition, they were regularly called on to provide auxiliary troops for the Ottoman campaigns and certain quantities of goods and raw materials constituting their principal wealth (salt, cattle, wool). The voivodes ruled only with the sultan's approval, whether granted a priori or a posteriori, and only so long as it pleased him. They were chosen from among the offspring of the country's great families. These children spent their youth and received their training in the sultan's capital, where they were held hostage. They were therefore more or less "Ottomanized" before their reigns began. Ottomanization from above developed further in the eighteenth century when, after the defection of Dimitrie Cantemir, prince of Moldavia, the Ottomans stopped appointing voivodes from the Romanian aristocracy, replacing them with Phanariots, that is, the important Greek or Hellenized families of the Phanar district of Istanbul.

As of 1541, Transylvania was also a tributary state, but its tribute was lighter and the situation unusual. In addition to Ottoman suzerainty, Transylvania recognized that of the Habsburgs with the Treaty of Szatmár (Satu Mare) and the Treaty of Speyer (Spire) of 1570, signed by the voivode John Sigismond Zápolya. Moving back and forth between these two vassalages, the voivodes sometimes sought to become autonomous, for example, during the Thirty Years' War. The population was organized into three "recognized" nations (the Hungarians, the Saxons, and the Székelys, or Sezklers, Hungarian-speaking peoples distinct from the Hungarians). The Romanians, despite their large numbers, were not recognized as a nation. Multidenominationalism was officially established, with four different "accepted" religions: the Hungarians were Catholics or Calvinists; the Saxons were Lutherans; and the Székelys were Unitarians, with the creation of that new church by Francis Davis, bishop of Kolozsvar (Cluj). The Orthodox faith was tolerated but not "accepted."

Central Hungary, as well as the Banat of Temesvár, Slavonia (the countries between the Sava and Drava), and certain parts of Croatia, were in principle part of the empire. These were Ottoman provinces that had administrators and military staff representing the central power and that possessed the institutions specific to the empire. But the region displayed very distinctive features, associated with its distance from the center, its relatively late integration (which would also be limited in time), and its lasting situation as a border zone (serhadd). There the Muslim element was reduced to a narrow stratum of administrators, soldiers, merchants, and artisans, confined to a few chief cities (Buda, Pest, Pécs, Székesfehérvár, Szeged). Furthermore, these Muslims were often not Turks but Islamized Bosnians. The rural areas and a good part of the cities remained wholly Christian and largely autonomous. A peculiarity of that situation was the dual tax system, set in place not only on the borders between Royal and Ottoman Hungary, but in localities within Ottoman Hungary itself. In addition to the Ottoman system, feudal lords, now living in the Habsburg part, continued to levy taxes on their subjects and even to enforce their own laws.

Greece, Serbia, Montenegro, Bosnia-Herzegovina, and Albania

Inside the outer circle just described was a transitional zone, bordered on the north by the Danube and Sava rivers, and on the east by northern Bulgaria and the Vardar Valley. These lands were Ottoman but still remained fairly remote from the center of the empire, and they had common borders with Venetian and Habsburg possessions. The Muslim population there was confined to certain cities and towns located on the former routes of Turkish penetration or on old border fronts. In addition, the proportion of Christian converts was higher than among Turkish settlers. Belonging to the zone thus defined were continental and Aegean Greece, Serbia, Montenegro, Albania, Bosnia-Herzegovina, plus a little appendix, perfectly autonomous but still a tributary of the sultan and in communication with the Christian world: the republic of Dubrovnik (Ragusa). That intermediate zone included many other enclaves, which were largely autonomous because of their location and natural conditions. These regions were not easily accessible and were the source of only mediocre revenues. Installing the *timar* regime of land grants in compensation for military service was therefore out of the question there. The ancient tribal systems continued to operate. That was the case for Montenegro, where the traditional cadres were under the authority of the *vladika*, the Orthodox bishop residing in Cetinje. It was also true of the northern mountains of Albania. For the most part, and increasingly from the sixteenth century on, the sultan drew contingents of warriors from these regions.

Greece also included mountainous districts, remote from Turkish authority and influence, such as the Mani Peninsula south of Peloponnesus, the district of Suli in Epirus, and that of Agrapha in the Pindus Mountains. In the Aegean Islands as well, and in the monastic republic of Mount Athos, on the Chalcidice Peninsula, various modes of self-administration occupied a large place.

Also associated with that second circle—because of their distance from the center and the absence of revenue distribution in the form of *timars*—were the provinces north of the Black Sea, neighbors to the khanate of Crimea and the Tatar steppes, the *sanjak* (and later the *eyālet*) of Kefe and Akkerman. Süleyman the Magnificent summed up the situation in June 1560 when he wrote to the khan of Crimea: "When the troops bringing victory are sent over there, they will encounter serious obstacles, since there are enormous rivers to cross and traverse." And he continued: "Given the distances, when troops are sent there, difficulties of all sorts emerge."[1]

Bulgaria, Thrace, Thessaly, Macedonia, and Dobruja

Finally, the innermost circle of Ottoman possessions in Europe included Bulgaria, Thrace, Thessaly, Macedonia, and Dobruja. The lineages of *akınji* beys, whose ancestors were the true conquerors of these zones when the Ottomans first came to live there, retained strong local prestige, as well as a secure and profound importance via ancient pious foundations. These were the Evrenos Oğulları in Macedonia; the Mihal Oğulları in northeast Bulgaria; the Turahan Oğulları in Thessaly; and the descendants of Ishak Bey in Skopje. But the heirs of these dynasties had become the sultan's loyal servants, like his other provincial governors.

This circle included the provinces that were conquered first and that were closest to the two successive capitals, Edirne and Istanbul. This was Rumelia in the strict sense, the part of Europe most firmly rooted in the Ottoman Empire, with no common borders with other European countries. It was only there that the Muslim population, whether converts such as the Pomaks of Bulgaria and Greece, or Turkish settlers from Anatolia, was of a considerable size, at least in some cities, such as Skopje, Niğbolu (Nikopol), Kyustendil, and Trikkala.

A MULTIFAITH EUROPE

A major feature of that Ottoman Europe was that Islam remained in the minority in terms of numbers, even in the parts most under Ottoman control. The dark predictions made in the letter that John Hunyadi sent to Pope Nicholas V on September 17, 1448 (and in other texts)—a formal epistle drafted by the Hungarian humanist János Vitéz—did not come true. In it, the hero of the anti-Ottoman struggle declares: "If my memory does not fail me, the spiteful weapons of the Turks have been lurking around Europe for a hundred years now. They conquered Greece, Macedonia, Bulgaria, Albania in quick succession . . . enslaving them, depriving them of their religion, forcing onto them foreign face, foreign morals, foreign laws and the language of the infidels. They showed no mercy either to the rights of the people or to those of God."[2]

These lines evoke the threat of systematic religious and cultural assimilation, combined with the desire to incite the recipient to energetic action; but that assimilation did not take place. In other words, what had occurred in Asia Minor between the end of the eleventh century and the thirteenth century did not occur in the Balkans of the fourteenth to fifteenth centuries.[3] In Asia Minor, even though Christian (Orthodox, Gregorian, Nestorian) and Jewish elements survived, the bulk of the population had gone through a rapid religious and cultural transformation—both Islamization and Turkification. The former Byzantine territory had become a single "Turkey," even though, at a profound level, heterogeneous substrata long persisted beneath that apparent unification.

We must not underestimate the enormous changes produced by the Ottoman conquest in the zones of Europe in question. They affected the countries annexed to the empire but also, to a lesser degree, the countries that were merely vassalized. New institutions, a new political and social configuration, replaced the prior order. The ethnic map shifted after the wars, as a result of spontaneous or forced displacements of the populations, but also because of the integration of these regions into a much vaster economic unit. A place must also be made for Eastern cultural contributions in areas such as architecture, furniture, clothing, and cuisine, along with the vocabulary to designate these new realities.

Nevertheless, these changes went hand in hand with strong ethnic and religious continuities, which prevent us from imputing a radical break to the Ottoman conquest. Alongside Islam, that newcomer in the conqueror's appurtenances, the previous faiths remained, with their respective beliefs, rites, and clergies. Although the Ottoman occupation established an Islamic political regime and haughtily asserted the superiority of Islam over other religions—as illustrated, for example, by the transformation of some of the churches into mosques—it also organized religious pluralism. The contrast between the two Europes can in no way be reduced to a simplistic opposition between a Christian Europe and a Muslim Europe. On one hand, there was a multifaith Europe where Islam was institutionally (but not demographically) dominant; on the other, a Europe with universalist religious aims, whose unity was dramatically shattered by the Reformation, and within which Judaism itself incarnated an alterity that was never totally accepted.

It is also not possible to claim that, within the coexistence of religions instituted by the Ottoman framework, each remained entirely closed on itself. On the contrary, it is very clear that, up to a certain point, that situation favored mutual influences, a cross-contamination of popular practices and beliefs. Saints, pilgrimage sites, and ceremonies were sometimes shared by several religions. But these phenomena of osmosis were not accompanied by shifting identities. The respective clergies made sure of that: everyone knew to which community he belonged, so long, at least, as he did not take the leap of conversion.

Let us consider a few statistics, insofar as the sources allow, about the persistent majority status of Christianity in Ottoman Europe. Ömer Lutfi Barkan's studies, based on the Ottoman census records from the sixteenth century, show that, in the years 1520–1535, the *beylerbeyilik* of Rumeli counted a total of 862,707 Christian households—most of them Orthodox—compared to 194,958 Muslim households, which therefore represented only 18 percent of the total population.[4] Three centuries later, if we are to judge by the census conducted on more modern foundations in 1831, that proportion had significantly increased. But it is still remarkable that, despite the shrinking of Ottoman Europe at the time and the immigration into this territory of Muslims fleeing the lost provinces, Muslims were still in the minority. At that time, out of a total of 1,334,691 adult males, there were 833,994 Christians and 500,697 Muslims, who therefore represented 37.5 percent of the population.[5]

Both before and after the Ottoman conquest, Europe under Turkish domination remained Orthodox in the majority. Although it had communities of Roman Catholics, called "Latins" or "Franks," these were established in border regions in Hungary, Croatia, and Albania, or in the Aegean world, where they were a legacy of medieval Latin colonization. In addition, there were missionaries from the Western religious orders, which became increasingly numerous from the seventeenth century on, especially with the creation of the Roman Congregation for the Propagation of the Faith in 1621. Western merchants residing in the large commercial centers of the empire also grew continuously in number; they were granted the status of *musta'min* and were under the protection of their respective consuls.

Compared to the Christians and the Muslims, the Jews were only small minorities, apart from the famous exception of Salonika, "city of the Jews," which had a Jewish majority between the early sixteenth century and the end of the Ottoman era. One of the consequences of the Ottoman occupation of the Balkans, however, was a proliferation in that zone of Jewish communities that were very diverse in their origins, languages, and rites. In fact, the Hellenophonic Jews (known as "Romaniotes") who remained from the Byzantine period—Sultan Mehmed II had deported most of them to Istanbul in the interest of populating his new capital—were later joined by Italiote, Askenazi, and especially Sephardic elements, as waves of persecution and expulsion measures followed one upon another in most of the European states. That last wave of immigration resulted from the far-reaching banishment decrees of the Iberian sovereigns in the late fifteenth century and, by contrast, the relatively welcoming policy of Sultan Bayezid II and his successors. These Sephardic Jews, and the *conversos* who succeeded them throughout the sixteenth century, settled primarily in a few large and small cities of southeastern Europe (Salonika, but also Vlorë, Patras, Trikkala, Niğbolu, Sofia, Skoplje, Serres, Kavala, Kastoria, Volos, Larissa, Sarajevo, Rustchuk, Brăila, and others).

THE LIMITS OF TURKISH COLONIZATION IN EUROPE

Two reasons may account for the relatively weak Islamization of Ottoman Europe. First, the conquest of eastern Europe was not on the whole accompanied by a significant emigration of Anatolians. A true colonization movement, composed both of voluntary emigration and of systematically organized deportations, existed only in the early part of the conquest, until about the mid-fifteenth century. In that phase, peasants from western Anatolia and nomads (the *yürük*) were deliberately relocated along the major roads in the principal strategic zones: the east-west penetration route leading to the Adriatic through Thrace and Macedonia, and all along the valleys of the Maritsa and the Tundza in the direction of the Danube. In addition, nomads were installed in the mountainous parts of the Balkan Peninsula, thereby creating Turkish villages distinct from the Christian ones. Following Barkan, some historians have emphasized the essential role that religious groups of dervishes played in the creation of these villages. Monastery-lodges (*zaviye*), coupled with attached farming operations, usually constituted their initial core.

Turks were also installed in the conquered fortified cities, which had a strategic value for the new state. Those strongholds that initially resisted the conqueror were emptied of a large part of their previous Christian population, becoming majority Muslim. The Christians who remained were relocated to segregated neighborhoods. Cities that followed that pattern included Niğbolu (Nikopol), Köstendil (Kyustendil), Vidin, and Silistra in Bulgaria; Tırhala (Trikala) in the Thessaly region of northern Greece; and Skopje (Üsküp) in Macedonia. For example, Skopje, conquered in 1391, had twenty-two Muslim neighborhoods (*mahalle*) some sixty-five years later, in 1455, compared to eight Christian neighborhoods. Other cities, those that had negotiated their capitulation, remained majority Christian.

After the mid-fifteenth century, by contrast, the newly conquered territories beyond the Rhodope Mountains and the Balkans gave rise to far less extensive colonization. Emigration was limited to state-ordered deportations to a few military centers on the new borders.

That reduction in the rate of displacement from Asia Minor to Europe has been associated with a weakening of the ethnic Turkish pool in Anatolia, itself attributable to the obstruction upstream, linked to the political situation, of communications between central Asia and Anatolia via Iran, a hostile Shiite zone.

The *yürük* registries studied by Tayyib Gökbilgin[6] provide a few notions about the number, at least approximate, of Turkish nomads and seminomads (the *yürük*) traveling from Anatolia to Europe who belonged to paramilitary organizations. In 1543, 1305 units (*ojak*) were counted, corresponding to some 160,000 individuals. Although the figures for the seventeenth century provided by later sources are higher (190,000 to 220,000 individuals), we must take into account the fact that, at the time, the *yürük* organization was supplementing its inadequate labor force by recruiting elements of various backgrounds (Tatars, Islamized Balkans, Gypsies, and others). The bylaws of the *yürük* of Kojajik, for example, mention emancipated *yürük* slaves, available elements unattached to a *timar*, who came from other regions or from Anatolia. It cannot be ruled out, however, that relatively large-scale emigration movements from Anatolia to the Balkans occurred after the mid-fifteenth century. There is information, for example, on a current—in all likelihood, limited in number—of *kızılbash* elements, that is, Turkomans from Anatolia who were considered heretics and were deported to Peloponnesus in the early sixteenth century. Other operations may have taken place in much later eras, though that history remains obscure. It has been argued, for example, that at the end of the Austro-Turkish wars in the late seventeenth and early eighteenth century, and then again after the emancipation of Serbia and Greece, the Ottoman authorities sought to reduce the disproportion between Christians and Muslims in the parts of the Balkans that remained under their control, by moving Turks (as well as Albanians) from Anatolia to the eastern part of Macedonia, generally along the left bank of the Vardar.[7]

THE *DHIMMIS*, "PROTECTED UNBELIEVERS"

The second major reason for the (at least relative) permanence of religious identities in eastern Europe after the Ottoman conquest had to do with the regime's policy concerning religion. Contrary to the discourses of the time—an emblematic example is provided by the previously cited letter from John Hunyadi to the pope—and contrary to an idea that is still very widespread, the conquerors did not conduct a systematic Islamization policy or, more generally, "cultural assimilation," to use a contemporary expression.

The Orthodox Church was therefore retained with its institutions, clergy, and hierarchy. The determining act of Mehmed II on January 6, 1454, that is, a few months after the conquest of the city, was to reinvest the patriarch of Constantinople in the person of George Scholarios, called Gennadius, a monk who had become known for his ardent opposition to the union with Rome. Through that appointment, the sultan was affirming the multifaith character of his empire. In addition, not only was the Greek church preserved, its authority was also broadened in a sense, through the abolition of the old autocephalous Serbian and Bulgarian churches that had emerged in the Middle Ages. Bayezid I had already suppressed the Bulgarian patriarchate in 1393, and the Serbian patriarchate of Peć, created at the instigation of Stephen Dušan, was suppressed in 1459. Only two institutions mitigated that Greek ascendancy over the Orthodox Church in the Balkans. As the last remnant of independence for the Bulgarian church, the archdiocese of Ohrid maintained a relative autonomy; and Sokollu Mehmed Pasha, even before becoming the last grand vizier of Süleyman the Magnificent, reestablished the Serbian patriarchate of Peć in 1557, granting it to a very close relative (perhaps even a brother). The measures taken by the Ottomans would only gradually produce their full effect. It was not until the second half of the eighteenth century that the elimination or subordination of the former autocephalous sees allowed the patriarchate of Istanbul, under the control of the Ottoman sultan, to become the head of the Orthodox Church as a whole.

The other large non-Muslim religious communities of the empire had more or less similar evolutions, though it is necessary to correct the chronology presented in certain historical myths, which tend to attribute everything to Mehmed II's conquest of Constantinople.[8]

It has been established, for example, that the head of the Armenians of Constantinople did not become patriarch under that sultan but in reality obtained that title of *patrik*, as well as a set of particular rights, only in the first half of the sixteenth century. In the case of the Jews, it was Mehmed II who recognized

Mosheh Capsali, leader of the Jews of Constantinople, as the *haham başı*. But what exactly does that title mean? Some have argued that it applied to the leader of the Jews of Constantinople but did not correspond to chief rabbi, whose authority extended to the entire empire. In effect, according to an autograph opinion of the *haham başı* who succeeded him, Elijah Mizrahi (1498–1526), Capsali's authority was confined to Istanbul and the surrounding area. But the question is largely theoretical, since during Capsali's time, Mehmed II had assembled most of the Jews within his empire in the capital. The dispersal of the Jews across Ottoman Europe would, on the contrary, be a consequence of the great immigration of the Sephardis after the 1492 expulsion. Nevertheless, the post of *haham başı* disappeared in 1526, reappearing only in 1835 in a completely different context. In addition, the Jews' aversion to any centralization did not prevent the Ottoman power from recognizing their community authorities, religious or not, as they did for all the other religions in the empire.

In that matter, the Ottomans based themselves primarily on Islamic canon law, the Sharia, especially its Hanefite version, which they embraced. They inherited the principle of *dhimma*, which had been applied by most Muslim regimes before them (as we have seen in part I), with the exception of the most radical. In doing so, like many of their predecessors they displayed pragmatism, even as they placed themselves within Islamic legality: they had to take into account the fact that, especially in Europe, they ruled over regions where Islam was by far the minority religion.

By virtue of the *dhimma* pact that bound the sultan to the *dhimmis*, non-Muslim subjects who had pledged their obedience, the *dhimmis* enjoyed religious freedom, while at the same time—the less positive side—certain obligations and specific forms of discrimination were imposed on them. They were compelled to pay a specific tax symbolic of their submission: a capitation called *jizya* or *kharāj* (or *bashkarāj*, to distinguish it from the tribute of vassal countries). The Ottomans added a few other royalties specific to the *dhimmis*, just as they imposed special rates for certain taxes that the *dhimmis* paid along with Muslim subjects. Under these circumstances, the conversion of a *dhimmi* to Islam—however laudable in principle in the eyes of the authorities—represented a tax deficit to be filled, and was as such regrettable. The *dhimmis* were the object of a number of prohibitions: they did not have the right to bear arms, to own slaves, or to ride horseback in town. Some garments and some colors were forbidden them, as well as all marks of ostentatious luxury. The list of prohibitions, in fact, had to be adapted to reflect changes in mores and fashions. Only the more austere—even unattractive and humiliating—clothing was allowed, appropriate to a fundamentally debased condition. There was to be no confusion possible between true believers and infidels. All the same, the insistent repetition of proscriptions on that subject is clear evidence of the difficulty in applying them, especially given that an elite of these *dhimmis* was quite wealthy. Initiatives calling the *dhimmis* to order generally came from the local

Muslim rank and file, whose virtuous indignation was probably not exempt from jealousy and resentment. In response to the complaints reaching it, the central authority could not fail to act as the guarantor of canon law.

Discrimination and harassment did not prevent the status of *dhimmi* from having one essential advantage: the right to claim to be the follower of any religion or sect whatsoever (so long as one remained outside Islam), to worship and perform rites. That was the difference between Christian Europe and Ottoman Europe, which therefore became a potential refuge for all those proscribed by European Christendom. That possibility had its limits, however. Public order was not to be disrupted, and the *dhimmis'* ceremonies had to be performed discreetly. All signs of ostentation were prohibited: the Christians, for example, could have no bells or processions. Their houses of worship could in no case surpass the height of those of the Muslims. Reparations had to be officially authorized and could be made only to return a restored or rebuilt structure to its initial configuration and dimensions. The construction of new places of worship was in principle not allowed.

It is clear, however, that on this point as well, the *dhimmis* discovered means for circumventing the law, especially by striking bargains with local judges. The writings of Machiel Kiel in particular demonstrate that not only were a great number of churches and monasteries, even relatively modest ones, restored, but new churches were founded and built during the Ottoman period, in Bulgaria and in continental Greece and the Greek isles.[9]

It is true that, apart from maintaining an Orthodox religious life in Ottoman Europe, the centers of high ecclesiastical culture—the Patriarchal Academy of Constantinople and the monasteries of Mount Athos—amounted to very little. The cultural centers that remained most vibrant were therefore located outside the empire: in Crete before the Ottoman conquest of the island and in Italy (Venice in particular), where the printing of religious and especially liturgical texts in Greek, as well as selections from profane Greek literature, proliferated.

The status of *dhimmi* also entailed a certain community autonomy, especially in judicial matters, since questions of personal law at least (marriage, divorce, inheritance, custody) belonged to the realm of the respective religious laws. Similarly, representatives of the different clergies quite naturally oversaw their respective communities of faithful and served as intermediaries with the Ottoman authorities, especially in matters of taxation, though the secular elites gradually came to compete with them for these functions. Moreover, these aspects of autonomy and self-government do not justify tracing the so-called *millet* system so far back in time, as is often done. The *millet* mode of administering the communities of the empire, which established special courts of "personal law" for religious minorities, was much more centralized and structured than what had existed in the previous periods. It would become a reality only in the nineteenth century, in the age of reform.

Conversions to Islam

The argument that the Ottoman conquest did not entail a systematic policy of forced conversion of the subject populations, but rather their reduction to the status of *dhimmis*, does not rule out the possibility that such conversions sometimes occurred, during particularly violent and troubled episodes of Ottoman history. In one of the accounts that attest to them, it is claimed that, at the conquest of Tirnovo in 1394, the only ones who escaped the massacre were notables who agreed to convert. Such accounts cannot necessarily be dismissed as anti-Muslim clichés in every case. Moreover, there is nothing implausible about such deeds within the context of invasions of Ottoman territory, during the wars of the late seventeenth and early eighteenth centuries. The Christian subject, always vulnerable to the suspicion that he was collaborating with the invader, found himself in an extremely critical situation after the invader withdrew. It is therefore understandable why, in 1689, Arsenije Crnojević, patriarch of Peć, who had previously preached insurrection against the Turkish masters, resolved to flee north of the Danube after the Austrians' departure and was followed by part of his flock—reportedly some thirty thousand families, though the matter remains controversial. In such a situation, the only way to prove one's loyalty to the sultan was truly to adopt Islam, since the religious and the political were inextricably mixed.

There was one case, moreover, when forced conversion was not "accidental" but rather at the foundation of an institution essential to the state: the *devshirme*. Through that procedure, which consisted of rounding up young Christian boys from the villages of Anatolia and especially Rumelia, then forcibly converting and circumcising them, the sultan recruited a large portion of his permanent army, especially Janissaries, and constituted a significant part of his ruling elite, political and military, at least until the late seventeenth century. But that procedure was a clear violation of Muslim law. The cavils made by certain jurists in an attempt to justify it scarcely conceal the fact that, in this matter, reason of state had prevailed. In addition, whatever the emotional trauma caused by the practice of tearing children away from their parents (the popular literature in that part of Europe provides ample depictions of it), and regardless of the tendency of Balkan historiographers to focus on that factor of de-Christianization and "denationalization," it is necessary to assess more accurately the real demographic impact of *devshirme* during the period it was in force. If we are to believe a late sixteenth-century Ottoman chronicler, Sa'adü-d-dīn, that policy was responsible for two hundred thousand conversions.[10]

In any event, to minimize the role of conversions imposed by force is not to claim that there were no conversions of any other kind.[11] Apart from violence and blackmail, other motivations, complex in some cases, could lead some people to opt, willingly or not, for Islam. These behaviors fall into the general category of social opportunism. Someone might have wanted to escape the taxes on the *dhimmis* or even a legal punishment (as in the emblematic case of the "Jewish messiah" Shabbetai Tzevi, who escaped execution by adopting Islam in 1666); or to advance in the social world and especially, gain access to public sector positions; or to survive banishment by one's community of origin and cut short one's prosecution; or finally, to obtain a reward, a job, or a pension. Moreover, for vulnerable persons—slaves, or even wives or orphans—pressure alone could make conversion inevitable. It seems that, in spite of everything, these individual acts were few in number. It has been calculated, on the basis of the *jizya* registries, that in sixteenth-century Rumelia, conversions of that kind did not number more than a few hundred a year. It is true, however, that not only the wartime situations noted earlier but also the evolution in the nature of Ottoman power itself may have had some influence on the volume of conversions. As that power became more closely identified with Islam, proselytism in ruling circles became more forward and insistent. That was especially the case in the second half of the seventeenth century under the reign of Sultan Mehmed IV and the grand vizierate of Köprülü Fazıl Ahmed Pasha, both followers of an Islamic radicalism of the "Salafist" type.

In certain parts of Ottoman Europe, conversions were much more massive in scope: in Albania, Bosnia, and Crete, and in the regions of Bulgaria and Macedonia inhabited by Pomaks. What causes are we to attribute to these phenomena? Without becoming involved in the often very sharp polemics, I shall confine myself to two remarks. First, the causes were certainly not the same everywhere or at all times. It is therefore necessary to seek out the dynamics at work in the contexts particular to each case. Second, Islamization seems to have occurred more slowly than people came to believe in retrospect. In the case of Bosnia, the Ottoman census records for 1489, that is, twenty-six years after the conquest, list twenty-five thousand Christian families and only forty-five hundred Muslim families. The conversion movement began among the elite in the Bosnian feudal system. The picture was completely different in the late eighteenth century: at the time, 265,000 Muslims, 253,000 Orthodox, and 80,000 Catholics were counted.[12]

UNDER THE DOMINATION OF THE CRESCENT

All in all, the Islamization of Ottoman Europe remained limited, but that centuries-old occupation produced a "Balkan Islam" whose legacy survives today, though the map was appreciably modified by the wars of national liberation and the Balkan Wars of the nineteenth and twentieth centuries.

Although Muslims were numerically in the minority in Ottoman Europe, Islam was the dominant religion there, in that it was the religion of the masters: the sultan and the civil and military representatives of his power. It was in terms of that one true religion that they judged the two earlier "religions of the Book": partly true but incomplete religions and, since the teachings of the ancient prophets had been forgotten, erroneous on several points. Followers of these religions, persisting in error, could not help but inspire a certain disdain. Conversion was the best thing that could happen to them, and though they could not be forced to take that step, they could only be praised for doing so. It was with Islam alone that the state identified itself; the resources of the treasury went to its buildings and charitable works through the pious foundations of the sultan, his family, and his dignitaries. Although in a sense the officiants of all faiths (the patriarch, his metropolitans, and his bishops, for example) could be considered cogs in the state machine, the ulemas took precedence and were the only ones who could benefit from the state's largesse and speak in its name.

THE PLACE OF NON-MUSLIMS

The traditionally accepted schema, according to which careers in the administration and in the military were for Muslims, while Christians and Jews were confined to economic occupations (farming, artisanship, and commerce) is not baseless in Ottoman Europe, but a few nuances need to be added. Apart from the fact that there were not only Muslim peasants and artisans but also merchants and even large-scale traders—even more than has been said—the state, in the interest of pragmatism, did not always systematically forgo the *dhimmis'* military service. After the conquests of the fourteenth and fifteenth centuries, local Christians of distinction could be granted *timars* without having to change religion. In Albania in 1431, that is, twenty years after the first Ottoman conquests in that country, 60 of the 335 *timariots* were identified as Christians (the region even had a Jewish *timariot* at the time). In 1455, in the district of Tırhala in Thessaly, 36 of the 182 *timariots* were Christian. At the same date, that is, sixty years after the conquest, the proportion was 27 out of 170 around Priština, Kosovo. Similarly, in the Serbian district of Braničevo, in the Timok Valley, 62 Christians were identified in 1468 among the 125 *timariots*.[13] Although there were still attributions of *timars* to Christians under Bayezid II, the phenomenon did become more unusual in the sixteenth century, and, in any case, the descendants of Christian *timariots* converted to Islam.

More long-lasting, however, was the persistence of old Balkan military organizations under the Ottoman regime. When necessary, the new masters modified their original character and function, reducing them to paramilitary organizations or auxiliary corps. But the Ottomans nevertheless retained them, along with their old hierarchies and their Christian composition, total or partial. Such was the case for the *voynuk*, which, under the name *voynici*, constituted a petty nobility in Stephen Dušan's empire and became, in the Ottoman armies, a corps specializing in the breeding and keeping of horses. Similarly, the role of border guards fell to the "Vlaches" of Serbia, and the *martolos* served as auxiliaries in the garrisons of fortresses or of local police forces.

To conclude, it is clear that the Ottomans radically altered the fates of the Balkan peoples, even while refraining, on principle or by necessity, from any true assimilation policy. They left in place a situation upon which, when the time had come, national rebirth would base itself in that part of Europe. In addition, the existence of these Christians, placed under the "Turkish yoke" in a lasting manner, would constitute an important factor in relations between the other Europe, the Christian one, and its infidel adversaries. On one hand, "captive" coreligionists would naturally be seen as potential allies and protected persons, whom fate would provide with pretexts for intervention; on the other, the *dhimmi* would come to be regarded as a potential traitor and, if need be, as a hostage.

CHAPTER 8

Antagonistic Figures

THE CHRISTIANS, first those of the East, then those of the West, had rejected Islam from its first appearance and continued to do so throughout the Middle Ages. Initially, they even denied it the status of religion, seeing it only as a heresy or a form of paganism or idolatry. When they had to consider Islam a religion, they could only denounce it, given that Christianity alone was true. In addition to being false, Islam was also a mortal danger: as a universal religion, it claimed to be superior to Christianity and intended to take its place. It was thus imperative to stand up to Islam and combat it by every means. The very survival of Christianity was at stake, and therefore humanity's salvation. Deep-seated hostility and ignorance combined in the Middle Ages to bring forth and spread the most negative and pejorative image of that religion and of the person of its Prophet.

IDEOLOGICAL BAGGAGE

The same aversion and the same prejudices predominated in Christian minds during the modern age as well. Theologians themselves were not generally better informed, or more nuanced in their criticisms, or more sophisticated in their arguments than their medieval predecessors. In fact, they did not refrain from printing old polemical treatises such as that of the late thirteenth-century Dominican Riccoldo da Montecroce titled *Contra sectam mahumeticam*, published in France for the first time in 1509. Works such as the *Debate between the Christian and the Saracen* by the Burgundian Jean Germain (d. 1460) or the treatise composed by the humanist Jacques Lefèvre d'Étaples against the religion of the "enemies of Christ's name," are evidence of that. The treatise in dialogue form by the Carthusian Denys Ryckel, titled *Against the Qur'an*, was published for the first time in 1533. The tone of that publication is apparent in its dedication to Ferdinand of Habsburg, who was fighting the Ottomans at the time. Among the major publishing ventures antagonistic to Islam during that time period, a place must also be made for that of a Zurich theologian, Theodor Buchmann, known by the pseudonym "Bibliander." In Basel, through the famous Oporinus Press, he published a set of texts on Islam under the title: *Life of Muhammad, Prince of the Saracens and the Whole Doctrine Known as the Law of the Ishmaelites and the Qur'an.* The book reprinted the twelfth-century Latin translation of the Qur'an by Robert of Ketton, complemented by the other translations commissioned by the twelfth-century abbot Peter the Venerable, an *Apology* written by Bibliander himself, a prefatory note by Martin Luther, and texts by Riccoldo da Montecroce and Nicholas of Cusa. As a compendium of relevant documents (of which Guillaume Postel would make very personal use), that Protestant venture displayed a new interest in documentation at its very heart. But the tone was still unconditional rejection and merciless combat.

Another example of antagonistic literature, this time Catholic in origin, appeared in 1589 within the context of the Wars of Religion. Written by the Celestine father Pierre Crespet, it was titled *Instructions in the Christian Faith against the Impostures of the Muhammadan Qur'an of the Great Sultan of Turkey.* That commentary, which accompanied the French translation of the letter from Pius II to Mehmed II, was composed by a fierce partisan of the Holy League. It is an apologia for the Christian religion and an incendiary refutation of the Qur'an, which, in accordance with tradition, is assimilated to a set of superstitions and impostures.[1] Once the issue at hand was to establish the falseness of that religion and the truth of Christianity, the same polemical arguments against Islam that had been made by medieval theology found their place even in Pascal's *Pensées.* All the old gossip about the person and life of the Prophet was still present in 1697, in *The True Nature of Imposture Fully Display'd,* by an English clergyman named Humphrey Prideaux.[2]

THE SACRALIZATION OF BATTLE

Other, very different views of Islam would appear during the period, but medieval discourse continued to serve as the backdrop.

The term "Saracen," which was still current in Jean Froissart's writings, and the other medieval terms faded away. It was now generally the term "Turk" in the various European languages that designated the Muslim. "To become a Turk," for example, became the ordinary expression for the act of converting to Islam.

The modern age began with the idea that the peril was greater than ever, since Europe, which had become a refuge for Christianity, by both the failure of the Crusades and the success of the *reconquista*, was in turn threatened at its very core by the Ottoman advance. If Islam was unacceptable in itself, Islam in Europe was doubly so, even though the divisions and compromises of the Christian princes had been of no little help in establishing it there. Particularly eloquent expressions of the anomaly of the situation can be found in many writings by one of the most clear-sighted observers of the mid-fifteenth century, Aeneas Silvio Piccolomini, who would become pope in 1458 under the name Pius II. He declared, for example: "In the past, wounds were inflicted on us in Asia and Africa, that is, in foreign countries. But now we are struck in Europe, our fatherland, our homeland."[3] In 1463, ten years after the taking of Constantinople, the same author declared before the cardinals of the Curia: "The necessary war against the Turks is imminent, and if we do not take up arms and meet the enemy head on, our religion is done for."[4]

Naturally, the reaction to the Turkish advance took the form of a Crusade, as that institution had developed in the Middle Ages: not just any expedition but a war decreed by the pope, involving a vow from participants and justifying the collection of tithes on the clergy's property, for example. Only the objective had to be adjusted somewhat: the liberation of the Holy Land was still the order of the day, but the defense of Constantinople and eastern Europe was becoming the main priority. In the early days of the Ottoman conquest, three neo-Crusades of that type had been set up in turn, with more or less success mobilizing Christian knights: the Crusade of Gallipoli in 1366; of Nikopolis in 1396; and of Varna in 1444. Apart from the difficulty in mobilizing the Christian princes, the last two of these were such resounding defeats, and the Turkish military superiority over the Crusader armies that had ventured into southeastern Europe became so obvious, that no further undertakings of that kind would be attempted.

Another obstacle to the organization of formal Crusades, even as the threat to Constantinople was becoming increasingly urgent, was the schism that continued to divide the Christians. The Turkish peril put the papacy in a position of strength for bringing about the unity of Christendom to its own advantage. That meant holding the Orthodox Church hostage.

In desperation, Basileus John VIII, who had come to Italy, agreed in July 1439 to sign the document concluding the long discussions of the Council of Ferrara-Florence. The union was consummated, even as Roman supremacy took root. Nevertheless, the violent reaction of most of the clergy and of the population in Constantinople completely undermined the implementation of that act, so that the question was left hanging. During that time, Mehmed II ordered the construction of the fortress of Rūmeli Hisārı on the Bosphorus and made ready for siege. The basileus attempted one last time to overcome Rome's reluctance to orchestrate a rescue mission, by having the end of the schism formally proclaimed in the Hagia Sophia on December 12, 1452. Isidore of Kiev, the Latin patriarch of Constantinople, had come from Rome for the occasion. But the opposition remained just as keen. It was then that the megaduke Lucas Notaras is alleged to have said: "Better the sultan's turban than the pope's miter."

When the city was taken, Nicholas V did order a Crusade, promulgating the bull *Etsi Ecclesia Christi* on September 30, 1453. In it, the Ottoman sovereign is portrayed as a prefiguration of the Antichrist. Tithes were to be collected throughout the Christian world; those who abetted the Turks were threatened with an interdict and excommunication. Several princes demonstrated their intention to join the Crusade, including the duke of Burgundy, Philip the Good. During a ceremony of knights held in Lille and called the "Feast of the Pheasant," he and others solemnly pronounced the oath to take up the cross. But ultimately, for fear of leaving the way clear for adversaries or of exposing themselves to the condemnation of the Turks, with whom some preferred to compromise, none of them made a move. Piccolomini made this bitter observation: "Each state has its prince, and each prince has his special interests." Once he became pope, Piccolomini would make a final attempt to mount a Crusade, before death overtook him in summer 1464.

Even so, though never actually realized, the *idea* of a Crusade did not fade away. "Turkish war" remained a duty for Christians and, in the representations of it, that fight more than any other was a holy war expressing divine will. Either God gave his benediction by granting victory to his faithful, or he displayed his wrath by inflicting defeats on them to expiate their sins. Special rites sought to appease that particularly redoubtable form of divine wrath: Turk prayers, Turk processions, Turk pilgrimages (*Türkengebete, Türkenprozessionen, Türkenwallfahrten*).[5]

One of the first stunning manifestations of the value placed on victories over the Turks accompanied the failure of Mehmed II's siege on Belgrade in 1456. The defense of that Hungarian border fort did not constitute a Crusade in the strict sense, but Pope Callixtus III nevertheless had his legate promise a plenary indulgence to all who participated in combat. John of Capistrano, a Franciscan famous for his fiery sermons against the Turks, sparked the passions of the city's defenders. When the sultan finally retreated after terrible massacres in both camps, there was immense relief and joy throughout Europe. The rumor even circulated in Rome and other cities that Constantinople had been retaken. Nearly everywhere there were magnificent feasts and bonfires as well as processions accompanied by thanksgiving and the exposition of relics. The pope went so far as to declare that the liberation of Belgrade was the most blessed event of his life.[6]

Subsequently, the Turkish defeats of the sixteenth and seventeenth centuries, independent of their real military significance—small, in the event—elicited similar or even more enthusiastic reactions. A famous case was the naval victory of the Holy League, uniting the pope, Spain, and Venice off the coast of Lepanto in the strait separating the Gulf of Corinth from the Ionian Sea, on October 7, 1571. The consequences were limited, since the Turks reconstituted their fleet within a few months, and Venice had to abandon Cyprus to Selim II. That did not prevent immediate and long-lasting celebrations of the event, duly orchestrated, first, in the capitals of the league members and then throughout Europe, where sumptuous festivities proliferated. All the arts—poetry, painting, sculpture, and music—paid their tribute.[7] In Venice in 1572, the composer Pietro Vinci published motets for five voices on the theme:

On the Destruction of the Turks. Among the great pictorial works inspired by that victory are the frescoes of Vasari in the Sala Regia of the Vatican Palace, and the paintings of Titian and Veronese. In the upper register of Veronese's work, the victory seems to have been awarded by the Virgin and the saints. A large number of books and engravings spread the happy news, which was also glorified in the altarpieces of modest churches in the most remote townships of Christendom.

A similar initiative had already occurred on the occasion of the recapture of Tunis by Charles V in 1535, following Barbarossa's takeover of that stronghold the previous year. Of that victory by the emperor in person, accompanied by the Infante Don Luis of Portugal, Gentile Virginio Orsini wrote, without illusions: "The sacking of Tunis is a paltry deed of little importance, with very minor gains, since all fled with their possessions."[8] Charles V was content to reinstall the Hafsid sovereign, Moulay Hassan, whom Barbarossa had thrust aside. Yet the episode was viewed as a sacred mission. Throughout the campaign on land and sea, Charles V had with him a standard bearing Christ on the cross; and, with the place evoking the memory of Saint Louis and the Eighth Crusade, he providentially discovered the weapons of the martyr king. Above all, that excessively orchestrated success was seen as the prefiguration of even more decisive accomplishments. In a letter to Charles V, Don Luis presents it as the prelude to the final major offensive against Constantinople, called the "holy venture" (*sancta empresa*), which he continually "longed for like a lover," and as the premonitory sign of the definitive expulsion of the Turks.[9]

The notion persisted that the most recent Christian success was the first act of a reversal that would put an end to the monstrosity of the Turkish presence in Europe. It was long the custom to celebrate any success against the Turks, even a minor one, by the *Te Deum*, processions, prayers, and donations: that would be the case in 1598, for example, at the victory of Raab, an episode in the Long War.[10]

In the late seventeenth century, the three jubilee years of 1669, 1670, and 1683 corresponded to periods of war between the Turks and Christendom. The respective popes, Clement IX, Clement X, and Innocent XI, let it be known that they were granting indulgences to all who would pray to "thwart the efforts and forces of the Turks, the cruel and irreconcilable enemies of the word 'Christian.'" The jubilee of 1683 began in a particularly tragic context, since it was decreed on August 11, just after Vienna was besieged, on July 14. The pope put out an anguished and tearful call in face of that new attack against "the strong and famous city of Vienna in Austria, which once vigorously repelled the impetuosity of Ottoman arms; and which, like a powerful dam, arrested their course." At stake was "the defense of the word 'Christian,'" while the Turk, "overlooking nothing that he could do to spread the abomination of Muhammad's perfidy everywhere . . . used all his strength to turn the church of the living God on its head."

On January 15, 1684, Innocent XI's appeal reached a distant audience, in the person of Louis de Laverne-Montenard du Tressan, bishop of Le Mans, who did not fail to pass it on to his flock. By then, the situation had changed: on September 12, the besiegers were defeated at Kahlenberg and had to retreat. Having compared the Holy Father to the "chaste Rachel" grieving the loss of her children, the prelate from Le Mans radiated joy: "Have we not already felt the effects of [God's] divine promises, since, when the Pastor of the universal church raised his hands to Heaven, that cruel enemy was put to flight . . . and the children of the chaste Rachel have come into possession of their inheritance."[11]

The Turkish wars were vested with a special sacredness. The coalitions to which they gave rise were so many "holy leagues" (sacra ligua). The victims were martyrs on the path of sainthood. Consider the example of Gedik Ahmed Pasha, who took Otranto in the summer of 1480. Eight hundred men, survivors of the siege on the city, were put to death at that time, in a massacre of a punitive nature intended to sow terror. These eight hundred victims became the eight hundred martyrs of Otranto who, it would be said, preferred to die rather than recant. They were considered blessed (though their official beatification was declared only three centuries later), and a series of miracles was attributed to them. Here again, paintings consecrated and perpetuated the event: many depicted the Martyrdom of the Holy Innocents, making implicit reference to Otranto. Other victims of the Turks were similarly the object of a popular cult. The shock produced by the landing of the Turks elicited fervor and excitement throughout Italy. In the following years, several apparitions of the Virgin were reported on the peninsula, especially in Tuscany: in 1482 in the Maremma and in 1484 in Prato.[12]

The ideal of Crusade was also perpetuated by the notion that at least part of the European nobility held about the war against the Turks: it was always meritorious to participate in it, whatever the flag under which one did so, since it was a supreme duty transcending national divisions. As a result, it offered an honorable path of escape—sometimes the only one—to all knights at odds with their own sovereigns. A good example is the French or Lorrainian nobles who, after the Wars of Religion or the Fronde, joined the Habsburg armies to go fight the Turks in Hungary (the duke of Mercoeur is an emblematic figure). Then there were those who, having joined the Order of Malta, participated in the corso maltese, hunting down Muslim ships in the Mediterranean.

The idea of Crusade also survived in the many writings by obscure or more illustrious authors. Addressed to sovereigns, these works exhorted them to rid themselves of the Ottomans, or predicted the destiny of the East and the eschatological mission of the blessed lineage from which the kings were descended. The "most Christian kings of France" in particular, given what their role had been in the Middle Ages, were the focus of hope both in Europe and among the sultan's Christian subjects, especially the Armenians of Syria and the Maronites of Lebanon. For example, a prophecy from an ancient Armenian saint, Nerses, declared that the king of France would be in Jerusalem in 1550.[13] Francis I, after initially corresponding with Pope Leo X to plan a mission against the Turks,[14] then took a diametrically opposed position, allying himself with the sultan. His successors, with more or less ardor, took the same path. But that in no way discouraged the illusions of the prophets or armchair strategists of the following centuries, who wagered first on the Valois and then on the Bourbons to realize the definitive victory of Christianity. In the early seventeenth century, for example, a certain Jean Aimé de Chavigny appealed to Henry IV to undertake grandiose adventures and turned to his own advantage ancient predictions supporting a "second Charlemagne": a king who "would stem from the extraction and stalk of the very illustrious lily" and would conquer the peoples of the East before going to die in Jerusalem. In 1632, an Italian, Silvestro Manfredo Vanino, dedicated a pamphlet to Louis XIII, reminding him that he was destined "to destroy all sects opposed to the Holy Church and above all that of the Great Turk."

Louis XIV was in turn the object of predictions and exhortations, from the time of his youth and throughout his reign. For example, in Louis XIV's "imperial horoscope," published in 1652, it is said that the young prince was given to France by God, "to reform France with new constitutions, to correct the vices and abuses being committed, to extirpate heresies and conquer the infidels, to this end as well that the Christian faith may be free throughout the universe." The king would receive the imperial title, which included the obligation to fight against the Ottomans.[15] In 1670–1672, the illustrious philosopher Gottfried Leibniz, part of the entourage of the archbishop-elector of Mainz—an influential figure in the politics of his time—also sent the Sun King a plan for the conquest of Ottoman Egypt.[16]

Seventeenth-century bishop and theologian Jacques-Bénigne Bossuet should also be mentioned in this context, since he pronounced the panegyric of Saint Peter Nolasco, in the church of the Fathers of Mercy, who were committed to ransoming captives taken by the infidels: "O Jesus, Lord of Lords, arbiter of all empires and Prince of the kings of the earth, how long will you allow your declared enemy, seated on the throne of the great Constantine, to support the blasphemies of his Muhammad with so many armies, to flatten your cross under his crescent, and every day weaken Christendom by such fortuitous weapons?"[17]

THE PROTESTANTS AND THE TURKISH QUESTION

It may have appeared for a time that the plans and prospects for reconquest of the Turk were irremediably compromised by the advent of the Protestant Reformation and the inexpiable divisions that followed within Christendom.

In their reciprocal imprecations, Catholics and Protestants used the Turk as the standard of ignominy, just as canonists and inquisitors had once declared heretics and schismatics worse than the infidels. The Protestants accused the pope and his entourage of being more vile, debauched, and dangerous than the Turks. And to discredit the Protestants, the Catholics could do no better than to discern their "resemblances" to the Turks.[18]

Apart from the fact that Christendom's unity was once again destroyed by that new fracture—following on the Great Schism—the Catholic sovereigns had reason to fear that the Turks would take advantage of the division and find allies among the dissidents. In a letter of May 10, 1552, Süleyman the Magnificent exhorted the Protestant princes, who were in fact allies of Henry II, king of France, to wage war against Charles V.[19] In any event, no formal alliance was needed for the Turks and Protestants to be objectively united against the emperor. Was it not true that Charles V, whose troops fought the Ottoman forces, did not have those needed to prevent Protestantism from spreading and gaining strength in his empire? That observation is the basis for the thesis of Stephen Fischer-Galati, who argues that the consolidation and ultimate legalization of German Protestantism was inextricably linked to the "Turkish peril" (die Türkengefahr). The thesis is not unfounded, at least until the Augsburg Confession in 1555. With that document, which marked the official recognition of Protestantism (and more precisely, of Lutheranism) in the empire, all tension between Protestants and Catholics surely did not disappear, but the struggle against the Turks became the best guarantor of the unity of the empire and the legitimacy of the Habsburgs' authority.[20]

At first, the thinkers of the Reformation, or close to the Reformation, maintained a troubling distance from the Turkish war. Erasmus did so in the name of his pacifism: in In Praise of Folly, he portrays all war as folly, including war against the infidel. In A Plaint of Peace, he maintains that the best way to fight the Turks would be for the Christian princes to begin by not making war against one another, which, Erasmus observes, had led some to ally themselves with the Turks against coreligionists. He adds that, even in combat that could not be avoided, people ought to maintain a Christian spirit. One of his adages eloquently expresses his thinking: "War is sweet to those who have never experienced it."

Others, such as Luther in the first place, then John Calvin, Phillip Melanchton, and the humanist Ulrich von Hutten, assumed a resigned defeatism toward the Turks: the Christians must not resist them but must rather submit to the punishment sent by God for their sins through the instrument of the Turks. That position, which is also sometimes found in Guillaume Postel, finds radical expression in Luther, who declared in 1520: "To fight the Turks is to oppose the will of God" (Gegen die Türken zu kämpfen, heisst dem Willen Gottes zu widerstehen).

The same authors, reasoning within an eschatological perspective, developed the idea, also tending toward demobilization, that the Turks' victories had to be accepted as part of God's plans. The "Muhammadists" or "Ishmaelites," as Postel calls them, had been incited by divine providence to rid the world of pagans and schismatic Greeks and thus prepare the way for the universal domination of the Roman church, since, he concludes, "Christendom . . . must be the sole and legitimate princess of the world, both in spiritual and in temporal things."[21]

These attitudes, inspired by philosophical and theological considerations, lasted only a little while, however, and most of these dissident thinkers later had no qualms about rallying behind a "Turkish war"—if not exactly behind the principle of Crusade in its traditional conception—especially after the successes of Süleyman the Magnificent in Belgrade, Rhodes, and Mohács, followed by his march on Vienna.

In his *Consultatio de bello Turcis inferendo*, printed in early 1530, Erasmus feverishly denounces the Turkish peril. "All of Asia Minor," he wrote at the time, "which contains no fewer than twelve peoples; all Thrace, with Constantinople . . . ; the two Mysies of Europe near the Danube; a large part of Dacia; all of Macedonia and all of Greece with the entirety of the Aegean Sea, part of it called Sporades and part Cyclades: all of these endure harsh servitude under Turkish domination."

Then there were the recent events in Hungary, which raised the philosopher's anxieties to their paroxysm: "What about all those murderous incursions into Hungary? What about the death of Louis, king of Hungary? And, in the current year [1529], this same country in its entirety is cruelly occupied, King Ferdinand driven from his throne, Vienna besieged with the greatest fury and all of Austria outside that city devastated with incredible ferocity."[22]

During the same period, Luther too went on the offensive.[23] Revising his earlier attitude, he became the ardent supporter of war against the Turks in a 1528 book titled *On War against the Turks*,[24] in various other pamphlets at about the same time (the *Türkenbüchlein*, or *Turkish Booklets*), and in the preface he wrote in 1530 for the first edition of George of Hungary's *Treatise on the Mores, Customs, and Perfidy of the Turks*.[25] The theme also appeared in his correspondence. In a letter of October 26, 1529, sent to Nicholas Haussmann from Wittenberg, Luther has these definitive words: "I will fight to my death the Turks and the God of the Turks." The culminating point of that conversion to passionate warmongering is indicated in Luther's 1541 work, *Admonition to Prayer against the Turks*.

In the following generation as well, Calvin was less impervious to the Turkish peril than some have claimed. What reformers continued to criticize were the institutional aspects the Crusade had assumed with the pontificate of Innocent III (1198–1203). At the time, the war against the infidel had become a powerful tool for managing—militarily, financially, and legally—the Christian world in the hands of the Roman Curia. The Curia had a powerful weapon at its disposal: someone who swore an oath to take up the cross and later delayed or avoided fulfilling his vow was liable to be excommunicated. He could liberate himself from his vow only by paying a sum of money or performing another mission decreed by the church to be a "cause of the cross" (*causa crucis*) or a "mission of the Cross" (*negotium crucis*). And Rome now had another spur to action: since the pontificate of Nicholas V in the mid-fifteenth century, those who came to the assistance of the Mediterranean islands threatened by Islam were granted specific indulgences in the afterlife. The first attested measure, from 1451, had to do with the island of Cyprus, which was still under the domination of the Lusignans. The first corresponding indulgences were printed in Mainz in 1454.[26] It was these various aspects that elicited the reformers' criticisms. As of 1517, therefore, Luther declared war on the practice of indulgences. Everyone now believed that, though the Turkish war should not be abandoned, it should be "depontificalized." François de La Noue would elaborate the idea with particular rigor in his *Political and Military Discourses*. That French Huguenot took up the pen during his captivity by the Spanish, after he had gone to support the rebel Calvinists of Flanders. Assuming a pragmatic stance, he did not claim that the pope's contribution—any more than the emperor's—to a future Crusade was completely without utility. The pope, he observes, "can work effectively," since his high position is still "much revered by the Catholic princes." As for the emperor, "though his power is not now commensurate with the title he bears," he can also provide valuable assistance because of "the sacred dignity with which he is vested" and which "must be held in great reverence by all Christian potentates."[27]

THE *MILITIA CHRISTIANA*: THE KNIGHTS OF MODERN TIMES

Whereas the Protestants rallied behind the cause of Turkish war and even, with a few correctives, behind the idea of Crusade, that same idea could be revived among the Catholics only by the advent of Tridentinism. One episode in 1616–1625 may serve as an example: the Crusade planned by the duke of Nevers, Charles Gonzaga, and by the Capuchin François Leclerc du Tremblay, Richelieu's right-hand man, better known by the name "Father Joseph" and the title "éminence grise." In Father Joseph's view, not only was the battle against the Turks necessary for the salvation of Christendom, but it also had the advantage of purging the Christians' hot-headed belligerence and therefore of introducing the reign of peace among them. As he wrote in a report to Louis XIII in support of his cause, "the certainty and stability of peace among Christians would follow from it, whereas the diversity of beliefs and the emulation of neighboring or domestic princes not engaged in something better can never allow peace to reign for long."[28] Trying to halt the Ottoman advance in Europe, as during the Crusades of the fourteenth and fifteenth centuries, was no longer at issue. Rather, at a time when that advance was running out of steam, the matter at hand was to combine the permanent objective of liberating the holy sites with the more pressing one of liberating the Christians, in this case most of them Orthodox, from the Ottoman yoke. In addition, Charles Gonzaga, by virtue of the fact that his grandmother was a Palaeologus, had claimed a right to Byzantium and therefore maintained relations with Greek notables. To realize their goal, the protagonists, having taken various diplomatic measures and obtained the pope's authorization, in 1616 founded a new military and religious order, the Christian Militia (*Militia Christiana*), with the support of part of the European nobility and of several sovereigns, such as Louis XIII and Sigismund II, king of Poland. In February 1618, the pope's secretary, Cardinal Borghese, sent instructions to the different nuncios living in the European capitals. But an event of great consequence, the "defenestration of Prague" on May 23, 1618, doomed the entire undertaking by provoking the outbreak of the Thirty Years' War between Catholic and Protestant states.

THE "TERRIBLE TURK"

Although the rejection of the Turks had religious motives and found justification in the alleged flaws and profound falseness of the religion that they professed and sought to impose, it also assumed other faces and was based on other reasons.

The Turks were not merely infidels. They were thought to lack any notion of civilization and morality: they were barbarians, a fact that corresponded to what people thought they knew about their origins. The scholars and thinkers contemporary to the Turkish advance had in fact pondered the origins of these invaders.[29] Their geographical origin, as well as the resemblance between the terms *Teucri* (the name of the Trojans in ancient literature) and *Turci*, initially led them to think that the Turks were none other than the descendants of the Trojans. That hypothesis was compatible with the sense of otherness they aroused, since the Christians implicitly identified themselves with the Greeks. But it quickly became incoherent since, according to Virgil's *Aeneid*, the Romans—with whom the Europeans identified as well—were also descended from the Trojans. Furthermore, in the flattering genealogies that several European princes of the time asked to have drawn up for themselves, they too could be traced back to Troy. That had the disadvantage of making them related to the Turks (a theme that persisted in diplomatic relations over the following centuries). The Trojan hypothesis, which simply entailed too many conundrums, was abandoned in favor of another, much more satisfying one. It appeared in 1456 in the treatise by Nicoló Sagundino, a Venetian from Eubea, titled *De origine et gestis Turcarum*; it was dedicated to Enea Silvio Piccolomini, who would use it to his own advantage. The same view is found again in 1538 in the *Commentario delle Cose de Turchi a Carlo Quinto*, written by Paolo Giovio, which claims: "Without a doubt, the Turkish nation drew its origin from the Scythians, now called Tatars, who inhabit the lonely regions above the Caspian Sea, near the course of the Volga."[30]

In assimilating (against all historical truth) the Turks to the Scythians of antiquity, Renaissance humanists were merely adopting a Byzantine custom, which designated as Scythians all the many peoples arriving in Europe from what is now the Russian steppes, including the Mongols and Tatars of the thirteenth century. In the twelfth century, to distinguish them from the other peoples of the steppe, Anna Comnena called the Turkomans in the Seljuk armies "eastern Scythians"; George Tornikes termed them "Persian Scythians" (*Persoskythai*). In addition, he says that they "live scattered in tents and migrate over the earth and . . . fly like sparrows in the field."[31] A dialectical relationship existed between the assimilation of the Turk to the Scythian and the European view of him. The success of that identification lay in the fact that it equated the Turks with barbarism; at the same time, it led Europeans to apply the ancient authors' discourses on the "barbarians" to these same Turks and thus shaped their image.

Commentators cite several privileged pieces of evidence attesting to their barbarism. In the first place, Turkish pretenders to the throne sometimes committed fratricide to rid themselves of their competitors, and sultans who were worried about their sons' ambitions sometimes killed their own children. (Süleyman, for example, ordered the execution of his sons Mustafa and Bayezid and their descendants, causing a great stir.) Such acts demonstrated the Turks' disdain for all the laws of nature and humanity. In his pamphlets on the Turks, Francesco Sansovino listed sultans who had been guilty of such crimes, under the title *Lords Who Murdered Their Own Blood and Usurped Power*.[32] The practice of polygamy and of other vices such as sodomy, portrayed as being very widespread, was another mark of their bestiality. Finally, commentators pointed out the Turks' ignorance and contempt for works of art, and especially, for books. In a letter from Lauro Querini, a Venetian from Crete, to Pope Nicholas V on July 15, 1453, shortly after the taking of Constantinople, he notes that more than 120,000 volumes were destroyed at that time, obliterating the work of many centuries. The conclusion to be drawn was that the Turks were "a barbarian people, an uncultivated people, living without clear laws or customs but in laxity, nomadism, and arbitrariness, full of perfidy and deceit."[33]

A number of Renaissance authors took up the theme first addressed in these lines. It is found in Montaigne, who speaks of people trained to "value arms and have contempt for letters." The theme would persist unchanged until the contemporary period: the religion of the Turks and Muslims in general was not only false, it was also synonymous with ignorance and with a militant contempt for science and the arts. That could not have been claimed without reservations in the Middle Ages, when the knowledge of antiquity was being transmitted to Westerners, at least in part, through the Arabs. But it was now freely asserted, since the transmission of knowledge was occurring in a single direction. Chateaubriand, along with many others, adopted that theme in 1807, making it one of the foundations of his *Itinerary from Paris to Jerusalem*: "Islam is a religion that burned down the library of Alexandria, that considers it meritorious to trample men and to hold arts and letters in supreme disdain."[34] The connection to the barbarians of antiquity was shored up in particular by descriptions of the Turks in battle. In reality, the Ottoman conquest had been gradual, with delays, breaks, setbacks; it had required organization and the adaptation of technology by its planners; it had privileged sieges of cities; and finally, it had sometimes had to combine force of arms with the use of a pragmatic policy of reconciliation and integration of the defeated. The rhetoric obscured all these realities, conforming completely to the descriptions of barbarian invasions from the past and even sometimes citing the ancient authors word for word. The Turks were simply hordes arriving in waves, birds of prey falling on fields, an irresistible torrent carrying off everything in its wake. Certainly such descriptions corresponded well to certain episodes in the Ottoman conquest, especially the raids of "privateers" (akınjı), which prepared the way for the arrival of the full army by terrorizing the population. "They are terrestrial corsairs, men who commit evil against Christians," the Genoese Promontorio de Campis wrote of them.[35] The Serb Konstantin Mihailović described them as follows: "The Turkish raiders, or 'those who flow,' like rainstorms, do not linger long, but wherever they strike they burn, plunder, kill, and destroy everything so that for many years the cock will not crow there."[36] In such evocations, it is only the shock images that appear, when the events were in reality more complex: other texts emphasize the sophistication of the Ottoman military apparatus as a whole, the specializations of the diverse units cooperating to achieve general effectiveness, and the rule of order and discipline.

But to return to the previous image, the barbarian is identifiable not only by the suddenness of his attacks but also, to an equal degree, by his cruelty in war: he massacres, inflicts horrible tortures, rapes women and children, and reduces his captives to the harshest slavery. He shows thereby that he is not only different but also, strictly speaking, outside humanity. Hence the Turk, used as the measure of deviance in the religious conflicts, was also the standard on the spectrum of evil: there was no better way for a Christian to stigmatize his enemy than by declaring him as bad or worse than the Turk.

A disturbing consequence of the Turks' perceived inhumanity is that it allowed the Christians to inflict the same abominable treatment on them that they were accused of reserving for their adversaries. The application of the principle of an eye for an eye to the Turks did not raise any moral questions. Without a second thought, witnesses therefore mention the conduct of the Christian army in Transylvania during the Long War in Hungary. At the victory of Raab in 1598, the Turkish governor's head was stuck on a pike and placed in a very visible spot. After the retaking of the Alba Regia stronghold, the heads of a number of Turkish chiefs were sent to Archduke Matthias "and then offered in exchange for a few Christian prisoners."[37] After a few other victories, "seventy-two heads of Turks" and then "eighteen Turkish heads" were collected in the same way.[38] Transgressions intended to terrorize could even go much further, if we are to believe an account of 1595: "The Tatars and the Turks have been beaten this year, and three times the Cossacks and Transylvanians forced some Tatar women to roast and eat their children, so that they would so be horrified of Hungary that they would flee, and through their accounts would put off others and even their posterity from coming here."[39]

But on the question of war, it is necessary to make a distinction between the peoples in the northern and western parts of Christian Europe, who had never seen and would never see a Turk or Muslim—for whom the threat, however terrible, was nevertheless theoretical and fantastical—and those in central Europe or on the banks of the Mediterranean, who were always at risk of seeing their *Türkenfurcht* materialize, whether as devastating raids, military occupations, or corsair attacks. "All'armi! All'armi! La campana sona, li turchi sunnu giunti alla marina" (To arms! To arms! The bells are ringing, the Turks have come to the shore), goes an old Italian popular song. In those regions, the representation of Turkish cruelties took on more precise and even tragic forms, accompanied, in the Germanic world, by strong biblical references: it was the arrival of Gog and Magog, the scourge of God who punishes humanity, especially the Germans, for their sins by making them fall under "the tyrannical yoke" (*das tyrannische Joch*) and into "bovine servitude" (*die viehische Servitut*).

Winfried Schulze has shown that, in the Germanic empire and throughout central Europe, the Turk was represented not only as the infidel and the barbarian but also as the hereditary enemy (*Erbfeind*) and a danger to the social order.[40] There, all-out resistance consisted not only of saving the Christian religion or attempting to deliver Jerusalem but also of defending the fatherland against an enemy hungry for conquest. The Catholic Johann Baptist Fickler thus wrote during the Long War at the very end of the sixteenth century: "If Hungary is occupied or conquered by the Turk, neither Italy nor Germany will be secure any longer, and the Rhine too will be unable to protect France."[41] It was not only the fatherland that was threatened but every person, home, and family, since the Turk kidnapped and raped women and children. As a result, not only holy war but a just, necessary, and even vital war was at issue.

That discourse was obviously not gratuitous. Its primary aim was to persuade the participants at the imperial diets to vote for allocations from Germany to the Habsburgs for the defense of Hungary and Croatia.

Official propaganda, whether it emanated from political or religious authorities, also had to fight another danger specific to those same regions: the "Turkish temptation" (*Türkenhoffnung*). That term referred to the illusion among the poorest and most oppressed classes of the population that their fate could not be worse, and might even be better, if the Turks were to become their new masters. When these oppressed peoples were not Catholic, they might also prefer the Turks to the Roman clergy: *eher Türkisch als Päbstisch* (better Turkish than popish). In that context, the Turks were not characterized solely by their unbelief, and in fact that trait was becoming relatively secondary. The actions taken throughout Ottoman history by "renegades," acting on their own with various motives, were now becoming a collective attitude inspired by despair. Veltwick, an envoy of Charles V to the sultan, confirmed the reality of such attitudes, when he reported to his sovereign what he had observed while traveling in Hungary: "The peasants of Hungary are wondrous pleased at the treatment [of the Turks toward them], and betray their lords to the Turks."[42] An echo of that same phenomenon could be heard at the end of the century, in the sermon the minister Salomon Gessner addressed to his flock in Wittenberg in 1597: "Many complaints and much agitation have been heard here that you have not put aside the opinion that you might perhaps live with less and not more difficulty under that race of Muslim dogs, and, if opportunity gave you that choice, who knows what you might and would venture to do, under the effect of folly and Satan's accursed influence."

Nor was joining the sultan ruled out in certain Italian circles, whether motivated by the "Turkish mirage" or as a form of blackmail. It could be found among the supporters of autonomy for medieval communities, against the centralizing tendencies of the Renaissance popes. In the early sixteenth century, for example, a deputy of the city of Ravenna declared to the pope's legate Cardinal Giulio de Medicis: "Monsignor, if the Turks come to Ravenna, we will surrender to them."

THE TURKISH TYRANT

Because the illusion existed and was in no way excluded a priori by the religious objection, it was important to dissipate it by giving the most repulsive image possible of the Ottoman regime: the sultan's subjects were governed by a terrifying and bloody tyrant who kept them as slaves and held over them the right of life and death. "All subjects in Turkey are slaves, actual serfs who have no access to the slightest freedom anywhere or to the rights of the bourgeoisie," declared Georg Mylius, another preacher speaking to a different audience.[43]

For the benefit in this case of the petty nobility, who might also be tempted to rally behind the Turks, the preacher Georg Scherer, among other critics, contrasted the benevolent attitude of the Kaiser and other German sovereign princes toward the nobility to the behavior of the sultan vis-à-vis his aides: "The Turk would not have so much patience with them, but at the slightest indiscretion would order straightaway all their heads to fall by the saber."[44]

That idea—that the divorce between Muslims and Christians was not necessarily radical in terms of religion and morality but remained so when it came to political notions, where the gulf could not be bridged—is brilliantly expressed in an anonymous work from the Spanish Golden Age (its attribution is a matter of controversy), the *Viaje de Turquia*, composed in 1557–1558.[45]

The work is as favorable toward Islam as prudence allowed. One of the characters declares of the Muslims: "During my travels, I never met a people more virtuous, and I believe that none could be found in the Indies either, . . . apart from their belief in Muhammad: I am well aware that the Turks will all go to hell, but here I am assuming solely the standpoint of natural law."[46] Another character categorically denies the accusation of barbarism: "Those people are called barbarians? It is rather we who are so in judging them such."[47] At the same time, the condemnation of the regime is absolute: "Turkey is a people of slaves, entirely subjugated to their leader, the Great Turk."[48] That diagnosis and verdict are omnipresent in the *relazione* of the bailis from Venice to Constantinople, at least in the late sixteenth and seventeenth centuries. After 1630, the Ottoman government was definitively stigmatized as *despotico*.[49]

JIHĀD AND GAZĀ IN EUROPE

Corresponding to these Christian representations, a no less antagonistic view prevailed among the Muslims: both posited an irreducible incompatibility between Muslims and Christians for reasons beyond the strictly religious. Islam, at least in the legal developments of the eighth and ninth centuries, projected a binary image of the world, which contrasted the "House of Islam" (*dār al-islām*) to the "House of War" (*dār al-harb*). It was the duty of sovereigns and of at least some of their subjects to expand the *dār al-islām* at the expense of the *dār al-harb* by conducting holy war, *jihād*—or, in a term often used by the Ottomans, *gazā*—against the infidels who had not yet submitted to Islam. The fate of Islam, at least virtually, was to spread throughout the world or, more exactly—in accordance with the cosmological notions in play—to the "inhabited quarter" (*rub'-i meskūn*) of that world. That was the messianic horizon toward which Islam was headed. In theory, then, there was no place for a peaceful coexistence between Muslims and infidel *harbīs*, or for the long-term survival of the Christian world. Temporary truces could occur between Muslims and Christians but in no case "perpetual peace." The Ottomans, who by virtue of their original position in a border region facing Byzantium, and because the European *dār al-harb* offered them their best chances for expansion, at least in a first phase, were quite naturally inclined to give a place of honor to that duty of jihad or, to use an expression that present-day historians have coined, that "gaza ideology" (which other Muslim princes in a less favorable position toned down). For these parvenus from the fringes of the Muslim world, the best means to acquire legitimacy in the eyes of the rest of Islam was to assign that label to their conquests. Upon taking Constantinople, at a time when the Mamluks had not yet lost their prestige and symbolic supremacy, the young Mehmed II, in his victory report to Sultan al-Malik al-Ashraf Inal, protector of the holy sites of Islam, defined his own place beside "the man who assumes the inherited suffering of his father and ancestors to revive the ceremony of the pilgrimage to Mecca." For his part, Mehmed was "the one responsible for equipping the men who work for *gazā* and *jihād*."[50] Elsewhere, Mehmed II styled himself the "lord of combatants for the faith" (*Sayyidü-l-ghuzzāt wa'l-Mujahidīn*). The chroniclers regularly call him the *gāzi* of *gāzis*, champion of the holy war.

These notions appeared continually in the official Ottoman phraseology. Members of the dynasty present themselves not as monarchs of a people or a particular state, but as the *pādishāh* of Islam, acting in the name of Islam as a whole. Their armies, according to another standard formulation, are the "armies of Islam destined for victory" (*'asakir-i mansūre-i islā*miyye). Their states were the "well-guarded territories of Islam" (*memālik-i mahrūse-i islāmiyye*)." And so on. Their adversary is designated primarily as an infidel (*kāfir*), even before the miscreant country from which he comes is specified (Venice, Hungary, Portugal), if in fact it is specified (this was not always done when evoking the fight against the Portuguese in the Red Sea and the Indian Ocean, for example). According to the same conventions, the term *kāfir* (pl., *küff*ār) is always accompanied by a pejorative, even insulting qualifier that rhymes with the noun to which it is attached, so that the expression will be more forceful: the infidels are worthy of scorn (*küffār-i haksār*); they behave badly (*küffār bedgīrdār*); they are full of tricks and ruses (*küffār hilekār*); they bear the marks of abjection (*küffār mezellet āsār*); they are in error (*küffār zalaet shi'ār*); and so on.

A large number of official Ottoman documents and chroniclers' narratives give considerable place to that rhetoric, which ascribes to the sultan, as his first priority, war against the infidel (or heretic), conquest of his territory, extermination if he resists, and, if he surrenders, subjugation and humiliation. The more a text claims to exalt a sovereign's greatness, the more it will use hyperbole, both pious and belligerent, even bloody. The dedicatory inscriptions on monuments, the elaborate titulatures of sultans, the victory reports (*fethnāme* or *fethināme*), the letters of imprecations (*tehdīdīdnāme*), and the preambles to formal orders are the privileged sites of that phraseology. Their authors try to outdo one another in Islamic erudition and stylistic virtuosity. Consider, for example, how Selim II (or more accurately, a scribe in the chancery) addresses one of his governors, the *beylerbey* of Egypt, in the preamble to an order of 1568. It commands him to study the possibility of digging a canal in the Isthmus of Suez, designed to facilitate the passage of ships sent against the Portuguese and the Shiite rebels of Yemen. His grandiloquence is all the more remarkable, given that the sultan's words are for internal use only, for a subordinate, albeit one of high rank:

Formerly, my glorious ancestors and my illustrious forebears who belonged to our dynasty, whose ambition is *jihād*, and to our lineage, for whom *gazā* is our lot—may God shine on their graves!—devoted their days, dedicated to victory, and every one of their moments, happy in its outcome, to *jihād* and *gazā*. They conquered and defeated a number of climates and territories, to the east and to the west, by their saber which brings victory, delivering them from associationism and error [*shirk ü delālet*], and reunited them to the well-guarded territories of the Ottomans.[51]

Another short draft in Persian, studded with multiple Qur'anic quotations, was written by a scribe from the chancery or a scholar badly in need of favor. It was to be used in the composition of a *fethnāme* celebrating the taking of Caffa from the Genoese in 1475. In accordance with Persian tastes, it is an even more astonishing purple passage. The expedition, it claims, is under the sign of the Qur'anic verse: "Make war on them until idolatry shall cease and God's religion shall reign supreme" (8:40). Its leader, Vizier Gedik Ahmed Pasha, became "the leader endowed with sharp judgment, destroyer of the subversives' base by means of penetrating thought and a sharp saber." When the fleet set out, "the resounding voices of those who dwell in the firmament [the angels], and who celebrated the verse: 'Embark,' said Noah. 'In the name of God it shall set sail and cast anchor' [Qur'an 11:43], arrived within hearing of the ships of holy war and within that of the residents of the kingdom of bold efforts." Once Caffa was taken, the significance of that victory was analyzed as follows: "We choke the law of tyranny and eliminate the shadow from the surface of the mirror by polishing our swords, whose pores contain divine assistance. We have devoted ourselves to brandishing standards of the gleaming law of Muhammad—may the best prayers and most perfect greetings be open to him—and by pushing toward the progress of the shining community of the Prophet."[52]

After Caffa, the other fortresses of southern Crimea fell one by one. Thus all of the former "Genoese Gazaria" passed into Ottoman hands, which the draft of the victory report proposes to formulate as follows: "The bride that is this kingdom, from the day of the Prophet's mission until today, had wrapped her slender figure in the costume forcibly worn by the infidels [an allusion to the fact that, since Islam had been preached, Gazaria had never been Muslim]. She was now adorned in the beautiful silk of the manifest Religion." In such a text, there is no discussion of the likely strategic and economic motivations of that Ottoman advance on the Black Sea: everything is represented in the most Manichaean religious terms.

The taking of the fortress of Szigetvár during the final campaign of Süleyman the Magnificent, who met his death there in 1566, is viewed the same way in the victory report that his son Selim II sent to Tahmasp, shah of Persia, though the writer's pen is less florid. Selim declares that his father "had gone to conduct illustrious holy war [*gazā*] against the Christians, as was his custom and ancient practice. . . . He had marched and launched an attack against the headstrong miscreants who brought harm to believers, endlessly causing damage and destruction in the Islamic countries."[53]

When a few later sultans adopted the tradition of their ancestors, placing themselves at the head of their armies, their successes, even of limited scope, were presented just as surely as victories of Islam over error and impiety. Such was the case for Mehmed III during the Eger campaign in 1596. At the most critical point of the battle of Keresztes, as a safeguard, he had taken care to put on the mantle of the Prophet, the most holy of relics, kept in the Palace of Topkapı. In addition, Mehmed IV's conquest of Kameniec-Podolski in 1672 earned the sultan the title "father of victory" (*Ebülfeth*), like his ancestor Mehmed II, and like "the one who demolished the edifice of unbelief and error" (*küfr ü zelāl bünyanının hādimi*).

THE QUEST FOR THE GOLDEN APPLE

Although the struggle between the Ottomans and the European states was officially expressed in terms of religious antagonism, that interpretation was not exclusive. Somewhat the same way that, in fighting the Turk, the Christian attacked not only the infidel but also the barbarian, and simply, the invader, jihad was not the only ideological motivation (setting aside the more concrete, strategic, and socioeconomic motivations factoring in) that pushed the sultan's troops toward the west. At the same time, that movement was impelled by a myth that did not contradict the Islamic motive, that occasionally combined with it, but that was nevertheless distinct.

The sultan's armies were setting out on a quest for the *Kızıl Elma*, the Golden Apple (or Red Apple). That fabulous fruit symbolized any city to be conquered, and in the end, the ultimate city, whose possession would signify that these armies had accomplished their task and that their master would now exercise the universal domination to which he had been called. The theme is clearly defined in what is the oldest attestation of it on the Ottoman side: a life of Sarı Saltuk (a *Saltuknāme*), semilegendary hero, patron saint of the first Turkish conquerors of eastern Europe, which was composed by Abū l-Hayr-er Rūmī at the request of Prince Jem, son of Mehmed II. The work dates to 1473, but the oldest manuscript extant is from 1590–1591. One passage evokes a dream of the glorious Sultan Murad I (1362–1389):

> In Iznik, Murad Khan Gazi saw in a dream His Lordship the Envoy [Muhammad]— may salvation be upon him!—And he said: "Go to the city of Edirne, it is your home, the place of the *gāzis*, the gate of victory, and the house of conquest. From there, to whatever place you go, conquest and victory will be yours; you will be in a position of strength. From there, you will conquer the east and the west, the north and the south, the four corners, on land as well as sea. You will defeat all who live in that land and will take those places. From there, you will march on, and your generation will also conquer the Red Apple. The whole world will be obedient to you," he said.[54]

Many later texts attest to the potency and popularity of the apple symbol. Depending on the period and phase of Ottoman conquest, various cities concretely corresponded to the objective the Golden Apple symbolized. But curiously, the most ancient city cited, and the one that would continue to be cited among the others, was Cologne. In the manuscript of the aforementioned *Saltuknāme*, Cologne is not expressly mentioned, but the city at issue might very well correspond to that Rhineland city: "They arrived in the prosperous places near Hungary, Germany, and Ayurusapur [Augsburg?]; they arrived in a large city where, inside a great fortress, was a large church whose door was shut. Above, on its dome, stood a golden globe; it had the shape of a golden or red apple. Then the sharif Sarı Saltuk spoke: 'What is that?' he said. They replied: 'It is called the Red Apple.'"

That reference to Cologne is surprising, given that the city never played any role in the Ottoman conquest. It very likely has to do with the intriguing and long-controversial question of the legend's origin, which was sought in Byzantium. In fact, the gilded copper globe held in the left hand of the equestrian statue of Justinian, erected on a column in front of the Hagia Sophia, may have served as a model for the Golden Apple, especially since that globe was interpreted as a symbol for the emperor's universal domination. It is much more likely, however, that the origin is to be sought, as Stéphane Yerasimos has argued, in a legend of the western Middle Ages, which accounts perfectly for the reference to Cologne. It was to Cologne that, in 1164, the Germanic emperor Frederick Barbarossa had the relics of the Magi transferred from Milan. A legend had formed around these relics, first mentioned in the *Liber de trium regum corporibus ad Coloniam translatis*, compiled by Johannes von Hildesheim in about 1370. According to that legend, Alexander had fashioned a golden apple by melting down the gold from the imperial tribute, and it was that apple that Melchior offered to the Christ Child. Jesus blew on it and reduced it to dust. But the relics of the Magi nevertheless preserved the spiritual power that the apple had initially borne within it. Transported to Cologne with the relics, that force now resided in the city, in possession of the Germanic emperors, who used it to good advantage in their rivalry with the Eastern emperors. The origin of the Turks' Golden Apple, then, may not have been the golden globe of Justinian but rather the *Reichsapfel* of Cologne. Furthermore, in the Turkish versions, the apple, identified from the start with Cologne, is never identified with Constantinople.[55] And the *Reichsapfel* became the *Kızıl Elma* only after many changes and adaptations, which in turn raise complex questions of origin.

Note as well that the Cologne cited in the Ottoman version is no longer the real city, site of the translation of relics; it has become a remote and mysterious city ("in the descending part of the earth," says one of these versions), which accords with the eschatological character of the legend. The final conquest would mark the end of history; therefore it was fitting to maintain a certain mystery, or at least a certain vagueness, about its identity. "What is the Red Apple?" inquires Baranyai Decsi János, a Hungarian poet of the late sixteenth century. "No one knows. . . . Only God and time will tell us."[56] When answers are provided, they always correspond to cities—with the exception of Cologne—that had been or remained objectives of conquest throughout Ottoman history: Buda, Vienna, or Rome. But they vary by author, and the same author may give several different answers. For Evliya Çelebi, the great traveler from the second half of the seventeenth century—and the Ottoman author who gave the largest place to that myth, perhaps because of the lack of progress in the Turkish conquest during his time—there were several "red apples." In a passage from his voluminous travel narrative, he cites two of them. The first is the "Red Apple of Vienna" (*Betch kızıl Elması*), a city he personally visited in 1665, in the retinue of an Ottoman ambassador, and which he predicted would be the object of a second Muslim siege, which would force the Viennese to make peace. The second was the "Red Apple of Rome" (*Irim papa kızıl Elması*), which prophecies said would also be conquered by the Ottomans (book 7). At another place in his work (book 6), Evliya Çelebi lists six "Red Apples." Four had already been taken by the Ottomans: Buda, Eger (Erlau), Esztergom, and Stonibelgrad (Székesfehérvár); the two remaining, Vienna and Rome, soon would be.[57]

In the investiture ceremonies of the new Ottoman sultans, one rite referred to the Red Apple and showed it exactly for what it was: the formulation of an ideology of conquest referring to notions that extended beyond Islam. The new sultan, returning to his palace from the sanctuary of Eyüp, where he had been girded with a symbolic saber in front of the sepulchre of the Standard Bearer of the Prophet, stopped outside the old barracks of the Janissaries, opposite the mosque of Chehzade. There the sovereign, supposedly thirsty from the long journey, received a refreshment from the colonel of the sixty-first company, namely, a cup of sorbet. The sultan brought the cup to his lips, then handed it to his saber-bearer, who returned it to the colonel filled with gold coins. The *pādishāh* then took his leave of the Janissaries, uttering these words, a pledge to lead them to new conquests: "We shall see each other again at the Red Apple" (*Kızıl Elma'da görüshürüz*).[58]

When it became known in (or indeed, when it returned to) the West, the Turkish legend of the Red Apple took on a modified and distorted form that inverted its meaning. It appears in the most famous and most widely diffused of the "Turkish prophecies," published in 1545 by the Dalmatian Bartholomeus Georgievicz (Barthol Djurdjevic).[59] He had been taken prisoner in Mohács in 1526 and remained in captivity among the Turks for about a decade. In one of the writings composed after his liberation, the *Vaticinium Infidelium lingua turcica*, he provides the text of a prophecy supposedly in force among the Turks, and he does so in the Turkish language, in a phonetic transcription, which confers a cachet of authenticity on it. He accompanies that text with a Latin translation and a short commentary. At the end of the prophecy, the *pādishāh* seizes the Red Apple, but his possession of it is very limited in time. It will last seven years if there is a reaction by the infidels; if that reaction takes some time to occur, it will last up to twelve years. But at the end of that time, "the Christian saber . . . will drive out the Turk." In his commentary, Georgievicz rightly says that the Red Apple "designates some imperial city of great scope and renown" and that there is a difference of opinion about its identity. By contrast, the hypotheses he attributes to the protagonists in the controversy do not correspond exactly to the names cited in the Ottoman versions: "There are some," he claims, "who judge that by that name the city of Constantinople is understood [on the contrary, it is omitted from the Ottoman versions]; especially since, in their books, it is read in two forms, namely, Kusul Elma and Urum Papai, one meaning 'Red Apple,' the other Greek 'priest' or 'patriarch'; and especially since, in ancient times, all Greece was subject to the Roman Empire."

There is no dearth of arguments allowing us to conclude that this Turkish prophecy is in reality a fake—though it is based in reality. It is only a pseudo-prophecy, probably invented to provide reassurance by announcing the final victory of the "Christian saber," a view diametrically opposed to that of the legend in force among the Turks. It is undoubtedly because it was somewhat reassuring for Christendom that the text of the prediction met with such great success there: no fewer than twenty-three editions are identified for the period 1552–1600 and eighty-two for the period 1544–1686.[60]

THE IDEA OF EUROPE OR THE IDEA OF ROME?

Was it Europe in the strict sense that the Ottomans sought to conquer, whether their aim was to integrate it into the well-guarded countries of Islam or to pluck the Red Apple there? To ask that question is to inquire into the role of the geographical notion of "Europe" in the Ottomans' view of the world. But that role was very limited. The word *Avrupa* appeared belatedly in Turkish and was derived from the Western term. An earlier Arabic term, *Urūfa*, did exist, but it was rarely used. The Ottomans, like the medieval Arabs, were the heirs to Greek geography and, like their predecessors, they adopted not the division of the world into continents but the Ptolemaic system dividing it into seven "climates" (*iqlim* in Arabic), that is, into horizontal bands running between the north pole and the equator (see figure 1). Under the circumstances, belonging to a region in Europe was no more a determining criterion in their view than it had been for the Greeks and Romans. By contrast, a different notion, geopolitical in this case, was fundamental: that of *Rūm*, that is, the Roman Empire.[61] But that empire, centered around the Mediterranean basin (*mare nostrum*), occupied three continents and was not limited to any one of them, though its capital was located in Europe. In classical Arab geography, the designation *Rūm* was given in particular to a part of Asia Minor, west of the line determined by the Taurus Mountains and the Upper Euphrates Valley, because that region constituted the borderland between Byzantium and the Arab empire, the gateway to the Roman countries. The term was retained to designate the Seljuk sultanate established over that zone in the twelfth century, with Konya as its capital: it was known as the Seljuk sultanate of Rūm. The Ottomans first styled themselves the successors of these Seljuks, but since their territory quickly surpassed that of their predecessors, it was not long before they played on the meaning of the designation "Sultan of Rūm" (very likely, this was already true for Bayezid I). The title certainly included the succession of the sultans of Konya but, much more broadly, also that of the Roman emperors. Although the center of Asia Minor was already named *Rūm*, and though the corresponding region would remain the province of Rūm (*Rūm beylerbeyiliği, eyālet-i Rūm*) throughout Ottoman history, the arrival of the Ottomans in Europe, beginning with Orhan's reign, was still a defining phase for them—not because they changed continents at the time, but because the part of the Roman world into which they were penetrating was of a different nature. No longer a zone that had been Roman in a remote past, it was rather one that, this time, still was so, and where the imperial capital (Constantinople, that is, the "new Rome") was still standing. That is what Süleyman Pasha expressed in the message he sent to his father, Sultan Orhan, when he established himself on the Isthmus of Gallipoli: "O happy one! Thanks to your wishes, we are making the conquest of the country of Rome!"[62]

For that new conquest, the Ottomans would also preserve the name "Rome," but they would distinguish it from the center of Asia Minor by no longer speaking, as in the previous case, of the "province of Rome" (*eyālet-i Rūm*) but rather of the "country" of Rome (*Rūmeli*).

Although the Ottoman conquest of Europe was theoretically destined to be total, it turned out to be only partial. It therefore split Europe in two, following in great measure a more ancient fracture line that had divided the Roman Empire itself and then Christendom. To the part of Europe that they could not (yet?) wrest from the *dār al-harb* (which, for its part, would now consider itself Europe as a whole), the Ottomans generally gave the name "land of the Franks" (*Frengistān*). Depending on the context, the referent of the expression varied: for the most part, it applied to the Italian states, but it could also encompass France and even England and the Netherlands. It applied, in short, to the countries of Latin Europe with which the Ottomans had diplomatic and commercial relations. It was a peaceful or at least a neutral expression. By contrast, the peoples of Europe with whom the Ottomans were at war were never simply "Franks": they were *harbī* infidels.

CHAPTER 9

THE ISLAMIC-CHRISTIAN BORDER IN EUROPE

BETWEEN OTTOMAN EUROPE and that other Europe, which saw itself as the only true one (Europe identified itself with Christendom), a line was drawn. It shifted with the Turks' advance, just as, at the end of the modern period, it would follow their first retreats. When the Ottoman Empire had reached its maximum extension, that line (or rather, that buffer zone) cut diagonally across the European continent, from roughly the Caspian Sea to the Adriatic. To the east, it ran through the northern steppes of the Black Sea, moving northwest of that sea toward central Europe, following the southern edges of Lithuania and Poland. It then crossed northern Hungary and returned south through Croatia. Farther to the west, opposite the western basin of the Mediterranean Sea, that "sea of fear"—in the striking expression of the Italian historian Giuseppe Bonaffini[1]—marked the separation between the "Land of the Franks" and the Maghreb of the Barbary regencies. The eastern basin, on the contrary, where the Ottoman possessions and the scattered fragments of Venetian Romania overlapped a great deal, became an "Ottoman lake," as these fragments were eliminated one after another.

In a Europe that also included many other cleavages of all kinds, that split became the major border, often compared to the "iron curtain" following World War II.[2] It was a political border separating a single state, that of the "well-guarded countries of Islam"— which also extended over a part of Africa and Asia—from several distinct Christian states. But it was much more than that: it was perceived on both sides as separating two worlds that stood opposed by their religions and more broadly, by their irreducibly different civilizations. That, at least, was the view arising from the respective ideologies previously described. On the Christian side, the Polish and Hungarian borders were so many ramparts or fortifications of Christendom. On the other side, three border fortresses were designated "Sedd-i islām" (barricade of Islam): one in Herzegovina; one in the *sanjak* of Qırqa near Zemūn; and one in the *sanjak* of Vidin. A fourth, also in the *sanjak* of Vidin, present-day Kladovo, was called "Feth-i islām" (Conquest of Islam). Belgrade was given the nickname "Dār ül-Jihād."

Simultaneously, a mysticism of the border (*serhādd*) developed among the Ottomans, sustained by the holy orders of dervishes. It made reference to the early glory days of Islam at war and gave rise, in the most prosaic everyday life, to holy figures in touch with the afterlife and endowed with supernatural powers. We therefore read in the *vita* of Sheikh Muslihuddīn of Smreska, a spiritual master of the border: "In his time, on all sides the governors and sovereigns acted with his support and, in confrontations with the enemy as in the expeditions of *gāzis*, in his presence and in his absence, they appealed to the departed one for help." One day, that sheikh was seen in the company of a man who looked like an irregular soldier (a *levend*), with whom he conversed on familiar terms. When the stranger left, the sheikh asked one of his dervishes: "Have you seen the *levend*? He is of the Seven." Referring to the mystic doctrine of Ibn 'Arabī, the biographer explains: "He meant by that that the sheikh was in the position of a pole (*kutb*), and that he knew the hidden saints (*rijāl*) who were beneath him. But God is the most knowing!"[3]

The symbols used to represent the two opposing sacralized worlds after the conclusion of peace treaties, when mixed commissions sought jointly to realize on the ground the line that separated them, were of the same register. In Dalmatia, crosses carved on tree trunks or on walls of rock delimited Venetian territory, crescent moons that of the Ottomans.[4] Similarly, during the Polish-Ottoman demarcation in 1680, four years after the truce of Żurawno between the two countries, stone mounds were erected on either side to mark the border. On the top of the mounds, the Poles planted crosses, and the Ottomans piled up pieces of wood shaped like turbans. A soldier in the escort of the Polish commissars reported: "When it came time to build mounds, the Turks, using spades they had attached to their saddles, built in a flash a mound of earth, after digging around a large trunk of an oak tree found in the middle. Once the work was completed, their superiors climbed on top of the mound and barked like dogs, their faces turned to the sky, thanking God for having conquered all that by their swords."[5]

That strong symbolic investment did not prevent the Islamic-Christian border from being, in actual fact, a border like any other in many respects, with the ambiguities common to border situations. A border is both a separation and a passageway, whether official or secret. It can institute an artificial break between ethnically and even religiously similar populations (for example, the Serbs and the Croats on either side of the Ottoman-Hungarian border), or those who, in any event, share a way of life. A border therefore makes no sense for transhumant shepherds or for fishermen in quest of waters full of fish. At the same time, in contrast to "the interior," it is a place of constant tensions, of "border incidents," and of contacts and exchanges of all natures.

That Islamic-Christian border, imposed by events, was fundamentally a scandal for both parties. Each saw it as the stigma of an unacceptable situation. For the Christians, it was the mark of an illegitimate presence that had amputated part of their continent, the painful materialization of a historical anomaly. For the Ottomans, the border signified the nonfulfillment of their mission. So long as it survived, it reminded them of their failure; it stood as a reproach. The fact is, it took them a long time to admit openly the reality of their borders. Only a painful learning process would persuade them that they did not rule over a virtually universal empire but over a particular state, which, like other states, had its limits. The preamble to a border demarcation act (sınurnâme) with Poland in 1680, inserted in the census registry of the Ottoman province of Podolia, took care to recall, in very stereotypical terms in fact, that though the document that followed had to do with borders, these were not to be taken too seriously, since only God entrusts kingdoms to the rulers of the world here below. A Hadith is evoked promising that, sooner or later, all the territories of unbelievers would become accessible to the warriors of Islam. Already, it was observed, the infidels had begun to desert by fleeing their ramparts, their fortresses, and their forts.[6] As other texts on the subject of diplomacy indicated, fixing the borders could follow only from the principle of "dissimulation" (mudara).[7] It was not until the late eighteenth century—1772 to be exact—that, drawing the lessons from the dramatic setbacks suffered at the hands of Russia, an Ottoman diplomat, Ahmed Resmi, ventured to send a "council treaty" (layiha) to Muhsinzâde, grand vizier of the time, expressly recommending that the empire be maintained within the defined borders and condemning dreams of excessive expansion.[8]

THE DEFENSIVE SYSTEMS

Rejected by both parties on principle, the Islamic-Christian border was a militarized border or, to borrow the expression that would be used for the Habsburg border after the Treaty of Karlowitz, a "military border" (Militärgrenze). It was not a continuous rampart over the entire length of the border, a "Great Wall of China"; rather, more complex defense systems appeared on several key segments of it. These were a combination of major fortresses several lines deep, built of stone, and following whenever possible the most modern principles of military architecture (the trace italienne, or bastioned fortress), and of a whole set of forts and guard posts possessing more rudimentary and much less burdensome alert systems. Such was the case for the stockades (palanques; the word, like the object itself, existed on both sides of the Hungarian border): forts surrounded by a defensive wall made of tree trunks into which loopholes had been cut, encircled by a moat. Such structures existed on the Ottoman as well as the Christian side, sometimes separated by very large distances, as in the steppes of the Black Sea. In both cases, depending on the circumstances, they could have an offensive as well as a defensive role: they were used as a base for launching occasional harassment raids in the Kleinkrieg but also for operations of greater scope in times of declared war. The border was never inert, even when, officially, it was peacetime. The very existence of a permanent military presence meant that local incidents would invariably break out in one place or another. In 1567, for example, Emperor Maximilian was moving toward peace with the Turks, yet he nevertheless wrote to one of his officers, captain of the fortress of Kiskomáron, south of Lake Balaton: "Keep your soldiers at the ready as if there were no peace at all."[9]

THE HABSBURG BORDER

In the center of Europe, the need to build a barrier against the Ottoman advance emerged in the fourteenth and fifteenth centuries. Sigismund of Luxemburg, king of Hungary, set in place a system whose cornerstone was Belgrade (Nándorfehérvár), ceded by George Branković, the despot of Serbia. One of his successors, King Matthias Corvinus (1458–1490), reorganized that old defense system to make it more coherent and unified. It was now divided into three sectors: to the west, the sector of Croatia-Dalmatia and Slavonia, placed under the authority of a single commander, or *ban*; in the center, a second sector called Lower Danube, under the authority of the "captain general of the lower regions of the kingdom of Hungary"; and finally, to the east, a third unit of defense under the authority of the voivode of Transylvania. Farther back from the border, the system was complemented by two other parallel fortress systems.

The conquest of Belgrade by Süleyman the Magnificent in 1521 dealt a fatal blow to that system. A few decades later, Ogier Ghiselin de Busbecq, Ferdinand of Habsburg's ambassador, would draw a military lesson from that event, which he judged key: "It is clear that this event threw open the flood-gates and admitted the tide of troubles in which Hungary is now engulfed. Its first approach involved the death of King Louis, the capture of Buda, the enslavement of Transylvania, the overthrow of a flourishing kingdom, and an alarm among neighboring nations lest the same fate should befall them also." And he concluded: "These events ought to be a lesson to the princes of Christendom and make them realize that, if they wish to be safe, they cannot be too careful in securing their fortifications and strongholds against the enemy."[10] But in the wake of 1521, it appeared that the kingdom of Hungary, threatened by such an adversary, did not have the means to assure its own defense. In a sense, Hungary had to "internationalize" it. The young king, Louis II Jagellon, appealed for the support of one more powerful than he, his brother-in-law and ally, Ferdinand of Habsburg, Charles V's younger brother. Ferdinand was archduke of Austria, and, after Louis II's accidental death, he would become king of Hungary and Bohemia. During the siege of Belgrade, he sent thousands of Germanic foot soldiers from the hereditary possessions of the Habsburgs to rescue the city. The Ottomans were victorious. In 1522, King Louis II granted Peter Berislavić, *ban* of Croatia (Croatia had been associated with Hungary by a personal union since 1102), permission to entrust the defense of the Croatian border to Ferdinand, which made Habsburg a de facto suzerain of Croatia. Subsequently, on January 1, 1527, following on the Battle of Mohács, Ferdinand was elected king of Croatia, in exchange for the pledge to defend the country against the Turks. So began the organization of the Habsburg border of Croatia, which would serve as a prototype for the very long Habsburg border generally. The line of that Croatian border with the Turks remained almost unaltered until the Treaty of Berlin in 1878, which would change the rules of the game by placing Bosnia-Herzegovina under Austrian administration. As for the Hungarian part of the border, it was first drawn with the tripartition of the kingdom in 1541: the center became an Ottoman province; the east a principality of Transylvania, vassal of the Ottomans; and the north and west a "Royal Hungary" in the hands of the Habsburgs. At that date, the border began east of the Maros and Temes valleys, then followed the northern edge of the Hungarian great plain to the center and southwest of Transdanubia, finally reaching Slavonia. But unlike the Croatian border, the Hungarian border, nibbled away by the Turks, continued to evolve during the rest of the sixteenth and seventeenth centuries. At the same time, the Habsburgs came to emphasize the Christian and therefore transnational character of the enormous border, which they defended over hundreds of kilometers, from the Carpathians to the Adriatic. In particular, the needs of a centralized organization impelled them to "denationalize" or "exterritorialize," and also to Germanize, the corresponding zones. German subsidies, obtained with some difficulty from the diets of the Reich, in large part financed that system. It was therefore not only the populations directly threatened or actually affected by the Turkish peril but others as well, across *Mitteleuropa* as a whole, who assumed the tax burden. The argument given to those for whom the peril was more remote tended to be more religious than national.

The agricultural zones entrusted to settlers behind the lines of fortresses, as well as the fortresses themselves, now escaped the influence of the magnates and traditional institutions, both Croatian and Hungarian. The Habsburgs placed them under Austrian military authority, which, as of 1556, took the form of the Wiener Hofkriegsrat, or Consilium Bellicum. That war council, established in Vienna, assumed the centralized command and military administration of the Turkish border, and also oversaw diplomatic relations with Istanbul. A bureau of experts and an administration, which developed over time and split into specialized bureaus, aided the council. Prince Eugene of Savoy, champion of the fight against the Turks in the late seventeenth and early eighteenth centuries (his martial statue would later be erected in front of the Habsburg Palace on Castle Hill), was war council president from 1703 to 1736. As of 1578, there was also a War Council of Inner Austria (*Inner-Österreichischer Hofkriegsrat*), established in Gratz until 1705, which controlled the border of Croatia and Slavonia.

The Hungarian and Croatian troops were not sufficient to cover the border, and the Habsburgs, like the authorities in charge of the other segments of the border with the Turks, and like the Turks themselves, were obliged to use every means at their disposal. As Sigismund of Luxemburg had done in his time, they used Orthodox Serbian settlers (*Soldatenbauer*) and many kinds of religious dissidents. Those attending the large military conference held in Vienna in 1577 even planned to establish the Teutonic Order in Hungary, which seemed logical, since that order, created in the Holy Land during the Crusades, had been installed in Prussia in the thirteenth century to fight the pagan Slavs. They never realized that plan, but they did establish German mercenaries alongside other elements in the Hungarian fortresses. That presence elicited the sharpest of criticisms from the diets of Hungary, which considered the Germans even more barbarous than the Turks. The crimes and impieties they attributed to them reached the level of atrocities. The "remonstrances" (*gravamina*) of the Diet of 1662 portrayed these German mercenaries as follows: "Against the peasants they have perpetrated homicide, torture, rape, even murder following rape, such that they have committed worse violence than the Turks. They have not even respected the sacred character of the churches but have acted out their guilty passions on prepubescent minors who took refuge in these churches; they even went so far as to cut children to pieces and threw others into the fire."[11] If these words are not merely an expression of xenophobia and the violence actually went that far—if, that is, some chose the churches to indulge in their abominations—we must believe that undesirables could be found on the ramparts of Christendom!

THE SEA BORDERS

Alert systems as well as forts and bastions were also set up on the coasts and islands, which the opposing fleets and pirates of all sorts threatened. In its *Stato da mare*, Venice especially undertook impressive fortification projects with state-of-the-art technology against the Turks. But that statement must be qualified, since one of Venice's finest accomplishments, the citadel of Nicosia in Cyprus, fell into the hands of the Turkish besiegers within two months; by contrast, the siege of Famagusta, which did not benefit from the same technical advances, lasted no fewer than eleven months.

In the marine zones, the notion of border was obviously hazier, and defense meant primarily control of strategic points.

In that sense, the entrances to the straits leading to Istanbul represented an essential "border" for the Ottomans. The first fortresses they built on the Bosphorus before the taking of Constantinople—Anadolu Hisārı, constructed by Bayezid I in 1394, and Rūmeli Hisārı, built by Mehmed II in 1452—were intended to blockade the Bosphorus and thus prevent any rescue by sea of the

besieged Byzantines. Once the city was captured, the sultan was anxious to preserve it from all external aggression. The threat came primarily by sea, usually from the eastern Mediterranean and the Aegean, since the Black Sea was
becoming an "Ottoman lake." Under these conditions, it was the entrance to
the Dardanelles especially that the conqueror was anxious to fortify, building
new fortresses on either side of the strait: Kal'e-i Sultāniye in Asia, near ancient
Abydos; and Kilid al-Bahr on the European coast. He also had the island of
Tenedos (Bozcaada) fortified. Süleyman the Magnificent would again restore
the two castles in the Dardanelles in 1551, but they gradually fell into neglect in
the late sixteenth and seventeenth centuries, since the decline of Venice left few
worries in that regard. By contrast, during the War of Crete, they once again
became a very sensitive zone. Mehmed II's two castles were again restored and
two new forts built at the entrance to the Aegean Sea: Sedd al-Bahr on the European bank and Kum Kal'e on the Asian side. During the Russo-Ottoman War
of 1768–1774, because the Russians had entered the Mediterranean, there was
a need for two new forts on the banks of the Dardanelles. A French volunteer
of Hungarian origin, Baron François de Tott, supervised their construction.[12]

In the meantime, the outlet of the Bosphorus onto the Black Sea had in turn
become a "border" to be defended: the danger began to appear in the early
seventeenth century, as a result of the sudden appearance in the strait of a new
and bold adversary engaged in worrisome exploits, the Cossacks of Ukraine.
To parry these blows, Sultan Murad IV built two new fortresses on either bank
of the Bosphorus, at its extremity, near the two present-day castles of Rūmeli
Kavağı and Anadolu Kavağı. Evliya Çelebi calls them the "padlocks of the sea"
(*Kilid al-Bahr kal'eler*).

With the rise of the Russian threat, which became in the eighteenth century
the chief peril to the empire's integrity, that end of the Bosphorus became the
most sensitive point of the Ottoman borders. In the Russo-Ottoman War of
1768–1771, even though the Russian fleet appeared in the Mediterranean and
not the Black Sea, the Ottomans felt the need to reorganize the defense of the
Bosphorus by building new fortifications on both its banks, and at the entrance
to the Black Sea. Selim III (1789–1807) would further develop and improve that
new defense system, known as the "seven fortresses" (*kilā'-i seb'a*).

THE BORDER OF THE TATARS

The mention of the Cossack incursions and of the Russian advance in the Black
Sea brings us back to another segment of the Islamic-Christian front in Europe,
the northeastern one. It was less visible than the Habsburg front because less
central to Europe, but it was also a theater for centuries-old confrontations in
the name of the Cross and the Crescent. In that enormous zone delimited to the
north by the fringes of the taiga, to the south by the Black Sea, to the west by

the Lower Danube, and to the east by the Volga, the conflict between Islam and
Christendom (Catholic and Orthodox) predated the Ottomans. It went back to
the Islamization of the Golden Horde, itself a legacy of the Mongol conquest of
the region. In 1475, Sultan Mehmed II became the suzerain of the Tatar khanate of Crimea, which had emerged some decades earlier from the dismantled
Golden Horde. In addition, the Ottomans would have direct access to a certain
number of strongholds and territories south of that entity, at the mouths of the
great rivers on the north side of the Black Sea. The kingdom of Poland and the
grand duchy of Lithuania, joined by the Union of Lublin in 1569, and the grand
principality of Moscow, which would gradually become the empire of the tsars,
stood opposite that Muslim region, beyond the steppes. Within that natural
environment, Muslim and Christian states were separated not by a more or less
linear border but by huge, almost unpopulated and undeveloped spaces. These
were the "wildlands" (*dikoe pole* in Russian; *dzikie pola* in Polish), a land border
that was in many respects more like a sea border. That vast territory would give
rise to the Ukraine, whose very name alludes to the fact that it was a border
(*krai, ukraina*).

North of that zone, Poland and Lithuania built a line of fortresses designed
to protect the southern border zones of their territories. These were the cities
of Bar, Kanev, Braslaw, Vinnitsa, Wlodzimierz, Kiev (former capital of the first
Russia), Kamenec, and Chmielnick. Farther to the northeast, the Muscovites
also built their line of fortresses between Bolhov and Tambov, but from the
sixteenth century on, that border began to advance to the south.

These fortresses were in the hands of representatives of great noble families,
who were both military governors (starosts) and very large property owners.
Included among these great Polish-Lithuanian names were the Sanguszkos, the
Sienawskis, the Ostrogskis, the Prońskis, and the Wiśniowieckis (Višniaveckis).
Some, such as a noble from Silesia, Bernard Pretwicz, starost of Bar, would
become semilegendary heroes in the fight against the Turks and the Tatars. In
1552, Süleyman the Magnificent expressly requested that Pretwicz be removed.
King Sigismund Augustus gave the sultan satisfaction, transferring the troublemaker to Trembowla, a stronghold farther from the border. But other champions of the anti-Turkish struggle immediately replaced Pretwicz on the border.

Altogether south of that zone, where the great rivers flow into the Black
Sea, stood the Ottoman fortresses: Kili (Chilia) on the Lower Danube, and
Aqkerman (Cetatea-Albă, Belgorod Dniestrovskij) on the Lower Dniester, both
conquered by Bayezid II; Bender (Tighina), farther upstream on the Dniester,
annexed by Süleyman; and Jankerman (Özü, Ochakov, Ochakiv) on the Lower
Dnieper, built by the khan of Crimea between 1492 and 1495 and occupied
by the Ottomans in 1538. To these were added Kefe (Caffa, Feodosija) and the
other Ottoman fortresses on the southern and southeastern coast of Crimea;
Kersh and Taman on the Cimmerian Bosphorus (the strait between the Black
Sea and the Sea of Azov); and, in the Sea of Azov, Azov (Azak) at the mouth of

the Don, which the Ottomans and the Russians would fight over from the end of the seventeenth century to the Treaty of Kuchuk Kaynarja in 1774.

As for the khanate of Crimea, it was within the purview of a tribal and clan organization and was based on a plunder economy. The Tatar hordes would raid the villages and cities on the border to bring back booty, especially slaves, who supplied the Ottoman market. Caffa was the hub of that traffic, as it had been in the Genoese period. The frequency and intensity of the raids were a function of the relations between the khan on one hand, the king of Poland and the prince of Moscow on the other. Depending on the period, the khan was sometimes the ally of Poland, sometimes that of Russia. The payment of a tribute governed these alliances; to the extent that it was actually paid, it served to compensate the loss of revenue resulting from the reduction in the number of raids. Beginning in 1513, therefore, Crimea was allied with Poland-Lithuania against Moscow, in exchange for the Polish king's pledge to pay an annual tribute of fifteen thousand florins, so that, as Khan Muhammad Giray wrote, "his kingdom may be spared."[13] There was nothing absolute about the guarantee, however, since the khan was far from in control of all that activity, which stemmed in large measure from a constellation of autonomous actors. As Khan Mengli Giray wrote to King Alexander Jagellon in 1506, in response to the king's complaints: "Hungry people, when they are on horseback, must feed themselves wherever they can find food." In addition, some Tatar groups were entirely independent of the khan. Wandering nomads north of the Black Sea, they are designated in the sources by the names of the Ottoman fortresses that they used, as needed, for bases and refuges.

As a result of all that, the "politics of the steppes" cannot be reduced to a binary confrontation between Islam and Christendom; it was the result of a complex game between protagonists acting at different levels. The rulers might be at peace, as the sultan and the king of Poland were continuously for the greater part of the sixteenth century, but that in no way prevented local actors—Polish-Lithuanian great lords on the border, Ottoman pashas or the chiefs of Tatar hordes, all at great distances from their respective capitals—from having their own interests and objectives. In fact, they had the upper hand in a very active *Kleinkrieg*, whose end was unlikely, particularly since the raids of one camp came in response to those of another.

A BORDER EPIC: THE COSSACKS

A new phenomenon emerged from a desire to respond effectively to the raids of the Tatars by returning them in kind: "Cossackry," or at least, the use the Polish-Lithuanian defense would make of the Cossacks.

The term "Cossack" comes from a Turkish word, *kazak*, which designates a dissident, a rebel, a bandit. It is especially used in the Ottoman sources to designate the groups of Tatars independent from the khan. And just as there were Muslim *kazak*, there would be Christian Cossacks. Within that context, the term was first applied to elements at odds with the established order of feudal society, particularly peasants fleeing the exploitation and oppression of the Polish-Lithuanian magnates. These dissidents settled, seasonally or permanently from the start, in the no-man's-land separating the Christian borders from the Tatar regions. Historians differ a great deal about the origins—in reality fairly obscure—of the phenomenon, and their respective interpretations are usually not devoid of ulterior motives, whether ideological, national, or social. In any event, the migrants took refuge particularly in what was called Niz, the Dnieper Valley beyond the river rapids. There they engaged in a kind of ideal life, rugged to be sure, but free and virile, combining hunting, fishing, the harvesting of honey, and out-and-out banditry. They lived in small groups but could also band together for actions on a larger scale, under the authority of charismatic leaders from their ranks or, paradoxically, under great border lords. Relations were ambiguous between the border nobility and these dissidents, who called into question the established order and, when necessary, struck blows to it, but who in other respects represented a labor force invaluable for opposing the Tatar raids. The Cossacks themselves could not be totally at odds with the interior, on which they remained dependent, if only for their necessary supplies of arms and gunpowder. In addition, once their leaders began to emerge, the Polish model of nobility did not fail to exert its attraction on them. The best illustration of these ambiguities is provided by a case that has greatly divided historians, that of the Lithuanian prince (of the Orthodox faith) Dimitrij Višniavecki, who was also the prototype for Bayda, the hero of Ukrainian popular tales.[14] Named starost of Kanev and Cherkasy by the king of Poland, Višniavecki was, in the 1550s and 1560s, one of the most visible successors of Bernard Pretwicz in the fight against the Tatars. In August and September 1556, he traveled down the Dnieper at the head of a private army and occupied the island of Malaja Hortica, fifteen kilometers south of the last rapids. There he built a fortress, the first milestone in the "camp" (*seč*) of Zaporogue Cossacks, or "Cossacks of the rapids," which somewhat later was set up on another island in the Dnieper, Tomakovka, some sixty kilometers farther south. The *seč* became a base for launching Cossack raids, whose troops were now more rigorously organized and structured. The Zaporogue army included regiments subdivided into tens and hundreds. Each regiment elected delegates to a council that itself chose a supreme leader, designated by two partly homophonic terms: *hetman* (from the German *Hauptmann*) and *ataman* (an old Turkish term).[15] The many lexical borrowings from the Turko-Tatars only illustrate the Cossacks' extensive imitation of their antagonists. They resembled each other, in fact, but only to better stand in contrast: it was said that any man who presented himself to the hetman to become a Cossack would be accepted only after a ritual consisting primarily of making the (Orthodox) sign of the cross.

After the major Tatar raid against Moscow in 1571, conducted by Khan Devlet Giray I, as a result of which the Russian capital was partly destroyed, not only Russia but the Poland of King Stephen Báthory felt the need to secure their hold over the Cossacks. They organized a new defense system that included guard posts manned by a special category of "Cossacks" who were better controlled by the states, the "registered Cossacks" (reestrovye). Relatively effective against the Tatar raids, they were more or less docile and maintained shifting relationships with the "true" Cossacks. The last two decades of the sixteenth century and the first four of the seventeenth century were the golden age of Cossack military power—a stateless army that had become an insuperable factor in regional policy. Their actions occurred by land and by sea. They had always been skillful at moving across the great rivers of the steppe, but in about 1600, they equipped themselves with an actual fleet of vessels, small but sturdy and easy to handle, by means of which they increased the number of their brilliant exploits. Venturing into the Black Sea, they attacked the Ottoman ports: Varna, on the Bulgarian coast, was plundered in 1614; Sinop, in northern Anatolia, met the same fate in 1614. At the same time, they momentarily occupied another neighboring stronghold, Trabzon (Trebizond), and attacked Beykoz, on the Bosphorus on the outskirts of Istanbul. The Cossacks seemed ready to repeat the assaults of the old Varegues against the walls of Constantinople in the early Middle Ages. In the early seventeenth century, the hetman Peter Sahaidchany, originally from western Galicia, fled Poland to seek refuge in Cossack territory, where he ultimately imposed his supreme authority. Like Višniavecki before him, he became a hero of legend, the inspiration for many anecdotes. (In one of these, extenuating circumstances led him to exchange his wife for a pipe and tobacco.) In 1617, he supported Poland in its war against Moscow, which earned him the position of commander of the "registered Cossacks." An indefatigable actor in the struggle against the Tatars on the steppe, he seized Ottoman Kefe in 1616 and took the opportunity to liberate the Christian slaves there. During the 1621 Ottoman campaign of Osman II in Khotyn, he again took Poland's side. But the emergence of that new power was ultimately a danger for Poland and for the Ottomans, though they did not fully realize it for some time. The two states therefore agreed to prevent the Cossacks from becoming in their turn a state that would disrupt the political balance of the region. The Ottomans, however, who had only limited confidence in the capacity for Polish resistance, did not believe they could forgo organizing a new defense system north of the Black Sea, rehabilitating some of their old fortresses and constructing new ones. Moreover, they placed the forts and cities of Bujak (the region between the mouth of the Danube and that of the Dniester) under the authority of a Nogay Tatar leader, Kantemir Mirza. In addition, the energetic Murad IV, wishing to increase his control over a khan of Crimea still inclined to shake off Ottoman tutelage, in 1624 dismissed Khan Muhammad Giray and named as his successor another member of the dynasty, Janibeg Giray, who had been waiting in the wings on the island of Rhodes. Yet Muhammad Giray refused to give in and attempted to remain in place. To carry out that bold plan to defy the Porte, he and his brother, the *qalgha* Shahin Giray, concluded an accord with the Zaporogue Cossacks in December 1624. The sultan seems to have yielded. The episode is noteworthy, since for once, these two buffer forces, Tatars and Cossacks, similar in nature and antagonistic in principle, came together, while the two "established" states, seeing their creatures about to escape their control, united to stop them. The Ottomans played their trump card, the Nogay leader Kantimir Mirza, against the rebel khan and once more removed Muhammad Giray. He and his brother tried again to resist by taking refuge in Poland, where they formed an army of forty thousand men, composed of Tatars but also of Polish adventurers and Zaporogue Cossacks. The two rebels were finally defeated. As a result, the khans of Crimea would more than ever be under the sway of the sultan of Istanbul, who appointed and dismissed them as he liked, until the Treaty of Kuchuk Kaynarja imposed the autonomy of Crimea, a prelude to the Russian takeover. As for the Cossacks, Poland and then Russia went on subjugating them. In 1638, the Polish armies, aided by the "registered Cossacks," stamped out the most intractable elements of Cossackry and eliminated their institutions. A large number of Zaporogue Cossacks then took refuge on the left bank of the Dnieper. There they came into contact with other Cossacks, known as the Don Cossacks. Finally, at the instigation of their hetman, Bohdan Khmelnicki, they came under the control of Russia, by the terms of the Treaty of Perejaslav (1654).

OTHER BORDER RESIDENTS: FROM ANTAGONISM TO IMITATION

This brief glimpse of the Cossacks has shown that their history is highly revealing of the complexities and ambiguities of the Islamic-Christian border. The inexpiable and chronic struggles for which that border was the theater were no doubt waged in the name of two antagonistic religions, but political interests inextricably combined with them: the lords of the Polish-Lithuanian border had irredentist aims on the coasts of the Black Sea and conducted their own policy, in concert with the Habsburgs when necessary. That policy was officially at odds with the one announced by the Polish Crown, which was compelled to exercise caution toward its troublesome neighbor. The Crown, however, did not neglect to give these lords their approval and support, but by necessity in secret. Economic interests were also present, since there was booty to be had on either side, and on this point the Cossacks and their potential silent partners among the nobility were not to be outdone by the Tatars.

At the same time, each of the two camps, in violent opposition with each other, was far from being as united as the Manichaean model of confrontation would suggest. On the Christian side, tensions existed not only between the

Russian and Polish states but also between Catholics and those of the Orthodox faith. At the social level, that is, between lords and peasants, these conflicts lay at the very heart of Cossackry, even if the movement was later co-opted to a certain degree.

The Muslim camp was also not unified. Grafted onto the Ottoman-Tatar tensions were all sorts of conflicts among the Tatars themselves: rivalries between members of the ruling clan and rivalries between tribes, as illustrated by the episode involving Kantemir Mirza, the ally of the Ottomans against the ruling Giray branch. These fissures on both sides opened the way for a complex play of alliances and oppositions that was not always overridden by the fundamental Islam/Christendom cleavage.

In addition, the Cossacks were the emblematic embodiment of a phenomenon—the one, perhaps, that left the most traces in Europe's collective memory (though we must take care to remember that each region of Europe has its specific memory)—that existed more or less, in various forms and with diverse fates, along every segment of the Islamic-Christian border in Europe.

As for the Habsburg border in Croatia and Slavonia, it too was separated from the Turkish lines by a no-man's-land similar to the Polish *dzikie pola*, though on a smaller scale. These were called the *nicija zemlja* ("empty lands"). They resulted from the border raids by Turkish forces but also from the scorched-earth policy conducted on both sides. Refugees leaving the territories ruled by the Turks came to settle on these marches near the Habsburg lines. They were given the name "Uskoks" (from a Croatian verb *uskociti*, meaning "to move by successive leaps"). They were primarily Serbs and Vlachs. (These Romanian-speaking Vlachs were also called "Arumanians" or "Kutsovlachs" or "Tsintsars.") The authorities granted them peasant holdings on uncultivated lands and on the prairies. In 1538, Ferdinand of Habsburg exempted them from paying taxes for twenty years, in exchange for their services guarding the border, and granted them the right to collect a third of the booty recovered from the Turks. Each Uskok captain had to maintain a standing army of two hundred settler-soldiers.

Over time, various elements joined these first Uskoks, not only Serbs and Vlachs from the Ottoman Balkans but also—moving us closer to the origins of the Cossacks—outlaws and peasants fleeing the oppression of the Hungarian and Croatian magnates in order to live under a different social arrangement. Their base cell was the *zadruga*, a community of members united by blood ties, collectively using goods held jointly and sharing the revenues among themselves. Several communities formed a village, which elected its own civil and military leaders. The rights and obligations of these "border guards" (*Grenzer, Granicari*) was ratified and elaborated in the very exhaustive charter on the military borders of Slavonia and Croatia, issued in 1630 by Emperor Ferdinand II, the *statuta Valachorum*. The term *harami*, an Arabic word meaning "outlaw" or "bandit," transmitted by the Ottomans, was used to designate these communities, whose military leader bore the Slavic title "voivode." Several "haramīs" formed a "kapitanat," commanded by a *kapitan*, who was under the "border general."

In addition to these land Uskoks on the Croatian border, there were maritime Uskoks along the edge of the other border zone, the Adriatic. Their base was the fortress of Senj (Segna), an aerie overlooking the sea. Some of these maritime Uskoks also came from the Ottoman territories, which they had fled, but others were from the Habsburg possessions and from Venice. Like the Cossacks, they were ardent defenders of Christianity and the inveterate enemies of Islam, but they would sometimes attack and pillage the ships of Christians living under the sultan's rule or in Venice. They justified themselves by arguing that these were bad Christians who collaborated with the infidel. They were officially dependents of the Habsburgs, but Venice sought to contain them, so as not to incite disputes with the Ottomans detrimental to its commercial interests.[16]

The Ottomans, of course, also had corsairs in the Adriatic. Intended on principle to respond to the attacks of the Uskoks, they did not overlook an opportunity to take the initiative. Nor did either side forgo attacking ships from their own camp on occasion. Similarly, when the two opposing camps wanted to settle their quarrels and enter a phase of peace, their respective corsair auxiliaries, deaf to all diplomatic considerations, continued to obstruct commerce and to precipitate incidents. They thus became a nuisance, against whom the two camps now united. For example, the minutes of a hearing held by the judge (*nā'ib*) of the fortress of Nova record that the representatives of Venice and those of the sultan reached an agreement to compensate merchants and other victims of corsairs, dependents of each of the two parties, as well as victims of Montenegro bandits (*Karadağ eshkiyaları*).[17] On the Hungarian border as well, the Habsburgs had to be very pragmatic in resolving the question of labor power. They appealed to German mercenaries, to the great displeasure of the populations they were supposed to protect, since in reality the Germans perpetrated the worst misdeeds. In addition, as their predecessors had already done in the fifteenth century, the Habsburgs recruited shepherds and serfs for their border needs. As in the previous cases, these elements were designated by a term of Turkish origin meaning "bandit": they were hajduks (Turkish, *haydut*). It is quite true that they often became bandits. In 1604, Stephen Bocskai, future prince of Transylvania, used that labor pool in his rebellion against the Habsburgs. Once his victory was assured, he fulfilled the promise he had made to the hajduks who had supported him: by the terms of an agreement reached with Vienna in 1610, he relocated them to the plain around Debreczen, where they would enjoy a great deal of autonomy. In 1608, the Hungarian diet recognized their privileges in exchange for the performance of military service for the king. Thereby established on the border of Ottoman Hungary and Transylvania, they maintained small strongholds between the course of the Tisza and the Transylvanian border. These elements, however, were overseen by Calvinist preachers and welcomed fugitive peasants, whom they refused to hand over. Once again, the Islamic-Christian border, by virtue of the need for troops to which it gave rise, became, with the complicity of the border officers, a social escape route for those in the hinterland and the site of an "alternative" society.

Another famous episode in the history of these communities with a special status, established on the border between the Habsburg Empire and the Ottoman, was linked to the wave of Serbian emigration in 1690. In 1689, the imperial army, having recovered Hungary, had broken through the Ottoman defense and penetrated into Serbia and Bosnia. Many Serbs had taken the side of the invaders and conducted guerrilla warfare against their Ottoman masters. Their religious leader, Patriarch of Peć Arsenio III Crnojević, after hesitating between placing himself under the protection of Venice or under that of Emperor Leopold I, finally opted for Leopold. On April 16, 1690, Leopold published a proclamation in which he asserted his desire to restore the ancestral freedoms of all peoples who were his subjects in his capacity as king of Hungary. He especially promised to ensure freedom of religion. That pledge favored the uprising of the Orthodox Serbians and Albanians, the sultan's subjects, by mooting their reservations about a regime known for its militant Catholicism. As a result, the imperial armies suffered setbacks that obliged them to retreat. The Serbian patriarch also decided on withdrawal, taking along a portion of his people, though their number is in dispute: he himself spoke of forty thousand families. They went first to Belgrade—in June 1690—a city the imperial forces still held. But the Ottomans recaptured Belgrade on October 9. The Ottoman victory forced the patriarch and his flock to negotiate with Leopold a move to Habsburg territory. On August 21, 1690, the emperor published a first diploma—others would follow in subsequent years—laying the foundations for Serbian autonomy, particularly in religious matters, in a kingdom of Hungary that had come under Habsburg domination. The Serbian peasant soldiers escaped the unbridled tax exactions of the noble large landowners and did not pay tithes to the Catholic clergy. They dedicated the equivalent sum to supporting their own clergy. The Hungarian magnates and the episcopate did not fail to protest these privileges. In addition, on May 1, 1694, the War Council of Vienna decided that the Serbs would receive lands in "Cumania," that is, between the Danube and the Tisza. After that, the Serbs came to populate the regions, desert at the time, of that zone along the Danube, from the lower Tisza and the Maros to the border with the Ottomans.

Since there were Serbs on the Ottoman side of that border as well, here, as along the border of Slavonia-Croatia, the Serbian people were split in two by the great fracture. Initially, the Serbian patriarch was also installed on the border, at the Krushedol Monastery (about fifty kilometers northwest of Belgrade), among his people. But in 1701, he received the order to move to Szentendre (about twenty kilometers north of Buda), this time far from his flock.

THE OTTOMAN BORDER GUARDS

On the Ottoman side of the border of central Europe, there were no exact equivalents of the Uskoks of Croatia or the hajduks of Hungary, but there was a similar need felt to complement the regular units (Janissaries sent from the capital, *sipāhī* who held local timars) by elements recruited, with extreme pragmatism, at the local level. A corps of "local Janissaries" (*yerli kul*) thus formed, made up of Islamized South Slavs and in particular, of emancipated slaves (*azadlu*). Another corps, the *'azab*, posted to the fortress garrisons but participating in naval expeditions as well, also recruited from among the local Slav peasants. Originally Christians, they usually—but not always—became Muslims. A Ragusan witness thus wrote to Emperor Maximilian I in the early sixteenth century, "possunt esse Assapi tam christiani quam Turcae et aliae nationes."[18] As for the corps of *martolos*, present in many Ottoman border fortresses, they were still composed primarily of Christians, though they included converts to Islam, and their officers, the aghas, were Muslims. They also displayed another similarity to the *Grenzener* on the other side: although some received pay, others were peasant soldiers whose land holdings had a special status, exempting them from most agricultural royalties. It is possible that, on this side as well, the Serbs were organized into extended family communities of the *zadruga* type. Ottoman regulations specified that those of their brothers and nephews who did not perform military service were not exempt from the ordinary agricultural royalties.[19]

THE BARBARY CORSAIRS

The acquisitions in North Africa of Süleyman the Magnificent and Selim II had made the coasts of Tunis, Algiers, and Tripoli an Ottoman border. This time, the western Mediterranean constituted the buffer zone with the Christian states. As on other borders, local representatives of the central power, from which they were far removed, had a tendency to conduct their own policies, which did not always coincide with that of the center. But things went farther here than elsewhere: the former provinces became quasi-independent states, though they never completely cut the umbilical cord attaching them to Istanbul. Like the other border regions, the "regencies" had at their disposal a labor force in the "intermediate buffer zone." This time they were Barbary corsairs.[20] Like the other "border men," these corsairs were unpredictable (opportunity could turn them into common pirates) and their motivations were mixed: they fought in the name of Islam, and it has been noted that the resentment of Muslims, then of the Moriscos driven from Spain, played a role in the growth of privateering and in the trafficking to which it gave rise.[21] At the same time, privateering and its booty were also their source of revenue, an alternative to regular commerce.²² The corsair captains and their own captains, like the officers of the Maghrebian *ojak*, occasionally rose from the ranks of these "renegades," whose Islamization generally took place for opportunistic reasons and did not always withstand every test. (But woe to those "Christians of Allah" if they returned to Christendom and fell into the clutches of the Inquisition!) Among the renegades were emancipated slaves, but also, since here again the border served as an escape valve, dissidents of all kinds who had an interest in fleeing Christendom: dissatisfied soldiers or sailors, peasants oppressed by their lords, habitual offenders and other outlaws, merchants in quest of brighter opportunities, and any specialist willing to cash in on his knowledge or expertise. There was no dearth of Venetians, Genoese, Sicilians, Calabrians, Neopolitans, Corsicans, and sometimes even Jews, who would "become Turks" and try their luck in Tunis, Algiers, or Tripoli. In part 1 of his *Don Quixote* (chaps. 39–41), Cervantes recounts that the bey of Algiers, a certain Hasan Pasha, demonstrated his friendship to the author during his captivity in the Barbary port— and that bey was a Dalmatian who had converted to Islam. Another famous example is the man who became bey of Tunis in 1637. The founder of a dynasty, the Muradids, which would rule the regency until the early eighteenth century, he was none other than a Ligurian by the name of Osta Morato. Another celebrated case is that of a Venetian, who would rule Algiers from 1638 to 1645 under the name Ali "Piccinino." Not all had such good fortune, but many of these renegades had astonishing fates: there was also Orzio Paterno Castello, from a noble family of Catana that he was compelled to leave, having killed his wife in a fit of jealousy. During his escape, he was captured by corsairs from Tripoli, and he converted to Islam, taking the name Ahmad. He would become a dragoman (interpreter) in Tripoli.

Beginning in 1650, the renegades who acquired high positions in the regencies were instead "Ponantines," seamen from the north, English and Flemish especially. The corsair threat poisoned Mediterranean navigation and had an impact on every nation. It affected populations who were in a position to see "Turks" only during a sea journey, generally to the greater misfortune of the passengers in question. European literature and theater are full of captives taken by the Barbary corsairs, who in an instant reversed people's best-laid plans and suddenly made the worst outcome seem possible, though not always certain. Molière describes such a fate in *The Bungler*, act 4, scene 7: "In feats of adventure it is common to see / Folks taken by Turkish corsairs at sea." Victims of the corsair attacks were reduced to slavery. How many destinies were thereby altered! They would toil and wallow in prisons, in convict galleys, or in the service of private individuals. The Christian states strove to redeem them, as did charitable institutions and religious orders that specialized in bargaining with the infidel masters. The most important of these were the Order of the Most Holy Trinity, or Trinitarians, founded in France in 1193 by John of Matha and

Felix of Valois, and the Order of Our Lady of Mercy, also called the Mercedarians, which Pedro Nolasco founded in Barcelona in 1203. But the slaves who were redeemed after a more or less prolonged captivity were in the minority. According to the estimate of Emanuel of Aranda, a Flemish gentleman soldier and himself a captive in Algiers, 600,000 Christians died in captivity in Algiers between 1536 and 1640.[23] Considering the Maghrebian slave trade as a whole between 1530 and 1640, a Trinitarian, Father Dan, declared: "It would not be stretching the truth to say that they [the Maghrebis] have put more than a million [Christians] in chains."[24]

Algiers was the principal center of the slave trade, but all the cities of the Barbary Coast between Sale and Tripoli participated in it. In the hundred years between 1580 and 1680, there were on average some twenty-seven thousand of these Christian slaves in Algiers (there would be fewer subsequently). At the same time, there were some six thousand in Tunis and perhaps two thousand in Tripoli. The grand total for these estimates nearly corresponds to the figures Father Dan indicates on that somber balance sheet:

> As to the slaves of both sexes that are in Barbary today, there are a quantity of them from all the Christian nations, such as France, Italy, Spain, Germany, Flanders, Holland, Greece, Hungary, Poland, Slovenia, Russia, and so forth. The number of these poor captives reaches about thirty-six thousand, according to the enumeration that I have carried out on the spot and to the records that have been furnished and sent to me by the Christian Consuls who live in the Corsair Cities.[25]

Such a grave phenomenon mortgaged the entire economic and social life of many coastal zones, such as those of Valencia, Andalusia, the Balearic Islands, Campania, and Sicily. But it also poisoned navigation as a whole, in both the western and eastern basins of the Mediterranean. In addition, in the late sixteenth and seventeenth centuries, the Maghrebis ventured as far as the Atlantic and into the English Channel. They then abducted their captives from off the coast of Cape Finisterre of Galicia, as well as near Belle Isle and Saint Malo, and even on the Banks of Newfoundland, where the French, Portuguese, and English cod fishermen were threatened. Iceland itself was attacked.[26]

Like all who sailed the Mediterranean, the French were targeted, despite their political alliance with the Great Turk. They thought they could remedy the difficulty by turning to him. Registering complaints with the Sublime Porte about the exactions by Barbary corsairs was a recurring mission of ambassadors to Constantinople. But apart from the fact that the pirates were by nature uncontrollable (like the Cossacks, Tatars, and Uskoks), such measures assumed that the regencies were still altogether an Ottoman frontier, when in fact they had become quasi-independent states. They had to be bargained with or combated directly. That realization came about gradually. By the early seventeenth century, an insidious war took hold between the French fleet and the Maghrebis.

Then, to end privateering, France signed treaties with Algiers in 1628 and 1640; with Tunis in 1665; and again with Algiers in 1666. But since the problems persisted, in the 1680s Louis XIV engaged in gunboat diplomacy against the corsair ports: in July 1681, Abraham Duquesne bombarded the roadstead of Chios, where he had pursued Tripolitan vessels. Algiers was shelled in 1682, 1683, and 1688; Tripoli in 1685. After that repressive phase, France signed a whole series of new treaties: in 1684 and 1689 with Algiers; in 1681 and 1685 with Tripoli. The corsairs of Sale were a special case, necessitating a negotiation with the Moroccan sovereign. A French captain, Lefebvre de la Barre, negotiated a first treaty, but Versailles refused to ratify it. An ambassador of Mawlāy Ismāʿīl named Temim, governor of Tetouan, had to travel to France before Louis XIV would finally sign a treaty, on February 12, 1682. The baron of Saint-Amans brought the text to Morocco, so that Mawlāy Ismāʿīl could ratify it in turn. Nevertheless, French-Moroccan relations rapidly deteriorated. In 1699, a new Moroccan embassy to France, that of Admiral Abdallah Ben-ʿAïcha, attempted to conclude another treaty, but negotiations fell apart.[27] The problem posed by the Barbary corsairs persisted into the eighteenth century, and there were further bombings from time to time.

THE CORSO MALTESE

Elsewhere, however, on that border as on others, the mirror effect was fully at play: Christendom's other response to the exactions of the corsairs was to retaliate in kind against the "Turks." The *corso maltese* was a large-scale privateering operation under the aegis of the Knights of Malta, freed from Ottoman pressure by the failure of the siege of the island in 1565. At the same time, the Knights of Saint Stephen established themselves in Livorno in 1562, at the instigation of the grand duke of Tuscany. That organization survived until the early eighteenth century, under the dual patronage of the grand duke and the eponymous saint. These Christian corsairs engaged in pillaging as well. They took booty and especially slaves, who were sold on the markets of Livorno, Malta, and Genoa. For the most part, Muslim captives were assigned to the various European galley fleets as oarsmen. In a letter to Colbert, the marquise of Nointel, ambassador to Constantinople, cites the figure of two thousand "Turks" rowing on French galleys in 1670 (not all came from the Mediterranean *corso*, however). In 1721, an ambassador of Sultan Ahmed III named Yirmisekiz Çelebi Mehmed Efendi arrived in France with great pomp to see the young Louis XV, having ransomed, at his stop in Malta, a captain by the name of Süleyman held prisoner there. He also brought with him a list of captives in Marseilles and asked the French authorities to liberate them or at least to allow them to be ransomed. The unwillingness he encountered impelled the ambassador to cause a very undiplomatic scene in front of his interlocutor, Minister Dubois:

While you claim to be the best friends of the Most High Empire, you are holding as slaves and in prison more than a thousand of my brothers in the Law. You make them pull the oars on your galleys. What are their crimes? For what reason are they held in that slavery? . . . The Germans, with whom we are sometimes at war and sometimes at peace, deliver our slaves in exchange for ransom. And there are many to whom they give their freedom without demanding anything! I have received from our people requests by which I see that you have them for thirty, thirty-five, forty years of slavery. Why not deliver them?[28]

That incident marred the festivities and undercut the friendly atmosphere. It peremptorily reminded people of something that everything else was intended to make them forget: that Europe was split in two.

CHAPTER 10

BREACHES IN THE CONFLICT

THE IDEOLOGIES WERE ANTAGONISTIC and irreconcilable on both sides. Had it been only the voice of ideology that had spoken during the modern period, the two camps would have remained at a standoff, each on its own side of the border. They would have fallen back into their respective certainties, and the relations between the two would have consisted solely of conflict. Even today, that is how relations between the Turks and Europe are frequently represented. But a study of the facts shows that many dissonant voices could be heard during that time. For both parties or for only one of them, these were the voices of political realism, commercial pragmatism, the appeal of exoticism, technological imitation, Orientalist scholarship, and philosophical speculation. Each of these voices was very different in nature and they should not be confused. Their consequences on the dominant ideology were uneven in their gravity. Some voices did no harm to the ideology because they merely bracketed it temporarily, without destroying it in any way: the ideology remained in the background but was never far off. That would explain, for example, the fluctuations of the most Christian king in his alliance—though very far-reaching—with the Turk, and the fact that the king could be his ally and at the same time loudly rejoice on the occasion of his defeats. It would also explain the intensity of the resentment by the merchant of Marseilles, rankled by the presumptuousness of the customs officer of Smyrna or Aleppo. Other voices were in principle more serious blows to ideology, but their effect remained limited, since only a few people heard them.

THE APORIAS OF ARMED STRUGGLE

The war took various forms. The Ottomans sometimes experienced delays and defeats during their conquests. And their adversaries sometimes took the initiative. Nevertheless, the Ottomans, whatever the ideological and material motivations for their behavior—the lure of booty, hunger for new lands to distribute to dignitaries and warriors—were on the offensive in Europe (and elsewhere), and the Europeans were in a defensive position. Again in the summer of 1577,

the major military conference in Vienna, headquarters for the Consilium Bellicum, in addressing the strategy to adopt toward the Turks, decided to give up
the offensive and opted for the best organized defensive strategy possible. On
the Ottoman side, however, the objective of complete conquest was not of long
duration. A border was established between the Turks and Christendom that
split Europe in two. The sultan had to convert to the reality principle, which
made him aware of the de facto limits of his capacity for action and led him,
in practice if not at the ideological level, to maintain other than belligerent
relations with his European protagonists, to integrate into the European order
instead of annihilating it.

The myth of Ottoman invincibility and indefinite expansion hit several snags,
even when the supremacy of the Sultan of Sultans was still intact. Political momentum and even, to a certain point, the direction of military operations in the
empire were concentrated in the capital, and the principal land and naval forces
were based within a limited zone, the *itch il* (interior of the country), the heart
of the empire. As a result, expeditions were still rigorously seasonal in nature;
distances became a major challenge, which had to be faced under the technical
conditions prevailing at the time, whether of transportation or communications.
Furthermore, difficulties attributable to the climate or terrain aggravated these
conditions. It is striking to observe, in the narratives of the Hungarian campaigns, the degree to which torrential rains, floods, the cold, and scarcity slowed
the advance of the troops, whatever the rather remarkable merits of Ottoman
logistics and supply systems. On the Iranian front, the heat and the dry climate,
along with the laborious crossing of dizzying mountain heights, broke down
the troops' resistance. These factors determined the "range of operation" of the
Ottoman forces and marked their limits. Several defeats resulted more from
these structural factors than from the adversary's efforts. The enemy, having well
understood the Ottoman conqueror's "Achilles' heel," systematically concealed
itself, and, when necessary, adopted a scorched-earth tactic: at the unsuccessful
siege of Vienna in 1529; at the semidefeat in the taking of Nice and at the conquest of Corsica by Franco-Ottoman fleets under the leadership of Barbarossa
and his immediate successors; and at the fiasco of the Astrakhan campaign on
the Volga in 1569. (Let us also note, outside Europe, Selim I's and Süleyman the
Magnificent's failure to conquer the Iranian plateau.) It was that same handicap
that hampered political, military, and economic control of the empire on its pe-
ripheries and forced it to be satisfied with compromise solutions, leaving a more
or less extensive degree of autonomy to vast border areas.

"General Frost," and natural obstacles in general, were not the only impediments to the Turkish advance, since the Turks certainly did not always face a
void. A not inconsiderable enemy, capable of resistance and even of counterof-
fensives, sometimes stood in the way of their plans and gave them trouble. Did
not Süleyman the Magnificent himself—at a time when the empire was supposedly at its apogee—experience moments of extreme irritation and a certain

anxiety, even during a campaign as profitable all in all as the conquest of the Banat of Temesvár in the spring and summer of 1552? He expressed his discontent in an order to Mehmed Pasha, *sanjakbey* of Bosnia, on May 24, 1552:

> Over the course of time, the *gāzi* of the governorate of Bosnia became accustomed to raiding and ravaging the country of the debauched miscreants. They carried out conquests and exploits in great number. They launched incursions and raids of plunder. In short, they were accustomed to imposing defeats of all kinds on the vile miscreants. Why, therefore, do these miscreants now take the license to act and subject the land of Islam [*vilāyet-i islāmiyye seğirdüb*] to incursions, and bring harm and destruction of that order to the subjects living in my well-guarded countries [*memālik-i mahrusen re'āysāsına*]? How is it, then, that measures are not taken to ensure a better defense?[1]

Two weeks later, in June 1552, the sultan exhorted the same *sanjakbey* "not to be negligent or fooled by the ruses and snares of the debauched miscreants, but always to display courage and valor in guarding and protecting the borders."[2] That edginess only became more pronounced when the military situation began to deteriorate further. If we are to believe a letter published in Paris in 1572, the disaster of Lepanto sowed panic in Istanbul. Selim II is reported to have had his treasury moved to Bursa, along with "the women and young male children in the seraglio." He and his Janissaries took refuge in Edirne while the defenses of Istanbul were being reinforced. The Muslim population fled the capital as well, leaving it populated only by Greeks and "Frankish Christians."[3] The Ottoman sources, by contrast, insist on the rapid reconstruction of the fleet, thanks to the sangfroid and energy of Grand Vizier Sokollu Mehmed Pasha.

In the counterattacks to the Ottoman advance, it is not always easy to distinguish between verdicts regarding their "range of operation," which imposed limits on them at a given moment, and the skill of an adversary who learned by experience, who became better organized, more modernized, and stronger. It is likely that, most often, the Ottomans were the victims of both. In any case, their rule was to absorb the blow in silence. They never openly recognized their failures, nor did they admit on principle the existence of their borders. In the official discourse, the *pādishāh* was "always victorious" (*muzaffer dā'imā*), and the enemy remained a contemptible miscreant, "destined for subjugation."

THE MESSAGE OF THE PROPHECIES

If doubts arose, therefore, they did so indirectly, between the lines of the official discourse or in the implicit language of the documentation.

An indirect expression of worry, or of a sense of weakness and vulnerability on the part of the Turks, can be discerned in the prophecies—or "pseudo-prophecies," as Jean Deny calls them—that circulated about them.[4] Of course,

not all the prophecies had the same status, nor do they all allow for the same interpretations. Some in fact came not from the Turks themselves but from their
Christian subjects. The Capuchin Michel Febvre, for example, in his *Present
State of Turkey* (1675), takes note of prophecies in effect in "most of the sects"
(that is, in the Christian faiths present in the Ottoman Empire), claiming that
the king of France would one day be victorious over Turkey. The same author
mentions in another work, *Theater of Turkey* (1682), a prophecy that the Armenians attributed to their fifth-century patriarch, Saint Nerses, "which gives
them hope that they will some day be delivered from the tyranny of the Turks."
Such prophecies express the hopes of subject populations and, since there is
no evidence they had any effect on the masters' morale, say nothing about the
Turks. In this context, the only prophecies that matter are those that the Turks
themselves believed in. We must also be cautious, since the case of the *vaticinium infidelium* reported by Brother Bartholomaeus Georgievicz has shown that
a prophecy that inverted the myth of the Red Apple could be falsely attributed
to the Turks. Nevertheless, these false attributions did not come from nowhere.
They only manipulated and distorted predictions that, elaborated on the basis
of ancient eschatological and apocalyptic traditions, Byzantine or Muslim, existed among the Ottomans and fostered doubt and anxiety about their own future. In one of these currents of negative predictions, a people called the "Banū
l-Asfar" or "Beni Asfar" (literally, the "sons of blonds" or "sons of redheads")
were destined to conquer the Ottomans and put an end to their domination.
In the medieval Arabic texts, the name "Banū l-Asfar" originally designated
the Greeks and Romans. In other contexts, it also applied to the native populations of Spain and to Europeans in general. Several genealogists present the
eponymous ancestor, Asfar, as the grandson of Esau and the father of Rumil,
himself an ancestor of the *Rūm*, that is, the Romans and Byzantines. An eschatological Hadith (reported in Ahmed ibn Hanbal's *Musnad* in the ninth
century) presents the breaking of a nine-month truce between the Beni Asfar
and the Muslims, followed by the conquest of Constantinople, as one of the six
signs announcing the end of time. These Beni Asfar also appear outside a prophetic context in several works of Ottoman literature.[5] The same peoples make
a spectacular reappearance in an anecdote Guillaume Postel reports about his
journey to Istanbul in the retinue of the first permanent ambassador of France,
Jean de la Forêt, in 1535. Postel deserves to be cited at length:

> The Turks have a special authority nearly equal to their Qur'an, a book of prophecies
> where it is expressly written that a prince and a people of yellow color shall destroy
> the Turks and all the other Ishmaelites and Muhammadites, who are commonly
> called Muhammadans. An indubitable testimony can be given of this, even though
> the Turks conceal said prophecy from strangers as much as possible.
>
> It so happened that, having been sent as ambassador to the Great Turk, Mr. Jean
> de la Forêt Auvergnat, and with him Postel, writer of the present work, who is a

trustworthy witness of what he will write here—It so happened, I say, that one of the pashas, governor of Constantinople, unrestrained at the first audience granted to Ambassador de la Forêt, during the absence of the Great Sultan (on a campaign against the Sophy of Persia), instead of flattering and receiving said ambassador in a friendly way, told him that he was a spy and a traitor who had come there not for the good but as an explorer of the kingdom. And to prove that it was so, he drew from his bosom said secret book of prophecies, as if the ambassador, who was Christian, believed in them as much as he, a Turk. And he started to say, in the presence of the other pashas and governors, that he was absolutely certain that Ibn Saphra, that is, the Son of the Yellow Man, was truly the Son of the yellow fleur-de-lis on the standard or shield of France. . . . When the poor ambassador, partly at a loss and astonished, seeing that it would be no use for him to deny the fact, asked to hear the words of said prophecy at greater length, the pasha explained that the Saphra had weapons that were yellow in color. Then the ambassador, knowing how ignorant the Turks were of cosmography and even more of foreign customs, told them: "Certainly your prophecy is true, but it is not the king of France who is the Ben Saphra, it is the principal people of Emperor Charles, who are the Germans, whose lansquenets all have yellow-colored breeches. And they are the enemies of your king as much as of ours." . . . And so the pasha, paying the price for his ignorance, and seeing that the ambassador spoke so much ill of the greatest enemy they had, calmed down and received us as the friend of the Great Sultan.[6]

The identity of the Bani Asfar—a shape-shifter, as suggested by this anecdote— varied among the Ottomans as a function of their situation. It was finally attributed to the Russians, the tsar being designated at the time as *al-malik al-asfar*: the "yellow king." In that prediction and in other similar ones, which echoed very ancient themes, there was a moral lesson to be drawn about the transitory nature of power and glory, as well as an expression of humanity's existential anguish and fundamental pessimism. But beyond that general significance, the prophecy, applied to the political and military context of the time, was the expression of and the spur for an anxiety, an edginess, a lack of self-confidence. The obsession with the spy, "explorer of the kingdom," and the mistrust of strangers are obvious symptoms of that. The Ottomans are generally represented as sure of themselves, of their superiority, and of their invincibility, and as a result as having nothing but contempt for their adversaries, "destined for subjugation," which in essence takes at face value what the official rhetoric proclaimed. But the pessimism of the prophecies allows us to hear a different tune.

THE SPACE OF DIPLOMACY

Diplomatic relations with the Christian countries had been natural and vital at the regional level in the early days of the Ottoman state, when Byzantium,

Venice, and Genoa still played a decisive role in its rise. Recall in particular the appeals for aid by Byzantine factions and the Ottoman hostages held in Byzantium. These relations continued when the *beylik* became an empire without peer, in possession of Constantinople. Even then, in fact, though complete conquest was impossible, though the infidel adversaries were in reality worrisome, and though, to believe the prophecies, total revenge on their part was under way, diplomatic avenues remained an indispensable recourse. But such avenues, despite what historians of international relations have often written, were in no way incompatible with Muslim law, which the empire aspired to observe scrupulously. In that case, the Hanafite version of the law was at issue: though not the only version accepted in the empire, it was that of the rulers. For the question of relations with the infidel states, it was therefore necessary to consult the precepts of the doctors who had founded that school in the classical age, primarily Abū Yūsuf (eighth century), Shaybāni (eighth century), and Sarakhsi, and of those jurists during the Ottoman period who expressly placed themselves within that tradition, such as Molla Husrev (d. 1480) and Ibrāhīm al-Halabī (sixteenth century). These authors and others after them enumerated and analyzed the various sorts of treaties that, following the example of the Prophet and his companions, it was lawful to conclude with the infidels (in this case, those populating Europe). It is clear both that the Ottomans were anxious to be faithful to those laws and that they adapted them for their own use. The first type of treaty was the *dhimma* contract, which granted the status of *dhimmi* to infidels who, after three notices (*da'wa, da'vet*), agreed to recognize the political domination of the Muslim conqueror, while at the same time keeping their own religion. These sorts of treaties (sometimes called *ahd al-dhimma* or *akd-i zimmet*) were perpetual. The Ottoman applications of them (for example, in the case of Galata in 1454 or Rhodes in 1521) show that such treaties could be the object of negotiations and could entail, in addition to the canonical status of *dhimmi*, certain privileges and exemptions specific to a particular city or region. That was the system of "Ottoman" Europe. It is now necessary to consider the types of treaties concluded with the European states that remained in the "territory of war," treaties that established other than belligerent relations with them.

That second possibility proceeded from a certain elaboration of Islamic law in contact with historical realities. Observing that the general expansion of the *dār al-islām* was encountering practical obstacles and hence delays, and that, though it certainly remained the only horizon possible, it was not an immediately accessible aim, jurists of the classical age agreed to suspend jihad and make truces with the infidel adversary. What was essential was the fundamentally provisional nature of these truces and of the coexistence they established, since it safeguarded the final objective of universal Muslim domination. Various terms were used to designate that type of truce: *sulh* seems to have been the most common during the Ottoman period, but there was also *hudna, muvāda'a,* and *muʿāhada*. Shaybāni and Sarakhsi were careful to distinguish them from true peace accords, for which they reserved the name *musālama* or *musālaha*.

Once the principle of time limits was set forth, the ancient authors displayed great flexibility in determining the duration of truces. Kalkashandi (1355–1418), illustrious secretary of the Mamluk chancery belonging to the Shafite school, cites a limit of four months, which could be extended to a year, if the Muslims were in a position of strength. If, on the contrary, they were in a position of weakness, the timeframe of the truce could be extended to ten years, renewable if necessary, to allow them to recover their strength. These arrangements could be accompanied by payments of money, but the terms *kharāj* or *jizya* tended to be avoided, because of their symbolism. More innocuous terms were used, ranging from the notion of a "ransom" paid to avoid being attacked (*fedāʾ*) to that of a "gift" (*armağan, pishkesh, hedāyā*), "contribution" (*vergi, kesim*), or "custom" (*ʿādet*). Abū Yūsuf even conceded that, when necessary, these sums could be paid by the Muslim party. The governing factor was the "utility" (*maslaha*) for the Muslim community (*ʿumma*), which resulted in an extreme pragmatism.

That explains why the peace treaties that the Ottomans concluded with the Christians from the "lands of war" were always for a limited duration. The Ottomans thereby marked their fidelity to the old Islamic principle of *hudna*. At the same time, however, the duration granted became longer and longer over time. That had to do with the transformation in power relations, which placed the Ottomans in a position of weakness relative to their partners and more vulnerable to their demands. Nevertheless, with the appearance of these constraints, the manipulation of time limits came to serve as a diplomatic instrument in the hands of the sultans, a way for them to woo certain Christian states, to favor them over others, and to demonstrate thereby (as by other means) their insertion within the European game of diplomacy.

The treaty that Bayezid II concluded in 1482 with the Grand Master of the Knights of Rhodes, Pierre d'Aubusson, was an exception during the period and a prefiguration of what would occur in the following century, since it was already a lifelong treaty (it was to end only with the death of one of the parties to the contract). Until the victory of Mohács (1421–1528), there were sixteen Ottoman treaties with Hungary, whose periods of validity were, depending on the case, four months, or one, two, three, five, seven, or ten years. Between 1444 and 1533, there were twelve treaties between Poland and the Ottoman Empire. Their duration could be for one, two, three, or five years. But when the treaty was renewed in 1533, Süleyman the Magnificent accomplished a diplomatic coup by granting his old partner, King Sigismund the Elder, a lifelong treaty. He would do the same twenty years later with Sigismund's son Sigismund Augustus, who ascended the throne in 1548. Through that very liberal application of the principle of *sulh*, Süleyman demonstrated his attachment to a sort of Ottoman-Polish axis against the Habsburgs. Polish diplomacy, for its part, made use of that favorable context in 1546 to fend off the looming threat of Süleyman's death, which seemed imminent at the time, by seeking in advance guarantees from his son and sole heir, the future Selim II. A treaty was in fact granted on October 17–26, 1564, by the man who was as yet only the imperial prince, entrusted with the governance of Kütahya. It survives in Latin translation.[7] From then on, all Polish-Ottoman treaties would be lifelong, four in the sixteenth century and ten in the seventeenth.

The period of validity for the treaties with the Habsburgs, the Ottomans' chief adversaries until the eighteenth century, reflected the situation proper to the Ottoman Empire and the evolution in power relations. Ten treaties have been identified for the sixteenth century. The first was concluded for five years in 1547. The others stipulated a duration of eight years but generally did not hold. The 1606 Treaty of Zsitvatorok marked a turning point, in this respect and others, in relations between the two states: it was concluded for twenty years. The following treaties would have the same duration, until the Treaty of Karlowitz, concluded in 1699 for twenty-five years, and that of Passarowitz, concluded in 1718 for twenty-four years. The Treaty of Belgrade in 1739 also had a limited period of validity, though for twenty-seven years. In the meantime, however, a new Ottoman-Habsburg treaty came into being in 1747, which for the first time was conceived as a perpetual treaty. The last connection to the Islamic principle of *sulh* was thereby broken, with the forced Westernization of Ottoman diplomacy finally prevailing over the last marks of fidelity to Islamic law.

The series of treaties with Russia is also instructive: it began late (though Ottoman-Russian relations went back much further), with the Treaty of Bahchesaray of 1681, which was concluded for twenty years. Stipulated for two years in 1699, the Treaty of Karlowitz with Russia was replaced in 1700 by a new treaty with a duration of thirty years. After Peter the Great broke it off with a new war, the treaties of Pruth (1711) and then of Adrianople (1713) replaced it. The latter of these was concluded for twenty-five years. With the Treaty of Belgrade of September 18, 1739, the Ottoman-Russian treaties became virtually perpetual.

Nevertheless, treaties of that sort, legitimate from the Islamic point of view so long as they were limited in time, suspended war only temporarily, by provisionally establishing peace. As such, they were not sufficient for governing all the kinds of relations the Ottomans maintained with the various European states. In fact, despite what is suggested by some studies (very useful in general but on this point too closely beholden to *fiqh* works), these relations cannot be reduced to the alternation between war and peace.[8] Some states in modern Europe never actually submitted to the Ottoman Empire and could therefore not be seriously considered tributaries of it (whatever the excesses of Ottoman rhetoric in that regard). They were also not actually at war with the Turks: either they were no longer so at a given moment or they never had been—though they might always be considered *virtually* at war, given that they were infidel states and were part of

the *dār al-ḥarb*. These same states maintained relations of a different kind with
the sultan: relations of alliance, more or less explicit and thoroughgoing.

Impium Foedus

As felonious and even scandalous as they appeared from the religious standpoint, these relations were part of the geopolitical realities of Europe, once the
Turks were present on that continent and the European states were too divided
to truly form a front against that "common enemy." On the contrary, each
would be tempted to use the redoubtable wild card of Ottoman support, or the
mere threat of that support, against its rival. The first examples were as old as
the Ottoman state itself, dating back to the fourteenth century. In the fifteenth
century, when Mehmed II had just conquered Constantinople and was said to
have designs on southern Italy, the flattery he received from Venice, Naples,
and Florence (not to mention Malatesta, lord of Rimini, who asked only to "collaborate"), with medals struck in his honor, for example, says a great deal about
the ulterior motives on both sides. The most emblematic case no doubt remains
that of France, whose successive sovereigns, beginning with the rapprochement
between Francis I and Süleyman the Magnificent, pledged far-reaching collaboration with the Turks against their chief enemy, the Habsburgs (ranging from
coordination in their respective undertakings to joint campaigns, at least in
the naval realm). The instructions that Chancellor Duprat drew up in 1534 for
Jean de La Forêt, Francis I's first permanent ambassador to Constantinople, are
ample evidence of the degree of military and political cooperation proposed
to the sultan. Furthermore, in the late sixteenth century there would be a convergence of interests between the France of Henry IV—but also the "northern
states," England and the Netherlands—and the Ottoman Empire against a common adversary, the "Catholic king" Philip II of Spain. Against that adversary,
Henry IV not only renewed the old alliance with the Ottoman sultan but also
bargained on several occasions with the Moriscos of Spain rebelling against
Philip II, which would lead to the torture and execution of one of his agents in
1605.[9] In fact, the same people who most vigorously condemned the collusion
of certain Christian states such as France with the infidel did not forgo, once
they were at war with the Turk, making contact with his enemy to the east, the
shah of Persia. Venice did so during its war with Bayezid II (1499–1502), arguing, to redeem themselves, that because of his Shiism, Shah Esmāʿīl was close
to Christianity and not really Muslim. Charles V, whose propaganda at times
went so far as to spread the rumor that Francis I, the Turk's ally, had become
Muslim, did not neglect to send emissaries to the shah in turn. Another, more
forgotten example of these alliances, unnatural at least from a religious point
of view, is that of the grand dukes of Tuscany, Ferdinand I and then Cosmo II,
with the Druze emir of Lebanon, Manʾoğlu Fakhr al-Dīn, in revolt against his

Ottoman suzerain. In 1613, the rebel emir went to Tuscany to rally support.[10] His rebellion lasted until 1635 and ended with his execution. The Ottoman sultan, for his part, could not fail to profit from these rapprochements with some on the European chessboard, whose complexity and divisions he always found a matter for astonishment. The immediately positive and remarkably warm reaction of Süleyman to Francis I's appeal for aid after the disaster of Pavia in 1525 is eloquent in that regard. The Great Sultan was himself a player in a rear alliance against the Habsburgs, whom he in no way underestimated. Furthermore, France offered him those naval bases in the western Mediterranean, such as Toulon, necessary for fighting against Spain and for gaining a foothold in the Maghreb. From the start, the king of France placed him in the position of protector, which could only suit Süleyman. He even underscored it by using a marked paternalistic tone in his correspondence with the king. That position preserved the principle of the supremacy of Islam.

Yet all these objective solidarities and more explicit agreements, duly prized by both parties, could not be formalized. The *fiqh*, though it stipulated peace with the infidel under certain conditions, opposed any idea of an alliance. In fact, the church's canon law equally rejected that eventuality. The *impium foedus*, or pact with the infidel, had been formally condemned since the ninth century. These legal particulars explain why both sides avoided applying to their relations terms that referred too precisely to the notion of alliance or, to adopt the terms of the time, "confederation" or "league." Among the Ottomans, the corresponding terms, *ittifak* and *ittihād*, were set aside. Both parties placed themselves by preference on a different register, that of feelings, devoid this time of any legal implications. The king of France thus evoked friendship, good terms, entente, the loyal affection that bound him to the sultan, adopting terminology that the sultan had been the first to use. He deployed the whole range of words for entente and affection: *dostluk, musāfāt, müsālaha, barıshlık, muʿāhede*. At the same time, in that onslaught of kindness and even affection, the sultan never failed to point out the difference in position between himself and his interlocutor "of the religion of Jesus," the king of France, for example. The king was only the obligee of the sultan, to whom he was supposed to pledge feelings of devotion and loyalty, expressed in terms such as *ihtisās, sadāqat*, and *istiqāmet*. The sultan, for his part, offered him aid and assistance (*muʿāvenet, muzāheret*) and lavished his favors and benefits on him.

ON THE PROPER USE OF CAPITULATIONS

In that situation, where de facto alliances, active and if necessary long-lasting, could not receive any legal sanction, another type of treaty—at least during a first long phase, from the fifteenth to the eighteenth century—played that role, though with something of a time lag. These were treaties well known in

Western parlance by the name "capitulations." Westerners borrowed that Latin term (*capitulatio, capitularium*) from the medieval chanceries, applying it, because of the organization of these documents into short chapters (*capitulum*; pl., *capitula*), to what the Ottomans designated more broadly as *'ahdnāme* (literally, written pledges by the sovereign). The principal aim of these capitulations was to define and ensure the guarantees and immunities granted to foreigners—merchants in particular—living in the Ottoman Empire. By providing indispensable legal guarantees, they thus made Western commerce possible within the Ottoman Empire. Each of the parties desired and had an interest in that commerce. It was in that sense that the capitulations prior to the nineteenth century were essential to the "commerce of the Levant" and not, as is generally claimed, because they were supposedly trade treaties in the strict sense. Furthermore, as of the seventeenth century, the kings of France took care to have chapters inserted that guaranteed not only the rights of their merchants but also those of Catholic religious serving as missionaries or parish priests in Jerusalem, Istanbul, and more generally, in all the sultan's possessions. In promulgating the capitulations, the Ottomans were merely following practices that had already been current among their former masters, whether Christian or Muslim, in the zones they had seized (Byzantines, Seljuks, Mamluks, Turkoman beys). Not all of them had their source in Muslim law—far from it—but in spite of everything, these sorts of treaties still had a foundation in the Islamic legal principle of *amān*.

In its dual meaning, pardon and favor on one hand, safe-conduct on the other (to offer safe-conduct is to grant favor), the concept of *amān* applied to different situations. First, it applied to the infidel who, for one reason or another, had brought the reproaches of the sultan on himself, but whom the sultan agreed to pardon. That was the case, for example, of the Genoese of Galata who provided aid to the besieged in Constantinople, despite their previous pledge of neutrality toward Mehmed II, and to whom the conqueror nevertheless granted a treaty, an accord of domination/protection (an *'ahd-i-dhimmet*). Second, it could apply to the *harbī* infidel residing in Muslim territory and, as such, liable to be killed or enslaved by the first Muslim to happen by. The *harbī* infidel was now accepted—provisionally at least—not only in his own territory, which he was temporarily allowed to hold in his possession, as during a state of truce, but also in Muslim territory. That principle of safe-conduct granted to the stranger was a legacy of the tribal rules of pre-Islamic Arabia. (The corresponding term in the Qur'an [9:6], is *jiwār*.) Islam then borrowed it on behalf of the *harbī* infidels especially. In principle, any Muslim could grant *amān*, but in practice it was the act of the local authority and by preference of the sultan himself. The *harbī* who was the beneficiary of *amān* became a *musta'min*. As such, he was untouchable for a limited span of time. The Hanafites set the duration for a maximum of one year; the Shafites, less liberal, for four months. The Ottomans did not depart from that practice: they provided safe-conduct (called *yol hükmi* or *yol tezkeresi*) to foreign Christians entering their territories and, in fact, to foreign Muslims and to Christian or Muslim subjects moving about within the empire. Ottoman and Western sources attest to them many times, but they also give a particular extension to the principle of *amān*, making it the legal principle at the foundation of the capitulations granted to certain Christian states. Yet these guarantees, instead of being the object of an individual concession granted on a case-by-case basis, as in the previous "letters of *amān*," were the consequence of an all-encompassing concession that the sultan granted to one of his Christian partners. Hence the concession was no longer granted at the individual level but at the state level. The sultan swore an oath to respect it, and it was valid for the entire length of his reign, provided there was no infringement on the part of the prince beneficiary. It had to be renewed upon the accession of his successor. The "great capitulation" granted to France through the marquess of Villeneuve, ambassador to Constantinople in 1740, was the first to be valid in perpetuity. After the late seventeenth century, the states benefiting from capitulations began to multiply: by the late eighteenth century, Austria, Sweden, Sicily, Denmark, the Hanseatic cities (1747), Prussia, Spain, and Russia were provided with them. These were now commercial advantages for the most part, granted, willingly or not, by a weakened Ottoman Empire. But before that, the capitulations had been granted by the sultan's express will, with entirely different intentions and to a smaller number: in a first wave, to Genoa, Venice, Florence, Dubrovnik, and Poland, and, in a second, to France, England, and the Netherlands, all states that had not only commercial but also political common interests with the sultan.

Despite what has long been claimed, these were far from mere trade treaties, and in fact were not so in the strict sense. Rather, they were vested with strong political significance. They conferred on the alliance the only legal recognition it could obtain, even though that recognition came with a time lag with respect to its object. The commercial guarantees granted by the sultan recognized and awarded political entente. They were the only acceptable expression of it. The preambles to the successive versions of capitulations clearly proclaim as much. The renewal of 1740, so favorable to France, followed directly on the great services France had rendered to the Porte during the marquess of Villeneuve's mediation in the peace of Belgrade. By contrast, should political relations deteriorate, the renewal of the capitulations (which were necessary so long as they were bound to the current reign) became problematic. The French ambassadors to the Porte had that bitter experience for a good part of the seventeenth century, throughout the period 1610–1673.

Because of the objects they dealt with, and because they were only an elaboration of the legitimate principle of *amān*, the capitulations, unlike alliance treaties proper, were not problematic in principle, either to the Christian or to the Muslim party. That did not exempt the sultan who issued them, however, from submitting the text for the approval of the *shaykh al-islām*, who could always raise objections to particular points. If we are to believe the emissary Claude du Bourg, that is what happened when he negotiated the first French capitulations with Grand Vizier Sokollu Mehmed Pasha in 1569. The mufti had found fault with something in an article (the seventeenth) that, in the event of the repression of Barbary corsairs, could have led the sultan to ally himself with the French infidel against other Muslims. Du Bourg prided himself on having on that occasion prevailed "with very great difficulty against the opinion of the mufti."[11] In any case, since capitulations were possible and alliance treaties were not, one of the functions of capitulations was to be a symbolic substitute for treaties, to the satisfaction of both parties.

There came a moment, however, when the agents of diplomatic life were no longer satisfied with symbolic substitutes, especially since, once the sultans began to increase the number of capitulations, these lost their initial significance, ceasing to go hand in hand with a political alliance. Such was the case for Frederick II, king of Prussia, in the 1760s, as Selâhattin Tansel and Kemal Beydilli have shown.[12] Frederick, very isolated at the time in his antagonism with Austria and Russia, sought the support of the Ottoman Empire. No doubt he was demanding capitulations for Prussia like those the other countries had obtained. But he would not be satisfied with that: he wanted a formal defensive alliance. The Ottoman rulers, though interested in his advances, hesitated to commit themselves, for fear of alienating Russia in particular. They temporized by soliciting advice beforehand from the grand ulemas of the empire. They met twice in "consultative assemblies" (*meshveret mejlisi*), where they exchanged legal opinions in favor of or opposed to the alliance. In actuality, the king of Prussia had asked for nothing more than what had been actively practiced vis-à-vis the king of France more than two hundred years earlier. But, in wanting to formalize the alliance (which the kings of France had never sought to do), he placed the problem in an entirely new light. A first meeting, which had dwelt especially on the political advantages of the alliance with Prussia, relegating the legal aspects to the background, reached a positive conclusion: "no obstacle or objection, either from the standpoint of the Law or from that of reason" (*sher'an ve aqlan hich bir hijnet ve mahzūr*). By contrast, a second meeting, run by a new *shaykh al-islām*, who, unlike his predecessor, was hostile to the alliance from the outset, gave much more weight to the legal obstacles. An archival document, reproduced at length in Beydilli's book,[13] sums up the various opinions (*görü*) expressed at the time. It is clear how distressed the participants were to find no analyses in the classical works of jurisprudence corresponding precisely to the situation about which they were being questioned. Some deflected the question to inquire whether it was permitted to make peace with the infidel. Thereby falling back on one of the most classic questions, they merely repeated the responses of the great Hanafite doctors, those I have summarized earlier. Others, anxious to confine themselves more closely to the precise question raised, sought a model in a different context, but one already treated by the jurisconsuls, that of Muslims placed under Christian domination and compelled to fight with their master against another Christian people. (That situation was possible, for example, in the Andalusia of the *reconquista*). That model raised a question similar to what they were being asked to resolve: Could Muslims join with infidels to fight against other infidels? The conclusion of that second assembly was negative. Given the opposition of the ulemas, decisive in Sultan Mustafa III's view, and in face of the accumulation of strictly political difficulties, the Porte denied Frederick II's request for an alliance. It simply took more customary measures, granting to Prussia what it had granted to a growing number of countries for centuries: capitulations. At most, an eighth article was appended to the seven articles of the treaty, one that held out a promise for the future, by stipulating that other articles beneficial to the two parties could be added later. It was not until 1790 that a first Ottoman-Prussian alliance treaty was concluded. What had still seemed impossible thirty years earlier was thereby realized.

Although I have distinguished among various sorts of accords concluded between the Porte and the Christian countries, corresponding to different situations, some documents were hybrids. For example, though the treaties with France were pure capitulations, since that country had never been officially at war with the Ottoman Empire (it would be for the first time in 1798, as a result of the Egyptian expedition), the case of Venice was more complicated. Some of the capitulations granted to the republic were pure, issued because of a change of reign, while others (the capitulation of 1540, for example) put an end to a conflict. They were thus peace treaties entailing the surrender of territories but also capitulations reiterating the different articles that defined the situation of the Venetians and their representatives in the Ottoman Empire, as well as the conditions for trade, which was to resume in earnest. The same was true for the treaty of 1494 between the Ottoman Empire and Poland. Like the previous treaties between the two countries, it renewed the truce; but since, for the first time, it also introduced a few articles concerning trade and merchants, it can be considered the first Polish capitulation.[14] The treaties with Dubrovnik represent another sort of hybrid. Like the *ahd-i zimmet*, they gave the merchant republic the status of a tributary; but they also granted the Ragusans doing trade in the empire a series of guarantees and privileges.[15]

Pera, a Diplomatic Microcosm

The Ottomans were an integral part of European diplomacy, which—as reasons of state required—in no way ended at the Islamic-Christian border. In reality, that border was constantly being crossed in both directions, with the requisite safe-conduct, by diplomats of all kinds, whether discreet emissaries or ambassadors sounding drums and trumpets, bearing messages, the texts of treaties, and, when necessary, rich presents. Historians who claim that the Ottomans were fundamentally resistant to the very notion of diplomacy have pointed out, as a major argument in support of their thesis, that the sultan had no ambassadors in European capitals. A distinction is necessary here, however. It is true that the Ottomans did not adapt to what was a new practice of European diplomacy, which appeared in Italy in the fifteenth century and took root only gradually and not without resistance in the rest of Europe: namely, permanent embassies in foreign capitals entrusted to ambassadors who would live there for several years. The Ottomans converted to that practice only belatedly; their first experiments did not take place before 1793. At the time, these clearly corresponded to a desire on Sultan Selim III's part to fall in line with Western practices. A long-lasting Ottoman "megalomania" no doubt explains that long delay as much as "Muslim prejudices." In fact, though their phenomenal ascent did not turn the Ottomans away from diplomacy, they sought to reconcile it with the somewhat contradictory concern to always assert their superiority over their partner. Hence, from the early sixteenth century on, they disclaimed official documents that had been written in foreign languages, a common practice until that time; and above all, their treaties always took a unilateral form. It appeared as if the treaties were the result of the sultan's will alone, even though the text had been negotiated beforehand every step of the way and would, at the end of the process, be ratified by both parties. The Ottoman-Venetian treaty of 1540, both peace treaty and capitulation, was thus issued only in the sultan's name on October 2, 1540. The text includes his oath swearing to respect it. Let us not be fooled by appearances, however: several Venetian emissaries in succession had been conducting talks in Constantinople since the spring of 1539. In addition, once the accord had been realized, the text established by the Ottoman chancery was sent to Venice, accompanied by an Italian translation, on October 8, 1540. The doge in turn swore an oath to respect that text during a ceremony in Venice on April 30, 1541, in the presence of thirty Venetian patricians and the sultan's representative, his ambassador, the interpreter Yunus Bey. Afterward, a version of the treaty was sent back to the sultan, sealed with the golden bull of the republic. In a letter of 1542 to the doge, the sultan made reference to that ceremony. He recalled the doge's oath, not considering it superfluous in any way, as complete unilateralism would have done.[16] In addition, that same treaty left a few questions hanging that would later be resolved by bipartite commissions.

The Ottomans, though refraining from establishing permanent embassies themselves, at the same time accepted—despite their acute "spy fever"—the presence in their capital of a number of resident ambassadors, representatives of their principal European partners. The first was the bailo of Venice in 1454. The French ambassador came in 1535 and was followed, in the late sixteenth and early seventeenth century, by English (1583) and Dutch (1612) colleagues. The ambassador of France, Harley de Sancy, wrote at the time to the lord of

Villeroy: "Although the vanity of that Porte is great and though they desire glory, to see here several ambassadors of great kings . . ."[17]

As for the Russian ambassador, destined to play such a large role on the Bosphorus in the nineteenth century, he made his appearance only in the eighteenth century, along with several other ambassadors, such as those of Sweden and Poland. A Polish embassy was stipulated in the treaty of 1621, but the implementation of that clause was delayed.

In addition, the Ottoman capital constantly welcomed special envoys, which these same countries and others continued jointly to dispatch.

For their part, the Ottomans sent, if not permanent ambassadors, then at least emissaries. Border countries such as Austria, Poland, and Venice were accustomed to welcoming these envoys *in nome del gran signore*, accompanied by a retinue, which became more numerous and more spectacular over time. They did everything they could to honor them and not to incur the risk of displeasing their master, "a worrisome and dangerous neighbor," as Sigismund of Poland called him. Ottoman missions to the more remote countries such as France, the Netherlands, or England were rarer, but the sultan did not hesitate to instigate them whenever the situation required. First welcomed discreetly, these Ottoman envoys were later received with great ceremony, when French sovereigns such as Henry III and Louis XIV came to understand that displaying their pomp before the eyes of the "exotic" ambassadors was the best way to spread the word about their power and glory to the most remote regions of the planet.

By the seventeenth century, European ambassadors no longer resided in Istanbul itself but had settled on the other side of the Golden Horn, in the old Genoese city of Galata and in the "Vineyards of Pera." Little by little, along the "main street of Pera," the palaces of the different embassies rose up, accompanied by the corresponding houses of worship. That cosmopolitan neighborhood, occupied by "Frankish" dealers and wealthy *dhimmis*, became one of the centers of European diplomacy: not only where ambassadors defended the political and commercial interests of their respective countries before the sultan's ministers, but also, more generally, where the European balance of power was played out. The first task at hand was to thwart those attempting to shatter that balance to their own advantage, by securing the support of the Turk, whether he took action or whether the threat remained implicit. That was the situation, depending on the period, of Venice against Genoa, of Dubrovnik against Venice, of France against the Habsburgs—under Francis I as well as Henry IV and Louis XIV—of Sweden against Russia, of Prussia against Austria, and so on. In a second phase, when the Turk had become weaker, the matter at hand for some was to prevent their rivals from taking advantage of that weakness to seize his spoils. They then intervened to mitigate unfavorable treaties imposed on the sultan, who became accustomed to that procedure, which he designated by the term *tavassut*. England and the United Provinces mediated negotiations for the Treaty of Karlowitz. In doing so, the two merchant powers, united under a single ruler, William of Orange, cut the ground from under the feet of French diplomacy. A few years earlier, at the height of the war in 1685, an emissary of Grand Vizier Hasan Efendi approached Guilleragues, ambassador of France, a traditionally friendly country, to find out whether it would be well disposed toward offering its mediation between the Ottoman Empire and its three adversaries: the emperor, Poland, and Venice. That scenario played out a few decades later, when the mediation of a later ambassador, the marquess of Villeneuve, allowed the sultan to recover Belgrade and northern Serbia during the peace of Belgrade concluded with the emperor in 1740.

Pera was therefore a microcosm where the different factions of Christendom came together and fell apart in infidel territory: each kept an eye on the other, plumbed its secrets by procuring through bribes copies of orders or secret correspondence. The enemy's intrigues were thwarted by every means possible. International tensions grew, and diplomats from all the European countries flocked to the Bosphorus. Ambassador Guilleragues took note of the situation in 1682, pointing out its disadvantages: "That multitude of eager ministers attests to an alarm from which the Porte will benefit and to a passion for peace that will make it difficult."[18] Pera was also an international showcase where everyone measured his prestige by the honors that the Great Sultan and his representatives bestowed and by the priorities in force on the Bosphorus. The ambassadors of France, duly chastised in instructions from their kings, were intractable on that point, and the anecdotes on the subject are legion. These ambassadors demanded precedence over all the other representatives of Christendom, beginning with those of the emperor and the king of Spain, and insisted that their privilege be inscribed in the capitulations and *exequatur* of the consuls of France. In the French capitulations of 1604, the reigning sultan, Ahmed I, ratifying the occasional guarantees of his predecessors, wrote as follows:

> And insofar as this emperor of France is, of all Christian kings and princes, the most noble and of the highest family and the most perfect friend that our ancestors acquired among said kings and princes of the faith of Jesus . . . in consideration of which, we desire and command that his ambassadors who reside at our blessed Porte shall have precedence over the ambassador of Spain and over all other kings and princes, whether in our public divan or in all the other places they may meet.[19]

Ambassador Guilleragues thus found in his instructions a reminder about "the priority that is generally due to France over the other crowns, but which is recognized, more than in any other place, so particularly at the Porte." That special recognition had to do with the fact that the habitual priority of the emperor was "dubious" in Constantinople, where the imperial ambassador was recognized only as a "minister of the king of Hungary."[20] The right to protection of the Catholic clergy officiating over the holy sites of Istanbul and in the rest of the Ottoman Empire, first granted to the ambassadors of France in the capitulations of 1604 and 1673, was a result of the good political relations between the two countries, and was also a way for royal propaganda to undo the damage of the violent criticisms roused, both within and without, by these same relations in the rest of Christendom. The royal instructions given to the marquess of Nointel in 1670, before his departure for Constantinople, recall with some exaggeration: "This lord ambassador must know that the chief reason for the good terms that the kings who were His Majesty's predecessors wished to establish among themselves and with the Porte of the Ottoman emperors was the piety and zeal they had for the advantages of the Catholic religion, which a great number of people profess in the Turkish empire, and also to preserve for all Christians in general free access to the holy sites."

In short, these concessions on the sultan's part were a matter of international prestige for the French monarchy and also one of the things at stake in the rivalry with the Habsburgs. They opened the way for the Russians, who in the eighteenth century styled themselves the protectors of the Orthodox Christians in the empire. The entire paradox of the situation lay in the fact that Christendom thereby made the infidel sovereign the fulcrum in its balance of power and the arbiter of its status. Regarding the sumptuous retinue of Ambassador d'Aramon, who was allowed to accompany Süleyman to Persia in the 1548–1549 campaign, Brantôme wrote: "What glory for his ambassador and for his French nation to have such standing with the greatest monarch in the world."[21]

A posting to Constantinople, though it varied in its importance depending on the international historical situation, remained one of the most prestigious in a diplomat's career, in France and in the other European countries represented. In that respect, it was one of the most enviable for the various officers, nobles, and prelates who pursued that career, with, it must be said, greater or lesser aptitude for the work and uneven success. The mission was one of the most dangerous as well, by virtue of its remoteness and the resulting difficulties in communication, the health risks (epidemics of plague especially), and the differences in customs and mores. "I am here among barbarians, without any civil conversation," lamented Ambassador François de Noailles in a dispatch of 1572.[22] Some twenty years earlier, the irascible Jean de la Vigne, Henry II's ambassador to Süleyman, had complained about having to tolerate the pashas' insolence: "It is shameful for the king and his subjects to endure such vileness from these barbarous dogs," he wrote to his colleague in Venice, the bishop of Lodève.[23] But there was something even more distressing than the blows to one's ego, which was especially sensitive because the attacks came from "barbarians" and "infidels." The chief peril was that the Ottomans, though not alone in this in Europe, were also not the least likely to take liberties with the status of diplomatic immunity being set in place at that time (and not without difficulty). When they went to war with a country, they immediately threw its ambassador (and its nationals in general) in prison or at least put them under house arrest. The slightest incident could earn an ambassador snubs and mistreatment, even the worst uncertainties (which the Ottomans skillfully dispensed drop by drop) about his ultimate fate. Did not Veltwyck, Ferdinand of Habsburg's envoy to Istanbul in 1544, claim that Aramon, Francis I's representative in the same capital, found himself "in such a bad way" following the Treaty of Crépy-en-Laonnois, by which his master again betrayed the Turk, that "many times there was talk of impaling him"?[24] Harlay de Sancy, ambassador of France, was imprisoned for a few days in 1617. More precisely, he was detained at the residence of the *chavush bashı* after Prince Korecki's prison escape, in which the ambassador was suspected to have played a role.[25] In 1682, after the bombing of Chios by the squadron under Duquesne's command, another ambassador of France, Guilleragues, feared "some intrigue" on the part of his Turkish hosts. Appearing at the grand vizier's audience, he was the object of breathless curiosity from all present and recounted: "I prepared myself somewhat to beat off the first violence."[26] There was in these crises, however, a certain amount of gesturing, and no Christian ambassador was ever put to death (though that was not the case for Muslim ambassadors or mere embassy secretaries or interpreters).

The Limits of Turkish Integration

As essential as the role of the Ottomans was in European diplomacy, that role was no more official in Christendom than were the alliances with the sultan. To recognize it formally would have been to accept and thereby legitimate it. But though it was impossible to disregard that ponderous Ottoman presence in Europe, and though it was even desirable to take full advantage of it, it remained an anomaly, an evil to be endured and not accepted. Charles IX's father and grandfather were Süleyman the Magnificent's greatest allies, and Charles himself corresponded amicably with him, but that in no way prevented him from publicly rejoicing at Süleyman's downfall at the siege of Malta. In a published letter to the duke of Nemours, governor of Lyons, Charles IX commanded him to announce the news everywhere by town crier and to order a procession from the Cathedral of Saint John to the Church of Saint Nizier. There, thanksgiving was to take place, "and in the evening, a bonfire will be built, as it is the custom to do on such good occasions."[27] The agreements that Christian states were led to reach with the infidel occupied a gray zone, between bald fact and law. They could not be theorized. Instructive in this regard are the different euphemisms by which the king of France designated the sultan in the instructions to his ambassadors in Constantinople. The *Grand Seigneur*, emperor of the Turks, His Highness, the Ottoman Emperor: these were all ways of characterizing him like any other emperor, circumventing the religious obstacle that in principle ought to have barred any relationship. In 1672, when Arnauld de Pomponne, Louis XIV's minister of foreign affairs, declared, regarding plans for holy war, that "they have gone out of fashion since Saint Louis,"[28] there was a great deal of realism in his remarks, and not necessarily religious relativism or skepticism of any kind.

Only a few anticonformists lifted the taboo. But—out of scruple or caution?—they did so only partly, and often changed their minds after the fact. Boldly setting forth things as they were, Jean-Baptiste Robinet wrote in his *Dictionnaire universel* (1778): "The Catholic priests band together every day with the same heretics against whom they once crusaded, and the Christian states have no difficulty allying themselves with the Turk." Emeric Cruce raised the question directly of the Turks' integration into the European system. In *The New Cyneas*, published in 1623, he imagines an assembly gathering in Venice, "where all the sovereigns would have their ambassadors in perpetuity, so that the disputes that may arise could be cleared up [there]." He makes a place for the sultan and his representative, and not an insubstantial one: in the hierarchical order, the sultan would come immediately after the pope and before the Germanic emperor. Twenty years later, however, that same Cruce set aside his boldness and championed traditional conflict. In the early eighteenth century, the abbot of Saint-Pierre took a direction similar to that of the early Cruce. In his *Plan to Establish Perpetual Peace in Europe*, he came up with a blueprint for a "society" where all the sovereigns of Christendom would be permanently represented, "to settle without war, by a three-quarters majority, their disputes to come and the conditions for trade." The abbot did not go so far as to integrate the Turks fully. He judged that "it would hardly be proper to give them votes in the congress." At the very most, he consented to make a concession to them: "In order to maintain peace and commerce with them, and to avoid having to stand armed against them," the Union "could make a treaty with them . . . and grant them a resident in the city of peace." From such an association agreement, even limited in scope, an advantage could be had regarding the primordial objective, the cause of Christianity: "The Church would gain thereby inasmuch as, the more enlightenment the Muhammadans have, the less attached they would be to their dogmas and the better disposed to sense the beauty and perfection of the Christian religion." That openness, despite being very cautious, was abandoned some years later when Saint-Pierre, at the end of a new work dedicated to the regent, now proposed in bald terms to "drive the Turk out of Europe and even Asia and Africa."[29]

Let us recall that it was not until 1856, on the occasion of the Congress of Paris, that the Turks were recognized as full-fledged members of the "European concert." After centuries of de facto participation, they thus achieved a de jure role. And in fact, does not that concession say more about the bitter rivalry among the Europeans at the time than about a real shift in thinking?

COMMERCE IN THE LEVANT

There was another realm where the weight of reality led Christians and Muslims to set aside the ideology of conflict and to peacefully cross the land and sea borders separating the two worlds: the realm of commerce. Even in the

Middle Ages, the attractiveness of precious commodities from the Middle and Far East—pepper, spices, silk—and the enormous profits anticipated from such trafficking (Venice's fortune rested in large part on that foundation) had always prevailed over the disadvantage of having to load the supplies in Beirut or Alexandria, that is, in Muslim territory. The fact that the hub for trade among the three continents was in the Muslim world was not enough to dissuade enterprising souls from taking part in that commerce. As for the Muslims, they did not discriminate in such matters, beyond setting higher customs duties for the *harbī*. The interested parties concluded trade treaties establishing the rules of the game and offering foreigners the security necessary. For both sides, relations of that kind appeared much more innocuous than political and military accords and therefore did not require the same kind of dissimulation from those who engaged in them. The only touchy point had to do with trade in strategic items (weapons but also raw materials), precisely because they were the equivalent of the kind of accords that were condemned. That is, they contravened the compulsory solidarity within each of the camps. Condemnations by the popes and councils, for example, targeted only trafficking of that kind, and with dubious success.

The framework remained by and large the same in the Ottoman period. The Ottomans, heirs to the Ayyubids, the Mamluks, the Seljuks of Rūm, and the Byzantines in the eastern Mediterranean, had the same attitude as the other Anatolian *beylik* (before they were absorbed into the Ottoman Empire) toward the Frankish merchants. The Ottomans granted them capitulations in turn, and these types of treaties would multiply, would be renewed and expanded, throughout the modern period. At the same time, those exports that risked weakening the country and strengthening the infidels, in open or potential war with the sultan, were condemned by the population and controlled by the authorities: they were prohibited without special permits. Wheat was foremost among these "sensitive" articles. In times of scarcity, the people saw the ban on exports as a religious obligation on the sovereign's part. Pragmatism was eclipsed and the ideology of conflict returned to the foreground. The bailo of Venice observed in a dispatch of November 1551: "All these ships that have loaded up in the canal [the Sea of Marmara] before everyone's eyes have led to protests from the people, who go about yelling that wheat was allowed to be loaded in front of the emperor's very throne, something that has never been done and which the Law and Commandment of the Prophet condemn." The same discourse still existed in the early eighteenth century, as attested by a French report: "The Turks, who find in the Qur'an everything they choose to look for there, . . . claim that their law does not in any manner allow granting to the Christians the transfer of wheat outside their states."[30]

The exportation of weapons and horses was also prohibited, as was that of various raw materials used in military and naval equipment: cotton, raw wool, hides, and metals such as iron, lead, gold, and silver. These prohibitions were not absolute, however: the Ottomans issued export permits, and a well-placed bribe could always facilitate their acquisition. The highest dignitaries were not above taking part in that trafficking for their own benefit. In addition, smuggling by sea continued apace. The Ottomans would play up the divisions within Christendom to obtain from the Protestant states the strategic articles that the Catholic states refused them: lead, tin, cannonballs, gunpowder. Writing to the king, Henry III's ambassador in Constantinople explained William Harborne's success in establishing cordial relations between the sultan and Queen Elizabeth, not without virtuous indignation: "What gave the Englishman the most favor vis-à-vis these people [the Ottoman rulers] is that he brought a great quantity of steel and broken pieces of images in bronze and brass for casting artillery, and secretly made a promise to bring more in the future, which is odious and pernicious smuggling for all Christendom."[31]

Although, in principle, trade was not supposed to strengthen the partner when he was becoming—or becoming again—an adversary, and though more or less solid limits were established to that end, both sides were perfectly aware of the advantages of commerce. So long as such trade was in surplus goods, it was seen on the Christian side as a factor of public and private enrichment, as the theory of mercantilism would posit. According to a formulation of the municipal magistrates and deputies of commerce in Marseilles in 1679, trade in the Levant was to be "the source of public abundance and individual wealth."[32] But the Ottoman side valued it as well, primarily from a fiscal standpoint, that is, for the customs duties and many other taxes that could be expected from it. In addition, commerce brought into the empire articles and goods they lacked but that were nevertheless an integral part of the luxury of the imperial court and the great houses. Also, certain imports, which by their very nature called for special arrangements, were indispensable for the sultan's armies. Finally, it was not unusual for high dignitaries to become "entrepreneurs" and to draw enormous profits from commercial speculation. The Ottomans therefore thought well of trade (which explains why, under certain circumstances, they united with the Venetians to battle both the Uskoks and the Muslim pirates, and with the French in efforts to neutralize the Barbary corsairs and the Maltese). It is true, however, that Ottoman power did not take measures to support, stimulate, and organize its merchants, as the mercantilist states of the same period did for the benefit of theirs.

In fact, there was always an obvious dissymmetry between the European merchants, who went to the Ottoman Empire in increasing numbers and founded multiple colonies there, and the sultan's subjects (Muslim or not), coming to trade in Christian Europe. These traders existed, however, which is sufficient to refute the idea some have advanced that Islam was an invincible obstacle to traveling to infidel territory. But it is true that their destinations were limited. Venice and its satellites particularly attracted them. They regularly visited the ports close to the Venetian Adriatic: Cattaro, Zara, Sabanico (Šibenik),

Spalato (Split). The local authorities, fearing espionage or the intermingling of people of different religions, strove to cut these foreigners off from the rest of the population: the city of Zara was thus gradually prohibited to Ottoman traders over the course of the sixteenth century. The authorities relegated the merchants to a place called San Marco, established as their lodgings and for their trading activities. Similarly, in 1622 the *conte* of Sebenico recommended that a special building, a *seraglio*, be constructed on the outskirts of the city, to assemble all the sultan's subjects present there.[33] Venice itself received the sultan's subjects, Jews and Christians as well as Muslims. These Muslims were from Anatolia, especially Bursa or, after the opening of the commercial port of Spalato in 1589, Bosnia and Albania. Unlike the Christians and Jews, the Muslims did not settle permanently on the lagoon, and their dispersal throughout the city worried the authorities. All sorts of misdeeds were attributed to them. They themselves complained of being the victims of assaults. The authorities therefore undertook to assemble and isolate them. After several fruitless attempts, they established the *fondaco dei Turchi* in 1621, in the former palace of the dukes of Ferrara on the Grand Canal. The building was renovated to suit its new purpose. There were only two doors: one on the Grand Canal and the other on the land side. The windows were reduced in number and covered with wire mesh. One regulation enacted says a great deal about the bias against the Turkish guests: neither women nor young men nor weapons were to go into the building, which was to be locked up tight at nightfall. That did not definitively solve the problem, however, and the authorities continued to denounce the dispersal of the Turks and its dangers. At the same time, they readily recognized, like the Senate in 1637, that "we are beholden to the Turks trading here for every comfort" and that it was necessary to make an effort to attract them and their valuable merchandise.[34]

Poland (especially the Galician city of Lvów) and Moscow, frequently paired in fact, were also Christian destinations for Ottoman merchants of all faiths, including Muslims. At issue in these regions was primarily "supply" trade, since the merchants, some of whom assumed an official status (these were the *hāssa tajiri* dispatched by the sultan), sought luxury articles, of which the palace was the foremost consumer: precious furs above all, as well as gerfalcons for hunting, narwhal teeth, amber, and other items.

The Rivalry among Nations

As for European commerce in the Ottoman Levant, though it had existed continuously since the medieval period, it underwent notable transformations and developments in the modern period, and in the first place, as to its agents. That trade had always been the business of Mediterranean merchants, primarily Venetians and Genoese, and this remained true under the early Ottomans. The Genoese initially obtained capitulations from them in 1352 (renewed in 1387) and the Venetians, between 1384 and 1387. But Genoa was rapidly eclipsed, its colonial settlements hard-hit by Mehmed II's conquests. Later, in 1566, the loss of Chios dealt a death blow to that "Genoese Romania." Venice held on for a much longer time (its capitulations were renewed twenty times between 1403 and 1641), even though the Ottomans placed them in competition with Florence and Pisa in the second half of the fifteenth century by granting capitulations to Tuscany in 1460, 1463, and 1483. Then the Most Serene Republic had to yield more and more place to the newcomers. First it was the Marseillais who tried their luck. In 1528, at the request of the joint consul in Alexandria for the Marseillais and the Catalans, Süleyman the Magnificent renewed on their behalf the commercial privilege that the Mamluk sultan Qansawh al-Ghawri had granted them on August 23, 1507. But it should not be claimed, as is still often done, that these same French benefited from the capitulations concluded between Francis I and Süleyman the Magnificent in 1536. There is no doubt whatever that the sultan did not ratify these capitulations, which as a result were never in force. It is true, however, that the French merchants benefited from the alliance that the sultan established with France, since that alliance was necessarily accompanied by special protection. In a letter to Francis I in February 1545, Süleyman the Magnificent writes:

> The lieutenant of that ambassador [Captain Polin, assistant to Ambassador Gabriel d'Aramon, who was away from Istanbul at the time] has also indicated that it was your wish that the merchants and traders in your country might continue to come and go in my well-guarded countries, as they have done up to the present. And, in conformity with the affection and friendship that have existed between us in the past and up to this time, inasmuch as your merchants have been in the habit of coming and going in my well-guarded countries, henceforth as well no one shall oppress them or further mistreat them. On the contrary, in accordance with friendship, they must be able to come and go and practice their trade in all safety and security. To respond to your wishes on that subject, sacred orders have been drawn up for the *beylerbey* of Egypt and Syria, as well as for all the beys and qadis of my well-guarded countries, so that none of the merchants coming from your country will be oppressed or mistreated in their comings and goings on land and sea.[35]

As a result, the French obtained their first valid capitulations only in 1569, following negotiations between Claude du Bourg, emissary of Charles IX, and Sokollu Mehmed Pasha, grand vizier to Selim II. The kings of France were therefore not the first "Christian princes" to obtain capitulations from the Porte, despite what royal propaganda would claim.[36] They had long been preceded not only by the Italian states mentioned earlier but also by Poland, which obtained, along with peace, initial guarantees for its residents in 1494. (The Polish capitulations would be renewed in 1553, 1577, and 1607.)

In 1570–1573, French trade no doubt benefited more from the troubles in Venice, at war with the sultan at the time, than from the strengthening of its legal foundations. But it was not long before the French encountered rivals of their own, whose advent on the scene would mark the entry of northwestern Europe to the Levant.

At first, the English presence was extremely modest. A first mention is made of an English merchant by the name of Jenkinson in Aleppo in 1553. But the ambitions of the English, who had no intention of continuing to travel to Venice to acquire Eastern goods, grew stronger in 1580. At that date, William Harborne, *factor* and emissary of two English traders (Edward Osborne and Richard Stapper), having arrived in Istanbul two years earlier, obtained capitulations similar to those of the French, who were greatly displeased thereby. But an incident at sea, the attack of two Greek ships by an English corsair, prevented their ratification. Returning to the Ottoman capital as first ambassador of England in 1583, Harborne made amends for his previous failure, this time obtaining ratified capitulations.[37] France consoled itself as it could by including in its own capitulations a so-called *droit de pavillon*, by which all countries wishing to navigate in Ottoman waters had to do so under the French flag, with the exception, however, of Venice and England. That *droit de pavillon* rapidly became the object of a bitter rivalry between France and England.

In 1581, the English created a Turkey Company, and in 1583 a Venice Company. The two merged in 1592, taking the name Levant Company, which, after a few vicissitudes, received a perpetual charter from King James I in 1605. In the meantime, in 1601, the English had obtained from the Turks what the French would not obtain until 1673: the reduction of their *harbī* customs duties from 5 to 3 percent.

The Netherlands, the other great sea power of the time, tried their luck in turn. In 1612, they sent a special ambassador to Istanbul, Cornelius Haga. As the representative of a nation that had fought so long and so hard against the Catholic Spanish monarchy, he received the best of welcomes at the Porte, and, despite the intrigues of the ambassadors of Venice, France, and England, who conspired against him, he also obtained capitulations and made his special embassy a permanent one. Just as Pera represented a capsule version of the political rivalries of the European states, the Ottoman ports became arenas for their commercial competition.

The Venetians and, to a lesser extent, the French, lost their standing in favor of the newcomers from the north. In the late 1660s, the volume of English commerce, which had managed to reduce its trade deficit by vigorously expanding its sales of cloth to the Levant, reached its peak, surpassing 400,000 pounds sterling. In the 1680s, the English and Dutch controlled, respectively, 43 and 38 percent of European trade in the Levant, whereas the French share represented only 16 percent and the Venetian share had fallen to 3 percent.[38] In general, French commerce in the Levant, promising in the sixteenth century, experienced hard times for the greater part of the seventeenth century. Not only a victim of its new competitors, it was also affected by the political troubles of the kingdom, the poor organization and internal dissensions of the French colonies in the Levant. In 1669, Minister Hugues de Lionne interpreted that slump in a rather unfair manner in the instructions drawn up for Ambassador Denis de La Haye-Ventelet. In it, he reproached the previous French authorities for having been unable to take sufficient advantage of the opportunities offered by the political alliance at the economic level, "our kings giving," according to him, "no application to commerce, and their council not realizing how advantageous it would be to the kingdom to reserve that commerce, which was so great and so considerable, for the French alone."[39]

THE PREEMINENCE OF FRANCE IN THE LEVANT

From the late seventeenth century on, the position of French commerce benefited from several favorable factors: Colbert's energetic measures, mercantilist in their inspiration, which established the monopoly of Marseilles through the charter of freedom granted to that city in 1669. By the order of 1681, they also assured control of the state over the institution of the consul. Similarly, an order of 1685 made residence in the Levant subject to a permit issued by the Marseilles chamber of commerce. In addition, the French took a lesson from the English, surpassing them on their own turf. Thanks to the dynamism of the Languedoc wool industry, duly overseen by detailed regulations, they were able to put high-quality products on the Ottoman market, particularly "London seconds" (*londrins seconds*), which would be a great success with the local elites. Finally, a little later, with the "major capitulations of 1740," the French had at their disposal a legal instrument more complete and precise than all the previous capitulations, which assured them all the protections desirable. They also had another advantage, namely, the retreat of the English and the Dutch, who in the eighteenth century were looking toward new horizons, more promising in their view: America and Asia. The English, however, would return in force to the Levant in the nineteenth century. The French continued to wager heavily on the Levant, which did not prevent them from taking an interest in turn, with some delay, in the new markets of the Americas, Asia, and Africa. The proportion of Marseilles trade in the Levant, which was 40 percent in the late seventeenth century, would be only 25 percent by the end of the eighteenth. In any event, from the 1720s until the late eighteenth century, European commerce in the Levant was dominated by the French. Near the middle of the eighteenth century, France represented more than 65 percent of that commerce, the English 15 percent, the Dutch 3 percent, and the Venetians 16 percent.[40]

NEW TRENDS IN COMMERCE IN THE LEVANT

That French preeminence went hand in hand with a diversification of trade and a change in its nature, compared to what it had been in the Middle Ages and during the first part of the Ottoman period. Until that time, trade in the

Levant had been a transit commerce, the Middle Eastern ports such as Alexandria and Beirut serving as stopover points for articles from much farther away, India and the Far East. The Portuguese's discovery of the ocean route for a time eliminated that traffic, which was partly reestablished later in the sixteenth century, only to disappear—or nearly so—in the seventeenth century. Other transit articles replaced the pepper and spices of earlier times: Yemeni coffee, beginning in the mid-seventeenth century, and Persian silk, transported to Syria by Armenian caravans. For the most part, that was the pattern of English trade in the Levant: Persian silk for English cloth. And the disaffection of the English with the Levant led them to prefer Indian and Italian silk.

The French, by contrast, placed the emphasis on "local" products, that is, on everything they could extract from Anatolia and Rumelia proper. That new orientation was accompanied by a proliferation of settlements. In addition to the old Middle Eastern ports, there was Alexandretta (Iskenderun) and Sidon (Saïda), as well as the large and small outlets for these local products. Smyrna (Izmir), on the Aegean side of Anatolia, having evolved from a modest harbor in the sixteenth century, gradually became the chief commercial center in the Levant, a large cosmopolitan city where the "Franks" felt more at home than in any other Ottoman port. Salonika, though it did not equal Smyrna, played a similar role in eastern Europe. And Istanbul, an unequaled center for consumption, also became a site of international commerce. The French and other "Franks" also frequented other, more modest places on land or sea: Canea, Adrianople (Edirne), Bursa, Angora (Ankara), Satalia (Antalya), as well as the ports of Morea (Patras) and those of the islands of the Archipelago.

The Marseillais came in search of raw materials for their industries. Cotton, from western Anatolia and Macedonia, held the foremost place and experienced a boom during the eighteenth century, increasing from about 860 metric tons annually in the early part of the century to 4,400 metric tons a year for the period 1786–1789, with raw cotton now far surpassing spun. But the extremely silky hair of the Angora goat was also much sought-after, as was horse and camel hair, and "local" silk from the region of Bursa, Peloponnesus, and Cyprus. Hides also played a large role, at least in the first half of the century. Usually imported raw and salted, they were tanned in the Marseilles region. Plant or mineral raw materials, indispensable for tanning and dyeing operations, were also in demand; alum, valonia, gallnuts, saffron, madderwort. The soap factories of Marseilles required imports of oil, as well as rocket and glasswort ash, barilla, saltwort, and potash. The importation of raisins and other dried fruits was also characteristic of that commerce.

The Marseillais traders strove to offset these imports by actively developing exports fed by the Languedoc wool industry. To this they added another category of exports, a further innovation in the structure of trade in the Levant— paradoxically so, since it reversed the former flow of exchanges. They took to the Levant what their predecessors had gone there to seek: sugar, now from the West Indies and Brazil; coffee from the Americas, a less expensive substitute for mocha; indigo from Saint-Domingue (now Haiti), which arrived in Marseilles via Nantes or Bordeaux; cochineal from Mexico, which Marseilles received from Qadiz before reexporting it to the Levant, where it replaced the old Eastern red dyes. Despite that dynamism, French imports from the Levant surpassed exports. It has been demonstrated, however, that there was no trade deficit: "Marseilles became richer by buying more than it sold." In fact, the trade imbalance was offset by "invisible" receipts from offshore maritime transport along the Ottoman coasts (the "caravan," which become a French monopoly) and from "banking commerce" (speculation on currencies and the negotiation of bills of exchange).[41] An expression used by Ambassador Choiseul-Gouffier in a 1788 dispatch to his minister reflects the place that Levantine commerce held in the French economy: "Although the Turks are the most inconvenient of allies . . . , they must also be considered one of the richest colonies of France."[42]

The Resistance of the Ottoman Economy

That startling expression must not be taken literally, however. It is obviously not possible to speak of a colony in the strict sense, or even, despite the claims of a major historiographical current in recent decades, of a "dominated" economy. A major argument in support of that view points out that the Europeans imported raw materials and exported manufactured goods to the Ottoman Empire. In the period under consideration, European commerce naturally had various repercussions on the Ottoman economy and society, but its importance must be relativized in terms of the other sectors of Ottoman trade—key to be sure, though largely unknown—both internal trade and trade with the East. The proportion of Western trade in Ottoman commerce must have been at most between 5 and 10 percent of the whole.[43] In addition, the activities of the Frankish traders were carefully kept in check, both by the authorities ("The Turks are the most inconvenient of allies . . .") and by their partners and local competitors: local brokers and merchants, Greeks, Armenians, Jews, and also Muslims. Finally, European industries were not yet able to strike a fatal blow to local artisanship, which remained vigorous, even though it was deeply affected by the rise in the price of raw materials occasioned by European purchases. In short, we must not commit the sin of anachronism and apply to this period the upheavals to come in the nineteenth and twentieth centuries.

It would also be easy to imagine that these Ottoman ports were a place where Franks residing for a long period of time, sometimes even establishing local roots, could meet and even grow close to Muslims. But in reality that was hardly the case, since these Franks (like the Turks of Venice) lived isolated from the rest of the population, in restricted neighborhoods or even special buildings, the *funduq*. They were therefore separated and protected by walls, just as they were, at another level, by the articles of their capitulations. These organized them into autonomous communities with their own institutions, under the authority of their own consuls, their religious freedom guaranteed by their status as *musta'min*. When young people married there—which the authorities on both sides proscribed (leaving aside their parents' wrath)—they of course did so only with local Christian women, Greek, Armenian, or Levantine (that is, European emigrants). In addition, business was almost never conducted directly with the producers but only through brokers and retailers, who were usually "minorities" as well. These same residents had neither permission nor even the temptation to venture outside the large ports to the interior of the country. A few French experiments in Bursa, Ankara, and Kirkagatch, the center of Anatolian cotton production, remained short-lived exceptions. The local intermediaries did their utmost to maintain the status quo that made them indispensable. Not only were contacts with the subjects of the Great Sultan nonexistent or limited, they were also governed by the tensions and disputes produced by often-conflicting economic interests. If there was one Ottoman institution with which the traders were well acquainted, apart from customs, it was the qadi's tribunal. In short, let us not harbor too many illusions about the role of Levantine ports in promoting knowledge of the other and in teaching mutual tolerance.

THE "NEW TRAVELERS"

The wall of antagonism and ignorance, however, was seriously breached in other ways during the modern period. That was the work of three categories of sappers, distinct in their appearance and objectives, who nevertheless influenced one another.

Let us begin with the travelers. Travel narratives multiplied and, when they were published, were often a great commercial success. The Ottoman Empire or, as it was commonly called, Turkey, was not the only desirable destination. (Persia, India, China, and the New World also fascinated visitors.) But in France at least, it occupied the foremost place: between 1480 and 1609 there were twice as many books printed on the countries of the Turkish empire, on the wars against the Turks, or on the "mores and manners of the Turks" than on North and South America, a world that had only recently been discovered.[44] Persia, with which Europe, and especially France, had only limited relations, was thoroughly treated in the seventeenth century, thanks to such best-sellers as the remarkable accounts of two Huguenots, Jean-Baptiste Tavernier (1630–1633) and Jean Chardin (1664–1670). That explains why, in the early part of the following century, in 1721, Montesquieu preferred that Persians and Turks serve as his "new eye" in his famous *Lettres persanes*.

Apart from the fact that they copied one another, travel narratives were of uneven quality. In the late fifteenth century and even after, there were still travelers who, in the tradition of the old anti-Muslim satires, found on their journeys only confirmation of their original prejudices. That was the case, for example, of a monk by the name of Nicole le Huen. Even in 1487, relating his journey to the Holy Land, he simply reiterated the vituperations against Islam of the fifteenth-century German pilgrim Bernhard von Breydenbach and of the thirteenth-century encyclopedist Vincent of Beauvais. He terms Muhammad a "stinking pig who calls himself a prophet" and all Muslims, whom he still refers to as "Saracens," "totally brutish, carnal, and bestial men."[45] Many narratives by missionaries during the classical period were of the same ilk, though in the best cases they offered a little useful information. For instance, in 1620 Father Boucher, an Observant Franciscan, could not recall without horror his visit to the Holy Sepulchre, "profaned by the reckless fondling of those despicable monsters": "O Great God." he wrote, "when I think of it and remember what I saw there, my hair once more stands on end, the sweat breaks out on my forehead, my blood runs cold, my mind goes blank, and I am struck dumb." His condemnation of the prophet of Islam is absolute: "Muhammad, monster of nature, plague of the earth, aborted runt of hell, scorn of heaven, ruin of men, horror of angels, cesspool of vice," and so on.[46]

But elsewhere, travelers of a different sort appeared in the fifteenth century and subsequently multiplied. They were observant and sought out information, anxious to give their readers a faithful—we would say objective—and serene picture of the realities they discovered. These travelers, like Postel, in turn asked readers to "strip away all preconceptions."[47] That did not rule out criticisms and reproaches when necessary, but without any systematic assumptions. Whether they evoked Islam in general, its prophet, its beliefs, and its rites, or the institutions and mores of the Turks, all these authors set aside exclusionary biases and the traditional sarcasm, in the aim of accuracy and precision. They then made this discovery, astounding when you think about it: not everything that comes from the other, from an other "outside our faith,"[48] is necessarily bad, and may even conform better to the good than what is found in Christendom. The other, far from being excluded from humanity by virtue of his alterity, may provide a more perfect embodiment of it. Such, for example, was the view expressed by Nicolas de Nicolay in the dedication of his book: he wanted to free himself from "that arrogant presumption usurped by the Greeks and Romans, to consider and call another man, or another nation, more barbarous than oneself or one's own. Better to reckon like the old man Terence, who said: 'Being a man, I believe that nothing human is alien to me.'"[49] Some of these works that called into question the prevailing opinions were published fairly quickly and could thus exert an influence on contemporaries, though only to small groups. Many others remained in manuscript form—and hence reached even fewer people— until the time, more or less recent, when scholars rediscovered them. Such works could hardly have had notable effects on their contemporaries, but they do bear witness to what their authors' state of mind must have been.

In retrospect, the first seems to have been Bertrandon de la Broquière, whose *Journeys beyond the Sea*, completed in 1432–1433 but not published until the late nineteenth century, attests to a remarkable open-mindedness. The next chronologically was Arnold von Harff, a young gentleman from the duchy of Juliers and Gueldre, who completed his pilgrimage in 1496–1499.[50] It too was not published until the nineteenth century. Their many successors came from various backgrounds, which is not inconsequential to the nature of their curiosity and therefore to the subjects they privilege. A few, enjoying a certain level of comfort, traveled for pleasure, but most did so for professional reasons. They were missionaries, diplomats, merchants, artisans, soldiers and sailors, literati, doctors, botanists, and so on. Also related to these texts are memoirs of captivity at the hands of the infidels (Schiltsberger, Angiolello, Menavino, Konstantin Mihailović of Ostrovića, George of Hungary) and accounts of embassies. Other writers, taking advantage of the craze, were not travelers in the strict sense but made use of the information provided by true travelers to compile historical and geographical works, some of which were also a success. The majority of these introductions to the East came from the various Italian states, especially Venice. The Venetians, for whom commercial relations—relations in good standing therefore—with the East were vital, could not simply repeat the same libelous fantasies knocked out by authors of the *Turcica* in central Europe. People needed to know as accurately as possible where they stood with these indispensable partners. It is therefore not surprising that the first solid and truly enlightening writings on the origins and history of the Turks had their beginnings on the lagoon. In the early sixteenth century, Donato da Lezze (related to the Zens, one of the patrician families very involved in relations with the East) wrote *A History of the Turks* in Italian, covering the fourteenth and fifteenth centuries. The Turks also appear in the writings of Marc'Antonio Sabellico, historiographer of the Most Serene Republic, and in the treatise of Giovanni Battista Egnazio, composed in Latin in 1516 under the title *On the Caesars*. Andrea Cambini's *Origin of the Turks and of the Ottoman Empire* was reissued several times between 1528 and 1541. Paolo Giovio's *Commentaries on Turkish Affairs* appeared in 1531 and would influence a number of other European authors. It was followed by Benedetto Ramberti's *Turkish Matters*, and above all by Francesco Sansovino's imposing *History of the Origins of the Empire of the Turks*. In the fifteenth and sixteenth centuries, Germanic informants were the second most numerous. In that world directly exposed to the Turkish peril, it took longer to achieve a serene perspective on the adversary. Among the remarkable authors from that region, let us mention, by way of example, Hans Dernschwam, who went to Istanbul and Anatolia in 1553–1555,[51] and Stephan Gerlach, whose journal covering the years 1573–1578 was published in Frankfurt-am-Main in 1674. Ogier Ghiselin de Busbecq's *Turkish Letters* is a special case: the author, ambassador to Constantinople of Ferdinand of Habsburg—Charles V's brother, whom Ferdinand would succeed as emperor of the Holy Roman Empire—was a Fleming who wrote in Latin. The work is a literary gem, studded with penetrating analyses, which, in its many editions, would significantly influence the view of the Turks in Europe.[52] During that same period, the French placed third in the number of accounts published. Then came the English, who would become numerous in the late sixteenth century, after William Harborne's embassy. Let us also mention the travel narratives of John Sanderson (1585–1588, 1592–1598, 1599–1602), which were not published until 1931,[53] and the 1585 text of Henry Austell, which was printed in London in 1599. Coming in fifth were travelers from Spain.

Let us reiterate the view of Frédéric Tinguely, for whom "the considerable volume of Italian and German accounts cannot conceal a sort of central kernel, toward which different trends converge and which unites the texts of seven French travelers."[54] He cites Pierre Belon (1547–1549), Jean Chesneau (1547–1552, 1553–1555), Jacques Gassot (1547–1549), Pierre Gilles (1547?–1552, 1553–1555), and Nicolas de Nicolay (1551–1552). Nicolay's work appeared in 1568, accompanied by engravings depicting the costumes of the different nations of the empire and those of the principal agents of the state. Tinguely's list continues with Guillaume Postel, who took two trips to Turkey (1535–1537, 1549–1550) and was also an astounding scholar. It ends with André Thévet (1549–1552): the first edition of his *Cosmography of the Levant* dates to 1554. What all these authors have in common is that they are associated in some way with the embassy to Constantinople of Gabriel d'Aramon (1546–1553). That brilliant embassy, the apogee of Frankish-Ottoman rapprochement, had as its complement a remarkable cultural dimension.

An inventory of travel narratives from the first half of the seventeenth century also finds Italy in the first position, but France comes in second this time, far ahead of Germany, England, Spain, or Poland.[55] Among the important seventeenth-century witnesses, let us cite the Roman Pietro della Valle, who traveled around the Ottoman Empire, in Persia, and in India, between 1614 and 1626; the Englishman Thomas Roe, who, after being ambassador to the Grand Mogul, was ambassador to Constantinople from 1621 to 1628; and the Frenchman Jean Thévenot, who passed through the Ottoman Empire as well as Ethiopia between 1655 and 1658 and gave a remarkably disinterested description of the rites of Sunni Islam in his *Account of a Journey to the Levant*, published in 1664. In the late seventeenth century, Paul Ricaut's *Present State of the Ottoman Empire* was particularly influential.[56]

The Enlightenment also had a number of perspicacious and insightful travelers, of whom we may cite, without being exhaustive in any way, James Bruce, Carsten Niebuhr, Henry Maundrell, Richard Pococke, Jean de La Roque, Claude-Étienne Savary, and Thomas Shaw. Lady Mary Montagu was a special case: the wife of an English ambassador to Constantinople in the early part of the century, she provided access, through the letters to her friends, to a mysterious world inhabited by myths and fantasies: the world of the Oriental woman.

With a certain propensity for paradox, she painted that world in terms of simplicity, humanity, and freedom.

THE OTHER AS MODEL

Of the insights of all kinds provided by these travelers, the one with the greatest intellectual import was the recognition of positive qualities in the Turks, even a certain moral superiority, since it called into question the most established certainties, less about the perfection of Christians than about the necessarily deep-seated and generalized depravity of the infidels.

The authors recognized the Turks' military qualities—the least they could do—but in this instance these lay less in their physical strength or technology than in certain virtues, which the writers thereby indicate were desperately lacking in their Christian adversaries. And these qualities—order, discipline, sobriety, modesty, silence—played no negligible role in Ottoman military successes. "All this shows you," notes Ogier Ghiselin de Busbecq, "with what patience, sobriety, and economy the Turks struggle against the difficulties which beset them, and wait for better times."[57] The visit he had the opportunity to make to a Turkish camp similarly inspired his admiration:

> The first thing that I noticed was that the soldiers of each unit were strictly confined to their own quarters. Any one who knows the conditions which obtain in our own camps will find difficulty in believing it, but the fact remains that everywhere there was complete silence and tranquility, and an entire absence of quarrelling and acts of violence of any kind, and not even any shouting or merrymaking due to high spirits or drunkenness. Moreover, there was the utmost cleanliness. . . . Moreover, you never see any drinking or revelry or any kind of gambling, which is such a serious vice amongst our soldiers.[58]

The same admiration and the same comparison at the expense of the Christian armies are found in a number of other travelers: "There is no city more orderly than that camp," wrote Louis Deshayes, baron of Courmenin, in 1621. And during that troubled time, he still retained his predecessors' regard for the discipline of the Janissaries: "There is an admirable orderliness among them, which I wish could be established in our own infantry."[59] In fact, the orderliness lauded by Deshayes was not only true of the army but also existed throughout that empire. He declared that "there is no monarchy where there is greater order, or where all things are better regulated than among them."[60] As a happy consequence of military discipline, the soldiers, as several authors pointed out, behaved "properly" toward civilians. Gassot, who had accompanied Süleyman's army to Persia in 1548, agreed: "I cannot omit to tell you of the greatest obedience they show the Great Sultan, by not stealing things around the villages, by not taking anything at all without paying, and they are very conscientious about it."[61]

Another oft-cited example of Ottoman military discipline came from foreign ambassadors received at the Palace of Topkapı. They note the spectacle of troops, as they were welcomed by the grand vizier and then allowed to kiss the sultan's hand. Busbecq went into raptures at the sight of "the silence and good discipline . . . [with] none of the cries and murmurs which usually proceed from a motley concourse."[62] The same was true for a Provençal (and Protestant) young gentleman allowed into the retinue of Ambassador François de Noailles, bishop of Dax:

> [We looked] with great pleasure and greater admiration at that frightening number of Janissaries and other soldiers standing along the wall of the yard, hands joined behind them like monks, in such silence that it seemed to us we were seeing not men but statues. And they remained motionless in that way for more than seven hours, without one of them ever making a gesture to speak or move. Of course, it is almost impossible to conceive of that discipline and obedience if one has not seen it.[63]

Another recurrent theme among travelers aspiring to be truthful was praise of the judiciary system, all the easier to make in that the link between that justice and the law of Islam was left aside. That enthusiasm casts into sharp relief the flaws in that realm in the authors' countries of origin. The foremost quality of that justice was to be swift (though some did acknowledge that such swiftness could also have its disadvantages). As Stochove, among so many others, observed in the mid-seventeenth century: "Furthermore, there is nowhere in the world where justice, both criminal and civil, is administered with such promptness, since the biggest trials last only three or four days."[64] That speed made justice much less onerous, as Du Loir, another traveler of that time, pointed out, not sparing the irony: "For myself, I wish that those who have a court case in France had a right of committimus to convene their trials in that Chamber. They would fare better to make the journey to Constantinople than to go back and forth to the courtroom, and their cases would be more promptly expedited at less cost."[65] The same author also points out the equality of all before the qadi, and more particularly, of all faiths: "There the Christian and Jew as well as the Turk is heard equally, for the smallest subject of complaint, without the necessity of an advocate's eloquence to defend the truth."[66]

Another pillar of the Ottoman system, meritocracy—as opposed to nobility of birth—is also praised by several fifteenth- and sixteenth-century authors, such as Spandugino, Busbecq, Postel, and Pierre Belon du Mans, who writes: "Nobility in the Turk's country is not like that in the countries of Christians, who inherit it from father to son. But the Turk who will hold the highest position vis-à-vis the Great Sultan is the one who does not know whence he comes or who his father and mother are; and anyone who is paid a salary by the Turk regards himself as a gentleman just as surely as the Great Turk himself."[67]

By relativizing notions in that way, Belon du Mans "deconstructs" the traditional discourse on slavery among the Turks. He adds in fact: "The greatest honor and good that a man in Turkey can have is to admit he is the Turk's slave, as in our country we say that we are the servant of some prince."[68] Another writer, Petremol, actually somewhat isolated in his interpretation, proposes a "rereading" of the "avarice" usually attributed to the Turks: "They do not value presents so much in terms of the need they have for them, or in terms of the greatness of the present, but rather as a sign of friendship, such that they delight as much or more in giving and presenting them as in receiving them."[69]

Travelers not only corrected on occasion the misunderstandings about the Turks, they also sometimes took a diametrically opposed view regarding several common allegations that were an integral part of the culture of antagonism. They invited accusers to examine their own consciences. The Turks were said to be barbaric and crude, but several travelers instead emphasized the cleanliness of their streets, their bodies, and their clothing, which Christendom, including great lords, could advantageously take as a model, and which made the Turks the true heirs to the Greeks and Romans. Postel expresses this in his own way: "I want the same availability of baths for the great personages and great cities of Christendom, as a very healthy thing, which has been the occasion to urge here what I wanted to write at greater length: for the great good that comes of it, and whereby the ancients, knowing this, avoided most of their illnesses."[70]

Cleanliness went hand in hand with decency in dress, a modesty that seemed far removed from the lewdness and debauchery ordinarily attributed to the Turks. Here again, the fault and the lesson to be learned were not on the side people thought. In Turkey, it was possible to assess what was shocking (and unflattering as well) about certain types of clothing that seemed natural in the West. Busbecq notes: "Our mode of dress seemed as strange to them as theirs appeared extraordinary to us. They all wear long garments down to their heels, which seems more decent, and their cut is much more becoming to them. By contrast, we wear them so short that, against propriety, it is easy to see the form and shape of the parts that nature wants to be covered, and to make men appear small."[71] Geuffroy had already noted the Turks' disapproval of the "codpiece on breeches, which displeases them greatly and seems very indecent to them."[72]

Just as several travelers point to the exceptional character of polygamy—reserved for the sultan and the very wealthy—which had so roused the Western imagination, they also call into question that other fantasy: the lasciviousness of the women. Postel, for example, ironically sums up the matter: "And of course, a recitation of the purity, simplicity, and decency that appears in the ladies from those parts, would, it seems to me, be a very odious thing to make many Christian ladies hear."[73]

It was commonly said that the Turks were incapable of "decency," used in a much broader sense, but several travelers dispute the validity of that reputation. According to Postel, it could be attributed solely to the testimony of peoples who had to suffer at the hands of some Turks but was not justified in general, if, in judging the matter, you were to "set aside all preconceptions like a good judge."[74] That was also the conclusion reached by Du Loir, who does not hesitate to reverse the usual scale of values by placing the decency of the Turks above that of the Greeks, those other Christians (schismatics to be sure):

> Naturally they are good, and it must not be said that the climate makes them so, since the Greeks were born in the same country, with such different propensities that they retained only the bad qualities of their ancestors: namely, deviousness, perfidy, and vanity. The Turks, by contrast, profess sincerity and especially modesty, with the exception of the courtiers, almost all of whom everywhere are slaves of ambition and avarice. Simplicity and ingenuousness reign among them with unparalleled freedom.[75]

The most astonishing thing is that they do not reserve their decency for their coreligionists alone: "It is worth remembering," exclaims Jean Chesneau, "with what loyalty the Turks behave toward the Christians, which the Christians do not do even among themselves."[76]

These few examples show the extent to which travelers, in light of an experience whose veracity they loudly proclaim, could attest to a new perception and could voice a discourse countering the age-old prejudices. Of course, they do not go so far as to praise Islam, but they are at least capable of lauding Muslims and their works. The authors thus potentially open a breach in the culture of conflict.

EVLIYA ÇELEBI AMONG THE FRANKS

Nothing equivalent was to be found on the other side. The dissymmetry we observed regarding merchants[77] was even sharper among travelers and can be attributed to the same deep-seated causes, whatever the analysis one might give (which is not our objective here). For the period concerned, only a very limited number of Muslim travel narratives to the countries of the "Franks" have survived, and they provide their potential readers or listeners with only meager information about the realities in these countries. That is true even of the most famous of the Ottoman travelogues, written by Evliya Çelebi in the second half of the seventeenth century. Evliya traveled primarily within the borders of the Ottoman Empire and, when he happened to venture beyond them—or when he claimed to have done so, since it is doubtful he personally went to all the foreign countries he talks about—the particulars he gives are so vague and fanciful that it is difficult to identify the sites in question. Several of the places he speaks of remain indecipherable enigmas for the modern commentator. What, for example, could correspond to the city of Karısh, which he presents as one of the most important in Holland? It is particularly surprising that he does not give more precise and reliable notions about that country, since he had no lack of opportunities to meet nationals from the Netherlands in several Ottoman cities.[78]

But precisely, is the aim of his narration to inform? Is it not rather to captivate and entertain? His description of Vienna is a case apart. We now know that, contrary to what used to be thought, it is very likely that he actually went to that city in 1665, in the retinue of the Ottoman ambassador, Kara Mehmed.[79] A number of indications he provides are accurate and attest to a thorough knowledge of the city and its inhabitants. His evocation of Saint Stephen's Cathedral, for example, is germane on several points, though on others, it is perfectly capricious. His recognition of the infidel's superiority in certain matters is telling: he vaunts the care taken in properly preserving the works in the cathedral's library and notes in passing the presence of Mercator and Hondius's *Atlas minor* and of Ortelius's *Geography*. Conversely, he condemns the disastrous neglect from which the most prestigious libraries of Islam suffered. In other words, for him, as often for his Western counterparts, praise of the other is a more or less explicit criticism of his own people, an exhortation to reform.[80]

THE BIRTH OF ORIENTALISM

To return to the Europeans: another category of go-betweens with the Muslim world stands apart from the travelers we have spoken of at some length, first, by their object but above all by their approach. These go-betweens were primarily concerned with the fundaments of Islamic culture in general, the Arabic language, and the scriptural sources of Islam, beginning with the Qur'an. Some were also travelers, but many were bookworms who had never gone to the countries where the manuscripts they relied on originated. These were the first Orientalists, who began to appear in the fifteenth and sixteenth centuries, though the term did not emerge until the very end of the period, in English in 1779 and in French in 1799. The word *orientalisme* did not even enter the dictionary of the Académie Française until 1838.[81] The Orientalists' primary intention was neither pro-Islam nor disinterested. At least at the beginning, their aims were apologetics and proselytism. In the tradition of Peter the Venerable and his team of Qur'anic translators in the twelfth century, they wanted to know Islam better in order to better combat it and to better curtail it by promoting the conversion of its followers. They wanted to learn the Arabic language, as well as Hebrew, Aramaic, and Syriac, for the purpose of biblical exegesis. They also needed to translate the holy scriptures into Arabic, for the sake of Muslims and, in the first place, of the Eastern Christians, whose state of ignorance they universally deplored. All the same, whatever their objective, knowledge emerged the winner and, having once been a means, tended to became an end in itself.

In the first half of the fifteenth century, John of Segovia (d. 1458), a cardinal *in partibus* who had retired to Savoy, produced (with collaborators) a trilingual Qur'an in Arabic, Castilian, and Latin, the text of which has been lost. In the same century, only Italy, particularly Florence, was a living center for the study of Eastern as well as ancient languages. Italy was the birthplace of the man who apparently launched the first Arabic studies in France, the Dominican Agostino Giustiniani (1470–1536). In 1516, he published in Genoa a psalter in seven versions, including one in Arabic, before being summoned to Paris. In the France of his time, knowledge of Arabic was becoming a component of a humanist education. In his famous letter to his son Pantagruel, Gargantua recommends, among other things, that he learn the "Arabicque" language. In 1539, Guillaume Postel received the title of royal lector of "Greek, Hebrew, and Arabic letters" at the Collège Royal (the future Collège de France), which had been founded a few years earlier. His contribution to Arabic philology is an important aspect of his vast and diverse body of writings. He published an Arabic alphabet within the context of a work devoted to the alphabets of twelve languages, and, for the first time in the West, an Arabic grammar (*Grammatica arabica*). In 1543, he provided a new translation of the *Fatiha*, the first sura of the Qur'an. He also worked on the Syriac version of the Gospels and probably also on an Arabic version. Simultaneously, he pursued his knowledge of Islam and of Judaism, with the objective proper to him: to lay a new foundation for Christianity in light of the other two forms of monotheism, in order to make it the universal religion and the basis of concord among all peoples. Whatever might be said about that idealism, that mysticism even, which often had disconcerting aspects, he attests particularly to a knowledge of Islam that is altogether impressive, in such works as *Quattuor librorum de orbis terrae concordia: On the Republic of the Turks and, When the Occasion Arises, on the Mores and Laws of All the Muhammadans*, which appeared in French, this time in Poitiers, in 1560. He would revise that work in 1575 under the title *On Eastern Histories and Primarily on the Turks or Turkites Both Scythian and Tartaresque*. In it he included a dictionary of "the most common" Turkish words.

Postel's Arabic teachings were perpetuated by the most famous of his students, François Juste Scaliger (d. 1609), who was appointed to the Arabic chair at Leiden University in 1593. In the late sixteenth and early seventeenth century, Arabic studies were represented in Italy (where Ferdinando de' Medici, cardinal and grand duke of Tuscany, set up an Arabic-character printing press in 1586), and in France, Germany, and the Netherlands. The indispensable work tools— grammars, dictionaries, editions of texts—began to appear. The role of the Netherlands, the sanctuary of Protestant culture, was preponderant at the time, with scholars such as F. Ravlenghien, or Raphelengus (1539–1597), who taught Arabic in Leiden in about 1593; and Thomas van Erpe, or Erpenius (1584–1624), and his student Jacob Golius (1596–1667). Over the course of the seventeenth century, that first Orientalist Europe expanded further: in 1627, Pope Urban VIII created the Sacred Congregation of Propaganda in Rome, which was an important center of learning on the fringes of missionary activity; and in 1638, Richard Pococke was the first to occupy a chair in Arabic at Oxford.

Along with knowledge of the Arabic language, promoted by Christian Arabs' stays in Europe, knowledge of Islam and of Arab history developed greatly, though within limited circles (academic or not), throughout the seventeenth and eighteenth centuries. That movement preceded, then went hand in hand with, the *Aufklärung*, or Enlightenment.

A first translation of the Qur'an into a European language—Italian, as it happened—was printed in Venice in 1547. The translator was Andrea Arrivabene, who based himself on the medieval Latin version of Robert of Ketton, greatly abridged and reworked. Shortly before, in 1530, the Qur'an had been printed in Arabic in the same city, but all the copies were burned on the order of Pope Paul III.[82]

In 1647, André du Ryer, former consul of France in Egypt, provided a first French translation of the Qur'an, *L'Alcoran de Mahomet*, which came out in a second edition in 1649. Somewhat skewed by the constant use of Christian terminology, it was nevertheless closer to the Arabic text than the Latin translations of the Middle Ages. The next French translation, by Claude Savary in 1783, was already much more satisfactory. In the meantime, in 1734 George Sale, an Arabist and lawyer, published a remarkable English translation of the Qur'an, accompanied by a high-quality "preliminary discourse" with sober and well-informed notes.

In 1691 and 1698, two volumes of the monumental opus of Ludovico Marracci, a priest from Lucca, were published in succession in Padua. They included a complete and excellent translation of the Qur'an into Latin as well as a refutation of Islam, in a new tone free of all aggressiveness. A collection of valuable historical works followed. In 1697, Barthélemy d'Herbelot's *Bibliothèque Orientale*, an overview of Muslim history with a telling subtitle—*Universal Dictionary Generally Containing Everything Having to Do with Knowledge of the Peoples of the East*—appeared posthumously, courtesy of Antoine Galland. In his substantial preface, Galland laid the foundations for the study of Eastern peoples and civilizations. In 1684, Richard Simon (1638–1712), in his *Critical History of the Customs of the Nations of the Levant*, gave a rigorous and objective description of the beliefs and rites of Islam, basing himself on the work of a Muslim theologian. Some twenty years later, the Dutch Arabist Adriaan Relan took up the question with greater proficiency, basing himself solely on Muslim sources, in his *De religione mahommedica* (Utrecht, 1705). Departing from the traditional invectives, other works reconsidered the personality and career of the Prophet: such was the case for the biography Pierre Bayle provided in his *Critical Dictionary* (1st ed., 1697), which he reworked in later editions to reflect the advance of knowledge. At the same time, Bayle presents Islam as a tolerant religion, rational and reasonable, humane and civilizing—all themes that would foster the philosophy of the Enlightenment and its battle against the Catholic church. In 1720, an anonymous pamphlet appeared in England with a title that announced its tone: *Mahomet No Impostor!* Another positive and even apologetic biography of the Prophet was written by a freethinker, Henri de Boulainvilliers (1658–1722). Left unfinished by its author, it would be completed by a friend and published posthumously in London in 1730.[83] At the same time in Germany, Johann Jakob Reiske (1716–1774) displayed incomparable erudition in Arab literature and history and did not conceal his admiration for Islam, meeting with incomprehension and attacks by those around him. The Oxford Arabist Simon Ockley (1678–1720) also made the shift from scholarship to admiration in a history of the Saracens published in 1708.

Dragomans and Erudite Diplomats

Among the initiators of that discovery of Arab Islamic culture, a place must be made for those professionals employed in the European embassies and consulates established in the Muslim world, especially in the capital and the ports of the Ottoman Empire: the dragomans. Necessarily possessing more or less extensive training in the three languages of the Islamic East—Arabic, Turkish, and Persian—they pursued practical activities for the most part, as translators and interpreters. Some of them, however, proved to be more interested in erudition and embarked on scholarly works. A precursor on that path was the interpreter from Lorraine in the service of Poland, François Mesgnien-Meninski, who in 1680 published an imposing *Thesaurus Linguarum Orientalium, Turcicae, Arabicae, Persicae* in Vienna. One undertaking destined for enormous success was the translation, between 1704 and 1717, of the *Thousand and One Nights*, by Antoine Galland (1646–1715), who, among other works, also left behind a translation of the Qur'an that has never been published. Galland was not a dragoman in the strict sense, but, attached to the embassy of the marquess of Nointel, he was a great traveler as well as a remarkable scholar. By contrast, Jean-François Pétis de la Croix, a genuine interpreter and the son of an interpreter, published a translation of the *Thousand and One Days* in 1732. At the end of the period, the most prolix representative of these dragomans by training, who played a great role in initiating his readers into the history of Islam, was the Austrian Joseph von Hammer-Purgstall. A student at the Oriental Academy in Vienna, author of a monumental history of the Ottoman Empire and of many other works dealing with the present as well as the past, he was also the founder of the first Orientalist review, the *Fundgruben des Orients* (1809–1818), precursor to other organs of the press that appeared in the various European capitals during the nineteenth century.

Compared to the Orientalists from other backgrounds, the dragomans and embassy secretaries were less likely to confine themselves to the fundamental texts of Islam and its early days. Their curiosity was more wide-ranging, in terms of the languages considered, the literary genres, and the periods concerned, including the most contemporary. They were impelled by the spirit of the eighteenth century generally, which, in its realism and optimistic and positivist approach, could not be satisfied with a totally disincarnated erudition, which in fact lost ground in the second half of that century. But in any case, the dragomans were predisposed to be open to the concrete and contemporary, by virtue of their professional practice and the circumstances of their training. Former students at the École des Jeunes de Langues, during their studies they had been induced to translate, as exercises, the various manuscripts collected in the royal libraries of their different countries. Such was the case for the French *jeunes de langues* in the period 1730–1750. The works they produced under these conditions, at the instigation of Ambassador Villeneuve, are the source of the translations of Eastern manuscripts housed at the Bibliothèque de France, a collection that remains in large part unpublished.[84] Since the requirements of their practical training led them quite naturally to focus on the Ottoman Turk, they brought to light a few works by a people that was truly the last from whom the West expected to find a literature of quality. La Haye, ambassador to Constantinople, dispelled all illusions in that regard, when he wrote in a dispatch to Mazarin on April 23, 1644: "As for Turkish and Persian books, I believe I am obliged to alert Your Eminence that there is nothing in those two languages but bad romances and fabulous stories, or commentaries on the Qur'an, worse than any kind of romance and fable, and which these people judge much greater than their worth."[85] A true connoisseur like Galland, a discerning and regular customer of the booksellers in Istanbul, reacted passionately against such an opinion. He administered the following lesson in 1697 in his preface to Herbelot's *Bibliothèque*: "We show some favor toward the Arabs, and they appear to have cultivated the sciences with great diligence. We attribute politeness to the Persians, and we do them justice. But the Turks, by virtue of their name alone, are so disparaged that ordinarily it is enough to name them to signify a barbarous, crude nation in complete ignorance." But that is an injustice dictated by ignorance and prejudice, for in reality the Turks "are in no way inferior to the Arabs or to the Persians in the sciences and belles lettres common to these three nations, and which they have cultivated almost from the beginning of their empire."

In the Turkish and Persian disciplines, the first works—dictionaries or conversation manuals—were for the most part practical in their objectives, though that did not exclude a scientific aspect to some of them. Such was the case for the work of Cosimo of Carbognano, dragoman of the Naples embassy in Constantinople, who published in Latin the *Principles of Turkish Grammar for the Use of Apostolic Missionaries in Constantinople* (Rome, 1794). Yet it was difficult for Galland's lessons on the plurality of the literatures of Islam to be heard, and the hierarchy he evoked continued to dominate Orientalism for a long time. This was still an embryonic discipline: Sylvestre de Sacy, professor at the École des Langues Orientales—created by the Convention in 1795—would finally fix its rules and methods for all of Europe in the early nineteenth century. For the moment, it had a tendency to confine itself to a philological approach to the founding texts and was therefore far removed from the living realities of Islam at the time.

Philosophical Reflection

Finally, it fell to a third category of actors to fully learn the lessons to be drawn from the empirical information that the observations of travelers and the discoveries of scholars provided. These were the philosophers. It was incumbent upon them to extract the meaning and import of these observations, to which travelers and scholars generally limited themselves. They then integrated them into more far-reaching reflections on Islam, Christianity, and religion generally; on the nature of political regimes and societies; and ultimately, on the human condition.

Well before the Enlightenment systematically called all the cultures known outside Christianity to serve as witnesses in its indictment against the established order, the political philosophy of the Renaissance sought to theorize the Ottoman case. It was a burning question at the time. In *The Prince* (1513), therefore, Machiavelli contrasted the Turkish and French regimes, noting: "The entire monarchy of the Great Turk is governed by a single master, the others are his servants. . . . The king of France, conversely, lives among a multitude of great lords of a very ancient lineage, recognized and beloved by their own subjects. Each has his hereditary privileges, which the king cannot touch without peril." On such premises, philosophers elaborated the conception of the Ottoman government as a tyranny, a view destined for great success at every level of discourse relating to the Turks. That tyranny was linked, implicitly or explicitly, to Islam. From 1630 on, the term "Oriental despotism" was in use. Nevertheless, an opposing theory appeared in the late sixteenth century in the writings of the jurisconsul Jean Bodin. The powerful author of *The Historical Method* (1566), *The Six Books of the Republic* (1576), and the *Colloquium heptaplomores* (*Colloquium of the Seven Scholars*; 1593?), which remained in manuscript form, he did not conceal his admiration for the political acumen of the Ottomans, whom he saw as the worthy successors of the Romans. He undertook to justify, in terms of political "engineering," their most violently denounced institutions, such as the perpetration of fratricide in the imperial family and the forced conscription of Christian boys. He even gave a legal justification for the latter practice, the *devshirme*, and for the sultan's ownership of all arable land, basing himself on the right of conquest. In addition, borrowing Aristotelean categories, he identified the Ottomans not as a tyranny, as in the generally held view, but as belonging in an intermediate category between tyranny and monarchy, to which he gave the name "seigneurial monarchy." Under such a system, "the prince is made lord of goods and persons by right of arms and the rules of war, governing his subjects as the family patriarch does his slaves."[86]

These distinctions, which also entailed a rehabilitation, no longer made sense to Montesquieu. In view of an Ottoman regime whose image had in the meantime continued to deteriorate, he revived and legitimated the theory of tyranny, which became that of despotism. Although *The Persian Letters* possessed an exotic charm and, in any case, took as its true subject not Islam but French society, unmasked by a withering gaze, Islam truly was condemned in *The Spirit of Laws*. Islam, by its fatalism and the passivity that resulted, catered to despotism. Montesquieu imposed that idea for a long time, and the scholarly and penetrating critique that Abraham Hyacinthe Anquetil Duperron made of it in his *Oriental Legislation* in 1778 was not enough to topple a view that would continue to be taken as self-evident in the following century.

Voltaire, as has often been pointed out, was more changeable and ambivalent about Islam. He provides a very negative image of it in his tragedy with a revealing title: *Muhammad and Fanaticism* (1742). There the Prophet is portrayed as a rogue and a cruel manipulator, an "armed Tartuffe." But in that play, which was quickly banned, was Islam the author's true target? Napoleon gave the response in a famous remark: "He attacks Jesus Christ in Muhammad." Voltaire evolved on the subject, however, as attested by several favorable estimations in his tales, especially *Candide*, and above all, in *Essay on the Mores and Spirit of Nations* (1756) and the *Philosophical Dictionary* (1764). A reader of Herbelot, Boulainvilliers, and Georges Sale, Voltaire understood Islam as a kind of deism, close to his own convictions, and he praised its spirit of moderation and tolerance. That more appealing image had infinitely less impact on public opinion than his *Muhammad*. In any event, it was intended primarily as an implicit denunciation of *l'infâme*, that is, clerical Christianity.

The image of Islam was more clearly positive in Rousseau, whatever the role played by his oft-cited familial bond with the Muslim world: the father of the "citizen of Geneva" was in fact a "clockmaker of the seraglio" in Constantinople, while his uncle practiced the same trade in Isfahan. In *Émile* (1762), Rousseau holds up the Turks, "generally more humane, more hospitable than we are," as an example for his pupil. In the *Social Contract* (1752), he praises the Prophet for the close bond he established between politics and religion.

Like Boulainvilliers, Rousseau admired Muhammad as a great lawmaker of lasting accomplishments. All in all, it is clear that the assessment is mixed. Although the Enlightenment broke away from the traditional culture of conflict, with a calmer and better-informed view of Islam, that view was far from uniformly positive, especially with regard to the sociopolitical effects of the Prophet's teachings. But the newest and most important contribution probably lay not in that realm but in the promotion of religious tolerance as a preeminent philosophical value. The underlying intentions had to do first and above all with Christendom itself, implying no judgment whatever of Islam or of any other religion at issue. The precursor in this matter was John Locke in his *Essay concerning Toleration* (1667), then in his *Letters concerning Toleration*, composed in Latin in Amsterdam in 1685–1686. Locke first set his sights on the politico-religious divisions of England and Europe. He utters this significant statement: "Neither Pagan nor Mahometan, nor Jew, ought to be excluded from the civil rights of the commonwealth because of his religion."[87] He had two major successors in the eighteenth century: Voltaire, and then, at the end of the century, the great figure of the *Aufklärung*, Lessing, author of *Nathan the Wise* (1779), *Education of the Human Race*, and the *Masonic Dialogues*.

For its champions, tolerance undoubtedly went hand in hand with a dose of skepticism and thus bore the mark of a certain de-Christianization. But others went even further. Another, more radical facet of the "crisis of conscience"— namely, atheism or the freethinking current—also targeted Christianity in particular but was obviously not inconsequential for an understanding of Islam as well. In fact, Islam provided a privileged opportunity for religious comparatism, which had the effect of relativizing Christianity by demonstrating that it obeyed the same historical and sociological laws as any other religion. Such was the—sulfurous—message of the pioneering work of Henry Stubbe (d. 1676), *The Rise and Progress of Mahometanism*, which circulated only in manuscript form but would be recopied until 1718.[88] That religious comparatism developed further in the eighteenth century, especially in Pastoret's *Zoroaster, Confucius, and Muhammad, Compared as Sectarians, Lawmakers, and Moralists* (1797). A charade by Anacharsis Cloots took to an extreme the relativization that results from comparatism. Responding to a book by the theologian Bergier, titled *The Certainty of the Proofs of Christianity* (1773), he parodied it point for point in *The Certainty of the Proofs of Muhammadism*, which he attributed to a certain Ali-Gier-Ber, alfaqui.[89]

TURQUERIES AND "FRANKISH FASHIONS"

What stood to be learned from foreign peoples with different mores and customs, and especially, from the Muslims, primarily the Persians and Turks, did not simply feed reflection. It sparked the imaginations of an undoubtedly wider audience. The fact that these peoples, especially the Turks, were generally as rejected at the religious level as they were feared in the field of arms, did not keep them from also eliciting insatiable curiosity and constant fascination. The number of travel narratives and, in several cases, their enormous success, attest to that, as does the favor enjoyed by certain translations, such as Galland's *Thousand and One Nights*. The appeal of all the figurative representations is evidence as well. These could be illustrations of certain travel narratives, such as that of Nicolas de Nicolay, or manuscript or printed collections of images. They might depict scenes from Turkish life or the different costumes of officeholders in the states, nations, and trades of the empire, as did the collection published by Charles de Ferriol (1637–1722), ambassador to Constantinople.

The Oriental pictures of first-rate painters such as the Swiss Jean-Étienne Lio-tard (1702–1789) and two Frenchmen, Jean-Baptiste Vanmour (1671–1731) and Corneille le Bruyn (1652–1711), fed the same craze. Although Europeans in the modern age no longer sought science in the Islamic East, as they had in the Middle Ages, they at least found it a source of inspiration (as they did India, China, and America).

What was happening on the other side during this time? Scientific and especially technical knowledge, now coming from the West, had no difficulty making inroads in the East during the early days of the Ottoman Empire. That was spectacularly true of artillery and firearms in the fifteenth and sixteenth centuries, and "renegades" going to seek refuge or their fortune with the Great Turk were key actors in these transfers. Busbecq notes in retrospect the Ottomans' capacity for adaptation, in a famous passage from the third of his *Turkish Letters*:

> For no nation has shown less reluctance to adopt the useful inventions of others; for example, they have appropriated to their own use large and small cannons and many other of our discoveries. They have, however, never been able to bring themselves to print books and set up public clocks. They hold that their scriptures, that is, their sacred books, would no longer be scriptures if they were printed; and if they established public clocks, they think that the authority of their muezzins and their ancient rites would suffer diminution. In other matters they pay great respect to the time-honoured customs of foreign nations, even to the detriment of their own religious scruples. This, however, is only true of the lower classes.[90]

Similarly, the artistic blossoming of the Italian *cinquecento* did not fail to have an impact in the Ottoman Empire. Mehmed II, "prince of the Renaissance" in some respects, requested a painter from Venice and had his portrait drawn by Gentile Bellini. Subsequently, the empire, steeped in its superiority and grown rigid by an increasingly prominent religious conformism, further closed itself off from European influences. That did not prevent the formation of small Istanbul circles, bringing together a few individuals present in the capital—foreigners or subjects of the sultan, Muslims or not—who were curious about science and who exchanged their information about the latest discoveries. A circle of that type formed around the geographer Kātib Çelebi.[91] But such phenomena remained rare and discreet. Later, in the eighteenth and nineteenth centuries, military defeats persuaded a few Ottoman rulers to once again open themselves to the technical progress of the infidels in well-defined areas: tactics, artillery, shipbuilding, and fortifications. "Volunteers" from allied powers, such as Bonneval Pasha, who became the chief of gunners (*humbaracı bashı*), or the Baron de Tott, who fortified the Dardanelles, were recruited to that end. In the early eighteenth century, under Ahmed III's reign, the aestheticizing and Epicurean climate of the "Tulip period" ensured a great success to the revelations that Yirmisekiz Çelebi Mehmed Efendi made about his embassy to France in 1721, both in his embassy report and in the unending torrent of words he uttered upon his return. At their country houses, the sultan and his entourage rushed to imitate in their fashion what the ambassador had taught them about the wonders of Versailles, Fontainebleau, and the many other palaces and gardens he had visited. Until the reactionary and puritan insurrection of 1730, there was thus a period of "Frankish fashions" on the Bosphorus. Brief as it was, it prefigured, in a light-hearted register, the Westernization of the nineteenth century. For the short time it lasted, it was a kind of counterpoint to the "Turqueries" of the same period in western Europe.

The term "Turqueries" has been used to refer to European works of all kinds that were closely or remotely inspired by Turkey. They are generally associated with the open-mindedness and taste for exoticism of the eighteenth century, as well as with the weakening during the same period of an empire that had supposedly ceased to inspire fear. In reality, though it is very true that these works changed in tenor over time, they began to appear much earlier and thus corresponded to a more deeply rooted tendency that transcended the historical context. In 1468, members of the court of Burgundy—where fourteen years earlier, during the Oath of the Pheasant, knights had pledged to go on Crusade against Mehmed II—donned sumptuous Turkish costumes on the occasion of the marriage in Brugge between Charles the Bold and Margaret of York. Olivier de la Marche left behind a description of the scene: "The first to arrive in the arena was Sir Jehan de Chassa, lord of Monnet, served by four gentlemen dressed in very rich robes in the Turkish mode . . . and there was a horse caparisoned with crimson velvet, embroidered with golden clouds, on which horse sat a maiden dressed in striped green silk cloth, with a large gold chain around her neck, dressed in the manner of Turkey."[92] These costumed interludes, in the tradition of the "medieval mummeries," would enjoy a long vogue in European princely celebrations. Sometimes, alongside the fascination they conveyed was an allegorical intention. In Lyons in 1501, during the betrothal of Claude of France to the young Charles of Ghent—the future Charles V—a "mummer" disguised as a Turk interrupted the ballet of the Christian powers and, out of spite, threw his bow at them.[93] In 1541, at the wedding of Jeanne d'Albret in Châtellerault, Francis I appeared, perhaps in a Turkish mask, among the dancers "who were dressed in the mode of the Turks in clothing of fine gold brocade."[94] A similar spectacle, which included an implicit and euphemistic homage to the power and pomp of Süleyman the Magnificent's Turkey, took place, notably, in 1548, during the wedding of Henry Balafré ("the Scarred"), duke of Aumale, to Anne d'Este.[95] Nor were such masquerades rejected by Louis XIV. At the Carrousel of 1662, the king, along with the prince of Condé and several other lords of the court, appeared dressed as Turks. At about the same time, M. de la Boullaye le Gouz, author of a travel book about Persia and the Indies, enjoyed real success in the Parisian salons by appearing there in "Levantine costume."[96]

A little later, it became the fashion to be painted as a sultan or sultaness. That was the case for Mme du Barry, among many others. As for writers, they went looking for images of luxury and refinement, and not only among the Turks. The conventional Orient where they set their romances or tragedies provided a more varied palette of emotions and sensations. The Orientalist novels of Madeleine de Scudéry, *Ibrahim, or the Illustrious Bassa* and *Almahide, or the Slave Queen*, immersed the historical dramas in a sentimentality imbued with the supernatural. Theater too seized on those events of Islamic history that contained the most pathos. Turkey was not the only source. Inspired by Guillen de Castro's *Youthful Deeds of Rodrigo, the Cid*, in 1636 Corneille gave the Moors of Spain, portrayed as loyal and magnanimous, a dazzling role in *Le Cid*. In 1587, Timur had inspired Christopher Marlowe's *Tamburlaine the Great*, and that terrible conqueror could be found again in 1658, in Jean Magnon's *The Great Tamerlane and Bajazet*. But from the Renaissance on, the most spectacular episodes of Ottoman political history turned out to be particularly productive in that Oriental gallery. They were echoed in many tragedies, where in reality the dual aim of giving the audience a fright and of making more or less veiled allusions to domestic current events prevailed by far over historical accuracy or local color. The execution of Mustafa by his father, Süleyman the Magnificent, and the intrigues of Roxelana to that end—an event that the correspondence of the ambassadors in Constantinople had widely disseminated—were the source for a series of plays: Gabriel Bounin's *The Sultaness* (1561), written eight years after the deed; the Florentine Prospero Bonarelli's *Il Solimano* (1619); Jean Mairet's *The Great Last Süleyman, or the Death of Mustapha* (1630); Desmarres's *Roxelana* (1643); and Abbot Gaspard Abeille's *Süleyman* (1680). The execution of Ibrahim, Süleyman's grand vizier and favorite, was portrayed not only in Mlle de Scudéry's novel but in three plays that appeared in quick succession: Mainfray's *Woman of Rhodes* (1621), Scudéry's *Ibrahim* (1643), and Desfontaine's *Perside* (1644). Yet another play, Jacquelin's *Süleyman* (1653), dealt with the rivalry for succession between the old sultan's two sons, Selim and Bayezid.

These works and others have now been entirely forgotten. But that is not true for the one that infinitely surpassed them all in style and dramaturgy, Racine's *Bajazet* (1672). The author was inspired for that play by an event that he himself noted was especially moving because it was contemporary. *Bajazet* is about the murder in 1635 of Murad IV's younger brother, Bayezid, on the sultan's order. That political crime, conforming to the "law of fratricide," was divulged in the dispatches of Harlay de Césy, ambassador to Constantinople. The play also stood apart from the other Oriental pieces by virtue of its meticulous documentation, which Racine set forth in his preface. That did not spare him the criticism of Corneille and others, who reproached him for showing characters onstage who were Turkish only in their costumes. Racine vigorously defended himself in his later prefaces, where he claimed, "I was intent on expressing in my tragedy what we know of the mores and maxims of the Turks." Furthermore, he preceded his text with this introductory note of great suggestive power: "The setting is Constantinople, in other words, Byzantium, in the seraglio of the Great Sultan." That famous tragedy contributed toward fixing in the public's imagination the notion of seraglio, a sensual and cruel world, the place of all pleasures and all crimes. In a much less circumspect manner, Michel Baudier had already laid the foundations for that fantasy in his *General History of the Seraglio of the Court of the Great Sultan* (1642). Many others would embroider on the theme.

The case of *The Bourgeois Gentleman* (1670), or more precisely, of the Orientalist finale of Molière and Lulli's comedy-ballet by that name, is entirely different. The Chevalier d'Arvieux reports in his memoirs that King Louis XIV, appealing to his personal experience of matters Turkish, had asked d'Arvieux to get in touch with the authors, so as to mount a spectacle that would parody the costumes and manners of the Turkish ambassador, Süleyman Aga Müteferrika, and his retinue. He thus took his revenge on a personage whose lack of tact during the formal audience that Louis XIV had granted him shortly before at the Château of Saint-Germain had irritated the king. The scene with the Grand Mamamouchi is distinguished both by a certain linguistic competence, unusual in the repertoire (the use of terms borrowed from Arabic, Turkish, and the *lingua franca*), and by its powerfully comic irony.

That buffoonery, still unusual in the seventeenth century, became one of the aspects of Turqueries in the eighteenth century. Mozart immediately comes to mind: Osmin in the *Abduction from the Seraglio*; the two gallants disguised as "Albanians" to test their fiancées in *Cosi fan tutte*; and the bounding, mocking rhythm of the *Turkish March*. The same spirit can be found in Rossini's *The Italian Girl in Algiers*. From another angle, the hero of the Turqueries can be seen as tender and good-hearted, a sensitive soul under his high turban and behind his long mustaches. He is "the Turk in love" painted by Lancret and mass-reproduced in countless curios. Or he is the "generous Turk" of the pantomime opening act of Jean-Philippe Rameau's *Gallant Indies* (1535): he grants freedom to his slave Émilie, with whom he is in love, and to Valère, her lover, whom a storm on the Barbary Coast had delivered to him. People took to imitating that kind character's art of living, building charming kiosks in the parks and drinking coffee, as Mme du Barry is doing in her "Turkish portrait," by preference from a precious porcelain cup. How did they arrive at that point? How did the "terrible Turk" turn into the "generous Turk"? The fading of *Türkenfurcht*, made possible by the Ottoman defeats, certainly played some role, as did the reassessment of the Turks and of Islam by certain travelers and philosophers. But it was a fragile achievement, which differences in the political and economic interests of Islam and Christendom could easily sweep away. Then all the themes of the ideologies of antagonism, all the demons of fanaticism and rejection of the other, would surface again and take on more force than ever.

PART III

◇◇◇◇◇◇◇◇◇◇◇◇◇◇◇◇◇◇◇◇◇◇

Europe and the Muslim World in the Contemporary Period

by
Henry Laurens

INTRODUCTION TO PART III

EUROPE AND THE ISLAMIC WORLD have a long, shared past. The very concepts "Europe" and "Islamic world" assumed meaning only in their opposition to each other. The conquests during the first Muslim centuries put an end to the Mediterranean unity inherited from the Roman Empire, creating a new geographical reality, and the first occurrence of the term "Europe" to name that reality appeared in reference to the Battle of Poitiers in 732. Of course, Europe had other borders, such as those with paganism, then with Orthodoxy, where the front lines of conversion, running from the Balkans to the Baltic, converged. In the same way, the "House of Islam" rapidly reached the conflictual borders of the Chinese and Indian worlds and their cultures, not to mention its first slow advance into sub-Saharan Africa. But because of its proximity to the vital cultural, religious, and political centers of the two worlds, the Mediterranean border has always been the most important.

From the seventh century to the eighteenth century, multiple military conflicts and exchanges were the rule. For centuries, vast territorial advances by one camp corresponded to the retreat of the other, back and forth in a zero-sum game. Geopolitics imposed its rules with its hybrid alliances, France with the Ottoman Empire, the House of Austria with the Persian Empire of the Safavids. The material culture represented by commerce in raw materials and manufactured goods constantly crossed borders. Large portions of the culture of antiquity, having been reworked by that of classical Islam, returned to Europe. Technological exchanges were a permanent part of the Mediterranean space, as attested by the many traces left in the linguistic vocabulary of the two worlds.

And yet the great rift took place in the second half of the eighteenth century.

CHAPTER 11

THE EIGHTEENTH CENTURY
AS TURNING POINT

THE REVOLUTIONS OF THE SECOND HALF
OF THE EIGHTEENTH CENTURY

The notion of "Europe" clearly existed in the eighteenth century. The term designated a cultural space and a political system, a balance of powers. Following on the terrible cycle of religious wars that ended with the Thirty Years' War, the European crisis of conscience restored the idea of a cultural unity transcending the cleavages among states, each with a single and official religion. The publishing industry, supplanting handwritten letters, created a space for books and newspapers: this was the European space proper, though it expanded to North and South America and to Europe's African and Asian trading posts. The printed word was closely associated with all things European, while the rest of the world was still the realm of the handwritten. The growth of literacy was a tangible reality, though it still affected only fractions of variable size of the populations concerned. Only Japan, having retreated to a voluntary isolation, had literacy rates comparable to those of Europe. Russia, despite questions about its true nature, was already part of Europe, because it had entered the world of the printed word. Its literacy rate was lower than in other places, however, and it was the first to come up with the innovation of remedial instruction.

The printed word had been the driving force of European exceptionalism since the late fifteenth century. Behind the appearance of a motionless history, a vast store of knowledge and technologies came to be constituted, giving rise to new modes of organization. The first beneficiary was the European state, whose chief activity was to wage war, which required not only new weapons, new disciplines, and new expertise but also new modes of financing and taxation, that is, new modes of social organization over the medium term.

Even in the early eighteenth century, the three great Muslim empires, the Ottoman, the Persian, and the Mogul of India, still seemed to be acting as a counterweight to the European powers and to be keeping them within their borders, as in the previous two centuries. The European discourse on Asian despotism was merely a translation of the deterrence effect of the great Muslim powers, and it exaggerated the organizational capacities and wealth of those powers. These gunpowder empires did not allow themselves to be outpaced during the great armaments revolution of the sixteenth century, and, though the Indian Ocean became a new space for exchanges and conflict, the Europeans were able to establish themselves there only on islands or in continental trading posts. From the Gulf of Bengal to the Mediterranean, the firearms were of the same nature as those in Europe (muskets and cannons) and were manufactured under the same system of small-scale production.

And yet, even before the true beginning of the industrial revolution, a power shift occurred, in seamanship in the first place, the sector where European technology and science were most advanced. That sector benefited from investments both by the state and by the commercial middle class. For the first time, the outlines of a true research and development strategy existed, with basic and theoretical science becoming a source for practical applications. The impetus came from ever more active transatlantic commerce and long-distance journeys to the Indian Ocean and already to the Pacific. The same was true for overland military arts: the eighteenth century witnessed the emergence of "smart weapons" and the first engineers, even as physical training found its fullest expression in Prussian discipline.

By the mid-eighteenth century, the military and maritime branches of European societies, without undergoing any major technological changes—which did not have an impact until after 1840—but thanks to a continuous series of modifications and improvements and the establishment of new disciplinary practices, far outshone the armed forces in other societies. The most glaring example was the Indian subcontinent, where, following the collapse from within of the sultanate of Delhi, the successor states appealed to European mercenaries to serve as officers in their armies, while the rival French and English companies in the Indies raised native armies. It all played out during the Seven Years' War: on June 23, 1756, an army of three thousand men, two-thirds of them sepoys (indigenous soldiers), defeated an army of several tens of thousands belonging to the Nawab of Bengal. That episode in the Franco-English struggle, meant to guarantee security and freedom of action for the British trading post of Calcutta, was the beginning of territorial conquest. By 1764, the East India Company controlled Bengal as a whole, perhaps 40 million inhabitants, that is, four times the total population of Great Britain. Within a few years, it would seize the entire subcontinent.

At the other end of the continental Islamic world, the Ottoman Empire, the traditional rear ally of France, launched a catastrophic war against Russia in 1768, to prevent the first partitioning of Poland. The defense line was breached, and a Russian fleet from the Baltic entered the Mediterranean and destroyed the Ottoman Mediterranean fleet near Chios on July 6, 1770. Finally, Russian troops occupied the Ottomans' Muslim vassal state, the Tatar khanate of Crimea. The Russians' financial difficulties and Pugachev's rebellion saved the Ottomans. With the Treaty of Kuchuk Kaynarja of 1774, the Ottoman Empire was obliged to recognize the independence of Crimea, where Russia maintained its army. The sultan retained his religious authority, priding himself on his title as caliph. In addition, the Russians obtained the right to build and protect an Orthodox church in Istanbul, which would later allow them to demand protection for all the Orthodox Christians in the empire. And finally, the Ottomans had to pay a heavy war indemnity. In 1779, Catherine II put an end to the fiction of Crimean independence by annexing Crimea to her other possessions. The Ottomans were obliged to recognize the annexation in 1784, even while maintaining the caliph's prerogatives in Crimea.

THE ENLIGHTENMENT AND ISLAM

The dizzying pace—made possible by the printed word—at which knowledge accumulated allows us to understand the essence of the Enlightenment as an effort at totalizing and deciphering that knowledge. Two distinct historical sources, moreover, provided the Enlightenment with its specific orientation. First, the European crisis of conscience in the wake of the Wars of Religion opened the way for a critique of religion, tending more in the direction of deism than of atheism. And second, the progress of the modern state tended to undermine the foundations of the old law-and-order societies.

All the large agrarian societies promoted a view of a stable social order founded on a qualitative and honorific hierarchy of groups divided by function, in which everyone had his place. Rank and distinction were defined permanently in terms of social roles, with notions of purity and impurity sometimes used as discriminating elements. The essence of that classification lay in the social function one performed and, in Europe, in one's bloodline. Absolute monarchy tended to subvert that order by concentrating the greater part of the powers around itself and by paring back privileges for fiscal reasons. The ideal for the monarchical bureaucracy was to have a population of subjects who were equal in their obligations, even though the king and his court remained the locus of the most firmly rooted distinctions. The aristocratic critique of absolutism unintentionally contributed to the ruin of the traditional social order by translating into historical terms what had at first been a functional division. It is likely that the weight assumed by inherited honors was the driving force behind that transition to history.

In monarchical France, therefore, the aristocracy, guarantor of freedom for all by virtue of its constitutive bodies, was said to be the descendant of the Germanic conquerors, and the Third Estate of workers, the result of the subjection of the Gallo-Romans. The freedom of the Roman commonwealth of antiquity thus gave way to the plural freedoms of feudalism. Absolute monarchy was a subversion of the traditional authorities, an Oriental and unnatural despotism that was taking root in Europe. Complementing that aristocratic critique was the egalitarianist demand for participation in power by "subjects," which tended rather to use ancient citizenship as its frame of reference. The two critiques merged in the political struggles of the short eighteenth century (that is, between the death of Louis XIV in 1715 and the onset of the French Revolution). The champions of Germanic liberties therefore took pride in citizenship. The ambiguity would be neutralized in the violence of the year 1789.

The first goal of the Enlightenment was to bestow a rational order on knowledge. But after 1750, the project to rationalize knowledge was paired with a plan to introduce rationality into the social order. The idea of progress took hold in the middle of the century, along with the advent of slow but continuous economic growth. If progress is movement, then points of reference are needed to measure it. The first frame of reference was the history of Europe, where many differences in wealth and knowledge had been clearly perceptible since the sixteenth century, a period that put an end to the barbarism of "Gothic" times. The second framework was non-European, that is, Eastern societies.

In the preface to *Bajazet*, Racine claimed that, in his tragedy, geographical distance compensated for the absence of temporal distance. Conversely, for thinkers of the Enlightenment, geographical distance made it possible to bridge temporal distance. The East implicitly but abruptly became a past within the present, the place where Europe's past could be recovered. As a result, the major controversies of the century played out in the various fields of Orientalism.

In the seventeenth century, when the first Orientalist disciplines took shape, their project was essentially humanistic: to universalize literature by adding Eastern literatures to the legacy of antiquity and to modern European literatures. These were initially the literatures of the Islamic world, which were the most accessible, followed by those of the more remote East: India, China, and Japan. In the following century, an ambition took hold to compose a universal history founded on the universalization of human behaviors. Hence a shift occurred: the Germanic invasions had previously been viewed as a singular occurrence, whereas invasions were now considered the driving force of Eurasian history. From the most ancient Scythians to the modern Manchus, great waves of conquerors from the steppes had put an end to great empires and constituted new states. Of all these waves of invaders, only one came from the south, all the other invasions having been carried out by peoples from the north.

The Arabs were the ones who came from the south, and a century of Orientalist research made it possible to write their history. Having originated on the Arabian Peninsula, they ruled the world between the Indus and the Atlantic and developed a brilliant culture. They were the past counterparts of contemporary Europeans, thanks to their acknowledged love for the sciences. As the *Encyclopédie* shows, the genealogy of all the exact sciences depended on the Arabs' improvements on ancient scholarship or on the invention of new sciences such as algebra. As a result, Enlightenment thinkers posited a relationship between Islam and Arab development. On one hand, the Prophet formed the Arabs into a people and provided them with the dynamic of conquest; on the other, the increasing weight of religious fanaticism and Turkish domination gradually neutralized them. Like all Easterners, the Muslims rejected the art of printing, though it had recently been introduced into a few Christian convents of the Lebanon Mountains.

Still, according to the principle of a universal history to be constituted, the Turks were a people of invaders from the north. Their invasions complicated the task of discerning a pattern in European history. Unlike the Germanic invasions, the Turkish invasions produced despotism, not liberties. The defenders of monarchy took that opportunity to demolish the thesis of the Germanic origin of liberties. Charlemagne's empire was an absolutist state, and feudalism rose from the ruins of that empire by dismembering the state's authority. The defenders of Germanic liberties responded with the new thesis of military despotism: the Turkish invaders did not enter into a dynamic of freedoms because they did not proceed to a distribution of wealth among equals, as the Franks had done with the division of their spoils. They remained within the framework of the preexisting state, becoming the recipients of the resources that the state collected from its subjects. That type of tax levy could adapt just as surely to an absolute monarchical system, such as that of the Ottoman great sultan, the "sophi" of Persia, and the great mogul of India, as it could to "military republics," such as the "regencies" of Barbary (the Maghreb). The immutable tendency of military despotism was to overtax society, leading to a decrease in its investment capacity and hence continuous impoverishment, which would also explain why the East increasing lagged behind Europe.

The old image of Oriental despotism was of a surplus of power resulting from the capacity to mobilize all the resources of society by means of terror, and that capacity for mobilization was attributable to the terrifying efficiency of the administration. The new image of despotism was the exact opposite of that view. Despotism was an oppressive system that obeyed the law of diminishing returns. Since it bankrupted the society it governed, its force inexorably declined, but it remained sufficiently strong to prevent the subjected peoples from emancipating themselves, even as they were led to their collective ruin.

The Enlightenment methodology was to grant meaning to the constituted bodies of knowledge. So it was with universal history. In the 1780s, thinkers constructed the trajectory of Mediterranean history, a construct that would have a lasting influence on school curricula. The Europeans clearly situated themselves at the end of history. Their immediate predecessors could not be the people of Gothic times. Knowledge came from the Arabs, who in turn had taken it from the Romans and Greeks. Since the Greeks named the ancient Egyptians as their predecessors, the native land of the sciences and arts turned out to be the mysterious ancient Egypt, a society certainly governed by sages who had fathomed the mysteries of death.

The Egyptomania of the last generation of the Enlightenment was an instrument in the struggle against Christianity, or more exactly, a substitute for it. The desire for de-Christianization on the part of the most radical fringe of the

Enlightenment was at odds with the powerful consolation provided by Christian death rites. It was indispensable to constitute a new funerary symbolism, and since there was a vague perception that most of the traces left by the ancient Egyptians were associated with funerary practices, Egyptian-style art came to compete with Christian funerary art, while Freemason esotericism increasingly embraced Egyptian sources.

POLITICAL TRANSLATION

In the last quarter of the eighteenth century, the deep-seated tendency of the Enlightenment was to transform knowledge into political action, resulting in a merciless renovation of human institutions. As would be said during the French Revolution, history ceased to be law, having been replaced by a rational reorganization of society. The criteria that were applied took into account individuality and the collectivity simultaneously: it was necessary to preserve or set in place what was both advantageous to the individual and beneficial to society. Happiness, a new idea in Europe, was the dual product of that individual and collective regeneration.

"Regeneration" was the watchword of the French Revolution. It led to the assertion of a new collectivity—the nation—made up of individuals equal before the law and participating equally in the exercise of sovereignty. Of course, the revolutionaries could not move beyond certain limits characteristic of their time, such as the exclusion of women and servants from the political body, but they set down principles whose application would serve as programs for the generations to come. In the interest of intellectual coherence, therefore, the members of the Constituent Assembly emancipated the non-Christians of French society, that is, the various Jewish collectivities in the kingdom. Since they were to participate in the body politic, everything was to be granted to them as individuals and everything refused them as a collectivity ("nation" in the old sense of the term).

During the 1790s, with its horrifying succession of events, the terminology became more precise. The regeneration of Europe was nothing less than a new stage in the historical process of civilization, and that process was not limited to Europe. Its destiny was to be universalized by spreading to humanity as a whole.

The Islamic world was the closest to Europe and the best known. It was Europe's immediate neighbor and stretched to the other end of the Old World, where the Europeans were building new empires. Intoxicated by their new power, which they already defined as the mastery of nature, the Europeans nevertheless knew that the European moment in the history of the New World was coming to an end. For France, the Seven Years' War entailed the loss of Canada. Although it held onto its Sugar Islands in the West Indies, it was rightly concerned about perpetuating its presence in that region. The Europeans correctly interpreted the

American Revolution as the beginning of an inexorable process of emancipation of the European colonies in the Americas. Europe had been split in two, and in the 1790s philosophers such as Condorcet marked that geographical threshold by systematically using the expression "the West" in its current sense.

The conquest of the New World had occurred in the name of Christianity. The Iberian conquerors had experienced it as the continuation of the *reconquista* against Islam. New England's original plan was to constitute a Protestant and English Christian society far from the depravities of European absolutism. The French colonization of Canada was accompanied by a permanent desire for the Catholic evangelization of the native peoples. The Enlightenment critique of the European colonial adventure thus became a vehement denunciation of the violence done in the name of Christianity. It marked the end of the European moment, which became one of the charges brought against Christianity.

The 1757 British victory in Bengal defined the Indian routes as the new geopolitical axes, which would dominate the next two centuries of history in the Old World. The sea route via Capetown was the object of a naval rivalry between France and Great Britain. Despite temporary difficulties during the American Revolution, the British were sure of their domination, thanks to their control of the seas. The overland route took longer to emerge. From the 1770s on, the Suez passage preoccupied the French and the British. They had to thwart the Ottomans' desire to keep the Red Sea closed to Europeans, an aim they achieved by the end of the century. Now the Isthmus of Suez had to become a canal. The troubled circumstances of the 1790s did not allow it, but the project was well within European prospects over the medium term.

The overland route was a virtual road that crossed through the entire continental Muslim world. Europeans were absent from the caravan routes in the Old World, but they dominated the seaways. The East India Company extended its network to the Persian Gulf, since the emirates in that region were the commercial partners of India. The British thus created settlements in Kuwait and Basra and studied the feasibility of delivering mail by caravan. The overland route was not a commercial thoroughfare, however, but a political prospect.

Great Britain would have lost interest in that route had it not been for the plans to partition the Ottoman Empire, tirelessly suggested by Catherine II of Russia and reiterated by Joseph II of Austria. The eastern Mediterranean, therefore, was to be divided in three, with a good part of the Balkans going to Austria, Constantinople and Anatolia to Russia, and the regions populated by Arabs (with the possible addition of Crete) to France. Great Britain was not invited to the table and still seemed far away. But when France bowed out because of its revolution, and when the Russians seemed once more ready to seize Constantinople (in the new war begun in 1787, when the Ottomans had to face the Austro-Russian alliance), London was obliged to intervene. In 1791, Great Britain issued an ultimatum to Russia, demanding that it not place itself on the overland Indian route, and made the requisite naval demonstration. A new partitioning of Poland and the formation of the First Coalition against revolutionary France provided a fortuitous diversion.

Although the Ottoman breach was temporarily closed, another threatened to open. For centuries, northern India had been menaced by Afghan invasions, the last of them in the eighteenth century. Now the Russians were outside Afghanistan. They could either spur another Afghan raid or take that path themselves and attack Great Britain, in what was considered at the time the base of its economic power, commerce with India. That trade still consisted of importing Indian cotton prints to Europe; it was not an export trade of manufactured European goods.

When the French Revolution prevailed in Europe, the overland Indian route seemed to mark the line of the major conflicts to come.

EUROPEANS IN THE ISLAMIC WORLD

The critique of European social and economic institutions was only one phase in the revision of human conduct undertaken by the Enlightenment. That transformation was supposed to spread to humanity as a whole and therefore, in the first place, to the Islamic world. Japan was closed off and little known. China was still too far away, and its mandarinate seemed to be the exemplary product of a regime founded on meritocracy—hence the positive assessment given it. India was a colonial extension of Europe, but it was already largely in the Islamic world, since the successor states of the sultanate of Delhi were at war with one another there.

Because of the costs of long-distance commerce, European activity remained centralized within large companies or, in the case of the French Mediterranean, within the Marseilles chamber of commerce. But the geographical boundaries were becoming hazy: Did Suez belong to Mediterranean trade or to that of India? In Persia, three English companies were active concurrently: the Levant Company (the Mediterranean), the Russia (Moscow) Company, and the East India Company. Governments had to arbitrate these conflicting interests.

The Persia of the Safavids had foundered in a cycle of civil wars that captivated Europe. Great war leaders, adventurers coming from out of nowhere, reemerged. Shah Nadir was seen as a new great conqueror and the builder of an empire, albeit a short-lived one. The restoration of order by the Qajars, which came very late in the century, appeared largely unachieved. In a Europe that was becoming increasingly civilized, the East more than ever seemed the place where a man could do "great things." The theme of Eastern violence free from European limits prefigured the romantic view of the East, a phantasmal protest against the bothersome impediments imposed by European civilization. The phenomenal enrichment of certain Europeans in India, by means of both commerce and war, made it possible to dream of something other than social ascent through work or savings. Since the European presence in India was male for the most part, these adventurers generally participated in an Eastern society for which they felt no disdain and whose mores, such as the constitution of harems, they easily adopted, at least in part. What was known about harems in Europe fueled secret fantasies, protests against the moral and disciplinary order being set in place, in like manner to reports of the sexual generosity of the Pacific Islanders. Every relationship between Europe and the East was built on that ambivalence between a supposedly wretched backwardness and the richness of an imagined authenticity, a nostalgia for a world that no longer existed in Europe, or that never had.

Nevertheless, these adventurers' pillaging of the Indies could not last long. The scandals became too apparent, and England cleaned house. High-profile trials took place, exposing all the moral and financial turpitude. A relatively effective tax system was set in place in the conquered territories. In 1790, the tribunals of Bengal were reorganized: a Briton now presided over a supreme court, assisted by a Muslim and a Hindu. A new legal code, largely inspired by British practices, was instituted in 1793. Inexorably, the East India Company lost its commercial functions and became a state machine. The first Protestant missionaries arrived in 1793. The time of adventurers was over, replaced by that of bureaucrats. An increased presence by British women definitively put an end to the equality of and intermarriage with the native peoples. Distance and separation became the rule. Also in the 1790s, British textiles began to supplant Indian prints on the world market. The vast Indian artisan class was being destroyed. The rural economy turned to the production of raw materials. The time of dependence had begun.

The small "Frankish" nations (communities) of the Levantine ports and Barbary did not pass through this era of adventurers. Tradespeople lived under the strict supervision of the consuls, who were responsible for imposing respect for public morality and for preventing any clashes with the Muslim authorities. These Levantines in the strict sense of the term (Europeans permanently established in the Ottoman Empire) lived in symbiosis with a significant portion of local Christians. From the sixteenth century on, the Holy See worked to reopen communications with Eastern Christianity. The missionaries of the Sacred Congregation of Propaganda sought both to purge religious practices of ancient superstitions and to spread the new forms of spirituality of the Catholic Reformation. Indisputably, the graft took, though the Eastern Catholics recombined the new practices with their own religious heritage, and the first conflicts arose around the Latinization of the rites. The Christian elites were the first to move toward modern European education, to participate in the new mechanisms of exchange, and to serve as intermediaries between Europe and the Islamic world.

Whereas the Muslims could not and would not cross the Mediterranean barrier, the Eastern Christians—Greeks, Armenians, and Arabs—traveled to Europe, where schools and monasteries were open to them. For the most part, they came to know an Italian and, to a lesser degree, a French Catholic society. The European education they received was clerical in its inspiration, but these travelers also transmitted knowledge about their own cultures. Eastern preachers were the language tutors and instructors of European Orientalists. When they returned home, they took part in a literary renaissance of their native languages. And, with the advent of the printed word, they set in place the first elements for the great renaissances of the nineteenth century.

Their immediate rivals were other non-Muslims, the Jews of the Islamic world. But though these Jews maintained contact with the Italian Jewish communities, they were in large part outpaced by the Eastern Christians, who possessed a much greater store of modernity and a much wider network of relations with Europe. Inexorably, the Christians dispossessed the Jews of their positions of strength in the fiscal and financial system of the Ottoman Empire. Nevertheless, since the Jews were not dealing with the European powers, they could command the trust of certain Muslim leaders troubled by that strengthening of ties between the Eastern Christians and the Europeans.

At stake in the near term was the restructuring of the flow of trade. The great Eastern empires constituted largely self-sufficient economic groups, where, in any case, domestic commerce predominated over foreign trade. European commerce with the Ottoman Empire had largely consisted of transiting products such as Yemeni coffee or Indian prints, in addition to a few food items and artisanal products. But during the eighteenth century, the Europeans planted coffee in the Americas and monopolized the trade in Indian prints.

The modifications of the terms of exchange led to lasting changes. The Europeans increasingly purchased agricultural products and supplies in exchange for their textile products, which came primarily from the rural and urban industries of southern Europe. The relative underpopulation of the Islamic Mediterranean allowed it to export cereal grains and rice, while the start of the industrial revolution in the textile sector amplified the need for cotton, and soon, for silk. In the exporting countries, the result was a renewed interest in investing in the rural world, favored by changes in the rural tax system (for example, an extension in the duration of the tax farm). In the decentralized framework of the Ottoman Empire, that evolution favored the emergence of strong provincial powers that financed their armies with tax farms and with the tax on trade. The prototype may have been Ahmad Pasha al-Jazzar, who ruled the Palestinian and Syrian regions in the last quarter of the eighteenth century. For French travelers, he stood as the model of the Oriental despot, not only for his cruelty but also for his harsh taxation of foreigners and his determination to maintain the various monopolies.

In the new discourse of the European political economics, the Eastern tax system, with its many monopolies and the state's eminent domain over land, appeared to be a new monstrosity of Oriental despotism. For the French philosopher and Orientalist the comte de Volney, the hard-won freedom of the

Lebanese mountain dwellers and their relative prosperity were a further demonstration of the merits of economic liberalism.

THE FATE OF THE OTTOMAN EMPIRE

After the Treaty of 1774, the Ottoman Empire seemed condemned to be divided among the European powers. Its fate was a subject of debate in the world of European publicists. The most commonly used image was of an imposing, worm-eaten tree. Some said it was practically dead, others that a skillful gardener could revive it with attentive care. All agreed that maintaining the present situation would prove lethal to it. Rousseau's disciples pushed the paradox to the extreme, expressing regret for the possibility of the tree's disappearance. That delay on the path to civilization became proof of a lesser moral corruption. Muslim decency served to point out European hypocrisy.

The French monarchy was still intent on holding onto the empire, no longer as a rear alliance against the House of Austria, an alliance that had been anachronistic since the reversal that occurred during the Seven Years' War, but as an instrument for limiting Russian expansion. Charles Vergennes, former ambassador to Constantinople and now minister of foreign affairs, believed in the possibility of Ottoman reform. He sent military missions, whose aims were, first, to modernize the Ottoman Empire, and second, to create the educational institutions that would allow it to catch up with Europe. That policy was well received in Ottoman governmental circles, which were aware of the imbalance of powers. They established a government printing office in the imperial capital, parallel to the one that had begun to operate in the French embassy, and ordered the translation of military manuals and elementary science books. The European military specialists hired to serve the Porte were able to keep their religion and nationality, unlike renegades from earlier periods. A certain number of adventurers, however, converted to Islam to advance their careers. In the 1790s, the empire for the first time established permanent embassies in the chief European capitals. They were there to follow the unfolding political events of that tumultuous era, but they also took an interest in the economic transformations under way.

That policy of openness produced a great deal of opposition. The old military institutions such as the Janissaries were profoundly hostile to the creation of new units in competition with them. The autonomous provincial powers feared a policy of modernization that would inevitably entail recentralization at their expense. Finally, a large fraction of the Islamic religious institutions refused to borrow anything from Europe. The coalition of malcontents constituted a powerful check on the army's and state's modernization and prided itself on defending the true religion. In their discourse, the authorities were obliged to mark their attachment to Islam and to declare that the reforms under way were inspired at bottom by the empire's original institutions. The precautions taken limited the debate of ideas, which for the moment was confined to the ruling circles of the empire.

In Europe, where revolution was brewing, the political analysis of the majority party assimilated these ruling Ottoman classes to Turkish domination, comparable to a certain degree to the Germanic nature of the French nobility. There was now an Ottoman Third Estate composed of peoples subservient to the Turkish military class and administration. European thought, having destroyed the character of Old Regime institutions in Europe—which rested on social functionalities—in favor of a historicist interpretation of the origin of these institutions, now interpreted Islamic institutions in the same way. Only Rousseau's disciples, in power during the revolutionary Reign of Terror, considered the Ottoman Empire a "democracy," a regime where no hereditary aristocracy existed, a meritocracy. It is true that the Ottoman Empire was the only European state to maintain diplomatic relations with the newly conceived republic. The Committee of Public Safety had ordered the Declaration of the Rights of Man and the constitution of Year I to be translated into the Eastern languages, and in the first place into the languages of Islam, a treacherous enterprise requiring the creation of neologisms. The Convention, then the Directorate, hoped to restore the rear alliance against Austria, whereas the Porte asked primarily for guarantees of its territorial integrity. The validity of that alliance rested especially on the absence of geographical proximity between the two states.

The Wars of the First Coalition temporarily brought to the fore the debate on the Ottoman Empire's fate. Some French dreamed of liberating the Indies from the ruthless and selfish profiteering of British domination. London took the opportunity to accuse the last independent Indian states of Jacobinism, a convenient pretext for continuing the conquest of the subcontinent. For moralists, colonial conquest on the British model merely replaced one despotism with another. It was the Eastern counterpart of the partitioning of Poland, a manifestation of the cynicism of the great states. The British were beginning to invent the discourse of the enlightened despotism of colonial good government, but it was in fact only an outdated variation on the theme of reformist despotism.

The French revolutionaries proposed another route for legitimating colonial expansion, the liberation of the Eastern peoples. The Egyptian expedition would be its testing ground.

The Egyptian Expedition

The respite allowed the Ottoman Empire thanks to the Wars of the First Coalition ended with Napoleon Bonaparte's Italian campaign. In 1797, the young general seized the republic of Venice and the Ionian Islands belonging to it. The

French republic became a neighbor of the Ottoman Empire. Immediately, the great pashas of the Balkans sent letters of congratulation "to the commander in chief of the Great Nation's army." That Ottoman expression of courtesy, intended to make up for the absence of established protocol for addressing a republic, became the slogan of revolutionary France, which had entered a phase of territorial expansion. For a time, Bonaparte envisioned organizing an uprising of the Greeks in the Balkans, then began to consider a possible conquest of Egypt.

That undertaking was not the political maneuver of a regime in desperate straits wishing to rid itself of a troublesome general. Rather, it was the culmination of a century of reflection on the nature of Muslim society and on the ramifications of the geopolitical changes. The first justification was that this was an attack on England in the Indies, the supposed source of its commercial power. Once installed in Suez, the French army would be able to organize a naval expedition, whose arrival in the Indies would provoke a general uprising against British domination. If necessary, an expedition could be planned for the overland route, inciting to revolt a vast movement of people, who would surge over the Indus.

That frame of reference allows us to understand the use made of the call for liberation. Initially, the Egyptians were told that the expedition had occurred with the agreement of the Ottoman authorities, who wished to rid themselves of the rebel Mamluk regime. If the Ottomans went to war nonetheless, then the French would incite a general revolt of the Eastern peoples. That strategic view rested on general principles used in analyzing Eastern societies, but it was reinforced by cognizance of the rebel movements against the autonomous provincial powers, such as that of Ahmad Pasha al-Jazzar in Acre, and of the beginnings of Wahhabi expansion in central Arabia, which was poorly understood. (European travelers interpreted it as a form of armed deism characteristic of desert culture.)

The innovation specific to Bonaparte, apart from his personal synthesis of the ideas of the age, was to argue that Islam had within it a revolutionary content that could be turned against the conquerors or, on the contrary, channeled to their advantage. The French would present themselves as the enemies of the Christians, particularly the Catholics, assuaging at every turn the Islamic religious authorities. Bonaparte himself would style himself a messenger of God, in accordance with the logic of his already romantic view of the East.

Everything would be done in the name of civilization, which became the key word of expeditionary discourse. In the first place, "civilization" meant the development of the conquered domain in accordance with the rules of individual and collective happiness. Economic success would make it possible to replace the Sugar Islands, whose fate appeared increasingly precarious, and would lead to a permanent colony founded on a Franco-Arab synthesis, an expression that appeared for the first time in history in 1799. The scientific expedition accompanying the military enterprise would mark the return of the sciences and arts to their land of origin. In addition to the natural sciences, that expedition would focus on rediscovering the secrets of the ancient wisdom of Egypt and would take stock of the modern state, preliminary to any civilizing enterprise.

The British immediately took the danger to the Indian route seriously. From the Deccan to the Indus, the men of the East India Company hastened to bring the "Eastern Jacobins" in line. Diplomats urged the sultan of Constantinople to go to war, to proclaim jihad against the atheistic French. They asked him, in the name of his supposed powers as caliph, to address the Muslims of India and warn them against the false promises of the French. The sultan would thereby engage unawares in pan-Islamism. Austrians and Russians joined that second coalition, which had become the union of the revealed religions against revolutionary atheism. Against that discourse of religious propaganda, Bonaparte in turn called on the Arabs to revolt against the Ottoman yoke.

For the Eastern populations, that chaos was incomprehensible. To be sure, the ulemas of Cairo saw the French ideas as a resurgence of the ancient materialism of the *zindīqs* in the first centuries of Islam, but for the Egyptian masses it was primarily a foreign domination of Christian origin. In Constantinople, where Europe was better understood, the impious ideas of Voltaire and Rousseau were formally condemned, but the frame of reference for popular mobilization was the Balkan Wars against the Austrians, the Russians, and the local Christian uprisings. Nevertheless, the three-year collaboration with the British army and navy would be a powerful vehicle for introducing modern forms of armaments.

For Egypt, those three years were a period of terrible destruction and misfortune. As during any occupation, some components of society found the means to accommodate themselves and even to collaborate with foreign domination. Some admired the new scientific methods and the art of printing, or took an interest in the administrative reorganization undertaken by the French, particularly in matters of taxation. But above all, the years 1798–1801 were the worst of a troubled time that had begun beforehand and would continue afterward.

The geopolitics of Islam emerged completely transformed by these Wars of the Second Coalition. The survival of the Ottoman Empire depended on its integration into a European balance of powers that now extended to India along the overland route. The policies of the European powers took into account every modification of local power relations. Local political leaders saw the need to adapt to this new state of affairs or to ask for European protections. Hence Bashir Shihab II, emir of the Lebanese Mountains, was allowed to keep his post as a reward for his refusal to join the French, enemies of the Christians—this despite the hostility of his traditional enemy, Ahmad Pasha al-Jazzar (who, however, had been the comrade in arms of the British in the decisive battle of the siege of Acre in 1799). The Muslims' political survival therefore depended on integration at a general level into the European political system and on European political penetration at the local level. Local chroniclers took note of that new political reality by recording in their accounts the arrival of news about the major Napoleonic battles, even as they ignored the European conflicts of the eighteenth century.

THE ISLAMIC WORLD UNDER THE INFLUENCE OF THE NAPOLEONIC WARS

The fate of the Ottoman Empire was the great geopolitical question of the late eighteenth century. Not surprisingly, it remained an underlying issue in the Napoleonic Wars. The aftermath of the Egyptian expedition was the immediate pretext for breaking the peace treaty of Amiens: in 1803, the British refused to evacuate Malta as they had pledged to do. In Egypt, they supported the Mamluks against attempts to restore the Ottomans to power, but they respected their pledge to evacuate that country. European imbroglios hampered British policy. London had to be tactful with Russia to impel it to join the Third Coalition against France, even while ensuring that the overland Indian route was safe from the Russian threat, which materialized as multiple encroachments in the Ottoman Balkans. In 1805, London compelled the Ottomans not to recognize Napoleon's imperial title, which meant breaking off diplomatic relations with France and furthering Russian influence in the empire. After Napoleon's victory at the Battle of Austerlitz (December 2, 1805), Sultan Selim III reversed the alliances, recognizing Napoleon as emperor. The Russians supported the Serbian uprisings and in 1806 went to war against the Ottomans, invading the Romanian principalities of Wallachia and Moldavia. They had the support of the British, who attempted a naval operation against the Dardanelles and the Sea of Marmara. Repelled, the British then landed in Egypt in March 1807, but the sovereign of the region, the Albanian Muhammad Ali, forced them to reembark.

In Tilsit (July 7, 1807), Napoleon renounced the Ottoman alliance. The Russo-Ottoman War went on sporadically until 1812, whereas the British made peace in January 1809, forcing the closure of The Straits to European war navies in peacetime. As a result of the French threat, the Ottomans obtained a peace treaty advantageous to Bucharest in May 1812. The empire lost only Bessarabia and recovered the principalities, while pledging to recognize Serbian autonomy.

At the same time, the restoration of a relatively strong power in Persia, the dynasty of the Qajars, opened the new front of the Caucasus. The Persians attempted to reestablish their lost suzerainty over the kingdom of Georgia. Georgia appealed to the Russians, who annexed the kingdom in 1801. In 1803, Fath Ali Shah tried to make contact with the French. In 1806, the Russian advance resulted in the occupation of Baku and Dagestan. The ambiguous treaty of Gulistan in 1813 consecrated the loss of Georgia and northern Azerbaijan. It is therefore clear why the Ottomans and Persians sent embassies to central Europe to discuss an alliance against Russia in the wake of Austerlitz. Finkelstein's treaty made

France the guarantor of the integrity of the Persian Empire, if that empire were to fight against the British and the Russians. Tilsit put an end to such caprices. At that time, Great Britain appeared as the bastion against a Russia allied with Napoleon. The 1814 Treaty of Tehran made Persia the shield for British India in exchange for aid from London (in actuality from the East India Company).

Napoleon used these Eastern wars as a diversion for the Russian power, even as he sought to keep the Russians from seizing Constantinople. The French emperor even envisioned a new Eastern campaign, a French army marching on India with the agreement of the Ottomans and Persians. The Peninsular War put an end to these plans. Contrary to a tenacious and enduring legend, whose primary propagator was Alphonse de Lamartine, there was never any plan to support an Arab revolt of Wahhabi inspiration by sending agents for that purpose to the Near East. Reconnaissance missions in the Maghreb were organized, however, with the task of studying a potential military expedition. These never went beyond mere studies.

During that period, the Maghrebian regencies were attempting to position themselves in Mediterranean commerce, which had been completely disrupted by the Franco-British wars and by the disappearance of the merchant marines of Venice and Ragusa following the French occupation of these city-states. But the Europeans did not want to see Muslim commercial ships in their ports and would have done anything to avoid that risk, whereas they accepted the growth of a Greek navy under the Ottoman flag. Once the Napoleonic Wars were over, the Maghrebian merchant marine was banned from the European ports and the Maghrebian regencies attempted to return to traditional privateering. But those times were past. The British had banned the slave trade in 1807, as a result of the rise of the powerful Protestant evangelist current, which had made that ban its rallying cry. The 1815 Congress of Vienna generalized the prohibition, and for the first time Europe prescribed a universal norm. Yet slavery had been the principal economic driving force of Mediterranean privateering, both Christian and Muslim. The different treaties of protection and even of complicity with the regencies were now at an end.

The other pretender to Mediterranean trade was the merchant marine of the United States, which profited from its status of neutrality (at least until 1812). But the Americans did not sign any treaty of protection with the regencies and were therefore vulnerable to Maghrebian privateering. Assimilating the corsairs to pirates, the United States launched expeditions against the regencies and established a permanent war fleet.[1] That was the first contact between the Americans and the Islamic world. In the wake of the Treaty of Ghent of December 24, 1814, which put an end to the War of 1812, the Americans declared war on the regency of Algiers. In June 1815, the American war fleet destroyed a large part of the Algerian navy and imposed a treaty abolishing any form of tribute and allowing the exchange of prisoners. In July, the regencies of Tripoli and Tunis were obliged to follow suit.

In spring 1816, Lord Exmouth's British fleet was given the mission of informing the regencies of the Congress of Vienna's decisions. It ransomed a number of European captives for a rather high price and did not secure a pledge to end slavery and privateering. Since the result was considered inadequate, the British fleet, reinforced by a Dutch contingent, went on the attack in August 1816. On August 28, a terrible bombardment of cannons and rockets took several hundred lives in Algiers. The regency had to give in, liberate the captives, put an end to the slavery of Europeans, and pay war indemnities. But the conflict resumed the following year. The Congress of Aix-la-Chapelle in November 1818 established a "European" league responsible for ending privateering. Tripoli definitively yielded, but Algiers and Tunis maintained their claims. In actuality, however, privateering was finished. Maghrebian sailors spent the last part of their careers serving in the Egyptian and Ottoman fleets during the Greek revolt. The regencies sought to hold on by strengthening their tax system and attempting to become involved in African internal trade. They were terribly weakened, however, and vulnerable to European expansion.

Thus ended a history of the Mediterranean that had lasted several centuries.

These conflicts in the first decade of the nineteenth century set in place the pressing issues related to the Eastern question at the time: Serbia, the Romanian principalities, freedom to pass through The Straits, the Russian advance in the Caucasus. The fate of the last two great Muslim states was directly linked to their military apparatus. Sultan Selim III tried to build a modern army, the *Nizam Cedid*, with European-style armaments and discipline, while attempting at the same time to preserve former military institutions such as the Janissaries, closely associated with the trade guilds and the ulemas. The disproportion between their forces and those of the European states obliged him to resort to conscription, first imposed in a partial manner on the Anatolian Muslims in 1802. When the sultan attempted to impose it in the Balkans in 1806, the local notables successfully opposed it. That was the prelude to the conservatives' deposing of Selim III the next year. A period of reaction against the reforms followed, then a civil war. In 1808, the reformers prevailed, placing Mahmud II on the throne. He had to act cautiously vis-à-vis the conservatives, who were quick to revolt. He took it upon himself to restore the units of the new army in order to create a real power base for himself, while multiplying the signs of respect for Muslim institutions. He built new mosques and established new pious foundations. He had to disassociate, in people's minds, the conservatives from the defense of the Muslim religion.

In Persia, the Qajars did not possess such authority. Despite their desire to style themselves absolute sovereigns, the Qajar shahs had to compromise on a permanent basis with powerful tribal confederations with armed forces of considerable size. The provinces were governed by members of the dynasty, who had a tendency to behave autonomously. The central power was thus relatively weak, despite its pretensions. In face of the Russian threat, the shah attempted to build an embryonic modern army by appealing to deserters from the tsarist army, then to a short-lived French military mission in 1807 (the Gardanne mission). As of 1809, he turned to British officers, then, after 1815, to the half-pay officers in the Napoleonic army. The absence of systematic procedures and of parallel reforms in the state and in society made these actions rather futile.

The old contentiousness between Persia and the Ottoman Empire, and the differences between Sunnis and Shiites, prevented any concerted action between the two great Muslim states. In 1820, the Qajars launched the last of the Ottoman-Persian wars, between Anatolia and Iraq. After initial successes, their armies emerged weakened by cholera. In theory, the Treaty of Erzurum of July 28, 1823, reestablished the territorial status quo ante, but in actuality left border conflicts that would be reactivated in the twentieth century.

The India question remained a permanent aspect of geopolitics in the early nineteenth century. Until 1804, the East India Company, on the pretext of the French threat, had conducted a vigorous campaign of territorial expansion, followed by a ten-year consolidation period. India was already being used as a pool for levying soldiers. When the Netherlands were integrated into the Napoleonic Empire, it was Indian troops who occupied the Dutch possessions of Insulindia. They would also seize the islands of Réunion and Mauritius. After 1814, the expansion resumed and the border of the British possessions stretched to the Himalayas and central India.

Whereas Enlightenment thought had defined the Muslim states as instances of military despotism, the East India Company became in fact its most perfect incarnation. In 1813, it lost its monopoly—which had not been respected for a long time—on commercial transactions, becoming for the most part a tax collection machine based on a military apparatus, and one that increasingly excluded Indians from positions of responsibility. The company stood completely outside society, though at the local level it needed the cooperation of the notables. Lacking all legitimacy, it held onto the fiction of perpetuating the Mogul Empire in Delhi. Having honed the military function to its own advantage, it disarmed the Indian subcontinent after the wars among the successor states of the Mogul Empire. Its army of sepoys was recruited from a number of Hindu or Muslim castes and ethnic groups, but indigenous soldiers could no longer obtain a rank above noncommissioned officer.

The company aspired to be respectful of all faiths and was rather hostile toward Protestant proselytism. But as the nineteenth century advanced, the British in India were increasingly influenced by the Protestant revival in Great Britain. They had a tendency, especially in the officers' corps, to display hostility to native religions, resulting in a growing tension with Hindu and Muslim collaborators and servants.

CHAPTER 12

CIVILIZATION OR CONQUEST?

EGYPTIAN CIVILIZATION

In Egypt, Muhammad Ali, leader of the Albanian contingent, took power in 1805, driving out the Ottoman governor with the support of the notables of Cairo. The Porte was obliged to recognize that coup d'état. The new governor, whom the Europeans called a "viceroy," established his legitimacy in 1807 by driving out the English. He gradually reestablished order and definitively eliminated the Mamluks in 1811. In his heart of hearts, he was the founder of an Islamic empire, and his first actions moved in that direction: he established a state monopoly on land and imposed strict control over economic transactions. He put an end to the tendency of tax farms to gradually turn into actual private property. That policy can be interpreted as a resurrection of the authoritarian forms of the traditional Muslim state. Compared to the traditionalist reformers of the Ottoman Empire, Ali had the enormous advantage of beginning from scratch after a long period of troubles, and he had the support of the people of his house (*Bayt*), composed of Turks, Albanians, Circassians, and great Bedouin chiefs but also of Coptic and Armenian Christians. The men of the *Bayt* were primarily Ottomans in their language and culture, and though they supported their leader's desire for autonomy, their aim was to establish an independent regency similar to those of Barbary.

Like all Muslim leaders of his time, Muhammad Ali was chiefly concerned with constituting a modern military force. He initially attempted to impose a new discipline on the traditional military units, but the results were unsatisfying, despite the use of European military advisers, Napoleonic army veterans in particular. After considering an army of black slaves, he resolved to use the inhabitants of the Nile Valley. Although collectively called *fallah* (peasants), they included urban populations. Here again, Muhammad Ali was merely following the example set by Selim III, but the specific situation of Egypt allowed him to have at his disposal a particularly effective force from the start.

Even though the Ottoman government distrusted him, it found itself compelled to ask him to fight Wahhabi expansion, which was very dangerous for the empire's survival. The Ottoman-Saudi War, waged by Ali's son Ibrahim

Pasha, turned out to be a series of victorious campaigns, ending in 1818 with the destruction of the first Wahhabi state. Now in charge of central Arabia and the holy cities of the Hejaz, Muhammad Ali turned toward Sudan, which he quickly conquered between 1820 and 1822. He thus controlled the banks of the Red Sea, which could only distress the British, who had considered him an enemy from the beginning. The existence of an entourage of French advisers only reinforced these fears.

Muhammad Ali increasingly used European advisers, French and Italian especially. He did not grant any positions of authority to them, with the exception of those who converted to Islam and became members of the *Bayt*, like the famous "Colonel" Sève, Süleyman Pasha. A profoundly pragmatic soul, the viceroy was aware of the importance of learning what was happening in Europe, and not only in the political arena. European consuls and travelers became his regular interlocutors. In conversing with them, he understood that he not only had to stay informed but also had to direct propaganda at European public opinion. He was the first Muslim chief of state to attempt to turn European discourse against itself and to make it a means of public action. In about 1821, he seized on the theme of civilization, declaring that he was called upon to lay the foundations for Egyptian civilization, to which the European nations could not remain indifferent. In the following years, his propagandists in France went so far as to compare him to Napoleon, whose accomplishments in the East he was supposedly continuing.

Cultural relations between Europe and the Muslim world were now on equal footing. Europe elaborated a certain discourse on the East, generally fed by preoccupations specific to Europe's future. The East received that discourse, which at first it found relatively incomprehensible. Then the East turned that discourse to its own advantage, elaborating a version of its actions that would be compatible with the Western interpretation. The process did not end there. In the late 1820s, the viceroy sent the first Egyptian scholarly mission to France, composed of young people from the *Bayt*. The sole *fallah* participating was the imam, a young Azharian named Rifaʿat at-Tahtawi. The mission was well received by the veterans of the Egyptian expedition and the French Orientalists, the most illustrious of them Sylvestre de Sacy. The students witnessed the events of 1830 and the birth of the July Monarchy. Tahtawi, upon his return to Egypt in 1831, composed *Paris Gold*, a sort of portrait of France. In the first pages of the book, he seeks to translate the concept of "civilization" into Arabic. Having proposed several equivalents, he finally opts for *tamaddun*. That Arabic term refers to the idea of a settled and urban existence. In his later works, Tahtawi clarified the concept. For him, unlike the European thinkers, it did not entail the binarity of the individual and the collective, but rather the union between human reason, which produced science and technology, and divine revelation, which set the rules for life in society. He thus forged the concept of Islamic civilization that would become that of the later reformers of Islam.

In wanting to save the essential, the Islamic commonwealth, these reformers exposed themselves to another danger, that of a pure instrumentalization of science and technology that did not take into account the underlying logic of these entities and did not really master them.

The restored French monarchy of 1815 launched a major Mediterranean policy, which was sometimes very muddled and contradictory. It sought to maintain France's status after the disasters toward the end of the Napoleonic era and to bestow thereby a second form of legitimacy on itself. Since there could be no question of a military venture within Europe, the Mediterranean became the outlet. Within that context, the Egypt of Muhammad Ali seemed like a stroke of luck, given its desire to position itself within the legacy of the Egyptian expedition. France offered Ali diplomatic support, and made arrangements to send advisers to him (which also allowed the monarchy to rid itself of people suspected of Bonapartism).

For the younger generation of romantics, the civilization process under way in the East prefigured great things, as Victor Hugo indicated in his preface to *Les Orientales* in January 1829: "The whole continent is tilting to the East. We will see great things. The old Asian barbarism may not be as lacking in superior men as our civilization wishes to believe. We must remember that it produced the only colossus that this century can compare to Bonaparte, if, all the same, Bonaparte can have a counterpart: that man of genius, in reality Turkish and Tatar, that Ali Pasha, who is to Napoleon what the tiger is to the lion, what the vulture is to the eagle."

The Muslim East made its contribution to the vast "Oriental renaissance" characteristic of European literature and thought in the decades following Waterloo. Its principal component arose from the discovery of the kinship among the Indo-European languages, which seemed to provide the key to understanding the history of ancient Asia and hence the origins of Europe, as if the Orient were more than ever the origin (*Oriens/Origo* in Latin). The theory of invasions gained in strength, becoming, with the elaboration of the Aryan myth, the driving force of history. The discovery of the purity of Indian origins led thinkers to view the presence of Islam in India as the intrusion of a foreign element that had diverted its history. That interpretation, which ignored the degree to which Islam had been profoundly Hinduized in India, if only by becoming part of the caste system, would later be taken up by a radical Indian nationalism that rejected Islam as an attack on Indian purity.

The Europeans accepted the theory of invasions all the more easily in that it justified the entire colonial enterprise as consistent with the history of the Old World.

In the European world, which was entering the industrial revolution, the moral order of modern bourgeois civilization gave rise to the fantasy of escaping to the Orient, where unbridled passions could be satisfied. That fantasy can be found both in the Orientalist paintings of the early romantics, which constructed paradigms destined to last until our own era, and in the writings of novelists such as Alexandre Dumas in *The Count of Monte Cristo*. Alongside that oneiric literature, authors would develop genres of literary fiction derived from travel narratives, in which they sought greater authenticity by adopting the persona of the Oriental himself. Britons such as James Justinian Morier, or later, Richard Francis Burton, excelled in that register, as did the Gobineau of the *Asian Stories*.

In peacetime Europe, the appeal of the East was also that of the violence outlawed in Europe after the end of the Napoleonic Wars. It was therefore a region where European adventurers could find individual fulfillment, either by seeking power or military action or by passing as a "native" in the aim of scientific exploration. From the British agents of the Great Game against the Russians in Asia to the discoverers of forbidden places—Burton traveled to Mecca disguised as a Muslim pilgrim, and Arminius Vambéry later visited central Asia in the guise of a dervish—a Western mythology of crossing the racial barrier came into being. That new figure of the transgressive adventurer became a powerful literary theme and culminated in the twentieth century with T. E. Lawrence's sensational experiment.

THE UNCERTAINTIES OF THE NATIONALITY PRINCIPLE: GREECE

The Congress of Vienna had restored the notion of legitimacy as the principle governing international relations. States remained the property of the monarchies, and political representation by a voter base of citizens was accepted only for Great Britain and France, which were thereby defined as liberal powers, in contrast to the absolutism of the rest of Europe. But the French Revolution had defined the nation as the totality of citizens comprising the people. In its expansionist phase, the French republic had become the Great Nation, initiating a shift toward a more specifically ethnic definition. The discourse of the Egyptian expedition had marked that shift in its evocation of an "Arab patriotism." Resistance to the Napoleonic Empire accelerated that transformation. In 1813, the German nation was urged to revolt against the Napoleonic system. The later coalitions used ethnicity as the touchstone to put an end to the Napoleonic adventure. In the wake of Waterloo, the conservative powers thus had to confront national movements that were taking up the demand for political representation or even calling into question the state structures in Poland, Italy, and Germany. Nineteenth-century political liberalism seemed to be resuming the fight of the defeated French Revolution.

The Ottoman Empire had not been invited to participate in the Congress of Vienna, but it was well understood that the principle of legitimacy, backed by that of the globalized European balance of power, applied to that empire as well and guaranteed that it would be maintained. The Holy Alliance was in charge of enforcement, authorizing military interventions against liberal uprisings. But the opposition of Great Britain and the United States kept the alliance from intervening in the wars of independence in Latin America. European liberals applauded, and in some cases even participated in, the American triumph of the nationality principle, which was antagonistic to the legitimacy principle and demonstrated its fragility.

The Ottoman Balkans were populated primarily by Orthodox Christians. In the successive Russo-Ottoman wars, the Russians supported the autonomist Christian movements, particularly among the Serbs and Romanians. But the Europeans had a simplified view of Balkan complexities. Muslim and Christian populations intermingled a great deal after the immigration of Muslims from other parts of the empire, and a large number of local Christians converted to Islam. Since the notables were the first to convert, in many regions Muslim city dwellers and tax farmers ruled over an overwhelmingly large Christian peasantry, creating a social cleavage parallel to the religious cleavage. Muslim Albanians and Bosnians regularly provided military and administrative cadres for the empire as a whole.

The autonomous great pashas were more worried about the recentralization policy conducted by Mahmud II than about a possible uprising of the Christians. Upon the death of a governor, the Porte refused to choose a successor from among his heirs and instead designated a government official from the capital. In general, descendants were given the opportunity to serve in the administration in another region of the empire. In the event of resistance, an armed expedition took the region by surprise and reestablished the central government's direct authority. This same policy was carried out in Anatolia. Although the empire thereby acquired greater general cohesion, it lost the complex network of relations established among the different components of society at the local level.

That is very clear in the case of Ali Pasha of Ioannina, the powerful pasha of Albania and Greece. To hold on to his de facto autonomy, he maintained good relations with the Greek underground movements in the Balkans. For centuries, the Greeks of Constantinople, called Phanariots, from the name of the neighborhood where the ecumenical patriarchate was located, had been associated with the administration of the Balkans, particularly of the Romanian principalities. The loss of Crimea opened the Black Sea to international trade, and many Greek traders moved to the new Russian possession, since treaties allowed them to sail under the Russian flag. In the Mediterranean, the Greek navy, under the Ottoman flag, underwent an unprecedented expansion resulting from the eclipse of the European navies during the revolutionary and imperial wars. A very active Greek bourgeoisie was thereby created, one attuned to the new discourses coming from Europe, though it remained fundamentally Orthodox in its culture and identity. A Greek cultural renaissance, favored by the art of printing and by the Greek networks established in Italy, in the Ionian

Islands—which had become British possessions—and in Russia, thus sought to wed references to the glories of antiquity to the Byzantine and Orthodox heritage. Bonaparte had already considered using that cultural renaissance in 1797 to stir uprisings in the Ottoman Balkans but had immediately given up the idea. In the following years, secret societies of liberal inspiration formed in these bourgeois circles, as well as attempted uprisings, which were rapidly aborted.

In 1820, the Porte decided to put an end to Ali Pasha's government and to remove him and his sons from their positions of authority. The pasha concluded an alliance with the secret societies, having encouraged them to take root in his territories. The Ottoman army intervened and mounted a siege on his capital, Ioannina. After a year, Ali Pasha had to surrender, and, despite the promises made, he was executed. That adventure held Europe in thrall, as attested by the literary works of Balzac and especially Alexandre Dumas.

The siege of Ioannina gave the signal for Greek insurrection, which spread to the Morea (Peloponnesus), central Greece, and the islands of the Archipelago (the Aegean Sea). In the insurgent regions, insurrection immediately took on the aspect of an ethnic war between the Christian and the Muslim peasantries, with many massacres on both sides. In the rest of the empire, the Greeks, suspected of disloyalty, were removed from their posts in the administration, while the patriarch of Constantinople, accused of supporting the revolt, was hanged.

In Europe, liberal opinion took up the Greek cause. The Philhellenic movement saw it as the rebirth of ancient Greece and condemned the atrocities committed by the Muslims, passing over in silence those attributable to the insurgents. For the first time, various writers and personalities organized a powerful movement to influence governmental decisions. The cause was especially popular because half-pay officers in the imperial army and volunteers joined with the rebels. Lord Byron's death caused a great stir. The governments of the Holy Alliance were caught between their Christian sympathies and the groundswell of opinion on one hand, and the need to preserve the principle of European legitimacy and stability on the other, which led them to delay intervening.

The Ottoman armies managed to retake central Greece but failed to reconquer Peloponnesus, a hotbed of insurrection. Mahmud II resolved to ask for aid from Muhammad Ali, who sent his son Ibrahim Pasha to reconquer Crete, then Peloponnesus, in 1825. The revolt seemed to be running out of steam. In 1826, the sultan forcibly suppressed the Janissary corps, the conservatives' armed wing. The path was now clear for the reformers to establish a new unified army. The lack of qualified cadres called for the creation of modern military schools, which further delayed the emergence of a real armed force.

Tsar Alexander I's death in late 1825 and the accession to power of his brother Nicholas I changed the international context. The new sovereign, while a proclaimed enemy of the liberals, wanted to resume Russian expansion at the expense of the Islamic world. He styled himself the defender of the Balkan Christians and prepared for a new advance in the Caucasus. Following many encroachments into Persian territories, war resumed in 1826. The Persian army could not match the veterans of the Napoleonic Wars. The Treaty of Turkmenchay of February 22, 1828, enshrined the power relations. Persia had to acknowledge the loss of the territories of Erivan and Nakhchivan and pay a heavy war indemnity. The new Russian ambassador, the writer Aleksandr Griboyedov, wanted to push Persia into war against the Ottoman Empire and demanded the return of Russian deserters and renegades. That set off a violent urban riot led by the clergy of Tehran, which ended with the massacre of the Russian legation. Preoccupied with Ottoman affairs, Nicholas I accepted the shah's official apology.

Great Britain, which did not want to see a Russian intervention along the overland Indian route, asked France to join with it for a mediation between the belligerent parties in Greece. Mahmud II denied all legitimacy to the actions done in Europe's name on behalf of those rebelling against his authority. France and Great Britain organized a naval demonstration with only a vague mission. The Franco-British fleet was supposed to set up a naval blockade of Peloponnesus and the Dardanelles, but without engaging in combat with the Egyptians and the Ottomans. On October 20, 1827, the European squadron attacked the Ottoman and Egyptian ships gathered in the Bay of Navarino. Declaring they were provoked by a shot from a Muslim ship, the Franco-British vessels unleashed a merciless barrage of artillery that destroyed fifty-seven ships and caused eight thousand deaths. The Europeans had demonstrated their overwhelming superiority, even over the most modern elements of the Muslim armies at the time.

The Ottomans persisted in rejecting European mediation. Russia took the opportunity to declare war on them in April 1828. Once again, Russian armies penetrated into the Romanian principalities and central Bulgaria. A new front opened in the Caucasus, where the Russians advanced as far as eastern Anatolia, taking Kars in July 1828. France sent an expeditionary corps to Peloponnesus to oversee the evacuation of Ibrahim Pasha's army. The Treaty of London determined the fate of Greece, forming a small Greek state, theoretically under Ottoman suzerainty. In 1829, the Russians arrived in Adrianople, Thrace, and in Erzurum, Anatolia. The Treaty of Adrianople of September 14, 1829, limited Ottoman losses, however. The Russians returned most of their conquests, while the Ottomans had to demilitarize their Balkan borders; recognize the Russians' previous acquisitions in the Caucasus as well as Serbian, Greek, and Romanian autonomy; pay a heavy war indemnity; and grant Russia the same capitulary rights as the other European powers.

The autonomy of the Serbs, Greeks, and Romanians seemed at first to be an instrument of Russian influence over the Orthodox monks in the Balkans; at the same time, however, it entailed an acknowledgment of the application of the nationality principle in the diminishing Ottoman space. The essential question remained: Could that principle be applied to the Muslim populations?

THE UNCERTAINTIES OF THE NATIONALITY PRINCIPLE: ALGERIA

The Algiers expedition may appear to have been more accidental than the Egyptian expedition, in that it does not seem to have been the result of an intellectual and political debate of the same nature. The uncertainties of French policy, hesitating between several options and still dreaming of the left bank of the Rhine, are a good demonstration of this view. Although its execution may appear to have been relatively fortuitous, it partook in the general enthusiasm for European expansion and in the problematic of the Ottoman Empire's dismemberment, a pressing issue for more than half a century.

The origin of the conflict went back to attempts by the regencies to reorganize their economies during a time of revolution and empire, and was linked to the dubious channels that commercial transactions were taking at that time and to the confusion about the respective functions of the consul and the merchants. The insult done to France by the dey of Algiers when he struck the French consul with a fan contributed to the rise of national pride, which also occurred in Palmerston's England. For a time, the Restoration government offered to intervene in Muhammad Ali's behalf. But Ali was more interested in Syrian affairs.

In the first place, then, this was a military expedition to enhance the prestige of a government lacking Napoleon's panache. It was inspired by Bonaparte's speech in Egypt evoking Arab liberation and the advance of civilization. The proclamation of June 8, 1830, drafted by Sylvestre de Sacy, was in large part an exact copy of the proclamation of July 1798. It mentions avoiding snubs and respecting the Muslim religion. Unlike Bonaparte, the French now hastened to celebrate mass in the conquered city and spoke of reopening the door to Christianity in Africa, with the mission of reviving civilization, which had been snuffed out there.

The first years of the conquest were a time of great incoherence in French policy, linked in part to the vicissitudes of its domestic policy. The "Turks," that is, the representatives of the Ottoman ruling class, were expelled. The undeclared war against the Ottoman Empire lasted until the taking of Constantine in 1838.

The Algerian urban elite, represented by a certain Hamdam Khoja, who in 1843 published *The Mirror, Historical Abstract and Statistics on the Regency of Algiers*, attempted to make the French confront their own contradictions. The acts of violence committed against the populations, the destruction of Muslim institutions, particularly institutions of learning, ran counter to the project of civilization. The French could not defend Greek or Polish nationality while at the same time oppressing the inhabitants of Algeria. The price of conquest would not fail to be the extermination or expulsion of the native population. The only path open was to establish a local civilizing authority and friend of France on the model of Egypt.

Once they made the decision to remain for reasons of national prestige, the French attempted a "limited occupation," which could be achieved only with the backing of a local power assuring control of the territories of the interior. An "Arab kingdom," ally and partner of France, was needed. They seemed to have found that ally in the person of Emir Abd al-Qadir, who gathered the Arab tribes of the interior under his religious and political authority. The Treaty of Tafna was a step in that direction.

Within a few years, then, the French were led to define the population of Algeria as "Arab," despite the great heterogeneity of social categories. The same dynamic was at work in that designation there as in Egypt. Once the French had spoken of the existence of an Arab "nation," it began to appear in the discourse of the interested parties, who used it in their attempts to influence their adversaries. Thus the urban notable Bourderbah, addressing the French, presented the emir as the one who would regenerate the Arab race and defend civilization, a second Muhammad Ali.

The emir was the leader of a brotherhood who rallied his followers against the invaders in the name of jihad, and who imposed scrupulous respect for Islamic law in the territories under his control. At bottom, he was an adversary of the Ottomans, from whom he had received no investiture. He did not hesitate to apply the caliphal title of "commander of believers" to himself and had his followers call him "sultan," a dual usurpation of the Ottoman or Moroccan sultan-caliphs. He tried to rally the Berbers behind him but failed in his attempts. His base was certainly the great tribes of Arab lineage and Arabic language, but that did not constitute a nationality in the modern sense of the term.

His project was incompatible with French domination, and the ambiguities were dispelled after the Eastern crisis of 1840–1841, a French humiliation recalling Waterloo. To restore the dignity of France, the July Monarchy launched a particularly destructive total conquest. French soldiers used every instrument of terror to destroy the system of Abd al-Qadir, who had to surrender in 1847. The government justified its behavior by pointing out that philanthropy was incompatible with conquest and that the only language the native populations, barbaric by nature, could understand was that of the most violent methods.

Alexis de Tocqueville, who as a politician did not want the native peoples to be exterminated but only repressed, could do no more than issue a warning for the future, which was lost in the parliamentary centrism of the July Monarchy:

> If . . . ever we acted in such a manner—without saying so, since these things are sometimes done but never admitted—as to show that, in our eyes, the former inhabitants of Algeria were only an obstacle that had to be thrust aside or trampled underfoot; if we embraced their populations not to lift them up into our arms for their well-being and enlightenment but rather to crush and smother them, the question of life and death would arise between the two races. Believe it: sooner or later, Algeria would become a closed field, a walled-in arena, where the two peoples would

have to do battle mercilessly, and where one of the two would have to die. God spare us such a fate, Gentlemen.[1]

In Algeria, France and Europe established settlement colonies in the Arab world for the first time, inaugurating a repressive colonialism, as the Russians were doing with equivalent methods in Crimea and the Caucasus. Nevertheless, the European discourse inherited from the Enlightenment on the role of the Arabs in the history of humanity predisposed the French to recognize Arab nationality. But the exclusion of the Arabs and Muslims from the nationality principle was confirmed in the European debate accompanying the Syrian wars of the 1830s.

The Uncertainties of the Nationality Principle: Syria

The Ottoman social contract inherited from classical Islam was now profoundly undermined. Some of the elites were aware of the frightening reversal in power relations vis-à-vis the European powers. In order to survive, they had to adopt the principles of the modern state, based on the elimination of social hierarchy and the establishment of equality. The first functional division of society to be suppressed was the specialized order of warriors. Modern armies relied on recruitment from a broad swath of society, usually through more or less selective conscription. The same was true in fiscal matters, which required that a universal and nondiscriminatory system be set in place for levying taxes. And finally, the Greek revolt dealt a mortal blow to the old distinction between Muslims and non-Muslims.

Anxiety ran deep in the Mediterranean Muslim societies: the traditional frames of reference were being called into question and the social order inherited from the previous generations was in a state of upheaval. The new order was coming into being at the expense of ancient and consecrated freedoms.

Even as anxiety took root in the consciousness of Muslims, Christian society was far from being at peace. While placing itself under the standard of Napoleonic modernity, France of the restored monarchy acted as the emperor had, reiterating the traditional demand for a French protectorate over the Catholics of the Ottoman Empire. That demand had formerly been based on a misinterpretation of the capitulation treaties and on the de facto reality that French protection was simply one more in the tangle of protections characteristic of all traditional societies. It changed meaning with the new social order being set in place. Now entire collectivities were placed under protection, with the progress of Uniatism (which embraced the authority of the Roman See), even as French protection became part of a competitive system: Russia made equivalent demands on behalf of the Orthodox communities, and the first so-called biblicist American and British Protestant missions, whose tone was often millenarianist, arrived on the scene.

According to a certain theological interpretation known as the "fulfillment of prophecies," the advent of the millennium was conditioned on the gathering of the Jews in the Holy Land and their conversion to Christianity. Protestant proselytism did not limit itself to the Jews but extended as well to Eastern Christian communities of various obediences, who were considered ignorant and far from the true faith.

The Eastern ecclesiastical authorities were thus exposed to pressures and competition from many sides. After 1815, the great revival of European Catholic missionary zeal began. The Eastern Catholic religious leaders needed these missionaries to counter the worrisome proselytism of the Protestant missionaries and to give their communities access to modern knowledge. At the same time, they were wary of these newcomers' encroachments on their authority and of their tendency to want to Latinize the Eastern rites. As for the temporal leaders, they used French protection in their political maneuvers with both the local powers and the central power. The Porte was leery of French claims and broke new ground by officially recognizing the Catholic faith in 1831, in the form of a certificate of investiture to the Armenian Catholic patriarch that definitively removed the Eastern Catholics from the ecclesiastical authority of the Orthodox and Armenian churches. During that period, the conflict between Uniates and Orthodox Christians focused on the "miter quarrel," that is, on the question of whether Uniate priests could wear the same ecclesiastical costume as the Orthodox clergy, which facilitated their proselytism.

The Ottoman Empire of Mahmud II and the Egypt of Muhammad Ali were both projects for establishing the modern state, but they were antagonistic in nature. The ambitious viceroy had long had his sights on Syria and may have even considered overthrowing the Ottoman dynasty for his own benefit. While running a particularly oppressive and despotic regime in his own domains, to the outside world he touted his astounding successes, contrasting them to the Ottoman failures. He claimed to be the uniter of the community of Muslims (*millat muhammadiyya*) against the first Ottoman reforms, misleading people about the even more radical character of the measures taken in the territories under his authority. In a world where the art of printing was at best in its infancy, a secret propaganda war began, in the form of open letters and other handwritten documents, which circulated in the ruling circles of the provinces and in the capital.

In December 1831, on the pretext of a border dispute, the Egyptian armies, under the command of Ibrahim Pasha, son of Muhammad Ali, invaded Syria. Within a few months, they had conquered all the provinces. They moved on to Anatolia in autumn 1832. In December, Ibrahim Pasha's victory in Konya left the path open to the Ottoman capital. During these early months of war with Syria, Ibrahim Pasha used the traditional rhetoric of Islam: he had come to remedy the injustices perpetrated by the bad local governors, and he accused the sultan of betraying Islam and of wanting to impose the practices of the Christians on Muslims. Mahmud II for his part used his capacity as caliph to have Muhammad Ali and his followers condemned as traitors and rebels, whose blood it was lawful for Muslims to spill.

That so-called Egyptian enterprise, in calling into question the fate of the Ottoman Empire and in positioning itself on the overland route to India, could only incite European intervention. Aggravating the situation was the fact that this venture, coming less than twenty years after Waterloo, may have appeared to have the support of France and even to have been inspired by the French. In February 1833, a joint Russian and British intervention halted the march of Ibrahim Pasha's army, now halfway between Konya and Constantinople.

The question still had to be resolved politically. In Europe, many publicists, writers, and politicians believed that the solution was to constitute an Arab empire under the leadership of Muhammad Ali and his son, Ibrahim Pasha. The viceroy of Egypt vaguely perceived the need to address a discourse to Europe portraying his enterprise as the equivalent of Belgian and Greek independence. But though he may have been credible as a hero of civilization, he was not so as a spokesman for the Arab "race." He seemed too "Turkish" and too representative of the "alien" elements ruling the Egyptian population. The same was not true of Ibrahim Pasha.

That remarkable general was close to his men and, unlike his father, he spoke fluent Arabic. He also had a better sense of the rift that was occurring between Egyptian domination and the Ottoman Empire. It was civil war, and the members of the viceroy's house constituting the ruling class were divided between loyalty toward their master and allegiance to the Ottoman sultanate, with all its religious legitimacy. Within that context, Ibrahim Pasha had a tendency to rely on the youngest elements, trained from the beginning in the *Bayt*, whose most brilliant members were those who had just returned from academic study in France. Through them, he had firsthand knowledge of the most recent European, particularly Saint-Simonian, ideas, though he was primarily interested in translating them into concrete realities. At the same time, facing the risk of defection by senior officers of Ottoman origin, he sought out the support and friendship of the rank and file, whom the Europeans considered universally "Arabs."

For European observers, Ibrahim Pasha's general behavior made him the defender of the Arab cause. In spring 1833, he became cognizant of that view and elaborated an Arabist discourse addressed to European envoys, evoking the rebirth of the Arab nation. He did not express himself in the same terms with his Syrian interlocutors, who did not have the intellectual tools to follow him. But what he described in ethnic and national terms to the Europeans, he put into practice in Syria, by putting an end to the traditional distinctions among the functional groups of Arab-Ottoman society.

Above all, the European chancelleries supported the European balance of power and the Indian route. They refused to acknowledge the application of the nationality principle in the dubious case of Muhammad Ali's Arab empire. For the time being, they were satisfied with a shaky state of affairs that put Muhammad Ali in charge of the majority of the Arab provinces in the Ottoman Empire after the evacuation of Egyptian troops from Anatolia. An uneasy truce, though one guaranteed by Europe, was set in place, but it did not resolve any of the fundamental questions.

European opinion was divided about the undertaking by Muhammad Ali and his son. The romantics saw them as civilizing heroes bearing within themselves the regeneration of the Arab race. The realists and defenders of the integrity of the Ottoman Empire portrayed them as the restorers of a despotic and oppressive order, but one much more efficient than the old systems. Neither was wrong, since the establishment of the modern reformist state relied on an authoritarianism incommensurate with that of the traditional order. As in Europe, the Old Regime in the Islamic world was a realm of liberties recognized by specific entities and of rights granted to constituted groups. Iniquities or snubs were violations of that social contract sanctioned by religion, and could entail a right to rebellion acknowledged and approved by the religious authorities. Modernity entailed the suppression of these traditional freedoms, which were invoked by those advocating the rejection of the transformations under way.

This was clear in Syria under the administration of Ibrahim Pasha, who vigorously set in place a centralized system imposing tax equality, disarmament of the population, conscription, and the de facto emancipation of non-Muslims. That administrative modernity, based on the leveling of distinctions, was all the more intolerable for being effective and translated into a sharp increase in fiscal pressure. In 1834, it gave rise to a major revolt by the Palestinian populations, which was brutally quashed. In 1838, it was the Druzes' turn to revolt and to be repressed.

In 1839, the Ottomans, encouraged by the British, resumed hostilities. They were again beaten, but that merely served as a pretext for London to impose a European settlement that would isolate France. The Treaty of London, concluded on July 15, 1840, between Great Britain, Prussia, Austria, and Russia, required that the Egyptian forces withdraw from Syria; in exchange, it granted Ibrahim Pasha the governorship of Egypt as a family inheritance and the province of Acre (twentieth-century Palestine) for life. France attempted to oppose the treaty provoking the Eastern crisis, which nearly caused a European war against France, once again cast as the troublemaker in the European system.

The British incited a vast insurrection from Lebanon, where the mountain dwellers did not accept the disarmament imposed by Ibrahim Pasha's ally, Emir Bashir. The revolt, perpetuated and supported by the British fleet, rapidly extended to all the Syrian territories. In late 1840, Ibrahim Pasha was obliged to return with his forces to Egypt.

France displayed a warmongering spirit. Tocqueville aptly expressed the general opinion when he addressed the Chamber of Deputies on November 30, 1840:

Do you know what is happening in the East? An entire world is being transformed. From the banks of the Indus to the edge of the Black Sea, within that enormous space, every society is teetering on the brink, every religion weakening, every nationality disappearing, every light being snuffed out, the ancient Asian world disappearing: and in its place, the European world is gradually rising up. The Europe of our time is not approaching Asia only from one corner, as Europe did in the time of the Crusades: it is attacking it in the north, the center, the east, the west, from every side; it is piercing it, enveloping it, subduing it.

Do you believe, therefore, that any nation that wants to remain great can witness such a spectacle without participating in it? Do you believe that we should let two European peoples seize that vast inheritance with impunity? And rather than suffer it, I will say to my country, with energy and conviction: Let us rather have war! (Very good!).[2]

Wisely, Guizot's new government avoided war and obtained for Muhammad Ali the right to the succession of Egypt and Sudan.

The Eastern crisis of 1840–1841 definitively set in place a political culture of European interference, based on a dual manipulation, that of Eastern actors by Western actors and that of Westerners by Easterners. The logic of self-interest was transformed into effective policies through twin propaganda discourses. A century later, Egyptian historians would use Ibrahim Pasha's texts to define retrospectively Egypt's vocation as unifier of the Arab world; among the Palestinians, by contrast, the insurrection of 1834 would become the expression of an emergent Palestinian identity.

In about 1840, however, the question raised in the late eighteenth century still remained a pressing issue: Would the ancient Asian world vanish in favor of direct European domination, or would that world be regenerated through its confrontation with Europe?

But what did conquest mean when the movement of history, both for those who celebrated it and for those who deplored it, was toward the democratization of societies?

The Issue of Conquest

After 1840, the Islamic world split in two: one came under direct European domination, while the other was subject to indirect control exerted through the state apparatus and the protection systems.

European military superiority was assured, thanks to increasingly efficient armaments and improved modes of organization. Yet things were no easier. The Muslim societies being conquered resisted with a desperate energy, which turned the colonial wars into wars of terror. The final phase of the conquest of Algeria, which French painters illustrated with fiery canvases, was therefore a war of destruction. To destroy Abd al-Qadir's emerging state, the French army ruthlessly ravaged the Algerian countryside, destroying villages, setting fire to crops and granaries, and making multiple exactions, which were denounced in vain by European, especially British, philanthropists. The French authorities denied these accusations while acknowledging sotto voce that it was not possible to be both a conqueror and a philanthropist. The human cost of the conquest was particularly high, confirming the enduring difference between European wars—which became civilized by adopting customary laws seeking to limit the toll of violence to combatants—and colonial wars, which no longer had any limits because the enemy was defined as uncivilized by nature and hence unprotected by the mechanisms limiting the effects of violence. The native peoples became the guilty party in the violence perpetrated against them, since their resistance required that they be treated in a regrettable manner.

The same was true for the Russian penetration into the Caucasus, where the Russian armies met with the fierce resistance of the Muslim mountain dwellers, assembled into Sufi brotherhoods. The Muslims acquired a brilliant war chief, Imam Shamil, who led the fight for several decades. Russian military losses were terribly high, while in many of the episodes Russian violence veered toward extermination pure and simple. Nineteenth-century Russian literature, from Pushkin to Tolstoy, bears witness to these Caucasian Wars. Muslim Caucasians by the thousands found refuge in the Ottoman Empire. At the same time, the Russian advance into Siberia made the tsarist empire the close neighbor of the central Asian khanates. Encroachments immediately turned into conquests. But the Asians fought off the Russians in 1840 during their attempts to seize Khiva.

In India, the British, grown confident by the easy conquest of the majority of the subcontinent, underestimated the force of resistance of the mountain-dwelling Muslim populations in the northwest. Obsessed with the Russian threat that had materialized in central Asia, they decided to fend it off by taking control of Afghanistan. In 1838, a naval demonstration in the Gulf forced Persia to abandon any attempt at conquering (or recovering) the province of Herat. Great Britain sent in an invasion force in 1839 and seized Kabul without great difficulty, installing a sovereign under the British protectorate. It quickly became apparent that the British garrison of Kabul was isolated in a hostile region, which sank into rebellion in autumn 1840. In November 1841, the insurrection reached the capital, where the garrison became trapped. After futile and complicated negotiations, the British army evacuated the city under the worst possible conditions in early January 1842. The retreat turned into a rout, leading to thousands of dead among the British and Indian soldiers, and among the civilians accompanying them. After that disaster, the other British forces of Afghanistan engaged in terrible reprisals on the Afghan population before retreating to India.

The disaster of the first Anglo-Afghan war was partly offset in the following years by the conquest of Punjab and Sind. The last independent Indian states had managed to establish military discipline equivalent to that of the Europeans, but the British now possessed the technology for greatly superior armaments. As a result, the notorious northwestern border was established, with practically independent tribal territories and the policing operations of the Indian army. The Russian threat remained a permanent concern and influenced Afghanistan's fate. Again in 1856, the British prevented the Persians from seizing the region of Herat.

The tsarist armies, in possession of superior means, continued their advance into central Asia. The conquest took another quarter century, but Tashkent fell on June 7, 1865. Planning to create a vassal state of Russia, the tsar decided to annex the region in 1866. The following year, it became the government-general of Turkestan. The khanate of Bukhara became a vassal state in 1868, Khiva in 1873, and the khanate of Kokand was annexed in 1876, becoming the province of Fergana. Turkmenistan was the next milestone, and the conquest was completed in 1884.

Unlike those of the Caucasus, the wars in central Asia were not very bloody. The Muslim states, weakened by internal conflicts, did not have significant military means, and the Russians had the intelligence to respect local mores and customs. At least initially, they did not seek to interfere in the internal affairs of the population.

In addition to the difficulties encountered by the conquest when it faced an unyielding population, there was the permanent risk of revolt, the most representative of these being the revolt of the sepoys of 1857, the "Great Rebellion." The immediate pretext was the introduction of modern weapons that required their users to come in contact with fats considered to be of impure origin (beef fat for the Hindus, pork fat for the Muslims). The movement was a vast protest against the impact of colonialism, experienced as a threat to their religion and mode of life, especially since the colonial government had entered a phase of technocratic reforms. The European presence was seen primarily as a form of pollution. The movement, which began in Bengal, extended to northern India and sought to rally behind it the traditional authorities, including the last representative of the Mogul dynasty. It did not manage to find true leaders or a centralized leadership. Muslims and Hindus participated equally in the insurrection. A large part of the urban and rural world joined in. The rebels systematically massacred Europeans, including women and children. The repression was terrible. In addition to engaging in battles in which they took no prisoners, the British columns systematically burned villages and massacred the male population, to instill lasting fear. The British army made rape a regular practice. (For the rebels, rape was a sin for the one committing it and not for the victim.) The human losses counted in the hundreds of thousands. The use of terror followed the logic of deterrence, revenge, and a sense of racial superiority to be reestablished.

The British victory can be attributed first and foremost to tools emerging from the industrial revolution: steam-powered riverboats, the electric telegraph, the beginnings of a railroad network. The central years of the nineteenth century (1840–1860) witnessed the establishment of European domination, now founded on the technological progress under way and no longer merely on the capacity to mobilize resources, as in the late eighteenth century. Without that transformation, it is likely that the British would have been expelled from India.

From that time on, they isolated themselves even more from Indian society. All-white troops were maintained permanently, with a monopoly on artillery. The British preserved the princely Indian states to earn their goodwill. The East India Company was abolished in 1857, along with the fiction of continuity with the Mogul Empire.

Beyond their impact on literature and art, the violence that characterized the wars in Algeria, the Caucasus, and Afghanistan would leave lasting marks. A century and a half later, these fractures and wounds can still be found in relations between the Muslim world and Europe.

The combined role of archaic social structures (tribes, brotherhoods)—which the social transformations under way in the great Muslim states did not destroy—the bellicose traditions of peoples who refused to be subjected to a tax-imposing and oppressive state, and the terrain and climate, inhospitable to the European invaders, allows us to better understand the scope of that resistance. It took the form of a local jihad conducted by war chiefs, who emerged during the first battles. The modern Muslim state seemed much more vulnerable and yet, in bowing to indirect control, it managed to endure by learning to change. The resistance of the archaic societies facilitated that task, since, by virtue of its costs, that resistance tended to deter adventures of conquest.

War favored the acquisition of knowledge. The military needed interpreters, the first mediators with the conquered population, but these intermediaries sometimes proved inadequate. In the Algeria of the conquest, "Arab bureaus" were established, instruments for administering and learning about the indigenous society, whose structures had to be identified and the legal rules governing it defined. A culture of officers and administrators of "native affairs" was thus set in place. Orientalists were called on to assist in translating the classics of Muslim law or the discourse that Muslim societies elaborated about themselves. Ibn Khaldūn was therefore translated into the European languages, since he provided an explanation for the tribal and clan system and its role in history.

The constitution of a colonial science followed. It had practical and concrete aims but tended to archaize the societies, both by referring to bodies of law several centuries old, which were once again applied, and by projecting a European medieval image on the conquered peoples. In the imaginations of the conquerors, tribal and brotherhood chiefs from Afghanistan, the Caucasus, and the Maghreb were the counterparts of the feudal grandees of Europe between the eleventh and fifteenth centuries. Until the end of colonization, the colonials paradoxically aspired to be the bearers of civilization and progress, yet at the same time they were resistant to that progress, rediscovering with pleasure, in the conquered East, the world that no longer existed in Europe.

Even as European society became more democratic, increasingly leveling social conditions and continuously expanding political participation, the colonizers' values became more regressive. In the colonial world as in the vanishing Old Regimes, everyone had to know his place: the colonial master had to be just and the native loyal, touchstone values that were no longer current in the Europe of the industrial revolution. Victorian England, where the medieval frame of reference became omnipresent precisely because that society had become urban and industrial, moved the furthest in that direction. France, more bourgeois and more rural, identified to a greater extent with Rome. The ideologues of the French Revolution had had the Germanic invasions in mind, whereas those of the conquest of Algeria saw it as a new Gaul, which French civilization would Romanize.

By the 1850s, the medieval frame of reference proposing ethnic separation had become dominant in English policy, with a vindication of the archaic rebels' premodern authenticity. The French, by contrast, were oriented toward a notion of Romanization, that is, of assimilation. But they did not have the capacity to realize their program fully, creating instead the monstrosity that was colonial Algeria, both a part of the metropolis and a realm where the laws of conquest were applied with extraordinary severity. With the formation of a European settlement colony and the concerted repression of the native population, the old schema of the struggle between the races, beloved of European historiography in the previous centuries, found its most absolute realization, just as the British presence in India perfectly expressed the concept of military despotism.

The fate of the Muslim Mediterranean was thus clearly defined in the mid-nineteenth century. It consisted, first, of a Balkan peninsula, where the nationality principle took root to the benefit of the Christian populations; second, of North Africa, destined to fall completely under the yoke of direct colonial domination; and third, of a central Arab-Anatolian entity that would preserve its nominal independence but that it would be imperative to reform.

CHAPTER 13

THE AGE OF REFORM

THE PROBLEM OF REFORM

Since the Enlightenment, it had been well understood that, in order to survive, the Muslim state had to be reformed. That was the condition for its remaining within the framework of the European balance of powers, which had become global via the Indian route. Although the need for reforms was a European imperative, given the universalization of its norms, it also corresponded to the needs of the societies being transformed. We therefore need to discern, in the analysis of the processes under way, what was imposed collectively and forcibly by the great powers, what evolved in synchronism between Europe and the Muslim world (with the two finding similar solutions to similar problems), and what resulted from one side influencing or borrowing from the other.

What was specific to the classic Ottoman approach was that it prohibited, at least theoretically, transmitting by heredity the duties of the sultan's servants, that is, those belonging to the ruling class. Paradoxically, the servile ideology of being a member of the imperial house and of the houses subordinate to it culminated in a sort of meritocracy that astonished aristocratic Europe. From the eighteenth century on, that definition of society was in large part belied by the constitution, at least in the provinces, of a vast class of notables related by marriage: Islamic religious officials, wealthy merchants, and members of the military and administrative classes. The cement for that social alliance was their common exploitation of urban and rural tax farms.

Nevertheless, the sultan had the power of life and death over his servants and complete latitude in confiscating their possessions. When a dynamic sovereign such as Mahmud II arose, he did not hesitate to use these instruments of terror against his close collaborators. So it was for the emergent dynasties, such as that of Muhammad Ali in Egypt.

The Muslim ruling class needed a political program that would ensure the security of their property and persons and the opportunity for their children to attain high public office. The upheaval caused by the emergence of the modern state offered them a historic opportunity to realize that program, using European liberalism as an ideological cover. That was the meaning of the famous

Edict of Gülhane of November 3, 1839, proclaimed in the midst of the Syrian war, following the death of Mahmud II.

Security became the mainspring of the state:

> If there is an absence of security with regard to wealth, everyone remains impervious to the voice of the prince and the nation; no one attends to the growth of public wealth, absorbed as he is by his own worries. If, on the contrary, the citizen is confident that he owns his property of every kind, then, full of eagerness about his own affairs, whose ken he seeks to broaden so as to extend that of his enjoyment, he feels his love for the prince and the nation, and his devotion to his country, increasing in his heart every day. These feelings become the source of his most laudable actions.[1]

Although that program protected the interests of the ruling class, it was expounded as if it benefited the population of the empire as a whole. All those falling under the jurisdiction of imperial authority, even non-Muslims, ceased to be subject to the diversity of statuses and became Ottomans equal before the sultan.

That departure from the ancient principles of the state and society was sanctioned both by reference to Islam, through the claim that it was merely an application of the true principles of that religion, and through the immediate communication of a French version of the edict, having legal weight, to the European embassies. The act of reform had to take into account simultaneously that dual audience, the Muslim community and the European powers.

The Ottoman reformers took their inspiration from Europe. For a long time, the empire had delegated to the Christian dragomans of the capital the responsibility for maintaining relations with the Europeans. Dynasties of translators lasting for centuries had thus been established. Some were of European origin, constituting the group of "Levantines" (in the sense of Europeans settled in the empire), while others were Phanariots. They would continue to play their role as go-betweens in the nineteenth century. With the establishment of permanent embassies in Europe in the late eighteenth century, Muslim elements joined them. Just as the French language was the universal language of diplomacy, so too the knowledge of Europe was filtered primarily through French culture. These Muslims, unlike the dragomans, could attain the highest positions in the empire. Through diplomacy and work in the translation bureaus, they came to constitute the first reformist elites, and slowly French became a second language in the administration, at least in its most modern sectors.

Knowledge of Europe expanded. Every European country seems to have had its specialty: the French were the best administrators; the Prussians had the best army; the British had the best navy, and especially, the most advanced mastery of industrial and economic modernity. It was tempting to take the best of each system, at the risk of producing complete incoherence. In addition, the group of reformers who ruled the state as the sultanate weakened after Mahmud II's death had to come to terms on a permanent basis with the struggle for influence among the European powers. Camps, groups, or propensities, defined as pro-French, pro-English, or pro-Russian, came to the fore. The groups and personalities in question needed the support of one embassy or another in the struggle for power and had intellectual preferences for one or another European culture, which led them to lean toward that power. But the general orientation was certainly the survival of the empire through reform.

In suppressing social functions, the Edict of Gülhane did not borrow from Europe. That suppression was the result of the empire's internal evolution over half a century. It corresponded to the ruling class's needs and to the necessity of assuring the survival of the Ottoman state. It can therefore be viewed as a contemporary but independent development. Its mechanisms are perfectly obvious in the example of the emancipation of non-Muslims, which is intelligible only within the context of a comparative history of the Islamic world and Europe.

THE CHRISTIAN IMAGE OF EUROPE

We must first recognize that the emancipation of non-Christians in Europe was far from complete. Of course, the French Revolution had emancipated both non-Catholics (that is, Protestants) and non-Christians (Jews) on the principle of granting everything to individuals and refusing everything to groups. But the Napoleonic Concordat had also recognized Catholicism as the religion of the majority of French people, and it was not until the July Monarchy that Judaism became a Concordat religion.

The evolution had been slower in the rest of Europe. English Catholics had not been emancipated until 1820, and the emancipation of the Jews was far from complete in 1839. It was not until the 1850s and 1860s that the British, German, Austrian, and Italian Jews would possess full rights and be eligible for political office. And Russia, even more than the Ottoman Empire, remained the sanctuary of the European Old Regime, as indicated by the fact that serfdom persisted until the reforms of Alexander II and that the discriminatory status of the Jews was maintained and even exacerbated.

Since the emancipation of non-Christians was far from complete in Europe, the matter at hand in the colonial world was either to proclaim itself neutral in the matter of religion, like the British in India, or to respect the Muslim institutions, like the French in Algeria. In both cases, the policy drifted away from its stated intentions. Indian Muslims, who had ruled the subcontinent at the time of the Mogul Empire, were gradually dispossessed of their function as ruling class. The Persian culture of the Moguls was replaced by a more purely Indian culture, increasingly mixed with the contributions of the British. In Algeria, conquest was accompanied by the dispossession of the rural land and the urban wealth of Islamic institutions. Inexorably, and despite discourses to the contrary, Algerian Muslims, officially subjects and not French citizens, were reduced to the most humiliating status possible, protected minors subject to the most discriminatory regulations of the Native Code in the early days of the Third Republic.

The image of Europe that reached the Islamic world, particularly the Ottoman Empire as of 1840, was no longer truly that of triumphant liberalism stemming from the Enlightenment, as it had been in the previous period. Rather, that image was the result of Europe's nonrecognition of the nationality principle vis-à-vis the Muslims following the Balkan, Algerian, Egyptian, and Syrian episodes. As the industrial revolution advanced, with its disenchantment of the world and its dynamic of creative destruction, it seemed to give rise in the Muslim world to the invention of tradition.

In Enlightenment thought, the process of civilization, or the history of progress, was defined in terms of a logic of gradual emancipation from religious authority, as attested by Condorcet's writings. Even for the early Guizot, the conflict between religious and civil society was one of the dynamics in the history of European civilization; in his theory, the race struggle and then the class struggle were produced by invasions.

In the 1840s, conservative thought regained momentum by co-opting entire aspects of Enlightenment thought through an invention of tradition. Anglo-Saxon liberalism thus appropriated a dual genealogy, laying claim both to the Germanic and feudal freedoms and to the free inquiry of the Protestant Reformation. By finding new foundations in history, it was able to reject the absolute rationalism of the French Revolution, which had claimed to establish modern society on reason alone and which nascent socialism was in the process of reviving. The Catholicism of the first half of the nineteenth century, which condemned "modern civilization," nevertheless posited that contemporary Europe was a Christian civilization, understood both as a state and as a dynamic process.

Whereas Enlightenment thought, in its absolute secularism, defined the relation between Western society and other societies as a game of catch-up, achieved through access to a common and future universalized modernity, the new European thought made the Christian heritage the discriminating element, which prevented other societies from elevating themselves to the same status as triumphant Europe, at least in the near future.

A twofold paradox arose at this point. First, the idea of catching up to Europe was more appealing the wider the gap to be bridged. As of 1840, the date of the establishment of the modern Muslim state, with its embryonic modern administration and the spread of the printed word, some began to claim that the gap was in fact unbridgeable. Second, the advent of industrial society was accompanied by ideologies embracing the past, whereas the previous, so-called protoindustrial stage of society had set forth a discourse of progress and rupture. It was as if the first discourse anticipated the future (as indicated by the

Enlightenment of the French Revolution), while the second clashed with the reality of the society of the Other.

THE EMANCIPATION OF NON-MUSLIMS IN ISLAMIC REGIONS

The Christian self-image that Europe projected in the 1840s corresponded to the political tools it used in the Islamic world. Beginning in that decade, there were no longer zones prohibited to Europeans, with the exception of the holy cities of the Hejaz. The great powers had the right to open consulates anywhere, and freedom of movement was hindered only by the lack of security reigning in entire regions of the Islamic world. The central authority had a great deal of difficulty imposing obedience in some provinces, which were permanently under the sway of banditry by rural mountain dwellers, clan and village wars, depredation by Bedouins and nomads, and the local powers of notables with armed forces of various kinds at their disposal.

Very often, the European consulates could not hope for effective action from the civil police. They became actors on the local scene, incorporating elements from their society of residence. They would therefore grant consular protection to a tribal chief or a local notable who became part of their clientele. Taken in that sense, consular protection was no longer religious in nature, since it was directed toward both Muslims and non-Muslims. It was an instrument of power, and the conflicts between European powers also had repercussions for the conflicts between clienteles. In that new power system, the indigenous dragomans in the consulates played an essential role, since they had the advantage of an intimate knowledge of society and also held permanent positions, in contrast to European diplomats with their temporary appointments. Many influential Christian families in the Near East trace the origin of their wealth and influence to these posts held in the mid-nineteenth century.

At the same time, the great powers reasserted their religious protectorate, and their rivalries stirred up nascent religious conflict. Several different logics were at work. Non-Muslim communities, as distinct groups recognized by the state, had only recently come into being, even though they were supported by Islamic protective regulations. In the Ottoman Empire, they were in the first place fiscal entities, since they had to organize themselves to pay specific taxes. The only institutions that extended to the empire as a whole were the Orthodox and Armenian churches. In the nineteenth century, the empire was obliged to recognize the Uniate Catholic and Protestant churches (in 1831 and 1847, respectively). For centuries, these non-Muslim communities maintained privileged relations with Christian Europe, through which they very early on became familiar with European modernity and acquired a great cultural and educational advantage. They were also experiencing a high rate of population growth: the increase in their numbers was much greater than that of the Muslim population.

In the mid-nineteenth century, these communities benefited fully from the transformations under way. They were well situated in the new order of economic trade imposed by industrial Europe. The collapse of the traditional order changed their place in society, since they came to participate in the new institutions being set in place, such as the provincial councils. Finally, external religious protection became a concrete reality, with power relations now leaning overwhelmingly toward Europe.

Religious Protection and the Great Powers

In Jerusalem, at the request of the Protestant missions, eager to proselytize among the Jewish population beginning in 1839, British diplomats asked for British protection for the Jews of Palestine, then for those throughout the entire empire. The Porte responded by appealing to the principles of Gülhane, attributing to these principles a new meaning, the emancipation of non-Muslims. From the 1840s on, competition was keen between the principal European countries present in Palestine: an Anglo-Prussian Protestant bishopric was created in Jerusalem in 1841; the Orthodox patriarch of Jerusalem returned to his city of residence; a permanent Russian ecclesiastical mission was set in place; and the Catholic patriarchate was restored in 1847. A frontal battle began in the late 1840s between Catholics and Orthodox Christians, in other words, between France and Russia, regarding their respective rights to the holy sites, even as Europe was shaken by the revolutions of 1848, the "springtime of the peoples."

After the suppression of the Mount Lebanon emirate in 1842, the Druzes and Maronites faced off in the region, drawing in the British and the French. Although the clienteles were fighting for their own reasons, they had the capacity to manipulate their protectors by exerting influence on their local agents and by spreading propaganda in the metropolises. Hence Abbot Nicolas Mourad finessed an excellent invention of tradition by creating the myth of a letter from Saint Louis to the Maronites.

In the Balkans, the Orthodox communities were differentiating themselves on the basis of ethnicity. But the Russians' demand for a protectorate over all Orthodox Christians would have marked, quite simply, the end of what was called "European Turkey," since the majority of the population belonged to these churches. Such a demand was unacceptable to the empire.

As a result, the attention to reforms focused not on institutional changes but on the status of the non-Muslim communities. The Jews, who were not asking for anything and who tended to be vulnerable to virulent anti-Semitism on the part of the Orthodox Christians, were included in the general movement.

Tsar Nicolas I wrote to the British ambassador in Saint Petersburg in January 1853. According to the tsar, "Turkey is completely disorganized. We need to agree on that. *Look, we have a sick man, a gravely ill man on our hands. Let me tell you frankly that it would be a great misfortune if he were to slip away from us one of these days, especially before all the necessary measures are taken.*[2]

Russia thus unofficially proposed once again dividing up the empire among the European powers, along with granting Balkan independence. Since France and Great Britain did not seem interested, Russia publicly demanded recognition of its protectorate over the Orthodox Christians and the strengthening of their rights to the holy places. The Ottomans refused, and Russia went to war in 1853, provoking the joint intervention of France and Great Britain. This was the Crimean War of 1854 to 1856.

The aim of that war, like that of the war of 1798, was to prevent the partitioning of the Ottoman Empire. The last war without hatred by the Europe of nations, it was also the first war of industrial Europe. The Franco-British military encroachment into the Black Sea occurred with the aid of steam navigation, whence the importance of coal supplies. The conflict could be followed in real time thanks to the expansion of the telegraph network. Like the war of Italian unification in 1858, it was accompanied by a growing awareness of the health risks to the wounded and of the need to provide them with proper care. From Florence Nightingale to Henry Dunant, the new humanitarian came into being, culminating in the creation of the Red Cross.

At stake was, first, the maintenance of the empire's territorial integrity, and second, the status of non-Muslims. After the territorial question was settled by the taking of Sebastopol, and diplomatic discussions focused on the fate of the Principalities (present-day Romania), the second issue remained. Vaunting their Christian identity, many Europeans, such as William Gladstone, considered it a "political solecism" to see a Muslim sovereign ruling despotically over millions of Christians. For the victors, it was necessary to act in the matter: while they did not seek to call into question European protections, they also did not want to broaden them. In the end, the French and British had to save appearances by portraying emancipation as an act of pure will on the part of the Ottoman Empire prior to the Congress of Paris. Nevertheless, that act was accompanied by urgent advice from the two allies. Everyone agreed on the de jure equality and treatment of Christians and Muslims; the main point of disagreement had to do with the freedom to change religion, on which British diplomacy, at the request of the Protestant missionaries, insisted. The Ottomans flat-out refused because of the state's Muslim identity and the prerogatives of the caliphate. After exhausting negotiations, a compromise was reached by which religious freedom was affirmed and a ban was placed on compelling a person to change religion. That implicitly meant that a former Muslim could not be compelled to return to his original religion.

The *Hatt-ı Hümayun* of February 18, 1856, was the major text of emancipation.[3] Inasmuch as it applied to the Jews, it was an advance over what was happening in many countries of Christian Europe. Although the Europeans wanted the emancipation of the Christians, they did not intend to abandon their rights of protection, which would have been abolished by emancipation on an individual basis. The edict granted everything to the non-Muslim communities and only secondarily to individuals. Each community, in the name of its privileges and immunities granted ab antiquo, would enjoy a constitution befitting the progress and enlightenment of the time and would establish the respective powers of its clergy and laypeople. Personal status would be under the jurisdiction of the religious tribunals of each faith. The result was that, though all individuals were eligible for public employment and were equal in their tax status, representation in provincial and municipal councils would come about on the basis of religion.

The faith-based community, or "millet," was a product of modernity, stemming both from the internal evolution of Ottoman society and from European intervention. It proceeded from the emancipation of collectivities, not individuals, and led to political sectarianism. The Treaty of Paris of March 30, 1856, recorded the "generous intentions" of the sultan "toward the Christian populations." It was difficult for Europeans to acknowledge that the rights granted to the Jews in the Ottoman world were greater than those they possessed in much of Europe.

Incidentally in the *Hatt-ı Hümayun*, the Europeans imposed the right of foreigners to possess property in the Ottoman Empire. The reformers took the opportunity to push through their economic program: the abolition of tax farms in favor of direct taxation; incentives for public utility projects, particularly highways; the institution of a public budget that the state would pledge to respect; and the creation of banks and financial institutions. "To reach these goals," they wrote, "we will seek the means to take best advantage of European science, art, and capital, and to put them into practice one by one."

For some Europeans, the emancipation of the Christians was a step toward Islam's disappearance, which would inexorably occur with historical progress. Curiously, this view can be seen as the counterpart to the discourse of free-thinkers on the disappearance of religion in the modern world. It was supported by the steady decline of the independent Muslim powers and the higher rate of population growth of Christian societies, including those of Eastern Christians. Some clerical circles therefore imagined the Christian East rising up from the ruins of the Islamic world.

The Muslims had a related view, seeing the edict of emancipation, missionary work, and the various sorts of European interference as demonstrations of a vast conspiracy destined to destroy Islam, with the Eastern Christians representing its vanguard. Within that context, the Syrian provinces, which had lagged behind in reforms, constituted a realm where tensions between the different religious communities were likely to develop. The events of 1860 in Lebanon and Syria, where a social emancipation movement of Christian peasants sparked violence between Druzes and Maronites, and then a massacre of

Orthodox Christians in Damascus, caused an enormous stir in Europe, where the image of Islam became inextricably linked to that of the massacre. In France, Napoleon III decided to intervene and obtained a European mandate for what we would now call the "right of intervention." Closely overseen by the other European powers, the operation culminated in a conference of ambassadors, who decided to create a semiautonomous Mount Lebanon in the empire, with a Christian governor named by the Porte in agreement with the great powers, and a council elected by the community. The constitution of an autonomous Greater Syria on the model of Egypt was envisioned. Napoleon III sounded out Abd al-Qadir, who had distinguished himself in the defense of the Christians of Damascus, to learn whether he would consent to assume the leadership of an Arab kingdom of Syria, but the exiled emir refused. The British proposed handing over the leadership of that Syrian entity to a reformist Ottoman vizier, but the vizier's circle was intent on defending the integrity of the Ottoman Empire.

In Morocco, where the large Jewish community played an essential role in commercial transactions with Europe, the sultan attempted to ban consular protection for these traders, which would have removed them from his authority and tax system. France and Great Britain opposed him and did not hesitate to use naval demonstrations accompanied by the bombing of Moroccan ports, in 1851 especially. The Moroccan authorities were forced to give in and, at the same time, to accept a capitulary system similar to that which existed in the Ottoman Empire. The Anglo-Moroccan treaty of December 1856 enshrined that change, since it granted the Europeans freedom of commerce, set customs duties at 10 percent ad valorem, dispensed with all other taxes, and established a consular justice system.

As a result, the protected Jews (about three thousand of them, or 1 percent of the Jews of Morocco), benefiting from a sort of reverse discrimination, played the role of mediators between Europe and Morocco and became the agents for European penetration. The Spanish-Moroccan War over Tétouan in 1859–1860 precipitated the shift, which produced strong tensions between communities, similar to those that existed in the Levant. The sultan of Morocco, without going so far as an edict of emancipation, pledged in a rescript of 1864 to treat the Jews fairly: "To apply to them, in the administration, the same scales of justice as to those who are not Jewish, so that none shall be a victim of the slightest injustice, so that no ill shall afflict them, and so that neither the agents of the Makhzen [administration] nor anyone else shall harm them in their persons or in their property."

The European powers, soon joined by the United States, seized on the rescript and congratulated the sultan for having granted full equality to his Jewish subjects. At the same time, they made themselves its guarantors and thus granted themselves the right to protect the Moroccan Jews as a whole, a right of intervention *avant la lettre*. That protection was in turn limited by the powerlessness of the Moroccan state to impose its authority on part of its territory.

Unlike the Ottoman Empire, which was undergoing recentralization, the Sharifian empire was weakened by its contact with Europe.

After the taking of Algiers, Tunisia found itself in a position of semivas-
saldom vis-à-vis France, which guaranteed its independence from the Ottoman Porte. The bey of Tunis took advantage of that situation, refusing to apply
the Edict of Gülhane as well as the principal reforms of the Ottoman authority. He attempted to create a modern state and army, but the reforms, poorly
planned, failed miserably. Taxes became even more burdensome as the agricultural economy declined. Following the execution of a Jew for blasphemy in
1857, France and Great Britain, by means of a naval demonstration, imposed
reforms. The fundamental pact of September 9, 1857, reiterated the terms of
Gülhane and of the *Hatt* of 1856, and proclaimed the security of the life and
property of residents of the regency, equality before the law and with respect
to taxes, and the abolition of the Muslims' privileges, of restrictions on commerce, and of monopolies. Furthermore, it granted foreigners the right to own
property and to practice any trade. A constitution founded on these principles
was promulgated in 1861 with Europe's boisterous approval. It was suspended
in 1865 following an uprising of tribes, primarily against taxes. Although the
revolt was harshly repressed, the Tunisian state found itself in debt for a long
time. It declared bankruptcy in 1867, and a foreign financial commission
(France, Great Britain, and Italy) was imposed the next year to manage the
resources of the Tunisian state.

In Tunisia and Morocco, the semi-emancipation of the Jews came about
thanks to the tireless actions of representatives of the Jews of Great Britain and
France, Claude Montefiore and Adolphe Crémieux in particular. In addition
to the humanitarian aspect, which garnered them the support of the chancelleries in their home countries, the demand for reforms, backed by gunboat
diplomacy, served to assure European economic penetration and to establish
increased dependence on the Concert of Europe.

Perhaps the only person in Europe who understood the anomaly of emancipating non-Muslims while proceeding to subjugate Muslims within the colonial framework was Napoleon III. Aided by enlightened advisers such as Ismaïl
Urbain, he attempted to alter the course of the process under way in Algeria,
with his famous policy of an Arab kingdom. That kingdom was supposed to be
associated with France more than subject to it. As shown by his famous letter
to Marie-Edme MacMahon of June 20, 1865, he wanted to make treatment of
the Muslims in Algeria the new mode of influence for French policy in the East:

France, which sympathizes everywhere with the ideas of nationhood, cannot, in the
eyes of the world, justify the dependency in which it is obliged to hold the Arab people if it does not summon them to a better existence. When our manner of governing
a defeated people is an object of envy for the 15 million Arabs spread throughout the
other parts of Africa and Asia; the day our power, established at the foot of the Atlas

Mountains, appears to them as an intervention of Providence to elevate a fallen race; on that day, the glory of France will ring out from Tunis to the Euphrates and will assure our country the kind of preponderance that cannot rouse anyone's jealousy because it rests not on conquest but on the love of humanity and progress. An effective policy is the most powerful vehicle for commercial interests. And what more effective policy for France than to give the Muhammadan races, so numerous in the East and so unified with one another despite the distances, unimpeachable guarantees of tolerance, justice, and respect for the difference in mores, faiths, and races within its own states?[4]

That policy failed because of the resistance of administrative and military circles and the opposition of liberals and republicans to an enterprise too closely linked to personal power and dynastic activities. At the very end of Napoleon III's reign, French policy turned toward supporting Ottoman reform measures with, in particular, the creation of the imperial secondary school of Galatasaray in Constantinople to train the new Ottoman elites.

Napoleon III's discourse can be understood within the context of the transformations of space and identity proper to the 1860s.

Transformations of Space, Transformations of Identity

Ottoman reformers perfectly internalized the logic of development corresponding to the coming of age of the industrial revolution. The entire eastern Mediterranean space was being restructured. The old and new seaports became points of entry for the circulation of merchandise and raw materials. At first, the ports were linked to the interior by modern roads and no longer by caravan trails. Located at regular intervals, these ports thereby provided access to the inland regions. Later, a port hierarchy was set in place, with a vast hinterland that was soon defined by a network of railroads. It was the new urban areas such as Jaffa and Beirut, more than ancient cities such as Tripoli and Saida, that benefited from that change. These modern ports became stops on regular steamship lines and in the 1860s were linked to Europe by telegraph. The world of Jules Verne had come to pass.

The Mediterranean coasts experienced a true rebirth and, more than the cities of the interior, attracted the burgeoning population and the fruits of the rural exodus in its early stages. Modern roads supplanted the old caravan trade routes linking the cities of the interior and defined three different spaces: the interior, a space for the production of raw materials, usually agricultural; the port, a place of exchange; and Europe, which asserted its gravitational pull. Trade between Europe and the Muslim world largely prevailed over internal trade. A frontier of agricultural reconquest continuously pushed back the boundary between settled life and nomadism, because there was now a European market, a consumer of agricultural products, as well as a reformist state eager for development.

The Ottoman state, having learned its lesson from long experience and from its tax problems, now had the tools for recentralization. A combination army and police force allowed for concerted pacification of the internal space, which put an end to the old autonomy of local and tribal notables. The use of sea transport, roads, telegraphs, and soon railroads allowed for the rapid deployment of law-and-order forces. Public security became the order of the day; it too relied on involving the local elites in development, thanks to new land legislation. These laws permitted the constitution of large properties, thus integrating the local and the global and making it possible to channel investments toward agriculture. All hope of industrialization was abandoned because, given the capitulations and trade treaties, it was impossible to pass protective customs legislation.

The Egypt of Khedive Ismā'īl was the best example of that evolution. The cotton famine caused by the U.S. Civil War considerably enriched the country, to the advantage both of its ruling elite, founded on the co-optation of members of Muhammad Ali's dynasty and of local notables. The emerging large properties were primarily Muslim, whereas the bourgeoisie, the vast majority of them non-Muslim and even foreign, took their place within the circuit of trade with Europe. The modern state spent a great deal both on development and on prestige projects. It soon went into debt, the costs of which kept growing because its credit was not good, resulting in increasingly unfavorable lending conditions. The European investor proved fond of his high-yield Eastern bonds. The Ottoman state and Tunisia met the same fate, since the tax system did not allow them to meet the costs of defending their countries (the Crimean War), operating the modern state, and promoting development.

Beginning in 1880, the ports brought the eastern Mediterranean world fully into the first globalization ventures and promoted the major intercontinental migrations, made possible by the links between the railroad networks and the steam navigation lines. Inexorably, travel time was reduced, as symbolized by the opening of the Suez Canal in 1869, which shortened the Indian route. At the beginning of the nineteenth century, it took six months to go from Great Britain to India; at the end of the century, three weeks. The telegraph transmitted the most important information in real time.

In the port cities, a largely non-Muslim commercial bourgeoisie took advantage of that evolution. Its members acquired a modern education, thanks to the growing network of missionary institutions of learning, both Catholic and Protestant. As of 1860, the Jewish communities had the Alliance Israélite Universelle, which took on the task of emancipation through education, with an interest in placing these impoverished communities within the world of modern production. The reformed administration increasingly used French, which thus became the language of modernity among both Muslims and non-Muslims.

An unexpected consequence of the restoration of order and recentralization was the battle the Ottoman authorities waged against the abuses of consular protection. In practice, they allowed such protection for non-Muslims but rejected it for Muslims, who were supposed to recognize only the authority of the Islamic caliph. Since pacification forced the consulates to deal exclusively with the representatives of provincial authority on questions of public order, the consular protection of Muslims became much less important. A new implicit social contract took shape: non-Muslims went to the European consulates, Muslims to the Ottoman authorities. For reformers, that was only a temporary situation. The communalist solution was diametrically opposed to the spirit of modernity, and one day the entire population of the empire would be subject to uniform legislation, as was the case in western European countries.

The Ottoman Empire thus appeared to be engaged in a race where reforms, recentralization, and development were intended to restore its independence, even as they contributed in the first instance to its further subjection to the European order. By contrast, the Persia of the Qajars remained the sanctuary of archaic practices. The authorities were unable to secure recentralization and pacification, which meant that the foreign consulates maintained their power until a late date. The consulates even went so far as to keep armed forces at their disposal. Their protection networks could extend to large tribal groups once again within the context of the Great Game between the British and the Russians. The Persian state was caught between the two superpowers. It tried desperately to obtain British guarantees for its territorial integrity, which was threatened by Russian penetration into central Asia. What happened instead was a partitioning of the country into two zones of influence, the north to the Russians, the south to the British. Did not Shah Nasir al-Dīn (1848–1896) complain that he had to consult the Russians if he wanted to go north and the British if he sought to go south?

Intellectual life, particularly vibrant in religious circles, went more or less unnoticed by European observers, who knew only the accounts of Morier and Gobineau. But the messianic Babist movement attracted the attention of Europeans interested in how a new religion came into being. That religion, having become the Bahā'i faith, was persecuted in its native country, but in the West it fell under the category of Oriental received wisdom.

Morocco was an even more archaic society than Persia. It lacked a reformist elite versed in European ideas and seeking to establish a modern state. A few attempts were made, plans for public works projects in the ports, for example, but these were mere caprices. The financial means were lacking and the capitulary powers refused to authorize an increase in customs duties. The European advance, with its interplay of multiple consular protections and various interventions, weakened the traditional state's authority. In Persia, this consisted for the most part of a tug-of-war between two powers, but in Morocco all the Western consulates (about a dozen) acquired clienteles and faced off in a complex play of influences. The consular malady (*morbus consularis*), even the consular furor

(*furor consularis*), as the foreign affairs ministries called it, reached its paroxysm. England did try to limit abuses, holding an international conference on the subject in Madrid in 1880. The sultan obtained a few concessions, such as the recognition of the right to tax protected persons, but, by the very fact that a conference was held, the Moroccan question became internationalized.

Another consequence of the communications revolution was that the different Muslim populations became better acquainted with one another. Steamships, railroads, telegraphs, the press, and in general, the printed word suddenly put places in contact with one other that had previously had little communication because of geographical distance. The caliph of Constantinople began to worry about the fate of Indian or even Chinese Muslims. In symbolic terms, the opening of the Suez Canal in 1869 can be said to have given rise to a new and hazy reality, the "Muslim world." The career of Jamal al-Dīn-Afghani, a Shiite Persian who took his battle to Afghanistan, British India, Constantinople, and Egypt, perfectly embodied that new situation.

Even as communications transformed space, giving rise to a Muslim world, identities became territorialized. The loss of social functions, the emergence of the modern state, and the need to fall in line with European discourse were the essential components of that process, which belonged to the context of regional diversities. In Tunisia and in Egypt—an autonomous and almost independent province of the Ottoman Empire—the local state encouraged the phenomenon in order to mark its distance from the central power. Ottoman government elites took hold in the country and co-opted the notables who had been born there, a kind of nationalization from above. At the same time, the modern state in formation was obliged to use the country's native language and to create a class of civil servants from the local areas, leading to nationalization from below. The process was more advanced in Egypt, where the constitution of the state entailed the recognition and definition of the territory. That did not prevent the highest elements of the ruling class from attaining high posts in the Ottoman administration.

In the empire itself, the state's discourse tried to promote a common Ottoman identity transcending religious and ethnic cleavages. After the troubles of 1860, a vague consciousness, Syrian and Arab at once, emerged in the discourse of certain intellectuals, who reiterated European interpretations. Unlike in Tunisia and Egypt, the Ottoman state did not encourage these regional identities, which therefore took some time to be defined. Nevertheless, as a consequence of the events of 1860, the new definitions of identity sought to move beyond the framework of religious communities. The result was an Arab-Syrian specificity within the Ottoman context, where, as in Egypt, Muslims and Christians participated in defining new frames of reference.

In the rest of the Ottoman Empire, however, religion prevailed in the definition of new identities. The Balkans were naturally in the forefront of the process. After the Crimean War, there was no longer a single Orthodoxy that could serve as the frame of reference for all Christians. On the contrary, every Orthodox church became the matrix for a new identity, leading to the assertion of Serbian, Bulgarian, Greek, and Romanian nationalities, which were able to claim allegiance to great states predating the Ottoman conquest. As a result, violence between Christian peoples became the corollary of the territorialization process. Similarly, the Balkan Muslims, even when they had the same native language as a Christian group, were defined as nonindigenous and alien, leading to strained relations between Christians and Muslims. The Muslims rightly feared that any progress toward national independence would translate into their repression or even expulsion.

Ottoman reformers were perfectly aware of the processes under way and, addressing European representatives, they pled the case for maintaining Ottoman authority, the only recourse possible in the face of an outburst of inexpiable violence. That is what Ali Pasha explained in 1862 to the French minister of foreign affairs:

> The existence of the Ottoman Empire is important, it is said, for the maintenance of the European balance of powers. I believe it, and if you study thoroughly and without bias the spirit and state of the members of different nationalities that compose the population of Turkey, you will be convinced in the end that only the Turks can serve as the link between them, and that, to leave them to themselves, or to wish to subject them to the domination of one of them, or to consider creating something like a confederation would be chaos and civil war in perpetuity. In the East, therefore, nothing could replace that old empire, whose enemies enjoy saying that it is ill, and about which impartial observers can only affirm the opposite. . . .
>
> Italy, which is inhabited by a single race speaking the same language and professing the same religion, is experiencing many difficulties in bringing about its unification. For the time being, its current state has achieved only anarchy and disorder. Judge what would happen in Turkey if you gave free rein to all the different national aspirations that the revolutionaries, and with them, certain governments, are seeking to promote there. It would take a century and torrents of blood to establish a somewhat stable state of affairs.[5]

The European chancelleries did not absolutely understand that message, at a time when Italian and German unity was being realized, and when a perfect correspondence between territory and nation was imaginable. As this letter shows, the Turkish frame of reference was beginning to replace the Ottoman in the French discourse of the authorities of the Porte. Very often the use of the European language made it possible to say things that could not yet be articulated in the original tongue. Already a distinction was being made between the Turks and the Arabs, though no political character was granted to that linguistic differentiation.

In Anatolia, the same evolution took place as in the Balkans, but with a certain delay. The kingdom of Greece, in the name of the "Great Idea," conducted an irredentist policy toward all Christian Hellenophones, its ultimate plan being to restore the Byzantine Empire. The Armenian elites began to give voice to an Armenian nationalism, whose project could be realized only if Anatolia met the same fate as the Balkans. As a result, Anatolian Muslims, even those who originally spoke Greek or Armenian, were impelled to take refuge in an Ottoman, or already Turkish, Muslim identity. The influx of Muslim refugees from the Caucasus and the Balkans shored up that tendency. Although the coastal Mediterranean cities were marked by an intermingling of peoples, with some cities—including the largest of them—having a Christian majority, relations among communities in the Anatolian interior were increasingly strained. The advent of population growth added further factors of dissension, especially when a Christian peasantry was competing for the use of territories with semi-nomadic Turkoman or Kurdish herders.

Islamizing Reforms or Reforming Islam?

The Russian advance into central Asia, the new, short-lived efforts of the British in Afghanistan, and the struggle for influence between the French and the Italians in Tunisia made it clear that the Muslims faced a common fate, given the constant advance of Christian Europe at their expense. Abd al-Qadir's and Shamil's glorious resistance ended in appalling bloodbaths and the establishment of a particularly oppressive colonial order. By the tens of thousands, Caucasian and Algerian Muslims took refuge in the Ottoman Empire, where they were put to use guarding the fringes of the nomadic world and curbing nomadism in Anatolia and all along the Fertile Crescent.

In the early 1870s, the Ottoman reformers' momentum seemed to have been broken, and the practice of authoritarian reformism was being contested. The sultan attempted to recover his powers vis-à-vis the Porte, but he did not have the means, which led to a growing ministerial instability. In the ruling class and within the framework of the struggle for power, the need for a new system of government took root.

Until that time, the platform of the Ottoman and Persian modernizers was primarily the security of property and persons, the rationalization of the administration, the creation of a modern military apparatus, and the development of the territory. In their minds, these elements were closely linked and would allow them to assure the collective interests of the ruling class vis-à-vis the ruling dynasty: the individual careers of high officials, their personal enrichment, and the survival of the state.

Despite the formation of administrative councils at various echelons of the state and territory, the chief weakness of the program was that it did not take into account the participation of the general population.

Persian bureaucratic reformers, anxious to win the favor of the British and to develop the country's resources, in 1872 negotiated with Baron Julius von Reuter (founder of the agency by the same name) a concession encompassing the totality of unexploited mining resources as well as all the instruments of a modern economy (railroads, factories, irrigation, banks). The country's abandonment of its resources, the most complete known to history, was justified by the need to begin again from scratch. That concession was opposed by a coalition of notables and clergy, some embracing an authentic national spirit, others rejecting Western innovations that threatened the religious purity of Persia, and still others, local clients of Russia, acting at thet encouragement of that country. Supported by the urban masses, the opposition movement compelled the shah, who had just visited Europe, to backtrack and to revoke the concession in 1873. For the first time, a public opinion movement, a mix of traditional and modern, had succeeded in blocking the actions of reformers.

In that third quarter of the nineteenth century, there were Muslim opinion makers, their opinions defined by their social stratum, who had access to the world of the printed word. Alongside the traditionally trained clergy participating in that world were ruling class literati and a bourgeoisie composed of civil servants and merchants. What was new was the emergence of a category of writing professionals: publicists, literary writers, and essayists. They could not generally earn a living by their pens, and if they had no other sources of revenue, they depended on the subsidies granted them by important individuals in the government, within the context of their own struggle for power.

By the 1860s, the new intellectuals were closely involved in reflections on the state's future. Forming an opposition of sorts to the authoritarian reformers, they developed the theme of the indispensability of the people's participation in—even approval of—the reforms, if these reforms were to achieve their full effect. The despotism of power and the absence of a scientific worldview were considered the principal reasons why the Islamic countries lagged behind Europe. Naïvely, these first liberals held ethnic and religious conflicts responsible for the nonexistence of participation in power, that is, for the absence of political representation. The establishment of a European-style parliamentary system would resolve everything and immediately put an end to European interference and protections.

The true importance of these liberal reformers' actions lay in their awareness of the need to consult public opinion and thus to adapt the European political vocabulary to that of Islam. They attributed new meanings to the traditional terms. Hence the classic notion of *shura*, "consultation," originally referred to the prince's advisers; then authoritarian reformers made it a descriptor of the central and local administrative councils of the modern state. With the liberals, it assumed the meaning of parliamentarianism, even constitutionalism. They understood that the great failure of the reforms was that they shocked religious consciences and looked like Europeanization. In order to move forward, it was necessary to Islamize the reforms.

The liberals elaborated these new ideas in the press and in books. The Masonic lodges, with their European-type sociability, became their propagators, and important personalities did not hesitate to draw up—or to have drawn up—programs of reforms under their names and in that spirit.

That first current, of liberal European inspiration, was complemented by another, religious in its inspiration, though it too was based on a reflection on the history of Europe, which was becoming increasingly well known. The political and material decline of the Muslim world was self-evident, given the apparently irreversible rise of European domination. It had not always been so, however, and Islam had once been the dominant power of the Old World, bearing the message of science and civilization. Something had happened; at a given moment in history, a deviation had occurred. In order to resist Europe, it was necessary to return to the sources of the original power. Europe provided a demonstration of that, since one of the secrets of its power was the return to its religious origins, in the form of the Protestant Reformation. Islam thus awaited its Luther or Calvin, and Jamal al-Dīn al-Afghani was a candidate ready-to-hand for that role.

The implicit assumption behind that approach was the primacy given to religion as the driving force of history. Religion was necessary in the first stages of civilization. European superiority did not consist in critical thought or scientific deduction but in the religious reformation from which all the rest stemmed. It is difficult to know how sincere the first "Salafites" were when they articulated that thesis. It is clear they all agreed that religion constituted a weapon, both of social transformation and of resistance to European aggression. Through religion, it was possible to have an impact on society without depending on action from above, that is, from the state. In the end, the Salafites were less interested in religion as such than in society modeled on its inspiration and teachings. Without saying so explicitly, they brought about a shift in religion, from a practice of worship to the defining element of a society. In that respect, they invented in an enduring way an Islamic nationalism that defended the community of believers, elaborating a utopian project of reinvented community.

In 1884, Afghani wrote in a propaganda text:

The times have become so cruel and life so painful, in such great upheaval, that some Muslims—rare in fact—are losing patience and have difficulty tolerating the fact that their leaders are oppressors who, in their conduct, have given up applying the principles of canonical justice. These Muslims then turn to the protection of a foreign power, but they are overcome with regret at the first step taken on that path. They are like those men who want to commit suicide but who turn back and give it up with the first sign of pain. In reality, the sources of the schisms and divisions that have occurred in the Muslim states are solely the breaches of leaders who depart from the solid principles on which the Islamic religion was built and who distance themselves from the paths taken by their early ancestors. In fact, acting counter to solidly established principles and distancing oneself from the usual paths are the things most prejudicial to supreme power. When those who hold power in Islam shall return to the rules of their Law and model their conduct on those of the earliest generations, it will not be long before God gives them broader authority and grants them power comparable to that which the orthodox caliphs, the imams of religion, enjoyed. May God bestow on us the ability to be upright in our actions, and may he lead us on the path of righteousness.[6]

These first Salafites styled themselves an elite in possession of a quasi-esoteric knowledge, partly inherited from the rationalist traditions of classical Islam, partly borrowed from modern European ideas, at least when they conformed to the Salafites' views. The Salafites therefore culled from the European thought of their time everything that defined religion as a social phenomenon.

They had the ability to use the political language of Europe when they addressed European intellectuals and that of Islam when they were targeting the new public of the Muslim world. With equal sincerity, they could tell one audience that all religions were obstacles to reason, and, before the other audience, could condemn materialism, both ancient and modern (Darwinism, for example). Recalling the role of ancient Islam in the propagation of the sciences, they used it to explain the current superiority of Europe. They declared the reversibility of the European schema of historical progress, provided that Muslims would return to the study of science and philosophy. They posited the universality of science and philosophy, which belonged neither to Europe nor to the Islamic world. And they condemned the attitude of religious scholars of their time, who studied their texts by the light of an oil lamp, without wondering even once, "Why does the lamp smoke when it is covered?" Their scientism allowed them to assert that there was no incompatibility between the principles of Islam and knowledge and science.

Many conservative Muslims, condemned by these reformers for their ignorance of true knowledge, considered these themes heretical, especially the condemnation of popular religion—the cult of saints in particular—which came to include the majority of Sufi practices. Their rejection of superstition was certainly what linked the Salafites most to the Christian reformers of the sixteenth and seventeenth centuries.

For these reformers in the religious sense of the term, the matter at hand was no longer to Islamize reforms but to reform Islam. But the two currents ultimately produced fairly similar themes and tended to become indistinguishable. Arab Christians as well participated in these movements, as did a few European adventurers, convinced of the nobility of the cause, who became its defenders before European public opinion. Although the projects were articulated in a largely revised Islamic political language, the reformers refused to express themselves in terms of religious conflict. On the contrary, the most idealistic of them, such as the Egyptian Muhammad Abduh, declared that all the monotheistic religions converged toward the expression of the same truths.

Reread today, these texts seem to be of a great naïveté. But we must not underestimate the vast thought experiment represented by that desire to reframe Islamic culture within the new universal thinking defined by Europe, and the considerable task of naturalizing the new ideas, at times by finding the most reckless equivalents.

The importance of that mode of thought can also be measured by the resistance it encountered. For conservative circles, it was often a heresy that replicated tendencies already present in the medieval period.

RENAN: FROM FANATICISM TO SEMITISM

Discrediting Islam became a predominant feature of European thought. In 1862, in his inaugural lecture to the Collège de France, Joseph Ernest Renan openly called for Islam's destruction:

> The European genius is developing with a greatness beyond compare. Islamism, by contrast, is slowly decomposing; in our time, it has come crashing down. At present, the necessary condition for the spread of European civilization is the destruction of the Semitic par excellence, the destruction of the theocratic power of Islamism, and as a result, the destruction of Islamism. For Islamism can exist only as an official religion: when it is reduced to the state of a free and individual religion, it will perish. Islamism is not merely a state religion . . . it is a religion that excludes the state, an arrangement for which only the pontifical states in Europe provided the prototype. Therein lies eternal war: war will end only when the last son of Ishmael has died of desperation or been driven by terror into the heart of the desert. Islam is the most complete negation of Europe; Islam is a fanaticism the like of which Philip II's Spain and Pius V's Italy barely knew; Islam is contempt for science, the abolition of civil society. Islam is the appalling simplicity of Semitic thought, which shrinks the human brain, closing it off to any delicate idea, to any refined feeling, to any rational search, and placing it before an eternal tautology: God is god.
>
> The future, Gentlemen, belongs to Europe and Europe alone. Europe will conquer the world and spread its religion, which is law, freedom, respect for men, the belief that there is something divine within humanity.[7]

Renan's interpretive grid took hold in European thought for several decades, since it provided that thought with the backing of scientific methodology. The foremost objective of Renan's work was not to determine the nature of Islam, even though he wrote his thesis on Averroes. His great intellectual construct, produced both by the personal quest of a man who had lost his faith and by the great question of his time, had to do with the nature of the religious phenomenon, and especially, with its historicization. Renan's starting point was the discovery, more than half a century old at the time, of the kinship among the Indo-European languages. Philologists had not only constructed a grammar of Indo-European and inventoried the roots of its vocabulary but had also immediately attributed a set of civilizational values to the original Indo-Europeans.

They began with the idea that the expansion of Indo-European in eras immediately prior to the dawn of history could have occurred only on the model of the well-known Germanic invasions, the root of political discourses for several centuries. It followed almost automatically that feudalism was not a phenomenon unique to European history but had been reproduced every time there was an Indo-European invasion. According to the same interpretation, modern freedoms were derived from the feudal system. Nevertheless, the first Indo-European peoples were polytheists.

On that basis, Renan split the historical discipline in two by piecing together the existence of a group complementary to that of the Indo-Europeans: the Semites. He produced a linguistic and ethnographic inventory of them. From the start, the Semites thought in terms of the unique, which inexorably led them to monotheism and, in politics, to theocracy, despotism, or anarchy. Indo-European mythology was an original way of thinking the multiple, which in politics led to freedom and to an understanding of the state.

Christianity was both a conquest of that world of multiplicity by that of the unique and, at the same time, its transformation into a relatively harmonious synthesis. It culminated in the constitution of an intellectual tradition uniting the culture of science to that of freedom. The victory of modern Europe was therefore that of Indo-European thought, which developed in the purest peoples (Germanic, Nordic, Anglo-Saxon) or among the Latin peoples, who were produced by a fusion of races called "civilization." Adopting Guizot's interpretation of history, Renan made the struggle between a Semitic-style religious society and an Aryan-style civil society the driving force of human progress. In both cases, aristocracies in the strict sense of the term, not the masses, were at issue.

Renan replaced the Mediterranean origins of reason prized by Enlightenment thought with a genealogy going back to a deduced protohistory in central Asia. That made it possible to understand the definitive victory of the European genius in the nineteenth century: if the East was the origin, the West was the future.

The term "race" is extremely ambiguous in Renan's writings. It can mean either a quasi-biological reality or an intellectual heritage. Race is a primary phenomenon linked to the creation of language, an all-encompassing and immediate description of the universe. Within that context, and as a Frenchman, Renan immediately felt in a position of inferiority to the Germanic peoples, who had preserved the original bloodlines. Hence his insistence, in the case of France, on evoking the historical process of civilization and fusion, which gave rise to the nation as antagonistic to race. Judaism as a religion, moreover, had lost most of its original Semitism.

In the case of the Muslim world, the opposition between the Semitic and the Indo-European was inadequate. Renan therefore developed a tripartite scheme. Linguistic ethnography defined three population groups: the Arabs, who with the birth of Islam had restored the original Semitic genius; the Persians and other Indo-Europeans, who were able to hold on to the spirit of scientific inquiry ("there is nothing Arab about Arab science"); and the Turks and other Mongols, a dull-witted race lacking any intuition for philosophy and science.

Islam was now contributing to global civilization by converting the black races of the African continent to monotheism.

In 1883 Paris, Renan became involved in a courteous polemic with Afghani. On the whole, they were actually accomplices. The Orientalist saw Afghani as "the finest case of ethnic protest against religious conquest that can be cited." On that occasion, he defined his viewpoint one last time:

> I believe, in fact, that the regeneration of the Muslim countries will not come about through Islam; it will come about through the weakening of Islam, just as the great burst of energy in the so-called Christian countries began with the destruction of the tyrannical medieval church. . . . The Muslims are the first victims of Islam. Several times in my travels to the East, I have been able to observe that fanaticism comes from a small number of dangerous men, who compel religious practice in others through terror. The emancipation of the Muslim from his religion is the best service that can be rendered him.[8]

THE EASTERN CRISIS OF 1875–1883

The Eastern crisis began in Bosnia-Herzegovina in 1875 with an uprising of Christian peasants against the Muslim masters, in the aftermath of changes regarding the status of land in the Ottoman legal code on real property. From there, the movement spread to Bulgaria, where it assumed a specifically national character, based, in spite of everything, on the opposition between Christians and Muslims. The harsh Ottoman repression, conducted primarily by irregular troops, outraged European public opinion. The great British statesman William Gladstone, then the head of the opposition party, conducted one of the largest publicity campaigns in history, on the theme of "Bulgarian atrocities." Muslim public opinion, by contrast, no longer tolerated European interference. On May 6, 1876, a raging mob massacred the consuls of France and Germany in Salonika.

The Ottoman liberals, with as their leader Midhat Pasha, hero of the second generation of reformers, took the opportunity to stage a coup d'état on May 30 and to depose the sultan, who died a few days later under murky circumstances. His successor quickly displayed signs of mental instability and was in turn deposed on August 31, 1876, in favor of Abdülhamid. As the war against Serbia was getting under way, the reformers drafted a parliamentary constitution, which was promulgated on December 23, 1876. Its aim was to assure the participation of all elements of the Ottoman population, that is, to assure them a growing autonomy, the prelude to complete independence, thus rendering moot European demands for reforms on behalf of the Christians in the Balkans. When the new Parliament met in February 1877, Abdülhamid exiled Midhat, who seemed too dangerous a rival. Midhat would be recalled a few months later to assume the duties of governor of Syria.

In April 1877, Russia declared war on the Ottomans. Fighting occurred in the Balkans and the Caucasus. After initial defeats, the Ottomans succeeded in blocking the Russian advance into Bulgaria during the siege of Plevna. In January 1878, the stronghold fell and the Russian armies arrived within proximity of Constantinople. The Russians imposed the Treaty of San Stefano, which in practical terms put an end to the Ottoman Balkans, and they imposed Russian rule over what remained of the empire. That was too much for the British, who resumed their naval demonstration and threatened Russia with war, to save the Ottoman Empire and the Indian route. Germany then proposed that a congress be convened in Berlin. The final act of that congress, on July 3, 1878, reorganized all the Balkans, with heavy territorial losses for the Ottomans. It marked the confirmation of Christian independence movements and the occupation of Bosnia-Herzegovina by Austria. All that remained of the former Rumelia was a strip running from the Adriatic to Thrace, which would be called Ottoman Macedonia. Invoking the permanence of the Russian threat, Great Britain had the island of Cyprus ceded to itself, so that it could intervene quickly to assist the Ottomans.

In February 1878, Abdülhamid suspended the constitution of 1876, though it remained part of the Ottoman law code. His power was far from assured. The war effort had struck a terrible blow to the empire's economy. Only the Muslims provided conscripted troops (the non-Muslims paid a compensatory tax), and the human cost was tremendous. In Anatolia and in the Arab provinces, a very large number of adult men died on the battlefields of the Balkans and the Caucasus. With the loss of the majority Christian regions, the proportion of Muslims grew considerably. In addition, tens of thousands of Balkan and Caucasian Muslim refugees flowed into what remained of the empire. Religious tensions ran high, but outbreaks of violence were averted.

Clearly, the liberal reformers had failed in their political project. They had placed themselves under European intellectual patronage, but Europe did not intervene on their behalf. For a long time, the "Bulgarian atrocities" brought disrepute to the Ottoman cause. Only the exigencies of geopolitics led Great Britain to intervene, and the nation exacted a high cost for its aid. France was still "regrouping" after its defeat at the hands of Prussia in 1870–1871, and it drew back from defending its positions acquired in the Islamic world in the previous decades. Germany took advantage of the situation to style itself the European arbiter and honest broker of Ottoman affairs, since it was not directly involved in them.

After the Congress of Berlin, posters appeared in Damascus and Beirut criticizing Ottoman power and calling for Syrian autonomy, even independence. The whole affair has remained a mystery. Several series of posters surfaced, at intervals of a few months, and each series developed themes that were clearly different from the others. Contemporaries saw their appearance as a plot spearheaded either by Midhat Pasha, who had become governor of Syria and was supposedly pro-British, or by Abd al-Qadir, who was said to have finally agreed to carry out a plan for an Arab kingdom. Others interpreted it as the action of secret societies of Christian or Muslim inspiration. The general tone of the posters was pro-Syrian, but later historians would see them, no doubt wrongly, as the first manifestation of Arab nationalism. By contrast, diplomatic correspondence made multiple references to a vast "Arab" conspiracy, whose profile remained imprecise. These letters spoke of the constitution of an Arab caliphate, whose religious legitimacy would be greater than that of the Ottomans.

After the disasters of the war against Russia, disaffection with the Ottoman authority ran deep. It was exploited by a series of major figures in the empire, who opposed Abdülhamid's personal accession to power. In that political battle, all involved turned to the publicists and intellectuals developing liberal and Islamic themes. They also appealed to the diplomatic representatives of the great powers, in order to demonstrate to them that they were the best candidates for political office and would act in the interests of the European power in question. France and Great Britain had a tendency to take opposing sides, and the sultan was therefore in a position to take action if he obtained the support of one or the other of the two powers. But he was paralyzed if the Europeans formed a bloc.

In July 1880, Abdülhamid obtained France's support when he deposed Midhat Pasha, who was accused of wanting to promote a Jewish colonization project in Transjordan under British patronage. In Egypt, by contrast, France and Great Britain made common cause on the question of the country's debt. They imposed a "European" ministry (that is, a ministry comprising European ministers), and then a European condominium on Egyptian finances. Khedive Ismāʿīl, who attempted to counter the intervention by appealing to Egyptian nationalist feeling, was deposed in 1879.

Within that general context, in January 1880 the Europeans posited the existence of Muslim religious unrest. The French at first attributed it to the British, who were suspected of playing both the Arab and the Muslim card against a sultan who was proving resistant to their influence. The supposed leader of that movement was the sharif of Mecca, the only Islamic religious authority capable of opposing the authority of the caliph of Constantinople. In March 1880, the notion of Muslim unrest came into sharper relief. There was talk of a vast conspiracy affecting the Muslim world as a whole and entailing an uprising of the Arabs against the Turks. For a long time, the prospect of an Arab revolt led by a sharif of Mecca and supported by Great Britain was one of the possible stratagems of European policy in the Muslim East.

From August 1880 on, diplomatic correspondence spoke rather of an Ottoman conspiracy seeking to foment, from Tunisia, the Muslims of Algeria against the French and to incite the Indian Muslims against the British. Abdülhamid supposedly wanted to assemble under his caliphal authority all the Muslims of the world and to neutralize the action of the European powers through colonial revolts. In 1881, the diplomats began to use the term "pan-Islamism." Gabriel Charmes, a French publicist close to diplomatic circles, adopted the term and was later credited with inventing it.

A new specter began to haunt Europe, that of pan-Islamism, which in the twentieth century would become Islamism. The threat was put to good use: French proponents of the conquest of Tunisia systematically invoked it. Great Britain agreed to that conquest as compensation for its acquisition of Cyprus. Germany and Austria-Hungary pressed for it to incite a quarrel between France and Italy.

Tunisia was defined as the rear base of an Algerian uprising, and the French republic could not allow itself to lose Algeria the way the Second Empire had lost Alsace-Lorraine. The incipient colonial camp justified the enterprise as a preemptive operation intended to suppress an immediate threat. The Third Republic's resumption of French colonial expansion can be understood in terms of the desire to build a "Greater France" after the disaster of 1870–1871. Those who opposed it, on both the right and the left, saw it as a dangerous diversion, in view of the German threat and revanchism. In fact, the German empire encouraged the undertaking, which had the further appeal of estranging France from Italy in a lasting manner. It was within that context that France imposed its protectorate in Tunisia on May 12, 1881.

Attention then turned to Egypt, where the military was challenging the authority of the khedive and of European control, in the name of "Egypt for the Egyptians." The European debate was in need of clarification, both in a France governed by the republicans, and in Great Britain, which now had a liberal government. Would Europe embrace the national and constitutional movement that had taken power in Egypt in February 1882, or would its economic and geopolitical interests prevail? That was the subject of the great French parliamentary debate of July 1882,[9] during which Léon Gambetta and Georges Clemenceau in particular faced off. For Gambetta, there was no "national party" in Egypt, only Muslim fanaticism, the chimera of revolution, and the exploits of the army rabble. Conversely, Clemenceau evoked a "democratic policy" more intent on moral than material conquests.

The debate focused less on the need for European intervention than on the modality of the European presence. According to Clemenceau, "Yes, the national party calls on the Europeans, not to hand over the country to them at will so that they can develop it, but to bring European ideas, education, European culture, and a sense of justice, which are lacking in the East."[10] The opposition coalition rejected the French intervention, and Great Britain intervened on its own, occupying Egypt in 1883.

The French protectorate over Tunisia and the British occupation of Egypt demonstrated the futility of applying the nationality principle to Muslim peoples. Separation from the Ottoman Empire entailed falling inexorably under direct European domination, which explains why autonomy movements in the Muslim-majority provinces came to a halt. Constitutionalism did not eliminate religious tensions and was discredited by the war with Russia. The resurgence of Muslim feeling would serve to cement the Hamidian regime.

Reformists and constitutionalists had now returned to the ranks or been exiled to Europe, where they would voice their opinions in newspapers published there and clandestinely imported into the Ottoman Empire. The same was true for certain Persian reformers, disappointed at the powerlessness of the regime in place. Some of these protesters, exasperated by the resistance to their plans, even went so far as to speak publicly in favor of a direct European takeover of their country, the only thing capable of imposing true modernization. For most, this was a temporary reaction of spite, with the exception of a few people who came to serve French or British policies directly.

In the last two decades of the nineteenth century, the freedom of expression existing in Europe made it possible to canonize the ideology of modernization in Muslim political thought, against the authoritarianism of bureaucratic reforms and the conservatism of traditional social structures. Such was the case for Abduh's and Afghani's Salafism, which found its most radical expression during their European exile. These Muslims benefited from the receptiveness and support of radical leftist circles in Europe with a somewhat freethinking or atheistic orientation, an odd convergence that would not be the last of its kind.

Within the context of the Russo-Ottoman War, the Anglo-Indians, having once again seen the danger of collusion between the Afghans and Russians, in autumn 1878 launched a new invasion of Afghanistan. Thanks to their modern armaments, they quickly seized most of the country. The following autumn, the country rebelled once again, in the form of a jihad. Without encountering a true disaster as in 1842, the British troops had to face an exhausting succession of military operations, without the possibility of decisive success. In 1884, they evacuated the country.

In the following years, the Russians and British agreed to make Afghanistan a buffer zone between the two empires. In 1893, Sir Mortimer Durand drew the border (it would be redrawn in 1895), creating a long corridor extending to China, so that there would be no point of contact between the Indian empire and Russian central Asia.

That success of the Afghan tribal forces had its counterpart in the Sudanese Mahdist movement. That politico-religious uprising targeted Egyptian domination, but the British were now in charge of the country. In 1883, they sent the mystic adventurer Gordon Pasha to organize the evacuation of Khartoum, but once in place he refused to carry out his instructions and persisted in defending the city. He died during the capture of the city by the Mahdists. That affair caused an enormous stir in Europe.

For a time, the expansion of direct European domination was halted. The costs of conquest and administration, which greatly exceeded the benefits of colonial expansion, and the fear of pan-Islamism and its repercussions were essential factors. Nevertheless, struggles for influence and a nibbling away by European powers continued in the Muslim world until the end of the century, which marked the introduction of the logic of empire.

CHAPTER 14

THE AGE OF EMPIRE

THE LOGIC OF EMPIRE: FRENCH AFRICA

Even as the term "imperialist" came into current use in European political language, the progress of direct European rule in Islamic countries was coming to an end. The 1880s were devoted to the conquest and partitioning of sub-Saharan Africa. European competition had shifted geographically; new actors existed, Belgium and Germany in particular, but Russia was notably absent. It was completing the consolidation of its hold on central Asia. The division of Africa was formalized by the Conference of Berlin in 1884 and by a series of border-defining accords concluded in the following years.

France had the most at stake in sub-Saharan Muslim Africa. Its penetration followed two major axes. The first began at the African Atlantic coast, advancing inexorably to the east, while the second originated in the North African possessions, reaching the colonies of sub-Saharan Africa through the conquest of the Sahara. The logic of French policy was to occupy the "empty spaces" on the geographical map and thus form an enormous bloc. The agents on the ground were not the same along the two axes. The Army of Africa, its officers coming from Native Affairs, carried out the Saharan penetration, whereas colonial troops, especially naval forces, advanced into sub-Saharan Africa. When they united in the Sahel regions, a certain tension arose between these military forces with different cultures and approaches. Both columns sometimes recorded bloody defeats, even total destruction.

The conquerors of the Sahara saw themselves as peacemakers and were supported by a certain number of Tuareg elements. The formation of the Mehari troops gave rise to a specific mythology, the greatest examples of which could later be found in the novels of Pierre Benoît and in Joseph Peyré's *White Squadron*. These works contain an apologia for the adventure and for the personal dynamism specific to the new colonial ethos. In sub-Saharan Africa, colonial officers supervised troops levied locally, particularly the famous Senegalese infantry, and did not hesitate to use terror to establish their authority over the local populations. The two columns joined together in about 1900, but pacification would take a few more years. In 1895, French West Africa was created.

The constitution of French Equatorial Africa was understandably delayed, until 1910. On the eve of World War I, fighting was still going on in the deserts of Chad and Mauritania.

A new order was installed, with a ban on raids and the gradual abolition of slavery. Although that penetration also aspired to open the region economically, it destroyed the elements of a centuries-old economy, that of the black slave trade and raids. The dream of establishing a trans-Saharan railroad took hold, but it was a pure colonial fantasy, its profitability being almost nil.

According to specialists in Native Affairs, the soul of the resistance came from the major religious brotherhoods. The enemy most often named was the Sanusiyya, a brotherhood whose actions extended into the Saharan zone. It was seen as "an extremely active religious propaganda group tending to muster the Islamic races against the invasion of the Western powers. That unrest could easily reach Algeria and compromise our domination there" (report of Commander Alfred Le Châtelier in 1888).[1] More than ever before, the conquest was accompanied by the development of a colonial ethnography, which classified populations into ethnic and religious groups and determined real or virtual enemies. The brotherhoods were portrayed as the expression and instrument of the pan-Islamist threat, whose secret ringleaders were in the Ottoman Empire, close to Hamidian circles of power.

At the political level, French colonial activities were divided among several agencies—the Ministry of Foreign Affairs, the Ministry of the Interior (for Algeria), the Ministry of War, and the Ministry of the Colonies—setting in place a specific French model. Although the colonial conquest was considered a matter of prestige and power in the aftermath of the defeat of 1870–1871, there were no colonial mass movements in France equivalent to the large British and German colonial leagues. The "colonial party" was a pressure group with decision-making power, and it recruited from all social strata: Parliament, the military, diplomatic circles, academia, public relations, commerce. It set up institutions such as the Société de Géographie de Paris and the Comité de l'Afrique Française, created in 1890. That allowed it to define programs of action and to constitute more specific pressure groups devoted to precise geographic zones, such as the Comité de l'Égypte (1895) and the Comité du Maroc (1902).

Parallel to the conquest of the Sahara, the penetration of Moroccan territory, little known except for its coastal fringes, got under way. Military explorers such as Charles de Foucauld and Alfred Le Châtelier mapped the regions concerned and proceeded to inventory the tribes and brotherhoods. From their positions in the Sahara, French officers toiled to turn these regions into a French zone of influence. Around 1884, it seemed for a moment that the conquest of Morocco was about to begin, but the historical circumstances of European diplomacy conspired against it. In the early 1890s, the nibbling away of eastern Morocco resumed, and France expressed with increasing clarity its desire to complete the conquest of the Maghreb. The other European powers opposed France, though they implied that the affair could be settled within the framework of a vast bargaining session.

While constantly expanding its African dominion, France consolidated its domination over North Africa. The advent of the Third Republic ratified the victory of the settlers over the military forces, who aspired to be the paternalistic protectors of the Arab population. The Government of National Defense accepted the principal claims of the settlers, with the nine decrees of October 24, 1870. These decrees naturalized Algerian Jews, who suddenly became French citizens. The government also transformed Algeria into three French departments falling under the jurisdiction of the Ministry of the Interior and represented in French parliamentary assemblies.

The French defeat in Europe (in the Franco-Prussian War) was accompanied by a Kabyle uprising in March 1871. The repression was extremely harsh, and the confiscations of land dispossessed the native populations. An underlying colonial fear became a permanent part of the makeup of the so-called European population, which demanded a general policy of control over the Muslims. That policy consisted of a patchwork of rules determined by the local authorities and culminated in the law of June 28, 1881, known as the Native Code, which gave local administrators full power over the indigenous peoples. The rural population was subjected to a quasi-dictatorship. In addition, the tax system was completely inequitable, benefiting primarily the European population.

In 1892, Jules Ferry, heading a senatorial investigation committee, pronounced a merciless but ineffectual indictment of the Algerian situation:

> It is difficult to make the European settler understand that there are other rights besides his own in Arab territory, and that the natives do not constitute a race ready to do its master's bidding.... If violence is not in the actions, it is in the language and feelings. We have the sense that an unappeased torrent of rancor, contempt, and fear is still roaring in [the settler's] heart of hearts. Very few settlers are instilled with the mission of education and civilization belonging to the superior race; even fewer believe in any possible improvement of the vanquished race. They outdo each other proclaiming that race incorrigible and uneducable, without having attempted in thirty years to wrest it from moral and intellectual destitution.... The settlers do not have general ideas about the conduct to assume with the natives. They barely understand any policy other than containment toward those three million men. They probably do not envision destroying them and even deny wanting to repress them; but they are concerned neither with [the natives'] complaints nor with their numbers, which seem to increase with their poverty. They have a sense of potential peril, but they take no measures to fend it off.[2]

Ferry would not hear of political rights for the natives, who needed only a strong and just power, and he favored reestablishing the authority of the governor-general of Algeria, named by the metropolis and standing above local influences.

To give added weight to the European population, a systematic policy was conducted to favor French naturalization of European (especially Spanish) immigrants. The law of June 26, 1889, instituted the automatic naturalization of every foreign European born in the country. With that "fusion of races" and "Creolization," a specific French population was constituted: in 1896 the number of Europeans born in Algeria for the first time exceeded that of European immigrants.

The fusion of European races was also a rejection of the Muslim element. Both the settlers and the administration rejected naturalization of the indigenous peoples through the acquisition of European civil status. Those Muslims who might have been tempted also met with the radical hostility of their coreligionists, who considered the renunciation of Muslim personal status a betrayal of Islam. Algerian Jews were in an intermediate position. They had European civil status (those who rejected the Crémieux decree of 1870 had sought exile in Syria, settling near the Algerian Muslims of Emir Abd al-Qadir) and full political rights, and they participated both in Arab culture and in French culture. But in that world of de facto separation, they did not play any role as mediators.

Algeria did not project a favorable image of French policy. Tunisia was the showcase for what was called the colonial policy of association. The Tunisian state was kept in place, and French officials merely "oversaw" the native administration. Consular jurisdictions were abolished. The tax system was gradually transformed. The protectorate did not seem to be encountering major opposition.

The Tunisian protectorate made it possible to evade the question of political representation for the European population. The settlers protested in 1890 and demanded advantages equivalent to those of the French population of Algeria. The residency granted a concession by agreeing to the constitution of French chambers of agriculture and commerce, but their duties remained consultative and economic in nature. The essential political question was still the Italian presence. The Italians, who outnumbered the French three to one, were not encouraged to ask for French nationality, and the Italian government urged them to keep their original identity.

The apparent success of French policy in Tunisia allowed for a clearer definition of the doctrine of association, in contrast to that of assimilation. The repercussions of the Dreyfus Affair in Algeria launched the debate anew. The European population was overtaken by a wave of anti-Semitism of unprecedented severity. In 1898, actual riots took place, and anti-Semitic candidates won the elections. Some settlers went so far as to call for autonomy or even independence from the metropolis.

The Third Republic then conducted an intelligent policy, granting the three Algerian departments financial autonomy and a local assembly (known as the "financial delegations"), even as they increased the power of the general government. A local Muslim uprising reignited colonial fear and put an end to separatist temptations.

Although one section of the financial delegations was created to represent the native peoples, the delegates were elected by a very small voter base (fifteen thousand electors) and were carefully controlled by the administration, giving rise to their nickname, "Béni oui-oui" (Yes-men). The French doctrine became that of an association of Muslims within the assimilation of Algeria to France.

In 1900, Robert de Caix, spokesman for the Comité de l'Afrique Française, perfectly expressed the views of the colonial world. By nature, he said, colonialism produced an aristocracy vis-à-vis the native populations. When there was a large European population, there was no possibility of merging with the native peoples but only of coexisting with them. The model of the declining Roman Empire, with the Edict of Caracalla of the year 212 making all free men citizens, was out of the question:

> If we confer political rights on our Muslim subjects, we plunge our entire achievement, our entire Algerian colonization, into chaos. . . . If, conversely, without giving them these dangerous rights, we make the natives subject to legislation, to a procedure, to an administration designed for French people, we fall into another theoretical error committed by the supporters of assimilation, which allowed the practices in Algeria that have come to light in certain legal proceedings. With such a system, the native is exploited by the European, whom that very exploitation corrupts. . . . To ward off that danger, we must have an administration of natives that does not mix with that of the Europeans. In a word, we must accept the existence in our colonial territory of different personal *statuses*. No doubt the rigidity of our administrative logic is loath to do that; but let us not invoke our character as Latins to deny ourselves the capacity for political adaptation. Whether we are or are not Latins is a very disputable matter; but if we are, we descend from a people who ruled the world while accepting all local circumstances, all social, ethnic, and religious diversity. The Roman Empire was unified in its rule, but very heterogeneous in the various regimes of persons; it was only during its decline that it effected a legal fusion by granting the status of Roman citizen in an unlimited manner. A nation like our own, possessing an empire, must tell itself that there is no viable imperial policy that can fail to encompass, accept in practice, and even put to use the diversities of which we have just spoken. If we fail to recognize that truth . . . we run the risk, first and foremost, of introducing unrest, disorganization, in the native populations in the various parts of our empire; but above all, we risk later losing that empire and being overtaken by the subjected peoples. Perhaps that theory will be found very aristocratic, but there is no reconciling imperial policy with the exportation of democracy.[3]

Such was the French dilemma. The strong tendency of French culture was toward assimilation, but it clashed with the realities of settlement colonies. The not unrealistic fear of being thrown back into the sea gave rise to the institutionalized violence of the Native Code and fed colonial racism, which created an authoritarian paternalism. Once again, colonialism culminated in a regression of values. The native had to "know his place," which was subordinate to that of the settlers. Inexorably, France reproduced in the colonial construct its old interpretation of the nature of the ancien régime as a product of conquest and the juxtaposition of races.

The Logic of Empire: England in Egypt

Whereas France was concerned with constituting a huge African bloc with the primary and avowed motive of preserving its rank as a major power, Great Britain confined itself to the desire to control the Indian route. True, certain great imperialists such as Cecil Rhodes set forth the grandiose plan of establishing territorial continuity between Egypt and Capetown; but by the end of the century, efforts focused primarily on the southern part of Africa and culminated in the Boer War.

The occupation of Egypt conformed to that logic of control. Originally declared provisional, it based its legitimacy on the need to bring about reforms before making any other decisions. These reforms were not political in the liberal sense, since the British had intervened to put an end to the national Egyptian movement, which embraced constitutionalism. Despite a first discourse on establishing "institutions favorable for the development of freedom" (Dufferin report of 1883), the matter at hand was to restore public security and punish those responsible for the revolt, while reestablishing the khedive's formal authority. Beyond that, it was necessary to put Egyptian finances in order to assure debt payments to the Europeans and to institute a viable state.

In that dual program, Evelyn Baring, the future Lord Cromer, British agent general and consul from 1883 to 1907, clashed with the other European powers. The Caisse de la Dette Publique (Commission of the Public Debt), dominated by the French, rejected the British monopoly. Backed by the capitulations, the European powers conducted a policy of harassment, called the "pinprick" policy. The war fronts were reversed: the British wanted to put an end to the capitulations, an obstacle for good management, while the Egyptians defended them to hold onto their room for maneuvering against the omnipotence of the unauthorized occupiers. As for France, though it discreetly supported the Egyptian nationalists, it made the internationalization of Egypt its battle cry. Renan theorized it, asserting that Egypt was not a nation but the stakes of competing interests. "A region that is so important to the rest of the world cannot belong to itself; it is neutralized for the benefit of humanity; the nationality principle meets its death there."

French diplomacy had a partial success with the convention of Constantinople on the international status of the Suez Canal (1888), but the British would apply the convention only with reservations.

Interest in Islam increased with the Sudanese revolt against Egyptian domination. The death of Gordon Pasha on January 26, 1885, was the occasion for great anxiety, as Renan noted:

> The dangerous cyclones that central Africa will periodically produce, ever since we were so rash as to leave it Muslim, were repressed. European science had free rein in a country that in some sense fell into its hands as a field of study and experimentation. But some consequences ought to have been brought to bear on that excellent plan. There was an imperative not to weaken a dynasty by means of which the tip of Europe's sword penetrated almost to the equator. Above all, it was imperative to keep an eye on Al-Azhar Mosque, the center from which Muslim propaganda has spread to Africa as a whole. When isolated and given over to fetishism, the Sudanese races amount to very little; but, when converted to Islam, they become hotbeds of intense fanaticism. For lack of foresight, an Arabia was allowed to form west of the Nile that is much more dangerous than the real Arabia.[4]

Great Britain could therefore justify its presence by the need to counter the Sudanese Islamic threat and to eliminate the risk of a contagion of fanaticism. But the immediate danger came from Europe, with the colonial penetration into sub-Saharan Africa. A French column might therefore be able to establish its presence on the Nile, and the French government clearly expressed its intention of doing so. Gabriel Hanotaux, minister of foreign affairs from 1894 to 1898, pressed for the reopening of the Egypt question. The Marchand Mission was launched in summer 1896 and arrived at the Nile, in Fachoda, on July 10, 1898.

That mission precipitated Britain's decision to reconquer Sudan. An Anglo-Egyptian army, under the leadership of Sir Herbert Kitchener, marched on Khartoum. It crushed the Mahdists at the Battle of Omdurman on September 1, 1898. The mortal remains of al-Mahdī were profaned to avenge Gordon's death. Kitchener rushed to Fachoda and demanded that the French depart. It was a major international crisis. French public opinion was in an uproar, but the French government gave in.

Within France, the nationalist right, until then hostile to the idea of colonial expansion—for fear of seeing the Alsace-Lorraine question abandoned—was finally won over. Colonials such as Robert de Caix were ready to envision an alliance with Germany against Great Britain, given the state of power relations: "It has never appeared more clearly that diplomacy is much less the representation of laws than the power of influence, so to speak. When we have such power on our side, we will certainly find an excellent legal argument for reopening the Egypt question."[5]

Sudan became an Anglo-Egyptian condominium in which Egypt paid and England administered. Under the cover of restoring Egyptian authority, a new Islamic region fell under direct European domination.

As for the rest, it seemed that British domination would have to continue automatically, since the work of reform to be undertaken was enormous, given that the colonizers retained the khedivial state and British actions were carried out by advisers established in sensitive areas. According to Lord Cromer, the governance of a half-civilized people was a long-term moral mission. The British were there for the good of the masses, who had to be lifted up materially and spiritually from their present abjection. Islam was more than a religion; it was a social system totally unsuited to the modern world. It was impossible to reform because it would thereby cease to exist. Hence his famous formulation, "Reformed Islam is Islam no longer." The authentic Easterner did not want to be reformed, because he knew that to change even moderately would completely transform his understanding of the world. In assimilating civilization, Islam ran the risk of succumbing: hence its resistance to modernity. There were some shining exceptions, including Lord Cromer's friend Muhammad Abduh, who recognized the need for European assistance in the reform process. Cromer suspected he was agnostic or at least a philosopher, that is, someone who knew how to discern the difference between the seventh and the twentieth century. In point of fact, every Europeanized Muslim Egyptian was an agnostic. Access to modernity meant being uprooted and losing one's traditional values, resulting in a dubious morality, especially if one did not convert to Christianity, the source of morality and civilization. It would take several generations for Egypt to be capable of governing itself. The British therefore had to remain for Egypt's own good, despite the ingratitude of the population.

Anglo-Egyptians developed the tendency, already observed among the Anglo-Indians, of increasingly separating themselves from the population they were administering, and especially, from its modernized elites. Even while championing modernizing reforms, they rejected the results, which would have run the risk of reducing the distance between the conquerors and the conquered. They rejected a cultural policy of Anglicization and allowed the Francophone schools to train the new generations of the elite. That allowed the British to assert that the Gallicized Egyptian had all the vices of the French along with all those of the Egyptians, without any of their virtues. The pashas of Turkish origin were perceived with somewhat more indulgence, since they still had some of their original dynamism as conquerors. Duplicity, in combination with immorality, was characteristic of the modern Egyptian.

Two applications developed out of the cult of authenticity. The first was directed at the most traditional population possible, for whom the British administrator was sacrificing himself. That included the Sudanese and the Bedouins. The second application adopted the idea of a slow accession to modernity, thanks to an evolution within a preserved but purified authenticity. For the time being, the interpretation of the world by British colonials, even more than that by French colonials, was based on neo-feudal values: the justice of the ruler and the loyalty-fidelity of the ruled. In some sense, political reform was supposed to reproduce the European feudal process, relying on a progressive attribution of rights on the model of the Magna Carta. For Egypt, that would mean educating the population while accustoming them to local management of their own affairs.

The contradiction specific to the British was that they saw their colonials as a service aristocracy devoted to the good of the populations, whom they initiated into freedom by slowly reproducing the European trajectory, which had begun in the forests of Germania; yet the British were in fact the agents of a military despotism with increasingly technocratic aims.

A portion of the Egyptian elite, particularly among Abduh's disciples, was receptive to that theme of reforms to be undertaken, especially since Cromer provided some support in their battle against the most conservative elements of society. What they appreciated about British policy was the great freedom of expression that was granted them. At the end of the century, Egypt became an active laboratory of ideas, because censorship was practically nonexistent in that country, unlike in the large independent Muslim states. Conversely, the Egyptian nationalists pointed out the contradictions of British discourse: if the reforms were achieved, the British would have to leave; if they were not achieved, it was because they were ineffective, and therefore the British would have to leave.

THE OTTOMAN EMPIRE, OR THE CONJUNCTION OF EMPIRES

In the wake of the Eastern crisis, Abdülhamid's regime focused on a policy of reconsolidating the empire on the basis of a modernizing Muslim authoritarianism. In an empire where the share of the Muslim population had grown considerably, with the loss of the Balkan provinces and the continuous influx of Muslim refugees, there was a revival of caliphal as well as Islamic influence. At the same time, the authorities continuously developed the tools of modernity: an administration with an economic development plan; a private and public education system oriented toward the new disciplines; and a strengthening of the means of communication, such as the railroads and the telegraph network.

Integration into Europe advanced with the completion of the Orient Express, which put the Ottoman capital three days from Paris (1888). At that date, European Turkey was part of the European railroad system as a whole, whereas the Asian networks were discontinuous, consisting of lines between the coast and the interior.

Integration was also domination since, after the bankruptcy of 1881, the Caisse de la Dette Publique was set in place. It allowed the empire to restore its credit, at the price of foreign control over a considerable share of state resources. Lack of financial means was the principal weakness of a state whose responsibilities were continually increasing and that, to assure its survival, had to maintain large military forces. Citing the capitulations, the European powers opposed any increase in customs duties, which would also have made possible the beginning of industrialization. To assure its development, the empire, which in any case could not oppose it, became completely open to foreign investment, particularly in the communication infrastructures (ports, lighthouses, railroads). These investments strengthened both the empire's cohesiveness and the foreign presence. In them, the state found another means of survival, since the chief European powers now had a direct interest in maintaining the empire. France was its first investor; Great Britain its first commercial partner. Britain had to deal with growing competition from imperial Germany.

Abdülhamid was particularly interested in the Arab provinces. He catered to Muslim identity and opened the doors of the administration and the army to Arab Muslim elites. A subtle play of influences was exerted at the local level. The European powers had given up the Muslims' consular protections. (France conducted a rearguard action on its Algerian subjects.) Political dialogue took place between the consuls and governors, men of law and order. The principal risk was that religious violence would resurface. In the event of an incident, the consuls took responsibility for their protected Christians and Jews, the governor for the Muslim notables. Their common desire was to defuse the crisis while saving face on both sides. That first balance of power combined with struggles for influence among the Europeans. England was handicapped by the absence of a religious protectorate and of a cultural policy; for the most part, it was preoccupied with its commercial interests and the security of the Indian route. It therefore showed a special interest in Mesopotamia, an extension of the Gulf dominated by the Anglo-Indians, and in Persia, the stopover point for a Russian advance toward the Indian Ocean.

The Franco-Russian alliance of 1891 marked an important change. On the ground, competition remained keen between the two partners, but Paris and Saint Petersburg acted in concert to prevent any violent confrontation between Catholics and Orthodox Christians. Russia was competing with Greece for Orthodox churches. The high-ranking clergy, recruited from among the monks, was ethnically Greek, whereas the low-ranking clergy and the ordinary faithful were Arabs. The Arabs protested the domination of the Greeks and received Russia's support. Violent conflicts erupted around episcopal and patriarchal elections.

The Uniate Catholics were supported by the Latin missionaries, who were overwhelmingly French. Leo XIII proved favorable to the cause of Eastern rites and called a halt to their Latinization, but his successor, Pius X, went in the other direction. The end of the nineteenth century was the golden age for French missionaries, particularly in the field of teaching. Their more or less avowed dream was to re-create in the East a French Catholic Christendom uncontaminated by so-called modern ideas. They had at their disposal financing from the French Catholics, thanks in particular to the work of the Eastern schools, but also to subsidies from the French Ministry of Foreign Affairs, approved on an annual basis and not without debate by a majority Republican parliament. For the Republicans, the French language was the natural vehicle for human emancipation, as Renan told the congress of the Alliance Française in 1888: "Everywhere the French go . . . the Revolution will ride behind them in the back seat. You mustn't have too much revolution, I know; but there are many countries in the world where, in certain doses, it would still do some good. Let's not press for it; but let our little bugle do its job. At certain times, who knows how, it turns into the trumpets of Jericho."[6]

By about 1880, French was by far the chief foreign language used in the empire. Several factors explain the birth of Eastern Francophonism. The state and society needed a language that would provide access to modernity. The Ottoman reformers were recruited from diplomatic circles, where French was the professional language, and they had a tendency to impose it in the reformed sectors of the administration. The Catholic missions and the Alliance Israélite Universelle made French the primary language of private instruction. Non-Muslims, the first clients of that education, benefited from their privileged access, but the Muslims followed. Public secondary education and the non-Catholic Christian schools thus contributed a great deal to the use of French.

Only the American Protestant missionary schools could really compete with the French schools in Syria and Anatolia, but since 1880 they had often served as a first stop on the way to emigration to North America. In that early globalization prior to 1914, the populations of the Ottoman Empire widely participated in the great human migration from the Old World to the new countries (North and South America, South Africa, Australia). That emigration was primarily Christian and came in response to the overpopulation of their own communities (the number of Christians was growing much faster than that of the Muslims), resulting in a large-scale rural exodus from the mountain zones. By contrast, the Muslim peasants were very active in the development of new lands taken from the Bedouins' domains.

The eastern Mediterranean metropolises moved to the rhythm of the world. They were the expression of Europe's openness and the starting point for intercontinental migrations. They became centers of culture. The study of French was accompanied by a vast translation movement with encyclopedic ambitions. The Eastern literary renaissances were inseparable from that movement and from the creation of so-called modern literary languages linked to the printing of newspapers and particularly active magazines.

Eastern Francophonism arose through that conjuncture of supply and demand. The mobile civilization proper to the Eastern Mediterranean gave a new meaning to the word "Levant." With great pride, the French publicists (but not the diplomats) spoke of a France of the Levant consisting of islets from Salonika to Alexandria and including Galata, Smyrna, and Beirut. That Levant was not only on the coast but existed wherever missions were involved in education, within the context of a demand for access to modernity.

The French were touched by that spontaneous adoption of their culture, often framed by the conservative interpretation of the Catholic missions. They were ready to see it as the voluntary choice of a French identity, especially since the consuls liberally granted consular protection to non-Muslims. By contrast, that Levantine growth appeared to be almost an abomination to the British, who considered it immoral and unnatural. According to Cromer, the ethnological status of the Levantine individual could not even be properly assessed. The British traveler developed a cult of authenticity based on the rejection of Levantine corruption. The idealization of the pure Bedouin Arab became a central element of the Anglo-Arab saga.

THE NEW EASTERN CRISES

During that period, the chief originality of the Arab provinces within the Ottoman Empire as a whole was that they did not move in the direction of ethnic conflict. Hamidian policy strengthened Islamic and Ottoman identity, and the Arab literary renaissance was the joint achievement of the Christian and Muslim Levantines. As a result, that sense of identity, of belonging, developed unopposed between the Ottoman frame of reference (the only one besides religion to have a legal definition), the Arab frame of reference, which was cultural in nature, and the Syrian frame of reference, which was geographical. The process of constituting a specific national identity seemed to have been halted.

The same was not true in the rest of the empire, where nationalism combined irremediably with religion. The religious cleavage prevailed over the linguistic: a Muslim whose native tongue was Greek or a Slavic language would not be considered Greek or Slavic but rather a Muslim who had betrayed his (supposed) native people. A Turkophone Armenian would be defined as Armenian and not Turkish. Territorialization was accompanied by the adoption of a revolutionary outlook.

Armenian nationalism, based on the transformation of the religious community into an ethnic identity, lagged behind that of the Balkans. The Treaty of Berlin (article 61) spoke of "improvements and reforms" to be applied "in the provinces inhabited by the Armenians," whose security would have to be guaranteed against the Circassians and Kurds. That rather weak pledge marked the confusion between two problems: that of the coexistence of populations in eastern Anatolia—where the resurgence of agriculture clashed with pastoralism, and where Muslim refugees from the Caucasus and the Balkans were setting down roots; and that of the territorialization of Armenian claims, beyond the status of a religious community.

Like the Syrian provinces, Anatolia went through a time of unrest in the early 1880s. The Kurds organized to reject the constitution of an Armenian state. This period was followed by a crackdown, with a policy for integrating the Kurds similar to that conducted for the Arabs. In the early 1890s, the revolutionary Armenian nationalist militants attempted to organize the peasants against the Kurds. In spring 1894, unrest erupted between Kurds and Armenians. The central power saw it as the beginning of an uprising that would trigger a new Eastern crisis. The regular army was sent in to impose a harsh repression on the Armenians. Mobilized by sympathizers for the Armenian cause, European public opinion raised its voice. The Porte had to accept a consular committee of inquiry, which, even while acknowledging the existence of Armenian revolutionary movements, primarily denounced the excesses of the repression. Projects for reforming the Anatolian vilayets (provinces) were again launched, on the model of the autonomous province of Mount Lebanon, with a division of "the populations into ethnographic groups that are as homogeneous as possible," that is, the beginning of Balkanization.

Abdülhamid equivocated and tried to stir dissension among the European powers. Russia was wary of the contagion of Armenian autonomist movements, and France believed that its interest lay in preserving the Ottoman political structure. Only Great Britain was on top of the matter.

In early autumn 1895, the revolutionary militants held demonstrations and sparked disturbances in Istanbul, to force the great powers to intervene in favor of the Armenian reforms. Clashes with the law forces ensued, and the Muslim population attacked the Armenians, causing many deaths. On October 16, the sultan gave in to European pressure and announced a program of reforms. In the following days, eastern Anatolia erupted in an outburst of violence between religious communities, leading to tens of thousands of dead. The official Ottoman position provoked spontaneous violence when the reform program was announced. The Armenians accused the imperial palace of premeditated organization of the violence, but that does not tally with Abdülhamid's cautiousness and with the fact that certain regions were spared the unrest. It appears that most of the responsibility lay with the Anatolian Muslim populations threatening open rebellion against the central authority.

After a relatively calm period in early 1896, the Armenian revolutionaries launched an attack against the central headquarters of the Ottoman Bank (funded by Franco-English capital) and took hostages, to force the Europeans to intervene once again. Although the revolutionaries evacuated the premises and were transported to France, thanks to the intervention of European diplomats, the event gave rise to a new outbreak of violence in Constantinople, producing several thousand Armenian dead. In the European press, the "red sultan" who massacred Christians became a popular image.

The Europeans once again found themselves at an impasse. They naturally considered deposing the sultan, but that would have done nothing to resolve the problem. The recent evolution had made the Ottoman state the instrument of European action. Should that instrument fail, the Europeans would have no other means available. Gunboat diplomacy would not allow them to resolve the question of eastern Anatolia. It would take a true partitioning of the empire, which the Russians were considering; but for Great Britain, that once again raised the question of the Indian route, and for France that of the security of its economic investments.

European paralysis allowed the Hamidian regime to survive, at the terrible cost of destroying the mechanisms of coexistence among the different communities in Anatolia. Distrust and hostility took root, and the authors of violent acts became heroes in each of the communities. At any time, after the slightest incident, all of Anatolia could sink into murderous violence. This consisted less of state action against an ethnic-religious minority (though a large portion of the administration was complicitous with the violence or passive in regards to it) than of mindless conflict between so-called civil societies.

In the Balkans, the dissolution went even further. The Christians split into ethnic groups on the basis of language. Balkan Orthodoxy, therefore, was divided between "patriarchist Greeks" (those who recognized the authority of the patriarchate of Constantinople) and "exarchist Bulgarians" (those who recognized the authority of the Bulgarian exarchate). In this new phase of Balkanization, religious violence between Muslims and Christians combined with ethnic violence between Christian groups. The Macedonian Revolutionary Organization earned the Bulgarians infamy.

Ottoman Macedonia (the vilayets of Kosovo, Monastir, and Salonika) had many ethnic groups and sects, and more than ever, "Macedonia" became the synonym for a heterogeneous mixture. The Christian Orthodox Balkan states (Greece, Serbia, Bulgaria, and Romania) all had interests in the region, given their historical rights and ethnic kinship. Each of them more or less clandestinely supported secret terrorist societies, which in the late nineteenth century attacked the other communities' public and religious buildings, as well as civilians. It was in the Macedonia of the 1890s that modern terrorism clearly had its origin (the sacking of entire villages, abductions for ransom, holdups, the torching of mosques and churches, attacks against the Orient Express). In fact, Armenian nationalists were inspired by the methods of Bulgarian terrorists. The Armenian "fedayi" followed the model of the terrible Macedonian "komitadji," and like them saw themselves as revolutionaries.

The Armenian crisis relaunched the question of Crete. Muslims and Christians were combating and massacring one another. In 1897, the Christian insurgents proclaimed the return of Crete to Greece and arranged for a Greek expeditionary corps to be sent out. The authorities intervened with a naval demonstration: they demanded the autonomy of Crete within the Ottoman framework and the departure of the Greek troops. Urged on by the nationalists, the Greek government declared war on the Ottoman Empire in April 1897. The Ottoman army easily crushed the Greek troops, but the European powers imposed an armistice immediately.

Territorially, this was another Ottoman setback, since the autonomy of Crete quickly became quasi-independence, which would lead to the island's return to the kingdom of Greece. The Cretan Muslims, usually Hellenophones, fled the island and swelled the refugee contingent in Anatolia. Politically, however, the Ottoman victory, the first for decades over a Christian power, was universally hailed in the Muslim world, even in India and China, to the great displeasure of the European powers. The prestige of the sultan-caliph was at its height. Nevertheless, the effective loss of Crete encouraged the Christian nationalists of Macedonia to increase their violent activism. The Macedonian question came to be the order of the day in European chancelleries. In 1902, the Bulgarians launched a true uprising, which the Ottoman army had difficulty containing. The Europeans pushed the need for "new reforms" that would place the region under financial oversight. Abdülhamid equivocated. In exchange for an increase in customs duties, he had to accept expanded European financial control of the entire empire.

Within the context of the European balance of powers, the events of 1878–1882 produced considerable changes. Although Russia remained the hereditary enemy, France, which had seized Tunisia, and Great Britain, which had taken Cyprus and Egypt, were no longer considered the protectors of the empire, as they had been during the Crimean War. Abdülhamid turned to the new Germany, which had not publicly claimed to have territorial ambitions at the expense of the Ottomans. In the 1880s, the sultan appealed to German military advisers to reorganize the Ottoman army, and they stood as the architects of the victory over Greece.

Bismarck had proved wary of any involvement in the Eastern questions, which he primarily used to make Germany the arbiter of European disputes. Wilhelm II, conversely, encouraged that political rapprochement, which corresponded to the growing role of his country in the commerce of the Ottoman Empire. At the start of his reign in 1888, Wilhelm made a first visit to the sultan, but the German emperor was still under Bismarck's sway. The pilgrimage to Jerusalem in autumn 1898 unfolded under the auspices of Germany's need to find "a place in the sun" within the global policy framework. Wilhelm II stayed for more than a month and did not confine himself to diplomatic and religious activity. He appealed to Muslim public opinion, particularly during his trip to Damascus to visit Saladin's tomb at the Umayyad mosque: "The three million Muslims living in the world must know that they have their best friend in me."

That appeal to the Muslim world as a whole, its population without question greatly overestimated, was taken as an encouragement of pan-Islamism. The first concrete result was the concession given to Germany to build a railroad from Istanbul to Baghdad, which immediately became the object of European rivalries. For Great Britain, the concession called into doubt its own economic domination of Mesopotamia and the Gulf. The first reaction of the British was to establish a protectorate over Kuwait, in order to bar access to the Gulf by the future railroad, but the engineers demonstrated that the railroad could still reach the sea from Basra and the Shatt al-Arab.

The Germans, short on capital, hoped to obtain the participation of the French and the British, but that turned out to be impossible. The result was a failure to establish European consortia for developing the Ottoman Empire and a strong tendency to constitute economic and hence political zones of influence.

The final balance sheet of the Hamidian regime is mixed. The last great sultan managed to strengthen the state and developed a modernizing administration. The loss of territories was limited, to Crete essentially. A complex relationship took root between strengthening the central power's authority over the provinces and expanding financial and economic oversight of the empire by Europe. The Macedonian and Armenian crises called into question the difficult internal compromises of Anatolian and Balkan society. Although the nationalism with territorial aims of the Christian communities was the product of developments within the populations, their political strategy was to incite tensions in order to provoke a European rescue mission. Despite the protests of certain components of European public opinion, the logic of the European balance of powers now made it impossible to undertake a new territorial dismemberment similar to that of the Congress of Berlin. In addition, the Ottoman political structure, which allowed an almost total openness of the Ottoman space to European interests, appeared of more interest to the great powers than a fragmentation of that space into national states or colonies, which would have been less accessible to them.

CHAPTER 15

THE FIRST BLOWS TO EUROPEAN DOMINATION

ISLAM AND REVOLUTION: PERSIA

In the 1890s, a portion of Ottoman society shifted toward a revolutionary outlook, but that faction consisted for the most part of nationalist Christian militants. In traditional Islamic political thought, the idea of revolution was considered a negative, since it shattered the unity of the community (or of society). The reformists of the years 1870–1880 had instead adopted a critique of the existing political system, defined as "despotic," and had sought to Islamize European liberal constitutional discourse. The sultan agreed to the Ottoman constitution of 1876, even though it was the result of a coup d'état, and he retained major powers in accordance with it. Although the constitution was later suspended, it remained part of the Ottoman legal codes. By contrast, in the Ottoman Empire as in Persia, any reference to "revolution" was strictly banned by official censorship, especially at the end of the century.

It was in Persia, precisely because modernization was less advanced there and the state weaker, that the first revolutionary Muslim tendencies arose. That is, modernizing intellectuals again found themselves part of a popular movement of which they were not the only organizers. Shah Nasir al-Dīn had shown a certain interest in reformist ideas and had spent time in Europe and Russia, where he was impressed with modern achievements.

After the failure of the concession granted to Julius von Reuter, British diplomacy did not wait long to ask for new concessions. Some were granted them. This time, Jamal al-Dīn al-Afghani worked to unite the reformist opposition to European encroachments with the opposition of the clergy. Secret societies formed. In 1891, Afghani was expelled from Persia. His followers focused their attacks on the tobacco monopoly, which had just been granted to a British company. The theme was particularly popular, since this was no longer a modern activity such as the railroads, created with foreign capital, but a traditional sector that affected thousands of peasants and small tradespeople. The clergy rallied behind the protest, and a mass movement spearheaded a boycott on the consumption of tobacco. In early 1892, in the face of popular demonstrations, the government was forced to cancel the concession, at the cost of heavy indemnities. That movement was considered the first national Iranian movement, organized in part from the holy Shiite cities in Iraq. In 1896, a follower of Afghani assassinated Shah Nasir al-Dīn, the last powerful figure of the Qajar dynasty.

Under his successor, the weak Muzaffar al-Dīn, the financial crisis grew perilously worse, with growing debts to the British and the Russians. Joseph Naus, a Belgian (that is, neither a Russian nor a Briton), was assigned to reorganize finances, spurring opposition on all sides. Again, the secret societies protested.

The Japanese victories over Russia in 1905 seemed to show that an Eastern constitutional state could successfully challenge Europe. In late 1905, a vast popular movement supported by the clergy defied the shah's authority in Persia. The reformers demanded that a constitution be set in place. The authorities were obliged to convene a constitutive assembly in summer 1906. The basic law was drafted and amended in the following months. Persia officially became a constitutional monarchy with equal rights for all, including non-Muslims.

Contrary to expectations, the constitution did not make it possible to resolve the problems. Muhammad Ali Shah, who ascended to the throne in January 1907, resumed the struggle against the constitutionalists. He obtained the support of part of the conservative clergy, who were hostile to Westernization. That led to a civil war between the revolutionary *mujahidin*, or *fidayin*, and the royalist troops supported by the Russians, who sent an armed contingent to the north of the country, officially to protect the Europeans. Following the Russian intervention in 1911, the assembly was dissolved and the central power collapsed.

Despite the sympathy of British public opinion for the Persian liberals, the new European alliances led the British government to align itself with Russian policy. Persia ceased to be a buffer state between the two empires. Russian troops occupied the northern part of the country, while the south came under the de facto tutelage of the British.

A fairly clear rule emerged from the Persian example: geopolitical constraints dictated that the European powers would have no interest in supporting attempts to establish a liberal regime in the Muslim world.

EUROPEAN INSTABILITY AND THE FATE OF THE MUSLIM WORLD

In the early twentieth century, European political alignments changed, with tragic consequences for the Muslim world under European domination, despite theoretical independence. The essential factor was the Anglo-German naval competition within the context of the German empire's global policy. The construction of a powerful modern war fleet directly threatened the British

Isles. Although Great Britain had a large numerical advantage, the needs of its empire required it to disperse its fleet over all the seas of the world, whereas Germany could concentrate its own in the Black Sea.

As a result, London rationalized its deployment and, in addition to launching new modern units, emerged from its splendid isolation to confront the German threat. The 1902 treaty with Japan allowed the British to limit its naval presence in the Pacific. The Entente Cordiale with France had more far-reaching consequences. It liquidated colonial disputes by putting an end to France's claims on Egypt, in exchange for support of its action in Morocco. France found it easy to end its discreet encouragement of the Egyptian nationalists, especially since it was itself worried about the pan-Islamist discourses being freely voiced in Egypt.

The Russo-Japanese War of 1904–1905 shook the world. The crushing defeats that an Asian country inflicted on a European Christian power looked like a promise of liberation for the entire European-ruled world. The Muslim press conceived a passion for the cause of Japan, which appeared to have pulled off the tour de force of preserving its identity intact even as it achieved perfect modernization. For the first time, a non-European model took shape. Some went so far as to evoke the imminent conversion of the Japanese to Islam.

The Russian defeats paralyzed the Franco-Russian alliance. Germany attempted to take advantage of the situation to isolate France and put an end to its growing interference in Morocco. On March 31, 1905, stopping in Tangier during a pleasure cruise, Wilhelm II made a declaration in which he recognized the sultan as the only authority in Morocco. A major European crisis followed, with Great Britain joining forces with France, whose views prevailed at the Algeciras Conference (January–March 1906). The independence of Morocco and the principle of equal treatment of the European nations were recognized, but France retained priority in the country.

In the same context, Abdülhamid reopened the question of the status of Sinai by establishing a military position in Taba. Great Britain reacted forcefully with a naval demonstration at the entrance to the Dardanelles. The Ottomans were obliged to give in, but Egyptian public opinion proved favorable to the Ottoman outlook. European diplomacy saw that crisis as the resurgence of pan-Islamism supported by Germany.

In the wake of the Taba crisis, Great Britain considered itself under threat in Egypt. It no longer had the means to exert pressure on the Porte, especially since, more than in Mesopotamia and the Gulf, the controversy of the Baghdad railroad—another pan-Islamist German-Ottoman conspiracy—was raging there. Britain had to assure the security of Egypt while increasing its influence in the Red Sea and Palestine. In the event of war, British strategists planned a landing on the Syrian coasts to overtake from the rear the Ottomans marching on Egypt. Reconnaissance missions to that end were carried out in 1906.

After its defeats in the Far East, Russia cut its losses and turned back to the Mediterranean and Europe. That coincided with British interests, in that it assured the security of the Indian route. The Anglo-Russian convention of August 31, 1907, divided Persia into two zones of influence, the north going to the Russians, the south to the British, with a neutral zone between them. We have already seen the consequences of that division for the constitutionalist Persian revolution.

The new European political alignment, founded on a de facto alliance between France, Great Britain, and Russia, came about directly at the expense of the Muslim world in Morocco, Egypt, and Persia. By contrast, imperial Germany, which felt threatened by a supposed desire to encircle it, more than ever looked like the major power protecting Islam.

The three empires in question considered themselves "Muslim powers," since they had millions of Muslim subjects.

France was permanently haunted by the specter of an Algerian uprising like the one in 1871. The North Africa–sub-Saharan Africa bloc was near completion. Although it was considered a source of power and a way to recruit soldiers, it appeared vulnerable to internal subversion by pan-Islamism. The colonial fear of a native uprising was a permanent reality, though official discourse usually concealed it. Nevertheless, many colonials, such as Louis Lyautey, harshly criticized the behavior of European civilians in North Africa, who heaped scorn on the Arab population. A whole Arabophile current was taking shape, deeply committed to respecting Arab mores and culture. Its finest expression came from Isabelle Eberhardt, who died at twenty-eight and whose friends posthumously published her *In the Hot Shade of Islam*. These Arabophiles were far from adversaries of French colonization and even recruited from political and military circles. We would now say that they wanted to put a "human face" on French colonization.

Russia completed its conquest of the Caucasus and central Asia. It even appeared about to add northern Persia, thus moving closer to the Indian Ocean. At the same time, the Muslims in the empire were in the midst of an evolution. The most dynamic factor came from the earliest conquered elements, the Tatars of Kazan and Crimea, whose influence extended to central Asia. Possessing a better knowledge of European culture, some Tatar intellectuals redefined Turkish identity.

The European Orientalists had determined the existence of two major ethnolinguistic groups, the Aryan and the Semitic. They gradually defined a third group, called "Touranian." The great Hungarian Orientalist Arminius Vambéry (1832–1913), a personal friend of Abdülhamid, became its theorist. He included within the Touranian group the Estonians, Finns, Hungarians, and all the Turkophone peoples, even the Siberian populations. He argued that there was a great Touranian civilization that, as a result of the vicissitudes of history, almost completely surrounded Russia. That sufficed to make Vambéry look like an agent of Great Britain, with its desire to contain Russia along the Indian route.

Whereas the French and German Orientalists were primarily concerned with the opposition between the Aryan and the Semitic, Russian Orientalists focused on the Touranian question, seen as a tool for devaluing the Slavs, who had supposedly intermarried with the Touranians everywhere. (German Orientalists often expressed that view.) They claimed both an autochthony for the Russians, supposedly descended from the Scythians of antiquity, and their proximity to the primitive Indo-Europeans of India. (The Russians therefore had a greater purity than the Germans and Celts of western Europe.) The Russian conquest of Siberia and of Muslim Asia, from the Caucasus to rural Asia, was only a reconquest of the original birthplace of the Aryan race. The Russian version of the Aryan myth played the same role as references to the Roman Empire by French colonizers, who saw the colonization of North Africa as a restoration of its former Latin character.

The writings of Vambéry, those of the Frenchman Léon Cahun (1841–1900), as well as the responses of the Russian Orientalists, immediately became known to the Turkophone intellectuals of the Russian empire, whose aim was to constitute a common Turkish language from the Mediterranean to central Asia, or even to China. This pan-Touranist movement sought to emancipate itself from Russian domination by reversing the terms of the discourse. They championed the unity of all Turkish, even all Touranian, peoples. These ideas spread to Ottoman territory via the constant immigration of Muslims from the Russian empire. Abdülhamid, deeply attached to the caliphate and to Islam, opposed them. But he could not prevent the creation of the modern Turkish language, a natural product of the diffusion of education and the printed word, and distinct from classical Ottoman Turkish. As everywhere, the modern language was a simplification, which entailed a gradual suppression of the many borrowings from Arabic and Persian. Turkophone intellectuals of the Russian empire played a large role in that process. Hence pan-Islamism combined with a pan-Turkish nationalism, a factor contributing to the rebellions against Russian rule.

Outside that Touranian current, there was an affirmation among Muslim intellectuals of the Russian empire of a more classic Muslim reformism, which combined pan-Islamism with a certain penchant for liberalism.

In Great Britain, the occupation of Egypt and Sudan, along with the vast Indian empire, made the colonial administration a growing outlet for educated young people. A colonial career provided guaranteed social ascent for members of the middle classes, and the power elite was also increasingly interested in that almost aristocratic opportunity. Although the colonial officers were recruited from the British public schools, those in the upper colonial administration were educated in the prestigious universities of Oxford and Cambridge, with significant instruction in the Eastern languages. That large caste was composed of the thousand members of the Indian Civil Service emerging from the upper classes of British society.

Rudyard Kipling became the voice of that milieu, with both an ideology of dedication incarnated in the "white man's burden" and a provincialist reproduction of the metropolis, represented by Simla, the summer capital of the Indian empire. In *Kim*, he expresses better than anyone the colonial fantasy of concealing oneself within the indigenous population, while placing that fantasy within the context of the Great Game between the Russians and the British in Asia. But the "native" cherished by the British colonial was the one who preserved his authenticity and therefore knew his place. Colonial ideology was coupled with a Victorian medievalism, which had its apogee in the great "durbars," ceremonies held in Delhi that made the British the direct heirs of the Great Moguls. These theatrical spectacles, during which the Indian princes paraded with great pomp, were intended to mark the continuity of Indian history in its British expression.

Colonialism had introduced modernity and found its justification therein, but it was also the victim of modernity. And though the Anglo-Indians ultimately aspired to be the just and moral restorers of the ancient order of the Great Mogul, they undermined its foundations. The upper classes of Indian society had access to modern education and began to contest the Europeans' monopoly on the modern professions. These beginnings of competition provoked a visceral reaction on the part of the British service aristocracy: The Hindu, regardless of his educational level, could never accede to the moral dignity of the Briton. The Hindu preferred words to action, lacked natural authority, was inclined toward venality, and foundered during a major crisis. The rejected Indian elite returned to the Congress Party, which initially sought only to make adjustments to the British system.

Whereas the early Congress Party aspired toward modernization, even Westernization, placing itself within a liberal and secular perspective and therefore opening its ranks to Indian Muslims, other currents aspired to be the defenders of a Hindu character that would call into question the rise of the Anglicized elites. The Sepoy War had marked the end of the last vestiges of Muslim domination, with the disappearance of the shadow sultanate of Delhi. Within that context, Muslim reformism was very well received by the Muslim elites, some of whom were leaning toward a liberalism in collaboration with the British. That gave rise to criticism from Afghani, who condemned them as "materialists." (Afghani actually agreed on the content of the doctrine; what he rejected was collaboration with the English.) More hard-line tendencies expressed a desire to return to Islam, whose doctrine was interpreted literally in the rigorous Wahhabi or Hanbalite mode.

Muslim reformism, like the revival of a Hindu identity movement, sought to purify religion of its supposed superstitions, which were often forms of religious practice common to Muslims and Hindus. That translated into an increasing uneasiness about the practices of the Other. In northern India, a vast movement developed in the 1890s to forbid Muslims from slaughtering cows, leading to conflicts of unprecedented scope between the two communities. In the same region, the cleavage took on a cultural aspect. The Hindus tended to reject the legacy of the sultanate of Delhi and to turn toward the purity of their Sanskrit origins. A so-called Hindi language and written culture developed. It used Sanskrit characters and became increasingly distinct from Urdu, the culture and language of the Muslims. Northern India thus underwent a process of cultural renaissance preliminary to the affirmation of a national body of knowledge, similar to that occurring elsewhere in the world. Hindu nationalists began to perceive the Indian Muslims as exogenous elements or traitors to Indian culture. They fought both British domination and the Muslim part of their own culture.

Indian Muslims gradually found themselves in the same situation as the Balkan Muslims, considered strangers and traitors in their own countries, which they had formerly ruled.

With Lord George Curzon, the greatest of the viceroys, the Indian empire reached its pinnacle (1899–1905). Curzon tried both to shake up administrative routines and to impose his imperial and aristocratic vision, even while combating the Congress Party. He also became the architect of the empire's expansion into Persia and the Gulf. Despite his tremendous energy, his political vision remained profoundly conservative.

His successor, Lord Minto, was cognizant of the need to put an end to the European monopoly on government institutions. With the agreement of John Morley, secretary for India, he spearheaded a vast reform program that opened all posts in the public sector to the indigenous people and in 1908 put elected native representatives on the government councils responsible for drafting laws, though only in a minority capacity. As is often the case in such situations, political openness was accompanied by unrest and protests in various regions of India, for the most part by Hindu elements.

Within that context, in 1906 Lord Minto came out in favor of constituting a Muslim League, which, in reaction to the Hindus' attitude, expressed its loyalty to the British from the start. Its first concern was to assure Muslim representation in the new institutions. In 1908, the league obtained in principle a separate electorate. Although the British had not sought to divide and conquer and had not created the antagonism between Muslims and Hindus—which was the product of new formulations of identity within the context of access to modernity, as the Ottoman example has shown—they noted with favor the massive support the Muslims provided for their rule.

From 1907–1908 on, Indian policymakers were firmly persuaded that the support of the Muslims was indispensable for maintaining British domination. As a result, they claimed, any event in the rest of the Muslim world involving the British would have damaging consequences for the Indian empire. That view was tirelessly repeated in the government councils.

The de facto alliance concluded in 1907 between France, Great Britain, and Russia was naturally intended to contain the supposed ambitions of imperial

Germany. It was also an alliance of the three great colonial empires with the largest Muslim populations, all of which were troubled by the specter of pan-Islamism. The fourth colonial empire with large numbers of Muslims was Dutch India (now Indonesia). Its leaders and Orientalists were also worried about the pan-Islamist danger, but that empire enjoyed relative calm, given its neutrality in the new European political alignments.

With the Tangier crisis of 1905, the disordered state of the European political system carried with it the risk of a general war in Europe, though the principal conflicts leading to crises, or at least to tensions, occurred within the Muslim world.

THE YOUNG TURKS

In early 1908, Alfred Le Châtelier's *Revue du Monde Musulman* inquired:

> Does it not seem that this struggle, so passionate, so shrewd to be sure, being waged against destiny from the Yildiz Kiosk, gives the impression of a last act soon to come, conditioned by so many conflicts that there are no longer enough diversions to change the outcome?
>
> If Europe wants to maintain the balance, which it worries will be destroyed, it will not suffice to focus its attention on the Balkans. Let it not forget the mediators provided it by Asia Minor, Armenia, Syria, and Arabia.[1]

All these geographical regions returned to the political horizon with the Young Turk revolution of 1908. In July of that year, the army of Macedonia, at the urging of the Committee of Union and Progress (CUP), marched on the capital and forced the sultan to restore the constitution of 1876. It was the end of Hamidian "despotism" and the triumph of the ideas of freedom and equality. Never had a great Muslim state gone so far in adopting European ideas.

Reality rapidly intervened. On October 5, 1908, Bulgaria declared its independence and rejected the sultan's theoretical sovereignty. The next day, Austria-Hungary proclaimed the annexation of Bosnia-Herzegovina, which it had administered since the Congress of Berlin, and Crete announced its intention to unite with Greece. All of a sudden, the new regime had lost more territories than Abdülhamid since 1878. Throughout the empire, the CUP orchestrated a powerful boycott against Austrian goods. Largely embraced by the working classes, it was also a de facto protest against the capitulation system. Diplomacy discreetly took on a role and, between February and March 1909, the Ottoman Empire received financial compensation, while the caliph's right to control the religious life of Muslims in the lost territories was acknowledged.

The essential thing was to establish a modern political life revolving around elections, the first of which occurred in November–December 1908, with a two-round voting process. The Muslim populations of the Balkans and Anatolia elected the candidates backed by the CUP. In the Arab provinces, by contrast, the important families of notables prevailed. Although they sought and obtained the backing of the CUP, these families for the most part represented very strong local influences, even engaging in logrolling. They thus returned to the forefront after being relatively marginalized under Abdülhamid's personal reign. The liberals from the same Young Turk current as the CUP, but who were proponents of full equality with non-Muslims based on extensive decentralization, were defeated everywhere by the Muslim electorate. The liberals were primarily represented by non-Muslim deputies, while the non-Turkish Muslim deputies (Albanians, Arabs) were naturally sympathetic to the idea of decentralization.

The question of equality therefore arose. In the CUP's view, a Jacobin orientation favored the disappearance of community-based privileges and the establishment of full equal rights and duties between Muslims and non-Muslims. For the millets, conversely, the matter at hand was to strengthen their nonterritorial autonomy or even to undertake a movement toward nationhood.

In conservative Muslim circles, the notions of freedom and equality seemed to run counter to Muslim traditions. Besides, the Young Turks were evoking a form of women's emancipation. By the very fact that political freedom of a sort had been instituted, the reactionaries were able to develop their propaganda campaign against a "handful of atheists" who were leading the empire to its ruin. A powerful movement called the "Islamic Union" came into being, the first modern form of Islamic populism, whose cadres recruited minor ulemas and students of religion. In April 1909, the soldiers in the Istanbul garrison mutinied and drove the Islamic Unionists from the capital. In the provinces, the movement evolved into a terrible massacre of Armenians in Adana. The army of Salonika immediately marched on the capital and imposed a harsh repression. In May, Abdülhamid was deposed and replaced by his brother, Mehmed Reshad. That marked the end of the sultanate's political role.

The events of April–May 1909 were the culmination of a vast debate of ideas that began with the revolution of July 1908. It is now possible to clearly discern two major currents of thought. The first was represented by the "Occidentalists." According to Abdullah Cevdet, one of their spokesmen, "there is only one civilization, and that is European civilization. It must be imported with its roses and its thorns." Mentalities had to be changed through the adoption, with the help of education, of the principles of modern life, freedom, and critical and scientific thought. The second current, which can be called Islamist, embraced the Muslim reformism of the previous generation and proposed to follow the model of Japan, which had been able to adopt Western science and technology without losing its identity. The decline of the empire was linked not to religion but to its corruption. Hence the need to restore the original principles of Islam. Other tendencies were more conservative and more blunt in their condemnation of modern mores imported from Europe.

Both Occidentalists and Islamists were fervent defenders of the empire and were committed above all to its survival. In these circles, Turkish nationalism, inspired by ideas coming from the Muslims of the Russian empire, exerted a growing appeal. Turkish culture could form a synthesis with European modernity. The nation was the modern receptacle for civilization. For a time, however, these ideas influenced only small circles in Istanbul and Salonika.

The Young Turks naturally turned to the liberal European powers: Great Britain, the mother of parliamentarianism, and France, land of positivism and modern ideas. At the same time, these nations were the two great colonial powers of the Muslim world, and they worried about the repercussions of revolution. In Egypt, the nationalists and liberals demanded a parliamentary constitution, the first phase of a British evacuation.

Cromer was recalled in 1907 and replaced by Sir Eldon Gorst, whose mission was to restore amicable relations with the khedive and to re-Egyptianize an administration overrun by British civil servants. At issue was not liberalization but an "indirect rule" policy, which produced direct hostility on the part of Anglo-Egyptians whose positions were threatened. The man behind that policy was the Coptic prime minister, Boutros Ghali. The Egyptian nationalists, who had lost the khedive's support, became radicalized and assumed a militant Islamist tone. On February 23, 1910, Boutros Ghali was assassinated. His murderer was considered a national hero among the Muslims, which led to strong religious tensions. Balfour, the former Conservative British prime minister, a member of the opposition at the time, declared in June 1910: "The Eastern peoples were not made for constitutional government. English authority in Egypt must remain intact, and everything must be done to maintain its prestige." The government defended itself by asserting "that no progress can be realized in Egypt so long as the protest against the occupation has not ended."[2] Gorst remained in office, but he was gravely ill.

It was not until Gorst's death in July 1911 that his successor, Sir Herbert Kitchener, was named and given the task of conducting a policy of repression against the nationalists and of restoring the British Empire's prestige. The new consul and British agent publicly styled himself the protector of the Egyptian peasantry and maintained that the nationalists were of no account. He bluntly explained in his first annual report that the Easterners were a long way from having the maturity necessary for a liberal political life:

> Upon my return to Egypt, I was deeply affected upon observing that the masses of enlightened Muslims who formerly constituted a collective community based on fixed social laws are at present divided into parties and factions of a political character.
>
> Whatever the value of a party system in Western political life, it is obvious that its application is misguided and can produce only division and weakness in a community . . . whose social system is based on the brotherhood of men, combined with respect for the knowledge and experience of age.

The development and elevation of a people's character depend on the respect individuals have for themselves, on the power to control their natural impulses, on a discreet personal confidence combined with a rational determination. In no way can elements of progress be advanced through dissension and party quarrels. A calm and well-considered interest in political affairs is good for both the governed and the governors, but imaginary interests presented in a false light and maintained with the aid of tactics and funds from these parties can in no way elevate or develop the intelligent character of an Oriental race.[3]

He launched a private war against the khedive, slighting him many times, and became increasingly interested in the political evolution of the neighboring Arab provinces.

There was also a risk that the Young Turk revolution would contaminate the Indian Muslims, who had become one of the essential pillars for maintaining the Indian empire. The British embassy in Constantinople was quick to see the Young Turks not as the natural offshoot of liberal European ideas, but as the fruit of the dark machinations of a Jewish and Freemason plot.

The French had the same anxiety about North Africa, especially since they had resumed the penetration of Morocco. Others had fears about the French influence. The new regime tended to display a supercilious nationalism, and nearly everywhere disputed the capitulations and their indirect effects.

For France and Great Britain, the absolute priority was to maintain the European alignment with Russia against the German threat. But Russia, ejected from the Far East by the Japanese, more than ever looked like the Ottomans' hereditary enemy.

The "Le Châtelier Moment"

A true debate opened among French experts on Islam. The CUP represented the triumph of Europe over Asia, represented by Abdülhamid's Arab entourage. Beyond that, the form of modernization of the Young Turk regime raised new issues: if Islam could not be reduced to a mere religious practice and had to be considered a social fact, then an Islamic nation and an Islamic nationalism distinct from the religious phenomenon might emerge. In addition, did not the hostility to the Young Turk regime translate into autonomist aspirations among the non-Turkish Muslims of the empire, the Albanians and the Arabs? Within that context, French policy could not confine itself to keeping track of its usual clients. It had to take an interest directly in Muslims who, in the Hamidian compromise, were located outside its zone of influence.

A year after the revolution, in July 1909, the French government issued instructions to those posted in the Muslim world to conduct a review of the press in their districts and to send it to Paris, a first stage in a general reflection on the situation. The next year, in the September issue of the *Revue du Monde Musulman*, Alfred Le Châtelier recommended the creation of a "Muslim policy" within the framework of a "consultative institution, as indispensable in our time to the political order as to the administrative order." He took the opportunity to draw a portrait of the Muslim world: European Islam was in full political retreat, but full Europeanization and modernization was under way. The European Muslims, "in renouncing their privileges of religious isolation, in participating in the movement of the European peoples . . . have gained in opportunities what they have lost in traditions." He was the first to analyze "the spread throughout Europe of a Western Muslim colonization with intellectual tendencies, but completely Islamic in its political objectives." These tendencies were represented primarily by students and political refugees from the Muslim world generally, now living in England, France, Switzerland, and Germany. In the case of that Muslim enclave,

> in becoming modernized, its civilization, a short time ago inert and somnolent, has become singularly active and robust in its new mode of being. It provides the meaningful spectacle of an Islam fighting and defending itself, not retreating but transforming itself, and in which a communal attraction to ideas, and resistance to the domination of the West, are becoming more pronounced. The same inspiration seems to preside over the efforts of the Hindu, Persian, Tunisian, Egyptian, or Turkish student, the Balkan komitadji, and the Russian Tatar: an aspiration for a twofold deliverance, through the progress of education and the demand by Muslims for the rights of every people. How better to define that stage of evolution except by the expression "state of civilization"?

During that time, an "African Muslim civilization" was developing, and it "manifested [itself] in the assimilation of the native to the foreigner, along with the absorption of the foreigner into the African environment." That end of isolation translated into raised consciousness for a vast Muslim community that extended as far as China, even as it was increasingly affirming national consciousness and was making progress within Africa.

When Le Châtelier spoke of the Ottoman world, the idea of movement always prevailed. It was

> dominated from above by a sincere fervor for intellectual, political, and social emancipation, but it culminates in the imperialism of authority, in Albania and in Syria, and in the request for alliances, solicited sometimes from France and England, sometimes from Germany. All things considered, Europe finds itself in the presence of a movement where the impulses of Turkish nationalism and Ottoman imperialism combine with those of a liberal and modern outlook, still rather young, and showing it is so through its ambition to exactly assimilate the civilization of Islam to that of Europe, leaving the former sufficiently Muslim so that there can be no mistaking it.

The Persian revolution marked "the vital force of rebirth by a civilization transforming itself in order to come back to life."[4] In India, Le Châtelier insisted on the primacy of the conflict with Hinduism.

To summarize a relatively complex notion, the confrontation with Europe and modernity gave rise to tendencies that were not contradictory: an increased awareness of belonging collectively to Muslim civilization, the affirmation of national identities, and the desire to emancipate oneself from European domination, even if that meant playing on the rivalry among the European powers.

Within that context, France had to acquire a "social science of the Muslim world," which would be used to develop a policy for fending off the danger of a "clash of civilizations."

Le Châtelier's writings constituted an essential turning point in the history of European Orientalism. Rejecting any idea of a fixism or specific essence, he introduced into the study of the contemporary period the central notion of "social science," applied to the study of "movement." The chair he held in Muslim sociology and sociography at the Collège de France was created in 1902, scarcely ten years after Renan's death. It is therefore clear how strong and quick the break with the past was.

In 1911, the French government endorsed Le Châtelier's conclusions by creating the Commission Interministérielle des Affaires Musulmanes.

THE ZIONIST QUESTION AND THE ARAB QUESTION

Zionism's existence as an effective movement depended on the linkage between western European railroad networks and those of eastern Europe, which allowed for connections to be made in the ports to the regular steamship lines. This linkage occurred in about 1880. That indispensable material contingency corresponded chronologically to the increasing harshness of discriminatory laws in the Russian empire and to the appearance of anti-Semitism in western Europe.

Although the first Zionist groups appeared in Russia in the early 1880s and attempted a first emigration to Palestine, they quickly met with failure. The risk was that the English Protestant missionaries, still intent on the conversion of the Jews within the context of the fulfillment of prophecies, would launch a religious propaganda campaign, offering material incentives to these migrants. Worried, the leaders of the Alliance Israélite Universelle made contact with the French baron Edmond de Rothschild, who initially offered one-time assistance, then later became enthusiastic about the project. He therefore established a whole series of agricultural colonies. He asked for French consular protection, which he obtained, in part because the agricultural colony administration was composed of French Jews, who therefore benefited from French protection.

Edmond de Rothschild was rapidly persuaded of the need to act discreetly, given the wariness of the Ottoman authorities, who saw that immigration movement as a European colonial project. He also had to somehow make these colonies economically self-sufficient, which led to a series of costly stumbles, until a "plantation economy" using an Arab labor force was set in place.

Those belonging to the first wave of immigration (*aliya*) integrated quite naturally into Levantine society. The administrative language of Rothschildian colonization was French and, apart from a few neighborhood skirmishes with the Arab peasants, there was no particular violence. In the cities, the Jewish immigrants participated in the community life of the Levant. The sociability of the elites occurred across communities. The young Hajj Amin al-Husayni, for example, learned French at the schools of the Alliance Israélite Universelle and under the tutelage of the baron's representative in Jerusalem.

With the beginning of Theodor Herzl's public activities in 1896, the situation changed. Rothschild rejected the political activism of the founder of political Zionism, who was making a mistake in drawing public attention to the Jewish immigration to Palestine. Herzl wanted a "charter" guaranteed by the European great powers, which would allow for the creation in Palestine of a homeland for the Jewish people. At the international level, he sought to obtain the support of imperial Germany. (He accompanied Wilhelm II on his famous journey to the East in 1898.) Herzl opened negotiations with Abdülhamid, promising to pay off the Ottoman debt with Jewish finances. The sultan was a shrewd partner, who used Herzl as a means to apply pressure as he negotiated for another Ottoman loan. After that dual failure, the founder of the Zionist organization turned to Great Britain, which declared it was interested in a Jewish concession in Sinai. But Cromer resolutely opposed it. At the time of Herzl's death in 1904, he had obtained nothing, though he had succeeded in organizing a powerful political movement known on the international scene. His successors at the head of the Zionist organization moved closer to Germany. The leadership of the movement was primarily German in composition, whereas most of the militants came from the Russian empire.

It was not until 1908 that the organization directly took root in Palestine, at a time when the most politicized militants were arriving, often socialist in their inspiration and having lived through the Russian Revolution of 1905. This was the second *aliya*. The interests of these militants converged with those of the Zionist organization, if only in their efforts to circumvent Rothschildian colonization.

The Arab elites became aware of the existence of the Zionist movement by reading the European press. At first, reactions were mixed. Some saw it as an opportunity to attract European capital for developing the regional economy, but they worried about its political aspirations. In Palestine itself, the first directly political clashes came about in early 1908. It was at that moment that the term "Palestine" entered into common use in the Arabic language. Like "Syria," the Europeans had originally used it throughout the nineteenth century to designate those regions of the Near East.

Membership in the Ottoman Empire slowed the emergence of a new regional consciousness, unlike in quasi-independent provinces such as Tunisia and Libya. Inasmuch as these new identities had no legal status, they were vague and often better formulated in the language of the Other. In the late nineteenth century, for example, ordinary discourse clearly distinguished the Turks from the Arabs, but without positing any political ramifications. At the start of the twentieth century, however, marginal individuals, whether Muslims like Abd al-Rahman al-Kawakibi or Christians like Najib Azouri, evoked a distinct Arab political identity. There was even talk of an Arab revolt to come. It was in fact in 1905 that Azouri made his famous prediction:

> Two important phenomena, of the same nature and yet opposed, and which have not yet attracted anyone's attention, are coming to light at this moment in Asian Turkey: these are the reawakening of the Arab nation and the latent effort of the Jews to reconstitute the ancient monarchy of Israel on a very grand scale. These two movements are destined to be continually at odds, until one of them prevails over the other. The fate of the entire world will depend on the ultimate result of that struggle between these two peoples representing two contrary principles.[5]

The idea of an Arab revolt was primarily identified with the Bedouin movements of the Arabian Peninsula and with the reconstitution of a third Saudi-Wahhabi state from central Arabia, undertaken by Abd al-Aziz al-Saʻud (Ibn Saʻud).

The great success of Hamidian policy was to integrate the Arab provinces politically in the wake of the Treaty of Berlin. From Syria, the elites from families of notables, usually members of the younger branches, provided an important contingent for high posts in the Ottoman government. From the Iraqi provinces came a large number of officers belonging to the Sunni population. The proclaimed Islamic character of the state cemented that unity.

The Young Turks put an end to that success, despite the return in force of the local notables, who prevailed in the parliamentary elections. Arab high officials were associated with the Hamidian regime. Modernizing discourses were interpreted as a rejection of Islamic traditions. Young, college-educated Arabs no longer received the same welcome in the Ottoman administration. The centralization measures of the CUP were viewed as elements of a Turkization policy, though they had been perfectly well tolerated under Abdülhamid. The same was true for the use of the Ottoman language in the administration and the justice system.

The growing disaffection of the Arab elites led to the reappearance in political discourse of the theme of an Arab caliphate, the only legitimate kind. The constitutional revision of June 1909 that accompanied the deposing of Abdülhamid made the caliphate a magistrature created by a national delegation and responsible to it, that is, to the Ottoman Parliament. But that Parliament included non-Muslims, both Christians and Jews. Those opposed to the Ottoman caliphate also rejected the idea of turning a Muslim community into an Ottoman nation that combined Muslims and non-Muslims.

That debate rapidly turned into a conflict between Turks and Arabs. The young French Orientalist Gaston Wiet analyzed it with acumen in summer 1910:

> The Arabs declare that they are tired of seeing the Turks be *everything*, and, though some of them claim only the right to proportional representation (in the Senate, in the Parliament, and in various public offices), some go much further and declare quite simply that they want to be everything in their turn. The battle, waged in that way, can only be violent, since the men in power and the public employees do not seem in any way inclined to yield their places to the Arabs. For their part, they attack with gusto.[6]

The protest, first expressed in religious terms, evolved into concrete political demands: greater Arab participation in the administration, but on a local basis, which translated into "administrative decentralization" and a critique of "Ottoman mismanagement." In Syria, the ancient richness of the country and its future promise of development was contrasted to its present-day poverty. For the Young Turks, such demands were unacceptable. The Balkan, Tunisian, and Egyptian examples stood as a reminder that any process leading to autonomy culminated inexorably either in independence (in majority Christian regions) or in colonial conquest over the medium term (in Islamic territories).

That interpretation was only corroborated by the new European expansion at the expense of Muslim independence.

Morocco and Libya

At the Algeciras Conference, France had received acknowledgment of a de facto preponderance in Morocco, even as the Moroccan state was about to collapse. In the name of protecting the Europeans, the French troops of Algeria, commanded by General Louis Lyautey, undertook the conquest of the neighboring regions of Algeria, while the French navy occupied Casablanca (1907). In 1911, after a period of relative calm, also marked by Franco-German economic cooperation, the French undertook a regular expedition intended to take control of the principal cities in the country, so as to "restore order" there.

Germany responded with a demonstration of force, sending a gunboat to Agadir on July 1, 1911. In face of the "Agadir crisis," Great Britain joined forces with France. The press in the various countries stirred up nationalist passions. Despite a difficult environment and after several months of negotiations, diplomats arrived at a compromise. France yielded a part of the Congo to Germany, in exchange for the renunciation of German claims.

France now had a free hand to impose its protectorate, which it did with the Treaty of Fez on March 30, 1912. At the same time, Spain directly administered a territory of 28,000 square kilometers. The news gave rise to general insurrection in the country, which General Lyautey, the new resident-general, had to address. The conqueror's genius consisted of abandoning the civilizing and contemptuous discourse of the French Republicans and of affirming that the French protectorate was a restoration of an old order threatened with collapse by colonial and European modernity. Lyautey pledged to maintain the traditional hierarchies, to keep Islam as the organizing principle of society, and to reestablish the authority of the dynasty. He thus made a pact with the administration of the Moroccan state, which allowed him to neutralize the insurrection, thanks to an army numbering 76,000 men in 1913. A pacified and homogeneous Morocco now stood in contrast to a rural, mountainous region still in rebellion.

Given his aestheticism and Orientalism, Lyautey sometimes tended to invent, for the needs of the cause, a tradition where it did not exist. He wanted to make Morocco an anti-Algeria, or even an anti–Republican France. He worked to isolate European modernity and to safeguard the Muslim city. Segregating the populations also meant rejecting any Europeanization of the Moroccan elites, which would have made them "the uprooted" in Barrès's sense. Everyone had to know his place, but at the same time people were supposed to establish relations of self-interest with one another, and these might have an emotional aspect. A shift therefore occurred from the "policy of respect" to a "bit of love" (*parcelle d'amour*). The resident-general, all-powerful master of the country, styled himself the servant of the sultan. In transposing a feudal view of society onto Morocco, he secretly assumed the role of a Cardinal de Richelieu: he built an absolutist state with technocratic leanings on behalf of the Moroccan monarchy, which was destined one day to reclaim its independence.

That tremendously original experiment embraced the doctrine of association, as opposed to that of assimilation. It replicated, in an even more aristocratic mode, the differentialist outlook of the British. It belonged to the tradition of thought characteristic of the "indigenophiles" or "Arabophiles" and to the aesthetic approach of Pierre Loti, Fromentin, and Isabelle Eberhardt. The Moroccan elites appreciated that attitude, which kept them safe from the Algerian catastrophe. For the French colonial party, Lyautey was the great man who knew how to wed an applied Islamology to the imperial interests of France.

In a public speech in late 1912, Célestin Jonnart, a high-ranking politician, former governor general of Algeria and Lyautey's political boss, noted the conclusions to be drawn regarding Algeria from the actions taken in Morocco:

> France, a great Muslim power, currently possesses a method and an experience—attained at great cost—which will simplify its task. . . .

Our Algeria, Gentlemen, after many groping hesitations, after half a century of ordeals, has found its way. We now have a clear view of the problems that its destiny raises and of the solutions to be adopted.

No one dreams any longer of making Algeria a vast military camp or an Arab kingdom or simply French departments. It is a land where our race must firmly take root, not with the brutal idea of repressing the native race or with the chimerical notion of assimilating it, but with the firm will of assuring it its place—every place befitting it—that is, of welcoming our Muslim subjects into the French family as the best of collaborators and partners. . . .

The governor-general in Algeria is the guardian of the native populations and, more than ever, our Muslim policy must be imbued with the perspectives of the nation, must subordinate itself to the nation's hopes and aims.

The policy requires a great deal of tact and competence. I am not surprised that it has given rise to passionate polemics; never before have the problems it stirs up appeared so formidable to French consciousness. . . .

On one hand is the thesis of the emancipation of the native populations; on the other, that of their evolution beforehand, prudently guided, readied, through economic, intellectual, and social development. Between the two tendencies, there is no opposition on principle, only one of method. . . .

The natives must see us as something other then policemen or merchants, and here and there, visible to all, a symbol of French goodness must rise up. . . .

Remember Renan's response to the question: "What makes a nation?" The constitutive element of a nation is the desire to be together. That is also the constitutive element of good marriages. Let the leader of each of our colonies say to his subordinates: "My instructions can be summed up as follows: Act in such as a way that the last to come into the great French family will feel the desire more each day to live alongside us!"

The security of our empire depends on the directions taken by Muslim policy. If overcautious and tactless, that policy would expose us to perilous complications, should the day come when we need all our resources and all our strength for a supreme struggle. If firm, benevolent, and just, it prepares magnificent reserves of men for us; it participates in the growth of our military might, at well as in the influence of our civilization, that is, in the prestige and greatness of France.[7]

The recently unified Italy was a latecomer on the imperial scene. In 1881, it found itself divested of Tunisia but was able to acquire Eritrea within the framework of the partitioning of Africa. Its expansion was halted by the defeat of Adoua in 1896 at the hands of the Ethiopians. To assert its ranking as a European power, it had to acquire a true colonial patrimony that would allow it to channel to its own advantage the permanent hemorrhaging of emigration overseas. It had long had its sights on the Ottoman province of Tripolitana, where it was the primary European investor. The Moroccan affair gave it the opportunity to act. On September 29, 1911, Italy declared war on the Ottoman Empire. It succeeded without too much difficulty in seizing the coastal zone of Cyrenaica and Tripolitana, from which practically all the troops had been withdrawn. The British forbade Ottoman reinforcements from passing through Egypt, which was still theoretically a province of the empire. But the Young Turks managed to smuggle through officers, who collaborated with the tribes in an exhausting guerilla war against the Italian troops.

Powerless to achieve recognition of their conquest, the Italians turned to the eastern Mediterranean and occupied the Dodecanese Islands. Dealing at the same time with an Albanian revolt that united Christians and Muslims against Ottoman domination, the Young Turk regime was in crisis. Even though it obtained an overwhelming victory in the elections of early 1912, thanks to the massive involvement of the state apparatus, it found itself discredited. In the summer of that year, facing the threat of a military coup, the regime was obliged to cede its power to the liberals. The new government granted quasi-independence to Albania in September 1912 and established peace with Italy by signing the Treaty of Lausanne on October 15, 1912. The Ottoman Empire recognized the annexation of Tripolitana and of Cyrenaica, where the sultan, in his capacity as caliph, retained his spiritual authority over the Muslims. The Italians pledged to evacuate the Dodecanese. In the following days, the principal European powers recognized Italian sovereignty over what had become Libya. Now the task was to secure the conquest of the interior, where the guerilla war continued. The large Sanusiyya brotherhood became the chief adversary.

The empire had yielded to the Albanians and the Italians only because its survival was at stake: a new conflagration was brewing in the Balkans.

The Balkan Wars and the Fate of the Ottoman Empire

The Tripolitanian War provided the opportunity to the enemy brothers in the Balkans to liquidate the Ottoman presence there. Despite their contradictory ambitions, they succeeded in forming a coalition, officially to resolve the question of Macedonia. When the Ottoman Empire rejected their demands, war was declared on October 17, 1912. The empire, completely isolated, suffered defeat after defeat. The Balkan provinces were dismembered. On December 3, an armistice was reached, to allow a European conference to convene in London. The Ottomans refused to abandon Thrace and Adrianople. On January 23, 1913, the CUP staged a coup d'état and returned to power. War resumed on February 3, and Adrianople fell into the hands of the Bulgarians on March 28. At the signing of the Treaty of London on May 30, 1913, the Ottomans held only a thin strip of European territories around the capital.

The victors could not agree on the division of the spoils. War began again in late June, this time with the Bulgarians against the Serbs and Greeks. The

Ottomans took the opportunity to recover Thrace and Adrianople. The Treaty of Bucharest of August 10, 1913, put an end to the conflict, and a whole series of complementary treaties redrew the map of the Balkans.

The war, with all its violence, gave rise to new waves of Muslim refugees, most of them headed toward Anatolia. All the Balkan states were officially Christian and Orthodox—with the exception of Albania, which was majority Muslim but did not include Kosovo and some possessions of Austria-Hungary. In the Balkans, the Muslims had become minorities; considered foreign or alien by nature, they were excluded from plans to form a nation. They were accused of being "Turks," even if they spoke a Slavic language. The liquidation of European Turkey did not put an end to Balkanization and ethnic cleansing. The history of that peninsula in the twentieth century would remain particularly bloody and tragic.

The European powers had attentively followed the Balkan Wars. Talk of partitioning what remained of the Ottoman Empire resumed, especially since the Moroccan question was now settled. But Europe's division into two large allied blocs made any amicable accord difficult. In addition, the naval competition between Britain and Germany had direct repercussions in the Mediterranean. Imperial Germany launched the naval armaments race in 1898, forcing Great Britain to pursue closer ties with France and Russia.

The competition had as much to do with the use of the most modern technology as with the number and might of the ships. At issue was the shift from coal to oil fuel. And though Great Britain was one of the major global producers of coal, it did not possess petroleum resources, even in its empire. To refuel, it had to depend on American and Russian production. That dependence was unacceptable. The British first took an interest in Persia, which had begun to produce petroleum in 1980, and the Admiralty became the primary shareholder in the Anglo-Persian Oil Company. It was suspected that the Ottoman Empire had comparable oilfields, and the British began competing for concessions.

It became clear that, in the event of conflict, Great Britain would have to withdraw its Mediterranean fleet to strengthen the Home Fleet. The naval conversations of 1912 culminated in a Franco-British accord. If a European war were imminent, France would move its fleet from the Atlantic to the Mediterranean, where it would meet the British fleet moving in the opposite direction, in order to assure protection of the Army of Africa on its way to the metropolis. The British, even in the case of undeclared war, would assure protection of the French Atlantic coasts and of the English Channel. Kitchener vehemently protested: over the medium term, the departure of the Mediterranean fleet would mean the loss of Malta, Cyprus, and Egypt, and the weakening of the British positions in India, China, and the Pacific.

Most concretely, the fate of the Arab provinces was at stake. The Balkan War dealt a terrible blow to Ottoman authority. There was open talk of deep reforms, even of reuniting Syria with Egypt, thereby extending the direct influence of the British. That was unacceptable for French diplomacy, which wanted to see the results of the naval conversations translated into political terms. After a clarification from the British government, Prime Minister Jules-Henri Poincaré was able to declare to the Senate on December 21, 1912, that Great Britain recognized the predominance of France in Syria and Lebanon.

France thereby opened the debate about the future of what remained of the Ottoman Empire.

The autonomist Arab movements were among the first to draw the conclusions of the Poincaré declaration. Having had a large margin of freedom after the Ottoman defeats in the Balkans, they now had to deal with the desire of the Ottoman government, in practice now a CUP dictatorship, to restore the authority of the central power. They realized that the application of their program of decentralizing reforms could come about only with the support of the great powers, in other words, through an internationalization of the "Syrian question." They even wanted to appeal to foreign—that is, European—advisers who would be granted broad powers.

The risk of such internationalization was that it might lead to the loss of France's privileged position in Syria. Beginning in early spring 1913, the French strategy, defined in the Syrian Affairs Commission of the Ministry of Foreign Affairs, was in essence to give the foremost role to the Ottoman government. The Balkan Wars had marked a diminution in French influence, since, in the former European Turkey, capitulations, the religious protectorate, and consular protections were abolished all at once. Although the victor states were compelled to take on a portion of Ottoman debt, the Caisse de la Dette Publique did not exert control over Ottoman finances. Any additional partitioning would mean a further reduction in French influence.

The French strategy consisted of obtaining recognition for a privileged zone of influence in Syria, while preserving an active presence in the Ottoman Empire as a whole. France was obliged to agree to an Arab congress in Paris, but it refused to support a secession movement.

The Arab Congress of Paris opened on June 18, 1913. Its president made a famous appeal to the West and to Europe, which he contrasted to Ottoman domination:

> The West is at present the guide to the East. However great the danger of assimilating all the ideas of the West may appear to some, it is less serious than that of remaining perfectly rigid and motionless. Since we ourselves are going to profit at no cost from an experience and expertise that Europe acquired at the price of great sacrifices, we owe the West a great debt of gratitude.
>
> We will be grateful for everything we take from it, as it was grateful to our ancestors for everything it owes them.

Those in Europe who prevent us from raising our voices are wrong. They have only themselves to blame for having taught us freedom! If any of you judge our success impossible or improbable, remember what the West was before becoming what it is.[8]

Just as the Congressists refrained from speaking of an independent Arab state, so too did French diplomacy confine itself to discreet approval. In the months that followed, it was clear that a triangular relationship had been established between the Ottoman authority, the Arab reformists of Syria, and France, whose predominant influence was recognized. Through a series of accords, theoretically of a commercial nature and including railroad concessions and potential petroleum resources, the powers divided up de facto what remained of the Ottoman Empire: to France, Syria; to Germany, Anatolia and the northern part of Mesopotamia; to Great Britain, all the regions bordering the Red Sea, the Indian Ocean, and the Persian Gulf. Nevertheless, it was in everyone's interest to maintain the Ottoman authority. The CUP, which governed in a quasi-dictatorial fashion, was increasingly oriented toward a form of Turkish nationalism, while seeking at the same time to relaunch the Ottoman economy through both new European investments and the constitution of a Turkish and Muslim middle class.

The management of economic and political interests sometimes clashed with other imperatives, such as reopening the Armenian question. On the model of the former Macedonia, the Europeans attempted to impose control on the eastern provinces of Anatolia.

CHAPTER 16

THE GREAT WAR AND THE BEGINNING OF EMANCIPATION

THE OTTOMAN EMPIRE IN WORLD WAR I

European rivalries in the Muslim world were one of the aggravating factors in the march toward war, but in 1914 all the conflicts appeared to be resolved. Imperial Germany, not possessing colonies in that vast region of the world, had largely refrained from intervening in the Balkan Wars. It returned to its posture as the friend of Islam and the protector of the Ottoman Empire, giving rise, among the Franco-British, to the specter of a pan-Islamism of Germanic inspiration.

The assassination in Sarajevo of Archduke Francis Ferdinand was a remote consequence of the Treaty of Berlin, which placed Bosnia-Herzegovina under Austrian administration, making the dual monarchy the enemy of Serbia, whose historical aim was to unify the "southern Slavs." The mechanisms of the alliances, combined with national passions and the sense among many that war was inevitable, allow us understand how, this time, European diplomacy was unable to avoid a war whose intensity and capacity for destruction was unimaginable.

Control of the Muslim world was secondarily at stake in the "European civil war," as it was designated by the last generation of the twentieth century. France and Great Britain conceived of themselves as great Islamic powers because of the millions of Muslims living in their colonial empire. The same was true for Russia. That colonial integration had been the result of a century and a half of recent history. Although the French Army of Africa and the British Army of India could levy large contingents from these populations, the Islamic peoples under domination nevertheless appeared to make the allies vulnerable against a Germany that was now openly protective of Islam, and which succeeded in drawing the Ottoman Empire into its camp and into the war on November 2, 1914.

The desire for emancipation from European rule was the primary driving force behind the Young Turk regime's decision. Russia was more than ever the hereditary enemy, and there was a desire to liberate the Muslim peoples of the Caucasus. France and Great Britain, because of their control over the economy, were considered the major obstacles to economic emancipation. On September 9, 1914, the Ottoman Empire unilaterally denounced the capitulations, a move that was rejected by the powers of the Triple Entente. They nevertheless proved ready to open discussions leading to greater equality, provided the Ottomans would maintain strict neutrality in the conflict under way. After the Battle of the Marne, the Entente Powers took a much tougher stance, which precipitated the rift.

As a consequence of these events, the Triple Entente again found itself in a defensive position against the pan-Islamist threat. Of course, the Muslim populations proved particularly loyal to the Europeans during calls for holy war launched by the sultan-caliph, but anxieties remained. It should be noted that the Ottoman Empire launched its jihad against the "oppressive entity that bears the name 'Triple Entente' . . . whose national pride takes extreme pleasure in the subjection of thousands of Muslims." Because the Ottoman Empire belonged to the Central Powers, it could not make any reference to a Christian enemy, which was in keeping both with nineteenth-century reformist thought and with the increasingly national character of the war.

The first use of counterpropaganda consisted of denouncing the Ottoman caliphate for being illegitimate because it was non-Arab. *Fatwas* were issued to that effect by various religious authorities of the colonial empires. But caution prevailed. In British India, the Friday prayer still invoked the name of the caliph of Constantinople, even among the troops levied to combat his armies.

The question of the caliphate preoccupied the French in particular. The Commission Interministérielle des Affaires Musulmanes collected various notes on that subject. In 1915, Lyautey boldly proposed the constitution of a "Western caliphate," with the sultan of Morocco as commander of believers. That caliphate was to encompass the French colonial empire as a whole. There would therefore be a "French Islam." That proposal elicited protests from the other colonial proconsuls of North Africa, who did not want to be answerable to Morocco.

The French also considered inciting a Syrian revolt, but that would have entailed sending precious troops to the East, at a time when all the available men were needed on the French front. For a time, the Allies were content to maintain the Ottoman Empire under their tutelage. But the decision to launch the Dardanelles expedition, which was believed capable of putting an end to the war, raised the question of the territorial goals of the conflict. The Russians demanded Constantinople, their historical objective for at least two centuries. The Franco-British were obliged to acquiesce and to accept a partitioning of the empire.

Although French and British interests were of the same nature, their ways of approaching the future of the Arab provinces were totally different. For French decision-makers, the pre-1914 "France of the Levant" constituted the frame of reference and was to be preserved and extended. That voluntary assimilation of French culture made it possible to dream of a greater France, whose universal vocation would be harmoniously wed to its imperial designs. Adopting the discourse of the French geographers, who evoked a "natural Syria," the colonial faction became a "Syrian faction," integrating a certain number of exiles from that region into the Comité Central Syrien and its press organ, the *Correspondance d'Orient*.

For the British of that generation, by contrast, Levantinism represented the worst of moral flaws. The British specialists on Cairo, as a result of their naturally differentialist view of the world, and in view of the scope of French advantages, had fallen under the spell of the cult of Arab authenticity and purity. That purity was incarnated first and foremost in the desert Bedouins, gradually dissipating in the settled peasant populations and in the city dwellers.

The French and British immediately considered countering the Ottoman jihad by appealing to an authority other than the sultan-caliph. Hussein bin Ali, emir and sharif of Mecca and head of the Hashemite family, was naturally the best candidate. He had the ability both to incite an Arab revolt and to call into question the religious authority of Constantinople. Sir Henry MacMahon, who succeeded Kitchener—now minister of war—in Cairo, was assigned the task of negotiating. Coming from the Indian administration, he had no particular familiarity with the Near East and relied on the advice of the Anglo-Egyptians, small groups of specialists and amateurs such as the archaeologist T. E. Lawrence, who wanted to expand the Egyptian experiment to the region as a whole.

The negotiation unfolded via a secret exchange of letters. The possibility of an Arab caliphate for the sharif was suggested to him. The risky circumstances of the exchange were coupled with semantic ambiguity. As good Britons, the men of Cairo contrasted the Levantines to the "pure" Arabs, a notion incomprehensible to their interlocutor, who held the genealogical view that the Arabs all descended from the same ancestor. No map was drawn up, and major points remained to be resolved. According to London and Cairo, the Arab state or states to be constituted would be located in the interior of the countries. The coastal Levantine regions would be under the direct control of the French and British.

The subsequent negotiation between the British representative, Sir Mark Sykes, and the French representative, Georges Picot, unfolded on that foundation. The aim was to establish the cartography of the French plan, called "Syria," and of the British plan, named "Arabia." After some vicissitudes, the result of their work was ratified through an exchange of correspondence between Paul Cambon, French ambassador to London, and the British Foreign Secretary, Edward Grey, in May 1916. Everything was approved by Russia, which received a large part of Anatolia, and later by Italy.

The Dardanelles expedition, from April to December 1915, became one of the bloodiest episodes of the war, with 200,000 dead and wounded among the Triple Entente forces, versus 120,000 on the Ottoman side. On the western fronts, regular armies fought terrifying battles; but from the Baltic to the Red Sea and even to the borders of India, civilians were the first victims of violence, which continued until the early 1920s and caused millions of deaths.

Even though, proportionally, Eastern Christendom paid the heaviest human cost during these terrible years, millions of Muslims were also victims of the conflicts arising from the European civil war.

In the Ottoman space, one of the main causes was the Allied blockade, supposedly directed at the enemy's war effort. The previous communications network had largely used sea routes, and the Ottoman army had requisitioned pack animals; as a result, the blockade undermined the entire resupply circuit. Many regions of Anatolia and Syria were stricken by scarcity, which in some sectors, such as Mount Lebanon, turned into a famine primarily affecting Christians.

Throughout that period, the Young Turk regime conducted itself ruthlessly. After the terrible defeat of the Caucasus during the winter of 1914–1915, using as a pretext the immediate danger of a Russian invasion of Anatolia, the Ottoman government gave the order to deport the Armenian populations to Syria. In a large portion of the regions concerned, that deportation became the occasion for massacres in which the authorities and the local populations were directly involved. About two-thirds of the Armenians of Anatolia died in that upheaval. In the following years, military operations and epidemics associated with the conditions of scarcity gravely affected the Muslim populations, though to a lesser extent than they did the Armenians. In Syria, the Mount Lebanon famine raised the question of the Ottomans' direct responsibility, which is still a matter of debate.

The Ottoman authority, represented by Jamal Pasha, conducted a harsh repression of the Arab autonomists, who were accused of treason on behalf of France. A number of notables were executed in Damascus and Beirut, while those under less suspicion were interned in Anatolia. Those who could escape went back to Egypt. That repression played a major role in the people's disaffection with the Ottoman regime, though a significant portion of the elites remained faithful to the empire to the end.

In Mesopotamia, the British landed in the Basra region, securing the protection of the Gulf and the neighboring oilfields. The British army then began to advance up the Indus Valley. But its vanguard went too far and, finding itself surrounded in Kut, it had to surrender. That conquest of Mesopotamia was achieved by the Army of India, which already saw that region annexed to the Indian empire, with the importation of millions of Hindu workers to develop it through major hydraulic projects. Its architects saw the plan as a noble mission destined to feed the rest of the world.

THE REST OF THE MUSLIM WORLD

Persia, which knew it was particularly vulnerable, proclaimed its neutrality on November 1, 1914, without having the means to repel foreign interference. Russian troops, however, had been present in the southern part of the country since 1912, and the British were forced to acknowledge the expansion of the Russian zone of influence. The Ottoman armies penetrated that region without declaring war, portraying themselves as liberators. They were well received at first, but came to be despised because of the taxes they imposed and the devastation of the war. Anatolian Christians also took refuge in these regions and went over to the Russians' side. After the Russian revolution of February–March 1917, the Russian troops scattered and anarchy increased, with Muslim massacres of Christians in the Urmia region.

It was a sign of the times that the British coupled their traditional defense of the Indian route with protection of oil resources. In the south, they organized local forces headed by British officers, but met with an uprising of the tribes in the province of Fars, encouraged by a German mission commanded by the famous Wilhelm Wassmuss. The Germans tried to stir up other regions of Iran, as well as to incite an Anglo-Afghan war. They sent in agents to that end, in what was one of the last episodes of the European Great Game, which had begun in the late eighteenth century. For part of 1915, a good share of the Persian territory was in the hands of the pro-German dissidents. The shah refused to join a pro-German government and remained in Tehran, but his supposedly pro-English government now controlled only the capital. The Anglo-Indian army intervened en masse to repress the pro-German and pro-Ottoman movements. After the Russian collapse, the British troops headed back to the Caucasus and temporarily occupied Baku.

These troop movements and various uprisings devastated the country. Inevitably, famine and epidemics took hold, claiming tens of thousands of lives. The state no longer existed and, after the Russian retreat, Great Britain seemed to have assumed control in a lasting manner.

Russian central Asia experienced relative calm for the first two years of the war, but there were rumblings of discontent, caused by the advance of Russian colonization at the expense of the nomadic populations. The announcement in June 1916 that men not required to do military service would be mobilized into work units set off the explosion. The Russian agricultural settlers were the initial target of the revolt of summer 1916. Two thousand were killed, and the repression was very harsh. A third of the Kirgiz took refuge in China. Many lands were confiscated. After the Russian revolution of February–March 1917, the conflict between the Russians and the indigenous people increased, especially since the provisional government was speaking only in vague terms of the region's future. The Muslims attempted to organize political movements in preparation for the future elections and distanced themselves from the conflicts between Russians. After the October Revolution, they refused to recognize the Bolsheviks' power. In February 1918, the Soviets forcibly established their authority, but central Asia gradually sank into anarchy, concurrent with the Russian civil war.

In Egypt, the Ottoman Empire's entry into the war gave the British the opportunity to depose Khedive Abbas Hilmi and to proclaim their protectorate over Egypt. Egypt became a sultanate, entrusted to a member of the khedivial family of Hussein Kamil, a sign of its emancipation from the Ottoman Empire. The British also made a vague promise to move Egypt toward "self-government," a form of association in which the governed assumed some of the tasks of governance.

Egypt became the major rear base of the British. The Ottomans boldly launched an offensive on the Suez Canal in February 1915. The artillery of French and British warships positioned in the canal successfully repelled the attack. Then the British undertook a slow and methodical conquest of Sinai, consisting of short advances followed by long halts, which allowed them to establish a railroad line and a freshwater pipeline. At that rate, it took them almost two years to reach the Palestine border.

Despite their noble proclamations about their interest in the well-being of the Egyptian population, the British repeatedly requisitioned pack animals and peasant labor to deal with the logistics of the troops' advance. Although, officially, the Egyptians did not fight, most of those whom the British used found themselves under fire. The Egyptian peasantry suffered greatly throughout those years, but the urban milieus took advantage of the first stages of a necessary industrialization to produce what could no longer be imported from Europe and to resupply the British armies of Egypt and the Dardanelles.

In Libya, the Sanusiyya resumed war against the Italian occupiers, who quickly lost control of a large part of the territory. The insurrection turned against the French of Tunisia and the British of Egypt. The war also spread to Chad and Niger, which were under French domination. The insurrection received assistance from a small Turko-German military mission that arrived by submarine. The French, also using modern means of transportation such as trucks, managed to block the brotherhood's advance. In Egypt, after initial successes, the Sanusiyya was pushed back into the Western Desert. The Allies negotiated a compromise. In 1917, the brotherhood was granted a form of territorial autonomy over the territories it controlled. This was a suspension of conflicts more than a true political settlement.

That desert war was the concrete realization of the great colonial anxiety about an Islamic uprising. That fear had led the colonials to repress the independent brotherhoods as a preventive measure and thus to push them toward revolt.

In Morocco, Lyautey refused to evacuate the interior of the country, even though a good share of the French troops had been recalled. He established a permanent deployment to use his remaining forces to best advantage, wagering on the movements and surveillance of the rebel tribes. Beginning in 1917, the French resumed their "oil-spot" territorial expansion.

North Africa played an important role in the French war effort: 173,000 Algerians, 80,000 Tunisians, and 40,000 Moroccans were mobilized. Of the nearly 300,000 men, 260,000 fought in the trenches, and 45,000 of them met their death there. In addition, 180,000 conscripted or volunteer workers were sent to toil in the metropolis, in factories, transport ships, or the fields. That fellowship in bloodshed foreshadowed a change in colonial relations.

The scarcity of transport ships resulting from the submarine war demonstrated the inadequacies of economic development in the French possessions, including Algeria. Far from taking advantage of the historical circumstances to become industrialized, the three countries ran into a number of bottlenecks, which resulted in a drop in industrial, mining, and agricultural production.

A Change in Perspectives

The strategy of the combatants was to promote uprisings of Muslims in the other camp. They thereby toppled the colonial or Ottoman order and opened the way to the rise of national movements. The first priority of the Triple Entente strategists was to thwart the Ottoman jihad by pandering to Arab sentiment. Such was the content, for example, of a proclamation by scholars from Al-Azhar University, made at the instigation of the Allies on January 21, 1916, and addressed to "our brothers, soldiers of Arabia, Syria, Iraq, and the Hejaz":

> You are being deceived by the Turks, who are using you to realize their own aims. A few of them, who have sold out to Germany, lure you with false promises. These individuals hate France and England only because these two countries have supported and continue to support the Arab element in Turkey, and because their representatives are always ready to stay the hand of criminals who want to destroy the Arab element.
>
> Consider the part of Iraq currently occupied by the English; consider the fate of Lebanon and of the Western Arabs protected by France; then you will perceive the difference existing between the conduct of the English and French, and that of the Turks.
>
> The Turks have a grudge against the Arabic language, the language of the Prophet and the Qur'an, the language of prayer, and seek to destroy it and substitute their own. Therefore our language, hunted down everywhere in Turkey, was able to find asylum only in two regions that have escaped the hold of the Turks, thanks to France and England: Syria and Egypt.
>
> In Syria, the Lebanese, through their many writings, and the Jesuits, by their talent, have become the propagators of the Arabic language. In Egypt, thanks to the assistance of the English, that language has thrived. These two powers never refused their protection to the Arab element; just recently, when the Arab Congress met in Paris, France offered it all its solicitude. What did Turkey do? It hanged a dozen Arabs. If you ask me why Turkey bears a grudge against our element, I will reply that it is because Turkey senses it is the usurper. The Qur'an, the Prophet, and Islamic law belong to us; Turkey wants to deprive us of them. It committed a first crime, and it will not recoil from others.[1]

The Arab revolt of June 1916 was the culmination of that strategy. The original discourse of the revolt, represented by Sharif Hussein's first proclamations, was more Islamic than Arabist in nature; what was rejected was the Young Turks' modernizing atheism.

One of France's first actions, in September 1916, was to organize a pilgrimage of Maghrebian Muslims to Mecca. Si Kaddour Benghabrit, a Muslim personality from Algeria who had already rendered considerable services to France in Moroccan affairs, was assigned to lead it. A permanent hotel was set up to serve the pilgrims from the French empire. The idea of a Western caliphate was abandoned in favor of a "French Islam" that would bring together the populations of the empire and the Muslims who were beginning to have a significant presence in the metropolis. Benghabrit became the advocate of moderate reforms in Algeria to emancipate the indigenous peoples from the unjust treatment they suffered and to allow them to better assert their Arab and Muslim personality, without calling French domination into question. That was the message of a memorandum he sent to the prime minister in April 1917.

The absence of unrest in Algeria and the subsequent participation of the local population in the war effort was a happy surprise for French policymakers, and Benghabrit was sharp enough to allude to it. In the colonial view, the subject people's loyalty had to be rewarded, and the argument for French gratitude became a particularly strong theme. The indigenophiles wanted to move forward, but in the direction of association, so that the Algerian Arabs could benefit from the "very liberal regime," that of the Tunisians and Moroccans.

For Benghabrit, there could be no question of

> suddenly granting to more than four million subjects prerogatives that would make them ungovernable and would bankrupt colonization. To dream of the Arab's complete assimilation is the worst foolishness, which could arise only in minds steeped in Rousseau's theories. It is as impossible to train their minds as to turn a yellow man white. And, may I add, it is not even desirable. Progress can occur more harmoniously through the collaboration of the races, with each preserving its genius, than by fusion, whose results will always be mediocre.[2]

The issue at hand was to abolish discrimination, raise the level of education of the native populations, and make public employment more available to them.

From the perspective prevailing at the time, the Arab revolt did not call into question the colonial system and would lead to a more complex form of indirect government, with the new Arab state or states under the supervision of European advisers, in accordance with the movement's demand for reforms in 1912–1913. It was on that principle that the so-called Sykes-Picot Agreement was built: in the French zone of influence, the advisers would be French; in the British zones of influence, the advisers would be British.

Thanks to the Hashemites, the Franco-British would thus control the holy cities of the Hejaz. Similarly, through the conquest of Mesopotamia, the Shiite holy cities would come under British influence; and since Persia too would be absorbed by the British zone, there would no longer be any risk of pan-Islamism, even if the Ottoman caliphate survived.

The Russian Revolution of February–March 1917 and the United States' entry into the war in April 1917 threw these prospects into confusion. President Woodrow Wilson attempted to impose the right of peoples to self-determination, though he was primarily thinking of the European peoples. As the partner and not the ally of the Triple Entente, the United States was not bound by the secret accords reached between the European powers. It did not declare war on the Ottoman Empire, which for the time being it sought to treat with tact. The immediate concern of American missionaries, who had a great deal of influence with President Wilson, was the survival of the Armenians and the Arabs, who constituted most of their local clientele.

In January 1918, the twelfth of Wilson's Fourteen Points set out the American perspective:

> The Turkish portions of the present Ottoman Empire should be assured a secure sovereignty, but the other nationalities which are now under Turkish rule should be assured an undoubted security of life and an absolutely unmolested opportunity of an autonomous development, and the Dardanelles should be permanently opened as a free passage to the ships and commerce of all nations under international guarantees.[3]

Sykes was one of the first to understand the changes under way. As the British armies gradually made their advance in Mesopotamia and Palestine, his public declarations came to be marked with what looked increasingly like a right to self-determination. At least in discourse, it was necessary to abandon references to imperialism and to favor the new right to nationhood. In a memorandum from the first half of 1918 regarding Mesopotamia, Sykes was able to express himself forcefully:

> Our position in Mesopotamia if judged by pre-war standards is sound. Our armed forces are quite able to hold the ground. The population is tranquil. Our rule is popular. Our relations with the surrounding tribes are exceedingly friendly. If America had not come into the war, if the Russian revolution had not taken place, if the idea of no annexations had not taken root, if the world spirit of this time was the world spirit of 1887, there would be no reason why we should take any steps to consolidate our position against a peace conference, it would be good enough.
>
> However, we have to look at the problem through entirely new spectacles, Imperialism, annexation, military triumph, Prestige, White men's burden's, have been expunged from the popular political vocabulary, consequently Protectorates, spheres of interest or influence, annexations, bases etc, have to be consigned to the Diplomatic lumber-room.

If Britishers are to run Mesopotamia we must find up to date reasons for their doing so and up to date formulae for them to work the country on. We shall have to convince our own Democracy that Britishers ought to do the work and the Democracies of the world as well.[4]

The appeal to Zionism, which Sykes was the first to make, can be understood within that perspective. Here was a national movement that pleased the Anglo-Saxon Protestants. If the call for a national Jewish homeland in Palestine was answered, it could attract the favor of the very influential American Jews, who until that time had been considered pro-German, and of the Russian Jews, whose role in revolutionary Russia was poorly understood. Finally, Zionism was an instrument for calling into question the Franco-British accords, at least the part regarding the internationalization of Palestine. It must not be forgotten that the theory of differentialism defined the Jews of the world as constituting a "Jewish people"—it encountered no particular objections on that point— whereas the French assimilationist view rejected that perspective. The Israelite was the Jewish counterpart of the Levantine.

On that matter, Sykes had the support of the Anglo-Egyptians, who wanted above all to make Palestine a zone under British control, in order to better protect the Suez Canal. For some, such as T. E. Lawrence, who had thrown himself heart and soul into the Arab revolt—even running the risk of losing his way there—it was necessary to call into question all the Franco-British accords. Lawrence had taken on the mission of transporting Emir Faisal (Sharif Hussein's son, who commanded the southern army) to Damascus. With that fait accompli, the partitioning would be called into question. He clashed with Sykes, who was still intent on cooperating with France. Conversely, Lawrence refrained from any intervention in Palestine and opposed recruiting Arab Palestinians.

Lawrence and Sykes shared the same overall vision. They saw a sort of springtime for the Eastern peoples (Armenians, Kurds, Arabs, Jews), who would definitively emancipate themselves from the Ottomans and would live harmoniously under the accepted but temporary tutelage of the British. They did not perceive the danger stemming from the contradiction in the national goals of each of these peoples. And they fended off future conflicts by appealing for brotherhood among the different races and religions and, for the time being, caution in the expression of demands. Some French people, such as Louis Massignon, then an active member of the Picot mission assigned to represent French interests in the Near East, shared that political vision, though he wanted to replace the British with the French in the advisory mission.

Despite clear-headed warnings from those of the old school, such as Lord Curzon, and after several successive drafts, the British government adopted the so-called Balfour Declaration on November 2, 1917. Although the prospect of European domination remained in place, it was now accepted that the nationality principle, henceforth the right of peoples to self-determination, applied to the Muslim populations, or at least to some of them.

THE FIRST ARBITRATIONS

With the arrival of winter in 1917–1918, military operations in the Near East bogged down. The Ottoman army, led by German officers, mounted a heroic resistance, despite being increasingly at a disadvantage both in numbers and materiel. The British advance was also hindered by troops being transferred to the European western front, where the final battle would be played out. The same was true for the army of Salonika, called the Army of the Orient, which formed under French command after the evacuation of the Dardanelles.

The Russian withdrawal from the war and the conclusion of the Treaty of Brest-Litovsk on March 3, 1918, marked the end of the threat to the Ottoman Empire from the hereditary enemy. The empire recovered the Caucasian territories of Kars, Ardahan, and Batum, which it had lost in 1877. The Young Turks were greatly tempted to posit the unity of all Turkish peoples, from the Mediterranean to China, by adopting Touranian ideas. The first phase would be to establish Ottoman authority over the Caucasus as a whole, by overcoming the Christian states then being formed (Georgia and Armenia). Germany opposed the plan, citing the priority to be given to the British threat. But the arrival of British troops in Baku changed the situation on the ground. The final Ottoman offensive was launched in early September 1918 and managed to penetrate as far as Azerbaijan. Although it was already too late for the Ottoman Empire, the Caucasus became entrenched in a cycle of all-out wars.

The retreat of troops from the Russian front gave the Germans on the western front a numerical advantage, at least until the American forces arrived. The Franco-British had to resist the blunt force of the German army by using their abilities to rapidly move strategic reserves. As the war of position turned into a war of maneuver, the enormous advantage of receiving regular supplies of oil increasingly became the determining factor. The Allied armies of 1918 had massive numbers of trucks, tanks, and airplanes. In August 1918, the Allies began to take the offensive and continuously attacked on both sides of the front. According to Lord Curzon, their victory came on a wave of oil. French ruling circles thought more in terms of a "useful Syria," providing access to petroleum resources, than of a "natural Syria," which would have particularly high management costs and uncertain benefits.

Following on the first victories of the Triple Entente, the peripheral armies saw action in mid-September 1918, in Iraq and Palestine as well as in Salonika. The collapse of Bulgaria on September 26 isolated the Ottoman Empire, and its capital became vulnerable. In early October, the Ottomans attempted to open armistice negotiations, but the British wanted to seize the maximum territory beforehand, so as to be in a position of strength during the final settlement. In Syria, Emir Faisal's troops entered Damascus on October 1, 1918. The French established their authority in Beirut on October 10.

In many respects, the Armistice of Moudros of October 30, 1918, was a capitulation that the British imposed unilaterally, without consulting their allies. It unconditionally opened the Ottoman territories as a whole to the Allied forces. In the weeks that followed, the capital was occupied, as was a portion of the Anatolian provinces.

At a time when the Ottoman Empire was foundering, the political weight of the United States became increasingly apparent. Wilson clearly let it be known that he opposed the constitution of zones of influence and preferred the tutelage of the conquered regions by a neutral power on behalf of the League of Nations. To satisfy the U.S. president (and to play for time), France and Great Britain, after consulting him, published a joint declaration on November 7, 1918:

> The goal that France and Great Britain have in mind in pursuing the war in the East, unleashed by German ambition, is the complete and definitive emancipation of the peoples long oppressed by the Turks, and the establishment of national governments and administrations that draw their authority from the initiative and free choice of the native populations.
>
> To carry out these intentions, France and Great Britain have agreed to encourage and aid the establishment of native governments and administrations in Syria and Mesopotamia, now liberated by the Allies, and in the territories whose liberation they are pursuing, and to recognize these entities as soon as they are effectively established. Far from wanting to impose one kind of institution or another on the populations of these regions, the only concern of France and Great Britain is to assure, through their support and efficacious assistance, the normal functioning of the governments and administrations that the populations will have freely bestowed upon themselves. To assure impartial and equal justice for all, to facilitate the country's economic development by pressing for and encouraging local initiatives, to favor the spread of education, and to put an end to the divisions too long exploited by Turkish policy, such is the role that the two Allied governments claim in the liberated territories.[5]

The reference to Syria had multiple consequences on the ground. For example, Palestine, occupied by the British, claimed to belong to "southern Syria," in order to benefit from the promises in the declaration and to use them against Zionist ambitions. In Syria itself, the situation was particularly muddled. Faisal's adversaries proclaimed themselves Syrians and rejected the Arabs as uncivilized Bedouins. The same was true for the pro-French Christians. The Franco-British declaration made no reference to the Arabs. Faisal and his advisers acted intelligently, portraying themselves as nationalists who rejected a religious identity ("religion for each, the nation for all") and constructing an all-encompassing discourse addressed to the "Arab Syrian nation."

But on December 4, Clemenceau went to London to meet with Lloyd George. His aim was to work out the difficulties emerging in the Near East within the framework of an overall resolution of the war. During a private interview, Clemenceau abandoned Palestine and the vilayet of Mosul to the British, in exchange for assurances regarding the petroleum issues and the general settlement.

When the peace conference met, the Americans seemed to be the arbiters of the situation. President Wilson enjoyed enormous popularity. Although he was opposed to the fundaments of European imperialism, he was convinced that the non-European populations were not ready for independence and that they needed temporary oversight. The principle of the right of peoples to self-determination was transformed quite simply into the consent of the governed. It was on that basis that Versailles adopted the famous article 22 of the League of Nations covenant of April 28, 1919:

> To those colonies and territories which as a consequence of the late war have ceased to be under the sovereignty of the States which formerly governed them and which are inhabited by peoples not yet able to stand by themselves under the strenuous conditions of the modern world, there should be applied the principle that the well-being and development of such peoples form a sacred trust of civilisation and that securities for the performance of this trust should be embodied in this Covenant.
>
> The best method of giving practical effect to this principle is that the tutelage of such peoples should be entrusted to advanced nations who by reason of their resources, their experience or their geographical position can best undertake this responsibility, and who are willing to accept it, and that this tutelage should be exercised by them as Mandatories on behalf of the League. . . .
>
> Certain communities formerly belonging to the Turkish Empire have reached a stage of development where their existence as independent nations can be provisionally recognized subject to the rendering of administrative advice and assistance by a Mandatory until such time as they are able to stand alone. The wishes of these communities must be a principal consideration in the selection of the Mandatory.[6]

The principle of mandatories gave concrete form to the final push of European imperialism in the Muslim world, while at the same time condemning it. This was a result of the evolution in international relations during World War I. That transformation can be understood in several ways: first, in terms of the long evolution of independent Muslim societies and their complex process of modernization; second, as the aftereffect of the policies of the combatants during the war, who sought to stir up the "native" populations of the enemy empires; third, in terms of the difficult affirmation of a new international right founded on the equality of peoples; and fourth, in relation to the redefinition of the great powers' economic interests, with the emergence of petroleum interests.

For the time being, the great colonial empires remained in the Muslim territories, but colonial expansion ended, both because it lacked legitimacy and because the ruling powers realized that these empires were becoming increasingly difficult to manage, both in terms of their administrative costs and as a result of the growing burden of maintaining internal order and external protection. In the early postwar period, the British system was the first casualty.

The Birth of the Middle East

In early 1919, British power in the Muslim world seemed irresistible. Nearly a million soldiers were encamped from Egypt to Afghanistan, in countries that were theoretically independent or aspired to be so. But even though these consisted in large part of colonial troops, that burden became unbearable for British finances after the enormous expenditures of the war. In addition, the "white" troops who had volunteered for the war effort, or who had been conscripted to defend their homeland, would not tolerate being kept under military conditions. Nearly everywhere, the delay in demobilization gave rise to particularly worrisome mutinies. It took a few months to realize that the empire was overextended, and that it was necessary to begin a withdrawal, or at least a redeployment.

The debate pitted the defenders of a classic form of imperialism, based on the white man's burden, against the proponents of a "new imperialism" that would entail a rapid devolution of powers to the local authorities, while assuring the preservation of vital British interests. For the boldest in the second group, such as T. E. Lawrence, it was even possible to envision over the medium term the constitution of a Muslim "brown dominion" within the commonwealth under formation. The idea was truly to constitute states and nations. The Egyptian revolt of 1919 and the political impasse that followed, the withdrawal of British troops from Syria, the unrest in Palestine in 1920, and the Iraqi revolt during the same period all demonstrated the impossibility of continuing to apply the old imperial formula. Winston Churchill's arrival at the Colonial Office in 1921 and the creation of the Middle East Department institutionalized the new perspective.

The Middle East, which some ironically defined as the space between the Colonial Office and the Indian Office, would stand outside the institutional structure of the British Empire. It would be composed of "independent" states linked to Great Britain by bilateral treaties. These treaties would assure the security of the "imperial communication routes," defined as the seaways (the Suez Canal, the Red Sea, the Persian Gulf), the airways (a network under construction of military airports that would allow people to travel from England to India while remaining continuously in territories under British control or influence), and the oil pipelines to be constructed. Significantly, unlike at the beginning of the century, there was no mention of railroads. The new armies would be under the control, at least temporarily, of the British officers who organized them. Local military deployment would be considerably reduced, in favor of aviation capable of striking anywhere zones in a state of rebellion.

Empire by treaty was a radical innovation. It abandoned the traditional notion of territories in favor of networks designed to preserve the "useful" part of the new spaces. It entailed a change of mentalities on the part of colonial administrators, who had to accept the idea of a more or less rapid transfer of powers to the local elites. But though direct authority was destined to decline, interventionism remained a constant given. The high commissioner, then the British ambassador, would be a permanent actor on the political stage, responsible for making sure that personnel favorable to British interests remained in power.

The testing ground was the British mandate in Iraq, with the creation of a monarchy in 1921 entrusted to the Hashemite Faisal. Transjordan was created the same year, separated out from Palestine, and became an emirate with Faisal's elder brother Abdallah as its leader. In 1922, Egypt was granted independence, subject to conditions to be established by a treaty. The Arab countries of the Gulf coast remained protectorates, with little British intervention in internal affairs. The Kingdom of Saudi Arabia under formation was locked within the British defense system, and Ibn Sa'ud turned out to be an attentive partner of the ruling power.

In the Levant, the French both admired and feared the British model. At first, they sought to move in the same direction, seeking a partnership with Faisal. Extremists in both camps precipitated the failure of the compromise considered in late 1919, and the French army occupied Damascus in July 1920. As a result, Arab nationalism was defined as the enemy, not only for its capacity to do harm in the Near East but also because there was a risk it would spread to North Africa. The French opted to partition the territory. But for the medium term, the prospect was access to independence, with a transfer of technical skills and political powers.

ISLAM AND NATIONALISM

The Turkish war of independence illustrated the impossibility of establishing direct European domination. During the Peace Conference, the Europeans showed little appetite for administering Anatolia and were ready to entrust it to the Americans as a mandate. The Treaty of Sèvres of August 10, 1920, stipulated that Anatolia would be divided between the European powers and the Kurdish and Armenian states, leaving the Turks only the center of the Anatolian Peninsula. The national movement, led by the dissident Mustafa Kemal beginning in 1919, took the opportunity to form a coalition of all Muslims. An exhausting war of independence followed: it pushed the French back to Syria and drove out the Greeks. The Treaty of Lausanne of July 24, 1923, marked the death of the Ottoman Empire and ratified the existence of a completely independent Turkey (the capitulations were definitively abolished), after the elimination of the Ottoman sultanate and then of the Ottoman caliphate. The Republic of Turkey was proclaimed on October 29, 1923.

Kemalism planned to build a Turkish nation-state populated primarily by Muslims but belonging fully to Europe. This was a cultural revolution imposed from above, and it followed a systematic and coherent plan. The Kemalists proclaimed their desire to be modern. Population exchanges with Greece eliminated the large Anatolian Christian populations, which had suffered terribly from the massacres and forced displacements of the previous period. The aspiration was to break completely with the past. Secularism was imposed as a sign of progress. Turkey banned many outward displays of religious practice and subjected what remained of the religious institutions to close supervision, so much so that it is possible to speak of a state takeover of religion. The country adopted the Latin alphabet in 1928. Western-style patronymics became obligatory. Women in Turkey won the right to vote in 1935, ten years before women in France. In 1932, when a Turkish woman was named Miss Universe, it was considered a great national victory.

The people's fatigue after more than ten terrible years, and the prestige of the nation's savior, made it possible to impose a new national mythology, according to which the Turks were the descendants of the oldest inhabitants of Anatolia (the Hittites). This myth, however, denied the many thousands of years of that region's history. The plan was to reconstitute a nation on the basis of the Anatolian peasantry and of the many populations that had taken refuge in the Balkans and the rest of the vanished empire. That mythification became more extreme in the 1930s, now painting the Turks as the trustee of humanity's primordial civilization. The non-Muslim minorities, or rather, what remained of them, were marginalized; non-Turkish, even non-Sunni, Muslims were refused any identity proper to them. The government harshly repressed Kurdish revolts in defense of Islam and ethnic particularisms.

Europeanization involved adopting Western clothing as well as entire legal systems. The new regime proved particularly authoritarian, and its nationalism hypersensitive to any sign of foreign encroachment. Kemalism led to a national unanimism that rejected all pluralism.

The Republic of Turkey, with its nationalism and exclusivism, was altogether similar to the Balkan states, the successors of the Ottoman Empire. In fact, the republic signed the Balkan Pact of 1934. Although its population was Muslim, it thoroughly rejected the Muslim heritage, which it confused with that of the Arabs. Secularism and modernism created a new image for the country in Europe, both in the democracies and in the authoritarian systems.

As for Persia, in 1919 the British had attempted to take advantage of the historical circumstances and the eclipse of Russia to impose a quasi-protectorate there. Although the government accepted that accord, the Parliament would not ratify it, and the country seemed about to disintegrate after the ordeal of

World War I. A national uprising culminated in a coup d'état on February 11, 1921, under the leadership of Reza Khan, commander of the Cossack Brigade. The army became the principal organized force and gradually reestablished the country's territorial unity. In 1925, Reza Khan deposed the Qajar dynasty and founded his own. (The religious element was hostile to the idea of a republic because of the Kemalist example.)

The new shah, Reza Pahlavi, also styled himself an authoritarian modernizer. His first great success was to abolish the capitulations in 1928, thanks to the adoption of a civil code and penal laws inspired in great part by European models. The new regime attempted to establish nationalist feeling, based in large part on references to glories that predated Islam. In 1935, the country took the name "Iran," which, though already in common use among the population, primarily made it possible to impose an image in the outside world that was more modern than that of Persia. Secular education, for girls as well as boys, was set in place. The Shiite clergy who opposed these reforms were harshly repressed. In 1936, Iran banned the wearing of the veil. Unlike the Republic of Turkey, however, the new regime did not adopt a discourse of Westernization. Europe's contributions were defined in terms of tools and technologies, but the cultural touchstone was pre-Islamic Iran. For example, the solar calendar Iran adopted was a reference to Iranian history.

Reza Shah did not go nearly so far on the path of secularization as Mustafa Kemal. The shah's extremely brutal government made major cultural and economic changes. He succeeded in restoring the Iranian state and of extending his authority over the territory as a whole. The Soviet Union replaced tsarist Russia as the northern enemy. Wishing to limit British influence, Shah Pahlavi undertook a first test of strength of the petroleum concessions of the Anglo-Persian Oil Company, which would become the Anglo-Iranian Oil Company. In the 1930s, he sought a certain rapprochement with Nazi Germany, to better assure his country's independence, thereby stirring up Great Britain's anxieties.

As in the case of Kemalism, Iran's political independence from Europe seemed to depend on a voluntarist modernization and Europeanization policy, at the expense of the traditional religious institutions. This policy was also in continuity with the elitist reforms of earlier times. The Turkish and Iranian experiments represented the apogee, even the extreme limit, of earlier authoritarian reformism on the part of the state. These experiments had the merit of reestablishing the self-respect of the respective nations, thanks to their recovered independence and the extolling of largely mythified national glories. The price to be paid was heavy nonetheless. Even more than in the nineteenth century, authoritarian reformism marked a traumatic divorce between the continuity of Islamic culture and modernity, while stripping modernity of its essential component, the consent of the people expressed through liberal and democratic institutions.

A redoubtable trap was thereby constructed. The slightest slackening of authoritarianism risked eliciting an Islamic reaction that might contest imported modernity as a whole.

British India and the Trap of Communalism

In the second half of the nineteenth century, British India had been a focal point for Islamic reformism, which evolved alongside a similar reformism of Hinduism. That return to the origins entailed a growing reliance on the Arab sources of Islam. As in the rest of the Muslim world, the reformism at the start of the twentieth century tended to be divided between modernism and fundamentalism.

Until World War I, the Indian Muslims appeared to be the firmest supporters of British domination. The war against the Ottoman Empire and the recognition of the Sunni Islam caliphate were a formidable test of that support. In 1919, for the first time, a powerful popular movement united the Indian Muslims under the banner of maintaining the caliphate. There were several episodes of violence before the movement faded away, having been forced to face the reality of Mustafa Kemal's suppression of the caliphate. The Congress Party, led by Mahatma Gandhi, gave the movement its support, but the results were very mixed. The caliphate issue was linked to that of constituting a purely Islamic state, and the possibility of Indian independence raised the question of the Muslims' future status. The demand made at the time was to constitute a separate Indian Muslim electorate, which would allow the Muslims and the Hindus to share power.

Although some Muslims participated in Ghandism, in the name of the message of universal justice contained in the Qur'an, the strongest tendency was communalism, which united the Muslims based on their particular interests, at the expense of regional or national identifications linking them to the Hindus. Muslims also took an interest in pan-Islamist issues, particularly the Palestine question.

The British began the process of devolving powers by providing the indigenous people access to high public posts and by increasing the powers of the regional elected assemblies. In 1935, provincial autonomy became a reality. The proclaimed objective was gradual accession to the status of a Dominion. In the new political structures, separate electorates were constituted for minorities, including Muslims. Depending on their numerical importance, the Muslims sometimes played an essential role—in the provinces (Bengal, Punjab), for example, where they represented a significant share of the population—while elsewhere they were obliged to ally themselves with the Congress Party. Muslim identity was no longer merely cultural but took on a political reality. Nevertheless, it did not manage to find expression within a perspective encompassing India as a whole. The result was a lasting malaise, which translated into a defensive attitude and the reassertion of Muslim demands for a status of their own, with personal status laws and political guarantees vis-à-vis the Hindu majority. The proliferation of violence between the Hindu and the Muslim communities reinforced that separatist sentiment, but it did not yet take the form of a demand to constitute a distinct territory.

The discourse of the Congress Party was twofold in nature. For Gandhi, Indian nationalism had to return to its religious sources; under the reign of God, all religious groups would be protected and the poor elevated. For Jawaharal Nehru, by contrast, the adoption of the socialist and secular model would make it possible to move beyond religious oppositions. These orientations were not enough to calm the fears of minorities, who saw the Congress Party as the political expression of the Hindu majority.

The Hindu nationalists held the British responsible for dividing the society into communities, even as the British were doing their best to manage an increasingly difficult situation. In reality, what produced the new community consciousness was the modernization movement accompanying the spread of education: on one hand, religious reformism, which entailed a return to the sources; on the other, a political use of history. For the Indian radicals, Islam was defined as a foreign entity violently imposed on India; conversely, some Muslims exalted the glory days of the Timurid and Mogul empires, in order to demand recognition for the existence of two separate nations.

Wherever Muslims were greatly in the minority, the tendency of fundamentalists was to preach the existence of a Muslim culture and society constituting a totality in itself and based on the imitation of the Prophet's example. The purification of religion depended on the rejection of popular religious culture, accused of superstition, and of colonial culture. Stemming from that rejection was a form of pietism based on strict respect for religious norms. Paradoxically, though separatism advocated isolation from the rest of the world, it made possible the abandonment of any political or territorial frame of reference and a life apart within a majority non-Muslim society.

The Indian situation served as a counterexample to what was happening in Turkey and Iran. The absence of authoritarian modernism and the gradual establishment of liberal institutions within the context of religious pluralism encouraged the formation of political and even social separatism. To be sure, the same tendency could also be found in Hinduism: a rejection of traditional customs; the establishment of a religious practice based on a sacred text and with an idealized era as its frame of reference; and recourse to new means of propaganda, dissemination, and communication (the printed word for the most part). Hindus as well as Muslims affirmed a spiritualism with political aims (Muhammad Iqbal, Gandhi), and, in both groups, modernists attempted to find solutions that would reconcile a purified religious heritage with European culture. It was because they were so similar that Muslims and Hindus came to be at odds with each other within the increasingly disabled British system.

THE CONSTRUCTION OF STATES IN THE MIDDLE EAST

The recognition of the right of peoples to self-determination, even translated into the bastard form of a mandate, entailed a contract for building states destined to become independent. In legal terms, the mandate structure suspended the capitulations without abolishing them, but it was clear that returning to the past was not a possibility. From the start, there were two major constraints: the end of the Ottoman Empire and its consequences, and the presence of a unified Arab nationalism.

The Ottoman Empire's Sunni religious administration did not recognize the existence of non-Sunni Muslims, whereas the state had approved the status of separate non-Muslim communities. When the empire disappeared, the Sunni religious organization had to be redefined within the framework of the state's new territorial space. "Grand muftis" or "muftis of the republic" occupied the place once held by Istanbul centralization. At the same time, non-Sunni Muslims sought to emancipate themselves from Sunni tutelage. And ultimately, the state was controlled by external rulers, at least temporarily. The consequences of that de facto situation led the Muslims to adopt the communalist model, which until that time had been reserved for non-Muslims. The evolution came about gradually and was enshrined by orders from the mandatory authority, then by the independent state.

The process of communalizing the Muslims was not the result of manipulation by the external power, though its policy necessarily played a role. France saw its Levantine states as the means to counter unified Arab nationalism and to take on a noble mission, that of emancipating human groups held in contempt until that time and kept in a subjugated condition. Great Britain conducted the opposite policy in Iraq, entrusting the workings of the new state to Arab Sunni nationalists. The majority Shiites had expressed their resolute opposition to the mandatory structure and did not appear to possess the elites necessary to run the new administration.

By establishing a definition of the territories and a capital city, the mandatory powers, whose actual presence was slight (a few hundred public employees), defined the context for the local elites' political action. The elites had to take control of the space thus defined by achieving the subordination of the territory as a whole to the new capital. The preeminence of Beirut over all of Lebanon had to be recognized, as did that of Damascus over Syria, that of Jerusalem over Palestine, and that of Baghdad over Iraq. Two complementary logics were at work. The mandatory administration itself hierarchized the territory into administrative districts. The political class, waging the nationalist battle against the mandatory power, was working at the same time to establish the authority of the capital city over its competitors (Damascus versus Aleppo, Jerusalem versus Nablus or Haifa). The struggle for independence depended on discrediting the various regionalisms, which were accused of compromising with the foreign ruler.

The economic evolution moved in the same direction. The suspension of capitulations made it possible to continually raise protective customs duties and to make the shift from an agricultural tax system to one based on levies on imports. Through that mechanism, the Near Eastern space was partitioned into distinct, even competing, economic units. (France, by means of "common interests," maintained the economic unity of Syria and Lebanon.) The communications revolution also made it possible to strengthen the supremacy of the leaders in the capitals, who could now transmit their voices everywhere by telephone and could intervene quickly via automobile.

Arab nationalism regrouped during the 1920s, recovering its momentum in the 1930s. New pan-Arab structures were set in place. Iraq, independent since 1932, saw itself as the "Piedmont" or "Prussia" of Arab unity. But the elites, in adopting the plan for fusional unity, refused in their discourses to take into account the new territorial and religious realities, on which they nevertheless based their political action. They even went so far as to discredit these realities, as they had done for regionalism.

Unlike the new states, Arab nationalism possessed neither a defined center (a capital city) nor a determinate territory. As a result, competition for power inevitably pitted one group against another. During the interwar period, the Hashemites portrayed themselves as the defenders of unity, while their adversaries, who sometimes set forth even more unitary discourses, were in reality working to affirm the new realities of the states.

With Iraq's independence in 1932 and the treaty with Egypt in 1936, which led to the abolition of the capitulations in 1937, Great Britain confined itself to defending the "security of imperial communication routes." France attempted a compromise with the nationalists in 1936 but returned to direct management in 1939. The two imperial powers hardened their positions beginning in autumn 1938 (the Munich Conference). The colonial empires were ready to go to war before the metropolises.

With all its complexities, the mandatory experiment belonged both to the colonial past and to the future of the various parties involved (through the transfer of powers). A new form of social engineering was under way, in preparation for relations after independence. An equivalent situation existed in Egypt, which was increasingly emancipated from the outside. Although it was still too early to speak of "technicians of decolonization," a store of new expertise was being constituted.

Ticking Time Bombs: Palestine, Oil, Islamism

The mandatory era was not a period of calm. The European withdrawal occurred in fits and starts, giving rise to growing impatience on the part of the peoples being emancipated. Colonial violence remained a permanent dimension, particularly during the Great Syrian Revolt of 1926 and the Palestinian revolt of 1936–1940. "Anti-imperialism" entered the vocabulary of local nationalist movements in the 1920s. The longer the European withdrawal dragged on, the greater the hostility toward Europe.

Political contingency and cultural sympathies had led the British to agree to the Balfour Declaration in 1917. By the early 1920s, they could see the implacable contradiction of their pledges. The establishment of a Jewish national homeland ran counter to the "self-government" promised to the Arab population. The British attempted by every means to keep their dual commitment, but the reality ascertained by royal investigatory committees prevailed. No mechanism for the devolution of powers was possible. At most, the British were able to transfer certain powers to Jewish and Arab community structures. Hajj Amin al-Husseini, grand mufti of Jerusalem, thus became the recognized political leader of the Arabs of Palestine.

What was called the Wailing Wall Uprising in August 1929 extended the dangerous question of the holy sites, heretofore confined to the Christians, to the Muslims and Jews. Both groups played on religious feeling, giving rise to a new and lethal opposition between the Jewish and Muslim worlds. All the Jewish communities in the Muslim world found themselves destabilized; the mechanisms for their destruction were inexorably set in place, putting an end to a coexistence dating back more than a millennium and rich in exchanges between the two groups.

The Nazis' rise to power put Great Britain in an impossible situation. The "Jewish question" took on a tragic dimension. Although Palestine was able to serve as a refuge for the Jews of central Europe, the rise in immigration caused tensions that erupted into violence, first during the general strike of 1936, then during the revolt lasting from autumn 1937 to late 1939. Hajj Amin al-Husseini, in exile in Lebanon, assumed the political leadership. The "Arab world" (the term entered the vocabulary in 1936) backed the Arab Palestinians, who were being subjected to an extremely brutal repression. In autumn 1938, world war became a certainty, and the British Empire could not allow itself the luxury of having the security of imperial communication routes compromised. In spring 1939, it set draconian quotas on future Jewish immigration. The war against Nazism would mean the abandonment of the Jews of Europe. Although promises of Arab independence were again made, Arab political activity was practically banned.

Europe of the industrial revolution had enjoyed total self-sufficiency in energy resources (coal, then electricity). The advent of the internal combustion engine and oil fuel changed that situation. In the interwar period, oil was primarily a strategic product indispensable for waging war. But France and Great Britain had no oil. The Near Eastern settlement reached after the war was largely inspired by that new reality.

In large part, cartels controlled the oil industry, because of the size of investments and the desire to keep the selling price constant. The petroleum map of the Middle East was defined in the 1930s. In Iran, the Anglo-Iranian Oil Company (AIOC, now BP) held the monopoly on Iranian concessions. In Iraq, the Iraq Petroleum Company (IPC), a consortium made up of the Compagnie Française des Pétroles (precursor of the Total group), the British companies Shell and the AIOC, and American firms had received the concession. In the late 1930s, consortia comprising British and American companies began operating in the Gulf (Bahrain, Kuwait), while an American consortium undertook exploration of Saudi Arabia.

The British seemed to have a lock on the oil system (payments were made in pounds sterling), though the French and the Americans also participated. New "oil cities" appeared (Abadan in Iran, for example), true Western enclaves that adopted the model of the Universal Suez Ship Canal Company. As the importance of the Indian route declined (but not that of the junction between Europe and the Indian Ocean), the oil-producing Middle East, with its pipelines and refineries, became vital for the French and British empires, and the Americans also began to take an interest in the region.

The emerging reality went counter to the logic of European withdrawal, by creating a mutual dependence (of Europe on the region's producers, and of these producers on Europe). Reza Shah was the first Muslim head of state to subject oil production profits to a test of strength. In the Arab world, petroleum revenues were still too recent and too small to change economic conditions. The identification between Islam and petroleum production was already being set in place. (The first version of Hergé's comic book *Tintin: Land of Black Gold*, which also contained allusions to Palestine, appeared as a serial beginning in September 1939.)

What was called the "liberal Egypt" of the interwar period appeared in the first place to be the political expression of Muslim modernism, stemming from the reformism of the previous period. By establishing a modern education system in the process of Arabization, the country aspired to be the most active cultural center of the Arab world, or even of the Muslim world. But many disillusionments followed. The British intervened constantly, and the political system functioned poorly. In the name of Islam, King Fuad's monarchy disputed the popular legitimacy of the majority party, the Wafd.

The abolition of the caliphate created a new situation. Until then, the "sultanates" had implicitly retained a Muslim dimension. That was not true of the "kingships" (*mamlakat*) that proliferated during and after World War I. The first was that of Sharif Hussein, whom the Allies recognized as king of the Hejaz. In Iraq, his son Faisal also took the title of king, and Egypt followed suit in 1923. But some Muslim thinkers did not believe in adopting a fully Western form of state. They began to evoke the specific nature of the Islamic state to be created.

In 1928, Hassan al-Banna created the Muslim Brotherhood, which rapidly spread throughout Egypt. Like Indian fundamentalists, the brothers saw Islam as an all-encompassing system of life, extending into the political realm. The fight for social justice went hand in hand with the battle (jihad) for the liberation of Muslim countries under foreign domination. The rejection of anything that "denies the teachings of Islam" implicitly included European culture. Very early on, the Muslim Brotherhood militated for the Palestinian cause and attacked the Jewish community of Egypt. It was the first to develop a form of anti-Semitism similar to European anti-Semitism.

Unlike the other Arab Muslim fundamentalist movements, often modeled on Anglo-Saxon Protestant organizations, the Muslim Brotherhood's mission was to take power, by force if necessary, but its institutional program lacked clarity. The doctrine embraced a "Muslim" nationalism, giving rise to a conflict with Arab nationalism.

The political Islam of Hassan al-Banna revolted against what remained of European political domination, and beyond that, against the notion that the price of the Muslims countries' emancipation would be the Europeanization of their political institutions and even of their social culture. Through his use of the political language of Islam, his puritanism, and his appeal for social justice, he seized on a powerful potential for popular mobilization.

COLONIAL NORTH AFRICA

During the interwar period, North Africa remained the strong expression of colonialism and therefore found itself lagging behind the rest of the continental Muslim world, which was in the process of emancipation. Fascist Italy resumed in earnest the conquest of Libya, which had been halted by World War I. Once achieved, that conquest was accompanied by an attempt to establish settlement colonies. The "pacification" of Morocco continued apace, ending only in 1933. One hundred thousand Moroccans lost their lives in the process, along with twenty thousand French soldiers, half of them indigenous Moroccans.

In 1923, the Rif revolt, which began in Spanish Morocco, spread to the French protectorate. The "Rif Republic," headed by Abd al-Krim, was both a tribal league and the forerunner of a modern state. It received the support of anticolonialists of various ideological persuasions. In 1925, Lyautey was replaced by Philippe Pétain, who crushed the revolt, at the cost of enlisting an army of 150,000 men. In 1926, Abd al-Krim was forced to surrender. He did not have the support of urban Moroccan society, which was anxious about the tribal and rural aspect of the movement.

In the terms of the French historian Daniel Rivet, the two protectorates of Tunisia and Morocco grafted an authoritarian technocracy onto a traditional state.[7] In a collusion of interests, they rallied to their side the old government elites. At the same time, the two countries accepted fewer settlement colonies than Algeria.

The colonial contradiction quickly came to light. Modernization, urged on by the external ruler, created new social groups that protested against the colonizer, who tended increasingly to be supported by the most archaic structures of society. In Tunisia and then in Morocco, there emerged both a small elite that had received a modern education, and an increasingly large urban proletariat. The native people's demand for political participation in the government, and even for independence, began to be formulated. It was taken up by college graduates who had opted for professional careers rather than public administration, where they felt they had no place beside the Europeans.

In Algeria, the participation of Muslims in World War I for a time created the impression that discrimination would be abolished. And indeed, the Clemenceau government considerably improved the legal status of the Muslims, but without abolishing the Native Code. Disappointment rapidly set in, despite the creation of the body of Muslim elected officials, who demanded full equality with the Europeans. In the 1930s, the Association of Muslim Ulemas made Islamic reformism a political program, rescuing Muslim and Arab identity from the temptation of Gallicization, but also setting aside the Berber heritage.

In France proper, the war had led to the permanent establishment of a proletariat of Algerian origin. Under the patronage of the French Communist Party, Messali Hadj's Étoile Nord-Africaine moved from championing the anti-imperialist struggle to militating for Algerian independence.

The colonizer's conduct became more hard-line in the 1930s. The centennial of the Algerian conquest and the Colonial Exposition of 1931 celebrated imperial glory. The settlers opposed any further expansion of the rights of the native peoples and applauded the repression measures taken against the nationalists. Only "liberal" elements, recruited from intellectual circles, repeatedly warned of the dangers of a violent confrontation between the races.

The Third Republic in decline had no clear course of action. The European elements in the protectorates pressed for the abandonment of "association" in favor of "assimilation," inspired more or less by the Algerian model. But the administration was unable even to coordinate action in the three French possessions. (Algeria rejected anything that might entail falling under Foreign Affairs or the Ministry of Colonies.) No one anywhere showed much inclination for developing a curriculum promoting Arab culture and the Arabic language. But even as the French sought to spread their own culture, they opposed bringing the native peoples into the French commonwealth. With the global crisis, it was the metropolis that kept the economy of its North African possessions afloat (Algeria included), while at the same time declaring that these possessions were a source of power. The North African rural exodus resulted in a constant migration of the labor force to the metropolis, a migration favored by the imperial structures and deplored by French demographers with eugenist leanings.

THE POLITICAL SPACE OF THE MUSLIM WORLD

Although the Great War had given the Europeans a sense that their civilization might be mortal, the appeal of their culture remained strong in the Muslim world. The essential transformation in that period was that the European model was no longer unique. For a time, the prestige of the victors consolidated the image of the liberal institutions. For the mandates, such institutions remained the price of admission to the League of Nations and the most prominent sign of modernity.

But the crisis of liberal democracies was already perceptible in the 1920s. The Soviet Union had spread the watchword of anti-imperialist struggle, which the various Muslim nationalist movements adopted. Moscow, however, held little attraction during that period. The Sovietization of what were becoming the "Muslim republics" of the Soviet Union occurred with extreme violence and produced a new exodus of residents, who dispersed throughout the Middle East (a small current settled in Europe as well). Kemalist Turkey and Reza Shah's Iran maintained cautious relations with their powerful neighbor, who was still also their hereditary enemy. The first Turkish and Iranian Communists were considered traitors.

In the Arab East, the first Communists were recruited from among minorities (especially Jews and Armenians) and did not manage to make inroads in Muslim circles. The first labor unions were offshoots of the nationalist movements. Although some Muslim intellectuals had socialist leanings, they were more attracted to democratic socialism than to Bolshevism.

It was through the migration of Maghrebian labor to France that the Communists were able to reach the North African population. But relations between the French Communist Party and Étoile Nord-Africaine rapidly reached the point of collapse. Even as Messali Hadj radicalized his pro-independence discourse by giving it a more Islamic dimension, the Communists, in shifting toward anti-Fascism, found it indispensable to moderate their own anti-imperialist struggle in order to constitute popular fronts. Although some European intellectuals supported the anticolonial struggle, by far the majority current among the so-called progressive forces merely sought to correct the "abuses" of colonialism and not to abolish it. Only the North African settlers equated pro-independence nationalism with the international Communist movement.

European nationalism remained the most appealing element. Although the Italian nationalism of the Risorgimento had traditionally been a source of inspiration for the nationalist movements in the Arab world, there was considerable mistrust of Fascist Italy, because of its brutality in Libya and its proclaimed designs on the Mediterranean as a whole. Nazi Germany appeared more effective and less dangerous. In the Arab world, it was the beneficiary of the Germanophilia left behind by Wilhelm II's Germany. In the 1930s, the Fascist model seemed to be working much better than the tired liberal democracies in retreat all over Europe. Everywhere, nationalist youth movements adopted the garb of politicized European youth (blue or green shirts). But the borrowings remained superficial: above all, "the enemy of one's enemy" was seen as a potential "friend." The fact that, until the war, Nazism left the monopoly on Mediterranean policy to Fascist Italy fostered the mistrust.

In 1934, with the Arabic broadcasts of Radio Bari, Fascist Italy launched a propaganda war in the Arab world. In 1935 (the Italo-Ethiopian War), the attacks against British policy turned violent. In response, in January 1938 the BBC began to broadcast in Arabic as well. The network was particularly anxious to maintain its independence from the government. In March 1938, it was Nazi Germany's turn for Arabic broadcasts.

Fascist Italy sought primarily to exploit the Palestinian issue in order to embarrass the British. It succeeded in that respect, but without creating a particularly favorable climate for its own cause. By contrast, the German broadcasts on the eve of war were openly anti-Semitic (even though Berlin was simultaneously encouraging the Jewish emigration to Palestine), but within the broader context of identifying the Jews with liberal democracy (plutocracy) and proletarian internationalism.

People tuned in to these broadcasts primarily because they broke the monopoly on information that the Franco-British had held in the Middle East.

CHAPTER 17

CONTEMPORARY ISSUES

THE MUSLIM WORLD IN WORLD WAR II

The French and British sought to draw Turkey into their camp by providing it with major benefits. France completely ceded the *sanjak* of Alexandretta, part of its mandate in the Levant, leading to lasting resentment among the Syrians. The German-Soviet Nonaggression Pact changed the situation. Moscow called on the Ankara regime to remain neutral. It complied, even after the German invasion of the Soviet Union. In 1943–1944, the English-speaking countries tried to persuade Turkey to join the war on their side, but Ankara quietly refused, using as a pretext the weakness of its army, which lacked modern materiel, and the geographical vulnerability of its territory. (The Axis powers controlled all of Greece, the Balkans, and the islands in the Aegean Sea.)

Turkey was the chief Muslim country to be spared by the new war that had begun in Europe. The populations of the French and British colonial empires were not consulted when the European countries joined the war in September 1939. The Indian nationalists protested the decision, which called into question the dyarchy of the previous years. With the Japanese invasion of 1942, military operations reached the borders of India. The Congress Party actively opposed the war and was subjected to harsh repression. The Indian Muslims, by contrast, were patently "loyal." In a context where the British were compelled to draw on India's resources to the maximum extent, and to promise the status of Dominion or even complete independence after the war, the Muslims obtained a true veto right over the future. In those terrible years, the idea developed of constituting a "Pakistan," a "Muslim nation" uniting northern India into a federation with rather loose ties to the rest of the subcontinent.

The war in North Africa began in June 1940. The French possessions fell under the provisions of the Armistice agreement, later constituting, under Maxime Weygand's command, the sole instance of unified management of the Maghreb. In 1943, the "Western Desert," covering Libya and Egypt, became one of the main battlefields. For a year, the British Empire fought the Axis Powers with almost absurdly inadequate means, but also with unflagging resolve. The conquest of the Balkans, then of Crete, by the German forces in spring 1941 brought the threat dangerously close. The Arab nationalists in Iraq staged a coup d'état and made contact with the Germans. The British counterattack was swift. With rough-and-ready forces, they reoccupied Iraq in May 1941. Because Vichy France had authorized the Germans to use the Levantine airports to bring aid to the Iraqis, the British imperial troops, while they were at it, penetrated the French Mandate, with the cooperation of the Free French Forces and a contingent of Zionists. That miniwar, which on the French side took on the aspect of a civil war, also created the oddity of Arab nationalists fighting on Vichy's side. In mid-July, the Vichy forces obtained an armistice that allowed them to return to metropolitan France on a voluntary basis.

To calm tensions, on May 29, 1941, Anthony Eden, British secretary of state for foreign affairs, made a declaration expressing his country's sympathy for the cause of Arab unity, without mentioning Zionism. On June 8, 1941, the French general Georges Catroux announced, in General de Gaulle's name, the principle of independence for Syria and Lebanon, based on treaties to be concluded.

The German invasion of the Soviet Union changed the strategic game. The Iran of Reza Shah seemed to have moved too close to Germany. The Soviets and the British called on Tehran to expel the Germans present in Iran and jointly invaded the country in late August 1941. Reza Shah was deposed and replaced by his son. The imperial regime seemed on the point of collapse, but above all, the country was for the first time under complete occupation.

In early 1941, the Italo-German threat to Egypt became more acute. King Farouk and his entourage attempted to make contact with the enemies of the British. On February 4, 1942, the British staged a true coup d'état, which forced Farouk to recall the Wafd to power. The Egyptian public felt a real national humiliation. On June 27, 1942, the Italo-German forces entered Egyptian territory. They arrived on July 1 in El Alamein, sixty kilometers from Alexandria. Simultaneously in Russia, the Germans took Crimea and proceeded toward the Caucasus. With the Japanese advance in the Pacific, the Middle East seemed to be the point of convergence for the three major offensives of the Axis Powers.

The British mobilized the entire economic potential of the Middle East to sustain the rising power of their war machine in the Western Desert. They would soon have at their disposal more than a million soldiers, from Iran to Libya, restoring the illusion of power that had existed in 1918. That war effort was financed on credit and favored the industrialization of the region as a whole. Great Britain rapidly went into debt, with hundreds of millions of pounds sterling owed to every country between India and Egypt . Inflation was high, which worked to the advantage of all debtors. Rural debt, the traditional scourge of the Arab countryside, was practically liquidated. Although, overall, the Middle East enriched itself during these war years, food rationing was imposed. It was substantially less restrictive than that existing in Europe at the same time and far from the famine conditions experienced during World War I.

Caught up in a fight to the death with Nazism, Great Britain proved steadfast in its opposition to all forms of nationalism (Zionism included) suspected of serving German interests, whether intentionally or unintentionally. The British violated all the political compromises of the interwar period. For the time being, they seemed to have an overpowering force at their disposal, but in practice they destroyed any possibility for political collaboration in the following period. They did try to conduct an ideological war of propaganda against Fascism, but any discourse promoting the defense of human freedoms could only turn against their colonial practices.

With the fall of France, emotion ran high in North Africa. A real feeling of unity briefly brought together Europeans and Muslims. But the Vichy regime abolished democratic freedoms and proved particularly paternalistic toward the indigenous Arabs. It applied the anti-Semitic laws with particular rigor (the Algerian Jews lost their status as French citizens), without even the excuse of pressure from the Occupation forces. In Algeria as in the two protectorates, the Muslims had a rather negative view of that state-sponsored anti-Semitism.

Nazi Germany had no political ambitions in the Muslim world. The Mediterranean was supposed to be an Italian zone of influence. Germany was tempted to support Arab nationalist movements in Iraq. Paradoxically, the existence of the Vichy regime paralyzed the Nazis' actions in that direction. If German support of the Muslims were too overt, it would risk pushing all of North Africa into the camp of de Gaulle and the Allies (the United Nations, as of 1942). The Arab nationalists who had taken refuge in Nazi-dominated Europe attempted to obtain a clearer declaration than that of the Allies in World War I, but Hitler and Mussolini equivocated. The best they could offer was a secret declaration, dated April 28, 1942, recognizing the sovereignty and independence of the Arab countries of the Near East and accepting their union, insofar as it was desired by the countries concerned, and the destruction of the Jewish national homeland in Palestine.

Fascist and especially Nazi propaganda broadcast over the radio waves elaborated anti-Semitic themes and pointed out the contradiction between the proclaimed doctrine of the United Nations and their colonial policy. It had a clear impact in the Middle East but did not lead to political mobilization. The Muslim countries from Iran to Egypt, legally independent or under mandate, did not take part in combat. Their military potential was low and their loyalty dubious. Some volunteered, but they primarily served in logistical positions for the Allied forces. (A few Syrians and Lebanese joined the French Free Forces.)

THE AMERICANS' ARRIVAL ON THE SCENE

The nationalists had primarily seen the Axis Powers as the means to liquidate Franco-British domination, though they had also been receptive to the nationalist radicalism of their discourses. Gradually, the Americans took the place of the Italo-Germans.

It was the British who, during the crucial year of 1941, made the United States aware of the strategic importance of the Middle East. Desperately lacking in means, they insisted on the direct delivery of American war materiel to the forces engaged in the Western Desert. When Saudi Arabia appeared at risk of collapse because of the drop in its revenues (resulting from the de facto suspension of the Muslim pilgrimage), Great Britain asked the U.S. government to grant the kingdom financial aid. After the Soviet Union entered the war, the Americans took direct control of the "Persian corridor," supplying materiel to the Red Army from the Gulf ports. More than twenty thousand American soldiers participated in that vast logistical operation, which in September 1942 became the Persian Gulf Command. The Americans became involved in the overall economic management of the Middle East.

In summer 1942, the American military realized that if the Egyptian and Caucasian fronts collapsed, the deciding battle would unfold in southern Iraq, near Basra, and the U.S. army would be part of it. The Allies made the decision to proceed to a North African rear landing. This was Operation Torch, which took place on November 8, 1942.

Franklin Delano Roosevelt was firmly opposed to European colonialism. In his view, the aim of the war for the United States was not only the liberation of the European peoples from Nazi domination but the general application of the right to self-determination. He recognized that the colonized peoples were not immediately ready for independence and considered setting in place a system of international trusteeship for the interim period. Its application was supposed to be more rapid for peoples of the "brown" or "yellow" races than for those of the black race. Roosevelt had to take into account the exigencies of the war, to the point of accepting the "temporary expedient" of maintaining the Vichy regime in North Africa under the leadership of Jean-Louis Darlan and then Henri Giraud. The war spread to Tunisia until the surrender of the German forces on May 13, 1943. Once French reunification had occurred, with the constitution of the "government of Algiers" and de Gaulle's victory, the Americans did not interfere in North African affairs, but their show of force had been overwhelming.

Once the war had shifted away from the Muslim world, politics returned. The Americans pushed for the rapid independence of Syria and Lebanon, despite the resistance of the Free French Forces and then of the Provisional Government of the French Republic.

The war demonstrated the strategic importance of Middle Eastern oil, especially since the reserves on the American continent were expected to be exhausted over the medium term. Saudi Arabia, defined as an American "national interest," became the privileged partner of the United States in the Middle East. The kingdom took the opportunity to emancipate itself from British influence.

Everywhere, the Americans opposed maintaining the economic and honorific privileges of the British in the Middle East. American-Arab relations were defined in terms of cooperation and fraternity, in contrast to the hierarchical view held by the British.

But the Palestine question was still not settled. The British had in mind a new partitioning, with an Arab part based in a future "Greater Syria." They gave up that idea in late 1944. In the United States, the question had become an internal policy issue. Roosevelt envisioned making Palestine the testing ground for the new policy of trusteeship, but his premature death kept him from carrying out his intentions.

In 1945, all the Middle Eastern states declared war on the Axis Powers, the price of admission for participating in the constitution of the United Nations. The prestige of the United States was at its height in the Muslim world, whereas the European powers seemed to belong to the past.

THE END OF THE "BRITISH MOMENT"

The tensions sparked by World War II definitively bankrupted British domination in India. The British had neither the means nor the will to reestablish their authority. Their aim was to leave India in a peaceful and honorable manner. For the most part, the Muslims in the north were leaning toward the constitution of Pakistan, whereas the Congress Party wanted to hold onto one strong state. Agreement was impossible, and the country slipped into bloody conflict between communities. The last viceroy, Lord Mountbatten, expedited matters and effected the shift to two states within an atmosphere of massacres and forced population transfers.

The departure of the British was the conclusion of the administration's Indianization policy. British taxpayers had assumed the army's costs, and Great Britain found it owed India 1.3 billion pounds sterling. The Indian market ceased to be significant. In the wake of World War I, Great Britain had provided two-thirds of Indian imports; by the 1940s, it was only 8 percent.

The British legacy in India proper had been positive, allowing for the establishment of the "largest democracy in the world." The essential problem was that, by its very nature, the colonial state had no inclination to become a national state, since nationalism had arisen in opposition to colonialism. The British Empire therefore left to its successors a linguistic and ethnic pluralism that they would have a great deal of trouble managing. That was particularly true of Pakistan, a belated and poorly planned project for a kind of Muslim national homeland. Although its identity as a religious community was self-evident, its principle of organization was undetermined. Would it become a less secular Republic of Turkey of a sort, or, on the contrary, the testing ground for a political Islam stemming from the reformist and fundamentalist discourses of the previous period?

Although the Indian route disappeared with the British Raj, Middle Eastern oil played an essential role in the economic reconstruction of Europe. The architects of the Marshall Plan made it the substitute for coal energy. The Labour government, which came to power in 1945, wanted to inaugurate a new period of relations with the peoples of the Middle East. They would no longer interfere in internal affairs but would establish a partnership in the service of economic and social development.

Although they aspired to be generous, their outlook collided with the sad reality that Great Britain, economically exhausted by the war and heavily in debt to its former dominions, did not have the means for such a policy. A good share of the region was in the sterling area, but the metropolis was unable to provide them with the commodities demanded or with the dollars indispensable for procuring them on the outside, and that became a new source of frustration.

The cold war looked like a way to maintain the British system. To be sure, it required heavy economic sacrifices in order to maintain the military apparatus from World War II, but it also led the United States to finance in large part that deployment, since the Americans did not have forces capable of replacing it.

For Western strategists at the time, the Middle East seemed to be the rear base indispensable for reconquering Europe in the event of a Soviet invasion. (They were replaying the game plan of the previous war.) The deciding battle would take place in Sinai, then in Palestine, Syria, and finally Turkey.

In fact, the Republic of Turkey found itself directly threatened by the Soviets, who were making territorial claims, thus reigniting nineteenth-century conflicts. Turkey obtained American protection in 1947 (the Truman Doctrine and the creation of the U.S. Sixth Fleet). It negotiated its role in Western defense in exchange for recognition that it belonged entirely to Europe, which made it a full member of NATO, a status refused every other Muslim state. With the Western rearmament in the early 1950s, the deciding battle would take place directly on its borders.

Elsewhere, Great Britain met with the obstinate refusal of the nationalists to maintain the empire by treaty. What had appeared in the 1930s as an advance on the path toward liberation was now resented as an intolerable foreign presence. Egypt and Iraq demanded that the treaties be renegotiated, so as to move Britain toward evacuation. Public pressure was exerted in that direction. The negotiations of 1946–1948 failed. Great Britain tried to find a solution by opting for multilateralism, making the Middle Eastern states equal partners in alliances with the Western countries. The nationalists would not hear of that false equality. The crisis culminated in violence in Egypt in 1951 and was a major factor in the Free Officers Revolution of July 1952.

The Labour government, however, was faithful to its pledge of nonintervention. It was rather averse to the Hashemites' plans for Arab unity (Greater Syria, the Fertile Crescent), which would have risked contaminating its Arab allies with Syrian Francophonism. But it could not publicly disavow its most faithful allies (Jordan and Iraq). The adversaries of the Hashemites took the opportunity to discredit their unification plans by portraying them as the instrument of British imperialist policy.

The Palestinian tragedy followed the Indian pattern. Despite the presence of a hundred thousand British soldiers, the mandatory power was unable to impose a solution. The Zionists had the support of American public opinion and of President Harry Truman, and the Arabs were opposed to any partitioning. The British made the decision to leave Palestine, transferring the matter to the United Nations. Great Britain, a member of the Security Council, refused to apply the partitioning plan of November 29, 1947, because the plan did not have the agreement of the Arabs. There was nothing left to do but evacuate the country, which was sinking into civil war. During the Arab-Israeli War, London's support of Jordan was limited, because of the constraints imposed by the Americans. In observing the armaments embargo passed by the United Nations, Great Britain further undermined what remained of its military commitments to the Arabs.

In Iran, the nationalists decided to nationalize the petroleum industry. Still refusing to intervene in any way, the British had to evacuate the country in 1951. Winston Churchill's Conservative government attempted to return to a policy of force, but it was the Americans who staged the coup d'état in Iran reestablishing the shah's authority. Anthony Eden, secretary of state for foreign affairs and then prime minister, attempted to reinstate a policy of cooperation, as indicated by the treaty of 1954 with Gamal Nasser's Egypt. But Nasser turned out not to be an accommodating partner. The Suez Crisis of 1956 led to a Franco-British military intervention in association with Israel and was a further political setback.

In the following years, the British struggled to hold onto what remained of their positions. They "lost" Iraq during the revolution of July 1958. In the 1960s, they were subjected to an exhausting guerrilla war in south Yemen and had to abandon Aden in 1967. In the Gulf, Kuwait became independent in 1961. In January 1968, after the devaluation of the pound sterling, Great Britain announced its definitive withdrawal from the Gulf by 1971 and took action in December of that year.

Empire by treaty was thus at an end. London nonetheless managed to maintain advantageous relations with the countries of the Gulf.

NORTH AFRICA ON THE ROAD TO INDEPENDENCE

World War II had put an end to Italian domination in Libya. After hesitations about who should be granted the trusteeship of that country, occupied in part by French and British forces, international constraints led to the recognition of its independence.

French rule was no longer accepted in North Africa. In the protectorates, the elites were ready to take over for the colonial state. They managed to oversee a powerful popular movement intent on driving out the foreigners. Bourguiba and Muhammad V threatened the use of force to successfully negotiate an orderly colonial withdrawal. They were fortunate to have French interlocutors who were resolved to avoid the worst outcome. There was, of course, no dearth of violent episodes. The general pattern consisted of a first period of reforms immediately following the postwar period, then their failure in the face of reaction from the conservative colonial circles. A violent test of strength between pro-independence forces and colonials would follow. It would culminate in the compromise of "internal" autonomy for Tunisia in July 1954 and the "independence within a framework of interdependence" for Morocco in November 1955. In March 1956, agreements put an end to the two protectorates and led to the international recognition of independence for both states.

Developments were much more tragic in Algeria, which was considered part of metropolitan French territory. The Sétif riots, followed by a repression that turned to massacre in May 1945, isolated the European and Arab communities from each other. The administration repeatedly engaged in electoral fraud against the nationalists. That ended up favoring the most radical element emerging from the Messalist movement. Recruits came largely from the working class, even the proletariat. That movement led to the insurrection of 1954, followed by the terrible war of independence, which lasted until 1962 and culminated in the departure of the European population. The violence claimed countless civilian casualties. The French army's reign of terror faced off against the terrorism of the pro-independence forces, who rejected any pluralism in their ranks. The war between "Europeans" and "Arabs" was coupled with a civil war among the French and another, much bloodier one among the Algerians.

Although the French army felt that it had won the war militarily, creating an inner turmoil, in practice it was politically doomed from the early years. Charles de Gaulle, in accepting the inevitable, reshaped French destiny.

The three successor states, with significant nuances among them, launched a prodevelopment program of an authoritarian nature, while maintaining a special relationship with the former colonial power. The Fifth Republic made that relationship a major political issue through "cooperation in substitution," whose aim was to train the postcolonial state cadres and promote the spread of Francophonism. As that cooperation came to an end, the Arabization plan became a competing model. A poorly conducted plan promoting Arab identity, it also opposed claims to a Berber identity. At the end of the twentieth century, the result was a conflict between "Arabophones" and "Francophones" within the educated classes. One side embraced their authenticity, the other their proficiency.

DECOLONIZATION, IMPERIAL CITIZENSHIP, AND
THE BIRTH OF A EUROPEAN ISLAM

Decolonization restored the collective dignity of the dominated peoples. It left development, as envisioned in the late colonial era, an open question for the new ruling groups. One of the factors at the end of external rule was the irresistible population growth, which made it necessary to redefine the state's missions, with continuous expansion of social services (education, medicine, employment) to provide for the people. The distinction between the "metropolis" and "dependencies" made it difficult to effect massive financial transfers to the former colonies. In France, the view favoring separation was called "Cartierism," and its watchword was "plutôt la Corrèze que le Zambèze" (Corrèze rather than the Zambeze).

During the transitional phase toward independence, the colonial power attempted to modify imperial relations by defining the empire as a "community": Overseas France, the French Community, the Commonwealth, which was opened to nonwhites when India and Pakistan joined. France's ambition was to build a new relationship by relying on the existence of a more or less long common history and a shared language. The former ruler saw that as the means to maintain an influence that would carry weight in world affairs. The former ruled discovered therein access to different forms of cooperation and the transfer of technical skills.

Paradoxically, the result was that, at a time when the independent states were defining their new borders, the circulation of people had never been so intense. The hope for a better life impelled a portion of the indigenous peoples to leave, in what was called a "labor" migration but that usually culminated in permanent settlement. That migration was facilitated by the existence of the so-called community structures, which gave the former colonized, now aliens, a privileged status in what actually became a metropolis for them. There was a kind of "imperial citizenship," maintained after the existence of the empire itself. The need for labor power associated with the rapid economic growth during the thirty years following World War II (the *trente glorieuses*) accounts for that phenomenon in terms of both supply and demand. (The availability of immigrants from within Europe, especially Italy, Spain, and Portugal, gradually declined.) During the 1970s and 1980s, growing restrictions were imposed on that migration, which was theoretically limited to family groups and "regularization" measures.

The French census of 1975 counted 710,000 Algerians, 260,000 Moroccans, and 139,000 Tunisians, not to mention those who had obtained French nationality. Because of the absence of statistics on ethnicity and intermarriage, it is impossible to determine the real size of the so-called Muslim population in France. In Great Britain, the 2001 census, which included details on declared religious identity, indicated the existence of 1.6 million Muslims, most of them from the successor states to the British Indian Empire. Turkish immigration to Europe came later and assumed a massive dimension only in the 1960s, when West Germany played the role of metropolis. In 1983, 1,552,000 Turks were counted in the Federal Republic of Germany, 154,000 in the Netherlands, 144,000 in France, and 63,000 in Belgium. The Iranian revolution of 1979 also created a large Iranian diaspora in Europe as a whole.

To these figures from the Middle East and from Europe must be added the growing share of Muslims from sub-Saharan Africa. In the 1990s–2000s, Spain and Italy became by turns destination countries for Muslim immigration.

That inversion of the migratory flow within the context of decolonization allowed for intensifying human relationships between Europe and the Muslim world within the framework of the new transportation and communication revolutions. Although the first migrants intended to stay only temporarily, the move eventually became permanent. The process of "metropolitanization" differed from one European country to the next, as a function of anthropological realities.

What is most noteworthy is that the disappearance of colonialism was accompanied by the end of the personal status associated with it. Settlement and naturalization entailed accepting the general civil status of the European populations; but the social and political practices of the states concerned were directly shaped by the anthropological views held by the metropolises. Hence the old French mission of civilization became the problematic of integration/ assimilation, and British differentialism became multiculturalism, whereas Germany long maintained the fiction of a foreign status perpetuated over several generations.

The Muslim migration to Europe affected in the first place rural and urban proletarians, but at the same time, and increasingly, college graduates also participated in it. Although the economic motivation was foremost, some groups rejected as accomplices in imperialism also migrated, and other individuals sought in Europe (and also in North America) possibilities for professional and personal fulfillment impossible in their own societies. Those of the "first generation" tended to keep their distance from the host society, because of its very foreignness and the myth of return. The problem of acculturation began with the "second generation": a social process of differentiation occurred, along with an economic evolution tending to obliterate the working class as the standard model, and the "ethnicization" of a number of social behaviors. Within the atmosphere of persistent economic difficulties, the descendants of immigrants were linked to an original identity, which they were simultaneously invited to leave behind. The many kinds of discrimination they suffered locked them dangerously into fixed identities. The risk is that "ethnoclasses" will arise, a mix between social determination and ethnic or even religious determination. The solution will entail accepting multiple identities within each individual (ethnic and religious origin, regional, national, and European identity), fighting discrimination, and promoting upward mobility (the emergence of a middle class of immigrants and their descendants). Although some of the contemporary conflicts borrow the vocabulary of colonization, the fundamental difference lies in the absence of laws applied on the basis of personal status, which allows for real social mixing, particularly in marriage. The first mixing entails that of Muslims from various regions and backgrounds.

The "metropolitanization" of Muslims culminates in an infrastructure of religious worship, which can prove difficult to establish. The affirmation of an Islam specific to Europe will depend on social demand itself. The diversity of origins implies a de facto pluralism similar to that of the Protestant churches.

NATIONALISM, THE THIRD WORLD, AND ACCESS TO UNIVERSALITY

The Muslim state, emancipated from direct European domination, ran up against the problem of development, which it had to take completely in hand. Its approach aspired to be voluntarist and usually entailed authoritarianism. The new groups in power also used development to eliminate the economic base of the old elites, who were accused of compromising with imperialism. An essential phase was the nationalization of foreign economic interests, usually European. That voluntarist process most often involved state control of the economy, sometimes with the beginnings of a welfare state. Adoption of a socialist vocabulary has been common.

In contradistinction to the First and Second Worlds, the so-called Third World states have a shared sense of identity, because of their common experience of colonialism and their common needs for development. The Bandung Conference in 1955, at which all the independent Muslim states were represented, proclaimed the principles of nonintervention in internal affairs and neutralism. The aim was both to make the independent state a sacred privilege and to demand aid from the industrialized countries—as much aid as possible but provided unconditionally. The cold war context lent itself to that policy, inasmuch as a certain number of states possessed geostrategic importance.

Neutralism evolved into nonalignment. The independent states demanded development aid from the industrialized countries as their due, especially since it was supposed to make up for a "deterioration in the terms of trade" between manufactured products and raw materials from the Third World countries. Anti-imperialism was seen as cementing that "tricontinental" coalition of more and more openly "progressive" countries.

Progressivism and developmentalism accompanied the nationalist approach toward achieving true independence, allowing the new states to participate fully in world affairs and on an equal footing. Emancipation allowed for a form of modernization and Westernization that was well accepted, especially since it broke away from the old European ruler and was therefore liberating. In choosing a path inspired by socialism, a certain number of Muslim states could therefore affirm their modernity and their access to universality without being accused of betrayal.

In the face of that progressivism, with which many Europeans could sympathize, the Franco-British governments attempted in 1956 to "demonize" their adversary, Nasser, by portraying him as the emulator of Mussolini or even Hitler. Antifascism was being used to contest the anti-imperialism that had succeeded it. In the same way, the North African independence movements were accused simultaneously of being antisecular Muslims, Fascists, and Communists. The completion of decolonization led to the disappearance of these discourses in favor of an accommodating view of the realities resulting from independence. In the field of Arabic and Islamic studies, the writings of Jacques Berque, and, within a more critical perspective, Maxime Rodinson, express that way of conceiving the historical moment of decolonization.

Once the decolonization of the Muslim world was completed in practical terms, the question of Israel remained the principal sore point. For the Arab nationalists, "the Zionist entity" was the "citadel" or "base" of imperialism in the Arab world. It was a replay of the Crusades, that earlier attempt on the part of an empire to establish itself in the region. The Jewish state was an artificial reality that drew its strength from the outside but constituted a dangerous threat by virtue of its "expansionism." In the 1950s, Israel was in large part viewed as a European colonial state, a reality demonstrated by the "tripartite collusion of 1957" and the United States' role in resolving the Suez crisis.

But between 1965 and 1967, the European countries stopped providing armaments to Israel, making the United States the principal supplier of the Jewish state. The 1967 war accelerated that shift. On the question of the occupied territories and the application of resolution 242, the European countries began to mark their distance from American policy. The progress of the European construct in Israel was accompanied by the difficult elaboration of a joint position by the Common Market countries. During the 1973 war, Europe more clearly distinguished itself from the United States, and it appeared more vulnerable to the pressures of the oil-producing Arab states.

The joint foreign policy of European politics, particularly regarding the Arab-Israeli conflict and the question of Palestine, aspired to be "declaratory" in nature, that is, to arrive at a definition of a joint position on the basis of a political settlement. That policy required, prior to any active diplomacy in the Near East, an intensive political coordination among the Europeans themselves, which accounts for its vagueness and relative ineffectiveness. Nevertheless, the Europeans took a secret pleasure in turning back against the United States the accusations of imperialism that had been directed at them during decolonization.

Beyond the "Arab policy" inaugurated by Charles de Gaulle in the last years of his presidency and elaborated by his successors, a sort of third way was desired, according to foreign policy theorists. It consisted of proposing to the Arab countries that they move beyond the alternative between the United States and the Soviet Union and of offering them potential access to modern—including military—technology developed in France, in exchange for a portion of their oil revenues. Since 1968, Ba'athist Iraq had shown particular interest. The other partners tended to use the French advances to provide themselves with a wider margin for maneuvering vis-à-vis the two superpowers. Arab policy was not conducted only by France. Italy took a similar approach. Spain and Greece, destined to join the Common Market after their democratization, adopted the same perspective. All of Mediterranean Europe proved favorable to a rapprochement with the Arab countries. But though a Euro-Arab dialogue was attempted at the institutional level after the 1973 war, the Arab-Israeli conflict was too grave a matter for the talks to end in concrete results.

Islamism, the Culture of Resentment, and Human Rights

The institutional success of the progressive approach toward European unity stands in contrast to the repeated failures of a unified Arab nationalism. Beginning in the 1970s, the Common Market set up a practical model, but the Arab states did not succeed in following it.

When Nasser took power, he engaged in a frontal attack on the Muslim Brotherhood, which was accused of not having a concrete political plan. Forcibly eliminated in 1954, the brothers were called "reactionary forces in the service of imperialism." In the Arab cold war against Saudi Arabia in the 1960s, Nasser made constant use of that argument. His enormous prestige and his capacity to unify the masses allowed him to marginalize the Islamist movement. By contrast, the United States tended to display a certain sympathy for these anti-Communist forces opposed to the Soviet Union. For their part, the Europeans ignored them, believing they belonged to the past.

During that entire period, the Islamists refined their body of doctrine, shaping it into the radical expression of a nationalism based on authenticity. Western domination was not only economic and military, it was above all cultural, a permanent cultural aggression that contaminated Muslim societies. Islamism aspired to be a global response on the part of the endogenous, who were expelling the exogenous imposed on them. That allowed the movement to discredit modernizing nationalism, defined as an instrument of Westernization. Ironically, independence became the "ultimate phase of imperialism." Islam was defined as an inalterable essence to which it was necessary to return, since it could provide the solution to all problems. Every Western action from the start was merely an evil plot.

Paradoxically, progressive, even postmodern thought contributed to that viewpoint. In his seminal 1978 book, *Orientalism: Western Conceptions of the Orient*, Edward Said condemned the Western discourse on the Arab and

Muslim worlds as an essentialist, derogatory, and domineering definition. In doing so, he in turn constructed a Western essence very close to that of the Islamists, while considering any critical approach to the Muslim world a venture of domination. True, he sought to place his perspective within all the battles of the Third World against imperialism, and many of his arguments hit the mark. Nevertheless, his was an effort to discredit the West, the dangers of which Maxime Rodinson pointed out in his time.

Among certain of Said's epigones, the critique of Orientalism veered toward the constitution of a vast catalogue of resentment, even though, in the last years of his life, Said argued rather for the constitution of a scientific Occidentalism in the Muslim countries.

Beginning in the 1980s, when Islamism—as a result of the impact of the Iranian Islamic revolution—became a prominent discourse in Muslim societies, Europeans saw it as a "return of the religious," or even a "revenge of God." It was assimilated to other forms of religious fundamentalism, such as colonialist messianism in Israel, Protestant fundamentalism in the United States, and fundamentalist forms of dissident Catholicism. The radicalization of Hinduism based on a notion of authenticity could be added to that list. In a Europe in the process of de-Christianization, which has domesticated the religious phenomenon without suppressing various forms of religiosity, Islamism inspired great fear, especially since it was expressed as a justification for jihad. When that jihad was waged in Afghanistan against the Soviets, it was of course attributed to "freedom fighters," but when it spread to Lebanon after the Israeli invasion of 1982, then to Palestine in the 1990s, it assumed the role of the enemy.

The state apparatus of the Muslim countries were defined as "moderate" and in need of support against the Islamists, who replaced the Soviet Union in decline. The states knew how to play that card to obtain various assistance, including cooperation in maintaining security. In their armed confrontations with the Islamists, Saddam Hussein's Iraq in the 1970s and Algeria during the civil war of the 1990s enjoyed general support from European and other Western powers.

At the same time, the protective mechanism arising from the Bandung Conference had ceased to function. Third-Worldism had been part of the general paradigm of those liberation struggles that accepted the necessity of the use of violence and of authoritarianism. But as of the late 1970s, that paradigm was replaced by that of human rights, which placed the emphasis on the defense of victims. Various European and Western human rights nongovernmental organizations (NGOs) challenged the dictatorial aspect of the regimes in place in Muslim countries. European governments were obliged to defend their support policies based on the exigencies of reason of state.

Subject to different forms of protest transmitted to Europe via the diasporas, the political regimes of the Muslim countries saw their images constantly deteriorating. These protests returned to the cultural question, an ironic reprise of the question raised by Islamists. Might modern and emancipatory democracy be incompatible with the nature of Muslim societies? At the time, the perspective of Western believers in the "clash of civilizations" converged with that of the different Islamist movements.

Europe: Preoccupations with Power and Security

The logic of expansion gradually led the European Union to cover the entire north bank of the Mediterranean, with the exception, for the moment, of Croatia, Albania, and Turkey. Within that framework, in 1995 the EU launched what was known as the Barcelona Process of Euro-Mediterranean partnership. Association agreements were reached with most of the so-called south-bank countries. Reform programs moving toward free trade were financed by the European Union, with efforts to develop relations between civil societies on the two banks. On its tenth anniversary in 2005, the EU defined the Mediterranean as a strategic priority for the union as a whole.

At the same time, within the context of the peace process, the European Union took over a large share of the financing of the Palestinian Authority, thus moving beyond the purely declaratory framework of its previous policy. It was also a member of the Quartet, along with the United States, Russia, and the United Nations, charged with finding a political solution to the Palestine question.

There is no denying that the most important concern of the European Union and its member states is security. The farther the EU expands geographically, the more Muslim its neighbors become. Although it speaks of necessary reforms, its first priority is conservative in nature: to assure stability in its immediate vicinity, since conflicts internal to the Muslim world have repercussions on its own soil. In the 1980s and 1990s, for example, terrorism linked to the Iraq-Iran conflict and to the Lebanese and Algerian civil wars cast its shadow over France. The security aspect requires a stronger collaboration with the Muslim states.

The same issue can also be found in the migration question. The Muslim world provides a good share of the undocumented workers trying to reach Europe, and most of the rest of them pass through those same countries. There again, the Muslim states have made the emigrants an instrument for exerting pressure on a new Fortress Europe seeking to build impenetrable walls around itself. Drug trafficking of various kinds and terrorism are also pertinent issues.

After September 11, 2001, Europe was the victim of jihadist terrorism on its own soil, in Madrid and London especially. The antiterrorist struggle requires constant cooperation in the field of intelligence between Europeans and the law forces of the Muslim countries.

All these constraints are pushing the European countries to take a rather conservative view of their relations with the Muslim world. They claim to be adopting a long-term perspective. In favoring reform processes, in financing them and providing technical assistance, Europe is working for a transition toward a more democratic Arab world. Nevertheless, the Europeans' Arab and Muslim interlocutors have only an instrumental view of their relations with Europe. Europe is there to contribute toward improving the performance of the state apparatus and of the economy, in order, precisely, to perpetuate the status quo. Only the future will tell which of the two parties will prevail.

The cultural question remains essential, however, at least in discourse. European leaders, particularly the French, are committed to rejecting the trap of the clash of civilizations. Dialogue between cultures is the order of the day. But the question of whether Turkey will join the European Union is rousing violent passions.

Those who have a culturalist interpretation of the European construct deny that Turkey belongs to Europe as a whole. They do not want to see that, if there was ever any cultural and religious reality in Europe, it was when it was composed of countries embracing the Catholic or Protestant tradition. But when Greece entered the Common Market in 1981, a Balkan, Orthodox, and formerly Ottoman country that had become part of European culture only in the nineteenth century—despite its claim that it was the heir to classical antiquity—joined the European group. The same was true for the successive expansions following the collapse of the Eastern Bloc. Practically all the former Ottoman Balkan countries, with the exception of Albania, Serbia, and Macedonia, are or will become part of the European Union.

In its history and culture, the Republic of Turkey belongs in large part to the Balkans, which include many Muslims. The question of religion is more complex. Hostility toward Turkey feeds on an Islamophobia incited in great part by the manifestations of various forms of Islamic radicalism (jihadist terrorism, hypersensitivity to anything that could be considered an attack or even a critique of Islam).

The real problems raised by the question of Turkey's membership in the European Union are more on the order of politics: Turkish ultranationalism in its mythified continuity with Kemalism; its complex entanglements in Middle Eastern affairs (the Kurdish problem; the use of water from the Euphrates; proximity to Iran and Iraq; the settlement of the Cyprus question; Armenian affairs). Demographics play a significant role as well: Turkey may be destined to become the most populous country in the EU. That will entail, at minimum, a redefinition of European institutions. Yet the European Union seems incapable of reforming its institutions.

But Turkey is not a population bomb. Its synthetic fertility rate (the number of children per woman) was 1.92 in 2006, that is, lower than that of Ireland or France. A good part of the south bank of the Mediterranean has already achieved most of its demographic transition (Tunisia: 1.74; Algeria: 1.89). Iran is at 1.8 (but Egypt is at 2.83, Syria at 3.4, and Morocco at 2.68). These indications show that, over the medium term, Europe will not be able to find in the nearby Muslim countries the immigrant labor force it will need as its population ages. It is even possible that these countries will become in turn destinations for emigration from farther away.

SHARED INTERIORITY

The violent acts of the early twenty-first century must not conceal the shared destiny that has been built up between the Muslim world and Europe over two and a half centuries. From the second half of the eighteenth century on, Europe, because of its extreme power, defined the shifting rules of a new universality that accompanied the expansion of its domination. In the twentieth century, Europe was replaced in part by North America. Despite the vicissitudes of politics, the elaboration of new norms with universalist aspirations has continued. These include women's emancipation and the legitimation of homosexuality. Muslim countries find themselves constantly subjected to pressure to put into practice these new norms, which are causing upheaval in their fundamental anthropological structures.

Modernization is at once propelled by Europe or the West and produced by the evolutions internal to Muslim societies. Such was the case for the disappearance of hierarchized Old Regime societies, for the establishment of equal status as the norm, for the redefinitions of identity leading to the emergence of nationalism and the modern state. Moment by moment, it is impossible to determine what is borrowed from the outside and what is an internal recomposition.

Creative destruction, which originated in Europe but has taken on autonomy in the Muslim world, relies on multiple inventions of tradition, as also occurred in Europe. At every moment, it was necessary to justify innovation by linking it to a religious and cultural heritage. Contemporary Muslim discourse in its identity- and authenticity-based phase had its counterpart in twentieth-century Europe, including its darkest side, such as anti-Semitism.

Within present-day globalization, the Muslim world occupies a middle position between industrialized societies, old and new, and the least developed countries, as defined by the human development index. Its performance is mediocre but not disgraceful and does not imply an overall failure of the culture of its societies.

In producing the universal, Europe has itself become universalized. Its material culture has been imbued with contributions from the entire world, as indicated by its everyday cuisine. Its arts are incomprehensible without reference to other cultures. Its literature became universal with the translation of the *Thousand and One Nights* in the early eighteenth century. Its human composition has changed, its religious constitution has been transformed. It would be as pointless to define a European identity without taking into account the multiplicity of its components as to define a Muslim personality closed off from the rest of the world. The trap of authenticity, which excludes the other as a foreigner, is probably the most widespread danger in the world as a whole.

NOTES

FOREWORD

1. Francis E. Peters, "The Early Muslim Empires: Umayyads, Abbasids, Fatimids," in *Islam: The Religious and Political Life of a World Community*, ed. Marjorie Kelly (New York: Praeger, 1984), p. 79.

GENERAL INTRODUCTION

1. Samuel P. Huntington, *The Clash of Civilizations and the Remaking of World Order* (New York: Simon and Schuster, 1996), p. 21.

2. Alain Rey, ed., *Dictionnaire historique de la langue française* (Paris: Le Robert, 1992 and 1998), s.v. "Islam," "musulman"; *The Compact Edition of the Oxford English Dictionary*, 2 vols. (Oxford, UK: Oxford University Press, 1971 and 1985), s.v. "Islam," "Moslim, Muslim."

3. Richard Bulliet, *The Case for Islamo-Christian Civilization* (New York: Columbia University Press, 2004).

PART I: SARACENS AND *IFRANJ*: RIVALRIES, EMULATION, AND CONVERGENCES

Chapter 1: The Geographers' World: From Arabia Felix to the Balad al-Ifranj *(Land of the Franks)*

1. Isidore of Seville, *Chronica maiora*, ed. Theodor Mommson, *Monumenta germaniae historica, Auctores antiquissimi (MGH AA)* (Munich: Monumenta Germaniae Historica, 1981), vol. 11, part 2: 391–506, § 417. For a comparison of these periods to those of other chroniclers in the early Middle Ages, see Bernard Guenée, *Histoire et culture historique dans l'Occident médiéval* (Paris: Aubier, 1980), pp. 150–52. On the six ages of the world in medieval Christian historiography, see Guenée, *Histoire et culture historique*, pp. 148–54; R. Schmidt, "Aetates mundi: Die Weltalter als Gliederungsprinzip der Geschichte," *Zeitschrift für Kirchengeschichte* 67 (1955–1956): 288–317, esp. 306–8.

2. For the following passage, I draw in part from the first chapter of my *Saracens: Islam in the Medieval European Imagination* (New York: Columbia University Press, 2002), where I cite all the references.

3. Isidore of Seville, *Etymologies* 9.2.6, in *The Etymologies of Isidore of Seville*, trans. Stephen A. Barney et al. (Cambridge, UK: Cambridge University Press, 2006), p. 192. [Translation slightly modified—trans.]

4. Irfad Shahîd, *Rome and the Arabs: A Prolegomenon to the Study of Byzantium and the Arabs* (Washington, DC: Dumbarton Oaks, 1984), pp. 100–101: the first-century authors were Josephus and Polyhistor.

5. Jerome, *Commentarii in Ezechielem* (*Corpus Christianorum scriptorum latinorum* 75.25). [Except where an English-language edition is cited, quoted passages are my translation from the French—trans.]

6. Modern etymologists do not agree on the origin of the word "Saracens"; see Shahîd, *Rome and the Arabs*, pp. 123–41. For an overview of the early medieval Latin texts that discuss the term "Saracens," see Ekkehart Rotter, *Abendland und Sarazenen: Das okzidentale Araberbild unde seine Entstehung im Frühmittelalter* (Berlin: Walter de Gruyter, 1986), pp. 68–77.

7. Isidore of Seville, *Etymologies* 9.2.6; Isidore of Seville, *Chronica maiora*, § 13. For the other authors, see Tolan, *Saracens*.

8. *The Koran*, trans. N. J. Dawood (New York: Penguin, 1995).

9. See, for example, Qur'an 2:136–40; 3:84; 4:163; and 6:84–86.

10. André Miquel, *La géographie humaine dans le monde musulman jusqu'au XIe siècle*, 4 vols. (Paris: Mouton, 1967–1988), vol. 2: 60–61, 142, 232–33.

11. Ibid., p. 369.

12. See François Clément, "La cité des Femmes," in *Les mille et une nuits, contes sans frontière*, ed. Edgard Weber (Toulouse: AMAM, 1997), pp. 171–93, esp. 184–85.

13. Miquel, *Géographie humaine*, vol. 2: 35, 60; cf. p. 311 for Mas'ūdī.

14. Ibid., p. 258.

15. Ibid., pp. 56–60. Miquel notes that Mas'ūdī introduced an innovation by placing the fourth climate (that of Baghdad) at the center of the earth, surrounded by the other seven. See Mas'ūdī, *Kitāb al-tanbīh wa al-ishrāf*, translated by B. Carra de Vaux as *Le livre de l'avertissement et de la révision* (Paris: Imprimerie Nationale, 1896), pp. 50–55.

16. Quoted in Miquel, *Géographie humaine*, vol. 2: 37.

17. Mas'ūdī, *Le livre de l'avertissement*, p. 39; see Miquel, *Géographie humaine*, vol. 2: 321.

18. Miquel, *Géographie humaine*, vol. 2: 348.

19. Ibn Fadlān, *Kitāb ilā Mulk al-Saqāliba*, translated by Richard N. Frye as *Ibn Fadlan's Journey to Russia: A Tenth-century Traveler from Baghdad to the Volga River* (Princeton, NJ: Markus Wiener, 2005), p. 43. On this text, see Miquel, *Géographie humaine*, vol. 1: 132–39; vol. 2: 227–41, 267–79, 336–42.

20. *Ibn Fadlan's Journey to Russia*, p. 64.

21. Bernard Lewis, *The Muslim Discovery of Europe* (London: Phoenix, 1992).

22. Nadia Maria El Cheikh, *Byzantium Viewed by the Arabs* (Cambridge, MA: Harvard Center for Middle Eastern Studies, 2004).

23. Miquel, *Géographie humaine*, vol. 2: 381–481; Cheikh, *Byzantium Viewed by the Arabs*, pp. 142–57.

24. Miquel, *Géographie humaine*, vol. 2: 371–72.

25. Ibid., vol. 2: 372–77.

26. Idrīsī, *La première géographie de l'Occident*, trans. Chevalier Joubert, revised and corrected by Annliese Nef (Paris: Flammarion, 1999); these are excerpts in French from the *Book of Roger*, primarily the parts on the West.

27. Henri Bresc and Annliese Nef, introduction to Idrīsī, *La première géographie de l'Occident*, pp. 13–53, esp. 44–45.

28. Idrīsī, *La première géographie de l'Occident*, pp. 424 and 426.

29. Hugh of Saint Victor, *Descriptio mappe mundi*, ed. Patrick Gautier-Dalché (Paris: Études Augustiniennes, 1988), introduction, pp. 55–58. On Hugh of Saint Victor's geography,

see also Danielle Lecoq, "La 'mappemonde' du *De arca Noe mystica* de Hugh of Saint Victor (1128–1129)," in *Géographie du monde au Moyen Âge et à la Renaissance*, ed. Monique Pelletier (Paris: Éditions du Comité des Travaux Historiques et Scientifiques, 1989), pp. 9–31.

30. It is in the Bayerische Staatsbibliothek in Munich, ms. CLM 10058, folio 154v, reproduced in Patrick Gautier-Dalché's introduction to Hugh of Saint Victor, *Descriptio*, pl. 1 and p. 83.

31. Hugh of Saint Victor, *Descriptio*, p. 138.

32. Ibid., p. 133.

33. Ibid., p. 141.

34. Jacques Le Goff, *Time, Work, and Culture in the Middle Ages*, trans. Arthur Goldhammer (Chicago: University of Chicago Press, 1980), pp. 189–200, esp. 195.

35. Curiously, Hugh makes no mention of Eden in the *Descriptio*, but it is clear in other texts that he places earthly paradise at the eastern limit of the earth. See his *De Archa Noe*, in Migne, *Patrologia latina* (*PL*) (Paris: Garnier Frères, 1844–1891), 176.677B–678B, excerpt translated into French by Patrice Sicard, *Hugues de Saint-Victor et son école* (Turnhout, Belgium: Brepols, 1991), pp. 140–42.

36. Hugh of Saint Victor, *De archa Noe, PL* 176.677, Sicard trans. in *Hugues de Saint Victor*, p. 141.

Chapter 2: Conquest and Its Justifications: Jihad, Crusade, Reconquista

1. Andrew Palmer, Sebastian Brock, and Robert Hoyland, eds. and trans., *The Seventh Century in the West-Syrian Chronicles* (Liverpool, UK: Liverpool University Press, 1993), p. xxi.

2. See Tolan, *Saracens*, p. 43.

3. On the concept of jihad, see Alfred Morabia, *Le Gihad dans l'Islam médiéval* (Paris: Albin Michel, 1993); Reuven Firestone, *Jihad: The Origin of Holy War in Islam* (Oxford, UK: Oxford University Press, 1999); and Rudolph Peters, *Jihad in Classical and Modern Islam: A Reader* (Princeton, NJ: Markus Wiener, 1996).

4. Morabia, *Le Gihad dans l'Islam médiéval*, pp. 140–41.

5. Qur'an 25:52; see Morabia, *Le Gihad dans l'Islam médiéval*, p. 124.

6. Morabia, *Le Gihad dans l'Islam médiéval*, p. 126.

7. See Firestone, *Jihad*, esp. chap. 4, pp. 67–91.

8. Morabia, *Le Gihad dans l'Islam médiéval*, pp. 159–75, 200–204.

9. Firestone, *Jihad*.

10. Quoted in Morabia, *Le Gihad dans l'Islam médiéval*, p. 106.

11. See ibid., p. 164.

12. *Encyclopaedia of Islam*, 2nd. ed. (henceforth abbreviated *EI2*), 12 vols. (Leiden, Netherlands: Brill, 1960–2009), s.v. "ribat" (J. Chabbi); the term *ribat* sometimes designates a Sufi monastery, with no military dimension.

13. Muhammad Talbi, *L'émirat Aghlabide 184–296, 800–909: Histoire politique* (Paris: Librairie d'Amérique et d'Orient, 1966), pp. 380–536; Morabia, *Le Gihad dans l'Islam médiéval*, p. 109.

14. Armand Citarella, "The Relations of Amalfi with the Arab World before the Crusades," *Speculum* 42 (1967): 299–312, esp. p. 305; on Amalfi, see chapter 4.

15. See Roger Collins, *The Arab Conquest of Spain* (Oxford, UK: Blackwell, 1989), pp. 23–36.

16. Philippe Sénac, "Les Carolingiens et le califat abbasside (VIIIe–IXe siècles)," in *Chrétiens et musulmans en Méditerranée médiévale (VIIIe–XIIIe siècle)* (Poitiers: Centre d'Études Supérieures de Civilisation Médiévale, 2003), pp. 3–19.

17. See Philippe Sénac, *Les Carolingiens et al-Andalus (VIIe–IXe siècles)* (Paris: Maisonneuve et Larose, 2002); Lewis, *The Muslim Discovery of Europe*, pp. 10–12; and Mohammad Arkoun, ed., *Histoire de l'Islam et des musulmans en France du Moyen Âge à nos jours* (Paris: Albin Michel, 2006), pp. 6–15.

18. See John Tolan, *Sons of Ishmael*, chap. 10, "A Dreadful Racket: The Clanging of Bells and the Yowling of Muezzins in Iberian Interconfessional Polemics." Already in 953, the generals of Abd al-Rahmān III tore the bells out of the churches in the raided zones and sent them to Cordova. See Évariste Lévi-Provençal, *Histoire de l'Espagne musulmane*, 2 vols. (Paris: Maisonneuve et Larose, 1950 and 1999), vol. 2: 68.

19. Fredegar, *The Fourth Book of the Chronicle of Fredegar with Its Continuations*, ed. J. M. Wallace-Hadrill (Westport, CN: Greenwood, 1981).

20. On Bede and his view of the Saracens, see Tolan, *Saracens*, pp. 72–78.

21. Bede, *Ecclesiastical History of the English People*, ed. Bertram Colgrave and R. A. B. Mynors (Oxford, UK: Clarendon Press, 1969), 23.2, p. 157. [Translation slightly modified—trans.]

22. Bede, *In principium Genesis usque ad natiuitatem Isaac* 4.16, in *Bedae Venerabilis Opera, Corpus Christianorum Series Latina* (henceforth abbreviated *CCSL*), 118A (Turnhout, Belgium: Brepols, 1955–1980).

23. Theophanes, *Chronographia*, ed. Carolus de Boor, 2 vols. (Leipzig: B. G. Teubnneri, 1883–1885), pp. 333–34; *The Chronicle of Theophanes Confessor: Byzantine and Near Eastern History, A.D. 284–813*, ed. and trans. Cyril A. Mango, Roger Scott, and Geoffrey Greatrex (Oxford, UK: Clarendon Press, 1997), p. 464. The following paragraphs on Theophanes are drawn from Tolan, *Saracens*, pp. 64–66.

24. *Chronicle of Theophanes Confessor*, p. 464.

25. Ibid, p. 465.

26. Ibid., p. 592.

27. Ibid., pp. 470–471.

28. *Chronicon moissiacense* 1.290, *MGH Scriptores in usum scholarum* (henceforth abbreviated *MGH SS*) 1.282–313, 2.257–59; see Georges Martin, "La chute du royaume wisigothique d'Espagne dans l'historiographie chrétienne des VIIIe et IXe siècles," *Cahiers de Linguistique Hispanique Médiévale* 9 (1984): 210–33.

29. On the chronicles of the sack of Benevento, see James Waltz, "Western European Attitudes toward Muslims before the Crusades," PhD diss., University of Michigan, 1963, p. 47. On the description of the Battle of Tours, see Rotter, *Abendland und Sarazenen*, pp. 217–30.

30. Liutprand, *Anapodosis*, quoted in Waltz, "Western European Attitudes," pp. 114–16.

31. Adon speaks of "Loca sanctorum, quae impii Sarraceni ac perfidi christiani contaminaverant" (*MGH SS* 2.323); for John VIII, see Fred Engreen, "Pope John VIII and the Arabs," *Speculum* 20 (1945): 318–30.

32. *MGH Poetae latini*, vol. 3: 403–5; Engreen, "Pope John VIII and the Arabs," p. 320.

33. Citarella, "The Relations of Amalfi with the Arab World," pp. 308–9.

34. See the examples cited in Jean-Claude Cheynet, *Pouvoir et contestations à Byzance (963–1210)* (Paris: Publications de la Sorbonne, 1996), pp. 394–95.

35. H. Cowdrey, "Canon Law and the First Crusade," in *The Horns of Hattin*, ed. B. Kedar (Jerusalem: Yad Izhak Ben-Zvi, 1992), pp. 41–48; James Brundage, "Holy War and the Medieval Lawyers," in *The Holy War*, ed. T. Murphy (Columbus: Ohio State University Press, 1976), pp. 99–104, reprinted in James Brundage, *The Crusades, Holy War and Canon Law* (Aldershot, UK: Variorum, 1991).

36. See Christopher Tyerman, *The Invention of the Crusades* (Toronto: University of Toronto Press, 1988); Christopher Tyerman, *Fighting for Christendom: Holy War and the Crusades* (Oxford, UK: Oxford University Press, 2004); and Jean Flori, *Pierre l'Ermite et la première croisade* (Paris: Fayard, 1999), p. 209.

37. Robertus Monachus, *Historia iherosolimitana* 3.1, in *Recueil des historiens des Croisades, Historiens occidentaux* (Paris: Imprimerie Royale, 1844–1895), 3.763 (henceforth abbreviated *RHC Occ*).

38. See Jonathan Riley-Smith, *The First Crusade and the Idea of Crusading* (London: Athlone, 1986), pp. 140–42; Tolan, *Saracens*, pp. 115–16.

39. Robertus Monachus, *Historia iherosolimitana* 1.1 (*RHC Occ*. 3.727–28).

40. Petrus Tudebodus, *Historia de Hierosolymitano itinere*, trans. John Hugh Hill and Laurita L. Hill (Philadelphia: American Philosophical Society), p. 51; on this author, see Tolan, *Saracens*, pp. 111–18.

41. Petrus Tudebodus, *Historia*, p. 92. This same language is also found in the later abridged version of his chronicle, *Tudebodus abbreviatus* (*RHC Occ*. 3.194).

42. Fulcher of Chartres, *Historia de Iherosolymitana*, chap. 26 (*RHC Occ*. 3.357).

43. Raoul of Caen, chap. 129 (*RHC Occ*. 3.695–96); on this passage, see Tolan, *Saracens*, pp. 119–20.

44. Guibert of Nogent, *Gesta Dei per Francos*, trans. Robert Levine as *The Deeds of God through the Franks* (Woodbridge, UK: Boydell, 1997), p. 36. On this text, see Tolan, *Saracens*, pp. 135–47.

45. Guibet of Nogent, *The Deeds of God through the Franks*, p. 32.

46. William of Tyre, *Chronique*, ed. R.B.C. Huygens (Turnhout, Belgium: Brepols, 1986), pp. 105–6.

47. Gratian, *Decretum, causa* 23; the analysis that follows is drawn from Tolan, "'Cel Sarrazins me semblet mult herite': L'hétérodoxie de l'autre comme justification de conquête (XIe–XIIe siècles)," in *L'expansion occidentale (XIe–XVe siècles): Formes et conséquences* (Paris: Publications de la Sorbonne, 2003), pp. 65–74.

48. Carolina lo Nero, "*Christiana Dignitas*: New Christian Criteria for Citizenship in the Late Roman Empire," *Medieval Encounters* 7 (2001): 125–45. These ideas were reiterated by Romanist jurists in the Middle Ages; see Frederick Russell, *The Just War in the Middle Ages* (Cambridge, UK: Cambridge University Press, 1975), pp. 50–51.

49. Russell, *The Just War*, p. 92.

50. Ibid., p. 184.

51. Ibid., p. 255.

52. See Tolan, "'Cel Sarrazins me semblet mult herite,'" pp. 69–70.

53. See Thomas Deswarte, *De la destruction à la restauration: L'idéologie du royaume d'Oviedo-Léon (VIIIe–XIe siècles)* (Turnhout, Belgium: Brepols, 2003), pp. 5–12.

54. On the concept of *reconquista*, see Manuel González Jiménez, "¿Re-conquista? Un estado de la cuestión," in *Tópicos y realidades de la Edad Media*, vol. 1, ed. Eloy Benito Ruano (Madrid: Real Academia de la Historia, 2000), pp. 155–78.

55. Deswarte, *De la destruction à la restauration*, pp. 226–31.

56. Ibn Bassam, *Dhakhira*, excerpt translated into French in Pierre Guichard, *L'Espagne et la Sicile musulmanes au XIe et XIIe siècle* (Lyons: Presses Universitaires de Lyon, 1990), p. 123.

57. See Tolan, *Saracens*, pp. 174–93; Georges Martin, *Histoires de l'Espagne médiévale: Historiographie, geste, romancero* (Paris: Klincksieck, 1997); Martin, ed., *La historia alfonsí: El modelo y sus destinos, siglos XIII–XV* (Madrid: Casa de Valázquez, 2000); and Peter Linehan, *History and Historians of Medieval Spain* (Oxford, UK: Oxford University Press, 1993).

58. "Era mas razón de tener con los romanos, que eran de parte de Europe, que con de los de Carthago, que eran de Affrica." *Primera crónica general*, § 26. See Americo Castro, *La Realidad historica de España* (Mexico City: Porrua, 1973), p. 61.

59. J. López Pereira, ed., *Crónica mozárabe de 754* (Saragossa, Spain: Anubar, 1980), § 55. See Georges Martin, "La chute du royaume wisigothique d'Espagne dans l'historiographie chrétienne des VIIIe et IXe siècles," *Cahiers de Linguistique Hispanique Médiévale* 9 (1984): 210–33; Tolan, *Saracens*, pp. 78–85.

60. Yves Bonnaz, ed. and trans., *Chroniques asturiennes (fin IXe siècle)* (Paris: Éditions du Centre National de la Recherche Scientifique, 1987), pp. 5–6. The chronicler found that biography in the *Liber apologeticus martyrum* of Eulogius of Cordova; see Tolan, *Saracens*, pp. 98–100, 111.

61. That text is published in Patrick Henriet, "Hagiographie et politique à León au début du XIIIe siècle," *Revue Mabillon* 8 (1997): 77–82, discussion, pp. 64–76.

62. *Primera crónica general*, § 559, p. 313. Here is another passage about churches being turned into mosques: "E los moros . . . loauan el nombre de Mahomat a altas uozes et ante todos en la eglesia de los cristianos o el nombre de Cristo solie seer loado." Ibid., § 562, p. 316.

63. On the conversion of places of worship, see Pascal Buresi, "Les conversions d'églises et de mosquées en Espagne au XIe–XIIIe siècles," in *Religion et société urbaine au Moyen Âge: Études offertes à Jean-Louis Biget par ses anciens élèves*, ed. Patrick Boucheron and Jacques Chiffoleau (Paris: Publications de la Sorbonne, 2000), pp. 333–50; Amy Remensnyder, "The Colonization of Sacred Architecture: The Virgin Mary, Mosques, and Temples in Medieval Spain and Early Sixteenth-Century Mexico," in *Monks and Nuns, Saints and Outcasts: Religion in Medieval Society: Essays in Honor of Lester K. Little*, ed. Sharon A. Farmer and Barbara H. Rosenwein (Ithaca, NY: Cornell University Press, 2000), pp. 189–219; Deswarte, *De la destruction à la restauration*, pp. 311–12 (on the *restauratio* of the cathedral of León in 1073); for the example of the transformation of the mosque of Cordova during its conquest by Ferdinand III in 1236, see Tolan, *Saracens*, pp. 185–86.

64. Letter in F. Balme et al., eds., *Raymundiana seu documenta quae pertinent ad S. Raymundi de Pennaforti vitam et scripta*, 4 vols. (Rome: Domo generalitia ordinis praedicatorum, 1898–1901), vol. 4, part 2: 12–13.

65. M. J. Viguera Molíns, ed., *El retroceso territorial de al-Andalus: Almorávides y Almohades (siglos XI al XIII)*, in *Historia de España*, ed. R. Menéndez Pidal (Madrid: Espasa Calpe, 1997), vol. 8, part 2.

66. François Clément, "La rhétorique de l'affrontement dans la correspondance officielle arabo-andalouse aux XIIe et XIIIe siècles," *Cahiers d'Études Hispaniques Médiévales* 28 (2005): 215–41.

67. Al-Qālamī, *Letter on the Victory of Caracuel*, French translation in Clément, "La rhétorique," p. 238.

68. Clément, "La rhétorique," p. 229.

69. On the use of Christian mercenaries, see Simon Barton, "Traitors to the Faith? Christian Mercenaries in al-Andalus and the Maghreb, c. 1100–1300," in *Medieval Spain: Culture, Conflict, and Coexistence: Studies in Honour of Angus MacKay*, ed. Roger Collins and Anthony Goodman (New York: Palgrave, 2002), pp. 23–45; François Clément, "Reverter et son fils, deux officiers catalans au service des sultans de Marrakech," *Medieval Encounters* 9 (2003): 79–106.

70. Ibn Tūmart, quoted in Clément, "La rhétorique," p. 232.

71. 'Imād al-Dīn al-Isfahānī, *al-Fath al-qussī fī al-fath al-qudsī*, translated into French by H. Massé as *Conquête de la Syrie et de la Palestine par Saladin* (Paris: Librairie Orientaliste Paul Geuthner, 1972), pp. 54–57. See John Tolan and Philippe Josserand, *Les relations des pays d'Islam avec le monde latin* (Rosny: Bréal, 2000), pp. 161–64.

72. Maqrīzī, *History*, pp. 262–63.

73. See the excerpts from Ibn Wasīl translated in Anne-Marie Eddé and Françoise Micheau, *L'Orient au temps des croisades* (Paris: Flammarion, 2002), pp. 109–16.

74. See Ana Echevarria, *The Fortress of Faith: The Attitude towards Muslims in Fifteenth-Century Spain* (Leiden, Netherlands: Brill, 1999).

75. See, among others, Peter Edward Russell, *Prince Henry "the Navigator": A Life* (New Haven, CT: Yale University Press, 2001).

76. Gomes Eanes de Zurara, *The Chronicle of the Discovery and Conquest of Guinea*, trans. C. Raymond Beazley and Edgar Prestage (New York: B. Franklin, 1963).

Chapter 3: The Social Inferiority of Religious Minorities

1. On the legal status of religious minorities in the medieval world, see the website and text database of the European Research Council project "RELMIN: The Legal Status of Religious Minorities in the Euro-Mediterranean World"; available at www.relmin.eu (accessed February 13, 2012).

2. The following section is based primarily on Antoine Fattal, *Le statut légal des non-musulmans en pays d'Islam* (Beirut: Dar el-Machreq, 1958 and 1995); and Morabia, *Le Gihad dans l'Islam médiéval*, pp. 263–89.

3. Fattal, *Statut légal*, pp. 60–69.

4. Ibid., p. 62.

5. *EI2*, s.v. "Al-Hākim bi-Amf Allāh" (Maurice Canard).

6. Shlomo Goitein, *A Mediterranean Society: The Jewish Communities of the Arab World as Portrayed in the Documents of the Cairo Geniza*, 6 vols. (Berkeley: University of California Press, 1967–1988), vol. 1: 197.

7. See *EI2*, s.v. "Tudmīr" (L. Molina): the text of the treaty is translated in Lévi-Provençal, *Histoire de l'Espagne musulmane*, vol. 1: 32–33.

8. On the meaning and pitfalls of the term "Mozarab," see Thomas Burman, *Religious Polemic and the Intellectual History of the Mozarabs, c. 1050–1200* (Leiden, Netherlands: Brill, 1994), pp. 7–9; Mikel de Epalza, "Mozarabs: An Emblematic Christian Minority in al-Andalus," in *The Legacy of Muslim Spain*, ed. S. K. Jayyusi (Leiden, Netherlands: Brill, 1992), pp. 149–70; *EI2*, s.v. "Mozarab" (Pedro Chalmeta).

9. Mikel de Epalza, "Falta de obispos y conversión al Islam de los Cristianos de al Ándalus," *Al-Qantara* 15 (1994): 386–400.

10. *EI2*, s.v. "Mozarab."

11. Lévi-Provençal, *Histoire de l'Espagne musulmane*, vol. 1: 78–79.

12. Ibn 'Abdun, *Treatise of Hisba*, translated in Évariste Lévi-Provençal, *Séville musulmane au début du XIIe siècle: Le traité d'Ibn Abdun sur la vie urbaine et les corps de métiers* (Paris: Maisonneuve, 1947), pp. 108–9.

13. Alex Metcalfe, *The Muslims of Medieval Italy* (Edinburgh: Edinburgh University Press, 2009); Umberto Rizzitano, "Gli Arabi di Sicilia," in *Il Mezzogiorno dai Bizantini a Federico II* (Turin: Unione Tipografica Editrice Torinese, 1983), pp. 368–434; and Henri Bresc, "Arab Christians in the Western Mediterranean (Eleventh–Thirteenth Centuries)," in *Library of Mediterranean History*, vol. 1, ed. V. Mallia-Milanes (Malta: Mireva, 1994), pp. 3–45.

14. For a very helpful summary of that question, see Nurit Tsafir, "The Attitude of Sunni Islam toward Jews and Christians as Reflected in Some Legal Issues," *Al-Qantara* 26 (2005): 317–36.

15. Ibid.

16. See R. Arié, "Traduction annotée et commentée des traités de *hisba* d'Ibn 'Abd al-Ra'ûf et de 'Umar al Garsîfî," *Hespéris Tamuda* 1 (1960): 5–38, 199–214, 349–75 (here, pp. 206–8); Tolan and Josserand, *Relations des pays d'Islam*, pp. 169–72.

17. See *EI2*, s.v. "Khamr" (A. Wensicnk and J. Sadan); on the consumption of wine in Egypt, see Goitein, *A Mediterranean Society*, vol. 1: 122–23.

18. Vincent Lagardère, *Histoire et société en occident musulman au moyen âge: Analyse du Mi'yâr d'al-Wanšarîsî* (Madrid: Casa de Velázquez, 1996), p. 52.

19. Ibn 'Abdun, *Treatise of Hisba*, Lévi-Provençal trans., pp. 64, 127–28; Arié, "Traduction annotée."

20. Lagardère, *Histoire et société*, p. 476.

21. Ibid., p. 477.

22. Ibid., p. 53.

23. See James Powell, ed., *Muslims under Latin Rule, 1100–1300* (Princeton, NJ: Princeton University Press, 1990).

24. On the Muslims in Norman Sicily, see David Abulafia, "The End of Muslim Sicily," in Powell, ed., *Muslims under Latin Rule*, pp. 103–33; David Abulafia, *Frederick II: A Medieval Emperor* (London: Penguin, 1988); Henri Bresc, "Féodalité coloniale en terre d'Islam: La Sicile (1070–1240)," in *Structures féodales et féodalisme dans l'Occident méditerranéen (Xe–XIIIe siècles)* (Rome: École Française de Rome, 1980), pp. 631–47; Bresc, "Mudéjars des pays de la couronne d'Aragon et Sarrasins de la Sicile normande: Le problème d'acculturation," in Charles-Emmanuel Dufourcq et al., *Jaime I y su época: X Congreso de Historia de la Corona de Aragón* (Saragossa, Spain: Institución Fernando el Católico, 1979), pp. 51–60; Donald Matthew, *The Norman Kingdom of Sicily* (Cambridge, UK: Cambridge University Press, 1992); Alex Metcalfe, *Muslims and Christians in Norman Sicily: Arabic Speakers and the End of Islam* (London: Routledge Curzon, 2003); and Metcalfe, *The Muslims of Medieval Italy*.

25. Ibn Jubayr, *Rihla*, trans. R.J.C. Broadhurst as *The Travels of Ibn Jubayr, Being the Chronicle of a Mediaeval Spanish Moor . . .* (London: Camelot, 1952), pp. 335–63.

26. A. Turki, "Consultation juridique d'al-Imam al-Mâzarî sur le cas des musulmans vivant en Sicile sous l'autorité des Normands," *Mélanges de l'Université Saint-Joseph* 50, no. 2 (1984): 691–704; Tolan and Josserand, *Relations des pays d'Islam*, pp. 152–56.

27. Jean-Marie Martin, "La colonie sarrasine de Lucera et son environnement: Quelques réflexions," in *Mediterraneo medievale: Scritti in onore di Francesco Giunta*, ed. Francesco Giunta, 3 vols. (Soveria Mannelli, Italy: Rubbettino, 1989), vol. 2: 795–811.

28. On the place of Muslims in Frankish society in the Holy Land, see Maya Shatzmiller, ed., *Crusaders and Muslims in Twelfth-Century Syria* (Leiden, Netherlands: Brill, 1993); Ronnie Ellenblum, *Frankish Rural Settlement in the Latin Kingdom of Jerusalem* (Cambridge, UK: Cambridge University Press, 1998); Benjamin Kedar, "The Subjected Muslims of the Frankish Levant," in Powell, ed., *Muslims under Latin Rule*, pp. 135–74; Joshua Prawer, *Crusader Institutions* (Oxford, UK: Oxford University Press, 1980); and Prawer, *Histoire du royaume latin de Jérusalem* (Paris: Éditions du Centre National de la Recherche Scientifique, 1969).

29. *The Travels of Ibn Jubayr*, Broadhurst trans., p. 317; on this passage, see Tolan, *Saracens*, p. xvii.

30. Joseph O'Callaghan, "The Mudejars of Castile and Portugal in the Twelfth and Thirteenth Centuries," in Powell, ed., *Muslims under Latin Rule*, pp. 11–56, esp. 13–18.

31. See Jean-Pierre Molénat, *Campagnes et monts de Tolède du XIIe au XVe siècle* (Madrid: Casa de Velázquez, 1997).

32. See Clay Stalls, *Possessing the Land: Aragon's Expansion into Islam's Ebro Frontier under Alfonso the Battler, 1104–1134* (Leiden, Netherlands: Brill, 1995); Robert Burns, "Muslims in the Thirteenth-century Realms of Aragon: Interaction and Reaction," in Powell, ed., *Muslims under Latin Rule*, pp. 57–102, esp. 64–67.

33. O'Callaghan, "The Mudejars of Castile and Portugal," pp. 16–18.

34. See Pierre Guichard, *Les musulmans de Valence et la reconquête: XIe–XIIIe siècles*, 2 vols. (Damascus: Institut Français de Damas, 1990–1991); Maria Teresa Ferrer i Mallol, *Els sarrains de la corona catalano-aragonesa en el segle XIV: Segregació i discriminació* (Barcelona: Consell Superior d'Investigacions Científiques, 1987); Robert Burns, *Islam under the Crusaders: Colonial Survival in the Thirteenth Century Kingdom of Valencia* (Princeton, NJ: Princeton University Press, 1973); Robert Burns, *Moors and Crusaders in Mediterranean Spain* (London: Variorum, 1978); Robert Burns, *Muslims, Christians, and Jews in the Crusader Kingdom of Valencia* (Cambridge, UK: Cambridge University Press, 1984); John Boswell, *The Royal Treasure: Muslim Communities in the Crown of Aragon in the Fourteenth Century* (New Haven, CT: Yale University Press, 1977); and Mark Meyerson, *The Muslims of Valencia in the Age of Fernando and Isabel: Between Coexistence and Crusade* (Berkeley: University of California Press, 1991).

35. Benjamin Kedar, "De Iudeis et Sarracenis: On the Categorization of Muslims in Medieval Canon Law," in *Studia in honorem eminentissimi cardinalis Alphonsi M. Stickler*, ed. R. J. Castillo Lara (Rome: Libreria Ateneo Salesiano, 1992), pp. 207–13; Henri Gilles, "Législation et doctrine canoniques sur les Sarrasins," *Cahiers de Fanjeaux* 18 (1983): 195–213; Emilio Bussi, "La condizione giuridica dei musulmani nel diritto canonico," *Revista di Storia del Diritto Italiano* 8 (1935): 459–94; Peter Herde, "Christians and Saracens at the Time of the Crusades: Some Comments of Contemporary Medieval Canonists," *Studia Gratiana* 12 (1967): 361–76; and Andrea Mariana Navarro, "Imagenes y representaciones de moros y judios en los fueros de la corona de Castilla (siglos XI–XIII)," *Temas Medievales* 11 (2002–2003): 113–50. See the laws and translations included in the RELMIN database, available at http://www.cn-telma.fr/relmin/index/ (accessed February 13, 2012).

36. Alfonso el Sabio (Alfonso the Wise), *Las siete partidos* (Madrid: Real Academia de la Historia, 1807 and 1972), § 7.25.1. See Tolan, *Saracens*, pp. 174–75, 186–93; Robert

Burns, "Jews and Moors in the *Siete partidas* of Alfonso X the Learned: A Background Perspective," in Collins and Goodman, eds., *Medieval Spain: Culture, Conflict, and Coexistence*, pp. 46–62.

37. Ferrer i Mallol, *Els sarrains*, pp. 88–94.

38. Kedar, "The Subjected Muslims of the Frankish Levant," pp. 154–65.

39. Mariana Navarro, "Imagenes y representaciones"; O'Callaghan, "The Mudejars of Castile and Portugal," p. 37.

40. Alfonso el Sabio, *Siete partidas*, § 3.11.21.

41. Ibid., § 3.16.8. See also § 3.11.21: "En qué manera deben jurar los moros."

42. O'Callaghan, "The Mudejars of Castile and Portugal," p. 39.

43. Lateran III, canon 26, in *Concilia oecumenicorum decreta*, p. 223; canon reiterated in § 10.5.6.5 of *Corpus iuris canonici*, vol. 2: 773; Alfonso el Sabio, *Siete partidas*, § 4.7.8.

44. Mariana Navarro, "Imagenes y representaciones."

45. Kedar, "The Subjected Muslims of the Frankish Levant," pp. 159–60.

46. Gratian, *Decretum, causa* 28. For Gregory IX's confirmation of the decree in 1234, see *Responsiones ad dubitabilia circa communicationem christianorum cum sarracenis*, in Raymond of Penyafort, *Summae*, 3 vols. of the *Universa Bibliotheca Iurus*, ed. Xavier Ochoa and Aloysius Diez (Rome: Commentarium pro Religiosis, 1976–1978), vol. 3: 1024–36, chap. 11; and Tolan and Josserand, *Relations des pays d'Islam*, pp. 164–69.

47. Mariana Navarro, "Imagenes y representaciones," p. 144. Alfonso el Sabio, *Siete partidas*, § 7.25.10, 7.24.9.

48. David Nirenberg, *Communities of Violence: Persecution of Minorities in the Middle Ages* (Princeton, NJ: Princeton University Press, 1996), pp. 127–65.

49. Agapito Rey, *Castigos e documentos para bien vivir ordenados por el Rey don Sancho IV* (Bloomington: Indiana University Press, 1952), pp. 126–33.

50. James Powers, "Frontier Municipal Baths and Social Interaction in Thirteenth-Century Spain," *American History Review* 84 (1979): 649–67.

51. O'Callaghan, "The Mudejars of Castile and Portugal," p. 31.

52. Benjamin Z. Kedar, "On the Origins of the Earliest Laws of Frankish Jerusalem: The Canons of the Council of Nablus, 1120," *Speculum* 74 (1999): 310–35. See James Brundage, "Prostitution, Miscegenation, and Sexual Purity in the First Crusade," in *Crusade and Settlement: Presented to R. C. Smail*, ed. Peter W. Edbury (Cardiff, UK: University College Cardiff Press, 1985), pp. 57–65, reprinted in James Brundage, *The Crusades, Holy War, and Canon Law* (Aldershot, UK: Variorum, 1991), pp. 60–61.

53. Lateran IV, canon 68, in *Les Conciles oecuméniques: Les décrets*, vol. 2, part 1 (Paris: Cerf, 1994), p. 567; O'Callaghan, "The Mudejars of Castile and Portugal," pp. 30–31.

54. Lateran IV, canon 68. On the Crown of Aragon, see Elena Lourie, "Anatomy of Ambivalence: Muslims under the Crown of Aragon in the Late Thirteenth Century," in her *Crusade and Colonisation* (Aldershot, UK: Variorum, 1990), p. 52; Nirenberg, *Communities of Violence*. On Castile, see O'Callaghan, "Mudejars of Castile and Portugal," p. 44.

55. Alfonso el Sabio, *Siete partidas*, § 7.28.

56. Ibid., § 7.28.6. See Larry J. Simon, "Jews in the Legal Corpus of Alfonso el Sabio," *Comitatus* 18 (1987): 80–97.

57. See Robert Burns, "Renegades, Adventurers, and Sharp Businessmen: The Thirteenth-Century Spaniard in the Cause of Islam," *Catholic Historical Review* 58 (1972): 341–66; Nirenberg, *Communities of Violence*, p. 128 n. 4; Mikel de Epalza, *Fray Anselm Turmeda (Abdallah al-Taryuman) y su polémica islamo-cristiana* (Madrid: Hiperión, 1994); Dwayne E. Carpenter, "Minorities in Medieval Spain," *Romance Quarterly* 33 (1986): 257–87; and Dwayne E. Carpenter, "Alfonso the Learned and the Problem of Conversion to Islam," in *Estudios in homenaje a Enrique Ruiz-Fornells*, ed. Juan Fernández-Jiménez, José Labrador-Herraiz, and Teresa Valdivieso (Erie, PA: Asociación de Licenciados y Doctores de Español en los Estados Unidos, 1990), pp. 61–68.

58. Alfonso el Sabio, *Siete partidas*, § 4.21.8; see Dwayne E. Carpenter, *Alfonso X and the Jews: An Edition of and Commentary on Siete partidas 7.24 "De los judios"* (Berkeley: University of California Press, 1986), pp. 95–98. For the conversions of slaves in Aragon, see Nirenberg, *Communities of Violence*, pp. 184–85; Burns, "Muslims in the Thirteenth-Century Realms of Aragon," p. 79; and Benjamin Kedar, *Crusade and Mission: European Approaches toward the Muslims* (Princeton, NJ: Princeton University Press, 1984), pp. 76–78, 146–52.

59. See *EI2*, s.v. "Hārūn b. Yahyā" (M. Izzedin) and "Kustantinīyya" (J. Mordtmann).

60. Qur'an 47:4; see Raoudha Guemara, "La libération et le rachat des captifs: Une lecture musulmane," in *La liberazione dei "captivi" tra cristianità e islam: Oltre la crociata e il gihâd: Tolleranza e servizio unmanitario*, ed. Giulio Cipollone (Vatican City: Archivio Segreto Vaticano, 2000), pp. 333–34.

61. Youval Rotman, *Byzantine Slavery and the Mediterranean World*, trans. Jane Marie Todd (Cambridge, MA: Harvard University Press, 2009), pp. 36–39.

62. See Kedar, "The Subjected Muslims of the Frankish Levant," p. 153.

63. Charles Verlinden, *L'esclavage dans l'Europe médiévale*, vol. 1: *Péninsule ibérique, France* (Brugge: De Tempel, 1955), p. 186, quoting Abenalcoitía el Cordobés, *Historia de la conquista en España*, in J. Ribera, *Colección de obras arábigas de historia y geografía que publica la Real Academia de Historia*, vol. 2 (Madrid: Impr. y estereotipia de M. Rivadeneyra, 1926), p. 115.

64. Verlinden, *L'esclavage*, vol. 1: 194; Rafael Pinilla, "Aproximación al estudio de los cautivos cristianos fruto de guerra santa-cruzada en Al-Andalus," in Cipollone, ed., *La liberazione dei "captivi" tra cristiantià e islam*, pp. 311–31.

65. Lévi-Provençal, *Histoire de l'Espagne musulmane*, vol. 2: 35–36.

66. James Brodman, *Ransoming Captives in Crusader Spain: The Order of Merced on the Christian-Islamic Frontier* (Philadelphia: University of Pennsylvania Press, 1986), p. 2; Verlinden, *L'esclavage*, vol. 1: 241. For other examples of captives taken during military actions by the Almohads, see Verlinden, *L'esclavage*, vol. 1: 200–202.

67. See Rotman, *Byzantine Slavery*, pp. 47–51.

68. Jacques Heers, *Esclaves et domestiques au Moyen Âge dans le monde méditerranéen* (Paris: Fayard, 1981), pp. 39–43.

69. Ibid., pp. 44–50.

70. Citarella, "The Relations of Amalfi with the Arab World," p. 309.

71. Verlinden, *L'esclavage*, vol. 1: 195–98.

72. Brodman, *Ransoming Captives*, p. 7; Mariana Navarro, "Imagenes y representaciones," p. 117; and Verlinden, *L'esclavage*, vol. 1: 153–54, 158.

73. Verlinden, *L'esclavage*, vol. 1: 241.

74. Goitein, *A Mediterranean Society*, vol. 1: 328–29.

75. Rotman, *Byzantine Slavery*, pp. 49–50.

76. Goitein, *A Mediterranean Society*, vol. 1: 329.

77. Heers, *Esclaves et domestiques*, pp. 234–44.

78. Brodman, *Ransoming Captives*, p. 8; Verlinden, *L'esclavage*, vol. 1: 153, 165–66, 242.

79. Cipollone, ed., *La liberazione dei "captivi" tra cristianità e islam*; Alan Forey, "The Military Orders and the Ransoming of Captives from Islam (Twelfth to Fourteenth Centuries)," *Studia Monastica* 33 (1991): 259–79; Yvonne Friedman, *Encounter between Enemies: Captivity and Ransom in the Latin Kingdom of Jerusalem* (Leiden, Netherlands: Brill, 2002); and André Díaz Borrás, *El miedo al Mediterraneo: La caridad popular valenciana y la redención de cautivos bajo el poder musulmán, 1323–1539* (Barcelona: Consejo Superior de Investigaciones Científicas, 2001).

80. Usāma ibn Munqidh, *I'tibār*, translated into French by André Miquel as *Ousâma: Un prince syrien face aux croisés* (Paris: Fayard, 1986); see Paul Cobb, *Usâma ibn Munqidh: Warrior-Poet in the Age of the Crusades* (Oxford, UK: Oneworld, 2006), p. 29.

81. *The Travels of Ibn Jubayr*, Broadhurst trans., p. 323.

82. Guemara, "La libération et le rachat des captifs: Une lecture musulmane," p. 341.

83. Brodman, *Ransoming Captives*; Cipollone, *Cristianità-islam: Cattività e liberazione in nome di Dio:Il tempo di Innocenzo III dopo "il 1187"* (Rome: Pontificia Università Gregoriana, 1992).

84. Verlinden, *L'esclavage*; Heers, *Esclaves et domestiques*.

85. Rotman, *Byzantine Slavery*.

86. Lévi-Provençal, *Histoire de l'Espagne musulmane*, vol. 2: 122–30; *EI2*, s.v. "Sakāliba" (Pierre Guichard and Mohamed Meouak).

87. On the use of slaves in the production of sugar, see Heers, *Esclaves et domestiques*; Mohamed Ouerfelli, "Le sucre: Production, commercialisation et usages dans la Méditerranée médiévale," doctoral thesis, Paris, Université de Paris-I, 2006.

88. Heers, *Esclaves et domestique*, pp. 136–38.

89. Verlinden, *L'esclavage*, vol. 1: 145 (for slaves whose masters were Portuguese cobblers and smiths).

90. Lévi-Provençal, *Histoire de l'Espagne musulmane*, vol. 2: 126.

91. Heers, *Esclaves et domestiques*, pp. 125–26.

92. *EI2*, s.v. "'Abd" (R. Brunschvig).

93. *EI2*, s.v. "Umm al-walad" (Joseph Schacht).

94. Lévi-Provençal, *Histoire de l'Espagne musulmane*, vol. 2: 2.

95. Rotman, *Byzantine Slavery*, 147–48.

96. Ibid., pp. 160–64.

97. See Guemara, "La libération et le rachat des captifs: Une lecture musulmane," pp. 339–40.

98. *EI2*, s.v. "'Abd."

99. Rotman, *Byzantine Slavery*, pp. 129–34.

100. Goitein, *A Mediterranean Society*, vol. 1: 144.

101. Heers, *Esclaves et domestiques*, pp. 247–83.

102. Rotman, *Byzantine Slavery*, pp. 40–41.

103. *El Fuero latino de Teruel*, chaps. 361–62; see Tolan and Josserand, *Relations des pays d'Islam*, pp. 179–89; Mariana Navarro, "Imagenes y representaciones," p. 145.

104. Bernard of Angers, *Livre des miracles de Sainte Foy* (Sélestat, France: Société des Amis de la Bibliothèque Humaniste, 1994), pp. 50–52, 59–60, 67–68, 72–74, 82–85;

Angeles García de la Borbolla, "Santo Domingo de Silos y las milagrosas redenciones de cautivos en tierras andalusíes (Siglo XIII)," in Cipollone, ed., *La liberazione dei "captivi" tra cristianità e islam*, pp. 539–49.

105. See Rotman, *Byzantine Slavery*, 150–51.

106. Verlinden, *L'esclavage*, vol. 1: 233–34.

107. *Usatges de Barcelona*, edited from the Catalan text by J. Rovira i Ermengol (Barcelona: Barcino, 1933), § 96.

108. Heers, *Esclaves et domestiques*, p. 234.

Chapter 4: In Search of Egyptian Gold: Traders in the Mediterranean

1. Cyril Mango, *Le développement urbain de Constantinople: IVe–VIIe siècles* (Paris: De Boccard, 2004).

2. Jean-Claude Garcin, ed., *Grandes villes méditerranéennes du monde musulman médiéval* (Rome: École Française de Rome, 2000).

3. André Miquel, *L'Islam et sa civilisation* (Paris: Armand Colin, 1990), p. 78.

4. Goitein, *A Mediterranean Society*, vol. 1: 75.

5. Christine Mazzoli-Guintard, "De Damas à Cordoue: Espaces urbains de deux métropoles omeyyades," in *Culture arabe et culture européenne: L'inconnu au turban dans l'album de famille*, ed. François Clément and John Tolan (Paris: L'Harmattan, 2006), pp. 149–62; Christine Mazzoli-Guintard, *Vivre à Cordoue au Moyen Âge: Solidarité citadines* [sic] *en terre d'Islam aux Xe–XIe siècles* (Rennes, France: Presses Universitaires de Rennes, 2003); and Mazzoli-Guintard, *Villes d'al-Andalus: L'Espagne et le Portugal à l'époque musulmane, VIII–XV siècles* (Rennes, France: Presses Universitaires de Rennes, 1996).

6. Ibn Hawqal, *Kibāb sūrat al-ard*, translated into French by J. Kramer and G. Wiet as *La configuration de la terre* (Paris: Maisonneuve et Larose, 2001).

7. See Olivia Remie Constable, *Trade and Traders in Muslim Spain: The Commercial Realignment of the Iberian Peninsula, 900–1500* (Cambridge, UK: Cambridge University Press, 1994).

8. Henri Pirenne, *Mahomet et Charlemagne* (Brussels: Nouvelle Société d'Édition, 1936); Maurice Lombard, *Espaces et réseaux du haut moyen âge* (Paris: Mouton, 1972); Richard Hodges and David Whitehouse, *Mohammed, Charlemagne, and the Origins of Europe* (Ithaca, NY: Cornell University Press, 1983); Adriaan Verhulst, "Marchés, marchands et commerce au haut moyen âge dans l'historiographie récente," in *Mercati e mercanti nell'alto medioevo: L'area euroasiatica e l'area mediterranea* (Spoleto, Italy: Centro Italiano di Studi sull'Alto Medioevo, 1993), pp. 23–43; Peregine Horden and Nicholas Purcell, *The Corrupting Sea: A Study of Mediterranean History* (Oxford, UK: Blackwell, 2000), pp. 32–34, 153–60; and Gene W. Heck, *Charlemagne, Muhammad, and the Arab Roots of Capitalism* (Berlin: Walter de Gruyter, 2006).

9. See Constable, *Trade and Traders in Muslim Spain*, pp. 39–41; on this period in European economic history, see Michael McCormick, *Origins of the European Economy: Communication and Commerce, A.D. 300–900* (Cambridge, UK: Cambridge University Press, 2001).

10. Philippe Sénac, *Les Carolingiens et al-Andalus (VIIIe–IXe siècles)* (Paris: Maisonneuve et Larose, 2002), pp. 41–42.

11. Philippe Sénac, "Les Carolingiens et le califat abbasside (VIIIe–IXe siècles)," in *Chrétiens et musulmans et Méditerranée médiévale (VIIIe–XIIIe siècle)*, ed. Nicolas

Prouteau and Philippe Sénac (Poitiers, France: Centre d'Études Supérieures en Civilisation Médiévale, 2003), pp. 3–19.

12. See Évelyne Patlagean, "Byzance et les marchés du grand commerce, vers 830–vers 1030: Entre Pirenne et Polyani," in *Mercati e mercanti*, pp. 587–629, esp. 616.

13. Goitein, *A Mediterranean Society*, vol. 1: 61; on trade in the medieval Muslim world more generally, see David Abulafia, "Asia, Africa and the Trade of Medieval Europe," in *The Cambridge Economic History of Europe*, vol. 2: *Trade and Industry in the Middle Ages*, ed. M. Postan and E. Miller (Cambridge, UK: Cambridge University Press, 1987), pp. 402–73.

14. Goitein, *A Mediterranean Society*, vol. 1: 101–8.

15. Ibid., pp. 99–100.

16. Ibid., pp. 53–54; Shlomo Goitein, *Letters of Medieval Jewish Traders* (Princeton, NJ: Princeton University Press, 1973), pp. 145–74, 278–304.

17. Goitein, *A Mediterranean Society*, vol. 1: 209–10.

18. Ibid., pp. 43–44.

19. On the consumption of wine in Egypt, see ibid., pp. 122–23.

20. *Mediterraneum: El esplendor del Mediterráneo medieval, s. XIII–XV* (Barcelona: Institut Europeu de la Mediterrània, 2004).

21. Barbara Kreutz, "Ghost Ships and Phantom Cargoes: Reconstructing Early Amalfitan Trade," *Journal of Medieval History* 20 (1994): 347–57; Armand Citarella, "Patterns of Medieval Trade: The Commerce of Amalfi," *Journal of Economic History* 28 (1968): 531–55; Citarella, "The Relations of Amalfi with the Arab World before the Crusades," *Speculum* 42 (1967): 299–312; and Goitein, *Letters of Medieval Jewish Traders*, pp. 42–45.

22. On Venice, see Jean-Claude Hocquet, *Venise au Moyen Âge* (Paris: Belles Lettres, 2003).

23. John Pryor shows that the Venetians actually envisioned the conquest of Egypt; John Pryor, "The Venetian Fleet for the Fourth Crusade," in *The Experience of Crusading*, vol. 1: *Western Approaches*, ed. M. Bull and N. Housley (Cambridge, UK: Cambridge University Press, 2003), pp. 103–23.

24. Gottlieg Tafel and Georg Thomas, eds., *Urkunden zur älteren Handels- und Staatsgeschichte der Republick Venedig mit besonderer Beziehung auf Byzanz und die Levante*, 3 vols. (Vienna, 1856–1857; Amsterdam: Hakkert, 1964), vol. 2: 184–93; Louise Bunger Robert, "Venice and the Crusades," in *A History of the Crusades*, 5 vols., ed. Kenneth M. Setton (Philadelphia: University of Pennsylvania Press, 1955–1989), vol. 5: 379–451, esp. 441.

25. Citarella, "The Relations of Amalfi with the Arab World," p. 310.

26. See M. de Mas Latrie, *Traités de paix et de commerce et documents divers concernant les relations des chrétiens avec les arabes de l'Afrique septentrionale au moyen âge* (Paris: Imprimerie Impériale, 1866); on the presence of the Pisan and Genoese merchants in the Andalusian ports, see Constable, *Trade and Traders in Muslim Spain*, p. 42.

27. See Maria Teresa Ferrer Mallol, "El Mediterráneo de los siglos XIII al XV: La expansión catalana," in *Mediterraneum*, pp. 143–58 (and bibliography, pp. 600–603); Charles-Emmanuel Dufourcq, *L'Espagne catalane et le Maghrib au XIIIe et XIVe siècles* (Paris: Presses Universitaires de France, 1965); David Abulafia, *A Mediterranean Emporium: The Catalan Kingdom of Majorca* (Cambridge, UK: Cambridge University Press, 1994); and Damien Coulon, *Barcelone et le grand commerce d'Orient au Moyen Âge: Un*

siècle de relations avec l'Égypte et la Syrie-Palestine (ca. 1330–ca. 1430) (Madrid: Casa de Valázquez, 2004).

28. Goitein, *A Mediterranean Society*, vol. 1: 327–28.

29. Ibid., p. 331.

30. Ibid., pp. 70–79.

31. On the *sakka* or *saftaja*, see ibid., pp. 240–42.

32. Ibid., p. 327.

33. *The Travels of Ibn Jubayr*, Broadhurst trans., p. 328.

34. Goitein, *A Mediterranean Society*, vol. 1: 344–45.

35. *The Travels of Ibn Jubayr*, Broadhurst trans., p. 72.

36. Olivia Remie Constable, *Housing the Stranger in the Mediterranean World: Lodging, Trade, and Travel in Late Antiquity and the Middle Ages* (Cambridge, UK: Cambridge University Press, 2003).

37. Goitein, *A Mediterranean Society*, vol. 1: 220–22.

38. Ibid., pp. 339–43.

39. Ibid., pp. 219–20.

40. Michael McCormick, "New Light on the 'Dark Ages': How the Slave Trade Fuelled the Carolingian Economy," *Past and Present* 177 (2002): 17–54.

41. *Liber pontificalis*, ed. Louis Duchesne and Cyrille Vogel, 3 vols. (Paris: E. de Boccard, 1981), vol. 1: 433; see McCormick, "New Light on the 'Dark Ages,'" p. 28.

42. Rotman, *Byzantine Slavery*, pp. 57–81, 97; Yûsuf Râgib, "Les marchés aux esclaves en terre d'Islam," in *Mercati e mercanti*, pp. 721–63.

43. Kreutz, "Ghost Ships and Phantom Cargoes," p. 353.

44. Council of Meaux, in *MGH*, capit. 2, p. 419, c. 75; see Verlinden, *L'esclavage*, vol. 1: 216–17.

45. Verlinden, *L'esclavage*, vol. 1: 218–25.

46. Rotman, *Byzantine Slavery*, p. 73; Lévi-Provençal, *Histoire de l'Espagne musulmane*, vol. 2: 124–25; Miquel, *Géographie humaine*, vol. 2: 324–25.

47. Goitein, *A Mediterranean Society*, vol. 1: 138.

48. Verlinden, *L'esclavage*, vol. 1: 143–47, 167–71.

49. Heers, *Esclaves et domestiques*, p. 104.

50. Ibid., p. 174.

51. John Tolan, "Taking Gratian to Africa: Raymond de Penyafort's Legal Advice to the Dominicans and Franciscans in Tunis (1234)," in *A Faithful Sea: The Religious Cultures of the Mediterranean, 1200–1700*, ed. Adnan Husain and Katherine Fleming (Oxford, UK: Oneworld, 2007), pp. 47–63.

52. Ibid.

53. See Robert Burns, *Society and Documentation in Crusader Valencia* (Princeton, NJ: Princeton University Press, 1985).

54. Goitein, *A Mediterranean Society*, vol. 1: 126–27.

55. Ibid., vol. 1: 70.

Chapter 5: On the Shoulders of Giants: Transmission and Exchange of Knowledge

1. See Roshdi Rashed, ed., *Encyclopedia of the History of Arabic Science* (London: Routledge, 2002).

2. On medicine in the Middle Ages, see Rashed, ed., *Encyclopedia of the History of Arabic Science, s.v. "Medicine" (Emilie Savage-Smith)*; ibid., s.v. "Influence of Arab Medicine in the Western Middle Ages" (Danielle Jacquart); and Danielle Jacquart and Françoise Micheau, *La médecine arabe et l'occident médiéval* (Paris: Maisonneuve et Larose, 1990).

3. Jacquart and Micheau, *La médecine arabe et l'occident médiéval*, pp. 32–35.

4. Ibid., pp. 13–14, 229.

5. Ibid., pp. 36–45; *EI2*, s.v. "Hunayn ibn Ishāk" (G. Strohmaier).

6. Jacquart and Micheau, *La médecine arabe et l'occident médiéval*, pp. 236–39; *EI2*, s.v. "Al-Tabarī, Alī b. Rabban" (D. Thomas).

7. Jacquart and Micheau, *La médecine arabe et l'occident médiéval*, pp. 56–68; *EI2*, s.v. "al-Razī, Abū Bakr Muhammad b. Zakariyyā" (L. Goodman).

8. Jacquart and Micheau, *La médecine arabe et l'occident médiéval*, pp. 235–36.

9. Ibid., pp. 74–85; Nancy Siraisi, *Avicenna in Renaissance Italy: The Canon and Medical Teaching in Italian Universities after 1500* (Princeton, NJ: Princeton University Press, 1987).

10. McCormick, "New Light on the 'Dark Ages,'" p. 36.

11. Usāma ibn Munqidh, *The Book of Contemplation: Islam and the Crusades*, trans. Paul M. Cobb (London: Penguin, 2008), pp. 145–46.

12. *Constantinus Africanus (11th cent.) and His Arabic Sources*, ed. F. Sezgin (Frankfurt: Institut für Geschichte der Arabisch-Islamischen Wissenschaften, 1996); Gabriele Marasco, "Constantin l'Africain, l'abbaye de Montcassin et le développement de la médecine en Occident," in Clément and Tolan, eds., *Culture arabe et culture européenne*, pp. 59–80.

13. For the translation of this text, see Edward Grant, ed., *A Source Book in Medieval Science* (Cambridge, MA: Harvard University Press, 1974), pp. 35–38, or Charles Burnett, "The Coherence of the Arabic-Latin Translation Program in Toledo in the Twelfth Century," *Science in Context* 14 (2001): 249–288, 275–281.

14. Ms. Lat. 6912, vol. 1, fol. 1v; see Jacquart and Micheau, *La médecine arabe et l'occident médiéval*, ill. 8.

15. Jacquart and Micheau, *La médecine arabe et l'occident médiéval*, pp. 185–89.

16. For an introduction to the subject, see *EI2*, s.v. "'Ilm al-Ha'ya" (David Pingree); for a more exhaustive treatment, see Rashed, ed., *Encyclopedia of the History of Arabic Science*, vol. 1.

17. Marie-Thérèse d'Alverny, *La transmission des textes philosophiques et scientifiques au Moyen Âge* (Aldershot, UK: Variorum, 1994); Charles Burnett, "The Translating Activity in Medieval Spain," in *The Legacy of Muslim Spain*, ed. Salma Khadra Jayyusi and Manuela Marín (Leiden, Netherlands: Brill, 1992), pp. 1036–58; Danielle Jacquart, "L'école des traducteurs," in *Tolède, XIIe–XIIIe siècles, Musulmans, chrétiens et juifs: Le savoir et la tolérance*, ed. Louis Cardaillac (Paris: Autrement, 1991), pp. 177–91; and John Tolan, "Reading God's Will in the Stars: Petrus Alfonsi and Raymond de Marseille Defend the New Arabic Astrology," *Revista Española de Filosofía Medieval* 7 (2000): 13–30.

18. See Roger Arnaldez, *À la croisée des trois monothéismes: Une communauté de pensée au Moyen Âge* (Paris: Albin Michel, 1993); Alain de Libéra and Maurice-Ruben Hayoun, *Averroès et l'Averroïsme* (Paris: Que sais-je?, 1991); Alain de Libéra, *La philosophie médiévale* (Paris: Presses Universitaires de France, 2004).

19. Oleg Grabar, *The Shape of the Holy: Early Islamic Jerusalem* (Princeton, NJ: Princeton University Press, 1996).

20. See Anthony Cutler, "Everywhere and Nowhere: The Invisible Muslim and Christian Self-Fashioning in the Culture of Outremer," in *France and the Holy Land: Frankish Culture at the End of the Crusades*, ed. Daniel H. Weiss and Lisa Mahoney (Baltimore: Johns Hopkins University Press, 2004), pp. 253–81.

21. See P. Guichard and D. Menjot, eds., *Pays d'Islam et monde latin, Xe–XIIIe siècles: Textes et documents* (Lyons: Presses Universitaires de Lyon, 2000), pp. 100–103.

22. Amato di Montecassino, *L'Ystoire de li Normant*, ed. Vincenzo Barthomaeis (Rome: Tipografia del Senato, 1935), p. 175.

23. Tolan and Josserand, *Relations des pays d'Islam*, pp. 148–52.

24. Vladimir Goss, "Western Architecture and the World of Islam in the Twelfth Century," in *The Meeting of Two Worlds: Cultural Exchange between East and West during the Period of the Crusades*, ed. Vladimir Goss and Christine Bornstein (Kalamazoo: Western Michigan University, 1986), pp. 361–75.

25. See the articles by James Monroe and Roger Boasse in Jayyusi and Marín, eds., *Legacy of Muslim Spain*.

26. The bibliography on Alfonso, his reign, and the cultural activities of his court is vast. The following are merely a few recent studies: Manuel González Jiménez, *Alfonso X el Sabio, 1252–1284* (Palencia, Spain: La Olmeda, 1993); Francisco Márquez Villanueva, *El concepto cultural Alfonsí* (Madrid: Mapfre, 1994); and Joseph F. O'Callaghan, *The Learned King: The Reign of Alfonso X of Castile* (Philadelphia: University of Pennsylvania Press, 1993). Also still useful is the biography by Antonio Ballesteros Beretta, *Alfonso X el Sabio* (Barcelona: Salvat, 1963).

In 1984, for the seven-hundredth anniversary of his death, a large number of colloquia and collections of articles were devoted to Alfonso: Robert I. Burns, *Emperor of Culture: Alfonso X the Learned of Castile and His Thirteenth Century Renaissance* (Philadelphia: University of Pennsylvania Press, 1990); Burns, ed., *The Worlds of Alfonso the Learned and James the Conqueror: Intellect and Force in the Middle Ages* (Princeton, NJ: Princeton University Press, 1985); John E. Keller, ed., *Alfonsine Essays*, volume of *Romance Quarterly* 33, no. 3 (August 1986); *Homenaje a Alfonso X, el Sabio (1284–1984)*, volume of *Revista Canadiense de Estudios Hispánicos* 9, no. 3 (Spring 1985); Juan Carlos de Miguel Rodriguez, ed., *Actas del congreso internacional: Alfonso X el Sabio, vida, obra, y época* (Madrid: Sociedad Española de Estudios Medievales, 1984); and Francisco Márquez Villanueva and Carlos Alberto Vega, eds., *Alfonso X of Castile: The Learned King (1221–1284), An International Symposium* (Cambridge, MA: Department of Romance Languages and Literatures of Harvard University, 1990).

27. See Martin Accad, "Corruption and/or Misinterpretation of the Bible: The Story of the Islâmic Usage of *Tahrîf*," *The Near Eastern School of Theology Theological Review* 24 (2003): 67–97; *EI2*, s.v. "Tahrîf."

28. On this text, see Laura Bottini, "The Apology of al-Kindī," in *Christian-Muslim Relations: A Bibliographical History*, 5 vols., ed. David Thomas et al. (Leiden, Netherlands: Brill, 2009–2012), vol. 1: 585–94; Tolan, *Saracens*, pp. 60–64.

29. See Juan Pedro Monferrer Sala, "Ibn Hazm," in Thomas et al., eds., *Christian-Muslim Relations: A Bibliographical History*, vol. 3: 137–39.

30. See John Tolan, "Petrus Alfonsi," in Thomas et al., eds., *Christian-Muslim Relations: A Bibliographical History*, vol. 3: 356–62.

31. Oscar de la Cruz Palma and Cándida Ferrero Hernández, "Robert of Ketton," in Thomas et al., eds., *Christian-Muslim Relations: A Bibliographical History*, vol. 3: 508–19; Dominique Iogna-Prat and John Tolan, "Peter of Cluny," ibid., 604–10.

32. See Fernando de la Granja, "Fiestas cristianas en al-Andalus (materiales para su estudio," *Al Andalus* 34 (1969): 1–53, and 35 (1970): 119–42; Lagardère, *Histoire et société*, pp. 50, 176, 476.

33. See Tolan, *Sons of Ishmael*, chap. 7.

34. Riccoldo da Monte di Croce, *Pérégrination en Terre sainte et au Proche-Orient et Lettres sur la chute de Saint-Jean d'Acre*, Latin ed. and French trans. by René Kappler (Paris: Honoré Champion, 1997), pp. 172–73.

35. "Machometum dicunt nuncium Dei fuisse et ad se tantum a Deo missum. Hoc legi in Alcorano qui est liber eorum." Burcardus de Monte Sionis, *Descriptio Terrae sanctae*, § 15, ed. C. J. Lauren, in *Peregrinationes medii aevi Quatuor* (Leipzig: Akademie Verlag, 1864). On Burchard, see Aryeh Grabois, "Burchard of Mount Sion," in *Trade, Travel and Exploration in the Middle Ages*, ed. John Friedman and Kristen Figg (New York: Garland, 1990), pp. 82–83; Aryeh Grabois, "Christian Pilgrims in the Thirteenth Century and the Latin Kingdom of Jerusalem: Burchard of Mount Sion," in *Outremer: Studies in the History of the Crusading Kingdom of Jerusalem Presented to Joshua Prawer*, ed. B. Kedar et al. (Jerusalem: Yad Izhak Ben-Zvi Institute, 1982), pp. 285–96.

36. For example, Qur'an 14:4: "Each apostle We have sent has spoken in the language of his own people, so that he might make his meaning clear to them."

37. For that comparative description of the Saracens and the Latins, see Burcardus de Monte Sionis, *Descriptio Terrae sanctae*, chap. 33.

38. The first text to give a version of that legend is *Novellino*, ed. Gérard Grenot and Paul Lariavaille (Paris: 10/18, 1988), pp. 176–79; Boccaccio gives his version in the *Decameron*, day one, third tale. See John Tolan, "'Tra il diavolo di Rustico e il ninferno d'Alibech': Muslims and Jews in Boccaccio's *Decameron*," in *Images of the Other in Medieval and Early Modern Times*, ed. Lieselotte Saurma and Anja Eisenbeiss (Munich: Deutscher Kunstverlag, 2012).

39. Carlo Ginzburg, *The Cheese and the Worms: The Cosmos of a Sixteenth-century Miller*, trans. John Tedeschi and Anne Tedeschi (Baltimore: Johns Hopkins University Press, 1980), pp. 112–15.

40. John Tolan, *Saint Francis and the Sultan: The Curious History of a Christian-Muslim Encounter* (Oxford, UK: Oxford University Press, 2009).

41. See William of Rubruck, *Itinerarium*, translated by Peter Jackson and David Morgan as *The Mission of Friar William of Rubruck: His Journey to the Court of the Great Khan Möngke, 1253-1255* (London: Hakluyt Society, 1990); Antti Ruotsala, *Europeans and Mongols in the Middle of the Thirteenth Century: Encountering the Other* (Helsinki: Finnish Academy of Sciences, 2001); Michèle Guéret-Laferté, *Sur les routes de l'Empire mongol: Ordre et rhétorique des relations de voyage au XIIIe et XIVe siècles* (Paris: Honoré Champion, 1994); Jean Richard, *La papauté et les missions d'Orient au Moyen Âge (XIIIe-XVe siècles)* (Rome: École Française de Rome, 1977); and Richard, *Croisés, missionnaires et voyageurs: Les perspectives orientales du monde latin médiéval* (London: Variorum, 1983).

42. William of Rubruck, *The Mission of Friar William of Rubruck*, pp. 231–35. On that debate, see Benjamin Kedar, "The Multilateral Disputation at the Court of the Grand Qan Möngke, 1254," in *The Majlis: Interreligious Encounters in Medieval Islam*, ed. H. Lazarus-Yafeh et al. (Wiesbaden: Harrassowitz, 1999), pp. 162–83.

43. Robles Sierra, "Raymond de Penyafort," DS 86, 190; Laureano Robles, *Escritores dominicos de la Corona de Aragon, siglos XIII–XV* (Salamanca, Spain: Universidad de

Salamanca, 1972), pp. 12–57; José María Coll, "San Raymundo de Peñafort y las misiones del norte africano en la edad media," *Missionalia Hispanica* 5 (1948): 414–57; and Tolan, *Saracens*, chap. 10.

44. Ramón Martí, *De seta Machometi o de origine, progressu, et fine Machometi et quadruplici reprobatione prophetiae eius*, Spanish ed. and trans. by Joseph Hernando i Delgado, *Acta Historica et Archaeologica Medievalia*, no. 4 (1983): 9–51. Under the title *Quadruplex reprobatio*, this work was falsely attributed to John of Wales; parts of it were published in Strasbourg in 1550 by W. Dreschsler, under the title *Gamlensis de origine et progressu Machometis*. Hernando i Delgado's "Le 'De seta Machometi' du cod. 46 d'Osma" has shown that this was actually a work by Ramón Martí; see also his "De nuevo sobre la obra antiislámica attribuida a Ramón Martí."

45. See Robin Vose, *Dominicans, Muslims and Jews in the Medieval Crown of Aragon* (Cambridge, UK: Cambridge University Press, 2009). Vose argues that the mission to the Jews and Muslims played only a very small role in the life and activity of Dominican friars in Spain, compared to their mission to serve the Christian communities. The point is well taken, but, in his attempt to minimize the missionary efforts of Dominicans, Vose overlooks much of the evidence for the considerable impact that Dominican missions indeed had in Iberian society. See my review of Vose's book in *Islam and Christian-Muslim Relations* 21 (2010): 200–201.

46. On Riccoldo, see Tolan, *Saracens*, pp. xiii–xiv, 245–54.

47. Riccoldo, *Lettres*, vol. 3: 239.

48. Riccoldo, *Contra legem Sarracenorum*, chap. 15.

49. Ibid., p. 125.

50. Francesco Petrarcha, *Letters of Old Age*, trans. Aldo S. Bernardo, Saul Levin, and Reta A. Bernardo (Baltimore: Johns Hopkins University Press, 1992), vol. 2: 471–72, 580. See Francesco Gabrieli, "Petrarca e gli Arabi," *Al-Andalus* 42 (1977): 241–48; Nancy Bisaha, "Petrarch's Vision of the Muslim and Byzantine East," *Speculum* 76 (2001): 284–314.

51. On the debates in the medical world, see Danielle Jacquart and Françoise Micheau, *La médecine arabe et l'Occident médiéval* (Paris, Maisonneuve et Larose, 1996); Nancy Siraisi, *Avicenna in Renaissance Italy: The Canon and Medical Teaching in Italian Universities after 1500* (Princeton, NJ: Princeton University Press, 1987).

52. Siraisi, *Avicenna in Renaissance Italy*, pp. 70–73.

53. Giovanni Pico della Mirandola, *Oration on the Dignity of Man*, trans. A. Robert Caponigri (Washington, DC: Regnery Gateway, 1956), p. 10; Nancy Bisaha, *Creating East and West: Renaissance Humanists and the Ottoman Turks* (Philadelphia: University of Pennsylvania Press, 2004), pp. 166–73; Angelo Michele Piemontese, "Il Corano latine di Ficio e i corani arabi de Pico e Monchates," *Rinascimento* 36 (1996): 226–73; and Louis Valcke, *Pic de la Mirandole: Un itinéraire philosophique* (Paris: Les Belles Lettres, 2005).

54. Paul Zumthor, *La mesure du Monde* (Paris: Seuil, 1993), p. 334.

PART II: THE GREAT TURK AND EUROPE

Introduction to Part II: Continuity and Change in Geopolitics

1. C.H.H. Wake, "The Volume of European Spice Imports at the Beginning and End of the Fifteenth Century," *Journal of Economic European History* 15, no. 3 (1986): 633.

2. S. Har-El, *Struggle for Domination in the Middle East: The Ottoman-Mamluk War, 1485–1491* (Leiden, Netherlands: Brill, 1995).

3. Jean-Louis Bacqué-Grammont and Anne Kroell, *Mameluks, Ottomans et Portugais en Mer Rouge: L'affaire de Djedda en 1517*, supplement to *Annales Islamologiques* 12 (1988).

4. Çengiz C. Orhonlu, "Hint Kaptanlığı ve Piri Re'is," *Belleten* 34, no. 134 (1970): 235–54.

5. For a somewhat different point of view, see Palmira Brummett, *Ottoman Seapower and Levantine Diplomacy at the Age of Discovery* (Albany: State University of New York Press, 1994).

6. See Salih Özbaran, *The Ottoman Response to European Expansion* (Istanbul: Isis, 1994).

Chapter 6: The Ottoman Conquest in Europe

1. See Paul Wittek, "Les Gagaouzes: Les gens de Kaykaus," *Rocznik Orientalistyczny* 17 (1953): 12–24; A. Decei, "Le problème de la colonisation des Turcs seljoukides dans la Dobroudja au XIIIe siècle," *Türk Araştırmaları Dergisi* 6, nos. 10–11 (1968): 85–111; and Machiel Kiel, "The Türbe of Sarı Saltık at Babadag-Dobrudja," *Güney-Doğu Avrupa Araştırmaları Dergisi* 6–7 (1977–1978): 205–25.

2. Stephen W. Reinert, "The Muslim Presence in Constantinople, Ninth–Fifteenth Centuries: Some Preliminary Observations," in *Studies on the International Diaspora of the Byzantine Empire*, ed. Hélène Ahrweiler and Angeliki E. Laiou (Washington, DC: Dumbarton Oaks, 1998), pp. 125–50; and Michel Balivet, "Les Turcs dans Byzance avant 1453," in *Turcobyzantiae: Échanges régionaux. Contacts urbains* (Istanbul: Isis, 2008), pp. 115–16.

3. Balivet, "Les Turcs dans Byzance," pp. 120–21.

4. Elizabeth A. Zachariadou, "The Conquest of Adrianople by the Turks," *Studi Veneziani* 12 (1970): 211–17; Irène Beldiceanu-Steinherr, "La conquête d'Andrinople par les Turcs," *Travaux et mémoires* 1 (1965): 439–61; and Halil Inalcik, "The Conquest of Edirne (1361)," *Archivum Ottamanicum* 3 (1971): 185–210. It is the "brief chronicles" of Byzantium that make it possible to decide in favor of 1369.

5. See Colin Imber, *The Ottoman Empire, 1300–1481* (Istanbul: Isis, 1990), p. 29.

6. Stephen W. Reinert, "From Niš to Kosovo Polje: Reflections on Murad I's Final Year," in *The Ottoman Emirate (1300–1389)*, ed. Elizabeth Zachariadou (Heraklion: Crete University Press, 1993), pp. 169–211.

7. T. A. Emmert, "The Battle of Kosovo: A Reconsideration of Its Significance in the Decline of Medieval Serbia," PhD diss., Stanford University, 1973; T. A. Emmert, *Serbian Golgotha: Kosovo, 1389* (New York: Columbia University Press, 1990); N. Malcolm, *Kosovo: A Short History* (London: Macmillan,1998); and W. Vucinich and T. Emmert, *Kosovo, Legacy of a Medieval Battle* (Minneapolis: University of Minnesota Press, 1991).

8. See Dimitris J. Kastritsis, *The Sons of Bayezid: Empire Building and Representation in the Ottoman Civil War of 1402–1413* (Leiden, Netherlands: Brill, 2007).

9. Michel Balivet, *Islam mystique et révolution armée dans les Balkans ottomans: Vie du cheikh Bedreddin, le 'Hallâj des Turcs' (1358/59–1416)* (Istanbul: Isis, 1995).

10. See Oliver Jens Schmitt, *Skanderbeg, der neue Alexander auf dem Balkan* (Regensburg, Germany: Verlag Friedrich Pustet, 2009).

11. Colin Imber, *The Crusade of Varna, 1443–1445* (Aldershot, UK: Ashgate, 2006).

12. On the two reigns of Mehmed II, see Franz Babinger, *Mehmed the Conqueror and His Time*, ed. William C. Hickman, trans. Ralph Manheim (Princeton, NJ: Princeton University Press, 1978).

13. Louis Massignon, "Textes prémonitoires et commentaires mystiques relatifs à la prise de Constantinople par les Turcs en 1453 (=858 Heg.)," *Oriens* 6 (1953): 10–17, reprinted in his *Opera Minora*, vol. 2 (Beirut: Daar al-Maaref, 1963), pp. 442–50.

14. See the analyses of Stéphane Yerasimos in M. F. Auzépy, Alain Ducellier, Gilles Veinstein, and Stéphane Yerasimos, *Istanbul* (Paris: Citadelle et Mazenod, 2002).

15. *Epistola ad Mahomatem II/Epistle to Mohammed II*, ed. with translation and notes by Albert R. Baca (New York: Peter Lang, 1990).

16. See Theoharis Stavrides, *The Sultan of Vezirs: The Life and Times of the Ottoman Grand Vezir Mahmud Pasha Angelović* (Leiden, Netherlands: Brill, 2001).

17. Spandouyn Cantacasin, *Petit Traicté de l'origine des Turcqs*, ed. Charles Schefer (Paris: Leroux, 1896), pp. 47–48; see also Nicolas Vatin, "Macabre trafic: La destinée post-mortem du prince Jem," in *Mélanges offerts à Louis Bazin par ses disciples, collègues et amis*, ed. Jean-Louis Bacqué-Grammont and Rémi Dor (Paris: L'Harmattan, 1992), pp. 231–39.

18. See Nicoara Beldiceanu, "La conquête des cités marchandes de Kilia et de Cetatea-Albă par Bayezid II," *Südost-Forschungen* 23 (1964): 36–90.

19. Nicolas Vatin, "Le siège de Mytilène," *Turcica* 21–22 (1992): 437–59.

20. Sa'dü-ddīn, *Tādjü-ttevarīh* (Istanbul, 1280/1863), vol. 2: 388.

21. Joseph von Hammer-Purgstall, *Histoire de l'Empire ottoman*, trans. J. J. Hellert (Paris: Bellizard, Barthès, Dufour, and Lowell, 1836), vol. 5: 457–60.

22. Gülrü Necipoğlu, "Süleymân the Magnificent and the Representation of Power in the Context of Ottoman-Habsburg-Papal Rivalry," in *Süleymân the Second and His Time*, ed. H. Inalcik and C. Kafadar (Istanbul: Isis, 1993), pp. 163–94.

23. Ebru Turan, "The Sultan's Favorite: Ibrahim Pasha and the Making of Ottoman Sovereignty in the Reign of Sultan Süleyman (1516–1526)," PhD diss., University of Chicago, 2007.

24. See Nicolas Vatin and Gilles Veinstein, *Le sérail ébranlé: Essai sur les morts, dépositions et avènements des sultans ottomans, XIVe–XIXe siècle* (Paris: Fayard, 2003), pp. 107–8, 123–24, 130–32.

25. See Caroline Finkel, *The Administration of Warfare: The Ottoman Military Campaigns in Hungary, 1593–1606* (Vienna: Verlag des Verbandes der Wissenschaftlichen Gesellschaften Österreichs, 1985), p. 69.

26. Jean Nouzille, *Histoire des frontières: L'Autriche et l'Empire ottoman*, preface by Jean Bérenger (Paris: Berg International, 1991); Géza Dávid and Pál Fodor, *Ottomans, Hungarians and Habsburgs in Central Europe: The Military Confines in the Era of Ottoman Conquests* (Leiden, Netherlands: Brill, 2000).

27. Gustav Bayerle, "The Compromise at Zsitvatorok," *Archivum Ottomanicum* 6 (1980): 5–53.

28. See Antonis Anastasopulos, ed., *The Eastern Mediterranean under Ottoman Rule: Crete, 1645–1840* (Rethymno: Crete University Press, 2008); Nicolas Oikonomides, "From Soldiers of Fortune to Gazi Warriors: The Tsympe Affair," in *Studies in Ottoman History in Honour of Professor V. L. Ménage*, ed. C. Heywood and C. Imber (Istanbul: Isis, 1994), pp. 239–47.

29. See Michael Khodarkovsky, *Russia's Steppe Frontier: The Making of a Colonial Empire, 1500–1800* (Bloomington: Indiana University Press, 2002); W. H. McNeill, *Europe's Steppe Frontier, 1500–1800* (Chicago: University of Chicago Press, 1974).

30. Marc David Baer, *Honored by the Glory of Islam: Conversion and Conquest in Ottoman Europe* (Oxford, UK: Oxford University Press, 2008), pp. 164–69.

Chapter 7: Ottoman Europe: An Ancient Fracture

1. Istanbul, Archives of the Prime Ministry, Ottoman Archives, *Mühimme defteri*, vol. 3, fol. 423, no. 1265.

2. English translation of the letter in Pál Fodor, "The View of the Turk in Hungary: The Apocalyptic Tradition and the Legend of the Red Apple in Ottoman Hungarian Context," in *Les traditions apocalyptiques au tournant de la chute de Constantinople*, ed. Benjamin Lellouch and Stéphane Yerasimos (Paris: L'Harmattan, 1999), pp. 101–2.

3. S. Vryonis, *The Decline of Medieval Hellenism in Asia Minor and the Process of Islamization from the Eleventh through the Sixteenth Century* (Berkeley: University of California Press, 1971).

4. Ömer Lûtfi Barkan, "Essai sur les données statistiques des registres de recensement dans l'Empire ottoman," *Journal of the Economic and Social History of the Orient* 1 (1958): 9–36.

5. Cem Behar, ed., *The Population of the Ottoman Empire and Turkey: Historical Statistic Series*, vol. 2 (Ankara: State Institute of Statistics Prime Ministry Republic of Turkey, 1996), pp. 23–24.

6. Tayyib Gökbilgin, *Rumeli'de yürükler, Tatarlar ve Evlâd-i Fâtihân* (Istanbul: Osman Yalçın Matbaası, 1957).

7. Jovan Trifunovski, *Albansko stanovnistvo u socialistickoj republici Makedoniji: Antropogeografska i etnografska istrazivanja* (Belgrade: NIRO "Književne novine," 1988).

8. See Benjamin Braude and Bernard Lewis, eds., *Christians and Jews in the Ottoman Empire*, 2 vols. (New York: Holmes and Meier, 1982).

9. Machiel Kiel, *Art and Society of Bulgaria in the Turkish Period* (Assen, Netherlands: Van Gorcum, 1985); Kiel, *Ottoman Architecture in Albania* (Istanbul: IRSICA, 1990); and Kiel, "Central Greece in the Suleymanic Age: Preliminary Notes on Population Growth, Economic Expansion and Its Influence on the Spread of Greek Culture," in *Soliman le Magnifique et son temps*, ed. Gilles Veinstein (Paris: La Documentation Française, 1992), pp. 399–424.

10. Quoted in V. L. Ménage, "Some Notes on the Devshirme," *Bulletin of the School of Oriental and African Studies* 29 (1966): 76.

11. For an attempt to organize the data in view of creating a model tracking conversions to Islam in the Ottoman period, based on the schema established by R. W. Bulliet for the Middle Ages, see Anton Minkov, *Conversion to Islam in the Balkans: Kisve Bahası Petitions and Ottoman Social Life, 1670–1730* (Leiden, Netherlands: Brill, 2004).

12. *EI2*, s.v. "Bosna" (B. Djurdjev).

13. Halil Inalcik, *Fatih devri üzerinde tetkikler ve vesikalar* (Ankara: Türk Tarih Kurumu, 1954), pp. 144–66.

Chapter 8: Antagonistic Figures

1. Jean-Claude Margolin, "Réflexion sur le commentaire du père Célestin Pierre Crespet de la lettre du pape Pie II au sultan Mahomet II," in *Chrétiens et musulmans à la Renaissance*, ed. B. Bennassar and R. Sauzet (Paris: Champion, 1998), pp. 213–39.

2. H. Prideau, *The True Nature of Imposture Fully Display'd* (London, 1697).

3. Quoted in Jean Delumeau, *La peur en Occident (XIVe–XVIIIe s.)* (Paris: Fayard, 1978), p. 263.

4. G. Bernetti, "Appassionato discorso di Pio II ai cardinali per la guerra contro i Turchi," *S. Caternia di Siena* 17, nos. 4–5 (1966): 25.

5. See Maximilian Grothaus, "Zum Türkenbild in der Kultur der Habsburger Monarchie zwischen dem 16. und 18. Jahrhundert," in *Habsburgisch-Osmanische Beziehungen*, ed. Andreas Tietze (Vienna: Verlag des Verbandes der Wissenschaftlichen Gesellschaften Österreichs, 1985), pp. 69–70.

6. Babinger, *Mehmed the Conqueror*, pp. 140–44.

7. See the thesis, still unpublished, of Guy Le Thiec, "Et il y aura un seul troupeau . . . L'imaginaire de la confrontation entre Turcs et chrétiens dans l'art figuratif en France et en Italie de 1453 aux années 1620," Université de Montpellier, 1994; I. Fenlon, "In destructione Turcharum: The Victory of Lepanto in Sixteenth-Century Music and Letters," in *Andrea Gabrieli e il suo tempo*, ed. F. Degrada (Florence: L. S. Olschki, 1974), pp. 257–77.

8. Letter from La Goulette, July 28, 1535, in Ernest Charrière, *Négociations de la France dans le Levant*, vol. 1 (Paris: Imprimerie Nationale, 1848), p. 274.

9. See Sylvie Deswarte-Rosa, "L'expédition de Tunis (1535): Images, interprétations, répercussions culturelles," in Bennassar and Sauzet, eds., *Chrétiens et musulmans à la Renaissance*, pp. 75–132.

10. Winfried Schulze, *Reich und Türkengefahr im späten 16. Jahrhundert: Studien zu den politischen und gesellschaftlichen Auswirkungen einer äusseren Bedrohung* (Munich: C. H. Beck, 1978), p. 39.

11. Multimedia center of Le Mans, Maine, 102, posters; information generously communicated by A. M. Touzard.

12. See Franco Cardini, *Europe et islam: Histoire d'un malentendu*, trans. Jean-Pierre Bardos (Paris: Seuil, 2000), p. 200.

13. Michel Febvre, *Théâtre de la Turquie traduit de l'italien en françois* (Paris: Edme Couterot, 1682), p. 423.

14. Charrière, *Négociations*, vol. 1: 7–47.

15. *L'horoscope impérial de Louis XIV Dieudonné prédit par l'Oracle François et Michel Nostradamus* (Paris: Chez François Huart, 1652), quoted in Géraud Poumarède, *Pour en finir avec la croisade: Mythes et réalités de la lutte contre les Turcs aux XVIe et XVII siècles* (Paris: Presses Universitaires de France, 2004), pp. 119–20.

16. G. W. Leibniz, *Mémoire de Leibniz à Louis XIV sur la conquête de l'Egypte*, edited with a preface and notes by M. de Hoffmanns (Paris: Garnot, 1840).

17. Quoted in P. Hazard, *La crise de la conscience européenne*, vol. 1, *1680–1715* (Paris: Nouvelle Revue Française, 1968), p. 274.

18. See, for example, W. Rainolds, *Calvino-turcismus, id est, Calvinisticae Perfideae, cum Mahometana collatio* (Antwerp, 1597).

19. Joseph Matuz, *Herrscher Urkunden des Osmanensultans Süleymân des Prächtigen: Ein chronologisches Verzeichnis* (Freiburg im Breisgau: Klaus Schwarz, 1971), p. 80, no. 342.

20. S. Fischer-Galati, *Ottoman Imperialism and German Protestantism, 1521–1555* (Cambridge, MA: Harvard University Press, 1959).

21. Guillaume Postel, *De la république des Turcs*, vol 3. (Poitiers, 1560), p. 89.

22. Erasmus, "Utilissima Consultatio de bello Turcis inferendo," in *Opera omnia Desiderii Erasmi Roterodami*, ed. A. G. Weiler (Amsterdam: North-Holland, 1986), 3.3, pp. 48–50.

23. Martin Brecht, "Luther und die Türken," in *Europe und die Türken in der Renaissance*, ed. B. Guthmüller and W. Kühlmann (Tübingen, Germany: M. Niemeyer, 2000), pp. 9–27.

24. *D. Martin Luthers Werke*, vol. 30, part 2 (Weimar: Hermann Boehlau, 1909), pp. 81–148.

25. Georgius de Hungaria, *Traité sur les moeurs, les coutumes et la perfidie des Turcs*, translated from the Latin by Joël Schnapp (Toulouse: Anacharsis, 2003).

26. Cardini, *Europe et Islam*, p. 186.

27. F. de la Noue, "Discours XXII," in *Discours politiques et militaires*, ed. F. E. Sutcliffe (Geneva: Droz, 1967), p. 446.

28. Walter Leisch, "Père Joseph und die Pläne einer Türkenliga in den Jahren 1616 bis 1625," in Tietze, *Habsburgisch-Osmanische Beziehungen*, pp. 161–69.

29. A. Pertusi, "I primi studi in Occidente sull'origine e la potenza des Turchi," *Studi Veneziani* 12 (1970); 465–515; J. Hankins, "Renaissance Crusaders: Humanist Crusade Literature in the Age of Mehmed II," *Dumbarton Oaks Papers* 49 (1995): 135–44.

30. Paulo Govio, *Commentari della cose de Turchi a Carlo Quinto, imperadore augusto* (1538), fol. aiiv–aiiir.

31. N. Oikonomides, "The Turks in Byzantine Rhetoric of the Twelfth Century," in *Decision Making and Change in the Ottoman Empire*, ed. C. E. Farah (Kirksville: The Thomas Jefferson University Press at Northeast Missouri State University, 1993), pp. 149–154.

32. F. Sansovino, *Lettera overo discorso sopra la predittioni fatte in diversi tempi da diverse persone illustri le quali pronosticano la nostra futura felicità per la guerra del Turco con la Serenissima Republica di Venetia l'anno 1570* (Venice, 1570), fol. 6r.

33. Letter from Lauro Querini to Pope Nicholas V, Candia, July 15, 1453, in A. Pertusi, *Testi inediti e poco noti sulla caduta di Constantinopoli* (Bologna: Pátron, 1983), pp. 74–76.

34. R. de Chateaubriand, *Itinéraire de Paris à Jérusalem*, ed. Jean-Claude Berchet (Paris: Gallimard, 2005), p. 373.

35. Franz Babinger, *Die Aufzeichnungen des Genuesen Iacopo de Promontorio-de Campis über den Osmanenstaat um 1475* (Munich: Akademie der Wissenschaften, 1957), p. 61.

36. Konstantin Mihailović, *Memoirs of a Janissary*, ed. Svat Soucek, trans. Benjamin Stolz (Ann Arbor: University of Michigan Press, 1975), pp. 176–77.

37. *La deffaicte des Turcs par Monseigneur le duc de Mercoeur* (Paris, 1601), quoted in Clarence Dana Rouillard, *The Turk in French History: Thought and Literature (1520–1660)* (Paris: Boivin, 1942), p. 79.

38. *Advis trescertain de ce qui s'est passé entre l'armée Chrestienne et celle des Turcs* (Lyons, 1598); cited ibid.

39. *Discours de ce qui s'est passé en Transylvanie* (Lyons, 1595).

40. Schulze, *Reich und Türkengefähr.*

41. Ibid., p. 56.

42. Charrière, *Négociations*, vol. 1: 581.

43. Schulze, *Reich und Türkengefähr*, p. 59.

44. Ibid., p. 60.

45. F. Garcia Salinero, ed., *Viaje de Turquia (La Odisea de Pedro de Urdemalas)* (Madrid: Catedra, 1980).

46. Ibid., p. 457.

47. Ibid., p. 413.

48. Ibid., p. 414.

49. Lucette Valensi, *Venise et la Sublime Porte: La naissance du despote* (Paris: Hachette, 1987).

50. Bey Ahmed Feridün, *Münsheāt al-Selātīn*, vol. 1 (Istanbul: Takvimhane-i a'mire, 1857), pp. 228–31.

51. Istanbul, Archives of the Prime Ministry, Ottoman Archives, *Mühimme Defteri*, vol. 7, no. 721.

52. Istanbul, Archives of the Museum of the Topkapı Palace, E. 11 687, published in Mattei Cazacu and Keram Kévonian, "La chute de Caffa en 1475 à la lumière de nouveaux documents," *Cahiers du Monde Russe et Soviétique* 17, no. 4 (1976): 506–11. The document was translated from Persian into French by M. Mokri.

53. Nicolas Vatin, "Un exemple d'histoire officielle ottomane? Le récit de la campagne de Szigetvár (1566) dans une lettre du Sultan Selim II au chah d'Iran Tahmasp," in *Événement, récit, histoire officielle: L'écriture de l'histoire dans les monarchies antiques*, ed. Nicolas Grimal and Michel Baud (Paris: Éditions Cybèle, 2003), pp. 143–54.

54. Quoted in Stéphane Yerasimos, "De l'arbre à la pomme: Généalogie d'un thème apocalyptique," in *Les traditions apocalyptiques*, ed. Benjamin Lellouch and Stéphane Yerasimos (Paris: L'Harmattan, 1999), p. 173.

55. Ibid., pp.170–84.

56. Quoted by Pál Fodor, "The View of the Turk in Hungary," in Lellouch and Yerasimos, eds., *Les traditions apocalyptiques*, p. 123.

57. See Robert Dankoff, *An Ottoman Mentality: The World of Evliya Celebi* (Leiden, Netherlands: Brill, 2004), pp. 62 n. 45 and 105 n. 63.

58. J. von Hammer, *Geschichte des osmanischen Reiches*, vol. 3 (Pest, Hungary: C. A. Hartleben, 1828), pp. 474–75.

59. See W. Heffening, *Die türkischen Transkriptionstexte des Bartholomaeus Georgievitz aus den Jahren 1544–1548: Ein Beitrag zur historischen Grammatik des Osmanisch-Türkischen* (Leipzig: Deutsche Morgenländische Gesellschaft, 1942).

60. F. Kidrić, "Bartholomaeus Gjorjević: Biographische und bibliographische Zusammenfassung," in *Museion: Veröffentlischungen aus der Nationalbibliothek in Wien* 2 (1920): 19–24.

61. Paul Wittek, "Le Sultan de Rûm," *Annuaire de l'Institut d'Histoire et de Philologie Orientale et Slave* 6 (1938); and André Miquel, "Rome chez les géographes arabes," in *Académie des Inscriptions et Belles-Lettres: Comptes Rendus des Séances* 12, no. 151 (January–March 1975): pp. 281–91.

62. Achikpachazade, "Tevarih-i Āl-i *Osman*," in *Osmanlı Tarihleri*, ed. Çiftçioğlu N. Atsız (Istanbul: Türkiye Yayınevi, 1947), chap. 40, p. 124.

Chapter 9: The Islamic-Christian Border in Europe

1. Giuseppe Bonaffini, *Un mare di paura: Il Mediterraneo in età moderna* (Caltanisseta, Italy: S. Sciascia,1997).

2. For example, "the Austrian military border . . . was the 'iron curtain' of Christendom, Europe's rampart against Ottoman aggression, and a site of confrontation between Christian and Muslim civilizations"; see Nouzille, *Histoire des frontières*, p. 57.

3. Excerpted from Müniri Belgradî, *Silsiletü-l-mukarribîn ve menâkibü-l-müttakîn,* quoted in Nathalie Clayer, *Mystiques, État et société: Les Halvetis dans l'aire balkanique de la fin du XVe siècle à nos jours* (Leiden, Netherlands: Brill, 1994), p. 128.

4. Maria Pia Pedani, *Dalla frontiera al confine* (Venice: Herder, 2002), pp. 44–46.

5. "Relacja komisarsy Rzeczypospolitej do rozgraniczenia," Warsaw, AGAD, AKW, Dz. Turk, k. 77, t. 479, no. 803, quoted in Dariusz Kolodziejczyk, *Ottoman-Polish Diplomatic Relations (Fifteenth–Eighteenth Century): An Annotated Edition of Ahdnames and Other Documents* (Leiden, Netherlands: Brill, 2008), pp. 62–63.

6. Istanbul, Archives of the Prime Ministry, Ottoman Archives, TT 805, p. 378; quoted in Kolodziejczyk, *Ottoman-Polish Diplomatic Relations*, p. 62.

7. Mustafa Naima, *Naima Tarihi*, 3rd ed. (Istanbul: Tab'hâne-i 'âmire, 1864–1867), vol. 5: 21–22.

8. See Virginia H. Aksan, *An Ottoman Statesman in War and Peace: Ahmed Resmi Efendi, 1700–1783* (Leiden, Netherlands: Brill, 1995), pp. 195–98.

9. Quoted in Géza Palfy, "The Origins and Development of the Border Defence System against the Ottoman Empire in Hungary (up to the Early Eighteenth Century)," in Dávid and Fodor, *Ottomans, Hungarians and Habsburgs*, p. 40 and n. 3.

10. *The Turkish Letters of Ogier Ghiselin de Busbecq: Imperial Ambassador at Constantinople, 1554–1562*, translated from the Latin by Edward Seymour Forster from the Elzevir edition of 1633 (Oxford, UK: Clarendon Press, 1968), pp. 14–15.

11. Jean Bérenger, *Les "Gravamina," Remontrances des Diètes de Hongrie de 1665 à 1681: Recherches sur les fondements du droit d'État au XVIIe siècle* (Paris: Presses Universitaires de France, 1973), p. 76, *gravamina* 1662, art. 2.

12. See Ferenc Toth, ed., *Mémoires du baron de Tott sur les Turcs et les Tartares* (Amsterdam, 1785; Paris: Honoré Champion, 2004).

13. See the letter from the khan of Crimea, Muhammad Giray, to Süleyman the Magnificent, Archives of the Museum of the Topkapı Palace, E. 1308 (1301)/2, French translation in Alexandre Bennigsen et al., *Le khanat de Crimée dans les archives du musée du palais de Topkapı* (Paris: Mouton, 1978), p. 111. See also Alan Fisher, "The Ottoman Crimea in the Sixteenth Century," *Harvard Ukrainian Studies* 5, no. 2 (1981): 135–70.

14. See Chantal Lemercier-Quelquejay, "Un condottiere lithuanien du XVI siècle, le prince Dimitri Višneveckij et l'origine de la seč zaporogue d'après les archives ottomanes," *Cahiers du Monde Russe et Soviétique* 10, no. 2 (1969): 258–79.

15. Louis Bazin, "Antiquité méconnue du titre d'"ataman'?" *Harvard Ukrainian Studies* 3–4 (1979–1980): 61–70.

16. See C. W. Bracewell, *The Uskoks of Senj: Piracy, Banditry, and Holy War in the Sixteenth-Century Adriatic* (Ithaca, NY: Cornell University Press, 1992).

17. Venice, state archives, collection Bailo a Constantinopoli, Busta 333, doc. no. 3.

18. See Klaus Schwarz, *Osmanische Sultansurkunden: Untersuchungen zu Einstellung und Besoldung osmanischer Militärs in der Zeit Murâd III*, trans. Claudia Römer (Stuttgart: F. Steiner, 1997), pp. 90ff.

19. M. Berindei, A. Berthier, M. Martin, and G. Veinstein, "Code de lois de Murad III concernant la province de Smederevo," *Südost-Forschungen* 30T (1972): 153.

20. See Salvatore Bono, *Corsari nel Mediterraneo* (Milan: Arnoldo Mondadori, 1993).

21. Robert C. Davis, *Christian Slaves, Muslim Masters: White Slavery in the Mediterranean, the Barbary Coast, and Italy 1500–1800* (Houndmills, UK: Palgrave Macmillan, 2003), p. xxv.

22. The Tunisians finally decided it was time to convert to regular commerce, with the help of the Napoleonic continental blockade of 1806, but the effort ended in failure in 1813 because Westerners did everything they could to neutralize that competition; Daniel Panzac, *Les corsaires barbaresques, la fin d'une épopée, 1800–1820* (Paris: Centre National de la Recherche Scientifique, 1999).

23. Davis, *Christian Slaves*, p. 8.

24. Ibid.

25. Pierre Dan, *Histoire de Barbarie et de ses corsaires* (Paris, 1649), p. 284, quoted in Davis, *Christian Slaves*, p. 15.

26. Bartolomé Bennassar and Lucille Bennassar, *Les chrétiens d'Allah* (Paris: Perrin, 1989), pp. 199–200, 244–45.

27. Lucien Bély, *L'art de la paix en Europe: Naissance de la diplomatie moderne, XVIe–XVIIIe siècles* (Paris: Presses Universitaires de France, 2007), pp. 347–52.

28. Mehmed Efendi, *Le paradis des Infidèles: Un ambassadeur ottoman en France sous la Régence*, ed. G. Veinstein (Paris: François Maspéro, 1981), pp. 144–45.

Chapter 10: Breaches in the Conflict

1. Istanbul, Library of the Museum of the Palace of Topkapı, *KK 888*, doc. no. 1036.

2. Ibid., no. 1092.

3. *Copie d'une lettre de la Sainte Ligue* (Paris, 1572), quoted in Rouillard, *The Turk*, p. 72.

4. Jean Deny, "Les pseudo-prophéties concernant les Turcs au XVIe siècle," *Revue des Études Islamiques* 10 (1936): 201–220.

5. See Stéphane Yerasimos, *La fondation de Constantinople et de Sainte-Sophie dans les traditions turques* (Paris: Librairie d'Amérique et d'Orient J. Maisonneuve, 1990), pp. 190–91.

6. Guillaume Postel, *Thresor des prophéties de l'Univers*, quoted in M. Balivet, "Textes de fin d'Empire, récits de fin du monde: À propos de quelques thèmes communs aux groupes de la zone byzantino-turque," in Lellouch and Yerasimos, eds., *Les traditions apocalyptiques*, pp. 10–11.

7. Kolodziejczyk, *Ottoman-Polish Diplomatic Relations*, pp. 255–59.

8. Majid Khadduri, *War and Peace in the Law of Islam* (Baltimore: Johns Hopkins University Press, 1966); and Viorel Panaite, *The Ottoman Law on War and Peace* (New York: Columbia University Press, 2000).

9. Bély, *L'art de la paix*, p. 161.

10. P. Carali, *Fakhr al-Din principe del Libano e la corte di Toscana, 1605–1635* (Rome: Tipografia del Senato 1936); and Albrecht Fuess, "An Instructive Experience:

Fakhr al-Din's Journey to Italy, 1613–1618," in *Les Européens vus par les Libanais à l'époque ottomane*, ed. B. Heyberger and C. M. Walbiner (Beirut: Ergon Verlag, 2002), pp. 23–42.

11. Charrière, *Négociations*, vol. 3: 91 n. 1.

12. "Selâhattin Tansel, "Büyük Friedrich devrinde Osmanlı-Prusya münasebetleri hakkında," *Belleten* 10 (1946): 133–65, 271–92; and Kemal Beydilli, *Büyük Friedrich ve Osmanlılar: XVIII yüzyılda Osmanlı-Prusya münasebetleri* (Istanbul: Istanbul Üniversitesi, Edebiyat Fakültesi, 1985).

13. Istanbul, Archives of the Prime Ministry, Ottoman Archives, *Hatt-i hümāyūn*, no. 319A, quoted in Beydilli, *Büyük Friedrich*, p. 54 n. 117.

14. Kolodziejczyk, *Ottoman-Polish Diplomatic Relations*, pp. 110–11.

15. See N. H. Biegman, *The Turco-Ragusan Relationship, according to the Firmans of Murad III (1575–1595) Extant in the State Archives of Dubrovnik* (The Hague: Mouton, 1967).

16. Hans Theunissen, "Ottoman-Venetian Diplomatics: The Ahidnames. The Historical Background and the Development of a Category of Political-Diplomatic Instruments Together with an Annotated Edition of a Corpus of Relevant Documents," PhD thesis, Utrecht University, 1991, p. 161.

17. Harley de Sancy to Seigneur de Villeroy, March 10, 1612, BNF, Ms. fr. 16 145, fol. 100r–v.

18. Guilleragues to the king, October 3, 1682, in Gabriel-Joseph de Lavergne, comte de Guilleragues, *Correspondance*, ed. Frédéric Deloffre and Jacques Rougeot (Geneva: Droz, 1976), pp. 740–41.

19. G. Noradounghian, *Recueil d'actes internationaux de l'Empire ottoman*, vol. 1 (Paris: Cotillon, 1897), p. 99.

20. Pierre Duparc, *Recueil des instructions données aux ambassadeurs et ministres de France depuis les traités de Westphalie jusqu'à la Révolution française, Turquie* (Paris: Centre National de la Recherche Scientifique, 1969), p. 89; see also the instructions to Ferriol, pp. 173–74.

21. Pierre de Bourdeille, seigneur de Brantôme, "Discours sur les couronnels de l'infanterie de France," in *Oeuvres complètes*, ed. L. Lalanne, vol. 6 (Paris: Mme v. J. Renouard, 1873), p. 180.

22. Charrière, *Négociations*, 3:289.

23. Letter to M. de Lodève, May 24, 1557, ibid., vol. 2: 395, note.

24. Report of Veltwyck of Constantinople, November 10, 1545, in Lanz, *Korrespondenz des Kaisers Karl V*, vol. 2 (Leipzig: Brockhaus, 1845), p. 471.

25. BNF, f. fr., ms. 16 148, no. 66, fol. 177–78, quoted in Emmanuel Antoche, "Guerre et diplomatie en Europe orientale au XVIIe siècle: Le cas de la principauté de Moldavie (1606–1621)," unpublished thesis, École des Hautes Études en Sciences Sociales, 2008, pp. 270–71.

26. Guilleragues to the king, June 15, 1682, in Deloffre and Rougeot, eds., *Correspondance*, 659ff., quoted in Bely, *L'art de la paix*, p. 337.

27. Rouillard, *The Turk*, p. 67.

28. Arnaud de Pomponne to Feuquières, from the camp outside Doesburg, June 21, 1672, quoted in Poumarède, *Pour en finir avec la croisade*, p. 51.

29. Géraud Poumarède, "Les projets d'intégration européenne de l'Empire ottoman," in *Histoire de l'islam et des musulmans en France du Moyen Âge à nos jours*, ed. M. Arkoun (Paris: Albin Michel, 2006), pp. 356–57.

30. Paris, Archives Nationales de France, A.E.B.III, 236, quoted in Michel Morineau, "Naissance d'une domination: Marchands européens, marchés et marchands du Levant aux XVIIIe et XIXe siècles," *Cahiers de la Méditerranée* (1976): n. 16.

31. Jacques Germigny to Henri III, May 1580 in Charrière, *Négociations*, vol. 3: 907.

32. Quoted in Louis Bergasse, *Histoire du commerce de Marseille*, vol. 4 (Paris: Plon, 1954), p. 90.

33. Géraud Poumarède, "Venise, la France et le Levant (vers 1520–1720)," thesis, Université de Paris IV-Sorbonne, 2003, pp. 1151–52.

34. Ibid., pp. 1189–90.

35. Archives of the Museum of the Palace of Topkapı, E. 12321, fol. 98r, no. 226, in Halil Sahillioğlu, *Topkapısarayı arşivi H. 951–952 tarihli ve E-12321 numaralı Mühimme Defteri* (Istanbul: Research Center for Islamic History, Art, and Culture, 2002), pp. 179–80.

36. See the instructions to Ambassador Denis de La Haye-Ventelet, 1665, in Duparc, *Instructions aux ambassadeurs*, p. 26.

37. Suzanne Skilliter, *William Harborne and the Trade with Turkey, 1578–1582* (London: Oxford University Press, 1977).

38. Edhem Eldem, "Capitulations and Western Trade," in *The Cambridge History of Turkey*, part 3, *The Later Ottoman Empire, 1603–1839*, ed. N. Faroqhi (Cambridge, UK: Cambridge University Press, 2006), pp. 285–335.

39. Duparc, *Instructions aux ambassadeurs*, p. 27.

40. Eldem, "Capitulations," p. 300.

41. Charles Carrière and Marcel Courdurié, "Un sophisme économique: Marseille s'enrichit en achetant plus qu'elle ne vend (Réflexions sur les mécanismes commerciaux levantins au XVIIIe siècle)," in *Histoire, Économie et Société* (1984): 7–51.

42. Quoted in Paul Masson, *Histoire du commerce français dans le Levant au XVIIIe siècle* (Paris: Hachette, 1911), p. 279.

43. Eldem, "Capitulations," p. 305.

44. Geoffroy Atkinson, *Les nouveaux horizons de la Renaissance française* (Paris: Droz, 1935), p. 10.

45. Nicole le Huen, *Dessainctes peregrinations de Jherusalem* (Lyons, 1488), quoted in Rouillard, *The Turk*, pp. 43–44.

46. Père Boucher, *Le Bouquet Sacré composé des plus belles fleurs de la Terre Saincte* (Paris, 1620), quoted ibid., p. 239.

47. Guillaume Postel, *De la République des Turcs* (Poitiers, 1560), p. 3.

48. C. Schefer, ed., *Le voyage d'outremer de Bertrandon de La Broquière, premier écuyer tranchant et conseiller de Philippe le Bon, duc de Bourgogne* (Paris, 1892), p. 121.

49. Nicolas de Nicolay, *Dans l'empire de Soliman le Magnifique*, ed. Marie-Christine Gomez et Stéphane Yerasimos (Paris: Centre National de la Recherche Scientifique, 1989), p. 46.

50. *Die Pilgefahrt des Ritters Arnold von Harff* (Cologne, 1860).

51. Franz Babinger, ed., *Hans Dernschwam's Tagebuch einer Reise nach Konstantinopel und Kleinasien (1553–1555) nach der Urschrift in Fugger-Archiv* (Munich, 1923).

52. *The Turkish Letters of Ogier Ghiselin de Busbecq*, Forster trans.

53. William Foster, ed., *The Travels of John Sanderson in the Levant, 1584–1602, with His Autobiography and Selections from His Correspondence* (London: Hakluyt Society, 1931).

54. Frédéric Tinguely, *L'écriture du Levant à la Renaissance: Enquête sur les voyageurs français dans l'empire de Soliman le Magnifique* (Geneva: Droz, 2000), p. 17.

55. Elisabetta Borromeo, *Voyageurs occidentaux dans l'Empire ottoman (1600–1644)*, vol. 1 (Paris: Maisonneuve et Larose, 2007), p. 80.

56. On Rycaut, see Sonia Anderson, *An English Consul in Turkey, Paul Rycaut at Smyrna, 1667–1678* (Oxford, UK: Clarendon Press, 1989).

57. *The Turkish Letters of Ogier Ghiselin de Busbecq*, Forster trans., third letter, p. 111.

58. Ibid., pp. 149–50.

59. *Voyage du Levant fait par le commandement du Roy en l'année 1621 par le Sr. D. C. [Deshayes of Courmenin]* (Paris: Adrien Taupinart, 1632), p. 198.

60. Ibid., p. 286.

61. Jacques Gassot, *Le discours du voyage de Venise à Constantinople* (Paris, 1550), fol. 25r.

62. *The Turkish Letters of Ogier Ghiselin de Busbecq*, Forster trans., p. 61.

63. Philippe du Fresne-Canaye, *Le voyage du Levant*, ed. H. Hauser (Brassac, France: Le Poliphile, 1986), pp. 63–64.

64. *Voyage du Sr de Stochove faict es années 1630, 1631, 1632, 1633* (Brussels: Hubert-Antoine Velpius, 1643), p. 148.

65. Nicolas Du Loir, *Les voyages du Sr du Loir contenues en plusieurs lettres écrites du Levant* (Paris, 1654; repr. Paris: Hachette, 1976), p. 80.

66. Ibid., p. 79.

67. Pierre Belon, *Voyage au Levant: Les observations de Pierre Belon du Mans (1533)*, ed. Alexandra Merle (Paris: Chandeigne, 2001).

68. Ibid.

69. Excerpt from the register of letters written by M. de Petremol (Troyes, 1623); quoted in Rouillard, *The Turk*, p. 324.

70. Postel, *De la République des Turcs*, pp. 28–30.

71. Busbecq, *Ambassades et voyages* (Paris: P. David, 1646), pp. 145–47; Rouillard, *The Turk*, p. 304.

72. Antoine Geuffroy, *Estat de la Cour du Grand Turc, l'ordre de sa gendarmerie et de ses finances: avec ung brief discours de leurs conquestes depues le premier de ceste race* (Antwerp, 1542), fol. D1, verso; Rouillard, *The Turk*, p. 189.

73. Postel, *De la Republique des Turcs*, p. 10.

74. Ibid., p. 69.

75. Du Loir, *Les voyages*, p. 166.

76. Jean Chesneau, *Le voyage de Monsieur d'Aramon*, ed. C. Schefer (Paris, 1887), p. 109.

77. That dissymmetry is a central theme in Bernard Lewis's famous book *The Muslim Discovery of Europe* (London: Weidenfeld and Nicolson, 1982).

78. Suraiya Faroqhi, *The Ottoman Empire and the World around It* (London: Tauris, 2004), pp. 204–6.

79. Karl Teply, "Evliyâ Çelebi in Wien," *Der Islam* 52 (1975): 125–31.

80. Richard F. Kreutel, *Im Reiche des goldenen Apfels* (Graz, Austria: Verlag Styria, 1963).

81. Maxime Rodinson, *La fascination de l'islam* (Paris: François Maspéro, 1980), p. 81.

82. Guy Le Thiec, "La Renaissance et l'orientalisme 'turquesque,'" in Arkoun, ed., *Histoire de l'islam et des musulmans en France*, p. 417 n. 4.

83. M. le comte de Boulainvilliers, *La vie de Mahomed* (Amsterdam: P. Humbert, 1730); English translation *The Life of Mahomet* (London, 1731; repr. Piscataway, NJ: Gorgias Press, 2002); see J. Tolan, "European Accounts of Muhammad's Life," in *Cambridge Companion to Muhammad*, ed. Jonathan Brockopp (Cambridge, UK: Cambridge University Press, 2010), 226–50, esp. pp. 240–41.

84. Annie Berthier, "Turqueries ou turcologie? L'effort de traduction des jeunes de langues au XVIIe [*recte* XVIIIe] siècle, d'après la collection de manuscrits conservée à la Bibliothèque nationale de France," in *Istanbul et les langues orientales*, ed. Frédéric Hitzel (Paris: L'Harmattan, 1997), pp. 283–317.

85. Quoted in Henri Omont, *Missions archéologiques françaises en Orient aux XVIIe et XVIIIe siècle*, vol. 1 (Paris: Imprimerie Nationale, 1902), p. 2.

86. Jean Bodin, *Les six livres de la République* (Paris: Fayard, 1986), vol. 2, part 2: 35.

87. John Locke, *A Letter concerning Toleration*, 11th ed. (London, 1812).

88. Norman Daniel, *Islam, Europe, and Empire* (Edinburgh: Edinburgh University Press, 1966), pp. 24–25.

89. J. B. de Cloots (Anacharsis), *La certitude des preuves du Mahométisme par Ali-Gier-Ber* (London, 1780).

90. *The Turkish Letters of Ogier Ghiselin de Busbecq*, Forster trans., pp. 135–36.

91. Gottfried Hagen, *Ein osmanischer Geograph bei der Arbeit: Entstehung und Gedankenwelt von Katib Çelebis Ğihânnümâ* (Berlin: Klaus Schwarz, 2003).

92. Olivier de la Marche, *Mémoires*, quoted in Rouillard, *The Turk*, p. 24.

93. Cited in G. Le Thiec, "La Renaissance et l'orientalisme 'turquesque,'" p. 420.

94. Ibid.

95. Ibid.

96. Dominique Carnoy-Torabi, "Regards sur l'islam, de l'âge classique aux Lumières," in Arkoun, ed., *Histoire de l'islam et des musulmans en France*, p. 462.

PART III: EUROPE AND THE MUSLIM WORLD IN THE CONTEMPORARY PERIOD

Chapter 11: The Eighteenth Century as Turning Point

1. The U.S. Marine Corps Hymn recalls that episode at the beginning of its first stanza: "From the Halls of Montezuma / To the shores of Tripoli / We fight our country's battles / In the air, on land, and sea."

Chapter 12: Civilization or Conquest?

1. Report by M. Alexis de Tocqueville on the legislation relating to the special allocation requested for Algeria, May 24, 1847, in his *Oeuvres complètes* (Paris: Gallimard, 1962), vol. 3: 269.

2. Second speech on the Eastern question, in Alexis de Tocqueville, *Oeuvres complètes* (Paris: Gallimard, 1985), vol. 3: 290.

Chapter 13: The Age of Reform

1. Official French translation communicated to the embassies and having legal weight; Adel Ismaïl, *Documents diplomatiques et consulaires relatifs à l'histoire du Liban*

et des pays du Proche-Orient du XVIIIe siècle à nos jours, vol. 24 (Beirut: Éditions des Oeuvres Politiques et Historiques, 1980), pp. 50ff.

2. Edmond Bapst, *Les origines de la guerre de Crimée* (Paris: C. Delagrave, 1912), p. 314 (italicized portion in French in the ambassador's dispatch).

3. Text in Adel Ismaïl, *Documents diplomatiques et consulaires relatifs à l'histoire du Liban et des pays du Proche-Orient du XVIIIe siècle à nos jours*, vol. 29 (Beirut: Éditions des Oeuvres Politiques et Historiques, 1982), pp. 214–23.

4. French Ministry of War, *Tableau de la situation des établissements français dans l'Algérie, 1865–1866* (Paris: Imprimerie Royale, 1868), p. xxxi.

5. Bernard Lewis, "Ali Pasha on Nationalism," *Middle Eastern Studies* 10 (1974): 78–79.

6. See the complete anthology collected by Marcel Colombe, *Pages choisies de Djamal al-dīn al-Afghani, Orient*, vol. 21: 87–117 and vol. 22: 125–60, quotation p. 130.

7. Joseph Ernest Renan, "De la part des peuples sémitiques dans l'histoire de la civilisation," in his *Oeuvres complètes*, vol. 2 (Paris: Calmann-Lévy, 1948), pp. 317–35.

8. Joseph Ernest Renan, "L'islamisme et la science," in his *Oeuvres complètes*, vol. 1 (Paris: Calmann-Lévy, 1947), pp. 945–65.

9. Lengthy excerpts of this debate can be found in Henry Laurens, "La France et l'Égypte en 1882," in his *Les Orientales*, vol. 2 (Paris: Centre National de la Recherche Scientifique, 2007), pp. 13–52.

10. Ibid., p. 42

Chapter 14: The Age of Empire

1. Henry Laurens, "Le Châtelier, Massignon, Montagne, Politique musulmane et orientalisme," *Les Orientales*, vol. 2 (Paris: Centre National de la Recherche Scientifique, 2007), p. 252

2. Jean-Michel Gaillard, *Jules Ferry* (Paris: Fayard, 1989), p. 604.

3. Robert de Caix, "La situation de l'Algérie," *L'Afrique Française*, November 1900.

4. Joseph Ernest Renan, "Réponse au discours de réception de M. de Lesseps," in his *Oeuvres complètes*, vol. 1: 799–818.

5. Robert de Caix, "La leçon de Fachoda," *L'Afrique Française*, November 1898.

6. Joseph Ernest Renan, "Conférence faite à l'Alliance pour la propagation de la langue française," in his *Oeuvres complètes*, vol. 2: 1087–95.

Chapter 15: The First Blows to European Domination

1. *Revue du Monde Musulman* 2 (1908): 416.

2. Ministère des Affaires Étrangères (MAE; Ministry of Foreign Affairs), Paris, new series, Egypt, vol. 12, June 13 and 14, 1910.

3. MAE, new series, Egypt, vol. 12, part 15, June 2, 1912.

4. Alfred Le Châtelier, "Politique musulmane, lettre à un conseiller d'État," *Revue du Monde Musulman* 3 (September 1910): 1–166.

5. Najib Azoury, *Le réveil de la nation arabe* (Paris: Plon-Nourrit, 1905), pp. 1–8, reprinted in Henry Laurens, *Le retour des exilés: La lutte pour la Palestine* (Paris: Robert Laffont, 1998), pp. 94–101.

6. Gaston Wiet, "L'antagonisme des Arabes et des Turcs," *L'Asie Française*, August 1910.

7. "Un discours de M. Jonnart," *L'Afrique Française*, December 1912.

8. Adel Ismaïl, *Documents diplomatiques et consulaires relatifs à l'histoire du Liban et des pays du Proche-Orient du XVIIIe siècle à nos jours*, vol. 20 (Beirut: Éditions des Oeuvres Politiques et Historiques, 1979), pp. 226–27.

Chapter 16: The Great War and the Beginning of Emancipation

1. Archive center [*Service historique*] of the land army, army general staff, Africa branch, 7, no. 2104, Muslim policy, 1916–1917.

2. MAE, Commission Interministérielle des Affaires Musulmanes, report dated April 14, 1917, in which M. Benghabrit envisions certain reforms to be introduced in Algeria, and the establishment of a commission to that end.

3. "Primary Documents, Woodrow Wilson's 'Fourteen Points' Speech, 8 January 1918" ; available at http://www.firstworldwar.com/source/fourteenpoints.htm (accessed February 14, 2012).

4. English text in Helmut Mejcher, *Imperial Quest for Oil: Iraq 1910–1928* (London: Ithaca Press, 1976), pp. 177–79.

5. Antoine Hokayem and Marie-Claude Bitar, *L'Empire ottoman, les Arabes et les grandes puissances* (Beirut: Éditions Universitaires du Liban, 1981), p. 98.

6. League of Nations covenant, Peace Treaty of Versailles, Peace Conference; available at http://unispal.un.org/UNISPAL.NSF/0/6CB59816195E58350525654F007624BF (accessed February 14, 2012).

7. Daniel Rivet, *Lyautey et l'institution du protectorat français au Maroc, 1912-1925* (Paris: l'Harmattan, 2000); *Le Maghreb à l'épreuve de la colonisation* (Paris: Fayard, 2010).

Selected Bibliography

Part I: Saracens and *Ifranj*

Primary Sources

Ibn Hawqal, Abū al-Qāsim Muhammad. *The Oriental Geography of Ebn Haukal.* Translated by William Ouseley et al. Frankfurt am Main: Institute for the History of Arabic-Islamic Science at the Johann Wolfgang Goethe University, 1992.

Ibn Jubayr. *The Travels of Ibn Jubayr, Being the Chronicle of a Mediaeval Spanish Moor. . . .* Translated by R.J.C. Broadhurst. London: Camelot, 1952.

Idrīsī. *Explanations to the Proof of the Map of the World.* Translated by Konrad Miller. Stuttgart: n.p., 1928.

Jacques de Vitry. *Lettres de la cinquième croisade.* Turnhout, Belgium: Brepols, 1998.

Usāma ibn Munqidh. *The Book of Contemplation: Islam and the Crusades.* Translated by Paul M. Cobb. New York: Penguin, 2008.

Secondary Works

Arnaldez, Roger. *À la croisée des trois monothéismes: Une communauté de pensée au Moyen Âge.* Paris: Albin Michel, 1993.

Balard, Michel. *Les Latins en Orient.* Paris: Presses Universitaires de France, 2006.

Balard, Michel, and Alain Ducelier, eds. *Coloniser au Moyen Âge.* Paris: Armand Colin, 1995.

Burman, Thomas. *Reading the Qur'ān in Latin Christendom, 1140–1560.* Philadelphia: University of Pennsylvania Press, 2007.

Cipollone, Giulio, ed. *La liberazione dei "captivi" tra cristianità e islam: Oltre la crociata e il gihâd: Tolleranza e servizio unmanitario.* Vatican: Archivio Segreto Vaticano, 2000.

Constable, Olivia Remie. *Housing the Stranger in the Mediterranean World: Lodging, Trade, and Travel in Late Antiquity and the Middle Ages.* Cambridge, UK: Cambridge University Press, 2003.

———. *Trade and Traders in Muslim Spain: The Commercial Realignment of the Iberian Peninsula, 900–1500.* Cambridge, UK: Cambridge University Press, 1994.

Ducelier, Alain. *Chrétiens d'Orient et Islam au Moyen Âge.* Paris: Armand Colin, 1996.

Eddé, Anne-Marie. *Saladin.* Translated by Jane Marie Todd. Cambridge, MA: Harvard University Press, 2011.

Flori, Jean. *L'Islam et la Fin des temps: L'interprétation prophétique des invasions musulmanes dans la chrétienté médiévale.* Paris: Seuil, 2007.

Friedman, Yvonne. *Encounter between Enemies: Captivity and Ransom in the Latin Kingdom of Jerusalem.* Leiden, Netherlands: Brill, 2002.

Garcin, J.-C., ed. *Grandes villes méditerranéennes du monde musulman médiéval.* Rome: École Française de Rome, 2000.

Garcin, J.-C., Michel Balivet, Thierry Blanquis et al. *États, sociétés, et cultures du monde musulman médiéval: Xe–XVe siècles.* 3 vols. Paris: Presses Universitaires de France, 1995–2000.

Gervers, Michael, and Ramzi Bikhazi, eds. *Conversion and Continuity: Indigenous Christian Communities in Islamic Lands, Eighth to Eighteenth Centuries.* Toronto: University of Toronto Press, 1990.

Goitein, Shlomo. *A Mediterranean Society: The Jewish Communities of the Arab World as Portrayed in the Documents of the Cairo Geniza.* 6 vols. Berkeley: University of California Press, 1966–1988.

Grabar, Oleg. *The Shape of the Holy: Early Islamic Jerusalem.* Princeton, NJ: Princeton University Press, 1996.

Grypeou, Emmanouela, Mark Swanson, and David Thomas, eds. *The Encounter of Eastern Christianity with Early Islam.* Leiden, Netherlands: Brill, 2006.

Guichard, Pierre. *Al-Andalus: 711–1492: Une histoire de l'Espagne musulmane.* Paris: Hachette, 2001.

Libéra, Alain de. *Penser au Moyen Âge.* Paris: Seuil, 1991.

Meserve, Margaret. *Empires of Islam in Renaissance Historical Thought.* Cambridge, MA: Harvard University Press, 2008.

Miller, Kathryn A. *Guardians of Islam: Religious Authority and Muslim Communities of Late Medieval Spain.* New York: Columbia University Press, 2008.

Miquel, André. *La géographie humaine dans le monde musulman jusqu'au XIe siècle.* 4 vols. Paris: Mouton, 1967–1988.

Nirenberg, David. *Communities of Violence: Persecution of Minorities in the Middle Ages.* Princeton, NJ: Princeton University Press, 1996.

Rashed, Roshdi, and Régis Morelon. *Encyclopedia of the History of Arabic Science.* London: Routledge, 2002.

Rotman, Youval. *Byzantine Slavery and the Mediterranean World.* Translated by Jane Marie Todd. Cambridge, MA: Harvard University Press, 2009.

Riley-Smith, J. *Atlas of the Crusades.* London: Guild, 1990.

Sénac, Philippe. *Le monde carolingien et l'Islam: Contribution à l'étude des relations diplomatiques pendant le haut Moyen Âge, VIIIe–Xe siècles.* Paris: L'Harmattan, 2006.

Thomas, David, Barbara Roggema, Juan Pedro Monferrer Sala et al., eds. *Christian-Muslim Relations: A Bibliographical History.* 5 vols. Leiden, Netherlands: Brill, 2009–2012.

Tolan, John. *Saint Francis and the Sultan: The Curious History of a Christian-Muslim Encounter.* Oxford, UK: Oxford University Press, 2009.

———. *Saracens: Islam in the Medieval European Imagination.* New York: Columbia University Press, 2002.

———. *Sons of Ishmael: Muslims through European Eyes in the Middle Ages.* Gainesville: University Press of Florida, 2008.

Touati, Houari. *Islam and Travel in the Middle Ages.* Chicago: University of Chicago Press, 2010 .

———. *L'armoire à sagesse: Bibliothèques et collections en Islam.* Paris: Aubier, 2003.

PART II: THE GREAT TURK AND EUROPE

Aksan, Virginia H. *An Ottoman Statesman in War and Peace: Ahmed Resmi Efendi, 1700–1783.* Leiden, Netherlands: Brill, 1995.

———. *Ottoman Wars: An Empire Besieged.* Harlow, UK: Longman/Pearson, 2007.

Anderson, Matthew. *War and Society in Europe of the Old Regime, 1618–1789*. Stroud, UK: Sutton, 1998.

Andrews, Walter G., and Mehmed Kalpaklı. *The Age of Beloveds: Love and the Beloved in Early-Modern Ottoman and European Culture and Society*. Durham, NC: Duke University Press, 2005.

Bayerle, Gustav. "The Compromise at Zsitvatorok." *Archivum Ottomanicum* 6 (1980): 5–53.

Bennassar, Bartolomé, and Lucile Bennassar. *Les chrétiens d'Allah*. 3rd ed. Paris: Perrin, 2006.

Bisaha, Nancy. *Creating East and West: Renaissance Humanists and the Ottoman Turks*. Philadelphia: University of Pennsylvania Press, 2004.

Bono, Salvatore. *Corsari nel Mediterraneo*. Milan: Arnoldo Mondadori, 1993, 1997.

Borromeo, Elisabetta. *Voyageurs occidentaux dans l'Empire ottoman (1600–1644)*. 2 vols. Paris: Maisonneuve et Larose, 2007.

Bracewell, C. W. *The Uskoks of Senj: Piracy, Banditry, and Holy War in the Sixteenth-Century Adriatic*. Ithaca, NY: Cornell University Press, 1992.

Cardini, Franco. *Europe et islam: Histoire d'un malentendu*. Translated by J.-P. Bardos. Paris: Seuil, 2000.

Charrière, E. *Négociations de la France dans le Levant*. 3 vols. Paris: Imprimerie Nationale, 1850.

Cook, Michael, ed. *A History of the Ottoman Empire to 1730*. Cambridge, UK: Cambridge University Press, 1976.

Dávid, Géza, and Pál Fodor, eds. *Hungarian and Ottoman Military and Diplomatic Relations in the Age of Süleyman the Magnificent*. Budapest: Loránd Eötvös University, 1994.

———, eds. *Ottomans, Hungarians and Habsburgs in Central Europe: The Military Confines in the Era of Ottoman Conquests*. Leiden, Netherlands: Brill, 2000.

Davis, Robert C. *Christian Slaves, Muslim Masters: White Slavery in the Mediterranean, The Barbary Coast and Italy, 1500–1800*. Houndmills, UK: Palgrave Macmillan, 2003.

Duchhardt, Heinz. *Balance of Power und Pentarchie, 1700–1785*. Paderborn, Germany: Ferdinand Schöningh, 1997.

Duparc, Pierre. *Recueil des instructions données aux ambassadeurs et ministres de France depuis les traités de Westphalie jusqu'à la Révolution française*. Paris: Centre National de la Recherche Scientifique, 1969.

Eldem, Edhem. *French Trade in Istanbul in the Eighteenth Century*. Leiden, Netherlands: Brill, 1999.

Faroqhi, Suraiya. *The Ottoman Empire and the World around It*. New York: Tauris, 2004.

———, ed. *The Cambridge History of Turkey*. Vol. 3: *The Later Ottoman Empire, 1603–1839*. Cambridge, UK: Cambridge University Press, 2006.

Finkel, Caroline. *Osman's Dream: The History of the Ottoman Empire, 1300–1923*. London: John Murray, 2005.

Frangakis-Syrett, Elena. *The Commerce of Smyrna in the Eighteenth Century, 1700–1820*. Athens: Centre for Asia Minor Studies, 1992.

Goffman, Daniel. *Britons in the Ottoman Empire, 1642–1660*. Seattle: University of Washington Press, 1998.

———. *The Ottoman Empire and Early Modern Europe*. Cambridge, UK: Cambridge University Press, 2002.

Groot, Alexander H. de. *The Ottoman Empire and the Dutch Republic: A History of the Earliest Diplomatic Relations, 1610–1630.* Leiden, Netherlands: Istanbul Nederlands Historisch-Archeologisch Instituut, 1978.

Guilmartin, John Francis, Jr. *Gunpowder and Galleys: Changing Technology and Mediterranean Warfare at Sea in the Sixteenth Century.* Cambridge, UK: Cambridge University Press, 1974.

Hazard, Paul. *La crise de la conscience européenne, 1680–1715.* Paris: Arthème Fayard, 1961.

Kann, Robert A. *A History of the Habsburg Empire, 1526–1918.* Berkeley: University of California Press, 1974.

Khadduri, Majid. *War and Peace in the Law of Islam.* Baltimore: Johns Hopkins University Press, 1966.

Khodarkovsky, Michael. *Russia's Steppe Frontier: The Making of a Colonial Empire, 1500–1800.* Bloomington: Indiana University Press, 2002.

Kolodziejczyk, Dariusz. *Ottoman Polish Diplomatic Relations (Fifteenth–Eighteenth Century): An Annotated Edition of Ahdnames and Other Documents.* Leiden, Netherlands: Brill, 2000.

Kortepeter, C. Max. *Ottoman Imperialism during the Reformation: Europe and the Caucasus.* New York: New York University Press, 1973.

Kurz, Otto. *European Clocks and Watches in the Near East.* London: Warburg Institute, 1975.

LeDonne, John P. *The Russian Empire and the World, 1700–1917: The Geopolitics of Expansion and Containment.* New York: Oxford University Press, 1997.

Lewis, Bernard. *The Muslim Discovery of Europe.* London: Weidenfeld and Nicolson, 1982.

Mantran, R., ed. *Histoire de l'Empire Ottoman.* Paris: Fayard, 1989.

Naff, T., and R. Owen, eds. *Studies in Eighteenth Century Islamic History.* Carbondale: Southern Illinois University Press, 1977.

Norman, Daniel. *Islam and the West: The Making of an Image.* Oxford, UK: Oneworld, 1993.

———. *Islam, Europe and Empire.* Edinburgh: Edinburgh University Press, 1966.

Ostapchuk, Victor. "The Ottoman Black Sea Frontier and the Relations of the Porte with the Polish-Lithuanian Commonwealth and Muscovy, 1622–1628." PhD diss., Harvard University, 1989.

Panzac, Daniel. *Commerce et navigation dans l'Empire ottoman au XVIIIe siècle.* Istanbul: Isis, 1996.

Paris, Robert. *Histoire du commerce de Marseille.* Vol. 5: *1600 à 1789: Le Levant.* Paris: Plon, 1957.

Peri, Oded. *Christianity under Islam in Jerusalem: The Question of the Holy Sites in Early Ottoman Times.* Leiden, Netherlands: Brill, 2001.

Poumarède, Géraud. *Pour en finir avec la croisade: Mythes et réalités de la lutte contre les Turcs aux XVIe et XVIIe siècles.* Paris: Presses Universitaires de France, 2004.

Preto, Paolo. *Venezia e i Turchi.* Florence: Sansoni, 1975.

Rodinson, Maxime. *La fascination de l'islam.* Paris: François Maspéro, 1980.

Rothenberg, Gunter Erich. *The Military Border in Croatia, 1740–1881.* Chicago: University of Chicago Press, 1966.

Rouillard, Clarence Dana. *The Turk in French History, Thought and Literature (1520–1660).* Paris: Boivin, 1942.

Schulze, Winfried. *Reich und Türkengefahr im späten 16. Jahrhundert: Studien zu den politischen und gesellschaftlichen Auswirkungen einer äusseren Bedrohung.* Munich: C. H. Beck, 1978.

Setton, K. M. *The Papacy and the Levant (1204–1571).* 4 vols. Philadelphia: American Philosophical Society, 1976–1984.

———. *Venice, Austria, and the Turks in the Seventeenth Century.* Philadelphia: American Philosophical Society, 1991.

Skilliter, S. *William Harborne and the Trade with Turkey 1576–1582: A Documentary Study of the First Anglo-Ottoman Relations.* London: Oxford University Press, 1977.

Stavrianos, L. S. *The Balkans since 1453.* New York: Holt, Rinehart and Winston, 1958.

Steensgaard, Niels. "Consuls and Nations in the Levant from 1570 to 1650." *Scandinavian Economic History Review* 1, no. 2 (1967): 13–54.

Theunissen, H. "Ottoman-Venetian Diplomatics: The 'Ahd-names: The Historical Background and the Development of a Category of Political-Commercial Instruments Together with an Annotated Edition of a Corpus of Relevant Documents." PhD diss., Utrecht University, 1991.

Yerasimos, Stéphane. *Les voyageurs dans l'Empire ottoman (XIVe–XVIe siècles): Bibliographie, itinéraires et inventaire des lieux habités.* Ankara: Société Turque d'Histoire, 1991.

PART III: EUROPE AND THE MUSLIM WORLD IN THE CONTEMPORARY PERIOD

The set of themes developed in this section coincides in large part with the colonial history of Europe. The *Oxford History of the British Empire*, 5 vols. (Oxford, UK: Oxford University Press, 1998) is an irreplaceable source of information. There is no French equivalent, with the partial exception of the *Histoire de la France coloniale*, 2 vols. (Paris: Armand Colin, 1991), to be complemented by the *Histoire de la colonisation française*, 2 vols. (Paris: Fayard, 1991).

To these must be added the most recent edition of the *Histoire de l'Empire ottoman*, edited by Robert Mantran (Paris: Fayard, 2003); Yann Richard, *L'Iran, Naissance d'une république islamique* (Paris: Éditions de la Martinière, 2006); and Denis Matringe, *Un islam non arabe: Horizons indiens et pakistanais* (Paris: Téraèdre, 2005).

The English-language bibliography is vast. The list that follows is limited to a few major works by authors whose oeuvre as a whole ought to be consulted.

Hodgson, Marshall G. S. *The Venture of Islam: The Gunpowder Empire and Modern Times.* Chicago: University of Chicago Press, 1977.

Hourani, Albert. *Arabic Thought in the Liberal Age, 1798–1939.* Cambridge, UK: Cambridge University Press, 1983.

———. *A History of the Arab Peoples.* London: Faber and Faber, 2005.

———. *Islam in European Thought.* Cambridge, UK: Cambridge University Press, 1981.

Keddie, Nikki R. *An Islamic Response to Imperialism.* Berkeley: University of California Press, 2003.

———. *Modern Iran: Roots and Results of Revolution.* New Haven, CT: Yale University Press, 2006.

———. *Sayyid Jamāl Ad-dīn al-Afghānī: A Political Biography*. Berkeley: University of California Press, 1972; American Council of Learned Societies (ACLS) History E-Book Project, 2001.

Laurens, Henry. *L'Empire et ses ennemis: La question impériale dans l'histoire*. Paris: Seuil, 2009.

———. *L'Orient arabe: Arabisme et islamisme de 1798 à 1945*. Paris: Armand Colin, 1993; revised edition, 2000.

———. *Orientales I: Autour de l'expédition d'Egypte*. Paris: Centre National de la Recherche Scientifique, 2004.

———. *Orientales II: La IIIe République et l'Islam*. Paris: Centre National de la Recherche Scientifique, 2004.

———. *Orientales III: Parcours et situations*. Paris: Centre National de la Recherche Scientifique, 2004. The three volumes of *Orientales* were published as a single volume by the same publisher in 2007.

———. *Paix et guerre au Moyen-Orient: L'Orient arabe et le monde de 1945 à nos jours*. Paris: Armand Colin, 1999.

———. *Le royaume impossible: La France et la genèse du monde arabe*. Paris: Armand Colin, 1990.

Lewis, Bernard. *The Emergence of Modern Turkey*. Oxford, UK: Oxford University Press, 1981.

———. *From Babel to Dragomans: Interpreting the Middle East*. Oxford, UK: Oxford University Press, 2004.

———. *What Went Wrong? The Clash between Islam and Modernity in the Middle East*. New York: Harper Perennial, 2003.

Shaw, Stanford J. *History of the Ottoman Empire and Modern Turkey*. Cambridge, UK: Cambridge University Press, 1977.

INDEX

Note: Page numbers in italics indicate illustrations.

James I of England, 230

Jandar, 128

Janibeg Giray, 196–97

Janissaries, 117–18, 130–31, 159, 183, 201, 208, 239, 269, 275, 282

Jankerman, 193

János, Baranyai Decsi, 182–83

Japan: British treaty with, 340; isolation of, 259, 266; literacy in, 259; Muslim interest in, 340, 346; Russo-Japanese War (1904–1905), 339–40, 348; in World War II, 387–88

Japheth, 12–13

Jem, 135–36, 181

Jerez, 59

Jerome, 13, 39

Jerusalem: captured in the First Crusade, 35; as the center of the world, 20; establishment of, 113; importance for Islam, 46; preeminence over Palestine, 379; religious minorities in, 59–60; religious protection of non-Muslims in, 300; Saracens' sacrilege in, 36–37; taken by Saladin, 46; Umayyad authority in, 70–71. *See also* Palestine

Jesus Christ, 12, 34, 97, 182

Jews: in Algeria, 324–25, 389; Askenazic, 154; as captives, 65; in Christian states, 57, 60, 62; of Constantinople, 156–57; as constituting a Jewish people, 369; *conversos*, 154; descent from Abraham and Sarah claimed by, vii; as doctors, 60; emancipation of, 297, 300, 302; food and slaughtering methods of, 54; in France, 264, 297; Hellenophonic (Romaniotes), 154; homeland for (*see* Zionism); Italiote, 154; massacred in Granada (1066), 52; in Morocco, 303–4; vs. Muslims, 381, 383; in Ottoman Europe, 154, 156–57, 161, 268, 300, 302; in Palestine, 300; in Russia, 297, 369; Sephardic, 154, 157; slavery by, 67; status in Ottoman Empire, 268; in Tunisia, 304; in the United States, 369. *See also* Judaism; Zionism

jihad: to conquer *dār al-harb*, 29–31, 178; in Europe, 178–80; against Franks (8th to 9th centuries), 30–31; against Franks (11th to 13th centuries), 44–46; greater (internal) vs. lesser (external), 45; Hadith on, 29; Islamism as justification for, 400; Qur'an on, 28–29; raids to acquire slaves, 30; via war vs. preaching, 28–29; against the West, global, x

jizya (tribute), 28, 49–50, 55, 80, 157, 160, 212

João I of Portugal, 47

Johannes de Deo, 40

John III of Portugal, 116

John of Austria, 118, 143

John of Capistrano, 133, 166

John of Matha, 202–3

John of Segovia, 242

John the Soldier, Saint, 69

John VIII, Emperor, 131, 165

John VIII, Pope, 35

John V Palaeologus, 122

Jonnart, Célestin, 354–55

Jordan, 393

Joseph II of Austria, 265

Journeys beyond the Sea (Broquière), 236

Juan Manuel: *Conde Lucanor*, 96

Judaism: conflicts/convergences with Islam and Christianity, 97–105, 422n36, 423n45; during Ottoman domination in Europe, 153; Qur'anic criticism of, 97; Renan on, 316. *See also* Jews

July Monarchy, 278, 285, 297

Justinian, statue of, 182

Kaaba (Mecca), 13, 46

Kabul, 291–92

Kabyle uprising (1871), 324

Kal'e-i Sultāniye, 192

Kalīla wa Dimna, 96–97

Kalkashandi, 212

Kamenec, 193

Kamieniec Podolski, 145

al-Kāmil, 46, 57, 102

Kanev, 193

Kanizsa, 144

Kantemir Mirza, 196–98

Karaman, 126, 128

Karamanli dynasty, 118

Kara Mehmed, 242

Karasi, 121

Karlowitz, Treaty of (1699), 145–47, 213, 221–22

Kars, 283, 370

Kātib Çelebi, 250

Kazan khanate, 119

Kefe, 135, 151, 193, 196

Kemal, Mustafa, 374, 376–77

Kemalism, 375–76, 385, 402

Keresztes, Battle of (1596), 144

Kersh, 193

Khadīja, 34

Khan, Reza, 376, 382, 388

CPSIA information can be obtained at www.ICGtesting.com
Printed in the USA
LVOW10s1113131015

458050LV00002B/6/P